Muslim Peoples

v.1

Muslim
Peoples

A World Ethnographic Survey

Second Edition,
Revised and Expanded

Edited by **Richard V. Weekes**

Maps by John E. Coffman
Paul Ramier Stewart, consultant

Acehnese–Lur

Greenwood Press
Westport, Connecticut

Library of Congress Cataloging in Publication Data

Main entry under title:

Muslim peoples.

  Bibliography: p.
  Includes index.
  Contents: [1] Acehnese—Lur — [2] Maba—Yoruk.
1. Muslims.   2. Ethnology—Islamic countries.
3. Islamic countries—Social life and customs.
I. Weekes, Richard V., 1924-
DS35.625.A1M87   1984   305.6'971   84-   83-18494
ISBN 0-313-23392-6 (lib. bdg.)
ISBN 0-313-24639-4 (lib. bdg. : v. 1)
ISBN 0-313-24640-8 (lib. bdg. : v. 2)

Library of Congress Catalog Card Number: 83-18494
ISBN 0-313-23392-6   (set)

First published in 1984

Greenwood Press
A division of Congressional Information Service, Inc.
88 Post Road West
Westport, Connecticut 06881

Printed in the United States of America

10 9 8 7 6 5 4 3 2 1

CONTRIBUTORS

Partap C. Aggarwal
SHRI RAM CENTER FOR INDUSTRIAL
   RELATIONS
New Delhi, India

Irshad Ali
DEPARTMENT OF ANTHROPOLOGY
Gauhati University

Tahir Ali
DEPARTMENT OF ANTHROPOLOGY
Wesleyan University

J. C. Anceaux
University of Leiden

Jane Monnig Atkinson
DEPARTMENT OF ANTHROPOLOGY
Stanford University

Jerome H. Barkow
DEPARTMENT OF SOCIOLOGY AND
   ANTHROPOLOGY
Dalhousie University

R. H. Barnes
INSTITUTE OF SOCIAL ANTHROPOLOGY
Oxford University

Daniel G. Bates
DEPARTMENT OF ANTHROPOLOGY
Hunter College of City University of New York

Ulku U. Bates
DEPARTMENT OF ART
Hunter College of City University of New York

Lois Beck
DEPARTMENT OF ANTHROPOLOGY
Washington University

Burton Benedict
DEPARTMENT OF ANTHROPOLOGY
University of California, Berkeley

Henri Berre (*deceased*)
CENTRE NATIONAL DE LA RECHERCHE
   SCIENTIFIQUE
Valbonne, France

Peter J. Bertocci
DEPARTMENT OF ANTHROPOLOGY
Oakland University

U. B. Bhoite
DEPARTMENT OF POLITICAL SCIENCE
Maharathwada University

R. M. Blench
DEPARTMENT OF SOCIAL
   ANTHROPOLOGY
University of Cambridge

Christian Bouquet
DEPARTMENT OF GEOGRAPHY
University of Bordeaux III

John Bowen
HARVARD INSTITUTE FOR INTERNA-
   TIONAL DEVELOPMENT
Harvard University

James L. Brain
DEPARTMENT OF ANTHROPOLOGY
State University of New York at New Paltz

Harald Beyer Broch
ETHNOGRAPHICAL MUSEUM
University of Oslo

Philip Burnham
DEPARTMENT OF ANTHROPOLOGY
University of London

Robert L. Canfield
DEPARTMENT OF ANTHROPOLOGY
Washington University

B. M. Das
DEPARTMENT OF ANTHROPOLOGY
Gauhati University

Thomas R. DeGregori
DEPARTMENT OF ECONOMICS
University of Houston

Leland Donald
DEPARTMENT OF ANTHROPOLOGY
University of Victoria

Paul Doornbos
AFRICAN STUDIES CENTRE
University of Leiden

Vernon R. Dorjahn
DEPARTMENT OF ANTHROPOLOGY
University of Oregon

Louis Dupree
DEPARTMENT OF ANTHROPOLOGY
Princeton University

Svetlana Rimsky-Korsakoff Dyer
FACULTY OF ASIAN STUDIES
The Australian National University

Pat Emerson
DEPARTMENT OF SOCIOLOGY
University of Washington

Richard M. Emerson (*deceased*)
DEPARTMENT OF ANTHROPOLOGY
University of Washington

Janet Ewald
DEPARTMENT OF HISTORY
Duke University

James C. Faris
DEPARTMENT OF ANTHROPOLOGY
University of Connecticut

Golamreza Fazel
DEPARTMENT OF ANTHROPOLOGY
University of Massachusetts, Boston

Robert A. Fernea
DEPARTMENT OF ANTHROPOLOGY
University of Texas, Austin

Gregory A. Finnegan
UNIVERSITY LIBRARY
Roosevelt University

James J. Fox
DEPARTMENT OF ANTHROPOLOGY
The Australian National University

C. Magbaily Fyle
INSTITUTE OF AFRICAN STUDIES
University of Sierra Leone

David P. Gamble
DEPARTMENT OF ANTHROPOLOGY
San Francisco State University

Frederick C. Gamst
DEPARTMENT OF ANTHROPOLOGY
University of Massachusetts, Boston

Gene R. Garthwaite
DEPARTMENT OF HISTORY
Dartmouth College

William H. Geoghegan
DEPARTMENT OF ANTHROPOLOGY
University of California, Berkeley

Alfred G. Gerteiny
DEPARTMENT OF HISTORY
University of Bridgeport

Byron J. Good
SCHOOL OF MEDICINE
University of California, Davis

Mary-Jo DelVecchio Good
SCHOOL OF MEDICINE
University of California, Davis

Peter G. Gowing (*deceased*)
DANSALAN RESEARCH CENTER
Iligan City, Philippines

Kathryn Green
DEPARTMENT OF HISTORY
Indiana University

Gunnar Haaland
DEPARTMENT OF SOCIAL STUDIES AND
    DEVELOPMENT
The CHR-Michelsen Institute (Norway)

John Hamer
DEPARTMENT OF ANTHROPOLOGY
University of Alabama

Robert L. Hardgrave, Jr.
DEPARTMENT OF GOVERNMENT
University of Texas, Austin

Donn V. Hart (*deceased*)
DEPARTMENT OF ANTHROPOLOGY
Northern Illinois University

Robert V. Haynes
DEPARTMENT OF HISTORY
University of Houston

LeVell Holmes
DEPARTMENT OF MULTI-CULTURAL
  STUDIES
California State College at Sonoma

Svend E. Holsoe
DEPARTMENT OF ANTHROPOLOGY
University of Delaware

Ladislav Holy
DEPARTMENT OF SOCIAL
  ANTHROPOLOGY
University of St. Andrews

C. Edward Hopen
DEPARTMENT OF ANTHROPOLOGY
University of Toronto

William G. Irons
DEPARTMENT OF ANTHROPOLOGY
Northwestern University

Alfred Janata
MUSEUM FUR VOLKERKUNDE
Neue Burg, Austria

Allen K. Jones
TRANSCENTURY CORPORATION
Washington, D.C.

Lidwien Kapteijns
AFRICAN STUDIES CENTRE
University of Leiden

R. Lincoln Keiser
DEPARTMENT OF ANTHROPOLOGY
Wesleyan University

Martin A. Klein
DEPARTMENT OF HISTORY
University of Toronto

R. M. Koentjaraningrat
DEPARTMENT OF ANTHROPOLOGY
University of Indonesia

Kim Kramer
DEPARTMENT OF ANTHROPOLOGY
Stanford University

Ruth Krulfeld
DEPARTMENT OF ANTHROPOLOGY
George Washington University

Herbert S. Lewis
DEPARTMENT OF ANTHROPOLOGY
University of Wisconsin, Madison

William G. Lockwood
DEPARTMENT OF ANTHROPOLOGY
University of Michigan

Deborah L. Mack
PROGRAM OF AFRICAN STUDIES
Northwestern University

Paul Magnarella
DEPARTMENT OF ANTHROPOLOGY
University of Florida

L. K. Mahapatra
DEPARTMENT OF ANTHROPOLOGY
Utkal University

Clarence Maloney
Rajshahi University

Peter Mark
DEPARTMENT OF HISTORY
Yale University

Gail Minault
DEPARTMENT OF HISTORY
University of Texas, Austin

Mattison Mines
DEPARTMENT OF ANTHROPOLOGY
University of California, Santa Barbara

David C. Montgomery
DEPARTMENT OF HISTORY
Brigham Young University

H. S. Morris
University of Cambridge

Larry W. Moses
CENTER FOR URALIC AND ALTAIC
  STUDIES
Indiana University

Victor L. Mote
DEPARTMENT OF GEOGRAPHY
University of Houston

Satoshi Nakagawa
DEPARTMENT OF ANTHROPOLOGY
The Australian National University

Merun H. Nasser-Bush
Boulder, Colorado

H. Arlo Nimmo
DEPARTMENT OF ANTHROPOLOGY
California State University at Hayward

J. Noorduyn
ROYAL INSTITUTE OF LINGUISTICS AND
ANTHROPOLOGY
Leiden, The Netherlands

Jennifer W. Nourse
DEPARTMENT OF ANTHROPOLOGY
University of Virginia

S. R. Nur
FACULTY OF LAW
Hasanuddin University

Arye Oded
FACULTY OF HUMANITIES
Tel Aviv University

Robert Olson
DEPARTMENT OF HISTORY
University of Kentucky

Maxwell Owusu
DEPARTMENT OF ANTHROPOLOGY
University of Michigan

Stephen L. Pastner
DEPARTMENT OF ANTHROPOLOGY
University of Vermont

Barbara L. K. Pillsbury
DEPARTMENT OF ANTHROPOLOGY
University of California, Los Angeles

Ronald Provencher
DEPARTMENT OF ANTHROPOLOGY
Northern Illinois University

Lanfranco Blanchetti Revelli
INSTITUTE OF PHILIPPINE CULTURE
Manila University

S. P. Reyna
DEPARTMENT OF SOCIOLOGY AND
ANTHROPOLOGY
University of New Hampshire

Rosemary E. Ridd
DEPARTMENT OF ANTHROPOLOGY
Oxford University

Carlton L. Riemer
Iligan City, Philippines

Richard Roberts
DEPARTMENT OF HISTORY
Stanford University

Frank A. Salamone
DEPARTMENT OF ANTHROPOLOGY
Mount Saint Mary College

Jeffrey T. Sammons
DEPARTMENT OF HISTORY
University of Houston

Ruth Laila Schmidt
CENTER FOR SOUTH AND SOUTHEAST
ASIAN STUDIES
University of California, Berkeley

Henry G. Schwarz
CENTER FOR EAST ASIAN STUDIES
Western Washington University

Kerrin Gräfin Schwerin
DEPARTMENT OF HISTORY
University of Heidelberg

Ray Scupin
DEPARTMENT OF ANTHROPOLOGY
The Lendenwood Colleges

William A. Shack
DEPARTMENT OF ANTHROPOLOGY
University of California, Berkeley

M. Nazif Shahrani
DEPARTMENT OF ANTHROPOLOGY
Pitzer College

Moin Shakir
DEPARTMENT OF POLITICAL SCIENCE
Maharathwada University

J. C. Sharma
DEPARTMENT OF ANTHROPOLOGY
Panjab University

Abdi A. Sheik-Abdi
DEPARTMENT OF ANTHROPOLOGY
University of Massachusetts, Boston

Sergei A. Shuiskii
Princeton University

Carol Silverman
DEPARTMENT OF ANTHROPOLOGY
University of Oregon

Michael Sims
AFRICAN STUDIES ASSOCIATION
Brandeis University

Susan Rodgers Siregar
DEPARTMENT OF SOCIOLOGY AND
ANTHROPOLOGY
Ohio University

David H. Spain
DEPARTMENT OF ANTHROPOLOGY
University of Washington

Jay Spaulding
Kean College of New Jersey

William Spencer
DEPARTMENT OF POLITICAL SCIENCE
Rollins College

James C. Stewart
California State College at Sonoma

Richard F. Strand
Chicago, Illinois

Nina Swidler
DIVISION OF SOCIAL SCIENCES
Fordham University

Richard Tapper
SCHOOL OF ORIENTAL AND AFRICAN
STUDIES
University of London

Robin Thelwall
DEPARTMENT OF LINGUISTICS
New University of Ulster

Akbarali H. Thobani
Metropolitan State College, Denver

Elly Touwen-Bouwsma
DEPARTMENT OF ANTHROPOLOGY
Free University, Amsterdam

Joseph Tubiana
CENTRE NATIONAL DE LA RECHERCHE
SCIENTIFIQUE
Valbonne, France

Marie-José Tubiana
CENTRE NATIONAL DE LA RECHERCHE
SCIENTIFIQUE
Valbonne, France

Dennis Tully
DEPARTMENT OF ANTHROPOLOGY
University of Washington

Ch. F. van Fraassen
ROYAL INSTITUTE OF LINGUISTICS AND
ANTHROPOLOGY
Leiden, The Netherlands

Leo F. Van Hoey
DEPARTMENT OF SOCIOLOGY AND
ANTHROPOLOGY
Lake Forest College

Jacob Vredenbregt
Hasanuddin University

Sidney R. Waldron
DEPARTMENT OF SOCIOLOGY AND
ANTHROPOLOGY
State University of New York at Cortland

Harry H. Walsh
DEPARTMENT OF RUSSIAN
University of Houston

Peter R. Watson
Summit, New Jersey

Ava S. Weekes (*deceased*)
Houston, Texas

Richard V. Weekes
DEPARTMENT OF ANTHROPOLOGY
University of Houston

Robert Wessing
DEPARTMENT OF ANTHROPOLOGY
Northern Illinois University

Sigrid Westphal-Hellbush (*deceased*)
Bochorn, Germany

Ronald Wixman
DEPARTMENT OF GEOGRAPHY
University of Oregon

John A. Works, Jr.
DEPARTMENT OF HISTORY
University of Missouri, St. Louis

Robert M. Wren
DEPARTMENT OF ENGLISH
University of Houston

Donald R. Wright
DEPARTMENT OF HISTORY
State University of New York at Cortland

Theodore P. Wright, Jr.
DEPARTMENT OF POLITICAL SCIENCE
State University of New York at Albany

Inger Wulff
DANISH NATIONAL MUSEUM
Copenhagen, Denmark

Moshe Yegar
Jerusalem, Israel

CONTENTS

Volume 1

Volume 2

PREFACE

When *Muslim Peoples* first appeared in 1978, Muslim Arabs, Filipinos and some obscure unnamed peoples in Chad held center stage on the Muslim scene. Since then, many more Muslim ethnic groups have held the world's attention. Somalis fought Ethiopians for control of the Ogaden, and lost. A revolution in Iran affected the lives of not only Persians, but Kurds, Lur, Bakhtiari, Qashqa'i and others. The Soviet invasion of Afghanistan triggered armed rebellion by the Nuristanis (the first to rebel), Pushtun, Hazaras and more. Moments of violence struck in Nigeria and the Indian state of Assam. Tensions continued among the Somalis, Malays of Thailand, Filipinos and, of course, the Arabs.

It seems appropriate to extend our knowledge of people who are Muslim. The first edition of *Muslim Peoples* was limited to 96 groups whose sizes each exceeded 100,000. The second edition, with no group size limitation, now presents some 190 ethnic and/or linguistic groups, most of which are totally Muslim but many of which are only partly so. Indeed, the conversion to Islam (and Christianity) of peoples adhering to traditional, nonmonotheistic, non-universal religions, in Africa and Indonesia especially, is an intriguing story in itself. Many such groups are included in this second edition even though these Muslims are only a small minority within their ethnic group.

Field research in Muslim ethnology remains inadequate, but not as inadequate as I first thought when I began this effort ten years ago. This second edition is enriched by the work of a number of British, Dutch, French, German, Indonesian, American and other scholars whose research among more obscure groups has heretofore been reported only in highly specialized publications. It is an honor to be able to present the disappearing Tunjur, the already disappeared Funj, the poldar-inventing Kuri on Lake Chad, the hippopotamus-dependent Wayto and the Muslim half of the Tomini.

Most of the 400,000 words which follow were generously contributed by the scholars whose names appear at the end of their work. All materials following a contributor's name, whether appendixes or bibliographies, are the work of the editor, who takes full responsibility for the contents.

The first edition benefited from the skills of the late Ava S. Weekes, former Time-Life researcher. Nevertheless, the editor thanks many supporters, including

Russell Reid, former Chairman of the Department of Anthropology, University of Houston, and Richard Kittrell, friend, for helping bring the efforts of some fine scholars to the public.

Richard V. Weekes

INTRODUCTION

Every inch of land on which there resides a brother who subscribes to the religion of the Noble Quran is part and parcel of the general territory of Islam which requires all its believers to further the cause of its defense and welfare.
—Hasan al Banna, founder of the Society of Muslim Brothers, 1928

There are approximately 837 million Muslims in the world. This book attempts to provide some insight into who and where they are and how they live. It seeks to discover what they have in common, what distinguishes them from each other and what they feel is important.

The method of study is based upon the division of the world's people into ethnic and/or linguistic groups and the identification of those with populations which are wholly or partly Muslim. Some 300 have been so identified. The groups presented in this study include nearly 98 percent of all Muslims.

Muslims live in nearly every country in the world. They form the majority of the populations of 36 nations and are close to 50 percent of the total population in 4 other countries. In the Soviet Union and India, where they are small minorities, they number together more than 125 million.

As the entries of this study show, Muslims have much in common. They share a universal trans-ethnic religion, Islam, the third largest religion after Christianity and Buddhism. They worship the same God, recognize more or less the same religious laws, observe many of the same rituals and share distinguishable culture traits derived from their Islamic heritage.

They share more than this. The Muslim world, for various reasons, is largely a part of the underdeveloped, nonindustrial world. Muslims are essentially a rural people living on land that returns little to them. Many have not advanced beyond hoe agriculture, and the rest, except in a few areas, rely on animal power. The result is a common poverty stretching from the Atlantic to the Pacific oceans.

Urban Muslims, probably no more than 30 percent of the total, share the frustrations of all nonindustrial city dwellers: low income, high unemployment and crowded living conditions, but high, unfulfilled expectations. Most of them have inherited a past of colonial subjugation and today remain largely dependent upon the economic, social and political initiatives from the industrial, Western world, although for some who have access to petroleum this balance is shifting.

These frustrations and victimizations manifest themselves in a variety of ways which inevitably reach the world press and shape the world image of Muslims. Most notable are the violent reactions of the weak against the strong—hijacking of airplanes by Palestinians, civil war in Lebanon, rebellion of Philippine Muslims, periodic warfare between Pakistan and India, Somalia and Ethiopia. Externally imposed decisions of the past breed conflict among Muslims themselves, such as between Kurds and Arabs in Iraq, Arabs and Tebu in Chad and, until 1972, between Punjabis and Bengalis in what is today Bangladesh. War between Muslim Iraq and Muslim Iran in 1983 threatens to involve much of the world.

Within the brotherhood of Islam there are many personalities. As Islam spread from its original home in the Arabian peninsula nearly 14 centuries ago, it encompassed people with different languages, cultures and religions. Some "became" Arab. Most, however, maintained their identities so that today Muslims speak dozens of languages and exhibit many cultures through the 300 or so ethnic groups to which they belong.

An ethnic group is a collection of people who see themselves (or are seen by others) as culturally distinct from other groups. They share certain culture traits which usually, but not always, include language, religion, heritage and value systems which they consider right for them. The group may be large, such as the Arabs, who number more than 148 million, and may include many subgroups. Or an ethnic group may be small, such as the Wayto of Ethiopia, who number no more than 2,000. Some groups, such as the Berbers, do not even know they are an ethnic group and identify primarily with their tribal subdivision.

A general characteristic of ethnic groups is the pride members have in their culture. They wish to perpetuate the group and retain those cultural elements which they believe are important. They usually marry within the group. If possible, they want to consolidate and strengthen themselves politically in relation to neighboring ethnic groups. Keeping an ethnic group politically and socially divided has been a classic strategy in weakening ethnic effectiveness, as demonstrated by European rule in Africa and India among the Hausa and Somalis and the Pushtun and Bengalis. Even more effective has been the division of the Arabs into a number of often competing nationalistic states.

Other influences tend to weaken ethnic unity. Among these are religious conversion, such as the propagation of Islam and Christianity in Africa, and the inexorable advance of Westernization or industrialization, which tends to divide people into modern and traditional, secular and religious, progressive and conservative.

The identification of ethnic groups is a continuing research task fraught with obstacles. Ethnologists have not agreed upon a common, worldwide ethnic classification.

Most ethnic groups are identifiable by their common language, but exceptions to this rule are numerous. Chinese Muslims speak the same language as the majority of Han Chinese, yet they are identified as Hui. So, too, the Mappilla and Labbai of southern India speak the majority languages, Tamil and Malayalam, respectively. India also offers additional criteria for ethnicity in the pervasive caste system based upon occupation and descent as well as Muslim sectarianism, despite common language. The Muslim leatherworkers in Rajasthan unite and marry endogamously as an ethnic group; the highborn Rajputs and Shaikhs act as ethnic groups; Ismaili Khojas and Memons are distinct groups throughout northern India, Pakistan and East Africa.

Even when a community meets the criteria of an ethnic group, there may be such great differences within the group that a common label is deceptive. Perhaps the best example is the Arabs. The Alawi of Syria are Arab, as are Bedouin tribes in Oman and Sunni urban dwellers of Alexandria. At least they speak Arabic, follow the same religion, identify with the same heritage, and consider themselves Arab. Yet major aspects of their cultures are quite different.

Compounding the difficulty, many governments, such as those of Iran and Afghanistan, resist efforts to examine the heterogeneity of the national society. This is less of a problem in states with relatively homogeneous societies, such as Somalia and Bangladesh.

Language is basic to culture. Its words and structure express human thoughts, relationships and actions. Through language the heritage of a people and their culture are transmitted to new generations and perpetuate their particular ethnic identity. As Muslims are divided into dozens of ethnic groups, so do they speak dozens of languages. Among the eight major language families of the world, five, in hundreds of subfamilies and dialects, are spoken by the 790 million Muslims represented in this study.

The languages most widely spoken by Muslims belong to the Indo-Iranian (or Indo-Aryan) branch of the Indo-European family. The ancient people who developed this language lived in eastern and central Europe. Sometime before 2000 B.C., these people began to move, some westward carrying the basis of today's European languages. Others, called Aryans, spread eastward and south into what is now Iran (land of Aryans), Afghanistan, Pakistan, northern India and Bangladesh, supplanting existing languages with Indo-Iranian and implanting different culture systems. Among the major languages of this family are Persian, Pushtu, Punjabi, Urdu, Bengali, Baluchi, Kurdish and Sindhi.

The second most frequently spoken languages by Muslims are those of the Afro-Asiatic family, which encompasses peoples living in a 2,000-mile-wide band stretching east and west from Saudi Arabia to Senegal. The chief language in this family is Arabic, spoken by more than 148 million Arabs. Other languages include Berber, Hebrew, Hausa and Somali.

The third largest language family for Muslims is Malayo-Polynesian, whose languages are spoken by populations of Madagascar, the Malay peninsula, Indonesia and the Philippines. Before the rapid spread of Indo-European languages beginning about four centuries ago, no other language family was as widely disseminated as Malayo-Polynesian.

Ural-Altaic is the fourth largest group embracing languages spoken by Muslims. Rising among the peoples living in Central Asia east of the Ural Mountains, this is the language of the Turkic-speaking peoples—the Turks, Tatars, Uzbek, Kazakhs, Uygur, Kirghiz and many others.

The fifth linguistic family is the Niger-Congo, which includes dozens of ethnic groups in Africa. Chief among the languages of Niger-Congo are Bantu, Wolof, Fulani and Manding.

Ibero-Caucasian is a minor linguistic family in the Caucasus area of the Soviet Union. Numerous Muslim groups, such as the Daghestanis and Circassians, speak sublanguages of this family.

There are common culture traits among members of each major linguistic family, enough so that a survey such as this could be organized along language lines. Thus, all Turkic-speaking peoples would be identified as minor subgroups within a major rubric. Indeed, the Pan-Turanian movement after World War I was based upon this principle. So, too, are the occasional efforts by some leaders to promote an Aryan confederation among Indo-Iranian-speaking peoples of Iran, Afghanistan, and Pakistan. This survey recognizes a validity in a linguistic approach, as shown by the entries on the Manding-, Malayo-Polynesian- and Turkic-speaking peoples. However, as other entries demonstrate, differences within the larger linguistic groups are sufficient—and so felt by the members themselves—to justify the treatment of subgroups as separate ethnic identities.

The complexity of studying the Muslim world through hundreds of languages and ethnic groups may be simplified by identifying larger culture areas. Such a system assumes that ethnic groups within a single area will have some cultural commonality. To an extent this is feasible, especially where culture areas embrace a major linguistic area or encompass relatively simple physical environments.

It is possible to identify nine culture areas in which most Muslims live.

1. The drylands of Southwest Asia, often called the Middle or Near East, is the heartland of Arab culture. Largely semiarid with mountains and plains, but fertile river valleys, it includes the countries of Saudi Arabia, Jordan, Israel, Syria, Lebanon, Iraq and Turkey. Its people, almost totally Arab except for the Turks and Jewish Israelis, are largely rural, either as cultivators or nomads, but with strong and active urban populations in such cities as Beirut, Damascus, Amman, Baghdad, Mecca, Jerusalem, Tel Aviv-Yafo, Izmir, Istanbul and Ankara.

2. The lower Nile River delta is the home of nearly 45 million Arabs who were once non-Arab Egyptians. The narrow inhabited area along the Nile has a population density exceeding 2,000 people per square mile.

3. The Mediterranean coast of North Africa, called the Maghreb ("sunset" in Arabic), hosts a culture composed of pre-Islamic traditions overlaid by Arab culture. The people, Arab and Berber, follow coastal living patterns as well as arid mountian and fertile valley life-styles.

4. The Arabs called the area to the south of the Maghred *sudan*, meaning "black." It is a 1,000-mile-wide belt stretching 3,000 miles from the Red Sea in the east to the Atlantic Ocean in the west. The northern edge of the Sudan is desert, which becomes dryland plains (called the Sahel) and, finally, forest in the south. Western Sudan was

the site of the great empires of Mali and Songhay, whose people were converted to Islam by the Berbers and Arabs beginning in the ninth century. Central Sudan, around Lake Chad, is dominated by the Muslim Hausa and Kanuri, who farm the dry plains along the Niger River and in northern Nigeria. Eastern Sudan is the dry plains area around the upper Nile in the Republic of Sudan and southern Egypt.

5. The northeast Ethiopic dry plains, forest and sea coast constitute a culture area of semi-sedentary Muslims who were converted to Islam by Arab armies and missionaries soon after the advent of Islam. The people include the Afar, Somali, Tigre and Oromo (Galla), who are noted for their fiercely independent spirit.

6. The East African coast, forested and with numerous trading cities, is culturally heterogeneous. Arabs, Persians and many ethnic groups from South Asia settled here—some to intermarry with the native Bantu, others to establish endogamous societies.

7. The Central Asian steppes reflect a culture area whose people are primarily Turkic speakers. The highlands are dry and suitable to pastoralism, while the rivers and valleys support such famous Muslim cities as Samarkand and Tashkent. This is the land of the Uzbek, Kazakhs, Tatars and Turkmen.

8. The great Aryan migrations of 2000 B.C. established a broad culture area reaching from Iran in the west to the border of Bengal in the east. It is a land of mountains and plains adaptive to both pastoralism and sedentary farming. The people speak sublanguages of the Indo-Iranian family. Their cultures include elements of an occupational caste system.

9. Southeast Asia beginning with the rivers of Bengal is an area of rivers, forests, peninsulas and islands whose people have developed cultures based on wet rice farming and seafaring. Their conversion to Islam came later than in the western culture areas, and their religion is strongly syncretistic.

Throughout the nine culture areas there are three basic ways of living—nomadic, sedentary rural village and urban—with obvious overlapping and interaction among the three. The socioeconomic culture patterns of the three areas are distinct, and the interpretations of Islam differ, particularly between the urban and rural sectors.

Muslim culture areas include a number of ways in which people live among and relate to their kin. The nuclear family (parents and unmarried children) is basic to most but is not a common residential group except in cities where space is limited. More common is the joint and extended family in which parents and children are joined in residence by the husband's parents, sons' wives and their children. Close bonds, frequently cemented by endogamous marriages, are maintained with paternal uncles and aunts and the latter's husbands' families. More extensive lineal kin relationships form tribal systems which are common in nearly all Muslim culture areas, although less so in Southeast Asia. The tribal structure is based upon descent from a common ancestor, with each segment (sometimes called a clan) composed of a number of extended families. Inheritance, authority, loyalties, responsibilities and obligations are determined by a family's location within this segmented system.

Tribal, segmentary lineage systems predominate among nomadic peoples, and even when nomads settle, they usually retain the system for many generations. Most sedentary villagers live in extended families, which continue to exist but in smaller numbers among townspeople and urban dwellers.

Nomadism is an adaptation to a hostile environment which requires that its participants move to live. While some nomads may occasionally raise crops on a seasonal basis, their principal occupation is the herding of animals—chiefly camels, sheep and goats. The search for pasturage is continual, and nomads move seasonally to areas which can feed their herds. For some nomads, migration to pasturage is vertical—to higher mountains in the summer, to valleys in the winter. For others, movement is horizontal, as on a desert, where rainfall is haphazard, not seasonal, and movement is between watered areas.

For all there is a common pattern of living, despite nomadic variations in types of animals, distance of movement and kind of terrain. Muslim nomads live for some part of their year in tents and are socially organized around a group of tents. They are dependent upon agriculture and must interact in particular ways with sedentary farmers or town merchants with whom they trade their animals and animal products for farm products, manufactured goods or cash. Movement requires frequent decision making, hardiness, and a social structure fostering group unity, harmony and authority. This structure is typified by extensive tribal kin relationships. As best described in the entries on the Shahsevan and Afar, the culture makes a virtue of tribal membership, militancy and aggressiveness.

Nomadism is a disappearing way of life. Such nomadic groups as the Arab Bedouin, Berber Tuareg, Qashqa'i, Bakhtiari, Fulani, Pushtun and Afar are being forced by modern economic and political systems to abandon their trails and herds. Trucks are replacing the camel and donkey as means of transport. National governments try to settle the nomads, preferring that their taxpayers stay in one place and remain disarmed, as described in the Bakhtiari study. Recent drought has decimated many nomad herds, and new industry in the developing countries beckons young men to the cities, despite the traditional nomad contempt for sedentary living. Muslim nomads who once numbered in countless millions today are no more than 30 million.

The sedentary rural dwellers, who are most typical of the Muslims (68 percent), are usually farmers, although many are also fishermen and foresters. They live with their extended families in villages, most of which are relatively self-sufficient and able to feed the inhabitants with only occasional need for manufactured products from the cities.

While most villagers are totally sedentary, some are also transhumant, leaving their villages during slack growing seasons and moving to other areas to work the fields or to pasture animals. They become nomadic, but unlike the nomad, their principal interest is farming, as described in the entry on the Berbers.

Whereas life is dynamic among nomads, requiring movement and change, life for Muslim villagers is static and monotonous, broken only by the change of seasons and the life-cycle celebrations, or by calamities—drought or flood, pestilence, pillage and disease. These factors, together with perpetual indebtedness, conspire to make village life insecure. The life-style is characterized by conservatism and close kin ties. Whether the farmer is growing rice in Indonesia, wheat in Turkey or yams in Nigeria, the villager's desire for a better life for his family is thwarted by his illiteracy, the absence of rewards for harder work, the lack of technology, the inability to risk innovation and the neglect of more progressive institutions of society, particularly those in the cities. He is relatively isolated from the changes taking place around him.

A third division in the Muslim world is the urban sector, relatively small in population, but politically and economically dominant. Muslim city life, like urban living everywhere, is characterized by a multiplicity of occupations, multi-storied dwellings implying smaller living quarters, and a moneyed economy (in contrast to the barter system which remains common among villagers and no-mads). Cities contain the bureaucracy of government, hospitals, schools and complex commercial systems, which offer opportunities for social and economic mobility. While kinship ties remain strong and the individual's status continues to rely on that of his family, the social structure of the urban dweller is more open and permits a degree of alternatives.

City dwellers control the wealth of the society, the government (including the army), and the knowledge and technology of modern life. Whereas the villager is conservative, the townsman, and more so the urbanite, accepts more readily change and progress. The material and psychological chasm between the Muslim town and country is deep and wide.

Nowhere is this division within Muslim society more apparent than in the understanding and practice of religion. Some authorities identify two Islams, that of the city and the folk Islam of the village and camp. Among rural Muslims there exists the strong influence of pre-Islamic animism. Among educated Muslims throughout the world there is awareness of the formal structure of Islam and its basic tenets, despite the existence of sectarianism.

***

The word "Islam" means "submission" (to the will of God). Those who make this submission to obeying God's laws will live an eternal and enjoyable life in paradise. Those who accept Islam are called Muslims (often spelled Moslems) or, sometimes, Musulmans. The words "Muhammadan" and "Muhammadism" are eschewed as implying a similarity in doctrine to traditional Christianity which views Jesus as divine; Muslims do not claim divinity for Muhammad *or* Jesus.

Muslims believe the law of Islam was revealed to Muhammad, an Arab merchant in Mecca, over a period of years after the turn of the seventh century. Muhammad said that God, sometimes speaking through Gabriel, told him that he was the last of a long line of prophets beginning with Adam and including

Abraham (Ibrahim), Noah (Nuh), Moses (Musa) and Jesus (Isa) to reveal the Word. Essential to the Word is the oneness of God. This is the heart of Muslim belief, the *shahada*: "There is no God but Allah and Muhammad is the messenger (prophet) of God."

Mecca at the time of Muhammad was a shrine city for Arabs, who worshipped a pantheon of gods; it also contained many entrepreneurs who made their living selling religious idols and other religious paraphernalia at the many shrines. Muhammad's message proclaiming monotheism and denouncing idolatry aroused hostility among the Meccans, and in the year 622 Muhammad and a few followers fled to the more hospitable climate of Medina. This flight (*hijra*) begins the Muslim lunar calendar.

In Medina, Muhammad became governor, judge and general, acquiring a large following among the townspeople and rural tribesmen. He later returned to conquer Mecca and unify the Arabs for the first time, successfully redirecting allegiance from tribal loyalty to Islam. His government was based on the laws of God, which envision an Islamic community (*umma*) ruled and governed by God. No man is superior to another; all are subservient. The army is the army of God, as are all governmental institutions. There is no legislature—God's laws have already been legislated. Man only applies the law.

By the time of Muhammad's death in 632, the form and structure of Islam had been established. His revelations were recorded in the Quran and his own exemplary conduct noted by his followers. His opinions and decisions are called *hadith*, or traditions, although it took more than two centuries to check and verify all of these (and some are not accepted yet by various Muslims). The group of *hadith* is called the *sunna*. Those who accept the most commonly recognized *sunna* are called Sunni (Sunnite) Muslims.

In the name of Allah, Muslim Arab armies captured Jerusalem and Damascus and fought northward into Central Asia, converting as they went. Others conquered North Africa and Spain. By the year 900 Arabs ruled from Cordoba and Casablanca in the west to Samarkand and Kabul in the east. Islam had become established.

Islam, like Judaism and Christianity, is based on three elements. One is revelation. God's word was "revealed" to Muhammad and is now recorded in 114 chapters (*suras*) in the Quran. These revelations are parables and stories which parallel those of the Old and New Testaments.

A second element is the confessional (*shahada*) that there is only one God, who "does not beget, nor is he begotten. . . and there is like unto him no one" (*sura* 112). To Sunni Muslims the Christian concept of the Trinity (the union of God, Christ and the Holy Ghost in one Godhead) is unacceptable, although Muslims believe in the virgin birth of Jesus. This does not mean that there is not a host of supernatural creatures. Islam recognizes angels and good and bad *jinns* (creatures of God) as well as the Devil (Iblis).

The third element of Islam is the body of duties a believer must perform, laws he must follow in order to be a good Muslim and so enter paradise. On the Day of Judgment, God will weigh one's good and bad actions (which are recorded during one's lifetime in the Book of Deeds) and decide a person's final destination, Heaven or Hell.

The four principal duties for Muslims are to pray, to give alms, to fast, and to make a pilgrimage to Mecca if possible. These four duties, plus the confessional, constitute what is called the Five Pillars of Islam. All Muslims, whatever their sect, ethnic group, or place of residence, accept these basic duties, although they may differ in the details or degree of performing them.

Prayer, *salat*, is the supreme duty, performed in a simple, disciplined ritual. While most Muslims recognize the obligation of five prayers a day, others limit them to three a day. One prays directly to God without intermediaries, while facing Mecca. Formal Islam does not recognize the role of saints as intercessors. Prayer also involves the cleansing of the body (ablutions), especially on Fridays, the chief day of prayer.

Almsgiving, *zakat*, calls for an annual payment of an alms tax for the poor. Voluntary charity, *sadakat*, increases one's chances of going to Heaven.

Fasting, the personal sacrifice to demonstrate one's faith, is in Islam a month-long ordeal performed in the ninth Muslim month, Ramadan. Among several rules the primary one is to refrain from eating or drinking from sunrise to sunset.

To make the pilgrimage, the Haj, to Mecca (during the month of Dhu al Hijja) is the dream of all Muslims. For those who make it and perform the rituals at the Kaaba (a large stone considered holy since the days of Abraham), the experience reinforces not only the faith but the pilgrims' awareness of the community nature of Islam. Pilgrims call themselves *hajji* and gain prestige when they return home.

A further duty, sometimes considered one of the pillars, is *jihad*, meaning "exertion" but often called holy war, whereby a Muslim must protect the faith, overcome nonbelievers and purify the practices of those who have fallen away. Various Muslim leaders on their own authority have conducted *jihad* in the past, such as Uthman dan Fodio, who led the Fulani against the Hausa in Nigeria in 1802. Other *jihad* have been called against the Allies in World War I and against Israel in 1967.

Islam, like Judaism, is a religion of laws so comprehensive that it has rules for nearly all human activity, personal and interpersonal. It sets forth rules for government, fighting wars and settling disputes. It decrees who not to marry and what foods not to eat. There being no area of activity not covered by law, there is no accommodation in theory for a separate secular, as against religious, jurisdiction.

Islamic law is called Shariah (*sharia* or *shariat*), meaning "the straight path." It derives in varying degrees from four sources, the primary one being the Quran, recognized as supreme by all Muslims. Second is the *sunna*, the collection of *hadith*, traditions and sayings of Muhammad, about which there are disagreements. Third is the body of opinions, *qiyas*, determined by jurists whose decisions on various cases were based on analogous elements in preceding cases. A fourth source is *ijma*, the consensus of a group of judges representing the community.

The Shariah is administered by religious courts, classically the only courts in a Muslim society. The *ulama* is a group of judges who make the legal interpretations for the community, and the laws are then applied by the individual judge or *qadi* (sometimes spelled *qazi*). A superior judge is called a *mufti*.

Not all laws require the same degree of observance. Islam recognizes five categories of obedience ranging from that which is obligatory (such as prayer) to that which is forbidden (such as incest and alcohol). Between are those which are desirable, optional or objectionable. Among these are the ritual slaughter of animals (desirable) and slavery (objectionable).

With such a comprehensive body of laws and a variety of sources and categories of observance, it is not surprising that there are a number of interpretations of the Shariah. In the early days of Islam, fighting between proponents of one or another interpretation or school of law (*madhabb*) was not unusual. Each school placed different emphasis on the four sources of the Shariah, none, of course, denying the primacy of the Quran.

Four schools of law, sometimes referred to as "rites," have retained their influence to the present. Each is identified with its founder.

The most widespread *madhabb* (because it was promoted by the Ottoman Turks) is the Hanafi, founded by Abu Hanifa (d. 767). The Hanafi school places a relatively liberal interpretation on the Quran and emphasizes the *qiya*, utilization of reason and analogy. For instance, Hanafi judges permit marriage of a Muslim male to a Christian or Jewish female (but not to a Shia Muslim). Followers of the Hanafi predominate in Turkey and Central Asia.

Al-Shafi (d. 829) also applied a more liberal interpretation and stressed consensus (*ijma*) and the prerogative of the community through the *ulama*. His school, which does not permit Muslim and non-Muslim marriage, has many followers in lower Egypt, western and southern Arabia, East Africa and Indonesia.

Malik ibn Anas (d. 795) founded a judicial system based essentially on the *hadith* with only limited use of *ijma*. The Maliki school finds adherents in North and West Africa, upper Egypt and the Sudan.

The Hanbali school is the most conservative and is found only in central Arabia. Ahmad ibn Hanbal (d. 855) rejected all innovation beyond the literal Quran and *sunna*, admitting personal interpretation only in cases of absolute necessity.

Each of the four founder-jurists is credited by Muslims with competence to formulate an application of the Shariah. Each school is thus held equally valuable, and divergences among them are considered to be matters of practice rather than principle. The orthodox Muslim is free to adopt any one of the systems for himself.

There is today no central authority in Islam for interpreting or enforcing the Shariah, nor has there been since the day of Muhammad and his caliphs (representatives), although there have been many claimants. Political and ecclesiastical divisions within the Muslim world have left to local leadership the responsibility of pursuing the ideals of Islam. At the lowest level, leadership resides with the individual religious cleric, who may or may not have formal training and may or may not be part of a formal clerical structure within a country. He is important in Muslim life, for he lives among the mass of Muslims, rural and urban, influencing their lives and representing their religion. He is often the only person in the community who can read and write.

Among Arabs, the cleric is known as a *faqi* or *shaikh*, sometimes *imam*, although some *imams* and *shaikhs* rise to considerable prestigious heights as heads of great mosques. Among Turks, the major cleric is called a *hoja* (*hoca*); among Persians and northern Indians and Pakistanis, a *mullah*. The Javanese call him *penghulu*; the Chinese, *ahong*; and in West Africa he is known as *mallam*. The North and West African *marabout* has the additional distinction of possessing exceptional spiritual powers, *baraka*. All perform the traditional functions of presiding at prayers, births, circumcisions, weddings, divorces, funerals and festivals. For their services, they receive compensation from their followers or, if in a country ruled by the strong Islamic government, from the government (as in Indonesia).

With the development of nation-states in the past century, administration of the Shariah is on a country-by-country basis. Each Muslim-majority country has its own *ulama* and system of clerics, and each has its own conflict between the roles of secular and religious law. Perhaps the only remaining prominent source of religious authority in the Sunni world is the group of scholars at Al Azhar University in Cairo, the oldest religious educational institution in the world.

Modernization of the Shariah, if indeed, as some believe, it needs modernizing, is the goal of few scholars. For most Muslims, innovation is synonymous with heresy—the Shariah as revealed by Muhammad cannot be "updated." Those who speak out for change find no channel of communications open to them. In each country, the Shariah is observed, placated or ignored. In the Soviet Union it is ignored; Soviet secular law is supreme and exclusive. In Turkey, some laws are ignored (polygyny is illegal but still practiced), and some placated (no pork is served in Muslim restaurants). In Saudi Arabia, where the influence of the eighteenth-century fundamentalist reformer, Muhammad abdu Wahhab, remains strong, Shariah is the law of the land, as it is in Iran. Most Muslim-majority countries accept two sets of laws: secular, which presumably does not infringe on the Shariah; and religious, which presumably does not greatly inhibit economic and social change.

Major events in Muslim life are the festivals and commemorations related to Islam. While they serve their function of affirming the dedication of the believer, they also help in relieving the monotony of village life. First in importance is the celebration of Ibrahim's offer to sacrifice his son, Ishmael (not Isaac as Christians and Jews believe), to God. It occurs on the tenth day of the twelfth Muslim month of Dhul Hijdja and is called Id al Adha (Sacrificial Feast) or Id al Kabir (Great Festival) in Arab countries, Bakr Id in India and Kurban Bayram in Turkey. Public prayers are held and animals are sacrificed.

A second important festival comes on the first night after the end of the fasting month of Ramadan. Called Little Id or Id al Fitr (Break the Fast), Id al Saghir (Minor Festival) or Şeker Bayram (Candy Holiday, among Turks), it is time for celebration, as Muslims don their finest clothes, exchange gifts and attend public prayer.

Other universal commemorations include Maulud al-Nabi, the birthday of the Prophet on the twelfth day of the third Muslim month of Rabi' al Awwal; Lailat al Qadr (Night of Power) on the twenty-seventh day of Ramadan, the date God first revealed his messages to Muhammad; and Lailat al Miraj, the night (in the month of Rajab) Muhammad died and ascended to Heaven.

All Muslims accept the *shahada*, the revelation of the Quran and most of the *sunna*. Some, however, and they number perhaps 10 percent of the Muslim population, disagree with the Sunni majority on certain aspects of theological interpretation and practice.

Sunnis believe that Muhammad's successors as leaders of the faithful, caliphs, were to be elected from among the Prophet's closest followers. On Muhammad's death, most of these followers selected Abu Bakr (Muhammad had married Abu Bakr's teenaged daughter, thus confirming a tradition of child marriage). Others objected on the grounds that leadership should fall to Ali, who was Muhammad's cousin and also husband of his daughter, Fatima. This was the beginning of the Shiat Ali, the Partisans of Ali, today called Shia or Shiites.

Abu Bakr was succeeded as caliph by Umar and then, following his assassination, by Uthman, Muhammad's cousin and a member of the Umayyid tribe. Uthman also was murdered (in 655), and Ali finally achieved leadership. He, too, was murdered nearly five years later. The Sunni mantle fell on the house of Umayyid, whose leader, Muawaiya, established his caliphate in Damascus. Warfare between the forces of the Sunni caliphs and the followers of Ali created a schism between the two sects which continues today.

Shiism is the major divergent sect of Islam, although Shias say that the Sunnis are the divergent ones. The heart of Shiism is the Imamate, the belief that the Divine Knowledge and Light that God granted to Muhammad continued—and continues—through a number of pure and sinless leaders, called Imams (not to be confused with an *imam*, a religious functionary). Behind this notion is the belief that there is an esoteric, hidden meaning to the Quran, inner mysteries which only a person with Divine Knowledge can understand.

Shias believe that Muhammad passed this Divine Knowledge to his cousin, Ali, a pious and beloved follower, and that Ali should have been the first caliph. As it turned out, Ali became the third caliph. After Ali was assassinated ("martyred," to the Shias), his son Hasan became Imam, only to be poisoned ("martyred") ten years later. The Imamate passed to Ali's other son, Hussain, who was killed ("martyred") at Karbala (in what is now Iraq) 11 years later. Hussain (and his family and followers) were massacred by troops of Yazid, the son (and eventual successor) of the Umayyid caliph, Muawaiya. Hussain was succeeded by his son, and for most Shias this succession continued until the twelfth Imam, who went into occultation in A.D. 939. Those Shias who accept this succession are called Imamis, Ithna Ashari, or Twelvers. They believe that the twelfth Imam will return as the Mahdi (Messiah) to institute divine rule on earth. Meanwhile, temporal authority for interpreting the religion or assuring that Islam's laws are being observed rests in the hands of highly educated religious leaders, selected from the *ulama*, called *ayatollahs*. Imami Shias are the overwhelmingly dominant sect in Iran, which in 1984 is ruled by the Ayatollah Khomeini. Iraq, where Shias are about 60 percent of the population, has a Sunni-controlled government.

While Shias accept the Quran, they recognize a *sunna* of their own, drawn not only from some of the *hadith* accepted by the Sunnis but also from the behavior and sayings of the Imams. Whereas Sunnis tend to interpret Islam in relatively legalistic and severe terms, Shias involve themselves in their religion passionately, mourning their martyrs with great emotion, particularly the death of Imam Hussain on the tenth day of the month of Muharram.

While in general Sunnis and Shias recognize the same rituals, festivals and religious practices, Shias demonstrate a number of distinctions. One of these is *taqiyya*, or dissimulation, the practice of hiding one's religion. Shias lived as minorities in a violent, intolerant world; it became acceptable to pretend to be something other than Shia just to stay alive. As described in the entry on the Qizilbash, *taqiyya* is observed today.

A second distinction among Shias is *mut'ah*, or temporary marriage, which Shias believe has Quranic validity. *Mut'ah* recognizes the need for men to satisfy their sexual urges but permits them to do so only under strict rules in order that they do not commit the sins of adultery or extramarital fornication.

In prayers, Shias include the sayings of the Imams and in certain other details differ from Sunnis. Shias also give religious justification to pilgrimages to shrines other than Mecca, such as the tombs of the Imams. Some Shias would rather make the Haj to Karbala, the center of Shiism and the tomb of Hussain, than to Mecca.

The major offshoot of the Shias occurred over the identity of the seventh Imam. While the Twelvers accepted the sixth Imam's youngest son, Musa, as successor, a smaller group accepted his eldest son, Ismail (who died while his father still lived). The Ismailis, called Seveners, then split over the identity of their eleventh Imam. One group followed al-Mustali, another his brother, Nizar. The Mustali Ismailis, called Bohras, believe their Imam, like that of the Twelvers, also went into hiding, to return as the Mahdi. (The Bohras are particularly numerous in western India, as described in the entry on the Maharashtrians.) The Nizari Ismailis believe the Imams must always be physically present in the world. The present living Imam is the Aga Khan, Karim, spiritual head of the Nizari Ismaili community. (As Prince Sadruddin, he also served as United Nations High Commissioner for Refugees.) A close-knit, highly organized community, Nizari Ismailis, sometimes called Khoja, are found chiefly in Pakistan,

India and East Africa (and are described in the entry on Asians in East Africa). The former Aga Khan is buried in a mausoleum on the banks of the Nile River, where nine centuries ago the Ismailis ruled the great Fatimid Empire (908–1171).

Another branch of the Shias, strongly influenced by Ismailis and also Christianity, is the Alawi (Alawites) who live along the Mediterranean coast in northern Lebanon, Syria and southern Turkey. They believe not only in the divinity of Ali but in a trinity which includes Muhammad and a Persian named Salman. Their tenets, which are mostly secret, include seven reincarnations (the number "7" has significant theological meaning to Ismailis). Alawi exclude women altogether from formal religious activity. Another departure from the usual Islamic practice is the partaking of wine during religious ceremonies. Numbering more than 1 million, they have no mosques, are usually poor sedentary farmers and maintain a tribal-like segmentary lineage system. Some Alawi have become powerful in the Baath Party of Syria (including the president of Syria in 1984, Hafez Assad).

Another group of Shias, the Zaidis, is dominant in Yemen. This group believes that the Imamate succeeded from Hussain's grandson after the Kerbala massacre and that the Imams have no supernatural (Divine Light) qualities.

Early in the controversies over the rights of succession, one group broke away from both the Sunnis and Shias (indeed, one of their members killed Ali). Called the Kharijites (Khawarij), or the Seceders, they disagreed not so much on dogma as on the degree of fervor in practicing their religion. Fiercely puritan, they believed that it was the duty of every Muslim to convert the nonbeliever and to exhort, even to kill, the backslider. Their leaders were those considered most worthy among them, elected by the community as a whole. From the eighth century they moved across North Africa in missionary fervor, converting the Berbers, in whom they infused their religious ardor. Fanaticism, however, was not in the mainstream of orthodox Muslim practice, and the Kharijites diminished in numbers. Today one Kharijite group, the more moderate but still fundamentalist Ibadis, remains active in the Mzab oases of Algeria and in Libya, on the island of Djerba in Tunisia and in Zanzibar.

Two early Ismaili sects so diverged from orthodoxy that they ceased to be Muslim. One is the Druze, who live in Lebanon, Syria and Israel. They deified one of the Fatimid rulers, rejected the Quran and developed an exclusive and largely secret doctrine with strong pre-Islamic influences. A second is the Bahai, a pacifist and ecumenical group originating in Iran, which became an independent religion in the mid-nineteenth century. It has many followers in the United States today.

The most recently evolved Muslim sect is the Ahmadiya, whose founder was Mirza Ghulam Ahmad (1835–1908), born in Qadian in the Indian Punjab. Most Ahmadis do not consider themselves a sect but followers of a contemporary interpretation of Sunni Islam, as pronounced by their founder. Other Ahmadis claim Ahmad was a true prophet, that Muhammad was the giver of perfect law, but Ahmad was the greatest interpreter of the law. Most Muslims, particularly in Pakistan, consider the Ahmadi heretical. They are barred by Saudi Arabia from making the Haj. As the entry on the Akan describes, the Ahmadiya is a modern, progressive movement in Islam, active throughout the world, but especially in West Africa. Its leaders are educated and enterprising, its followers seek modern, secular education while piously accepting the basic duties of Islam.

In the seventh and eighth centuries there developed the tradition of Muslim mysticism which came to be called Sufism, after the coarse woolen mantle, *suf*, worn by early ascetics. Emphasizing the love, rather than the fear, of Allah, the mystical movement spread rapidly, flowering in Baghdad in the last half of the ninth century. From there it spread to the farthest reaches of the Islamic world, each people and area contributing something of itself to its adopted form of Sufism.

The ultimate goal of a Sufi is to achieve direct communication with God through a series of ecstatic experiences. The *murid*, or aspirer, attempts to obtain release from illusion by awakening his inherent but dormant emotional and intuitive spiritual faculties under the guidance of a *murshid*, a preceptor, who himself has achieved communion. The *murid* may live a secular life, consulting his *murshid* on occasion, or he may commit himself entirely by joining a Sufi brotherhood, or *tariqa* (way), founded by a saint, or *pir*.

Because of Sufism's appeal to the emotions, its emphasis on direct experience of Allah and its tendency toward pirism, the movement came into early conflict with the scholasticism of the *ulama*, the Islamic jurists. Even so, Sufism and the brotherhoods flourished, primarily among the Sunnis, and today more than 70 Sufi orders survive in varying strengths (some have membership in the millions) throughout the Muslim world. They provide concrete bonds among Muslims of different ethnic groups that in some areas, such as West Africa, engage in political activity.

The major active brotherhoods of Sufism (*turuk*; sing. *tariqa*) are the Alawiyya (Algeria, Morocco, Palestine, Syria, Jordan, Aden, Ethiopia); Bektashiyya (Balkans); Bhaniyya (Egypt); Chistiyya (India, Pakistan); Darqawiyya (Morocco, Algeria, Egypt, Lebanon, Sri Lanka); Khalwatiyya (Egypt, North Africa); Madariyya (India, Pakistan); Mawlawiyya (Turkey and various parts of the former Ottoman Empire, the so-called whirling dervishes); Naqshbandiyya (throughout the Muslim world); Ni'matallahiyya (Iran); Qadiriyya (throughout the Muslim world); Rahmaniyya (Algeria); Riga'iyya (Iraq, Syria, Egypt); Sanusiyya (Arabia and North Africa, especially Libya); Shadhiliyya (throughout the Muslim world); Shattariyya (India, Bangladesh, Malaysia, Indonesia); Suhrawardiyya (Iraq, Afghanistan, Pakistan, India, Bangladesh); Mourid and Tijaniyya (North and West Africa, Sudan).

Islam imposes, or at least sanctions, a number of social values, institutions and practices which are found throughout the Muslim world, although as the entries in this survey show, not without some inconsistencies. Many of these elements existed in pre-Islamic Arabia and exist today among non-Muslims and thus do not require the convert to abandon significantly his basic beliefs and practices in order to become a Muslim.

Chief among Muslim values are piety and equality of male believers. To these might be added a strong sense of honor and a commitment to hospitality to friends and strangers alike.

Islam has traditionally exalted the role of the male in society, although the Shariah requires that this role be played compassionately and fairly. The traditional Muslim family is patriarchal, the eldest male having full authority to make decisions for the good of all. Descent is traced patrilineally through the father; this system is protected by an inheritance procedure which assures that sons receive the lion's share of the father's wealth.

The position of women in Islam is inferior to that of the male, yet it is far superior to their position among animists prior to the coming of Islam. In Arabia, Islam stopped the common practice of female infanticide, reduced the multiplicity of legal wives to four, and stipulated that each wife must be treated equally. The Hanafi school requires that a husband offer his wife freedom if he marries a second wife or if he stays away from home too long. In addition Islam granted women the right to own their own property (there is no community property in Islam) and inherit property (at one-half the amount received by the sons).

Deep concern for the sexual purity of their daughters and the constancy of their wives prompts Muslim men to guard the women in their family, a custom sanctioned by the Quran. Techniques of guarding vary with the traditions of the ethnic groups and conditions of environment. Except in more modern cities, women are secluded in the home (*purdah*), and in some areas, particularly in South and Southwest Asia, women veil themselves when they are outside the home.

Marriage in Islam is a contractual affair whereby the rights and duties of each partner are spelled out in detail and theoretically approved by each before witnesses. The contract usually involves the bridegroom (or his family) promising money, animals or goods to the bride (*mahr*, sometimes called bridewealth or brideprice) and making other agreements to care for her in return for her joining his family and raising his children. Marriage contracts may also spell out conditions for taking a second wife, separation, and divorce.

The Quran does not designate whom a man may marry, only whom he may not marry, such as sisters and milk kin (those nursed by the same wet nurse). Custom gives preference to such endogamous marriages as cross- or parallel-cousin marriage (father's brother's offspring or mother's brother's offspring). Cousin marriage is practiced more among ethnic groups of the Middle East than in Africa or Southeast Asia. Extended endogamy may apply to marriage within the clan, the tribe, the village, the occupational caste, the religious sect or the ethnic group. Exogamy (marriage outside the group) is practiced by many ethnic groups which are wholly or partly Muslim and is increasing among urban Muslims.

Muslim tradition, not ordained by Shariah and not observed among all ethnic groups, calls for patrilocal or virilocal residence for bride and groom. Generally it can be expected that Muslim newlyweds will move into the home of the groom's parents or at least live nearby. They will remain there as part of the patriarchal family until the father dies or the compound or village becomes so overcrowded that some must move away. This custom becomes increasingly difficult to observe in cities.

Other Muslim traditions widespread among the ethnic groups include circumcision of male children (only rarely female as well), a practice not mentioned in the Quran but carried forward from pre-Islamic times. Muslim dietary laws follow the Old Testament and include ritual slaughter of animals and not eating pork.

Folk Islam, followed by rural Muslims, contains many more traditions which lack Quranic sanction. An almost universal custom is the placing of a blue bead on a child's head to protect it from the evil eye or the wearing of amulets with words inscribed from the Quran. Blood from a sacrificial animal is often considered to have curing powers. The burial of a newborn child's placenta is an important aspect in Arab and Jabarti folk culture. And even among urban Muslims, some women hang handkerchief hammocks on sacred trees in the courtyard of a mosque in hopes that they or their daughters will become pregnant.

As Islam spread among the many ethnic groups, it encountered a variety of customs which were treated by the people as law. As long as these customary laws (called *adat*) did not conflict directly with Shariah, Muslim proselytizers made little effort to change them. Today in nearly all Muslim societies there is both *adat* and Shariah, as best described in the entries on the ethnic groups of Indonesia.

The entries of this survey show two trends in Islam. One is the expansion of the religion, particularly in Africa, where conversion from animism to Islam is proceeding rapidly. A second trend is the increase in orthodoxy. The transistor radio brings information from the outside world into once relatively isolated Muslim communities. New roads facilitate the importation of ideas as well as goods into small villages from the cities. National independence has fostered growing political activity so that villagers become more knowledgeable. There is a growing sense of Muslim community among the Meo of India and the Maguindanao of the Philippines, the Diola of Senegal and the Batak of Indonesia. With this new feeling of membership and new awareness of the urban world has come an appreciation of Muslim orthodoxy. Many are abandoning their nonorthodox practices and adhering more closely to a common way of Muslim living.

This study emphasizes patterns of living rather than an analysis of Islam, but from the evidence presented there does not appear to be a trend away from religion. There is evidence that more young urban Muslims, both male and female, are attending secular schools, that national societies are becoming more secular as they become more industrialized, that urban kin ties are becoming weaker and that urban women are becoming freer. This evidence, however, does not include either the abandonment of Islam on the one hand or a significant reinterpretation of Islam on the other. If anything, religious reformers today seek fundamentalism and neo-orthodoxy, not liberalism.

***

This survey of the Muslim world is designed primarily for the English-speaking nonspecialist, whether academician or layman. As such, it has limitations which need explanation.

An author or editor faces innumerable decisions when transliterating into English words originating in a language written in a non-Latin alphabet. The English spelling of words relating to Islam presents a particular problem when this spelling varies among scholars of so many different ethnic groups. Most of the words derive from Arabic and Persian, which are written in their own rather than Latin script. These words then come into English from another language, say Turkish, which has its own modified Latin alphabet.

One alternative is to follow the transliteration of Arabic scholars, but this involves a myriad of diacritical markings, which tend to confuse more than help the general reader. Another is to follow the transliteration of ethnic group specialists, but this involves a variety of spellings for the same word, also somewhat confusing.

This survey follows another course, that of using simplified English spelling with few diacritical marks as close as possible to actual pronunciation, with ethnic variations shown in parentheses. The object is to make an extensive survey as readable to as many people as possible, and the chief aim is consistency. Each bibliography contains entries with the more scholarly spellings.

The bibliographies concentrate on works related to current patterns of living— the theme of this survey. Materials published within the framework of a narrower academic discipline—history, economics, political science, linguistics—are largely omitted on the assumption that they can be found readily in the library or are included in the bibliographies of the entries given.

Statistics can sometimes be a guessing game with no referee. When considering the number of Muslims in a subgroup of an African tribe, one person's thousand may be another's million. In societies where census taking is a new art, population estimates of Muslims are haphazard at best. Yet this survey attempts to establish at least relative group memberships on a country-to-country basis, drawing on a variety of sources.

Country populations mostly are those given by the Population Reference Bureau, Inc., of Washington, D.C. The breakdown of ethnic group populations in the various countries derives from a number of sources: government census figures when ethnic groups are identified (which is seldom); ethnic group studies by specialists; U.S government foreign area handbooks; U.S. Department of State "Background Notes"; and for Africa, *Black Africa: A Comparative Handbook*, edited by D. G. Morrison et al. (New York: Free Press, 1972). Considerable use was made of *The World Christian Encyclopedia*, edited by David B. Barrett (New York: Oxford University Press, 1982). Where population figures are dated, they have been made current by identifying percentages of country populations, modified in some cases by known growth rates (generally relatively high among Muslims).

The number of people who adhere to Islam in any ethnic group is often a guess. First, Muslim communities do not have organized, officially recognized "churches" with membership lists. Second, in some countries, particularly in Africa, conversion is a continuing process, with Islam finding adherents in nearly every ethnic group. For example, in Nigeria the Hausa are almost completely Muslim, while the Yoruba are only partly so. The national census provides no clear indication of the extent of Islamization. Third, there are millions of Muslims in the Soviet Union who may have been born of Muslim parents but disclaim any religion. In this study, it is assumed that traditional Muslim groups, such as the Kazakhs, Uzbek and Daghestanis, remain 100 percent Muslim.

The results of these population studies appear in appendixes 1 and 2 of this survey. They show what a wide variety of people inhabit the Muslim world. As Malcolm X noted after his visit to Mecca in 1964, "I saw all *races*, all *colors*—blue-eyed blonds to black-skinned Africans—in *true* brotherhood! In unity! Living as one! Worshipping as one!"

BIBLIOGRAPHY

Books

Bates, Daniel G., and Rassam, Amal. *Peoples and Cultures of the Middle East*. Englewood Cliffs, N.J.: Prentice-Hall, 1983.

Berger, Morroe. *The Arab World Today*. Garden City, N.Y.: Doubleday, 1962.

Brockelmann, Carl. *History of the Islamic Peoples*. Translated by Joel Carmichael and Moshe Perlmann. New York: Capricorn Books, 1960.

Broeck, Jan O. M., and Webb, John W. *A Geography of Mankind*. New York: McGraw-Hill, 1968.

Coon, Carleton. *Caravan: The Story of the Middle East*. New York: Holt, Rinehart and Winston, 1951.

Gaudefroy-Demombynes, Maurice. *Muslim Institutions*. London: Allen & Unwin, 1950.

Gellner, Ernest. *Muslim Society*. Cambridge: Cambridge University Press, 1981.

Gibb, H.A.R. *Mohammedanism*. London: Oxford University Press, 1949.

———— et al., eds. *The Encyclopedia of Islam*. Leiden: Brill, 1960.

Greenberg, Joseph H. *The Languages of Africa*. Bloomington: Indiana University Press, 1966.

Guillaume, Alfred. *Islam*. Rev. ed. Baltimore: Penguin Books, 1956.

Hunter, Guy. *Modernizing Peasant Societies*. New York: Oxford University Press, 1969.

Johnson, Douglas L. *The Nature of Nomadism: A Comparative Study of Pastoral Migrations in Southwestern Asia and Northern Africa*. Chicago: University of Chicago, Department of Geography, 1969.

Kritzeck, James, and Lewis, William H., eds. *Islam in Africa*. New York: Van Nostrand-Reinhold, 1969.

Levy, Reuben. *The Social Structure of Islam*. Cambridge: The University Press, 1969.

Little, Malcolm. *The Autobiography of Malcolm X*. New York: Grove Press, 1965.

Murdock, George P. *Africa: Its People and Their Culture History*. New York: McGraw-Hill, 1959.

Redfield, R. *Peasant Society and Culture*. Chicago: University of Chicago Press, 1956.

Stoddard, Philip H.; Cuthell, David C.; and Sullivan, Margaret W. *Change and the Muslim World*. Syracuse: Syracuse University Press, 1982.

Tabataba'i, Muhammad Husayn. *Shi'ite Islam*. Albany: State University of New York Press, 1982.

von Grunebaum, G. E., ed. *Unity and Variety in Muslim Civilization*. Chicago: University of Chicago Press, 1955.

MAPS SHOWING LOCATION OF MUSLIM GROUPS

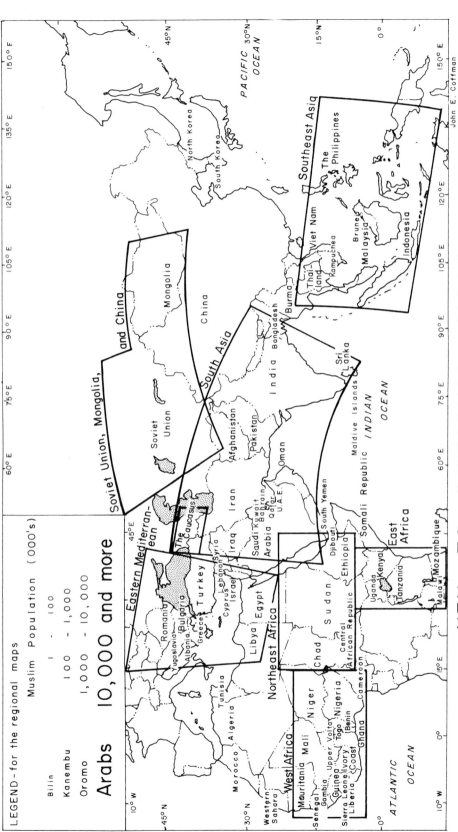

KEY TO REGIONAL MAPS

LEGEND – for the regional maps

Muslim Population (000's)

Bilin   1 – 100

Kanembu   100 – 1,000

Oromo   1,000 – 10,000

Arabs   10,000 and more

Soviet Union, Mongolia, and China

Eastern Mediterranean

South Asia

Southeast Asia

Northeast Africa

West Africa

East Africa

John E. Coffman

EASTERN MEDITERRANEAN

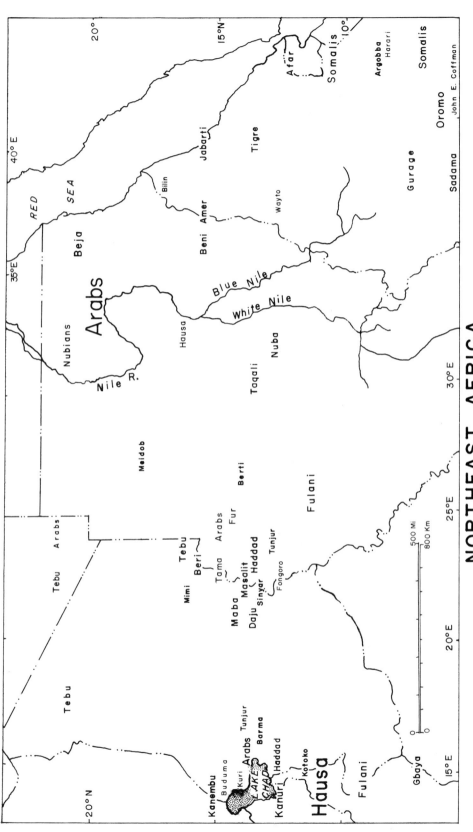

NORTHEAST AFRICA

John E. Coffman

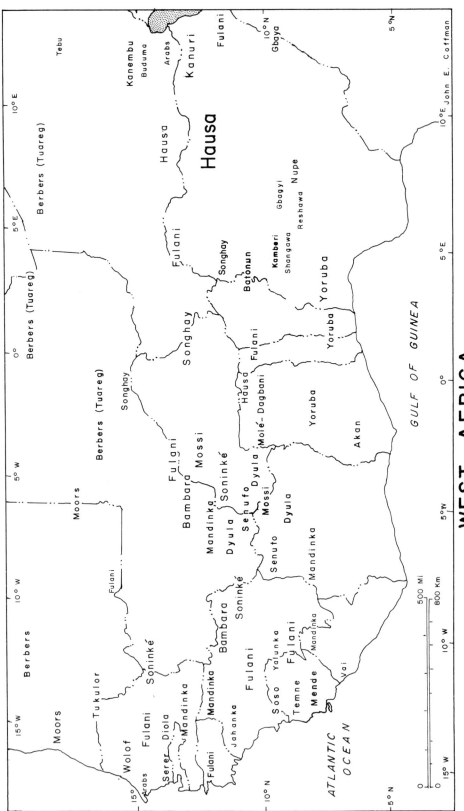

WEST AFRICA

John E. Coffman

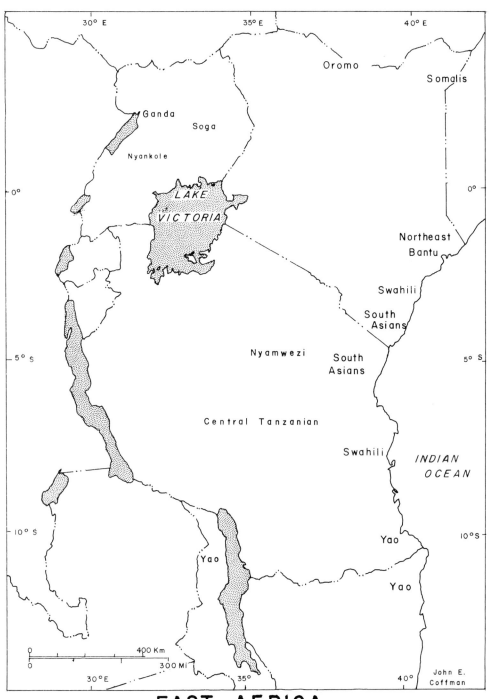

Oromo

Somalis

Ganda
Soga

Nyankole

*LAKE
VICTORIA*

Northeast
Bantu

Swahili

South
Asians

Nyamwezi

South
Asians

Central Tanzanian

Swahili

*INDIAN
OCEAN*

Yao

Yao

Yao

Yao

30° E   35° E   40° E

0°

5° S

10° S

0°

5° S

10°S

400 Km

300 Mi

30°E   35°   40°

John E.
Coffman

EAST AFRICA

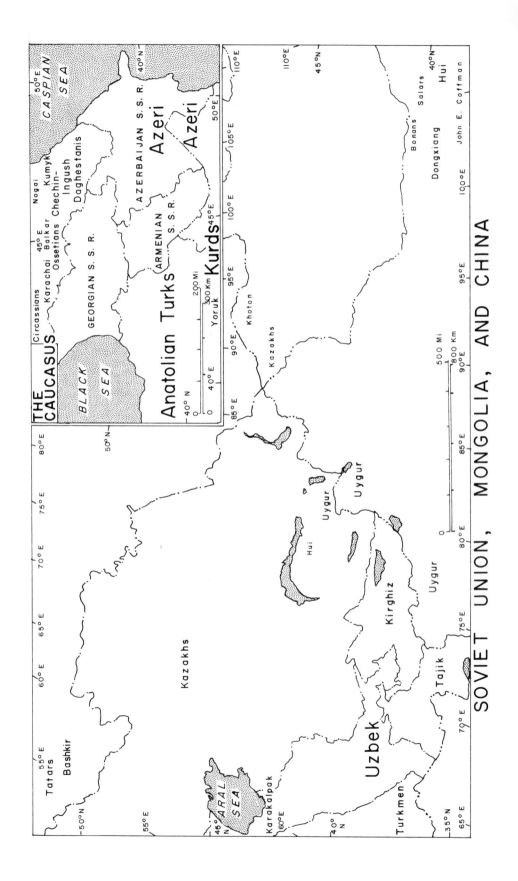

THE CAUCASUS

CASPIAN SEA

50° E

40° N

Nogai

Kumyk

Kabar Chechin-

Karachai Ingush

Circassians Ossetians Daghestanis

45° E

GEORGIAN S. S. R.

AZERBAIJAN S. S. R.

Azeri

BLACK SEA

ARMENIAN S. S. R.

40° N

50° N

Azeri

Anatolian Turks

Kurds

Yoruk 45° E

0   100   200 Mi

0   100   200   300 Km

50° E

Tatars

Bashkir

55° E

60° E

65° E

70° E

75° E

80° E

85° E

90° E

95° E

100° E

105° E

110° E

40° N

45° N

40°N

Hui

Salars

Bonans

Dongxiang

John E. Coffman

100° E

Kazakhs

Khoton

Kazakhs

Uygur

Uygur

Uygur

Uygur

Kirghiz

Tajik

Uzbek

Turkmen

Karakalpak

ARAL SEA

50° N

45° N

40° N

35° N

50° E

55° E

60° E

65° E

0   500 Mi

0   800 Km

80° E   85° E   90° E

SOVIET UNION, MONGOLIA, AND CHINA

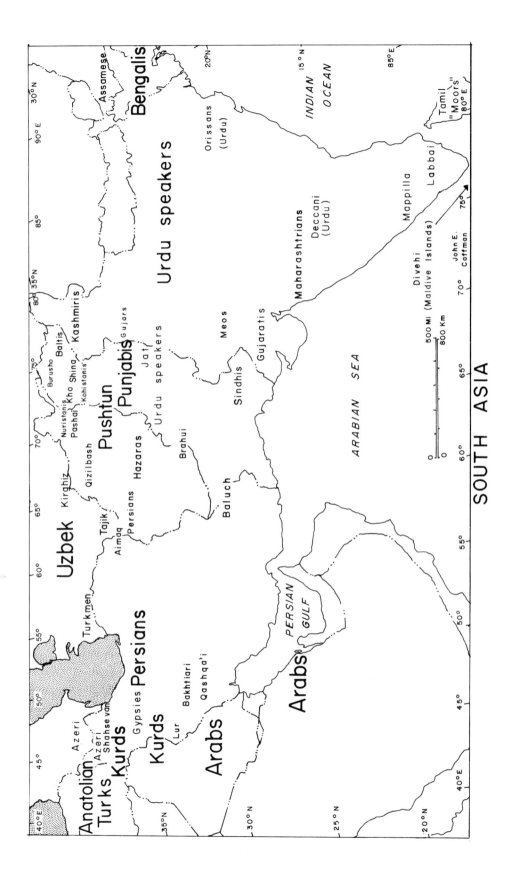

SOUTH ASIA

John E. Coffman

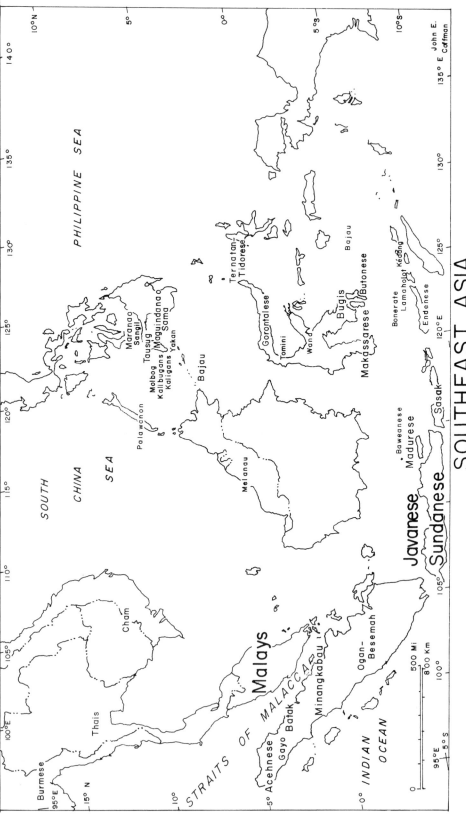

SOUTHEAST ASIA

Muslim Peoples

A

ACEHNESE   Adherence to Islam is perhaps the primary factor in a person's self-identification as Acehnese, one of the indigenous peoples of the northernmost part of the island of Sumatra in Indonesia. This devotion to the religion takes precedence over language and custom (*adat*).

The Acehnese or Ureung Aceh (pronounced ''Atcheh'') number more than 2.6 million and dominate the province of Daerah Istimewa Aceh, which includes the islands of Pulo Weh and Simeulue. Other ethnic groups in the area are the Alas and Gayo, who live in the mountainous central and southeastern regencies of the province (see Gayo). There are other small groups throughout the region, many brought to Aceh via the government's transmigration program to relieve population pressures elsewhere in the country.

Awareness of other Indonesian ethnic groups is low, except in the area where Aceh borders on the province of North Sumatra. Acehnese opinion of the Batak who live there is particularly low, as many Batak are Christian and eat pork (see Batak). People from the city of Medan are considered to be crude and the source of thievery and prostitution.

The Acehnese language has been classifed as Austronesian and seems to be related to Cham (see Cham). Acehnese, however, has been strongly influenced by Malay, which was used both as a court language and the language of trade. Modern Indonesian, Bahasa Indonesia, which is taught in schools and is the language of official discourse, continues this trend. While Acehnese lives as a spoken language, most people communicate readily in Indonesian as well.

As in many Indonesian languages, ideas of social status differences are expressed in the language. However, unlike Sundanese or Javanese, these distinctions are only made in the choice of pronouns (see Javanese).

Acehnese adhere strongly to traditional values. They often do not distinguish between Islamic and pre-Islamic ideas. Behavior which can clearly be shown to antedate Islam is often considered to have been initiated by persons who introduced Islam into a particular area. In this way the traditional behavioral code (*adat*) and the Islamic way have become almost completely merged. Modernist

Islamic movements, such as the Muhammadiya, have since the 1930s been trying, with varying success, to purify Islam.

Much of the Acehnese *adat* is said to have been initiated by Sultan Iskandar Muda (1607–1636), although in reality he only codified certain state regulations. As elsewhere in Indonesia, the *adat* aims at maintaining harmonious relations between people. There are rules governing relations in the family and in the *gampong* (village), between equals and unequals. All these rules are placed in an Islamic context. While these are all social rules, the Acehnese tend to be an individualistic people among whom conflict regularly occurs. To restore harmony, a ceremony (*sayam*) is performed in which those directly involved in the conflict as well as their relatives are made to restore the peace between them. The emphasis in this ceremony is on community harmony rather than on individual retribution.

In urban centers and other areas influenced by modern development, these values of harmony, *adat* and Shariah (Islamic law) still hold. But they are modified by the individualizing effects of a monetary economy, the increased anonymity (and personal freedom) which urban life allows and a more "modernist" or reformed interpretation of Islam free from syncretic and traditional restrictions. From this urban group have come the leaders—political and religious—of Aceh, men who adapt to secular education and the other paraphernalia of development.

Islam (Sunni) seems to have arrived in the area about the middle of the twelfth century, although there is speculation that it may have arrived as early as the seventh century, when Chinese sources indicate the presence of "Arab" settlements on the west coast of Sumatra. It is, however, an arguable point whether such a presence can be interpreted as Islamic influence, if indeed these outsiders themselves were Muslims.

The kingdom of Pasai (1270) appears to have been Islamic, although the Hikayat Raja Raja Pasai (Chronicle of the Kings of Pasai) still shows considerable Hindu influence in this kingdom. From Pasai, Islam spread to other parts of Aceh. The first sultan of Aceh appeared in the sixteenth century. His sultanate has been characterized as a harbor kingdom in which the sultan controlled the port region but the hinterland was in the hands of his *uleë-balangs* (lords). In the early seventeenth century Sultan Muda unified Aceh and incorporated into it the area of Pidië, which until that time had either dominated Aceh or been independent of it. This was Aceh's golden age. After the surrender of the last sultan, Tuanku Muhamad Dawud, to the Dutch in 1903, the state underwent a steady decline.

European influence was first felt in the sixteenth century with the arrival of the Portuguese (ca. 1509) and the Dutch (ca. 1599). By 1601 Dutch influence prevailed, although Holland's relationship with Aceh never became stable. As the Acehnese resisted colonization, a state of war continued officially until 1903, although in reality conditions remained turbulent long after.

At the beginning of World War II, Acehnese leaders actively invited the

Japanese with the aim of using them to drive out the Dutch. Soon, however, disenchantment arose with the Japanese as well. After the war, Acehnese were semi-autonomous, although in theory they were part of the Republic of Indonesia, which declared its independence on August 17, 1945. After the traditional leaders, some of whom had sided with the Dutch, were killed or driven out in what is known as the Cumbok affair, and until sovereignty was transferred, Aceh was governed by Islamic leaders such as Daud Beureueh. Until 1961 conditions in Aceh remained unstable as various factions vied for influence and power in the area. In 1961 Aceh was recognized as a special area and designated Daerah Istimewa Aceh by the government of Indonesia.

Acehnese generally live in villages, which are also called *meunasah* (prayer houses) because each village has at least one. In the past a mosque would be built centrally to several villages. The village head (*keuchik*) is assisted in the administration of the village by a scribe, religious leaders such as the *imeum meunasah* (the person in charge of the *meunasah* activities), four or five elders (*tuha peut* or *tuha pakat*) and the man in charge of the LKMD, an official organization looking after the general welfare of the village. These men are in charge of day-to-day affairs and village development. They also settle disputes, coordinate agricultural activities in conjunction with the *kecamatan* (district government) and mediate between the villagers and the government.

The function of the *tuha peut* is quite formalized. This group should ideally consist of experts in agriculture, religion and *adat*. They are the primary advisors to the *keuchik* and will give advice, whether it is requested or not, whenever they feel it is necessary.

Aside from these more or less formal leaders there often are also those who because of wealth or special skills have a voice in the running of the village. Especially when conflict occurs between necessities as perceived by the villagers and the development priorities of the government, the influence of these men is often crucial.

Farming is the principal occupation of Acehnese villagers. For Aceh as a whole, according to the 1980 census, 246,550 people work their own land while 123,554 people either sharecrop or do both. A further 54,472 people are agricultural laborers. Fisheries, either in the form of fish ponds or deep sea fishing, employ 30,837 people, and 135,782 are involved in animal husbandry.

Agricultural labor is in short supply and is one of the limiting factors on the amount of land a family can farm. Because Aceh does not have a pronounced dry season, as, for instance, do parts of Java, rice cannot safely be left in the fields after harvest. Even limiting the amount of land cultivated, the farmer's harvested crop often suffers losses due to sudden rains.

One important socioeconomic pattern is the practice of men, especially those from the Pidië and Aceh Besar areas, to leave their home villages to trade and seek a different life elsewhere. The practice is called *merantau*. When a young man is married it is expected that he will do this during the first year of his marriage. These men return home only occasionally, mostly during the holidays.

Merantau involves the Acehnese in the money economy and is an important source of cash. As elsewhere in Indonesia, cash is in short supply in the villages. To supplement their income from rice farming, people engage in small trade, handicrafts or services. Nonetheless, mechanization is coming to Acehnese agriculture. In some areas land is now plowed by large tractors, it being cheaper for the farmer to pay the tractor operator and repair the bunds to his rice field than to pay a crew of laborers.

The Acehnese recognize ascending and descending relatives to the seventh generation. They distinguish between paternal (*wali*) and maternal (*karong*) relatives, each group having distinct rights and duties vis-à-vis any particular person. Post-marital residence, with some minor exceptions, is matrilocal, a pattern which creates a localized group of related women which by its nature forms the female core of an individual's *karong*. (The *wali* here should not be confused with the Islamic concept of *wali*—guardian—as this involves a much wider range of individuals.)

Early writers recognized a patrilineal descent pattern in the *kawom*, a grouping primarily involved in matters of security, revenge and conflict. More recently bilateral descent has been shown to exist in certain areas with a strong position of women. The *kawom* seems to have lost its significance as only traces of its existence can now be found. Although it is not completely clear, the *kawom* may well have merged with the *wali*.

Given the distinction between the *wali* and the *karong*, it could be argued that Acehnese descent is reckoned bilineally with the *wali* and the *karong* performing distinct functions. As such it would conform to the more general Indonesian pattern of female-inside, male-outside. Security and revenge, functions of the old *kawom*, are typically matters taking place outside the home. Child care and housekeeping are the responsibilities of the woman. In the case of the death of the father, continued care of the children tends to fall to the mother and her relatives, the children's *karong*, even though according to Islamic rules this ought to be performed by the *wali*, the father's relatives.

The basic kin group is the nuclear family. After marriage the couple usually lives with the bride's parents until one or even two children have been born. The bride's parents will, if possible, at this point build a house for their daughter or help the groom in the construction of one. The youngest daughter inherits her parent's house. When she has a family, her parents give her the house and take up residence in the kitchen.

Demands of modern occupations are introducing neolocal residence, especially in the urban centers. While this gives the man a greater amount of financial security, it places the woman in a weaker position than she was in before, as she now loses the control she had over the agricultural land which she gained when her husband was on *merantau*.

At the age of seven, sons begin to sleep in the *meunasah*. Travelers and married men who for some reason are not spending the night with their wives sleep here also. In general men do not spend much time at home. During the

day, if they are not working, they may often be found in coffee shops, a place
not commonly frequented by women. Women's activities focus on the home to
the point where the men typically do the shopping as well.

Women run the household and are in charge of rearing the children. While a
father may fondly play with a newborn child, he has only a minimal role in the
day-to-day care of the children and is perceived as a distant figure by them.
Children approach him through their mother.

Marriage follows Islamic rules with certain *adat* taboos added to them. For
instance, in addition to the Islamic restrictions, patrilateral relatives who fall in
the *wali* category are prohibited as marriage partners for a man. In addition to
the Islamic contractual aspect of the marriage, which is performed in the *meunasah* or, depending on the social status of the couple, in the bride's home, an
adat ceremony is performed in the bride's home. This latter ceremony focuses
on, and is attended mainly by, women.

Marriage is arranged by the parents, although the children have some say in
whom they will marry. Polygyny is allowed, although it is relatively rare and
is made more difficult by the 1975 revision of the Indonesian marriage laws.

Inheritance also follows the Islamic rule of two parts to the male versus one
part to the female. Women, however, do receive the house when they are married
and, if it is plentiful, may receive a share of land as well. All this, however, is
predicated on a measure of economic welfare. Poorer women may find themselves
in dire financial straits, especially when abandoned by their husbands.

In daily life, the mother and her female relations form the context in which
the children are socialized. The father as well as males in general tend to operate
outside this context. This can be seen in the practice of sending sons off to sleep
in the *meunasah* and in the men's coffee shop. When the father does eat at home
he again has his meal in a special place.

Children are expected to be polite and obey their parents. Discipline tends to
be the mother's responsibility. If the children are excessively noisy their father
will tell the mother to do something about it. Conversely, if the child has a need,
it will approach its mother, who then conveys the request to the father. Generally,
children say that they are closer to their mother than to their father. With the
mother, they say, they have a *batin* (spiritual, or soul) connection.

This separation between the sexes is carried through to many aspects of life.
Men relax with men, while women visit female relatives and neighbors. For a
man to visit a house while the husband is absent is considered a grave breach
of etiquette which might result in a fight.

The Acehnese are known throughout Indonesia for the zealousness of their
belief in Islam. Many consider them fanatics. Most follow the Shafi juridical
rite, although younger people tend to mix rites. Aceh itself is known as Serambi
Mekah (the front porch of Mecca). The "fanaticism," however, is mostly a
matter of emphasis on the necessity of being a Muslim rather than a faithful
observance of all the tenets of the faith. Islamic duties in Aceh are often observed
in the breach. While modernist reform movements such as the Muhammadiya

have been active since the 1930s, the practices of many people, both urban and rural, are still far from the ideal espoused by the reformers. Many *adat* practices, such as visits to graves and mystical practices, continue, having been incorporated into Islamic belief. This latter phenomenon was aided by Sufism, the form in which Islam arrived in Aceh. Among South Aceh villages, the Naqshbandiyya *tariqa* (Sufi brotherhood) is the most active and is deeply involved in politics, particularly the PERTI political party.

The *ulama* (leading clerics) may exhort the faithful to shun non-Islamic practices, but the attitude of many is expressed in the story of an old men who left the mosque after the Friday prayer before the sermon was given. When asked why he was leaving, he answered that he had heard all that before. It is ironic that, while the modernist movement has produced the major Acehnese leaders, recent research shows that the villagers often still look for aspects of *keramat* (the mystical or sacred) in these leaders.

The reason for Acehnese zeal is difficult to pinpoint. In the days of the sultanate, Islam was adhered to, although the literature does not depict an especially fanatical people. This fanaticism may have arisen due to the European influence in Acehnese affairs, especially the war against the Dutch, which was declared to be a *jihad* (holy war) against the infidel. In this way the defense of Aceh as a state became fused with the protection of the faith. Thus the emphasis on Islam may well be as much an expression of a person's Acehneseness as an expression of faithful adherence to the religion.

BIBLIOGRAPHY

Books

Anderson, J. *Acheen and the Ports on the North and East Coasts of Sumatra*. London: Oxford University Press, 1971.

Boland, B. J. *The Struggle of Islam in Modern Indonesia*. Verhandelingen van het Koninklijk Instituut voor Taal-, Land- en Volkenkunde, 59. The Hague: Martinus Nijhoff, 1971.

Gibbons, D.; de Koninck, Rodolphe; and Hasan, Ibrahim. *Agricultural Modernization, Poverty and Inequality: The Distributional Impact of the Green Revolution in Regions of Malaysia and Indonesia*. Westmead: Teakfield, 1980.

Hiliry, Mas'ud. *The Role of Social and Psychological Factors on Family Size in Aceh*. SEAPRAP Research Report, 24. Singapore: Institute of Southeast Asian Studies, 1977.

Kennedy, R. *Bibliography of Indonesian Peoples and Cultures*. New Haven: Yale University Press, 1962.

Koninck, Rodolphe de. *Aceh in the Time of Iskander Muda*. SerieInformasi Aceh, 4. Banda Aceh, Indonesia: Pusat Dokumentasi dan Informasi Aceh, 1977.

LeBar, Frank M., ed. *Ethnic Groups of Insular Southeast Asia*. New Haven: Human Relations Areas Files Press, 1972.

Peacock, James L. *Indonesia: An Anthropological Perspective*. Pacific Palisades, Cal.:
    Goodyear, 1973.
Reid, Anthony. *The Blood of the People: Revolution and the End of Traditional Rule in
    Northern Sumatra*. Kuala Lumpur: Oxford University Press, 1979.
De Rijk, Pieter A. L. *The Climate and Its Implications for Agricultural Planning*. Ag-
    ricultural Sector Report, 8. Banda Aceh, Indonesia: Badan Perencanaan Pemban-
    gunan Daerah Istimewa Aceh, 1982.
Siegel, James T. "Acehnese." In *Muslim Peoples: A World Ethnographic Survey*, edited
    by Richard V. Weekes. Westport, Conn.: Greenwood Press, 1978.
————. *The Rope of God*. Berkeley: University of California Press, 1969.
————. *Shadow and Sound: The Historical Thought of a Sumatran People*. Chicago:
    University of Chicago Press, 1979.

Articles

Alfian. "The Ulama in Acehnese Society: A Preliminary Observation." *Asian Journal
    of Social Science* 3:1 (1975): 27–41.
Arif, Abdullah. "The Affairs of the Tjunbok Traitors." *Review of Indonesian and Ma-
    layan Affairs* 4/5 (1971): 29–65.
Castles, Lance and Alfian. "Some Aspects of Rural Development in Aceh." *Berita
    Antropologi* 7:24 (1975): 4–14.
Cowan, H.K.J. "An Outline of Acehnese Phonology and Morphology." *Bulletin of the
    School of Oriental and African Studies* 44:3 (1981): 522–549.
Jayawardena, Chandra. "Acehenese Marriage Customs." *Indonesia* 23 (1977): 157–173.
————. "Women and Kinship in Aceh Besar, Northern Sumatra." *Ethnology* 16:1
    (1977): 21–38.
Koninck, Rodolphe de. "The Integration of the Peasantry: Examples from Malaysia and
    Indonesia." *Pacific Affairs* 52:2 (1979): 265–293.
Reid, Anthony. "The Japanese Occupation and Rival Indonesian Elites: Northern Sumatra
    in 1942." *Journal of Asian Studies* 35:1 (1975): 49–61.
Siegel, James T. "Prayer and Play in Atjeh: A Comment on Two Paragraphs." *Indonesia*
    1 (1966): 2–21.
Sjamsuddin, Nazariddin. "The Achehnese Rebellion of 1953: Some Outlines." *Solidarity*
    10:6 (1975): 60–66.

Unpublished Manuscripts

Aziz, Muhammad. "Entrepreneurial Behavior Among Achehnese Farmers." M.A. thesis,
    University of the Philippines at Los Banos, 1973.
Bowen, John. "Land Tenure and Village Structure in Aceh." Banda Aceh, Indonesia:
    Development Alternatives, 1981.
Hasan, Ibrahim. "Rice Marketing in Aceh." Ph.D. dissertation, University of Indonesia,
    1976.
Hiliry, Mas'ud D. "The Assimilation of Migrants in Aceh, Indonesia, with Special
    Emphasis on Cultural and Social Change." M.A. thesis, Australian National
    University, 1981.

Siegel, James T. "Religion, Trade and Family Life in Aceh." Ph.D. dissertation, University of California, 1966.

Sugihen, Bahrein T. "Socio-Cultural and Attitudinal Change in the Modernization Process: A Study of Acehnese Society in Transition." Ph.D. dissertation, Louisiana State University, 1982.

Robert Wessing

AFAR   Among the least-known people in the eastern Horn of Africa are tribal Muslims who call themselves Afar, better known to outsiders by their Arabic name, Danakil, or their Amharic name, Adal. Their forbidding desert homeland and their reputation for ferocity (it is widely reported that an Afar male cannot be considered an adult until he has killed an enemy) prevented successful exploration of their country by Europeans until the early 1930s.

The 55,000-square-mile territory occupied by the Afar, the so-called Afar Triangle, includes the eastern lowland desert parts of the Ethiopian provinces of Shoa, Wollo and Tigre, as well as northern Harar Province, southern Eritrea and the country of Djibouti (formerly the French Territory of the Afars and the Issas). Within this area lies some of the grimmest desert in the world, including the Danakil Depression, a vast plain of salt pans and active volcanos, which in parts is more than 300 feet below sea level and the hottest place on earth. Population estimates for the Afar vary, but a reasonable estimate is that 375,000 Afar live in Ethiopia, while another 120,000 are found in Djibouti.

Although they claim descent from Arabs—their most celebrated mythic ancestor being Har-al-Mahis, a Yemeni—the Afar speak an eastern Cushitic language. Beneath their universally professed adherence to Sunni Islam, remnants of Cushitic animist cults persist.

Some coastal Afar are fishermen, but most are pastoral nomads herding, in varying proportions depending on the terrain, sheep, goats, cattle and camels. Afar nomads live in camps called *burra*, generally made up of kinsmen by blood or marriage. Descent is patrilineal. The portable tortoise-shaped palm-mat houses (*ari*) of the camps are generally surrounded by thorn palisades as a deterrent to predators, both two- and four-legged. Like their Somali neighbors to the south, the Afar often graze their camels at some distance from the main camp in the care of young warriors, while the rest of the group remain closer to water sources with the less hardy livestock. Afar do not appear to migrate widely with their herds and instead try to stay near assured water supplies.

Although they have been increasingly controlled by national governments, traditionally the Afar were divided into four paramount sultanates—Tajoura and Raheito in Djibouti and Aussa and Biru in Ethiopia—each of which was in turn composed of smaller confederate chiefdoms. Afar overlords had powers of taxation, but their main role was as arbiters of disputes over grazing and water rights. Beyond the areas of immediate control by the chiefs, Afar society seems to be fairly egalitarian. However, throughout Afar territory a distinction is drawn between Asayahamara (the "red ones") and Adoyahmara (the "white ones"). In some cases the terms appear to apply to the descendants of different apical ancestors and in others to status differences within a descent group. This distinction may ultimately have an ecological basis in that the "whites" traditionally predominated in the saline coastal areas while the "reds" were more numerous in the reddish-soil deserts of the hinterland. Although the two sectors today are intermingled territorially and do not seem to have any distinguishing behavioral characteristics, traditionally the "reds" were generally accorded more prestige and power.

The Afar are divided into numerous named groups, or *mela*, which is often translated as "tribe." However, this concept is rather ambiguous. Some of these groups are based on shared territory; in others on descent from a common ancestor; and in still others on clientage, with a core lineage giving its identity to satellite groups.

Prior to the late nineteenth-century expansion of Amhara domination under King Menelik II, contacts between Muslim Afar and the Christian farmers of Ethiopia's central plateau and eastern escarpment were sporadic and predominantly hostile. During periods of dynastic strength on the plateau, Christian rulers tried to expand their power into the Afar lowlands. Conversely, whenever it seemed possible, Muslims attempted to overrun the highlands. Afar fought in the vanguards of such Muslim rulers as Mahfuz of Zeila (who ruled Adal, a coastal Afar-Somali kingdom) and the Amir of Harar, Ahmad Gran, both of whom devastated the highlands in the sixteenth century.

A major East Africa–Arabia slave route traversed Afar country, and as recently as 1928 the Afar were active participants in the trans-Red Sea slave trade, mainly as guides to the Arab slavers. On the whole, though, in comparison to Middle Eastern nomadic peoples, the Afar were relatively self-sufficient economically. They lived mainly on meat—both domestic and wild—and dairy products supplemented by agricultural produce stolen or, less frequently, obtained in peaceful trade from villagers of the adjacent Rift Valley escarpment and the highlands.

The building of the railroad from Addis Ababa to the city of Djibouti in what was then French territory in the late nineteenth and early twentieth centuries and the resettling of highlanders on the fringes of Afar country under the "Pax Amharica" served to weaken somewhat the economic and cultural insularity of the Afar, as more trade goods and agricultural produce became available to them. Today Afar engage regularly in peaceful trade with Christian farmers of the Abyssinian plateau to the west, exchanging butter, hides, livestock and wild sisal rope for agricultural goods. But most Afar are still very much on the fringes of national life on the Horn.

Modern technology increasingly enables what outsiders saw as a useless oppressive piece of terrain populated by savage nomads to appear rather more desirable real estate. For example, the Awash River, harnessed by the Koka Dam, irrigates thousands of acres of cotton in Afarland under the British-owned Tandaho and the Aussa cotton plantations, the latter controlled by the Sultan of

Aussa, one of the hereditary Afar rulers. Likewise the saline lakes of the sub-sea-level Danakil Depression in northern Afar territory, which have for centuries supplied salt to the highlands in the form of crude blocks (*amole*) borne to the plateau by highland camel caravaneers, now see salt trucks increasingly plying to motorable roads. An as yet unsuccessful scheme to mine potash there has also been attempted.

Even more fundamental recent attractions of Afarland to Ethiopia are its potential as a place in which to settle the large number of landless, disaffected highlanders and its location astride the road from the oil port of Asab to the highlands. Recognizing the economic and strategic importance of the Afar and the country they control, the Ethiopian government prior to the revolution of 1974 attempted to woo powerful Afar chiefs by granting them titles in the Amhara civil military hierarchy, with accompanying power perquisites. Cases in point are the Sultan of Aussa, who was designated as a *bitwoded*, or "beloved of the emperor," and the Sultan of Biru, on whom was bestowed the title of *dejazmatch*, or "general of the king's gate."

But despite this upsurge of governmental interest in the harsh desert home of the Afar, attempts to incorporate the tribesmen more fully into the national life of the states within which they are enclaved have so far met with dubious success, and the future of such efforts is even more uncertain. An attempt to transform nomadic Afar into sedentary cotton farmers on the Tandaho plains has been largely unsuccessful.

Alongside their own cultural conservatism, a series of crises in the past decade has raised barriers to the Afar's smooth transition into less insular ways of life. In the early 1970s the drought which ravaged the Sahelian zone of northern Africa hit the Horn as well. Centuries of overgrazing and the failure of rains for several years created famine conditions for the Afar and Somali of a severity rivaling the better publicized famine among the Tuareg and Fulani in northwest Africa.

The failure of the Ethiopian government to respond effectively to the famine's victims in both the desert and the highlands was a major factor in the overthrow of Haile Selassie's regime in the autumn of 1974. The Afar, in the early stages of drought, received some aid from their hereditary rulers, notably the wealthy Sultan of Aussa, who as of 1973 was sending various forms of transport, from jeeps to tractors, deep into the desert to carry drought victims to the banks of the cotton-rich domains along the Awash River. But subsequent journalistic accounts describe dead and dying Afar with little in their stomachs but the mud of drying waterholes from which they had tried to suck the last remaining moisture.

Political as well as natural forces have created problems for the Afar. The long-standing war between the Ethiopian central government and the Eritrean secessionists continues in the post-Selassie era, and the sympathies of many Afar, and often their outright military support, have generally been on the rebel side. If the Afar were a little-known and hard-to-study people under the Selassie regime, they are a virtual lacuna in "revolutionary" Ethiopia, especially since the death, in the mid-1970s, of a young British anthropologist who in the course of a study of the Aussa region was caught in crossfire between government troops and Eritrean guerrillas.

In Djibouti, independent since June of 1977, the Afar comprise about 40 percent of a population dominated by Issas and other Somalis. The rise of Somali irredentist nationalism, manifested in the Ogaden conflict between Somalia and Ethiopia with its Cuban allies, coupled with Afar's own truculence and cultural pride, guarantees tensions there for a long time to come.

The Afar, then, have increasingly become drawn into the intrigues of the nation-states of the Horn of Africa. As overseas powers, such as the Cubans, get drawn into such squabbles, it seems likely that the people, long a virtual ethnographic cipher, will find themselves at center stage in an international conflict.

BIBLIOGRAPHY

Books

Bulliet, Richard. *The Camel and the Wheel*. Cambridge: Harvard University Press, 1975.
Lewis, I. M., ed. *Islam in Tropical Africa*. London: Oxford University Press, 1966.
———. *Peoples of the Horn: Somali, Afar and Saho*. London: International African Institute, 1955.
Murdock, George P. *Africa: Its Peoples and Their Culture History*. New York: McGraw-Hill, 1959.
Pankhurst, Richard. *Economic History of Ethiopia*. Addis Ababa: Haile Selassie I University Press, 1968.
Thesiger, Wilfred. *Arabian Sands*. New York: Dutton, 1959.
Thompson, Virginia, and Adloff, P. *Djibouti and the Horn of Africa*. Stanford: Stanford University Press, 1968.
Trimingham, J. Spencer. *The Influence of Islam Upon Africa*. New York: Praeger, 1969.
———. *Islam in Ethiopia*. 2d ed. London: Frank Cass, 1965.
Weissleder, Wolfgang. "The Promotion of Suzerainty Between Sedentary and Nomadic Populations in East Ethiopia." In *Nomadic Alternative*, edited by Wolfgang Weissleder. World Anthropology Series. The Hague: Mouton, 1978.

Articles

Englebert, Victor. "The Danakil: Nomads of Ethiopia's Wasteland." *National Geographic Magazine* 147:2 (1970): 186–212.
Gardner, Robert. "Herders of Ethiopia." *Newsletter, Program in Ethnographic Film* 22:3 (1971): 1–3.
Mesghinna, H. J. "Salt Mining in Enderta." *Journal of Ethiopian Studies* 4:2 (1966): 127–135.
O'Mahoney, Kevin. "The Salt Trail." *Journal of Ethiopian Studies* 8:2 (1970): 147–154.

Parker, Enid. "Afar Stories, Riddles and Proverbs." *Journal of Ethiopian Studies* 9:2 (1971): 219–287.

Pastner, Stephen. "Lords of the Desert Border: Frontier Feudalism in Southern Baluchistan and Eastern Ethiopia." *International Journal of Middle East Studies* 10 (1979): 93–106.

Savard, George. "Cross Cousin Marriage Among the Patrilineal Afar." In *Proceedings of the Third International Conference of Ethiopian Studies*. Addis Ababa: Institute of Ethiopian Studies, Haile Selassie I University, 1966.

Stephen L. Pastner

AIMAQ   The term "Aimaq" is not an ethnic denomination. Its contemporary meaning in western Afghanistan and adjacent Iranian Khorasan is "tribal people," in juxtaposition to the nontribal population in the area, the Persians (Fariswan) and Tajik. Linguistically, there is no difference between the Aimaq and the majority of Persians surrounding them. The local dialects of the Aimaq tribes are very close either to eastern Khorasan Farsi or to Dari, the Herati dialect of Farsi. In Afghanistan all of the 478,000 Aimaq (3.4 percent of the population) are Sunni (Hanafi school), in contrast to the Shia Persians. Approximately 120,000 Aimaq live in Iran.

Most numerous among the 20 Aimaq groups is the Char Aimaq (*chahar*—four), an administrative grouping of four semi-nomadic or semi-sedentary tribes. They live in a continuous area reaching from the central hills of Badghis north and northeast of Herat to the mountains of Ghor in the west of central Afghanistan. The area is drained by the headwaters of the rivers Kushk, Heri-rud, Murghab and Farah-rud and their respective tributaries.

The Char Aimaq include 42,000 Jamshidi, 62,500 Aimaq-Hazara (Sunni Hazara of Qala-e nau), 104,000 Firuzkuhi and 187,500 Taimani. The tribes of Char Aimaq are ethnic formations of the sixteenth and seventeenth centuries. Ethnic groups of various origins, sometimes mere splinters, such as Chagatai Turks, Uzbek, Kipchak, Baluch and others, were unified by chiefs coming from outside the area. Descendants of these founders are still an influential tribal aristocracy, although they have lost their absolute power. Among the Jamshidi these are the Keyani or Mir, Persians from Sistan (tracing their descent to the legendary ruler, Jamshid, from whom the tribal name was derived). They were invested some 300 years ago in Badghis as Wardens of the Marches by the Safavid ruler, Shah Abbas II.

Taiman, a Kakar Pushtun from Baluchistan, built a coalition in the mountains of Ghor around 1650. In this case, the tribe bears the name of the de facto founder. The Zai Hakim, traditional rulers of the northern Firuzkuhi, claim descent from Durrani Pushtun ancestors (see Pushtun). This tribe takes its name from Firuzkuhi—Mountain of Turquoise—the twelfth–thirteenth-century capital of the Ghorid dynasty on the upper Heri-rud River.

After the downfall of Safavid power in Persia in the eighteenth century,

Badghis became the prey of marauding Sunni Turkmen hunting for Persian Shia slaves in Khorasan, whom they sold on the markets of the Uzbek khanates of Khiva and Bukhara. The Jamshidi joined them, whereas the Aimaq-Hazara retreated farther to the east. Jamshidi fought Hazaras, and the three contending factions of the Firuzkuhi took part in these conflicts. As far as history can be traced, the Char Aimaq have never been politically united (see Hazaras).

In the nineteenth century the situation in Khorasan and Badghis provoked more than one international crisis. The Persian quest for Herat was backed by czarist Russia, which intended to incorporate Badghis into the newly acquired Central Asian territories. The British were anxious to maintain their influence in Afghanistan, where two branches of the reigning Durrani Pushtun clan were fighting for supremacy. Herat, the traditional economic, political and spiritual center for all the Aimaq, was the focus of activities in all these affairs. The Aimaq leaders sided, at one time or another, with either of the contending parties in order to retain their power and to secure the homesteads of their people.

During the second half of the nineteenth century and early in this century, the Jamshidi were forced to lead a nomadic life. All of the tribe or greater parts of it had been exiled in Persia, in Khiva and in northeast Afghanistan. Thousands of Taimani and Tajik of Ghor were forcibly transplanted to the north of Herat, and the most populous of the other Aimaq tribes, the Timuri, suffered a virtual diaspora.

The situation calmed down only after the delineation of Afghanistan's northwestern border in 1886. Amir Abdur Rahman (1879–1901) cruelly, but successfully, had gained power even in the most outlying areas. The power of the traditional tribal leaders had been weakened, if not smashed. A new type of tribal chief supplanted the hereditary aristocrats. Leaders of the patrilineal lineages started to compete. This segmented structure of Aimaq tribes is a consequence of their ethnogenesis. There are 67 subtribes (taifa) forming the Jamshidi, 38 the Aimaq-Hazara, 42 the Firuzkhuhi and 100 the Taimani.

Around the end of the last century, exiled Taimani chiefs undertook raids on Afghan police posts from Turkmenistan. Their heirs and successors represent political power today. One leader, Mullah Rahman, was an elected member of the Afghanistan parliament during four successive sessions from 1957 to 1973. In Kabul, he represented his tribe more than the county of Kushk. His power is based on marriage bonds with other influential Jamshidi.

One prominent heir of the Aimaq-Hazara's aristocracy was a senator of Qala Nau elected despite strong Pushtun opposition. Members of the once-reigning families of Firuzkuhi and Taimani were high-ranking government officials or were elected representatives of their counties. The most renowned personality among them was Masha'al of the Nili branch of Khanzada Taimani, one-time mayor of Herat and senator and a well-known miniaturist.

Of all the non-Pushtun tribes in western Afghanistan, the Jamshidi have maintained a high degree of independence from the central government. But tribalism is strong among the other Aimaq as well. For instance, feuds—even blood feuds—tend to be settled by tribal institutions rather than by government authorities. Their traditional concept of honor and shame, governing also tribal law, still is stronger than Islamic rules or state legislation.

Among the Aimaq, the position of women is exceptional when compared to other societies in rural Afghanistan. Women sit with men and raise their voices in discussion, even if strangers are present. Girls not married until about age 18 (a frequent occurrence in Ghor) are free to reject a groom proposed by their father. In many instances among the Taimani and Firuzkuhi the young groom moves to the compound of his future bride's parents and serves for a contracted period (two years or more) before the wedding ceremony is performed and marriage can be consummated. These traits are less pronounced, or could not be recorded at all, among Jamshidi, Aimaq-Hazara and the "lesser" Aimaq of Badghis, where the influence of the orthodox Muslim clergy of the city of Herat is much stronger than that of the *mullahs* of Ghor.

Pre-Islamic traits are also more pronounced in Ghor than in Badghis, such as the veneration of the tombs of saints (*ziyarats*). Visited especially by women, the shrines often disclose their pagan character by their names, such as "Saint of the Caves." There is seldom evidence of a grave. Devotees give offerings and deposit sheets of paper on which their wishes are written or drawn. Another pre-Islamic feature, observed among Firuzkuhi, is a dance of unmarried girls asking for rain after a period of drought.

The economy of the Char Aimaq is based on agriculture and animal husbandry. Jamshidi and Aimaq-Hazara in the hills of Badghis might be classed as semi-sedentary, whereas Firuzkuhi and Taimani in the valleys of the central mountain ranges are semi-nomadic. All four tribes use temporary housing during summer months to varying degrees. The Jamshidi have shifted in the past five decades from the yurt to the cheaper Pushtun nomad's black tent. Aimaq-Hazara and Firuzkuhi are chiefly yurt dwellers. Among the northern and central Taimani, a peculiar type of black tent prevails. The southern Taimani, on the Pushtun border, have adopted the same tent as the Jamshidi (see Uzbek [Afghanistan] for yurt construction).

Badghis is one of the most fertile areas of Afghanistan. Water for irrigated agriculture usually is plentiful, and in lower regions, rice, cotton and grapes can be grown. Dry farming, chiefly of wheat and melons, is also practiced. Conditions for herding are optimal. Sheep of the fat-tailed variety, including karakul, can be kept grazing all year. During spring and summer, the herds graze on pastures near the village, cared for by one of the brothers in an extended family, the social and economic core of all the Aimaq. In autumn and winter, professional shepherds take the cattle to the lower steppes along the Soviet border. Conditions in Badghis permit the production of a considerable surplus of agricultural products that can be sold in the nearby markets of Herat or Qala Nau. Carpet weaving brings additional cash.

The narrow defiles in mountainous Ghor provide only limited space for irrigated agriculture. There is less rainfall than in Badghis. Yields in dry farming are much lower than in Badghis, and during the severe winters the cattle must be kept in stables, which limits the number of animals. Fodder must be grown on the limited irrigable lands.

Although Ghor (as a province it is now called Chakhcharon) is less densely populated than Badghis, the Firuzkuhi and Taimani always have been economically more restricted than the population of Badghis. After two years of drought followed by the severe winter of 1971–1972, the population of Ghor and adjacent E-Badghis (where the Firuzkuhi live) was virtually decimated. Recovery was slow. West and central Badghis have been affected heavily, too, but because of the existing economic infrastructure in the vicinity of Herat, the worst was prevented.

Besides the Char Aimaq, there are half a dozen other semi-sedentary, semi-nomadic or nomadic Aimaq in western Afghanistan, chiefly in Herat Province, among them, 34,000 Timuri, 18,500 Tahiri, 15,500 Zuri, 12,400 Maleki and 5,000 Mishmast. Still other now fully sedentary groups who consider themselves or are classified by Heratis as Aimaq are 17,000 Kipchak, 6,000 Chenghizi, 2,000 Chagatai, 1,500 Mobari, 1,000 Badghisi, 1,000 Ghuri, 1,000 Kakeri, 200 Damanrigi and 200 Khamidi.

The Timuri were once the most powerful and most numerous of the "lesser" Aimaq. Their homeland can be traced to western Badghis, where now in the county of Gulran a part of this tribe borders Jamshidi country. It is here that the best qualities of the so-called Herat Baluch rugs are woven by the women of some of the Timuri subtribes, such as the Kaudani, Shirkhani, Yakubkhani and Zakani.

During the eighteenth and nineteenth centuries an important part of this tribe moved to what is now Iranian Khorasan, where today there still live 25,000 Timuri who have incorporated various small groups of Jamshidi, Zuri and other Aimaq. Only some 250 Jamshidi and perhaps 1,500 Aimaq-Hazara live in the vicinity of Meshed and preserve the traditions of their origins. Many of the Timuri in Iran and some of those in Badghis are nomadic, while others, especially in the oases around Herat and near Shindand, are settled. A group of Pushtunized Timuri pastures its herds near Baghlan in northeast Afghanistan. The Timuri-Hazara to the north of Ghazni stem from the same tribe. There are only a couple of hundred Jamshidi and Aimaq-Hazara in Soviet Turkmenistan, where they live near Kushka.

Since the invasion of Afghanistan by Soviet troops in 1979, there is evidence that the Aimaq are cooperating with the resistance to the central government attempts to control the country.

BIBLIOGRAPHY

Books

Aslanov, A. G., et al. "Ethnography of Afghanistan." In *Afghanistan: Some New Approaches*, edited by George Grassmuch and Ludwig W. Adamac. Ann Arbor: University of Michigan Press, 1969.

"Herat and Northwestern Afghanistan." In *Historical and Political Gazetteer of Afghanistan*. Reprint ed. Vol 3. Graz, Austria: 1974.
Schurmann, Herbert Franz. *The Mongols of Afghanistan: An Ethnography of Mongols and Related Peoples of Afghanistan*. The Hague: Mouton, 1962.

Articles

Ferdinand, Klaus. "Preliminary Notes on Hazara Culture." *Historisk-Filosofiske Meddleser, Kongelige Danske Videnskabernes Selskab* (Copenhagen) 37:5 (1959).
Janata, Alfred. "On the Origin of the Firuzkuhis of Western Afghanistan." *Archiv fur Volkerkunde* (Vienna) 25 (1971): 57–65.

Unpublished Manuscripts

Barry, Michael. "Western Afghanistan's Outback." USAID report. Kabul, Afghanistan, September 1972.
Kuhn, Martin. "A Report on Village Society in the Chakhcharan District of Afghanistan." Manuscript, London School of Oriental and African Studies, 1970.
Singer, Andre F. V. "A Study of the Impact of Social and Cultural Change Upon Ethnic Identity in Eastern Iran." Ph.D. dissertation, Exeter College, Oxford, 1976.

Alfred Janata

AKAN   The Akan-speaking peoples of West Africa inhabit the tropical rain forest and the transitional savanna in the southern half of Ghana, the western part of the Volta region, Togo and the Ivory Coast. Despite a high degree of cultural homogeneity, they may be divided into four major linguistic subgroups of the Kwa branch of the Niger-Congo family: the Twi, the Fante, the Nzema and the Anyi-Bawle. Each of these is subdivided into dialect groups or individual ethnic groups (called tribes in Ghana), the largest of which is the Twi-Asante (population 1.6 million), the best known and most influenced by Islam.

Historians disagree on the precise ethnogenesis of the 6.6 million Akan. Evidence indicates that no one particular locality can be described categorically as the cradle of the Akan. Multilineal development seems to have occurred in the northern Brong savanna, in the Adanse forests and along the Etsi coastline.

Akan civilization apparently evolved in stages, beginning about A.D. 1000 among agricultural communities based on iron technology and moving through the development of urban settlements and small principalities between 1400 and 1600. It crystallized in the rise of large kingdoms between 1600 and 1850, the most illustrious being the Asante Empire, stemming from profitable long-range international trade, the spread of firearms, Islamic influences and European imperialism.

Six basic institutions distinguish the Akan-speaking peoples from their neighbors, the Molé-Dagbane, Ewe, and Ga-Adangme. These are 1) traditional military organization, 2) laws of succession and inheritance, 3) the kinship system (*abusua*), 4) religion, 5) the calendar system and 6) festivals.

The Akan military formation, which is still the basis of the organization of Akan states, has as its major feature the division of the state into several wings, each headed by a chief. The king was traditionally the commander-in-chief of the state armies.

Succession to office and inheritance of property is matrilineal. A deceased man, for example, is not succeeded by his son but by his brother, maternal cousin or his sister's son in order of seniority.

The rule of matrilineal descent and the matrilineal clan has been the basis of Akan social organization. Members of the matrilineage, both men and women, trace their descent in the female line to a common female ancestor. Members of the *abusua*, or lineage, used to live in the same town or village or in the same section of town. Today migrations associated with rapid urbanization, population pressures and basic socioeconomic changes in Ghana have led to the dispersal of lineage members throughout the country. In some Asanta and Kwawu towns, however, members still live close together, a majority of the members of the *abusua* occupying the same *brono*, or ward. Each *abusua* is headed by an *abusuapanyin*, the custodian of family lands, who settles disputes between members and officiates at funerals of members.

The lineage is a branch of a still larger kinship unit, an exogamous clan. There are seven of these clans among the Fante and eight among the Asante. The clans, of which all members are considered ''brothers'' and ''sisters,'' are found among all Akan-speaking peoples throughout Ghana.

Ancestor worship has been the central focus of the Akan religious system. The Akan recognize a wide hierarchy of gods with corresponding powers and functions. At the apex of the deistic order is Nyame, the supreme being, creator and giver of all things. Other gods derive their powers from him. Nyame cannot be the object of direct worship and is approachable only through intermediaries, the *abosom* (lesser gods). The latter may inhabit lakes, streams, rivers, or trees. Below the *abosom* are *asuman*, minor deities, who in turn derive their powers from the *abosom* and when personalized in the form of talismans or charms worn on the body are believed to give protection and help to their wearers. The spirits which affect the life of the average Akan more directly are the *nsamanfo*, or ancestral spirits. These are regularly consulted, offerings given to them, libations poured for them and their guidance and protection sought in all important family and personal matters.

The underlying principles of major Akan festivals derive from their religious beliefs. Many of the festivals such as the Western Fante Nyeyi or Ahobaa Kakraba (little Ahobaa) mourn dead ancestors, especially those who died in the recent past. These are sad occasions, marked by beating drums, gunfire and wailing women. Other festivals, such as the Yam Festival, celebrate the harvest of new yams and other foodstuffs. These are festive occasions with feasting and merry-making throughout Akanland. It is during these periods that the gods are given thanks for protecting the peoples of the various Akan states. Most of the Akan festivals and ceremonies emphasize the continuous dependence of the living on the dead ancestors.

In recent years the Akan have reported a high percentage of Christian affiliation and a low percentage of Muslim commitment; 62.7 percent of adult Akan in 1960 claimed to be Christian against 4.3 percent Muslim. The figures are at best crude estimates and are misleading. They do not, for instance, reflect the extent to which both Christianity and Islam have adapted to local religious traditions and customs. No figures were collected for Muslim sects other than the Ahmadiya, who were estimated in 1948 to be .5 percent of the population. The 1960 census figure of 4.3 percent for Muslims does not distinguish clearly the sizes of the various Muslim sects, although that percentage applied to Ghana's 1983 population of 13.9 million would show 264,000 Muslim Akan. What is even more crucial is that all the religions in Ghana exhibit high degrees of syncretism.

Despite the militant expansion of Islam in West Africa, especially in the early nineteenth century, its success does not seem to have affected the majority of ethnic groups in Ghana. Nevertheless, Islam in one form or another and some degree of Arabic scholarship have managed to penetrate far into the savanna country and even to the tropical forest to such places as Salaga and Kumasi in the northern and Ashanti regions, respectively.

One of the principal means by which Islam spread was the trading journeys of Muslim merchants, particularly Dyula (See Dyula). Wherever they settled or established trading centers or staging posts on a trade route, for example in Kumasi, schools were founded to teach Muslim children to read and write Arabic to enable them to study the Quran. In the nineteenth century functions of the literate Muslims at the Asante court included the writing of charms for the king and his courtiers and the making of talismans to protect his soldiers in combat. The superiority of Islamic magic and the awe in which Arabic characters were— and are—held made Muslims much in demand at the courts of the chiefs in Akanland. Throughout Ghana Hausa *mallamai* or *marabouts* still enjoy the prestige accorded great spiritualists. Muslim culture generally is synonymous with Hausa culture (see Hausa) throughout Ghana. The phrase ''those Hausa people'' is often applied indiscriminately to all Muslims from the north.

Akan Twi has also absorbed a number of words of Arabic origin, although usually at second or third hand through languages employed by their Muslim neighbors. These loan words include Arabic terminology related to religion, trade and commerce, military, politics and words and phrases associated with literacy—all of which readily demonstrate the degree of Islamic influence in West African societies.

In the popular Ghanaian mind, especially in the Akan, Islam is connected culturally with its more obvious outward manifestations—mosques, Quran schools, Arabic script, turbans and skull caps, flowing gowns, veils and titles, such as *al-hajji*, *imam*, *mallam* and *shaikh*. It is also popularly identified by the outward observance of public prayer, ablution, fasting and pilgrimage. Many ethnic groups in Ghana, the Akan included, have adopted some facets of Muslim culture as they understand it without formally adopting the faith. There are a few Akan who have formally adopted the faith but still retain customs which contradict it. (This, incidentally, is also true of the adoption of Christianity in Ghana.) Others have accepted Islam and maintained many of their traditional practices and beliefs while giving them Islamic flavor. Then again, there exist parallels between Akan religious beliefs and some basic Muslim cosmological beliefs. Examples are the Akan conception of Nyame and the Muslim belief in Allah; the Akan *abosom* and the Muslim *jinn*; the Akan cult of the ancestors and the great Muslim reverence for the founders of the two Sufi orders, the Qadiri and the Tijani.

Muslim amulets are commonly worn by non-Muslims in Ghana. There is hardly an Akan chief who does not place great confidence in the reputed efficacy of Islamic talismans. And there is not a soccer team in Ghana hoping to win league matches that does not hire the services of a *mallam*. Islam, no less than Christianity, is an overlay to the indigenous religious beliefs of the Akan, not eliminating them but complementing them.

A large majority of orthodox Muslims in Ghana are Sunni of the Maliki school; others follow Shafi rites. There are hundreds of parochial Muslim organizations scattered all over the country, many serving villages, towns and districts. Within the orthdox communities of southern Ghana, sectarian, ritual, ethnic and other differences hamper the unity of all Muslims. In fact, one of the problems of Muslims in Ghana which has been a major concern of the government has been the almost endemic factional strife, litigations and disputes having both sectarian and ethnic undertones, often leading to lawlessness and unrest in the *zongos* (segregated residential quarters where immigrants, usually Muslim, settle, although Islamized Akan and other indigenous ethnic groups live there).

While disputes between different orders or factions of orthodox Muslims are, at least in theory, resolvable, the traditional cold war existing between orthodox, predominantly Hausa-speaking immigrant Muslims and the local, largely Fante Ahmadiya movement (Fante Nkramo) is difficult to arrest, for its causes relate to fundamental issues.

Orthodox Muslims consider the Punjabi founder of Ahmadiya to be a false prophet and refuse to accept Ahmadis as true Muslims. They disagree with the Hanafi practice, which Ahmadis follow, of folding the arms hand to elbow at the beginning of prayer. The orthodox of the Maliki school leave their arms at their sides. Ahmadis allow women in the congregational prayer and permit the bride to be present at her wedding to give consent: the orthodox do not.

The differences between orthodox and Ahmadiya Muslims are also largely differences between Hausa and Akan, notably Fante ethnic cultures; between what the Akan see as "lower status" and inferior northern immigrant *pepefo* cultures of the Hausa, Zambrama, Gonja, Mossi, Kotokoli etc. and the "higher-status" progressive, heavily Westernized cultures of the Fante and Asante. While orthodox Muslims have until recently resisted Western influence, particularly

Western secular education, the Ahmadiya in Ghana has from its very inception self-consciously imitated Christian missionary methods, institutions and even terminology. Ahmadis were the first Muslims in West Africa to establish Western schools combining their religion with secular study and education. Only intermittent efforts are made by the Ahmadis to foster interest in Arabic and Isalamic subjects. Since 1957 the Ahmadiya movement has built more than 150 mosques and has established numerous primary, middle and secondary schools in many regions of the country. However, a large majority of the students and teachers of the Ahmadiya schools are non-Ahmadis and are not required to be Ahmadiya.

The Ahmadiya movement has made some gains among the relatively educated Muslims in Ghana: mechanics, commercial and government clerks, even a few university graduates. However, the great majority of the estimated 30,000 Ahmadis are illiterate Fante agriculturalists who are mostly concentrated in the central region of Ghana and who form the largest single Ahmadiya community in West Africa. The widespread illiteracy of the Fante Ahmadis, however, contradicts the popular presentation of the faith as the religion of the enlightened and educated Muslim. The movement, no doubt, is in a position to profit from the spread of education and the general rise in the level of literacy among Muslims.

Although the Akan have on the whole accepted the efficacy of Muslim supernatural powers, including the ability of *mallamai* to effect, for good or ill, intended results through ritual words and actions, serious adoption by the Akan of the Muslim faith is fraught with a host of problems.

The negative stereotypes that the Akan hold about the dominant Hausa and other northern immigrant ethnic groups—the *pepefo* of the *zongos* who are identified with the Muslim religion—hamper conversion. Also, perhaps most important of all, the Hausa custom of patrilineal succession and inheritance is in direct opposition to established Akan rules of matrilineal descent, inheritance and succession, to which most Akan are still deeply attached. Again, Akan funeral practices, with their traditional stress on extended communal mourning periods, public exhibition of deep sorrow and particularly the conspicuous consumption of huge quantities of alcohol are all anathema to conscientious Muslims. In the final analysis, the popular view is that Muslims speak Hausa and few Akan speak this language; most do not even wish to. They seldom even associate with Hausa. Yet, when an Akan converts to Islam, he is expected to become culturally Hausa. There is the rub.

BIBLIOGRAPHY

Books

Ahmad, Mirza Mubarak. *Our Foreign Missions*. Lahore: Lion Press, 1961.
Bravmann, Rene A. *Islam and Tribal Art in West Africa*. London: Cambridge University Press, 1974.

Busia, K. A. "The Ashanti of the Gold Coast." in *African Worlds*, edited by D. Forde. London: Oxford University Press, 1963.

———. *The Position of the Chief in the Modern Political System of Ashanti*. London: Oxford University Press, 1951.

Christensen, J. B. *Double Descent Among the Fanti*. File No. 16. New Haven, Conn.: Human Relations Area Files Press, 1954.

Claridge, W. W. *A History of the Gold Coast and Ashanti*. 2 vols. London: Murray, 1915.

Dinan, C. "Socialization in an Accra Suburb: The Zongo and Its Distinctive Sub-Culture." In *Institute of African Studies, Legon. Family Research Papers No. 3. Changing Family Studies*, edited by Christine Oppong. Accra: Institute of African Studies, 1975.

Fisher, Humphrey. *Ahmadiyyah. A Study in Contemporary Islam on the West African Coast*. London: Oxford University Press, 1963.

Fortes, M. "Kinship and Marriage Among the Ashanti." In *African Systems of Kinship and Marriage*, edited by A. R. Radcliffe-Brown and D. Forde. London: Oxford University Press, 1950.

Ghana '76 An Official Handbook. Accra: Ghana Government Publications, 1976.

Hodgkin, Thomas. "The Islamic Literary Tradition in Ghana." In *Islam in Tropical Africa*, edited by I. M. Lewis. London: Oxford University Press, 1966.

Hunwick, J. O. *Islam in Africa: Friend or Foe*. Accra: Ghana Universities Press, 1976.

Lewis, I. M. *Islam in Tropical Africa*. London: Oxford University Press, 1966.

Mendelsohn, Jack. *God, Allah and Juju, Religion in Africa Today*. London: Thomas Nelson, 1962.

Meyerowitz, E. *Akan Traditions of Origin*. London: Faber & Faber, 1952.

1960 Population Census of Ghana. Special Report "E" Tribes in Ghana. Accra: Ghana Government Publications, 1964.

Owusu, Maxwell. *Uses and Abuses of Political Power: A Case Study of Continuity and Change in the Politics of Ghana*. Chicago: University of Chicago Press, 1970.

Trimingham, J. Spencer. *Islam in West Africa*. Oxford: Clarendon Press, 1959.

Wilks, I. *The Northern Factor in Ashanti History*. Accra: Institute of African Studies, University College of Ghana, 1961.

Articles

Anquandah, James. "State Formation Among the Akan of Ghana." *Sankofa, The Journal of Archaeological and Historical Studies* 1 (1975): 47–57.

Fynn, John K. "The Pre-Bor-Bor Fante States." *Sankofa, The Journal of Archaeological and Historical Studies* 1 (1975): 20–29.

Goody, J. "A Note on the Penetration of Islam Into the West of the Northern Territories of the Gold Coast." *Transactions of Gold Coast and Togoland Historical Society* 1:2 (1953): 45–46.

Hunwick, J. O. "The Influence of Arabic in West Africa." *Transactions of the Historical Society of Ghana* 7 (1964): 24–41.

Maxwell Owusu
Population figures updated by Richard V. Weekes

ALBANIANS   Albania is the only European state of which the majority of the population is Muslim. No religious census exists for contemporary Albania, but it is generally accepted that 70 percent (or around 2 million persons) are Muslim or the unpracticing descendants of Muslims. In northern Albania there is a Roman Catholic population (10 percent of the total), and in the south, an Orthodox one (20 percent of the total), with an almost exclusively Muslim Albania population in the central region. In addition, there are roughly half as many Albanians in Yugoslavia as in Albania proper. Some 70 percent of these reside in Kosovo (an autonomous province of Serbia), with most of the remainder in Macedonia, Montenegro and southern Serbia, but also scattered as migrant workers elsewhere in Yugoslavia. Nearly all of these Yugoslav Albanians are Muslim. There also exists an immigrant population of Albanian Muslims in Turkey, which continues to be replenished from Yugoslavia, and a still smaller group in Egypt. All other major communities of expatriate Albanians (in Italy, Greece, Bulgaria, the United States) are overwhelmingly Christian. The estimated total Muslim Albanian population is around 3 million.

The Albanian people are thought to be derived predominantly from Illyrians who inhabited the Dinaric region in classical and post-classical times. By the end of the Roman Empire, of which the area now Albania was a part, much of the region had been converted to Christianity. With the schism between Eastern and Western churches, the Albanians divided their allegiance accordingly. Later, following the Ottoman conquest in the late fourteenth century, great numbers converted to Islam. Many Albanian Muslims served in the Ottoman armies (often converting specifically for this purpose) and played a significant role in the Ottoman administration. A national consciousness developed relatively late, and an independent Albania was not created until 1912.

The majority of Albanian Muslims are Sunni. Over 200,000, however, are followers of the Bektashiyya Sufi order, a *tariqa* of the Shia branch of Islam. Most Bektashiyya live in southern Albania and historically constituted a more liberal and progressive group than their Sunni co-religionists. Although the Bektashiyya order is of central Anatolian origin, its most important sphere of activity in the modern period has been Albania. This arose because of the close association of Bektashi with the Janissaries, in which the Albanians were numerous.

There was in Albania an exceptionally high degree of tolerance between the different religious groups. Religion did not serve as a basis for ethnic differentiation as it did among the neighboring South Slavs. Social and cultural distinctions between Muslim and Christian were minimal. Intermarriage was common in many parts of Albania, and children, even of homogeneous marriages, were often both circumcised and baptized and given both Muslim and Christian names. There were Christian women who wore veils and Muslim women who did not. Crypto-Christianity—the continuation in secret of Christian belief and practice even after conversion to Islam—was not uncommon.

The Albanian language has two principal dialects: Gheg, spoken north of the Shkumbi River; and Tosk, spoken to the south. Gheg and Tosk are quite different, although still mutually intelligible, and each is divided into a number of subdialects. This linguistic boundary between north and south corresponds to major differences not only in physical type but, more significantly, in social structure and culture. Albeit more inaccessible, the mountainous northern area is the better known ethnographically. Both social scientists and laymen have long been fascinated by the perseverance there until World War II of an archaic social organization and a material culture frequently compared with the Halstatt Iron Age of early medieval Europe.

The Gheg present the only example of a tribal system surviving in Europe until the mid-twentieth century. People's lives were strictly organized in terms of kinship and descent. The population was divided into a number of patrilineal clans, the genealogies of which could be traced to founding ancestors some 13 or 14 generations earlier. The clan was an exogamous unit, and bridges were often exchanged traditionally between two clans over several generations, thus perpetuating an alliance.

The basic unit of Gheg society was the household, which was patrilocally extended and often very large, with more than 90 members in some cases. Groups of households which had a common descent formed a brotherhood, which constituted a village or sector of a village. Groups of villages made up a larger territorial unit, the *bajrak* (from the Turkish term for flag or standard), led by a *bajraktar* (standard-bearer) who served as a military leader. The *bajraktar* was usually a hereditary position, descended patrilineally from an original appointment by the Ottoman government. There was often a one-for-one correlation between clan and *bajrak*, but in other cases a single *bajraktar* led several different clans or a single clan had several different *bajraktars*. In some regions, the *bajraktar* vied for power with hereditary heads of clans. Social relations were governed according to an unwritten body of law codified by Leke Dukagnini in the fifteenth century. Blood feuds, which might occur between units at any level of social organization, were common and served as the principal mechanism of social control. Assemblies composed of *bajraktars*, village and clan elders and other important personages were called for various administrative and judicial purposes, especially the settlement of feuds.

Tosk social structure provides a sharp contrast. In the less mountainous and more productive lands of southern Albania, a feudal system developed early in the Ottoman period. An endogamous aristocracy, usually Albanian converts to Islam, developed as individuals were given titles and estates in return for their service to the Ottoman government. Gradually they expanded their control over free peasants of the lowland areas, many of whom remained Orthodox. During this process the large, patrilocally extended family households of the peasantry, previously the pattern in this area also, were broken up. As late as 1930, two-thirds of the land in southern Albania (some half-million acres) belonged to only 165 aristocratic families. Attempts at land reform between the world wars were largely ineffectual, and it was not until the post-World War II period that the feudal structure of southern Albania was finally altered.

The post-World War II government of Albania has made great changes in traditional society and culture, both north and south. Both the hereditary leaders of the former and the feudal landlords of the latter have been deprived of power and authority. The contemporary government has also strongly suppressed religion, both Islam and Christianity, and in 1967 eliminated by law all organized religious activity. Although making a valiant attempt to modernize and industrialize (with assistance first from Yugoslavia, then the Soviet Union and later China), Albania is still the least urbanized and least industrialized state of Europe. Approximately two-thirds of the population is rural and engaged in agriculture or herding, nearly all of which is now collectivized.

BIBLIOGRAPHY

Books

Coon, Carleton. *The Mountains of Giants: A Racial and Cultural Study of the North Albanian Ghegs*. Papers of the Peabody Museum of American Archaeology and Ethnology, Harvard University, 23, no. 3. Cambridge: Harvard University Press, 1950.

Erlich, Vera. *Family in Transition: A Study of 300 Yugoslav Villages*. Princeton: Princeton University Press, 1966.

Grossmith, C. J. "The Cultural Ecology of Albanian Extended Family Households in Yugoslav Macedonia." In *Communal Families in the Balkans: The Zadruga*, edited by Robert F. Byrnes. South Bend: University of Notre Dame Press, 1976.

Hamm, Harry. *Albania*. New York: Praeger, 1963.

Hasluck, Margaret. *The Unwritten Law of Albania*. Cambridge: The University Press, 1954.

Inalçik, Halil. "Arnawutluk." In *Encyclopedia of Islam*, edited by H.A.R. Gibb, et al. Vol. 1. London: Luzac, 1960.

Mamullaku, Ramadan. *Albania and the Albanians*. Leiden: Brill, 1975.

Pano, Nicholas C. *The People's Republic of Albania*. Baltimore: Johns Hopkins Press, 1968.

Skendi, Stavro. *The Albanian National Awakening, 1878–1912*. Princeton: Princeton University Press, 1967.

———. "Crypto-Christianity in the Balkan Area Under the Ottomans." In *Balkan Cultural Studies*, edited by Stavro Skendi. Boulder, Colo.: East European Monographs, 1980.

———, ed. *Balkan Cultural Studies*. Boulder, Colo.: East European Monographs, 1980.

Traerup, Birthe. "Albanian Singers in Kosovo: Notes on the Song Repertoire of a Mohammedan Country Wedding in Yugoslavia." In *Studia Instrumentorum Musicae*, edited by G. Hillestrom. Stockholm: Nordiska Musikoforlaget, 1974.

U.S. Senate. Committee on the Judiciary. *Church and State in Albania*. Washington, D.C.: Government Printing Office, 1965.

Whitaker, Ian. "Familiar Roles in the Extended Patrilineal Kin-group in Northern Albania." In *Mediterranean Family Structure*, edited by John Peristiany. Cambridge: Cambridge University Press, 1976.

———. "Tribal Structure and National Politics in Albania, 1910–1950." In *History and Social Anthropology*, edited by Ioan M. Lewis. London: Tavistock, 1968.

Articles

Balič, Smail. Eastern Europe: The Islamic Dimensions.'' *Journal of the Institute of Muslim Minority Affairs* 1:1 (1979): 29–37.
Byron, Janet L. ''Displacement of One Standard Dialect by Another.'' *Current Anthropology* 19 (1978): 613–614.
Costa, Nicholas J. ''An Ethnomusicological Study of the Land of the Eagle.'' *East European Quarterly* 15 (1981): 251–259.
Filipovič, Milenko S. ''The Bektashi in the District of Strumica (Macedonia).'' *Man* 54 (1954): 10–13.
Hasluck, Margaret. ''The Non-Conformist Moslems of Albania.'' *Contemporary Review* 127 (1925): 599–606.
Kastrati, Qazim. ''Some Unwritten Sources on the Unwritten Law in Albania.'' *Man* 55 (1955): 124–127.
Smajlovič, Ahmed. ''Muslims in Yugoslavia.'' *Journal of the Institute of Muslim Minority Affairs* 2:1 (1980): 132–144.
Whitaker, Ian. ''A Sack for Carrying Things: The Traditional Role of Women in Northern Albanian Society.'' *Anthropological Quarterly* 54 (1981) 3: 146–156.

Unpublished Manuscripts

Byron, Janet Leotha. ''Selection and Evaluation of Alternatives in Albanian Language Standardization.'' Ph.D. dissertation, University of Pennsylvania, 1973.
Grossmith, Christopher John. ''Marginality and Reproductive Behavior Among the Albanian Minority in Yugoslav Macedonia.'' Ph.D. dissertation, University of North Carolina, 1977.
Kolsti, John S. ''The Bilingual Singer.'' Ph.D. dissertation, Harvard University, 1968.

William G. Lockwood

AMERICAN BLACKS Islam among American blacks runs along two increasingly divergent paths. One is called the American Muslim Mission, directed by Wallace Deen Muhammad (Warithud-Din-Muhammad). The other is the Nation of Islam, with Brother Louis Farrakhan as its National Representative.

Although the American Muslim Mission is the lineal descendant of the original Nation of Islam, it differs greatly from the parent body. It considers itself orthodox Muslim, welcomes all races, and allows its membership to participate in the full range of American social and political institutions. It has incorporated many of the ideals of the late reformer Malcolm X (El Hajj Malik El-Shabazz). Its estimated 50,000–100,000 members look upon their group as primarily religious.

The ''new'' Nation of Islam, resurrected in 1978, adheres to the heterodox tenets put forth by the late Elijah Muhammad and promotes separatism (blacks only and withdrawal from white society). It advocates millennialism, maintaining that its members are a ''chosen people'' charged with establishing a Holy Kingdom on earth by ''correcting the wrongs.'' Its approximate 25,000–50,000 followers believe Brother Farrakhan's revelation that Elijah Muhammad is not dead. (Estimates of the number of American Black Muslims range from 100,000 to 2 million. *Ed.*)

While exact figures for the membership of either organization are unavailable, neither approaches the level of influence and size of the Black Muslim movement of the 1960s and 1970s, when Malcolm X and his disciple, heavyweight boxing champion Muhammad Ali (Cassius Clay), shook the nation and Elijah Muhammad established a small empire, amassing a fortune. Both groups are essentially urban phenomena.

Despite the splits, the changes and the diminished influence within the black American Muslim community, the legacy of those protest days lingers. This legacy is composed not only of the more sensational experiences identified with Malcolm X, Elijah Muhammad and the black nationalist movement, but it also includes the more basic but less publicized element of religion.

Black revolutionary and radical protest movements usually have had a deep religious component. The spiritual base of black people is so significant that any movement which plans to have substantial social impact must tap the religiosity of blacks. Throughout the history of the Nation of Islam, its leaders recognized that a move away from Christianity requires a more profound guy wire than a purely secular movement could provide. When, for example, Malcolm X left the Nation of Islam in 1964, he founded a religious organization, the Muslim Mosque Inc., before he founded the Organization for Afro-American Unity.

The Black Muslim movements were peculiarly American, attributable to the fact that they appeared in response to the unique American racial situation. While most of the beliefs emanated from the American experience, those which did not, such as Islamic names and some of the Islamic tenets, were "Americanized." Even Elijah Muhammad kept his original Christian name. The prominence of "Islamic" elements disguised the "Americanness" of the movements.

The Nation of Islam grew out of two early twentieth-century movements. One was the Marcus Garvey "Back to Africa" effort of the late 1920s. The other was the Moorish-American Science Temple movement of Noble Drew Ali (formerly Timothy Drew of North Carolina). Each called for a withdrawal from white society as a means of escaping a depressed sociocultural environment fostered by the harsh legacy of slavery and complicated by the process of urbanization.

The interest of black Americans in separation or colonization was especially pronounced in the period immediately following World War I, when Garvey, a black Jamaican, built his Universal Negro Improvement Association into an organization of worldwide significance. Claiming a following of several million blacks, Garvey spearheaded efforts to promote racial pride and to uplift the black race by redeeming Africa from the throes of white imperialism. While Garvey's movement was primarily political and economic, it contained a religious component. Garvey called upon blacks to reject worship of an alien white deity and embrace a truly black religion based on their African heritage.

During the same period, Drew Ali, allegedly on the authority of the King of Morocco, proclaimed that "Negroes" in the United States were actually Moors, whose forefathers had inhabited North Africa. He urged them to refer to themselves as Moors or Moorish Americans. According to him, the white man, by stripping blacks of their true names, robbed them of their religion, their power and their identity. Christianity was a white religion, but Islam was the religion for colored people. Drew Ali died in 1929 under mysterious circumstances.

Wallace D. Fard, of Detroit, claiming he was the reincarnation of Noble Drew Ali, assumed leadership of the Moorish movement and reinforced the Islamic belief system. Although some members refused to accept his claim, one faction led by Elijah Muhammad (Elijah Poole of Georgia) did, even to the point of deifying Fard. With racist and economic conditions facilitating his efforts, "Master" Wallace Fard Muhammad recruited 8,000 Detroit blacks, many of them recent, poverty-stricken, rural migrants overwhelmed by the alien urban environment.

Fard gave Islamic trappings to his movement, as evidenced by his references to Marcus Garvey and Noble Drew Ali as "fine Muslims," but he also borrowed heavily from Christianity. Among the most significant Christian influences were the Jehovah's Witnesses. Fard faced the dual problem of a shortage of Qurans and a largely illiterate or semi-literate following. As a consequence, he urged his flock to listen to the radio broadcasts of Judge Rutherford of the Jehovah's Witnesses. Although Christian, the Witnesses unleashed such radical, angry diatribes against other Christian sects that they reinforced Fard's contention that Christianity was the Negro's "graveyard" and "the slave holder's religion."

When Fard disappeared in 1934, after moving his headquarters to Chicago, Elijah Muhammad assumed leadership of the movement now called the Nation of Islam. He, too, leaned heavily on Christianity for preaching and guidance and borrowed heavily from other religious movements. Indeed, much of what appeared mysterious, alien and frightening about the Nation of Islam was (and is), in essence, something both very Christian and very American—millennialism. A concept derived from Revelation and a part of Christian theology, millennialism represents the power of good overcoming evil to establish a glorious and righteous kingdom on earth, led by Christ. According to some scholars, millenialism influenced the Puritans, the American Revolution and radical abolitionists. Moreover, millennialism has as a component the belief in the divine election of a group through whom the millennium will occur. Many Americans, from the Puritans on, have identified themselves as a "chosen people."

Elijah Muhammad, as the self-proclaimed Messenger of Allah, turned the notion upside down, by finding in it the basis for the "Devil" theory of white American civilization. According to the tenets of the Black Muslims, the original man was none other than the black man. Accordingly, all blacks represent Allah or at least participate through him and are therefore divine. With the destruction of white American civilization by Allah, a black millennium will be ushered in. Blacks are the chosen people. The notion has great appeal today to blacks seeking to salve an injured pride. Within the above context, the Nation of Islam grew as a nationalist/religious organization.

After Elijah Muhammad's takeover in 1934, the Nation of Islam grew slowly. During the early 1940s it suffered through a period of persecution because its members refused to serve in the armed forces. Elijah Muhammad spent five years in a federal prison, a blessing in disguise, for he demonstrated a willingness to suffer for his beliefs. After his release from prison in 1946, he built the Nation into a significant movement. By 1955 there were 15 temples scattered throughout the country. By the end of the decade the number had grown to 50 in 22 states and the District of Columbia with membership exceeding 100,000.

The 1960s saw a surge in membership, resulting largely from an increasing pride in the accomplishments of Africans, who were obtaining their independence, and a decreasing faith in the capability of the civil rights movement to obtain equality for black Americans.

Like the Garvey movement, the Nation of Islam stressed social separation and economic independence. It extolled hard work, thrift and accumulation of wealth. Members were required to contribute one-tenth of their earnings to support the work of the Nation. Over the years the Nation of Islam invested in a variety of businesses, including restaurants, supermarkets, clothing stores and farms. The Nation of Islam was considered the largest black economic enterprise in the country, with assets once estimated at $70 million.

The rapid growth of the Nation of Islam did not occur without internal dissension, increased problems of discipline and even assassination. The best-known Black Muslim was Malcolm X, a former pimp and drug peddler, who joined the Nation while still in prison. In 1954, Elijah Muhammad made him head of the movement in Harlem. As a skilled orator, Malcolm X won numerous adherents, but as a staunch foe of integration, he angered liberal whites and middle-class blacks. Moreover Malcolm X and Elijah Muhammad drifted apart as Malcolm started to steer the movement into a more politically radical posture. Malcolm X found the nonpolitical policy of the Nation self-defeating, especially when he witnessed the successes of Martin Luther King, Jr. (SCLC), Roy Wilkins (NAACP), Floyd McKissick (CORE) and Whitney Young (Urban League). Furthermore, he proposed a violent campaign against the established order. Such a departure, Elijah Muhammad believed, would only destroy the Nation of Islam. In December 1963, after Malcolm X described President John F. Kennedy's assassination as a case of "the chickens coming home to roost," Elijah Muhammad had a convenient excuse to rid himself of this charismatic man who threatened his movement. Elijah Muhammad temporarily suspended Malcolm and prohibited him from speaking publicly for 90 days. Malcolm X left the movement and in March 1964 formed the Muslim Mosque Inc.

A month after his break with the Nation, Malcolm X visited Mecca, where he gained new insights into Islamic teachings, and Africa, where he consulted with the heads of several African nations. While in Mecca he saw Muslim pilgrims practicing brotherhood, irrespective of race or color. He became an orthodox Muslim and rejected the idea of the white man as devil as well as other elements of the Nation's dogma. He denied that God was incarnated in the person of Master Wallace Fard. He pointed out the Islamic heresy of deifying a human. Malcolm came to believe that the impending racial holocaust could be averted if white Americans turned toward the spritual path of truth and embraced real brotherhood. He repudiated the Black Muslims' policy of separation, denounced their acquisitive thirst for money and property and insisted that the real conflict between the races was a class struggle.

Shortly thereafter, Malcolm committed the unpardonable sin of revealing Elijah Muhammad's extramarital affairs. While his break with the Nation had itself been an affront to Elijah Muhammad, Malcolm's scandalmongering sealed his fate. Malcolm X had barely begun the process of redefining the directions of the civil rights movement and of propagating his own gospel when he was shot and killed on February 21, 1965. (Recent disclosures indicate that the death orders came on high authority in the Nation of Islam and were carried out by three rank-and-file members.)

Through the posthumous publication of his autobiography, Malcolm X continued to exert influence on black Americans. His followers remained plentiful within the Nation of Islam, among them Wallace Muhammad.

Malcolm X's assassination was not the only retribution murder in Black Muslim history. In January 1973, a squad of armed Muslims burst into the home of Hamaas Abdul Khaalis, the leader of the secessionist Hanafi Muslims, and killed seven followers including four children. Five members of the Nation of Islam were convicted of the murders. Khaalis, like Malcolm X, had not only broken with the Nation but had denounced the Messenger as a religious charlatan.

The Hanafi sect, named for one of the four major schools of Islamic law, appeals to more educated and economically secure blacks. The most notable member of the Hanafi sect is Kareem Abdul Jabbar (Lew Alcindor), a professional basketball superstar.

The Hanafi sect will be most remembered for the "seige of Washington, D.C.," in March 1977. Believing that those ultimately responsible for his followers' deaths had gone unpunished, Khaalis vowed that the killings must be avenged. The Hanafis seized three Washington buildings in which they held 134 persons hostage, wounded numerous others and killed a reporter. While his men held the buildings, Khaalis demanded that Wallace Muhammad, his brother Herbert Muhammad and Muhammad Ali be delivered to him in order that justice could be served. Khaalis wound up in a psychiatric prison ward.

In 1975, Elijah Muhammad died, leaving behind some 70,000 followers in 73 temples throughout the nation. By the time of his death, the movement and attitudes towards it had changed considerably. The late Richard Daley, mayor of Chicago, called the death of Elijah Muhammad "a great loss to the City of Chicago and to the entire community." The Black Muslim thrift and moral code impressed many leaders who once only made disparaging remarks about the movement. Leading civil rights figures such as Jesse Jackson, Julian Bond, Roy

Wilkins and Vernon Jordan all heaped praise upon the departed leader, lauding him for providing blacks with a positive model of hard work, devotion to self and cleanliness of mind and body.

Upon Elijah Muhammad's death, Wallace Deen Muhammad emerged as the leader. He found that he had inherited $8 million in debts and a corrupt fiscal management. He began dismantling his father's empire on the grounds that Islam is a faith and not a conglomerate.

Wallace Muhammad then undertook to lead his flock towards a gentle, new orthodoxy, called the "Second Resurrection." To do so he had to shake out many of his father's dogmas, including his claim to having been the Last Apostle of Allah. Elijah Muhammad was reduced to mortal status. Another of Wallace's purgative acts was to dissolve the Fruit of Islam (FOI), the so-called moral right arm of the movement, a tough collection of enforcers.

He formally ended the use of the epithet "white devils" and welcomed white believers to membership. He denationalized the Nation, renaming it the World Community of Al-Islam in the West. The new name represented a break from racism and separatism. In 1979, to establish an even closer link to America, the group became the American Muslim Mission.

His followers were no longer to be known as blacks but as "Bilalians," after Bilal, an African convert to Islam who became the first muezzin of the Prophet Muhammad. The publication, *The Messenger Muhammad Speaks*, was changed to *Bilalian News*, and in 1979 it became *AM Journal*. Political activities were no longer discouraged, and American Muslims could even serve in the armed forces and salute the American flag.

No change was more irksome to a significant percentage of the sect than the dramatic move to restore Malcolm X to a place of honor. Not only did Wallace Muhammad rehabilitate Malcolm and demote his own father, he had Louis (Abdul Hareem) Farrakhan, the successor to Malcolm X, make the announcement. Rumors of dissent erupted.

In 1978, the schism between Wallace Muhammad and Farrakhan exceeded rumor status. Wallace Muhammad accused Farrakhan of preaching black nationalism and attempting to have the Muslims in Chicago align themselves with Uganda and Idi Amin. He demanded that Farrakhan not preach against the "new concept of God that we have accepted," namely, orthodox Islam.

In the thirtieth month after the death of Elijah Muhammad, Farrakhan claimed leadership of the revived Nation of Islam in the name of Prophet Elijah Muhammad. He announced that Elijah Muhammad still lives.

With the revival of the Nation of Islam, millennialism reemerged as Farrakhan proclaimed that his followers "are now living in the judgment or doom of the white man's world. Preparations have been made to meet every effort by the white man to oppose the setting up of Allah's new world of righteousness." He named the group's publication, *Final Call*, after the first newspaper of Elijah Muhammad, the *Final Call to Islam*.

If the new Nation identifies with any Islamic sect, it is Shiism. The relationship rests on Farrakhan's need to reinforce the validity of his claim to leadership. The point has been argued that Farrakhan, like Ali, cousin of Muhammad, had been unjustly denied his rightful place as heir to the last Messenger. Moreover, Shia Islam's survival as a splinter and minority sect of Islam is perceived as a symbol of the Nation of Islam's potential.

The new Nation of Islam resembles the former and for similar reasons. Farrakhan believes that national and world conditions are forcing blacks to think in terms of self-help. To prepare themselves for leadership, Black Muslims are required to live by a strict code of private and social morality appropriate for a divine black man. While some of the codes reflect Islamic doctrine, others are very American and have earned them the nickname "Black Puritans."

Followers of the Nation of Islam are to pray at least five times a day, facing east towards Mecca, but only after thoroughly cleansing the body. They are to refrain from eating certain foods, such as pork and cornbread ("slave diet"). Black Muslims are not to overeat and are encouraged to take only one meal a day. Tobacco and alcohol are absolutely forbidden. They are to observe a strict sexual morality. No Muslim woman is to be alone in a room with a man other than her husband. She is never to wear provocative, revealing dress or to use cosmetics. Any Muslim who engages in illicit sexual relations faces severe punishment and possible expulsion from the Nation. Marriage outside the faith is discouraged, and nonbelieving spouses are pressured to join the group. Although divorce is discouraged, it is permitted under certain conditions. The similarity between the old and new are remarkable, especially in the intensity, austerity and discipline which clearly filters down to the rank and file.

Only the most superficial changes have been made with regard to race attitudes. The white man is still viewed as a liar and oppressor. Nonbelieving blacks are also seen as "betrayers of the truth" because they seek "to lose their 'black identity' under the guise of 'humanity,' 'integration' and even 'religion.' " While the new Nation of Islam preaches a message of brotherhood, that message does not seem to include whites.

Since the formal and bitter split in 1978, the new Nation of Islam and the American Muslim Mission have purposely moved further apart. The former holds onto the past, while the latter distances itself from the past, without totally rejecting it. For the American Muslims, Elijah Muhammad's "social myths" are allegorical and transitional. His personalization of God seemed necessary in any appeal to the poor, uneducated urban masses, who had no concept of Islam but who knew Christianity was not serving their needs.

In contrast, the American Muslim Mission is open and moderate. This openness manifests itself in the welcoming of all types to the fold and in interracial and interfaith efforts to improve society. In the context of social service, American Muslims believe that common problems confront the poor and downtrodden, and they insist that religious differences must be forgotten.

The American Muslim Mission is decentralized and more democratic in structure than the Nation of Islam. A council composed of seven regional Imams directs the organization. Moreover, American Muslims are no longer institutionalized businesspeople and are free to engage in occupations with no link to the religion.

Despite their differences, the new Nation of Islam and the American Muslim Mission answer the desperate needs of a particular group of urban American blacks who are disenchanted with Christianity and the prevailing socioeconomic system. Both groups continue to work to improve the prison system, which has always been a fruitful area for proselytizing. They are involved in community service, food cooperatives and education. While some have predicted the increasing success of the moderate American Muslim Mission at the expense of the more radical new Nation of Islam, changing socioeconomic conditions bring such a prediction into question. The American Muslim Mission, which makes itself more acceptable to black and white alike, could be identified with a system that more and more blacks perceive as alien, distant and uncaring. If increasing disparity between rich and poor, black and white, continues, there seems a reasonable chance for the Nation of Islam to recapture at least some of the following and the influence of the past.

BIBLIOGRAPHY

Books

Breitman, George. *The Last Year of Malcolm X: The Evolution of a Revolutionary*. New York: Merit, 1967.
———, ed. *Malcolm X Speaks: Selected Speeches and Statements*. New York: Grove Press, 1966.
Clarke, John Henrick, comp. *Malcolm X: The Man and His Times*. New York: Macmillan, 1969.
Cronon, Edmund David. *Black Moses: The Story of Marcus Garvey and the Universal Negro Improvement Association*. Madison: University of Wisconsin Press, 1955.
Draper, Theodore. *The Rediscovery of Black Nationalism*. New York: Viking Press, 1970.
Essien-Udom, Essien Udosen. *Black Nationalism: A Search for Identity in America*. Chicago: University of Chicago Press, 1962.
Goldman, Peter. *The Death and Life of Malcolm X*. Urbana: University of Illinois Press, 1979.
Lincoln, Charles Eric. *The Black Muslims in America*. Boston: Beacon Press, 1961.
Little, Malcolm. *The Autobiography of Malcolm X*. New York: Grove Press, 1965.
Lomax, Louis E. *When the Word Is Given: A Report on Elijah Muhammad, Malcolm X, and the Black Muslim World*. New York: New American Library, 1963.
Muhammad, Wallace Deen. *As the Light Shineth from the East*. Chicago: WDM, 1980.
Wolfenstein, Eugene Victor. *The Victims of Democracy: Malcolm X and the Black Revolution*. Berkeley: University of California Press, 1981.

Articles

Geneson, Paul. "The Muslims in 1982: From Isolated Anger to Mainstream Involvement." *Houston Career Digest* 5:21 (1982): 7–10.
Gianckos, Perry E. "The Black Muslims: An American Millennialistic Response to Racism and Cultural Doctrination." *The Centennial Review* 23:4 (1979): 430–451.
Mahiri, Jabari. "Beyond Black Religion." *Black Books Bulletin* 4:2 (1976): 42–45.

Robert V. Haynes
Jeffrey T. Sammons

ARABS Numbering nearly 148 million and forming the majority population of 15 nations, the Arabs represent the largest, most diverse and most politically influential Muslim ethnic group in the world. Their involvement with the non-Muslim world, whether through oil or politics, is profound; their influence within the Muslim world is deep and broad. Arabic is the sixth most widely spoken language in the world as a mother tongue, but it is spoken by more than three-quarters of a billion people as a religious language. The Prophet Muhammad, who established Islam, was an Arab.

As no ethnic group this size can be homogeneous, there are no universal physical types. Arabs are tall and short, black-haired and blond, with skin colors ranging from fair to dark; the predominant physical appearance, however, is usually "Mediterranean"—swarthy, black-haired and of medium height.

There is also no single environmental adaptation. Arabs live on mountains, in valleys, on deserts and on seacoasts, in small villages and large cities. Nearly 2.5 million, of whom perhaps 10 percent are Muslim, live in the United States. Muslim Arabs, composing 92.7 percent of the ethnic group, belong to a number of sects—Shia (Ithna Ashari and Ismaili), Alawi, Zaidi and Sunni, the last group being overwhelmingly the largest. The other 7 percent of Arabs are largely Christian or Druze.

What "makes" an Arab is a combination of traits, which narrows down to whether or not a person "feels" he is an Arab. He probably speaks Arabic (with a dialect), although in Arab-minority countries, such as the United States, a second- or third-generation Arab may no longer speak the language. More importantly, he identifies with the heritage of Arabs and those cultural values and inspirations unique to Arabs, be they Moroccan or Syrian, Christian or Muslim, farmer or businessman. In non-Arab countries, again like the United States, social and political pressures (i.e., Israel) may encourage a person's feeling of "Arabness."

Arab culture draws upon a heritage several thousand years old that includes some periods of glory, but more of travail. Camel-riding Arab tribesmen fought in the armies of ancient Romans and Persians. Arab caravans and ships carried merchandise to trading centers of South and Southeast Asia before the birth of

Christ. Some Arab tribal kingdoms in southwestern Arabia were powerful and prosperous.

It was among Arabs, early in the seventh century and at first largely confined to the Arabian peninsula, that Muhammad preached his gospel of Islam. With remarkable rapidity Muhammad's successors spread the word of Allah into Southwest Asia, westward across North Africa and into Spain, eastward into Persia, Afghanistan and Central Asia and southward to the east coast of Africa. Wherever these new and fervent Muslims went, they implanted elements of Arab culture alongside the religion.

Muslim Arab leaders created great empires that lasted several hundred years. Following the original Caliphate of Muhammad, the Umayyid dynasty in Damascus (661–750) established a governing system whereby religious and ethnic minorities were given a large measure of self-rule, provided that they paid the taxes levied against them and remained peaceful.

The succeeding Abbasid dynasty ruled the Muslim world from its capital at Baghdad for nearly 500 years, the first 200 of which (750–950) are called the Golden Age of Arab civilization. Arab rulers encouraged scholarship by bringing to Baghdad and other centers of learning intellectual Jews, Christians, Greeks, Persians and Indians—all contributing from their own cultures to the development of Arab culture. Plato and Aristotle were first translated from Greek to Arabic, then later into European languages. Indian scientists brought the concept of zero to Baghdad; the Arabs combined it with Arabic numerals and transmitted to Europe the mathematical systems of algebra, geometry and trigonometry. While the Dark Ages blanketed Europe, Abbasid scientists were exploring the fields of optics (disproving Euclid's theory that the eye emanates rays), chemistry (introducing such words as alkali, alcohol and antimony to the world's vocabulary) and medicine (compiling the world's first medical encyclopedia; Ibn Sina's was the major medical work in Europe until the seventeenth century). Historiography became a discipline under the Abbasids, and what happened in most of the world then was told to later civilizations by Arab historians. Arab architecture, best exemplified in mosques, tombs and palaces, created styles popular to this day.

By the thirteenth century, Arab might and splendor were fading. With the discovery of sea routes around Africa and the later European colonization of North and South America, trade routes from Europe shifted from the Mediterranean Sea. Trade through the Arab world did not return until the opening of the Suez Canal in 1869. Meanwhile, outlying provinces broke away from the empire, with separate kingdoms appearing in North Africa. The Arab empire in Spain dwindled to a shaky foothold in the south, then disappeared from the peninsula completely. Elsewhere, Arab power was too weak to resist the incursion of outsiders. From the north came invasions of Turks and Mongols, destroying irrigation systems, cities and whole economies, from which the Arabs never recovered. By the sixteenth century first Seljuk, then Ottoman Turkish rulers had conquered the Arab homelands, ruling until World War I, when the Turkish empire was itself broken into European mandates.

Throughout this period Arab economic, political and intellectual initiative lay dormant under the domination of foreign imperialism. An awakening (*nadha*) appeared in the 1920s, manifested by the writings of intellectuals and political activism, but not until after World War II did Arabs once again rule most of their own lands. By then, however, the imported system of political nationalism had divided the Arabs into separate states, undermining the political unity of the ethnic group as a whole.

While Arab political unity is still a dream, language remains a common denominator. Arabic, written from right to left in a flowing shorthand script, is, like Hebrew, a Semitic language of the Afro-Asiatic linguistic family. Evidence of its first use appears in accounts of wars as long ago as 853 B.C. As the language of the Quran, it brings prestige to the Muslim who can speak and read it. Arabic has developed into two forms: classical Arabic, the religious and literary language, spoken and written uniformly throughout the Arab world and serving as a bond among all literate Muslims; and colloquial Arabic, the informal spoken language, which varies by dialect from region to region. Both forms are used by educated Arabs.

Arabs can be said to live on an island, or archipelago, stretching from the Atlantic Ocean eastward for 4,000 miles to the Indian Ocean, bounded on the north by a sea of water and on the south by a sea of sand. This analogy serves to distinguish the extremes of Arab culture—most Arabs live in between.

Arab culture developed on the desert side of the island among the peoples of the Arabian peninsula, who lived either as tribal nomads (bedouin) or town dwellers engaged in commerce but who were nevertheless greatly influenced by bedouin ways and values. While Muhammad himself was a town trader, his tribe, the Quraysh, included many bedouin, and Muhammad and his followers were deeply imbued with pre-Islamic, tribal traditions. These traditions, born in the harsh environment of the desert, included strict codes of proper economic and social behavior which became legitimized by Islam and accompanied the Arabs as they emerged from the desert and its oasis towns.

Arab bedouin live on land not good enough for year-round cultivation or dismal enough to abandon as long as there is water. They must move either constantly or seasonally, living in tents and earning their living as stock breeders, transporters or tradesmen and no longer as warriors—except as part of a nation's army. They produce the livestock for much of the sedentary Arab world (almost totally in the past, but less so today), raising camels, horses and donkeys as beasts of burden and sheep and goats for food, clothing and manure. As transporters, they move products from the countryside to towns and between settlements where no roads exist. As tradesmen, they provide a link between villages and towns, bringing to the villagers the manufactured utensils, cloth, coffee, tea and processed salt and sugar not available locally. Their relationships with the settled people are based on reciprocity following carefully defined rules of procedure and protocol. There is mutual contempt for each other's life-style, and intermarriage is rare.

Bedouin are tribally organized, with each family belonging to a patrilineal descent group, and that group to a tribe, which assures a measure of social and economic control of each segment. The family, which moves with others—mostly near relatives—as a semi-autonomous unit, is patriarchal, patrilocal and patrilineal. The individual is subordinate to the group and, in return, receives protection and security as long as the tribal mechanism functions. Marriage is endogamous except when a marital tie outside the lineage is important for political or economic reasons. The preferred marriage for males is to father's brother's daughter, and each marriage is carefully negotiated so that both families benefit from the new bonds.

Within this social structure, there is a strong element of egalitarianism. With few occupational variations, social distinctions are based on family membership, not job status. And among families there is no great social distinction, although some descent lines are considered more noble than others. The only true social distinctions at the extended family level are between sexes (men are dominant) and between young and old, the former deferring to the latter.

Unlike villagers, bedouin live an erratic life—on the move, deciding when and where to move next and concerned with daily care of animals and family needs. There is a continuing sense of insecurity in a physically hostile world. To meet the demands imposed on them, they must be tough, self-disciplined and aggressive, characteristics reflected in traditions of independence, hostility to compromise and a strong system of values.

The bedouin's life-style has become symbolic of basic Arab values. These values serve to ensure harmony in human relationships, solidarity of the family in the face of adversity and a continuation of the system. Seemingly contradictory, each value is operative in its own time and circumstance. For instance, the independent bedouin is defiant of outside authority, yet each bedouin lives in a tightly controlled social system which subordinates the individual to the group. Bedouin Arabs are generous and hospitable, yet they are hostile toward outsiders generally (as opposed to guests), or when the family honor is threatened. The blood feud is part of bedouin culture whereby transgressions against the family must be revenged. In their camps, bedouin recognize the equality of the individual, yet women play a subservient role to men. Courage and bravery bring status to an individual, yet wisdom to mediate disputes and the self-discipline to avoid bullying the weak are commendable traits. Observance of these values brings honor to the family and lineage; violation of them brings shame and loss of face to the group. Those who commit indiscretions against honor are punished severely, sometimes by banishment from the group, sometimes even by death.

To these ideal values may be added an attitude towards religion which is both fundamentalisticly Islamic and pre-Islamic in origin. The Shariah (religious law), when interpreted literally, gives divine support to bedouin values; indeed, Muhammad's teaching reflected the bedouin environment in which he lived. Any reinterpretation of Islamic law implies a questioning of these values. This conservatism in religious practices is best exemplified on the Arabian peninsula by Wahhabism, illustrated by the ban in Saudi Arabia, Kuwait and the Emirates on drinking alcohol, dancing and women drivers.

Bedouin live in an inhospitable environment of temperature extremes and capricious rains. They accept the harsh effects of the elements, as they do all unexplainable occurrences in their lives, as the will of God. Fate, however, is affected by a world filled with spirits who either help or thwart objectives. These spirits must be placated or avoided.

Today no more than 5 million Arabs, and fewer than 1 million of them pure bedouin, live in or along the desert "shore," continuing the traditions of the past and reminding the rest of the Arab world of the "true" nature of Arab culture. While roads and trucks usurp the role of the camel, bedouin still ply the old trade routes, seek pasture for their animals and maintain their tribal systems. Many have found work in the oil fields of Saudi Arabia, Kuwait and the Emirates, some have gone to universities, but the rigid codes of honor, revenge, hospitality, hostility, loyalty and resistance remain strong (see Arabs, Chadian).

The opposite extreme of Arab culture developed along the Mediterranean shore of the Arab "island," where Arabs met and mingled with the different cultures of Europe. Compromise with diversity replaced rigidity; religious fundamentalism gave way to accommodation to new ideas. In the cities of Beirut, Cairo, Alexandria, Tunis, Algiers and Casablanca, diversified economies offered new professions for the traditional Arab. Universities opened minds to change. Political nationalism replaced tribal allegiance and came into conflict with European imperialism.

About half of the Muslim Arabs live in cities and towns. They are distinguished by the variety of their occupations, the weakening of the broader family ties which characterize bedouin and rural kin relationships, the relative freedom of women to leave the home, the reduced practice of arranged marriages, endogamy and polygyny and the lessening of social pressures which enforce conformity in religious practices. The social structure of the urban Muslim Arab is considerably more complex than that of his desert or village counterpart.

New economic institutions and comparative release of the individual from family restrictions require new systems of interpersonal relationships which, while not replacing the role of the family and neighborhood, do call for new ways of determining status and prestige. Modernization, industrialization and political nationalism have increasing influence on urban life. A middle class is arising, composed of professional people, bureaucrats, clerical technicians and industrialists who, while not yet predominant, play a growing role in society. Among all there is a wrench as the old ways and values conflict with the changes demanded by urban life.

The town Arab, like the urbanist, lives in a changing world where traditional patterns of living are undergoing stress, only to a lesser degree. Life in the small

Arab town revolves around the *suq* (marketplace), where nomads, villagers and urban traders meet to exchange goods and products. In the towns, representatives of government agencies (tax collector, army conscriptor, police, irrigation officer) make contact with the bulk of the population.

Closer to the villager (but disdainful of him), the townsman is religiously conservative and intimately involved with his kin group. Ideal values exemplified by the nomad find minimal adherence. There is less concern with hospitality and defiance and more concern with economic symbols—property, wealth, education and prosperity. Family honor remains important, however, and women continue to live a secluded life under the watchful eyes of their menfolk.

Marginal to the urbanists and townspeople are Arabs who live in villages close enough to cities and towns to be influenced by the "modern" ways of urban life. The best examples of these urban-influenced villages are in Israel, Lebanon and the Nile delta and along the coasts of Tunisia, Algeria and Morocco. These villagers comprehend a degree of political nationalism and have a high level of economic expectation, although it is usually thwarted.

Between the two extremes of the desert with its ascetic rigidity and the city/town with its aura of change live most of the Arabs, those who cultivate the soil. The Arab village is usually a compact cluster of walled, mud-floored homes built of local products, most often mudbrick. Its intimate nature reflects the closeness of the family and the insecurity of its inhabitants, who hide their private world from strangers.

Characteristic of villagers everywhere, Arab villagers confine their work to a limited number of occupations, chiefly farming. Other jobs they might pursue, usually on a part-time basis, include being watchmen, midwives, storytellers and seamstresses. Each village will have a group of outsiders with special skills—carpenters, barbers, shopkeepers, tailors, religious leaders—and professionals, such as teachers and doctors, if they are there at all.

The work life of the Arab villagers is hard and seldom rewarding. They are able to grow only what they need to eat or trade—cereal grains, vegetables, livestock, cotton. There is seldom a surplus in food or money to pay off their heavy indebtedness or to save for investment in machinery, tools or fertilizers should they be so inclined, which usually they are not. Villagers live by tradition, without the incentives, knowledge or security necessary to take the risks that innovation entails. Change is disruptive and threatens the institutions the villagers have established to live in harmony with their environment as well as with fellow villagers.

Village values stem from the ideal values of the nomad. While tribesmen relate only to kinsmen, villagers do relate to non-kin, yet loyalty to the group (tribe or village) is strong. As tribal kin groups may be split by feuds, village segments may feud as well. Standards of hospitality are high among villagers, as is awareness of family honor.

The villager lives in an extended family with numerous kin residing together or in close proximity. Family life is tightly controlled. Each family member has a defined role with little room for individual deviation. Like the bedouin, the villager finds security in the family during times of economic hardship and in old age. Changes in individual roles, such as when a son goes off to work in a town, often weaken the family socioeconomic system.

Children are a villager's greatest asset. They are his work force and social security. Islamic rules of inheritance, which give more to boys than to girls, particularly in terms of real estate, and traditional patrilineal ties lend importance to having boys in the family. A girl's asset is in her function of tying one family with another through marriage and, of course, her primary role as a mother. The birth of children, particularly a boy, is cause for celebration. It is often surrounded by non-Islamic ritual, as in some Lebanese and Egyptian villages where the placenta is buried (either under the front doorstep or inside the mud-floored home) so that enemy spirits cannot enact magic against the child or mother. For the same reason, boys are often dressed as girls to deceive evil spirits; the first possession of a child is an amulet or blue bead to ward off malevolence. The first word a baby hears is the name of Allah whispered into its ear.

The naming of a child is important. Custom provides that a child's name will reflect the three dominant elements in Arab village life: kin, home and religion. Thus a boy will have a name such as Muhammad ibn Ibrahim al Hamza: Muhammad (religious name), son of Ibrahim (father's name) of Hamza (village name). Girls are similarly named and keep their name even after marriage, reflecting Muslim Arab tradition that even though they are subservient to men, Arab women retain their own identity, their separate legal rights and their family ties.

Circumcision for boys is universal and is a celebrated ritual around the seventh year; it formally initiates the boy into the religious community. Again, animistic ritual may accompany this ceremony. In Lebanon sometimes the severed foreskin is placed in a vent over the door along with the child's first soiled diaper. Girls are seldom circumcised except in upper Egypt, where sometimes the clitoris is excised.

Boys and girls, while raised together during early childhood, receive different treatment. Boys are given great affection and are pampered by the mother, who responds to every wish, including continued breast feeding on demand until the boy is past the age of two or three, sometimes longer if the mother has milk (or the boy is given to another woman for suckling). Girls are also shown affection but are weaned much earlier and are not pampered. The mother remains throughout the children's lives a symbol of warmth and love. For both sexes the father is a stern disciplinarian who administers corporal punishment and instills a degree of fear among his children. Boys are especially taught—often harshly—to obey and respect older males.

Children assume adult activities early in life and as soon as they are able take up separate sex roles, the boys going to the fields and the girls helping their mothers cook and care for siblings. Adolescents have no contact with the opposite sex outside the family, with special care taken to protect the girl's chastity. The primary protector of the girl is her older brother, who continues to watch over his sister even after she marries and leaves the household.

Marriage of village children is arranged by parents. Girls enter marriage between 14 and 19, boys a little older. Marriages are arranged to meet family kin needs, to establish ties either within the kin structure or with other lineages which will have economic or status advantages. The traditionally preferred Arab marriage is endogamous (between brothers' children). It is not unusual that bride and groom meet for the first time on the day of the wedding, when the bridewealth (*mahr*) is determined and the marriage contract signed.

Polygyny is accepted by Arabs, but its practice is limited by the high cost of the second wife and the Quranic command that each be treated equally. A man will marry another woman usually only when his first wife is barren or reaches old age or when it is especially important to establish new lineage ties. The major cause for divorce is childlessness. Divorce is easy in theory, difficult in fact, because the separation of two individuals implies the separation of two families, each with special interests in the success of the marriage.

The lives of Arab village men and women run on different tracks. Their work life is separate, with the men in the fields, the women in the home. Their social life is separate, the men in the coffeehouses and the women in the home, visiting with neighbors and relatives. They often eat separately, and they pray separately.

Arab villagers are deeply religious, following a composite of Islamic folk beliefs and rituals. Religion explains the many unknowns and uncontrollables which plague their lives. It provides divine authority for action, and God's name is invoked at all times; seldom does an Arab villager make a promise or plan without saying "*inshallah*" ("if God wills"). Religion confirms changes in social status, such as circumcision and marriage. It provides hope for a better life after death. Above all, religious festivals, such as Id al Adha, Id al Fitr and, for Shia Arabs, Muharram, break the monotony of village life.

For men the mosque is the center of worship. Women go less to the mosque (where, if they are allowed in at all, they must pray separately in the rear) and more to their own religious ceremonies conducted in a home by female religious leaders. Or they may worship at a saint's tomb, where there is not the physical segregation of the mosque.

Arabs follow all sects of Islam, although most are Sunni. All schools of law have Sunni Arab adherents. The Shafi predominate in Jordan, Egypt and western Arabia; Hanbali in central Arabia; Maliki in eastern Arabia, North Africa and Sudan and Hanafi in Syria and Iraq (areas with a long history of Ottoman domination).

More than one-half the Arab Muslims of Iraq are Shia, as are 20 percent of the Lebanese. Nearly 1 million Arabs in western Syria and northern Lebanon are Alawi, an offshoot of Shiism. The Shia and Alawi usually are the poorest people in the population, farming the least fertile soil and holding the least skilled jobs in towns and cities.

Sufi brotherhoods abound among town and urban Arabs. In Syria and Jordan (including Palestine) the Alawiyya is strong; the Darqawiyya has followers in Lebanon and North Africa; the Riga'iyya is active in Iraq, Syria and Egypt, while the Qadiriyya and Naqshbandiyya find adherents throughout the area. In Libya and Saudi Arabia the Sanusiyya is especially important, as the Khalwatiyya and Burhaniyya are in Egypt.

As a bedouin sees his life changing with the construction of roads, the introduction of trucks and the influence of the oil fields, so too the Arab villager notes evidence of change. Contemporary Arab governments are being led by new and younger men who at least make verbal commitment to economic and social development. While this usually means urban development, some of it affects the villager. Road building has decreased the degree of isolation of thousands of villages and increased the contact of the villager with the outside world. Transistor radios hang off the bedouin's camel saddle and blare loudly in the village coffeehouse, bringing in ideas from the outside world. Land reform in some Arab countries has brought new systems of land ownership, agricultural credit and new farming technology. Young village Arabs, reacting to overcrowded homes and uneconomic parceling of land, increasingly seek their fortunes in the towns and cities. International labor migration from poorer Arab countries to oil-rich states is becoming an important source of revenue to millions of families of all classes and backgrounds. Change comes slowly, but it comes.

BIBLIOGRAPHY

Books

Abraham, Sameer Y., and Abraham, Nabeel, eds. *Arabs in the New World*. Detroit: Wayne State University Press, 1983.

Ammar, Hamed. *Growing up in an Egyptian Village*. London: Routledge and Kegan Paul, 1954.

Antoun, Richard T. *Arab Village: A Social Structural Study of a Transjordanian Peasant Community*. Bloomington: Indiana University Press, 1971.

———, and Yarik, Iliya F., eds. *Rural Politics and Social Change in the Middle East*. Bloomington: Indiana University Press, 1972.

Asad, Talal. *The Kababish Arab: Power, Authority and Consent in a Nomadic Tribe*. New York: Praeger, 1970.

Atiyah, Edward. *The Arabs*. Beirut: Lebanon Bookshop, 1968.

Awad, Mohamed. "Nomadism in the Arab Lands of the Middle East." In *The Problems of the Arid Zone*. Proceedings of the Paris Symposium Arid Zone Research, 18. Paris: UNESCO, 1962.

Ayrout, Henry H. *The Egyptian Peasant*. Boston: Beacon Press, 1963.

Baer, Gabriel. *Fellah and Townsmen in the Middle East*. London: Frank Cass, 1982.

Barclay, Harold. *Buuri al Lamaab: A Surburban Village in the Sudan*. Ithaca: Cornell University Press, 1964.

Barfield, Thomas. *The Central Asian Arabs of Afghanistan*. Austin: University of Texas Press, 1982.

Bates, Daniel, and Rassam, Amal. *Peoples and Cultures of the Middle East*. Englewood Cliffs, N.J.: Prentice-Hall, 1983.

Beck, Lois, and Keddie, Nikki, eds. *Women in the Muslim World*. Cambridge: Harvard University Press, 1978.

Berger, Morroe. *The Arab World Today*. New York: Doubleday, 1962.

Blunt, Lady Anne, ed. *Bedouin Tribes of the Euphrates*. London: Frank Cass, 1968.

Bovill, E. W. *The Living Races of the Sahara Desert*. Papers of Peabody Museum of American Archaeology and Ethnology, Harvard University, 28, no. 3. Cambridge: Harvard University Press, 1958.

Charmichael, Joel. *The Shaping of the Arabs: A Study in Ethnic Identity*. London: Allen & Unwin, 1969.

Coon, Carleton S. *Caravan: Story of the Middle East*. New York: Holt, Rinehart and Winston, 1958.

Cunnison, Ian. *Baggara Arabs: Power and the Lineage in a Sudanese Nomad Tribe*. Oxford: Clarendon Press, 1966.

Dessouki, Ali E. Hillal. *Islamic Resurgence in the Arab World*. New York: Praeger, 1982.

Dickson, H.R.P. *Arabs of the Desert*. London: Allen & Unwin, 1949.

Eickelman, Dale F. *The Middle East: An Anthropological Approach*. Englewood Cliffs, N.J.: Prentice-Hall, 1981.

Ellis, Harry B. *Heritage of the Desert: The Arabs and the Middle East*. New York: Ronald Press, 1956.

Fernea, Elizabeth. *Guests of the Sheikh: An Ethnography of an Iraqi Village*. New York: Doubleday, 1965.

————, and Bezirgan, Basima Qattan, eds. *Middle Eastern Women Speak*. Austin: University of Texas Press, 1981.

Fernea, Robert A. *Sheikh and Effendi: Changing Patterns of Authority Among the El Shabana of Southern Iraq*. Cambridge: Harvard University Press, 1970.

————, and Fernea, Elizabeth W. "Variations in Religious Observance Among Islamic Women." In *Scholars, Saints and Sufis*, edited by Nikki R. Keddie. Berkeley: University of California Press, 1972.

Fuller, Anne. *Buarij: Portrait of a Lebanese Muslim Village*. Middle East Monograph Series. Cambridge: Harvard University Press, 1960.

Gulick, John. *The Middle East: An Anthropological Perspective*. Pacific Palisades, Cal.: Goodyear, 1976.

Hitti, Philip. *History of the Arabs*. London: Macmillan, 1960.

Ibrahim, Saad. *The New Arab Social Order: A Study of the Social Impact of Oil Wealth*. Boulder, Colo.: Westview Press, 1982.

Lancaster, William. *Changing Cultures: The Rwala Bedouin Today*. New York: Cambridge University Press, 1981.

Levy, Reuben. *The Social Structure of Islam*. Cambridge: The University Press, 1957.

Nelson, Cynthia, ed. *The Desert and the Sown*. Berkeley: University of California Institute of International Studies, 1973.

Patai, Raphael. *The Arab Mind*. New York: Scribners, 1973.

Peristiany, J. G. *Honour and Shame: The Values of Mediterranean Society*. Chicago: University of Chicago Press, 1966.

————, ed. *Contributions to Mediterranean Sociology*. Paris: Mouton, 1968.

Rodinson, Maxine. *The Arabs*. Translated by A. Goldhammer. Chicago: University of Chicago Press, 1981.
Sweet, Louise E., ed. *Peoples and Cultures of the Middle East*. 2 vols. New York: Natural History Press, 1970.
Tessler, Mark A.; O'Barr, William M.; and Spain, David H. *Tradition and Identity in Changing Africa*. New York: Harper & Row, 1973.
von Grunebaum, G. E., ed. *Unity and Variety in Muslim Civilization*. Chicago: University of Chicago Press, 1955.
Williams, Judith R. *The Young of Hoouch el Harimi, A Lebanese Village*. Cambridge: Harvard University Center for Middle Eastern Studies, 1968.

Articles

Abu-Zahra, Nadia. "Material Power, Honour, Friendship and Etiquette of Visiting." *Anthropological Quarterly* 47:1 (1974): 120–138.
Altorki, S. "Milk-Kinship in Arab Society: An Unexplained Problem in the Ethnography of Marriage." *Ethnology* 19:2 (1980): 233–244.
Antoun, Richard. "Social Organization and the Life Cycle in an Arab Village." *Ethnology* 6:3 (1967): 294–309.
Berque, Jaques. "Tradition and Innovation in the Maghrib." *Daedalus* 102:1 (1973): 239–250.
Chatty, D. "From Camel to Truck: A Study of Pastoral Adaptation." *Folk* 18 (1976): 113–128.
Cunningham, Robert B. "Dimensions of Family Loyalty in the Arab Middle East." *The Journal of Developing Areas* 8:1 (1973): 55–64.
Dodd, Peter C. "Family Honor and the Forces of Change in Arab Society." *International Journal of Middle East Studies* 4 (1973): 40–54.
Farsoun, Samih K. "Class and Patterns of Association Among Kinsmen in Contemporary Lebanon." *Anthropological Quarterly* 47:1 (1974): 93–111.
Ghanem, I. "Social Life in the Yemens and the Role of Tribal Law." *Middle East International* 18 (1972): 11–13.
Hansen, H. H. "The Pattern of Women's Seclusion and Veiling in a Shia Village." *Folk* 3 (1961): 23–42.
Hilal, Jamil M. "Father's Brother's Daughter Marriage in Arab Communities: A Problem for Sociological Explanation." *Middle East Forum* 46 (1970): 73–84.
Rosenfeld, Henry. "Changes, Barriers to Change and Contradictions in the Arab Village Family." *New Outlook* 13:2 (1970): 28–44.
Shokeid, M. "Ethnic Identity and the Position of Women Among Arabs in an Israeli Town." *Ethnic and Racial Studies* 3:2 (1980): 188–206.

Richard V. Weekes

ARABS, CHADIAN   The centuries-long movement of Arabs westward across Africa brought them into contact with innumerable ethnic groups, nearly all of whom they converted to Islam. Some were absorbed and "became" Arab, such as the Egyptians. Others resisted "Arabization," such as the Berbers. A dynamic confrontation occurred—and continues to occur—among the dozens of small ethnic groups along the southern reaches of the Sahel, where central Africa begins. Here, in western Sudan, southern Chad, northern Cameroon and northern Nigeria, Arab influence is considerable.

Inhabitants of the Chad Basin in the former states of Bagirmi, Bornu and Kanem call these Arabs "Shuwa." One of the plausible explanations of this term is that it is a deformation of the Arabic *shawiyat*, meaning semi-sedentary herders, which is indeed the pastoral adaptation of most Chadian Arabs. The term has the pejorative connotation of "bush yokel." An Arab answering to the question, What are you? will either respond with "Arab" or give the name of his specific descent group.

There are more than 1 million Chadian Arabs distributed between Darfur in western Sudan and Borno in northeastern Nigeria with the highest concentrations around Lake Chad. Myth attributes this location of tribes to migrations following a combat provoked over a stolen camel. A more likely reason is that the hydrological complex of Lake Chad and the Chari and Logone rivers contained abundant dry-season pasture and water, providing precisely those resources whose absence is threatening to animal survival, and thus appearing to herders as a sort of Sahelian "Garden of Eden."

Chad Basin Arabs divide themselves into two categories based upon putative differences in descent. Hassauna (or Bawalme) trace descent from Hassan el Gharbi. Their traditions have them arriving in Chad between the fourteenth and nineteenth centuries from the north out of Libya. There are relatively few Hassauna (perhaps 42,000), and they are found largely in the western portions of the basin near Lake Chad. Important Hassauna tribes include the Dagana, Bani Wail and Abu Krider.

The Djoheina are much more numerous (estimated at 776,000 in Chad) and claim descent from Abdallah el Djoheini. According to tradition they transhumed into the basin from the Nile between the fourteenth and nineteenth centuries. Tribes belonging to this group are widely scattered through the basin. Djoheina further subdivide themselves into those claiming descent from Ahmed el Adjedem, called el Djouzm, and Ahmed el Afser, called Fezera. Important El Djouzm tribes include the Salamat, Messiriya, Rizeygat and Awlad Rachid. The Fezera, few in numbers, are located east of the Chad Basin.

A key to past and present Chadian Arab social structure, as with Arab tribes everywhere, is the use of patrilineal descent to place individuals into systems where smaller descent groups are nested within larger ones. An Arab lives in a household (*bayt*) with a head (*syd al bayt*). A child inherits a patrilineal genealogy (*nisba*) from its father. It soon learns that, after ascending a number of generations in the geneaolgy, he or she will find an ancestor (*jid*) who founded a lineage (*khashim bayt*) to which only the patrilineal descendants (*ahl*) of that ancestor belong. The child also recognizes that there are other descent groups, founded by ancestors who are thought of as brothers or patrilineal cousins of its ancestors, that together make up the "kind" (*nafer*—frequently translated as "tribe" or "race") to which the child belongs. "Tribes" are collections of patriclans that consistently use a particular geographic area (*dar*, or "home"). A tribe may be conceived of as being founded by one or more ancestors. Tribes that conceive of themselves as sharing a remote ancestor at great genealogical depth constitute a confederation. However, in the past, confederations often included non-Arab tribes and usually functioned as military alliances.

Prior to colonization, Arab tribes were usually acephalous. The only position of leadership was that of *shaikh*. Important lineages had *shaikhs*. A *shaikh*, depending on his leadership·skills and wealth, might wield considerable influence but had little authority over any persons beyond his household. Tribes were incorporated into central Sudanic states, and much of their nineteenth-century history is determined by the nature of the incorporation. Usually, states extracted as much tribute as they could squeeze from tribes. Warfare and migrations were major ways by which Arabs dealt with these demands, revolting when they became too great and migrating if rebellion failed. States also insisted that Arabs provide them with military assistance in the form of cavalry. In certain areas where this occurred, Arabs eventually came to control client states. This was probably the case in sixteenth-century Wadai and nineteenth-century Kanem. Once Arabs dominated an area, their culture often surplanted that of its other ethnic groups. Such was the case immediately south of Lake Chad on the eastern side of the Chari River, where the Babelyia, whose small kingdom came to be dominated by the Arabs in the nineteenth century, gradually abandoned their language. This may also account for the disappearance of the Tunjur language (see Tunjur).

Agro-pastoral production systems in Chad appear to be influenced by their distance from Lake Chad and the Chari and Logone river systems. Herders whose rainy season villages are close to the hydrological complex find abundant dry-season pasture and water. This reduces seasonal transhumance. Such Arabs (i.e., Abu Krider) are essentially mixed farmers running dairy and cereal operations. Herders who spend their rainy season farther to the east and northeast, for example in the region around Massakory, perform longer transhumances. The Dagana spend the rainy season near Massakory and the dry season 60 to 120 miles to the south near the Logone between N'Djamena and Bongor. An opportunity cost of increased time spent transhuming is the decreased time that can be spent farming. The Misseriya, for instance, spend their wet season in the extreme Sahel north of Wadai and migrate hundreds of miles south to the pastures near Lake Iro.

Basin Arab experience with colonialism and independence varied widely. Colonial rulers found mobile, apparently leaderless pastoralists slippery to administer, so they frequently delegated the chore to officials from pre-colonial states. This "indirect" rule often insulated Arabs from economic opportunities introduced by colonialism. The situation continued into the first decade following independence and probably has implications both for attitudes toward change and certain supernatural beliefs.

Basin Arabs have been characterized as resistant to change because of a nomadic "wild spirit of independence." Yet there are only two realistic economic choices open to the average Arab: either continued agro-pastoralism or migration to jobs outside Chad. A high percentage of young males do in fact leave, seeking work as far afield as Lagos and Saudi Arabia. The so-called wild attitudes usually are values which investigators have shown contribute to personalities adapted to the rigors of pastoralism. Thus, a fair percentage of the population does seek change but does so in the only way it can—by leaving. For the remainder who stay, their "wild" values are not so much inhibitors of change as facilitators of the rugged, often dangerous pastoral work they perform.

Basin Arabs are Sunni Muslim and for the most part belong to the Tijaniyya *tariqa* (Sufi brotherhood). Around N'Djamena there is a form of sorcery (*sihir*) in which the sorcerer (*massas*) reputedly kills his or her victim, who is then taken to a glen and, deep in the night, cannibalized in a sorcerers' orgy. Arabs believe that the Kotoko indulge in such feasts, dining upon Arab victims (see Kotoko). During the early years of the twentieth century the Kotoko, who in pre-colonial times controlled a number of city-states in northern Cameroon, were delegated authority by the French to administer Arabs within their region. This they did to Arab disadvantage. It is likely that Arab concern about dining with the Kotoko, and serving as the main dish, is but a projection of their history.

Chad's civil war, raging since 1965, is often characterized as one between the Arab north and the Christian/animist south. It is true that Arabs generally have been against the central government. It is equally true that most non-Arab Muslims and a fair number of southerners have at times been disaffected. For example, in 1970 a sample of ethnic groups in N'Djamena was asked what occupation they desired for their children. The response was overwhelming. Everybody, Arabs as well as southerners, wanted their children to grow up to become bureaucrats. This attitude was also exemplified by the comment of an Arab herder who, as he watched a government vehicle speed past, said matter-of-factly: "There are two paths—those of the people and those of the bureaucrats."

In Chad, those who control the central government are assured of economic advantage. They are the only significant group assured of this advantage. When the government rules in a truculent fashion and deploys enough force by invoking military treaties with France to deal with the resulting dissension through violence, but lack sufficient force to achieve repression through military means, then Arabs revolt for the same reasons that Sara Christians burned government cotton trucks in the late 1960s and animist Hadjerai ambushed government Land Rovers during the same period. Civil war in Chad probably has less to do with ethnicity and religion than with the nature of the state in a desperately poor nation.

BIBLIOGRAPHY

Books

Asad, T. *The Kababish Arabs: Power, Authority and Consent in a Nomadic Tribe*. New York: Praeger, 1970.
Carbou, H. *La Région du Tchad et Ouadai*. Vol. 2. Paris: Leroux, 1912.

Cunnison, I. *Baggara Arabs: Power and the Lineage in a Sudanese Nomad Tribe*. Oxford: Oxford University Press, 1966.

Reyna, S. P. *Etude de l'économie et des populations de l'Assale-Serbewel*. N'Djamena: Commission du Bassin du Lac Tchad, 1974.

Yusuf, Fadl Hasan. *The Arabs and the Sudan*. Khartoum: Khartoum University Press, 1973.

Zeltner, Fadl Hasan. *Les Arabs dans la région du lac Tchad: Problèmes d'origine et de chronologie*. Ndjamena, Chad: Centre d'Etudes Linguistiques du College Chasks Lwanga, 1977.

Articles

Hagenboucher, Fr. "Les Arabes dites 'Shuwa' du Nord-Cameroun." *Orstom* (N'Djamena) (1973): 1–24.

———. "Magic et sorcellerie chez les arabes 'Suwa' (Rive sud du lac Tchad)." *Orstom* (N'Djamena) (1974):1–32.

Reyna, S. P. "Social Evolution: A Learning-Theory Approach." *Journal of Anthropological Research* 35 (3): 336–349.

S. P. Reyna

ARGOBBA   The cryptic Argobba, a Muslim people in Ethiopia now reduced to two small and separate populations, number less than 9,000. They pose some of the major historical and ethnological problems remaining among Ethiopia's Semitic-speaking peoples. Questions exist as to the very survival of the Argobba language, and no ethnography of the group has ever been carried out.

The two groups of Argobba are the Northern and the Southern. The former was carefully surveyed in 1973 by the late Volker Stitz, who located some 25 villages stretching 190 miles along the East African Rift escarpment, which defines the edge of the Ethiopian highlands from below Ankober to Dessie. Stitz reported:

The [Northern] Argobba today number some 6,000. They are living in a long chain of villages, some connected to each other, others isolated among different peoples. All of these villages are found in the hilly zone at the foot of the slopes of the Rift Valley. They are bordered in the west by Amharic-speaking Christians, in the east by Adal-speaking Muslims [usually referred to as Afar or Danakil]. The Argobba villages form the eastern fringe of the area of settled agriculturalists. They occupy the Wayna Ega zone (3,500 to 6,000 feet). Here the Argobba industriously till their own land and grow the lowland crops of sorghum and maize in addition to coffee, ch'at [a slightly narcotic leaf for chewing], cotton and tobacco as cash crops. Another important occupation is weaving. Some Argobba speakers are still occupied in short- and long-distance trade, especially in camels and cattle. . . . The long-distance trade to the east, which existed in the nineteenth century . . . has ceased.

The Southern Argobba, who number about 3,000, undoubtedly derived from the Northern group, although the specifics of the historical connections are far from clear. In 1975 there were 20 named Southern Argobba settlements, ranging in size from Kurumi, which had about 500 residents, to clusters of a few houses, such as Gende Hullo. These villages are located on a ridge which forms an arc southeast of the old Muslim city of Harar, the radius of which is about 10 to 14 miles from that city (see Harari).

Ecologically these Southern villages are similar to their Northern counterparts, being located in a chain-like distribution on the edge of a projection of the Rift, some 3,500 to 6,000 feet in elevation. They are surrounded by Oromo agriculturalists and in contact with Somali pastoralists (see Oromo; Somalis). Like the Northern group, the Southern Argobba utilize terracing to maximize their marginal agricultural potential.

Most of the Southern Argobba locales are at the very edge of the cultivable zone, and in years of short rainfall and drought, hunger is readily apparent. Health conditions in the villages with the poorest water supplies further reflect the marginal position of these Argobba. Parasitic infestations and eye diseases such as trachoma are common among the young. In the 1960s, before the World Health Organization's successful campaign against the disease, smallpox regularly swept through the Southern Argobba villages, affecting primarily the young and killing about 20 percent of those infected.

The origins of the Argobba, according to oral traditions reported in both regions, trace to Arabia. The Harari say that the name "Argobba" is an elision of "Arab *gaba*," which means, "The Arabs came," in Harari. One version of this was recounted in 1963 by Baba Haji Mume Bashir, then 97 years old.

"Long ago, before the Suez Canal was dug, a people called Beni Umayya were driven out of Arabia. They walked overland, coming south into Ethiopia and eventually to Harar. When people saw them, they said, 'Arab *gaba*,' and this became their name—Argobba."

Historical linguistics provides a means of linking the Argobba language with other Ethiopian Semitic languages and by so doing provides a clue to the depth of time involved. Robert Hetzron, in his comprehensive analysis of the Ethiopian Semitic languages, classifies the Argobba language as a close relative of Amharic, the national language of Ethiopia. Together, the two languages comprise one of the major subcategories of Transversal South Ethiopic. The other subcategory includes Harari and the Eastern Gurage languages (see Gurage). Argobba, then, is closely related to Amharic, but is distinct.

The language is disappearing. Among the Northern Argobba, it remains their first language, but most of the people are bilingual in Amharic and Oromo. Among the Southern Argobba, it is nearly extinct, having given way to Oromo ("Galla"). Although there is no current written literature in Argobba, there may be examples of written Argobba which have yet to be identified. Further research may uncover more about written Argobba.

There are three explanations of the problem of Argobba distribution. The first is that, in accord with the origin tradition of a migration of the Beni Umayya from Arabia, a very early Argobba presence, ca. A.D. 750, was established in Ethiopia, probably in the northern region. A further development of this possibility would allow for a continuous population of Argobba, encompassing the present locations and intermediate points. There is evidence that Argobba were more widespread than at present.

A second explanation connects the migration of the Argobba to their southern range with the fortunes of the sultanates which developed in the northern area. This hypothesis has strong circumstantial evidence in its favor, particularly if one connects the Argobba to the Walashima' dynasty. In A.D. 1277 one Wali Asma' began the conquest of the Muslim state of Shawa, completing his task in 1285 and establishing 'Ifat as the dominant state of the region. 'Ifat itself was conquered by the armies of Christian Ethiopian kings Dawit I and Yeshaq in 1415, and the Walashima' were driven towards the Red Sea, finally establishing Adal, which was to become the most powerful of this succession of Muslim polities. This explanation of the origin of the Southern Argobba notes that the capital of Adal was near the site of Harar and the present Argobba villages. Although there is no direct evidence, this hypothesis suggests that the Southern Argobba accompanied the Walashima' leaders on their flight from 'Ifat in the early 1400s. There is evidence to suggest that the Northern Argobba were the remaining population of 'Ifat after the conquest.

The third hypothesis for explaining the links between the Northern and Southern Argobba suggests relatively recent migration to the Harar region. Two major events in Ethiopian history affected the Adal kingdom. In 1529 Imam Ahmed Ibrahim al-Ghazi of Adal mounted a *jihad* from Harar which swept throughout highland Ethiopia, where the Imam is still remembered with trepidation as Ahmed Gragn, "the left-handed." He was finally killed in 1549 by the Portuguese troops of Christopher de Gama, who had come to aid the Ethiopian king. In reaction to the *jihad*, the Christian Ethiopians counterattacked, crushing the Adal kingdom. At this point Adal retreated to an oasis in the Danakil desert, leaving the city of Harar as the last remnant of the once powerful Muslim principalities of Ethiopia. Immediately following the collapse of the *jihad*, a major population movement took place which permanently altered the demographic and political balance of Ethiopia. This was the expansion of the Oromo from their homelands in southwestern Ethiopia northward until they occupied most of the Rift region, thus surrounding the Northern Argobba villages, and eastward until they isolated the city of Harar and occupied the environs of the Southern Argobba. The present Argobba villages in this region are, for the most part, situated on hilltops. The inhabitants explain that the sites were chosen to defend against the Oromo invaders. This would add plausibility to the second hypothesis, as would the mention of a still extant southern village, Afarduba, in the chronicles of the *jihad*, *Futu al-Habasha*, written by Shihabaddin Ahmed b. Abdalqadir Arabfuqih.

Just as the history of the Argobba presents more problems than solutions, so does consideration of Argobba society as it exists today. All now speak the

Oromo language, with the exception of the residents of the village of Kurumi, who speak Harari. This linguistic idiosyncrasy is particularly puzzling, as Kurumi is surrounded by Oromo-speaking Argobba villages.

The linguistic isolation of Kurumi indicates the degree of social isolation of the Argobba villages, not just from contiguous ethnic groups but from one another. Village endogamy is the preferred form of marriage, although as the village populations decrease, the number of exceptions increases. An Argobba man in Gende Adam explained the preference for endogamy as deriving from Muslim inheritance laws wherein males receive full shares and women receive half-shares. Among the Argobba, land is passed through the male line. "Since a girl gets a half-share from her father," he said, "it is best to marry a girl from your own village." A preferred type of wedding, called *au aziza*, is one in which two men of a village exchange closely related relatives as brides. These are designated "sisters" for the purpose of the wedding.

Beyond village endogamy, any marriage within the Argobba ethnic group is considered acceptable. Argobba men may marry Oromo women, although it is considered a disgrace to permit a daughter to marry an Oromo man. Occasionally the latter form of marriage occurs, but it is likely to provoke physical violence between friends of the Oromo groom and protectors of the bride.

The village of Umar Din typifies the defensive position of Southern Argobba villages, built atop a sheer-walled granite outcrop which surveys the entire Bisidimo Valley. Even in 1975 lookouts watched for strangers and yodelled their approach to fellow villagers. Umar Din is laid out in an ascending spiral, with walls and fences enclosing the path which winds through it and through which one must pass to get to Kurumi and other Argobba villages. On both ends of the chain are villages (Umar Kuli and Atero, respectively) in which both Argobba and Oromo reside. Whether or not this co-residence indicates acculturation is not known. However, in these villages, Argobba women retain their visible identity by wearing the distinctive Argobba dress, a black-topped, dark brown robe.

Southern Argobba men are farmers who utilize both ox-drawn wooden plows and stone-weighted digging sticks to turn the soil, depending on its characteristics. The staple crop, sorghum, is stored in hidden underground pits within the village. Terracing is utilized as in the northern population and seems to be a distinctive and ancient Argobba practice, probably ultimately traceable to Yemeni agricultural traditions. Some men make wooden chairs with traditional carved designs, and pottery is made in some of the villages. Both occupations may carry a stigma, since Argobba would not discuss them. Unlike their Northern brethren, Southern Argobba men do not seem to be involved in trade. Women, who walk to Harar's markets, weave hairnets, which they sell to Harari women as an ethnic specialty.

The link between the Southern Argobba and the Harari is important and indicates a long-standing relationship. Indeed, one of the five gates of the city of Harar is called Argoberi, "Argobba Gate." Harari manuscripts and oral traditions include many citations of the Argobba, referring to a period of Argobba emirs which preceded those of the independent Harari emirate, which began in 1551. Probably this is the period of the Adal sultanate of the Walashima' dynasty.

Harari children believe that the Argobba are were-hyenas and chant at Argobba women as they come to town, "Argobba, Argobba, nighttime hyena, daytime human!" Despite this stigma, Argobba women have an important ritual role in Harari weddings, that of officially confirming the virginity of the bride-to-be.

Evidence of the close link between Argobba and Harari is the similarity of their houses. Both are rectangular stone and mud-walled buildings, having raised earthen terraces for seating and many similar specifics in the interior. Stitz, who studied the Northern Argobba, pointed out that only the village of Shonke has Harari-style architecture, and he sees this as evidence of a return migration.

Certainly both the Northern and Southern Argobba deserve intensive study before they disappear. Acculturation to nearby ethnic groups is taking place, and changes in the nation of Ethiopia are also eradicating ethnic distinctions. Moreover, heavy fighting took place in the Southern Argobba range during the Ogaden War of 1978. The damage done to Argobba villages and the number of Argobba who fled as refugees has not yet been reckoned. Nonetheless, the chance to do significant research and thus solve some of the puzzles provided by the Argobba may still remain.

BIBLIOGRAPHY

Books

'Arabfuqih, Shihābaddīn Ahmed b. 'Abdalqādir. *Futuh al-Habasha.* Translated by Rene Basset as *Histoire de la conquête de l'Abyssinie (XVI siècle).* Paris: Publications de l'Ecole des Lettres d'Alger, 1897.

Cohen, Marcel. *Etudes d'éthiopien méridional.* Paris: Librairie Orientaliste Paul Beuthnen, 1931.

———. *Nouvelle études d'éthiopien méridional.* Paris: Librairie Ancienne Honoré Champion, 1939.

Hetzron, Robert. *Ethiopian Semitic: Studies in Classification.* Manchester: Manchester University Press, 1972.

Huntingford, G.W.B. *The Glorious Victories of 'Amda Seyon, King of Ethiopia.* Oxford: Clarendon Press, 1965.

Paulitschke, Philipp. *Harar: Forschungsreise nach den Somal-und Galla-ländern.* Leipzig: F. A. Brickhaus, 1888.

Shack, William A. *The Central Ethiopians: Amhara, Tigre and Related Peoples.* London: International African Institute, 1974.

Stitz, Volker. "The Western Argobba of Yifat, Central Ethiopia." In *Proceedings of the United States Conference on Ethiopian Studies, 1973,* edited by H. Marcus. East Lansing: African Studies Center, Michigan State University, 1975.

Trimingham, J. Spencer. *Islam in Ethiopia.* 2nd ed. London: Frank Cass, 1965.

Ullendorf, Edward. *The Ethiopians*. 3rd ed. London: Oxford University Press, 1973.
Wagner, Ewald. *Legende und Geschichte der Fath Madīnat Harar von Yahyā Nasrallāh*. Wiesbaden: Kommissionsverlag Franz Steiner GMBH, 1978.

Articles

Braukämper, Ulrich. "Islamic Principalities in Southeast Ethiopia Between the Thirteenth and Sixteenth Centuries, Pt. 1." *Ethiopianist Notes* 1:1 (1977): 17–56.
Leslau, Wolf. "A Preliminary Description of Argobba." *Annales d'Ethiopie* 13:1 (1959): 252–273.

Sidney R. Waldron

ASIANS OF EAST AFRICA   The Asian presence in East Africa can be traced back several centuries, but the bulk of the Asian settlement there has occurred within the last 100 years. At its maximum, the size of the Asian population of Kenya, Uganda, Malawi and Tanzania numbered about 850,000. The last ten years have witnessed a substantial exodus, voluntary and involuntary. More than 125,000 persons have left East Africa to resettle in other parts of the world.

The overwhelming majority, about 85 percent, of the Asian Muslims of East Africa (who number perhaps 295,000) are Shia and belong to one of three sects: the Ithna Ashari (Twelvers), the Nizari Ismaili (Khoja) and the Mustali Ismaili (Bohra). Sunni Muslims (Punjabi speakers) constitute about 10 to 15 percent of the Asian Muslims and include a large Ahmadiya community.

Linguistically, the Shia Muslims of East Africa speak either Gujarati or Kutchi. Among the Ithna Asharis, there are a few who speak Sindhi. The Shias of the Tanzanian and Kenyan coasts tend to be more Kutchi-speaking, but on the whole, perhaps about 60 percent of the Shia Muslim Asians are Gujarati speakers (see Gujaratis). Many who speak Kutchi also speak Gujarati, and quite a few Gujarati speakers are conversant in Kutchi. Kutchi is mainly a dialect and does not have a script, whereas Gujarati is used both orally and in writing.

Because the majority of Asian Muslims of East Africa are descendants of converts from Hinduism, one aspect of the Hindu past that many of them have retained is their Hindu family name, or *atak*. The Ismailis have assimilated numerous other Hindu customs and practices into their version of Islam. These are reflected in the *ginans* (hymns), *juro* (communion) and reverence of the book *Das Avatar*, which deals with ten incarnations of the Hindu god, Vishnu, the tenth incarnation being Ali and the succeeding Ismaili Imams, or Aga Khans.

Of the three Shia sects of East Africa, the Ithna Asharis are the most oriented to the Quran. They place a great deal of emphasis on Quranic education and the teaching of Arabic. Although the Ithna Asharis do not use Arabic as their main language of communication, many are literate in Arabic. Their general life-style is largely shaped by Quranic laws and Muslim traditions. In their mosques women are not allowed in the same section as men; many women observe *purdah*; the

Ithna Asharis do not charge interest on loans to other members of the community; and many of the devout donate to the community the interest they receive from their bank accounts. Their mosques are open to all, and they recite five prayers, but some of them combine them and pray only three times a day. The leader of the mosque, whom they refer to as *imam* or *aga*, must be a religiously trained and qualified person. Training is usually obtained in India, Iran, Iraq or Pakistan. Some of their other *furoo-e-deen* (principles) are obligatory fasting during the month of Ramadan; payment of *zakat* and *khums* (one-fifth of annual savings); pilgrimmage; and *jihad*. In recent years the Ithna Asharis have begun missionary activities through the Bilal Muslim Mission of Kenya.

The Khojas (Nizari Ismailis), on the other hand, believe that laws formulated in the past may be changed. The living Imam (Aga Khan) guides his followers according to worldly conditions that prevail at that particular time in history; therefore, different laws may be needed at different periods in history. The Imam, who is the direct descendant and successor of the Prophet Muhammad, provides guidance to the *momins* (followers) through *firmans* (pronouncements). The Imam is divinely guided and infallible, and his *firmans* supersede the Quran. Several excerpts from the Quran are included in the main prayer of the Khojas, the Du'a. Prayers are recited in Gujarati, but now they are also in Arabic. Apart from about half a dozen verses from the Quran included in their prayers, the overwhelming majority of Khojas have no other knowledge of the Arabic language. An Ismaili who has read the Quran from cover to cover is indeed rare. Religious readings are mostly confined to *Das Avatar*, *Nurum Mubin* (a two-volume history of the Imams), *ginans* and other works of a biographical nature.

The center of Khoja communal activities, religious and nonreligious, is the *jamat khana*, basically a prayer house existing wherever there are Ismailis. In larger towns there are libraries, community administrative offices and offices for socioeconomic organizations attached to the prayer house. A *mukhi* (chief) and a *kamaria* (deputy chief) and their counterparts for women are in charge of an Ismaili congregation. They are appointed directly by the Aga Khan for a term of one to three years. Their service to the community is voluntary, and for that reason most of them are from economically well-off families. In moderate- and large-size towns the service to the community can become very demanding of time and financial resources. Nonetheless, most Ismailis accept the appointment as *mukhi* or *kamaria* with great honor. Unlike the leader of the Ithna Ashari congregation, the leaders of the Khoja *jamat khana* do not have to be trained or qualified in religious education. Wealth, popularity, record of service to community, serious interest in religious activities and communal political connections are the most important variables in getting appointed to these positions.

Two of the better-known duties of Islam are generally not practiced by the Khojas. These are the Haj and the fast of Ramadan, but they celebrate the Ids with enthusiasm. Other important festivals are the birthday of the Aga Khan, the day of his accession to the throne, and Nauroz (the Persian New Year). Every month they also celebrate *chand rat* (the eve of the new month). On these monthly occasions, the Ismailis perform special and additional rituals to pray to Allah and the Imam for forgiveness for their transgressions, and many of them make payments of their *zakat*, or *dasond*, as the Ismailis refer to it. Perhaps there is no other sect or community in Islam whose members make as great financial contributions to their religion as do the Ismailis. Obligatory *dasond* and voluntary contributions associated with each of the many rituals constitute the main forms of these contributions. At the same time, community organizations under the guidance of the Imam have provided the Ismailis some of the best material services in East Africa, such as schools, housing and hospitals.

The Khojas also have missionaries, but they do not seek converts from among non-Ismailis. They are students of Ismailism and of Islam in general and are the ones most knowledgeable about Islam in the Ismaili sect. Serving as religious teachers, they are often employed by the community organization to travel to different congregations and lecture to the followers. Their role is to deepen the religious knowledge of the general congregation and to strengthen the members' faith.

The third and smallest Shia Muslim Asian community of East Africa is the Bohra (Mustali Ismailis). Most of the East African Bohras are Daudi Bohras, as opposed to Sulaimani Bohras, who live in India and Yemen. The Bohras (the name derives from the Gujarati word for "trade") are largely a Gujarati-speaking community, and among them there is more emphasis on the learning of Arabic than with the Khojas but not as much as the Ithna Asharis. Like the Khojas, their prayer house is the *jamat khana*, and they recite prayers only three times a day. The head of a Bohra prayer house, the *mullah*, is usually trained and educated in the doctrines of the sect before he is appointed to the post by the chief *mullah*, who resides in India. The Bohras also make substantial financial contributions to the *mullah* through *zakat* payments and other donations associated with religious rites. Like all Shias, the Bohras are secretive about certain aspects of their faith. In the absence of their Imam, who is hidden, their chief guide and leader is the Dai, whose judgments and decisions on religious and nonreligious matters are accepted as final.

The Asian Muslim communities of East Africa, whether Shia or Sunni, as a rule are endogamous and patrilineal. Kinship ties and extended family relationships are strong among all of them, rural as well as urban. While polygynous marriages are exceptional among all these communities, first cousin marriages are not uncommon. Marital customs of *dej* (dowry) and *mahr* (prearranged alimony to women in case of divorce) are quite common.

There is little religious interaction among these various sects. The only occasions when some unity is displayed and joint services may be held are the two Ids and the birthday of Muhammad. The three Shia sects commemorate Muharram, the martyrdom of Imam Hussain, but they do so in their separate ways. Each group feels strongly that its version of Islam is the correct one. This separateness is as strong in the rural areas as in the urban.

The Asian Muslims of East Africa are generally a commercially oriented group.

The Bohras are dominant in jewelry-related business and smith crafts. Commerce, religion and Westernized education are chief pursuits not only of the Muslims but also of the Asians in general.

In national politics of the East African countries, the Asian Muslims play little part as a unit. There have been some individuals in all three countries who have utilized their communal links in addition to their other resources for positions in the national political arena. During the Obote regime in Uganda, out of six Asians in the parliament, four were Muslims, and in Tanzania the only Asian to have been appointed a cabinet minister was a Muslim. The general Asian Muslim population remains disinterested in politics except when politics affect Asian commerce and business opportunities and citizenship status. It is the politics of the Indian subcontinent that arouse excitement among the Asians of East Africa. Asian Muslims, for obvious reasons, are very supportive of Pakistan, but India–Pakistan friction has not led to any violent hostilities between the Asian Hindus and Muslims of East Africa.

The religious differences among Asian Muslims and between Muslims and Hindus as a rule do not hinder interaction in many social relationships. Asian families from different religious sects who live in the same or adjoining buildings maintain neighborly relations and will come to each other's assistance in time of need. Interaction, such as visiting, sharing meals, attending weddings and going on picnics and to movies together takes place frequently. There are also numerous instances of mixed business ventures.

BIBLIOGRAPHY

Books

Amiji, Hatim M. "The Asian Communities in East Africa." In *Islam in Africa*, edited by James K. Kritzeck and William H. Lewis. New York: Van Nostrand-Reinhold, 1969.

Bharati, Agehananda. *The Asians in East Africa: Jayhind and Uhuru*. Chicago: Nelson-Hall, 1972.

Chattopadhyaya, Haraprasad. *Indians in Africa: A Socio-Economic Study*. Calcutta: Bookland Private, 1970.

Ghai, D. P., ed. *Portrait of a Minority: Asians in East Africa*. London: Oxford University Press, 1965.

Gregory, Robert G. *India and East Africa: A History of Race Relations Within the British Empire, 1890–1939*. Oxford: Clarendon Press, 1971.

Kuper, Leo, and Smith, Michael G. *Pluralism in Africa*. Berkeley: University of California Press, 1971.

Mangat, J. S. *A History of the Asians in East Africa, c. 1886–1945*. Oxford: Clarendon Press, 1969.

Morris, H. S. *The Indians in Uganda*. Chicago: University of Chicago Press, 1968.

Sagini, Lawrence, ed. *Racial and Communal Tensions in East Africa*. Nairobi: East African Publishing House, 1966.

Trimingham, J. Spencer. *Islam in East Africa.* Oxford: Clarendon Press, 1964.
Twaddle, Michael. *Expulsion of a Minority: Essays on Ugandan Asians.* London: Athelone Press, 1975.

Articles

Ghai, D. P., and Ghai, Y. P. "Asians in East Africa: Problems and Prospects." *Journal of Modern African Studies* 3:1 (1965): 35–51.
Nelson, Donna. "Problems of Power in a Plural Society: Asians in Kenya." *Southwest Journal of Anthropology* 28:3 (1972): 255–264.

Akbarali H. Thobani
Population figures updated by Richard V. Weekes

ASSAMESE   Like Muslim communities in other parts of India, the Asamiya-speaking Muslims of Assam are the product of prolonged interaction between Islam and local cultures. They are considered less orthodox than other Indian Muslims and share many culture traits with Assamese Hindus. Nevertheless, the basic values of Islam are the values of the Assamese Muslims.

The Assamese language, a derivative of Sanskrit, is called Asamiya. One of the 15 constitutionally recognized national languages of India, it is spoken by approximately 12 million people (out of a population of Assam Province of 20 million), mainly in the Brahmaputra Valley districts. Muslim Asamiya speakers number perhaps 2 million out of a province-wide Muslim population of 5 million.

Asamiya has two major dialects, eastern and western, which differ sharply in phonology, morphology and vocabulary. It is an unorthodox and borrowing language greatly enriched by acquisitions from Hindi, Persian, Arabic, English, Portuguese and local tribal languages.

The common name for Muslims of the Assam valley is Garia. There are various views of the word's origin. It could connote the introduction of the faith by invaders from the ancient Muslim Bengal capital of Gaura. According to another view, the term could refer to people who bury their dead (*gor*) in a graveyard. A third view is that the term refers to the traditional occupation of Muslim settlers, tailoring (*garia*).

As with language, there are slight regional variations in the culture of Assamese Muslims between rural and urban areas and also between eastern and western Assam. In parts of western Assam there are strong feelings not only against kin marriage but also against marriages between members of the same lineage. In eastern Assam, endogamous marriage is accepted by the Sayyids. Among western rural Assamese, wedding ceremonies continue through the night; in eastern Assam, the ceremonies are short and are performed in the afternoon. In parts of eastern Assam, women participate in both planting and harvesting crops; in the west, they take part only in the planting. More than 80 percent of the Assamese Muslims live in the west.

Assam came into contact with Islam for the first time in 1206, when a Turkish army led by Muhammad bin Bakhtiyar made an expedition to Tibet through the region. He was followed by other Muslim invaders. In 1532, a Muslim army under Turbak invaded Assam. The forces of the local Ahom king defeated the Muslims, and those who were taken prisoners were settled in different parts of the state. They married Assamese women and, after a few generations, their descendants immersed themselves so deeply into the indigenous culture that they lost whatever Islamic moorings their ancestors ever had. Descendants of these soldiers today are called Marias.

The history of Assam's contact with Muslims clearly suggests that they never really gained a significant foothold. However, these early encounters contributed towards the propagation and strengthening of the Islamic faith in Assam, and some traits of Islamic culture were adopted by the indigenous population. Furthermore, the prolonged wars between the Muslim and Assamese kings led to the growth of the Muslim population in Assam.

The consolidation of Islam in the Assam valley dates from the early part of the seventeenth century. A Muslim saint named Shah Milan, popularly known as Azan Faqir, was the chief patron of this consolidation. He is said to have come to Assam during the 1630s and to have proselytized and preached reform. Through his work, as well as that of other clerics who followed him, Islam was revived among those who were nominal Muslims, on the one hand, and some indigenous population converted to Islam, on the other. Presumably, these preachers were patronized by the Ahom rulers in their missionary work and in propagating the Islamic faith. (The Ahoms, a Thai or Shan peoples from northern Burma, entered eastern Assam in the thirteenth century and established a kingdom that eventually included the whole of the Brahmaputra Valley.)

The present-day Asamiya-speaking Muslims would thus appear to be composed of the descendants of 1) Muslim soldiers captured by the Ahom rulers in battles after 1532, 2) the Muslim artisans brought to Assam by the rulers of Assam from time to time and appointed to various departments of the state government, 3) Muslim clerics who propagated Islam and 4) converts to Islam at different historical times.

To these may be added numbers of Muslims who migrated to Assam over many decades. Between 1910 and 1931, thousands of Bengali Muslim peasants from eastern Bengal, particularly the district of Mymensingh, settled in the riverine tracts of the plains. Their descendants have adopted Asamiya as their first language and now identify themselves as Assamese; they are called Na-Asamiya Mussalman (Neo-Assamese Muslims). In the past 40 years, thousands more Bengali Muslims migrated to Assam, settling as rice farmers in the districts of Goalpara, Nowgong, Kamrup, Darrang and Cachar, in all numbering more than 1 million. Their presence has been resented by local non-Muslims as these Bengalis have maintained their language and culture. Other Muslims have arrived from other states of India, mainly Bihar and eastern Uttar Pradesh. Most of these are found in urban, non-agricultural occupations. They, with the Bengalis, number nearly 3 million.

About 70 percent of the Assamese Muslims are farmers. Their main crop is paddy rice of several local varieties. Other crops include maize and wheat, pulses such as black grams, oil seeds such as mustard, jute, sugarcane and seasonal vegetables. Many farmers supplement their income with wage labor and various types of petty trade and commerce. Some Muslims in eastern Assam produce agar wood oil (*aquilaria agalocha*), from which the choicest of perfumes are made. The trees are infected by a disease which creates the scent, especially appreciated by Arabs who purchase the oil in Bombay. Urban Muslims pursue a more diversified occupational pattern including the professions.

Rural Assamese Muslims live in clustered hamlets and villages surrounded by their fields. While Muslims and Hindus generally live in villages of their own, there are many villages and towns where both groups reside. In such cases, each community maintains its separate identity largely through its exclusive religious and social groups. At the same time, spatial proximity and sharing of a number of institutions have provided opportunities for social contact. Intermarriage, however, is rare. Towns are inhabited by both groups everywhere, but here, too, Muslims and Hindus maintain separate social and religious activities.

The basic unit of the kinship system among Assamese Muslims is the nuclear family household, unlike the extended family system so common in other parts of India and the non-industrial world. Although this household is a discrete socioeconomic unit, it often forms part of a wider kin group. The effective kin group would include a number of family households among whom mutual assistance is a recognized ideal and practice.

Assamese Muslim families are patriarchal, and descent is traced through the father. The rules of succession and inheritance are patrilineal, but these principles are sometimes modified by the wishes of the original owner. Women are entitled to inherit one-eighth of the father's property.

The family life of the Assamese Muslims exhibits a peculiar synthesis of Islam and the traditions of the local Hindus. The kinship terminology of Muslims is comparable to that of Hindus. Like the Hindus, certain types of coactive behavior patterns between certain categories of kin are also present among the Muslims. Avoidance in relations between father-in-law and daughter-in-law, and between husband's elder brother and younger brother's wife is found among both Muslims and Hindus.

The formalities of an Assamese Muslim marriage cover two separate ceremonies: the ring ceremony (*magni* or *angathi pindhua*), which is followed by the actual marriage ceremony (*nikah*). After finalization of the negotiations, a party consisting of close kin and the parents of the groom-to-be visits the future bride's home. The party carries a gold ring, silk clothes and sweets as presents. The negotiations are sealed with the presentation of the engagement ring to the future bride. In performing *nikah*, the proposal and acceptance are made in the presence of three elderly and respectable males, one of whom acts as *ukil* (chief negotiator) and two as witnesses. The *ukil* asks the consent of the bride and groom to the marriage. The *imam* then recites verses from the Quran.

By and large Assamese Muslims are Sunni and follow the norms of Sunni marriages. However, the practice of cross-cousin marriage is not encouraged. Marriage for men is between 21 and 25 years of age, while females marry between 16 and 20. Statistics show one-third of the males prefer to marry after 26, while one-third of the females marry before 16. Marriage among educated Muslim males is generally late, even later than their Hindu counterparts.

The marriage customs of Muslims are characterized by a mixture of Hindu and Muslim rituals. Muslims fix the date of marriage in consultation with both Hindu and Muslim almanacs. Among Assamese Muslims, the bride and groom take ceremonial baths on the day of marriage and exchange betelnuts with their respective family and friends. *Bianam* (songs sung by Hindu females during marriage) is prevalent among Muslims. A local custom known as *athmongola* is also observed by Muslims, whereby the bride and groom attend a feast given by the bride's parents on the eighth day following the wedding. Both Muslims and Hindus arrange marriages in all months except Puh (December/January), Chot (March/April), Bhado (August-September) and Kati (October/November). Muslims usually do not plan marriages during the lunar month of Ramadan. During the days of February and March the rural people are not engaged in agriculture and have enough leisure time to celebrate marriage.

An Assamese Hindu wife gives birth to her first child in her parent's home. Muslim wives follow this custom. Like Hindus, Muslim mothers protect the newborn baby from evil spirits by keeping a fire burning and iron implements in the room. Among traditional rural Assamese, the mother cuts the umbilical cord immediately after birth with a bamboo split. The cord is buried to protect the baby from sorcery. The part of the umbilical cord remaining attached to the baby dries out and detaches automatically. In many cases, this dried cord is used to quiet a crying baby by allowing the baby to drink a drop of water from a pot into which the umbilical cord has been dipped. Muslims bring a newborn baby out ceremonially to the courtyard in the presence of a gathering of women on a day following detachment of the umbilical cord.

Aqiqa is a naming ceremony of close kin and is performed on the seventh, fourteenth or twenty-first day after the birth of a baby. The head of the newborn in shaved. A cow or a goat is sacrificed. The circumcision (*sunnat*, *khatna* or *mussalmani*) ceremony calls for another gathering of close kin. A boy is usually circumcised between the ages of five and ten years. The person who performs the surgery is called a *badia* or *hajam*. Most *hajams* are non-Assamese Muslim barbers. The ceremony is performed early in the morning.

A Hindu girl is kept in seclusion during the time of her first menstrual period; so, too, is a Muslim girl. Muslims, like Hindus, perform post-mortuary rites on the third and between the seventh and tenth days after death (according to Islamic custom, post-mortuary rite is preferably performed on the fortieth day after death).

Elements of the Hindu caste system have also influenced the social structure of Assamese Muslims. Muslims in Assam are broadly divided into three "caste-like'' groups: Sayyids, Shaikhs and Marias. The Sayyids, who have the highest social status, claim to be descendants of the Prophet Muhammad. The majority of Shaikhs are presumably descendants of local peoples, including some who have been converted to Islam. The Marias, third in social status, are descendants of the Muslim soldiers captured during the Muslim invasion of 1532. Their traditional calling is brassworking. Shaikhs are most common, followed by Marias and Sayyids. Each of them maintains a large degree of autonomy on a social plane, and social relations, including marriage, are confined within the group.

Assamese Muslim women, compared to men, are more backward and sub-servient because of a number of factors, one of which is the influence of *purdah*, which keeps women in seclusion (although not to the degree that women must wear the *burqa*, a cloth shroud from head to feet excepting the eyes, as is required in other parts of the Indo-Pakistani subcontinent). The Muslim com-munity is apathetic about providing formal education to women, preferring in-stead that they get married. Large numbers of girls from Muslim families have no opportunity to continue schooling beyond secondary levels.

In recent decades, especially since Independence, many urban Muslim women have seen their opportunities increase measurably. Some have entered the profes-sions, and there are now a number of stage, screen and radio artists with popular followings. Social change is paving the way for many women to come out of the confines of the four walls of their homes.

The strong influences of Hinduism have distinguished the Assamese Muslims as being the least orthodox of Indian Muslims. While they are formally Sunni of the Hanafi juridical rite, they observe many local Hindu rites that conflict with Islamic practices. For instance, Hindus—and many Muslims—are attracted to the Vaishnavite philosophy preached in Assam by the sixteenth-century phi-losopher Sankardev. This brand of Vaishnavism is devotion to a shapeless Cre-ator, a philosophy easy for Muslims to appreciate. Devotional songs, even though embodying the teachings of Islam, were composed by Azan Faqir on a pattern of Vaishnava poetry.

The basic values of the Assamese Muslims are Islamic, despite regional and syncretistic variations. They observe Islamic rites, rituals and practices, al-though not as vigorously as Muslims in other parts of India. Above all, Assamese Muslims identify themselves with Assam, their homeland, and Asamiya, their language. While intermarriage with a Hindu is rare, an Asamiya-speaking Mus-lim feels more at home in the company of an Assamese Hindu than with a Muslim who speaks another language. Marriage to a non-Assamese speaker is considered ''a distress deal.'' Few Assamese Muslims speak Urdu or identify with Muslims in other parts of the subcontinent. To a great extent, Assamese Muslims identify with the common culture they share with Assamese Hindus. (Evidence of the intensity of nationalism among Asamiya speakers is the violence that occurred in Assam during the 1983 elections, when Assamese killed many Bengali immigrants in resentment over Bengali participation in politics. *Ed.*)

The Assamese Muslims exist in the Assamese society as an inseparable and non-isolated entity. Their culture operates within the social structure as segments of a common social system.

(The authors are grateful to Professor A. C. Bhagabati, Head, Department of Anthropology, Dibrugarh University, and Professor Md. Taher, Department of Geography, Gauhati University, for their contributions to this article.)

BIBLIOGRAPHY

Books

Ahmad, Imtiaz. "For a Sociology of India." In *Muslim Communities of South Asia*, edited by T. N. Madan. New Delhi: Vikas House, 1976.
Ali, A.N.M. Irshad. "Kinship and Marriage Among the Assamese Muslims." In *Family, Kinship and Marriage Among Muslims of India*, edited by Imtiaz Ahmad. New Delhi: Monoher Book Service, 1976.
———. "Marriage Among the Assamese Muslims." In *North East India: A Sociological Study*, edited by S. M. Dubey. Delhi: Concept Publishing House, 1978.
Bhuyan, S. K. *Anglo-Assamese Relations (1771–1826)*. Gauhati, India: Department of Historical and Antiquarian Studies, Gauhati University, 1949.
———. *Swargadew Rajeshwar Singha*. Gauhati, India: Asom Prakashan Parishad, 1975.
Das, B. M., et al. "The Assamese Hindus and Muslims: Their Biosocial Profile." Study No. 9. Mimeographed. Gauhati, India: Department of Anthropology, Gauhati University, 1980.
———. "The Assamese Muslims: Their Physical Features." Study No. 6. Mimeographed. Gauhati, India: Department of Anthropology, Gauhati University, 1980.
Gait, E. *History of Assam*. 3rd rev. ed. Calcutta: Thacker Spink, 1963.
———. *Report on the Census of Assam, 1891*. Shillong, India: Government Printing, 1893.
Hunter, W. W. *Statistical Accounts of Assam*. 2 vols. Calcutta: n.p., 1897.
Sarma, Benudhar. *Phul Sandan*. Gauhati, India: Asom Joyti, 1969.
Weiner, Myron. *Sons of the Soil*. Princeton: Princeton University Press, 1978.

Articles

Ali, A.N.M. Irshad. "Hindu Muslim Relations in Assam." *Man in India* 59:4 (1979): 261–381.
Malik, Syed Abdul. "Ashamiya Mussalmanar Gharuia Bhasha." *Asom Sahitya Sobha Patrika* 2 (1960): 51-54.
Sattar, Abdus. "Samajik Ashar Beboharar Khetrat Ashamiya Hindu Mussalmanar Ghanisthata." *Nilachal* 1:1 (1969): 228–230.

B. M. Das
Irshad Ali

AZERI   The Azeri Turks, sometimes called Azerbaijanis, occupy the land of ancient Media and are divided politically into two groups, one dominated by

Persians, the other by Russians. The Azeri of Iran form the largest ethnic group in the strategic grain-producing provinces of East and West Azerbaijan (see Azeri [Iran]). The Azeri of the Soviet Union are found principally in the Azerbaijan Soviet Socialist Republic, which is bounded by the Daghestan Autonomous Soviet Republic on the north, by the Georgian and Armenian Soviet republics on the west, by the Caspian Sea on the east and by Iran on the south.

The most common self-designations of the Soviet Azeri are Türkler and Azerbaijanlilar; however, tribal or regional appellations often replace the general designation. The Azeri of western Soviet Azerbaijan call themselves Airumy. They are mainly stockbreeders and farmers. The Azeri of the eastern part of the Azerbaijan S.S.R. call themselves Padar and for the most part are semi-nomadic pastoralists. The Shahsevan live mainly in Iran but also in the Mugon Steppe of the Azerbaijan S.S.R. (see Shahsevan). The Karapapakhi inhabit the western portions of the Azerbaijan S.S.R., a few locations in the Georgian and Armenian republics, Turkey and Iran. The Kardagi and Afshari are scattered over northwest Iran.

The Azeri language belongs to the Ogüz, or southwest branch of Turkic, and is structurally similar to Anatolian Turkish, although the two languages are not mutually intelligible (see Turkic-speaking Peoples). Azeri has a written tradition going back to the fourteenth century. It is written in Arabic script in Iran and in the Cyrillic alphabet in the U.S.S.R. Azeri serves as the lingua franca of eastern Transcaucasia, southern Daghestan and northwestern Iran.

There appear to be more than 15 million Azeri. In Iran they are estimated to be approximately 8.8 million, from 15 to 20 percent of the country's population. Some 190,000 live in the southern Kurdistan area of Iraq, and at least 6 million live in the Soviet Union, of whom 98 percent consider their native language to be Azeri. The Soviet Azeri are characterized demographically by extreme longevity and a high birthrate. Between 1959 and 1970 the number of Azeri in the Soviet Union increased nearly 50 percent, from 2.9 million to 4.4 million. Except for the Russians, who comprise only 7.9 percent of the population of the Azerbaijan Soviet republic, the Azeri are the most numerous nationality in the Caucasus. Within the Soviet Union 256,000 Azeri reside in the Georgian republic, 161,000 in the Armenian republic and approximately 65,000 in Daghestan. The Russian and Armenian minorities in Soviet Azerbaijan live mainly in the larger cities and towns. Fully one-fourth of the population of the entire republic lives in the capital city of Baku.

There do not seem to be any overt signs of irredentist sentiment between the Iranian and Soviet Azeri. The only attempts to unify the two groups, divided since 1813, have come on the part of the Russians, who occupied the Azeri provinces of Iran in the periods 1909–1914 and 1941–1946. The Soviet attempt to create an Azeri puppet state in northwest Iran did not receive widespread support among the Iranian Azeri. If anything, the replacement of Reza Shah Pahlavi's historical ethos based on Aryan particularism by the Muslim fundamentalism espoused by the Ayatollah Khomeini would seem likely to lessen, rather than exacerbate, tensions between the Persian and Turkic-speaking populations of Iran. There appears to be little indication of strong feelings of affinity for the Anatolian Turks, who are close linguistically to the Azeri but are divided by a different cultural tradition and a different Islamic sect. The Azeri are Shia; the Anatolian Turks, Sunni.

While the strategic importance of Iranian Azerbaijan rests in its position as the breadbasket of Iran, Soviet Azerbaijan is inseparably bound to the Soviet petroleum and petrochemical industries. Since 1870 the production and refining of oil have dominated the economy of Baku and the western shore of the Caspian Sea. In recent decades the importance of the Caspian oil fields has declined as new and larger finds in the Urals and Siberia have begun to be exploited, but the Baku fields were for many years of paramount importance not only for the growth of Soviet industry and agriculture but also for the transformation of the Azeri from a backward, feudal agrarian people to an industrialized, relatively advanced Turkic minority.

As the Azeri migrated to the Apsheron peninsula to take over skilled jobs in the oil fields, a bona fide urban proletariat, the first among Turkic peoples, was created. The Azeri rapidly became the most literate and culturally advanced Turkic nationality in the Russian Empire. The Azeri led all other Turkic peoples of czarist Russia in the publication of books, newspapers and journals. In their drive to attract the allegiance of all Asian people to the October Revolution, the Bolsheviks arranged to have the International Congress of Eastern Peoples take place at Baku in 1920. There the Azeri were cast as the model for transforming a backward, colonial people to an advanced proletarian nation. Baku today is the seat of Kirov State University, the Azerbaijan Academy of Sciences, numerous scientific and pedagogical institutes and a very active publishing industry. According to the latest Soviet census, two-thirds of the Azeri residing in the U.S.S.R. have had at least a high school education.

The Azeri remaining in the countryside were not as amenable to radical transformation as were the town dwellers. Most of the rural Azeri in Russian-occupied Azerbaijan were engaged before the revolution in animal husbandry, agriculture, viticulture and cottage industry. While in purely economic terms these industries have been reorganized through collectivization, certain vestiges of the feudal past persist to the present.

In the past the traditional family-clan type of organization was encouraged among the Azeri by their weakly developed social stratification. The clan, called *hoj, modiam* or *imejiklik*, was usually named after a common ancestor. The clan held pastureland in common, was bound to provide mutual aid to members and frequently acted as a unified entity in business dealings. The clan residential system consisted of large dwellings, called *gazma*, in which up to 40 members of an extended family lived together. A son was restricted to the *gazma* so long as either parent remained alive. Each clan had its own places of worship and sacrifice.

The landless peasants, called *tavyrga* or *nekameral'nye* (the latter term from the Russian word for "unenumerated," i.e., in the census), were at the lowest stratum of existence among the Azeri and formed the nucleus of the unskilled laborers who flocked to Baku after the discovery of oil in 1870.

In rural areas of Soviet Azerbaijan, pre-Islamic religious practices may still be encountered among the Azeri. Holy places, called *pir*, are still revered. The holiday Su Jeddim, in which Azeri seek communion with their ancestors through bathing in sanctified streams, has been observed in recent times. Certain trees, especially the oak and the iron tree (*Parrotia persica*), are venerated and may not be felled. Pieces of bark from the iron tree are worn about the neck of persons and horses as amulets and are tied to cribs in order to ward off illness and the effects of the evil eye. A cult of fire, which is regarded by the Azeri as the holiest and purest element in nature (from the influence of Zoroastrianism), has had many adherents, and there has been a cult of rocks, particularly of a certain kind of black rock to which curative powers are attributed.

The Persian influence is reflected in the continued celebration of the festival of Nauroz, marking the beginning of the Zoroastrian New Year on March 21. A substratum reflex of Zoroastrianism is seen in the Azeri predilection for endogamy, which contrasts radically with the practice in other parts of the Caucasus. Azeri settlements were traditionally divided into *makhelle*, or clusters of dwellings occupied by an extended family. Marriage within the *makhelle* was prescribed, unions between first cousins being considered the most desirable. Marriage with non-Azeri was almost unheard of prior to the Soviet period. Polygyny was not normally resorted to except in cases of infertility or through the application of the levirate or the sororate. In the arrangement of marriages the *mahr*, a deterrent to divorce, was paid to the bride. The family of the bride receive the *bashlyg*, or brideprice, also called *yol pulu* (money for the road), *atalyg pulu* (money for the father) and *sud pulu* (milk money).

While the religious practice of the Iranian Azeri has not been restricted, the Soviet authorities have mounted a strong anti-religious effort since the beginning of Soviet rule. In recent years the newspaper *Bakinskii rabochii* (The Baku Worker) has carried stories deploring the continued practice of Islam even by Communist Party members. There are also reports of unauthorized opening of boarded-up mosques in Baku and elsewhere.

An unusual honor was conferred on the Soviet Azeri in 1982 when, following the death of Leonid Brezhnev, the first secretary of the Communist Party in Azerbaijan, Geider Aliev, was elevated to full membership in the All-Union Party's Politburo and was named first deputy to the chairman of the Council of Ministers of the U.S.S.R. This was an unheard-of promotion for a member of the Turkic nationalities of the Soviet Union.

BIBLIOGRAPHY

Books

Bennigsen, Alexandre. "The Muslims of European Russia and the Caucasus." In *Russia and Asia: Essays on the Influence of Russia on the Asian Peoples*, edited by Wayne Vucinich. Stanford: Stanford University Press, 1972.

————, and Lemercier-Quelquejay, Chantal. *Islam in the Soviet Union*. New York: Praeger, 1967.

Cottom, Richard W. *Nationalism in Iran*. Pittsburgh: University of Pittsburgh Press, 1964.

Douglas, William O. *Strange Lands and Friendly Peoples*. New York: Harper, 1951.

Huddle, Frank. "Azerbaidzhan and the Azerbaidzhanis." In *Handbook of Major Soviet Nationalities*, edited by Zev Katz, Rosemarie Rogers, and Frederic Harned. New York: Free Press, 1975.

Menges, Karl. *The Turkic Peoples and Languages: An Introduction to Turkic Studies*. Wiesbaden: Harrasowitz, 1968.

Rywkin, Michael. *Moscow's Muslim Challenge: Soviet Central Asia*. Armonk, N.Y.: M. E. Sharpe, 1981.

Seton-Watson, Hugh. "The Regime's Nationality Policy." In *Soviet Society: A Book of Readings*, edited by Alex Inkele. Boston: Houghton Mifflin, 1961.

Tillett, Lowell. *The Great Friendship*. Chapel Hill: University of North Carolina Press, 1969.

Wheeler, Lowell. *Racial Problems in Soviet Muslim Asia*. London: Oxford University Press, 1960.

Wimbush, S. Enters. *Iran's Ethnic Factions Threaten to Split the State*. Santa Monica, Cal.: Rand, 1980

Articles

Burg, Steven L. "Soviet Policy and the Central Asian Problem." *Survey* 24:3 (1979): 65–82.

Karakashley, K. T. "A Contribution to the History of the Social Structure of the Population of the Lesser Caucasus." *Soviet Anthropology and Archaeology* 8:4 (1970): 304–354.

Pipes, Richard. "Demographic and Ethnographic Changes in Transcaucasia." *Middle East Journal* 13 (1959): 41–63.

Schweizer, G. "Tabris and Its Bazaar." *Erkunde* (Germany) 27 (1972): 32–46.

Stackelberg, George von. "The Tenacity of Islam in Soviet Central Asia." *Studies on the Soviet Union* 5:4 (1966): 91–101.

Tekiner, Suleyman. "Developments in Azerbaidzhan." *Studies on the Soviet Union* 2:3 (1963): 1117–1122.

Harry H. Walsh

AZERI (IRAN)   Azeri constitute the largest linguistic minority in Iran. They are a unique national minority, clearly Iranian in identity, culture and history. They are Shia, a distinctive characteristic of Iranian society, and live in the northwestern provinces of East and West Azerbaijan, in migrant communities of long standing in Tehran and in scattered towns and villages between Azerbaijan and Tehran. They call themselves and are called by other Iranians Azerbaijani, Azeri or simply Turk.

The characteristic distinguishing Azeri from other Iranians is their mother tongue, Azeri Turkish (see Azeri; Turkic-speaking Peoples). Many urban Azeri speak Persian. In the Azerbaijan provinces, one-half of the men and one-quarter of the women are considered literate in Persian as well. As with other regional minorities, Iran's Azeri are found in nomadic tribal groupings, in village communities, in small towns and in major cities throughout Azerbaijan (see Shahsevan). They are an integral part of Iran's economic, religious and political life and thus work and live throughout the country.

The Azeri are a group quite distinct from the Persian majority. They are perceived by other Iranians as associating mainly with each other, even outside Azerbaijan Province. And yet, in comparison with other ethnic and linguistic minorities in Iran, in particular contrast to the Kurds, Azeri have been centrally involved in Iranian dynastic and nationalist history and are culturally very Iranian.

The major Turkish migration into Azerbaijan dates from the eleventh century, with the Seljuk conquest of Iran; it was completed by the fifteenth century. From the establishment of the Shia Safavid Empire (1501–1722), which had its origins in Azerbaijan and was brought to power by the Shahsevan, through the Qajar dynasty (1796–1925), when the Qajar Crown Prince was based in Tabriz, and into the contemporary era, Azeri have been politically prominent in central government politics.

In contrast to Turks outside of Iran, the social structure of Azeri communities and their religious practices, family life and cultural traditions are Iranian and Shia in form. Azeri perceive themselves as Iranian *and* Azeri; they believe they hold a special place in Iranian society, culture and history. Although there have been dissident political and literary movements aimed at preserving their unique ethnic identity, separatist movements have successively failed. Literary movements flourish only among a small group of Azeri poets, writers and intellectuals. Thus, while they are Turkish in language and literature, Azeri are distinctively Iranian.

Precise population estimates of Azeri in Iran are difficult to obtain because the national census does not document ethnic origin. Incomplete census figures suggest that between 15 and 20 percent of the Iranian population of 42.5 million are Azeri. Perhaps 5 million live in the northwestern provinces; between 2 million and 4 million persons of Azeri background live in other provinces contiguous to Azerbaijan and in Tehran, Mashad and other cities of the country.

Azeri are noted for both their agricultural wealth and their commercial acumen and skills. The agricultural produce of Azerbaijan, where 64 percent of the people are rural, is exceptional in Iran. It is among the wealthiest areas in agricultural resources. Azerbaijan was the first province to undergo land reform instituted by Muhammed Reza Shah Pahlavi in 1962–1963 (many landlords owned scores of villages). The relative success of the program may be attributed to the quality of agricultural resources of the area as well as to the capabilities of Azeri peasants.

Tabriz, the capital of East Azerbaijan, was among the foremost commercial centers in Iran prior to Reza Shah's reign. Its position on the east–west and north–south trade routes from Turkey and Russia contributed to its preeminent commercial role, and thus to the commercial sophistication of Azeri merchants. Azerbaijani merchants and manufacturers suffered economically under the policies of economic and political centralization carried out by Reza Shah. Those who were most vigorous moved to Tehran to carry out commercial activities. They became central figures in the traditional bazaar. During the last ten years of Pahlavi rule, Azerbaijan and Tabriz once again began to flourish commercially and industrially as the central government dispersed economic development efforts to the region.

Two political issues—nationalism and regional autonomy—have been central to Azerbaijani politics. The wealth and strategic location of Azerbaijan and the relatively sizable middle class of merchants, religious scholars and intellectuals, particularly in Tabriz, contributed to the activism of Azeri in nationalist and liberal democratic politics in the twentieth century. Azeri from Tabriz were in the forefront of the Tobacco Protest of 1891–1892, the first significant popular protest against the encroachments of foreign interests in Iranian affairs. The Tobacco Revolt, which brought together the religious classes, merchants and intellectuals in joint political efforts, cast the pattern of protest and cooperation that marked successive developments of nationalist politics.

Azeri, in particular residents of Tabriz, were in the vanguard of the Constitutional Revolution of 1906, which sought to establish parliamentary government, limit the excesses of the Qajar shahs and restrict foreign influence in Iran's internal political and commercial affairs. The first parliamentary delegates from Tabriz constituted the core of the liberal, nationalist faction in the Majlis, the national assembly.

Movements for increased regional autonomy have been characteristic of Azeri politics from the post-World War I era to the present day. In 1917, following the withdrawal of Russian and Turkish troops, Azerbaijani nationalists rebuffed Turkish efforts at annexation and Bolshevik overtures of alliance, though they resisted control from Tehran and called the province Azadistan, "land of freedom," a term that reappears in Azeri politics. In 1945, Mohammad Pishevari led a Soviet-supported movement towards Azerbaijani autonomy. Although Azeri responded positively to increased independence, legitimation of Azeri literature and culture and social reforms, popular disillusionment followed Pishevari's failure to combine local autonomy with Iranian nationalism. During the Mossadeq era of Iranian nationalist politics (1951–1952) and the subsequent years of economic development and reform under Mohammed Reza Shah Pahlavi, Azeri continued pressing for more autonomy and increased development funds from the central government. Although there was dissatisfaction with the Pahlavi regime and the amount of money that was devoted to Azerbaijan's development, there was no evidence of Azeri flirtation with separatist movements. Liberal democratic movements flourished in Azerbaijan, and many National Front leaders were Azeri. Men such as Mehdi Bazargan, who later became Prime Minister in the first Islamic Revolutionary government after the fall of the Shah, and Ramatollah Moqaddam, a liberal member of the Assembly of Experts and the first Governor General of Azerbaijan in the Khomeini government, are Azeri with deep family roots in Azerbaijan.

The Islamic Revolution in 1978 once again brought the Azeri traditions of liberal nationalism and desire for local autonomy into focus. In the very early stages of the revolution, when popular protests against the Shah began to sweep Iran, riots in Tabriz, called for by the Azeri Ayatollah Sheriatmadari in February 1978, crystallized the opposition and focused protest on issues of human rights. Individual Azeri such as Bazargan and Moqaddam, through such dissident political movements as the Freedom Front and the Radical Movement, pushed for the liberalization of the Shah's human rights policies and for greater political freedom and participation.

After the demise of the Pahlavi government, the Azeri found themselves in opposition to the policies of the Khomeini regime, in particular to the elevation of Khomeini to the position of ultimate political judge and Faqi and to the infringement of Khomeini's Persian-speaking revolutionary guards and officials on Azerbaijan's local rule. This disagreement led to riots in Tabriz in December 1979 over the issue of the constitution and local autonomy. Because the Tabriz demonstrations were held under the banner of Ayatollah Sheriatmadari and called for Ramatollah Moqaddam to be reappointed Governor of the province, both of these Azeri lost favor with Khomeini's revolutionary regime. Sheriatmadari has been under virtual house arrest in Qom, stripped of his access to media and to his Azeri followers. Moqaddam was forced into exile, in spite of his support for the revolution. Former Prime Minister Bazargan has remained in Iran (as of Spring 1984) and continues to express hope for liberalization of human rights policies. He has urged granting increased autonomy to local regions in an effort to reacquire political loyalty not only from Azeri but also from the more alienated minorities, particularly the Kurds. His political position is nonetheless precarious.

Shia Islam has provided a unifying set of religious symbols, traditions and frames of meaning that has wed Azeri and Persian in Iranian culture. Azeri commemorate the same Shia holy days as do Persian Iranians, and with at least the same intensity. In sophisticated metropolitan circles, Azeri are often thought to be more intense in their expression of religious ritual than their Persian counterparts. The month of Muharram is devoted to commemoration of the martyrdom of Imam Hussain, the grandson of the Prophet Muhammad, who died at the behest of the Umayyid Caliph. The conflict between the followers of Imam Hussain and the Umayyids is portrayed as a battle of the just against the unjust. The liturgy of the Muharram rituals, symbolically contrasting the righteousness of the religious community with the injustice of secular rulers, has provided, at various moments of Iranian political history, an idiom for protest against local and national secular political authorities.

Muharram is commemorated in Azerbaijan through a variety of ritual forms. Passion plays reenact the story of Imam Hussain's martyrdom and are orchestrated and performed by local religious organizations. The city of Maragheh is noteworthy for its continuation of the more elaborate ten-day performance of the passion plays. They are performed in mosques and caravansarays set aside and decorated for the occasion. Mournful sweet singing, prayers and ritual crying by the audience characterize the performances. The tragedy of the Imam's mar-tyrdom is thus conveyed, and many participants relish the bittersweet emotions engendered and recollect their own troubles. Parades of men who wear black mourning costumes or Arab headdress accompany the performers, and each play is preceded and concluded with athletic displays of self-flagellation. Women participate in public rituals only as observers and mourners; however, they sponsor similar gatherings (*mersia*) to commemorate the events of Kerbala in their homes.

Family structure and the position of women among the Azeri are smiliar to those of other Iranians (see Persians). Kinship is bilateral in form; research indicates that about one-quarter to one-third of the Azeri marry relatives and of those, one-third marry maternal first cousins and one-third marry paternal first cousins. However, it is more common for extended family households to include paternal relatives.

Prior to the Islamic Revolution, the position of Azeri women had undergone important changes due to increase in educational attainment. In 1966, less than 10 percent of the female population of East Azerbaijan was literate. By 1976, over 20 percent was literate. Azeri women from cities and smaller towns were beginning to attend the university in greater numbers in the 1970s, and by 1976, 2,322 women were university graduates or students, in contrast to 656 in 1966. Women still tend to see their ideal role as being married and having a family. Women who combine career and marriage often decide to have children early in their marriage, thus showing proof of their fertility and worth as wives.

Since the Islamic Revolution, the restriction of employment of women in government offices has no doubt limited the opportunities of Azeri women, who were just beginning to experience modern role options. However, for the vast majority of Azeri women, who led quite traditional but not powerless lives, who veiled themselves in public and whose primary role responsibilities were as wives, mothers and household administrators, the restrictions brought by the revolution will have limited effect.

Social hierarchy in Azerbaijan reflects that of the rest of Iran, with sharp differences in wealth and power found between those at the apexes of the status system and those in the middle and lower classes. Under the Pahlavi dynasty, a dual system of social stratification emerged, with status groups and classes distinguished not only by wealth but also by the source of that wealth and by cultural orientation and life-style. Two status communities emerged. One had its roots in the traditional hierarchy, its wealth in the traditional economy of agriculture and the bazaar and its cultural values and rituals formed by Shiism. The modern status community, fostered by secular education and professional and civil servant employment and funded by an economy that was regulated and dominated by the central government, came to be characterized by a more cosmopolitan life-style, values and orientation.

Before the Islamic Revolution, these two status communities maintained a relatively peaceful coexistence, as many parents encouraged their children to achieve in the modern status community, to become doctors, engineers or at least teachers or civil servants. However, the Pahlavi government denigrated the more traditional urban classes of merchants and *ulama* in its political propaganda in an effort to undermine opposition. The resentment of the traditional status community to the Pahlavi government clearly took on elements of anti-modernism and anti-secularism. With the success of the revolution, the modern status community became the target for the Khomeini government and has been consistently denigrated. The cultural clash between the two status hierarchies continues.

Azerbaijan presents an interesting variant on the Iranian pattern of social hierarchy, as many of the bazaar merchants, members of the traditional middle class, are dissatisfied with the Khomeini regime and with its failure to allow greater local autonomy for Azarbaijan. Thus, the modern and traditional middle classes find themselves in political agreement. Khomeini's greatest support in Azerbaijan appears to come from the poorest segments of the population, from day laborers and from members of the Tudeh Party.

Committed both to Iranian nationalism and to regional autonomy, the Azeri might be expected to continue at the forefront of the struggle for more democratic forms of government in Iran. Rather than seeking separation from Iran, Azeri are likely to continue their efforts to play a central role in national politics.

BIBLIOGRAPHY

Books

Abrahamian, Ervand. *Iran Between Two Revolutions*. Princeton: Princeton University Press, 1982.
Cottam, Richard W. *Nationalism in Iran: Updated Through 1978*. Pittsburgh: University of Pittsburgh Press, 1979.
Fischer, Michael M. J. *Iran: From Religious Dispute to Revolution*. Cambridge: Harvard University Press, 1980.
Good, Byron. "The Transformation of Health Care in Modern Iranian History." In *Modern Iran: The Dialectics of Continuity and Change*, edited by Michael Bonine and Nikki R. Keddie. Albany: State University of New York Press, 1981.
Good, Mary-Jo DelVecchio. "The Changing Status and Composition of an Iranian Provincial Elite." In *Modern Iran: The Dialectics of Continuity and Change*, edited by Michael Bonine and Nikki R. Keddie. Albany: State University of New York Press, 1981.

————. "A Comparative Perspective on Women in Provincial Iran and Turkey." In *Women in the Muslim World*, edited by Lois Beck and Nikki Keddie. Cambridge: Harvard University Press, 1978.

Keddie, Nikki R. *Roots of Revolution*. New Haven: Yale University Press, 1981.

Articles

Good, Mary-Jo DelVecchio. "Of Blood and Babies: Popular Islamic Physiology and Fertility in Iran." *Social Science and Medicine* 14 B (1980): 147–156.

————. "Social Hierarchy in Provincial Iran: The Case of Qajar Maragheh." *Iranian Studies* 10 (1977): 129–163.

Unpublished Manuscripts

Good, Byron J. "The Heart of What's the Matter: Structure of Medical Discourse in an Iranian Provincial Town." Ph.D. dissertation, University of Chicago, 1977.

Good, Mary-Jo DelVecchio. "Social Hierarchy and Social Change in a Provincial Iranian Town." Ph.D. dissertation, Harvard University, 1977.

Byron J. Good
Mary-Jo DelVecchio Good

B

BAJAU Sometimes called the Sea People, the Bajau are a boat-dwelling, or formerly boat-dwelling, Sama-speaking population of southern Sulu in the Philippines, eastern Borneo and eastern Indonesia. Variant spellings of the name include Badjau, Badjaw, Badjo, Bajo and Bajoe. The name apparently comes from Indonesia, where it is more commonly used as a self-identification. In southern Sulu, and to some extent in eastern Borneo, the people usually call themselves Sama or Sama Dilaut ("Sama of the Sea"). Several local names, such as Luwa'an and Pala'u, are used by neighboring populations, but the Bajau consider these pejorative (see Sama).

The name "Bajau" is sometimes extended to Sama-speaking peoples of central and northern Sulu who occasionally use the boat as living quarters during fishing trips. However, certain cultural features distinguish these people from the southern people, and it has yet to be established that they were ever full-time boat dwellers.

Within southern Sulu, Bajau populations are found in the Tawi-Tawi and Sibutu islands. A related group is found near Semporna, Sabah. Wherever they are located, the Bajau represent a minority of the total population (4 percent in Tawi-Tawi and 23 percent in Sibutu) and are generally considered social inferiors by the surrounding people. Most of the Tawi-Tawi Bajau still live in houseboats and are considered non-Muslims by surrounding populations, while the Sibutu and Semporna people have become house dwellers in relatively recent years and are generally regarded as Muslims.

It is difficult to estimate the population of the Bajau since the name has been used differently by different investigators. Within the Philippines, fairly reliable census data exists for the late 1960s. At that time, the Tawi-Tawi Islands had a population of only about 1,600, whereas about 3,000 lived in the Sibutu Islands. A small village near Semporna, Sabah, related to the Sibutu people, had a population of about 700. Census data for Sabah lists 60,000 Bajau, but this is misleading since "Bajau" is used to include all Sama-speaking peoples. The number of Bajau in Indonesia is less well known, although a population of 10,000 to 15,000 has been estimated. At the most, there are possibly 25,000 people in insular Southeast Asia who can be called Bajau. (Ethnic indicators for Malaysia identify 105,000 "Bajau" in that country, but this may be misleading. *Ed.*)

The maritime environment of the southern Philippines Bajau consists of extensive coral reefs and low coral islands. In the past, in both Tawi-Tawi and Sibutu, Bajau moorages were scattered throughout these reefs and islands, where houseboats congregated and served as villages. Typically, the moorages were located near villages of land-dwelling Sama.

Fishing is the mainstay of Bajau life. It ranges from subsistence fishing among the boat dwellers to rather sophisticated commercial fishing among house dwellers. The collection of marine products, such as mollusks and seaweed, supplements both diets and income. The majority swap fish for vegetable produce or buy produce with income from their catches in the local markets. Fishing crews among the boat dwellers usually consist of one or two nuclear families, whereas among the house dwellers such crews often consist mostly of men. A few Bajau families cultivate small cassava farms leased from land-dwelling Sama.

The Tawi-Tawi Bajau houseboat typically houses a single nuclear family, usually about five members. The houseboats are planked dugouts, sometimes with double outriggers and averaging 35 feet in length with a beam of 3 to 4 feet. Built upon the hull is a frail house structure, consisting mostly of a nipa (palm thatch) roof. On most boats the house structure can be easily taken down and a sail erected when long-distance travel is necessary.

A family living on a houseboat is a very close unit and spends a good deal of its time fishing and traveling alone. Occasionally an elderly parent, an adult unmarried sibling of one of the spouses or, less often, another family joins the household. Although the nuclear family moves among the various houseboat moorages, it always identifies one moorage as its home; or, if the husband and wife are from different moorages, the family divides its allegiance and time between the two moorages. Frequently, the nuclear family fishes and travels with the boat of a married sibling, forming the second important social unit in Bajau society, the family alliance unit. Its primary function is that of mutual aid for fishing, ceremonies and any other activities that require group assistance. Each moorage consists of several of these family alliance units, and together they comprise a group of people from both the paternal and maternal sides of the family, the head of which is an older male. At the larger moorages, several such localized kindreds may be found, and the head of the kindred which first began mooring there serves as head for the entire moorage.

The traditional pattern of social organization among the Sibutu Bajau has been altered by the move to houses. As with the land-based Sama, Bajau houses are built over shallow reefs on piles driven into the reef floor. They range in size from 50-by-25-by-15 feet to 12-by-10-by-8 feet. All dwellings have extensive open decks which are used for outdoor household activities, such as drying fish, woodworking, preparing cassava, ceremonies and children's play. The interior is normally a single room used for daytime activities and sleeping, while a small house built on the deck serves as the kitchen. Bridges usually connect the house to other houses.

Although some nuclear families live together in single family households, more typically households consist of extended families, usually related through matrilineal ties. The size of such households varies greatly from two married couples with children to perhaps a dozen couples with as many as 50 members. Despite its membership in an extended household, the family unit retains its own living space within the house, buys and cooks much of its own food and usually has its own fishing equipment and boat. The men of such houses fish together in adjoining boats, while women form work groups at home. The household conducts ceremonies as a unit.

Several such related households cluster to form residential neighborhoods. In smaller villages, such a grouping may comprise the entire village, whereas in the larger communities there may be several such neighborhoods, each identified by the man recognized as its headman. Such groups include people who act as curers, midwives and shamans for the members.

The Bajau do not participate significantly in the politics of Philippine society. The boat dwellers of Tawi-Tawi are virtually detached from national politics. The house dwellers in Sibutu are somewhat more involved in local politics and have had members elected to the community governing board at Sitangkai.

As in the rural Philippines generally, a large family is the ideal, with the extended family the most important kinship group for day-to-day interaction. Marriage is often with a kinsman, and for some groups, especially the boat dwellers, this is an ideal. First cousin marriage occasionally occurs among the boat dwellers, but for most, second cousins or more distantly related people are considered more proper marriage partners. Parents and their siblings often arrange marriages between young people, but a marriage is never forced which is not desired by the partners themselves. Elopement is common in those cases where parents disapprove of marriage. The payment of goods and money to the family of the bride by the family of the groom is part of the marriage ceremony. Bajau women have high status within the family unit, although men act as family heads in external affairs. Divorce is common among Bajau, and little stigma is attached to it. Divorce may be initiated by either the husband or wife. If it occurs in the early months of marriage, part of the bridewealth is expected to be returned to the groom's family. Marriages tend to be stabilized with the birth of a child. Polygyny is permitted in Bajau society, but it is virtually nonexistent.

Formal education is limited among the boat-dwelling Bajau, and literacy is restricted to a few young people who have rudimentary reading and writing skills. Many of the house dwellers are literate, especially on Sitangkai, where they may attend public schools and even colleges. In addition, house-dwelling Bajau children receive religious instruction through the mosque.

The boat-dwelling Bajau of Tawi-Tawi are the least Islamized indigenous population in all of the Sulu Islands. They are viewed as pagans by other populations, although they consider themselves Muslims. Their religious life has been influenced somewhat by Islam, but they still largely follow their traditional religion. Some express belief in a supreme deity, usually called Tuhan, but their religious activities are concerned mostly with two large groups of spirits, namely the *unmagged* and the *saitan*. The *unmagged* are the spirits of once living people who dwell around the two cemetery islands. These spirits are generally indifferent to human affairs but may occasionally interfere in a malevolent way if offended. The *saitan* (an Islamic name, but the belief in such spirits obviously predates Islam in Sulu) are evil spirits who never lived as humans. Certain places throughout the area are known as their dwellings, but they move at random and may be encountered anywhere. Most illness and misfortune is believed the result of these spirits. Simple rituals and ceremonies for placating them are known by all Bajau; however, for more persistent illnesses or problems, a shaman is consulted. Bajau religion is more highly developed among the house-dwelling Sibutu Bajau.

Most of the house-dwelling Bajau are considered Muslims by their Muslim neighbors as well as by themselves. Mosques are found in their villages, and they are acculturated in varying degrees to Islam. They have their own *imam* who is knowledgeable in Islamic ritual. Some have made the pilgrimage to Mecca, and many attend the Friday mosque services and celebrate the calendrical ceremonies of Islam. Their life-cycle ceremonies incorporate Islamic ritual. However, much of the indigenous religious system has been retained, and the present religion of the house-dwelling Bajau is a syncretism of Islam. Virtually all the traditional religious ceremonies are still practiced by the house-dwelling Bajau, but these have been elaborated and enriched by the addition of Islamic ritual. An individual may act as shaman for traditional ceremonies and as *imam* for Islamic ceremonies, seeing little conflict in the two roles.

The civil war resulting from the Muslim secessionist movement in the southern Philippines has dramatically affected the Bajau of southern Sulu. Great dislocations of people have occurred. Many Tausug people from the Jolo area moved to Tawi-Tawi and Sibutu to escape the conflict, which perhaps reached its peak with the destruction of Jolo in 1974. Also, Sama-speaking peoples from the areas of greatest conflict in the north moved to the relatively peaceful southern islands of Sulu. During this same period, specifically, 1975, Sulu Province was divided. The northern islands remained as Sulu Province, whereas the islands of Tawi-Tawi and Sibutu in the south became Tawi-Tawi Province. The establishment of the capital of the new province at Bongao brought large numbers of people to fill civil service posts as well as to participate in the economy of the rapidly expanding city. The conflict also brought thousands of military personnel, concentrated for the most part in Bongao. The city grew from a small port town of about 5,000 in the late 1960s to more than 40,000 by the early 1980s.

The economy of Tawi-Tawi, and especially Sibutu, has been dramatically altered by the introduction of agar-agar cultivation. The commercial cultivation of this sea plant was introduced to the area in the early 1970s and rapidly became a profitable enterprise. The success of the new aquaculture brought many people, especially Tausug, from Jolo to the reefs of Tawi-Tawi and Sibutu (see Tausug).

The Bajau have always been intimidated by conflict and outsiders, especially the aggressive Tausug. As their home waters have been inundated by outsiders, many Bajau have dealt with the ensuing conflicts and tensions by leaving. This happened during the recent conflict, when many Bajau of both Tawi-Tawi and Sibutu moved to the more peaceful waters of Sabah. By 1982, probably half, possibly two-thirds of the Bajau of Tawi-Tawi and Sibutu had left the Philippines to reside on the coasts of eastern Borneo, especially in the Semporna area. Those who remain in Sulu experience great sociocultural change. For the most part these changes involve an adaptation to modernization as well as a greater acculturation to Islam.

If the current conflicts and trends continue in southern Sulu, probably even more Bajau will leave or become amalgamated into the general Sama Islamic culture. It is conceivable that there will be no traditional Bajau left in Tawi-Tawi and Sibutu by the end of the next decade.

BIBLIOGRAPHY

Books

Nimmo, H. Arlo. "A Functional Interpretation of Bajau Songs." In *Directions in Pacific Traditional Literature*, edited by Adrienne L. Kaeppler and H. Arlo Nimmo. Honolulu: Bishop Museum Press, 1976.

———. *The Sea People of Sulu*. San Francisco: Chandler, 1972.

Sather, Clifford. "Bajau Laut." In *Ethnic Groups of Insular Southeast Asia*, edited by Frank M. LeBar. Vol. 2. New Haven: Human Relations Area Files Press, 1975.

———. "The Bajau Laut." In *Essays on Borneo Societies*, edited by Victor King. Oxford: Oxford University Press, 1978.

———. "Kinship and Contiguity: Variation in Social Alignments Among the Semporna Bajau Laut." In *The Societies of Borneo*, edited by G. N. Appell. Washington, D.C.: American Anthropological Association, 1976.

Sopher, David E. *The Sea Nomads*. Singapore: National Museum, 1977.

Szanton, David. "Art in Sulu: A Survey." In *Sulu's People and Their Art*, edited by Frank Lynch. IPC Papers, 3. Quezon City: Ateneo de Manila University Press, 1963.

Article

Nimmo, H. Arlo. "Reflections on Bajau History." *Philippine Studies* 16 (1968): 32–59.

Unpublished Manuscript

Pallesen, Kemp. "Linguistic Convergence and Culture Contact." Ph.D. dissertation, University of California, Berkeley, 1976.

H. Arlo Nimmo

BAJAU (INDONESIA)   The Bajau of eastern Indonesia are an extension of the same Sama-speaking population of southern Sulu in the Philippines and eastern Borneo. These Muslims are of particular interest because of the wide distribution of their settlements, the fluidity of movement of individuals and families among these settlements and the migratory way of life that is still largely dependent on fishing and on gathering other products from the sea (see Bajau).

Ethnographic reports on Sulawesi note the existence of Bajau settlements on the island of Naim near Menado at Torosiaje in southwest Gorontolo, on many of the Banggai islands, around Kendari and along the Straits of Tioro, in the Gulf of Bone, especially around Luwu and at Ujung Pandang, and along the Makassar coast. Elsewhere Bajau are reported to be found in scattered settlements from Halmahera to as far as Aru. They are settled on both sides of the Sape Straits, which divide Sumbawa from Flores, and on the island of Komodo, on the north coast of the island of Flores, on Adonara, Lembata and Pantar, at Sulamu in the Bay Kupang on Timor and on the islands of Ndao and Roti. In the nineteenth century, Bajau were also reported on the north coast of Australia.

Various legends link the dispersal of the southern Bajau to events that occurred in the old kingdoms of the Bugis or Makassarese. Luwu, Bone and Makassar as well as Johore and Malacca are frequently alluded to in these tales. According to one legend, the Bajau originated from chips of wood that fell into the sea in the making of a Bugis trading *prahu*; according to another, the Bajau dispersed on the order of a raja to search for his lost daughter. Since they have never found this princess, the Bajau continue their migratory existence.

Historical records of the Dutch East India Company report the presence of a large number of Bajau located around Makassar who dispersed to various other islands, mainly Borneo, Lombok and Sumbawa, after the conquest of Makassar in 1667 by combined Dutch and Bugis forces. By 1728, company records note large fleets of Bajau as far south as Timor and Roti, and it is presumably sometime after this period that the Bajau reached the shores of Australia. Eighteenth- and early nineteenth-century accounts give good descriptions of the Bajau, who lived on small family boats or in temporary houses erected on posts set in the sea. Virtually all accounts described the Bajau as dependents of either Bugis or Makassarese. They make clear that the chief economic motivation for the Bajau dispersal was the search for valuable sources of trepang, a sea slug or sea cucumber found in coastal waters throughout the area and supplied to China as a culinary delicacy. Throughout eastern Indonesia, for almost two centuries, the Bajau were the principal gatherers and suppliers of trepang for their Bugis and Makassarese patrons (see Bugis; Makassarese).

The Bajau of eastern Indonesia are now undergoing a process of considerable change and are adapting their way of life to the various conditions where settlements are located. They still live chiefly from fishing and trade their fish for products of the land; they still maintain connections among scattered settlements in each locality where they are to be found. They still accord special respect to Bugis and Makassarese and, in many small communities, choose as their *imam* someone from one of these ethnic groups.

There is increasing official government pressure to get the Bajau to settle down permanently, allow their children to attend school and modify their methods of fishing with new nets and other equipment that will tie them to the modernizing economy of Indonesia.

BIBLIOGRAPHY

Articles

Fox, James J. "Notes on the Southern Voyages and Settlements of the Sama-Bajau." *Bijdragen to de Taal-, Land- en Volkenkunde* 133 (1977): 459–465.
Pelras, C. "Notes sur quelques populations aquatiques de l'archipel nusantarien." *Archipel* 3 (1972): 133–168.
Zacot, François. "To Be or Not to Be Badjo—This Is Our Question." *Prisma* 10 (1978): 17–29.

James J. Fox

BAKHTIARI   The Bakhtiari of Iran have historically had two major interrelated characteristics: nomadic pastoralism and tribalism, the former involving their economy and the latter dealing with their political structures, loyalty and identification. Changes have occurred to modify these traits. Most significantly, the central Iranian government under Reza Shah (1925–1941) removed the highest level of leadership in the tribal confederation. This change, together with increasing sedentariness of the nomads, improved communications and a host of government activities at the local level, is initiating the gradual transfer of loyalty and identification from the tribe to the nation-state.

Accurate Bakhtiari census figures are not to be found, but an estimate of 100,000 families, about 700,000 individuals, appears to be reasonable. The Bakhtiari, like their Luri neighbors (see Lur), are Shia Muslim.

The term "Bakhtiari" refers not only to the people but also to the territory they occupy, an area of approximately 20,000 square miles, some 60 percent of which encompasses the rugged central Zagros Mountains. Low hills along the narrow fringe of the northeast Khuzistan plain provide the tribes with their *kishlak* (winter) encampment and also fields and pastures for sedentary agriculturists; the intermontane valleys furnish the *yayla* (summer) pastures. The broad valleys at the western edge of the central plateau form the summer pastures for part of the tribes as well as the permanent habitat of a sedentary village population. Bakhtiari reside year-round in agricultural settlements throughout the territory except at the highest elevations.

The migratory quest for pastures underlies the central economic role of sheep and goats, the most important animals owned by the tribesmen. These animals provide the Bakhtiari not only with food and wool for their own subsistence but also with products for economic exchange with the sedentary society.

The basic unit of Bakhtiari society is the family. It is the unit of production and flock and land ownership, as well as the lowest level of political and social organization. At the next level, families cooperate in sharing of pastures and at successive levels of segmentation regroup and redefine themselves under a variety of political and/or kin headings and for different purposes. These aggregates are grouped successively and roughly, beginning with the smallest, under *rish safid* (white beards); *kalantars* (headmen); khans (chiefs); and an *ilkhani* (paramount chief of the entire confederation).

The confederation, Il-i-Bakhtiari (*il* means "tribe") is the inclusive unit and encompasses those who live or lived in the territory, speak a subdialect of the Luri dialect of Persian and acknowledge the leadership of the khans and the *ilkhani*. The Bakhtiari are divided into the two major sections; the Haft Lang and the Chahar Lang, each of which is further divided into a variety of named *tayafah* and/or *tirah* (tribes and subtribes). The larger and more important ones are headed by khans and the lesser by *kalantars* appointed by the khans. Since the end of the nineteenth century, however, the most significant division has been Ilkhani and Hajji Ilkhani—the moieties from which the *ilkhani* were chosen—and no longer Haft Lang–Chahar Lang.

The factors of the migration, competition for limited resources, and the necessity for exchange with sedentary society sharpen the potential for internal conflict in Bakhtiari society. These elements, added to the pressures generated by external conflict with other tribes, the defense of territory and the demands of the larger community, especially the central government, seem to necessitate the existence of khans as mediators and intermediaries. These leaders usually have common ancestors with their people. Or, lacking that, they possess the characteristics of wisdom, courage and generosity necessary for their chiefly function, which includes coordination of the migration, assignment of pastures, appointment of *kalantars*, mediation of intertribal disputes, leadership for raids, defense and battle and the awarding of levies, taxes, and fines.

Traditionally, the power of the khans and *ilkhani* is both personal and vested in their chiefly office. It is based on the benefits that they are able to dispense, the respect they may command through their birth, their coercive capabilities within the tribe as a result of loyal armed retainers and the support given them by the central government or outside sources of power (as in the past, provincial notables and the British).

The Bakhtiari political system differs from the customary segmentary lineage system by having a hierarchy of khans. But the Bakhtiari do share the division into segmented levels which function in balanced opposition with certain relationships, activities and responsibilities associated with each segment. Within the Bakhtiari the various tribes and subtribes use force against each other, against their khans, and against their *ilkhani*. Significantly, the highest authority at even the lower level can, in effect, negotiate treaties, form alliances and conclude peace independently of higher levels of authority. Thus, like a segmentary lineage system intergroup, and even intragroup, relations are based on a balance of power at each level. Groups that oppose each other on one occasion may unite on another in opposition to some third group.

The power of the Bakhtiari confederation was far greater in the past than it is today. The Bakhtiari played the leading role in the deposition of Mohammed Ali Shah and the restitution of the constitution during the Persian Revolution in 1909, but Bakhtiari attempts to dominate national politics in subsequent years were blocked by their own internal divisions and the opposition by the other tribal confederations and urban nationalists.

In the late 1920s, Reza Shah removed the threat to his sovereignty posed by the Bakhtiari through a series of military, economic and administrative maneuvers. The intensity of this campaign, and the single-mindedness of Reza Shah and his Western-type army, combined with the support of the urban classes on the tribal question, were forces that the Bakhtiari khans had never confronted. Thus, the khans lost administrative positions and their right to be accompanied by military retainers; the Chahar Lang were removed from the authority of the *ilkhani*; and the Anglo-Persian Oil Company was instructed to lease land through the government and not from the khans. The Bakhtiari and other tribal groups revolted, and the leaders, in this case minor khans, were executed. Finally, in 1933, the position of *ilkhani* was abolished. In 1936 the Bakhtiari territory was divided and placed in two separate administrative districts under civil administrators. Meanwhile, three of the major khans, including the Bakhtiari serving as Reza Shah's minister of war, were executed, and all the other major khans (with two exceptions) were imprisoned. In 1938–1939, Reza Shah exacted his last due by forcing the khans to sell their estates and oil shares to the central government.

With the disappearance of the traditional position of *ilkhani*, the family from which the last *ilkhani* was chosen has ceased to be a tribal power. A key element of this family, however, has continued to play an important role in Iran not unlike that of great nontribal families.

Although Reza Shah effectively destroyed the political power of the ruling khans, he was less successful in forcibly settling the Bakhtiari. The problem, as he perceived it, focused on pastoralism as the major factor in maintaining tribal loyalties. His government adopted a policy of forced sedentarization to fracture the tribal economy and identification as well and to insure that tribalism itself would never again threaten the unity of the nation. No provision was made for better use of much of the tribal lands, which were often ill-suited for agriculture, nor were sufficient capital and assistance provided to facilitate the process of creating settlements.

Voluntary sedentariness now appears to be taking place at a progressively faster rate. In the past, only the richest and the poorest entered sedentary society, but contemporary Bakhtiari not only settle in agricultural villages, they also find work in the oil fields, in urban centers or even in Kuwait. (For a description of central government policy and practices toward tribal minorities under both Muhammad Reza Shah Pahlavi, 1946–1978, and the Islamic Revolutionary government of Ayatollah Khomeini, see Qashqa'i. *Ed.*)

There is little solid information on the Bakhtiari in post-Pahlavi Iran, but when Khomeini returned to Iran, a delegation from each of the Ilkhani and Hajji Ilkhani factions appeared before him. In the summer of 1980, ten Bakhtiari were executed, charged with fomenting an anti-Khomeini coup. Others have been imprisoned, and many members of the major khan families are living in exile.

BIBLIOGRAPHY

Books

Coon, Carleton S. *Caravan: Story of the Middle East*. New York: Holt, Rinehart and Winston, 1951.
Digard, Jean-Pierre. *Techniques des nomades baxtyari d'Iran*. Cambridge: The University Press, 1981.
Douglas, William O. *Strange Lands and Friendly People*. New York: Harper, 1951.
Garthwaite, Gene R. *Khans and Shahs: A Documentary Analysis of the Bakhtiyari in Iran*. Cambridge: The University Press, 1983.
Johnson, Douglas L. *The Nature of Nomadism: A Comparative Study of Pastoral Migrations in Southwestern Asia and Northern Africa*. Chicago: University of Chicago, Department of Geography, 1969.
Vreeland, Herbert H. *Iran*. New Haven: Human Relations Area Files Press, 1957.

Articles

Case, Paul E. "I Became a Bakhtiari." *National Geographic Magazine* 91:3 (1947): 325–358.
Garthwaite, G. R. "The Bakhtiyari Ilkani: An Illusion of Unity." *International Journal of Middle East Studies* 8:2 (1977): 145–160.
———. "The Bakhtiyari Khans, the Government of Iran and the British, 1846–1915." *International Journal of Middle East Studies* 3:1 (1972): 24–44.
———. "Two Persian Wills of Hajj Ali Quli Khan Sardar Asad." *Journal of the American Oriental Society* 95:4 (1975): 645–650.
Lorimer, D.L.R. "The Popular Verse of the Bakhtiari of S.W. Persia." *Bulletin of the School of Oriental and African Studies* 16:3 (1954): 542–555; 17:1 (1955): 92–110; 26:1 (1963): 55–68.

Gene R. Garthwaite

BALKAR   The Balkar are a Turkic-speaking peoples who live along the northern slopes of the Caucasus Mountains in the Kabardinian-Balkar Autonomous

Soviet Socialist Republic. A few small groups of Balkar also live in the Kazakh and Kirghiz S.S.R.S. Based on the 1979 census, there are about 74,000 Balkar.

The name "Balkar" may derive from the word "Bulgar," which has applied to a number of people in a variety of spellings for many centuries. Other names and spellings which are used to refer to the Balkar include Balkarlar, Malkarlar, Malkarla, Taulu and Mallqarli. Regardless of these designations, the Balkar are linguistically identifiable as members of the Kipchak-Turkic subgroup of Turkish, and therefore as members of the Altaic family of languages. They share a written literary language with the Karachai, to whom they are closely related linguistically. This literary language has been written with Cyrillic characters since 1938 (see Turkic-speaking Peoples).

The Balkar have shared in the complex and troubled history of the peoples of the Caucasus and, as such, probably evolved out of the confused mixing of Persian-speaking and Turkic-speaking tribes which have swept with regularity across that area. Among the probable ancestors of the present-day Balkar are the Alans, Bulgars and Kipchaks. Although they were certainly pastoral nomads in their early history, the need to seek some protection from the waves of warring invaders from the east, especially the Mongols, most likely forced the Balkars to seek refuge in the higher elevations of the Caucasus, where their life-style evolved into more settled patterns of stockbreeding and agriculture. After the fourteenth century, the Balkar gradually divided into five groups, geographically determined: the Balkar, Bezengi, Chegem, Khulam and Urusbiev. In the later nineteenth century, some elements moved lower into the northern slopes and lowlands of the Caucasus along the upper Baksan, Chegem and Cherek rivers.

The exact time of the Balkar conversion to Islam is a matter of conjecture, although they were certainly converted by the mid-nineteenth century, at the time of the Shamil revolt in Daghestan (1834–1858). Whenever the time of conversion, however, the Balkar remained only superficially committed to the faith, retaining certain aspects of shamanism and animism with an incomplete knowledge of the Sunni belief system of the other peoples of the North Caucasus. Their commitment was slight enough to allow the Balkar to refuse to join the Shamil revolt, even though the call to join was plainly cast as a holy war against the Russians (see Daghestanis).

By the late nineteenth century, the Balkar lands had been caught in the wave of Russian settlement that followed the pacification of the Caucasus. Never a numerous people, the Balkar were unable to oppose the gradual conversion of their lands to agriculture, an occupation to which they themselves gradually adapted.

After the Russian Revolution, the Balkar eventually split from the Karachai, with whom they share a common heritage, and were placed in a separate administrative district—the Kabardian-Balkar A.S.S.R. (see Karachai). Although there is no substantial evidence of Balkar disloyalty during World War II, the Balkar were nonetheless uprooted as a people in 1943 and 1944 and scattered throughout Central Asia and Kazakhstan; their republic was abolished, and they ceased to be counted as a people. After 1956 and de-Stalinization, they were rehabilitated, their republic was recreated and certain select groups were allowed to return to it. Some remained in Central Asia and continue to live there today. There is little evidence to show that the Balkar of today are practicing Muslims.

BIBLIOGRAPHY

Books

Allen, William Edward David, and Muratoff, Paul. *Caucasian Battlefields*. Cambridge: The University Press, 1953.
Baddeley, John F. *The Rugged Flanks of Caucasia*. 2 vols. London: Oxford University Press, 1942.
Benningsen, Alexandre. *The Evolution of the Muslim Nationalities of the USSR and Their Linguistic Problems*. Oxford University, St. Antony's College, Central Asian Research Centre, 1961.
Geiger, Bernhard, et al. *Peoples and Languages of the Caucasus*. The Hague: Mouton, 1959.
Menges, Karl H. *The Turkic Languages and Peoples*. Wiesbaden: Harrassowitz, 1968.
Nekrich, Alexsandr M. *The Punished Peoples*. New York: Norton, 1978.
Smirnov, N. A. *Islam and Russia*. Oxford University, St. Antony's College, Central Asian Research Centre, 1956.
Wurm, Stefan. *Turkic Peoples of the USSR*. Oxford University, St. Antony's College, Central Asian Research Centre, 1954.
Zenkovsky, Serge A. *Pan-Turkism and Islam in Russia*. Cambridge: Harvard University Press, 1960.

Larry W. Moses

BALTIS   In the basin of the upper Indus River, the 170,000 or so Baltis are the downstream neighbors of the Buddhist Ladakhi of Tibet and the upstream neighbors of the Muslim Dards of Gilgit and Chilas. Over mountain passes to the north live the Burusho of Hunza and Nagar. China's Xinjiang Province is over mountain passes to the northeast, and to the south tracks lead into Indian Kashmir.

The land of the Baltis, once formally known as Baltistan but now only an administrative district of Pakistan, coincides exactly with the ecological intersection of arid climate with severe mountain terrain. As the Indus River descends from the Tibetan Plateau, high pasture lands give way to the arid, rocky gorges watered by melting glaciers in the high Karakoram Mountains. The region will not support pastoral specialization; agriculture is made possible only by transporting glacial melt-water to isolated soil deposits. Balti society is a hydraulic peasant society of oasis villages, based upon intensive irrigation agriculture at altitudes from 7,000 to 11,000 feet.

The Balti language is an early form of Tibetan. It is, in fact, the spoken version of literary Tibetan, colloquial Tibetan having evolved away from forms retained in contemporary Balti. It is the most extreme westerly extension of the Tibetan-Burman language. Since the Baltis became Muslims more than five centuries ago, some Persian, Arabic and Urdu have replaced Tibetan words, notably relating to religious matters. Balti is locally known as Purki.

Balti culture differs from that of its two neighbors, the Buddhist Ladakhi and the Dards, in that it is a true peasant culture. To the Baltis, the Ladakhi are called Mar-pa (Butter People) and the Dards are Broq-pa (People of the Mountain Pastures). There has been considerable speculation about the origin of the Balti people and the name "Baltistan." In the Balti language, *balti* refers to a basement chamber where animals are housed below the ground-level human dwelling space. Such protective housing for a necessarily limited number of animals marks the early Balti people as settled agriculturalists. These Tibetan-speaking farmers might have been known to their Tibetan pastoral neighbors as Balti-pa, "those who keep their animals in an underground chamber."

Due presumably to the high organizational and manpower requirements of the canal systems of Baltistan, the typical Balti village is a tightly organized corporate group notably larger than villages of neighboring regions. The percentage of villages having 200 or fewer people in Baltistan, Ladakh and Dardistan is 22.3 percent, 48.2 percent and 51.1 percent, respectively. Large villages of 1,000 or more constitute 14.3 percent, 2.8 percent and .0 percent, respectively.

A more important social-organizational correlate of Balti hydraulic ecology is seen in the history of state formation and alien rule in Baltistan. What are now the three most intensively irrigated regional centers in Baltistan—Skardu, Shigar and Khapalu—were, from as early as A.D. 750, the foci of major political development in the upper Indus Basin. Most likely under the sponsorship of Chinese imperial power in Turkestan, Turkestani dynasties established rulership in all three regions of Baltistan. The Amacha family ruled over the sovereign state of Shigar from some unknown date of origin (possibly around 750) until 1840. The Yabgo dynasty was ruling in Khapalu for some time well before 1500 until 1972, when Khapalu was fully annexed into Pakistan. There is reason to believe that "Amacha" derives from *amacas*, a title granted by the Chinese crown to the kings of Khotan; and that "Yabgo" derives from *yabghu*, the title of the eighth-century Turkic Buddhist rulers of Kundus in the Tokharistan region of Turkestan. In Baltistan, these dynasties came to rule under the title *cho* ("chief" in Balti/Tibetan). Thus a ruling class of ancient Turkestan origin (called Kha-Cho, brothers of the Cho) ruled over indigenous Tibetan-speaking culti-vators. The Balti states lost sovereignty and were gradually absorbed into the British-Indian empire beginning in 1840, when Zorawar Singh conquered all of Baltistan and Ladakh.

The Baltis were Buddhist prior to 1400. At approximately that time, Sufi teachers converted the Baltis to Islam. Local tradition attributes the origin of Islam in Baltistan to one or more visits from Kashmir by Sayyid 'Ali al' Hamadani (1314–1384). There is no historical record of his personal visit, but his influence, whether directly or through his disciples, is well established. Some of the oldest mosques in Baltistan are wooden *khanaqahs*, constructed on the unique design of the famous Shah Hamadan mosque in Srinagar. But most interesting, the Nurbakhshiyya Sufi order, derived from Ali al Hamadani through Isaq al Khuttalani to Muhammad ibn Abdullah (known as Nurbakhsh; d. 1465) was brought from Kashmir to Baltistan. Nurbakhshiyya Sufis still prevail in the eastern sections of Baltistan (Khapalu region) and are numerous in the Shigar region. The rest of the Balti population, notably in the Skardu area, is predominantly Shia. Shiism was brought from Kashmir to Baltistan by Mir Shams-u-din 'Iraqi', a Shia who preached in Kashmir under the cloak of the more acceptable Nurbakhshiyya Sufi order. When he fell from favor in Kashmir, he went to Skardu for a brief period.

Although the Baltis have been Muslim for more than 500 years, the Tibetan roots of their culture can still be seen in their language, animal husbandry, clothing, food and folklore traditions.

The villages of Baltistan perch on laboriously terraced and fertilized alluvial fans which extend from side streams onto the banks of the main rivers. A typical Balti village is a tight cluster of interconnected houses and narrow passageways. Houses are of stone and dried mud-brick with flat roofs of interlaced willow fronds overlain with mud. In winter the family occupies an 8-by-10-foot ground floor room with their animals quartered below in the *balti*. In summer much of the life and work of the household takes place on the roof. The village occupies as little space as possible in order to allow maximum amount of cultivation in this inhospitable soil.

The village is surrounded by small plots of privately owned land. Although new lands are developed through communally pooled labor, as the land comes into production it is divided into individually owned parcels, and villagers must travel farther and farther away from the village to work their fields. The people continue to reside in the main village, preserving its compact character.

The arid environment has kept Balti villages at a subsistence level. Wheat, barley, millet, apricots, peas and dairy products are the basic crops. Potatoes were introduced 20 years ago; since then turnips have been used mainly as animal fodder.

In the lower valleys, apricots are a major crop. Ancient Chinese documents refer to Baltistan as "Apricot Tibet," and Balti dried apricots were prized as far east as Lhasa. At the higher altitudes, where apricots will not grow, the main subsistence crops are wheat and dairy products, which are traded for apricots in the lower villages. The high villages have access to more summer pasture; they keep larger herds and even provide summer pasture for animals from lower villages, in return for winter care, a share of the milk and butter or use of the animal at plowing time.

Yaks, zos (a cross between the yak and the common cow), sheep and goats are the major domestic animals. The fertile yak-cow hybrid is preferred over the yak-yakmo as the milk of the female (zmo) is richer in butterfat and the male (zo) is a more tractable work animal. All households have at least one zmo, and every household has some sheep and goats. Although Baltis are meat eaters, animals are kept as producers of milk or wool and are slaughtered only on special occasions.

The Baltis are not migratory. Animals are taken to nearby high altitude pastures (*broq*) for summer grazing. The huts at the *broq* are temporary shelter only; people come and go from the village every day carrying butter, yogurt, milk, dung and wood down to the village.

The standard diet is *paiju cha* (salt tea made with butter in the Tibetan tradition), milk, soda and salt; coarse wheat flour either baked into a thick cake or boiled into a thick porridge, supplemented with an occasional egg; even more occasional meals of ibex or goat; buttermilk and yogurt. Butter is kept for barter or for special festivals. A very special treat is the parched barley flour which is mixed with the tea to make a thick paste. In recent years some sugar and black tea have found their way into the villages, but this "milk tea" is prepared only for special guests.

While their diet is clearly Tibetan, clothing is only faintly reminiscent of their Tibetan cultural origins. The indigenous clothing of Baltistan is wool, men wearing white wool and women wearing black. Both wear the distinctive round Balti skull cap, with braided silver cloth or filigree silver decorating the women's hats. Elderly women and mothers of infants wear a distinctively different red and black hat which resembles the Ladakhi woman's headgear. Infant headgear is clearly Tibetan-Ladakhi in origin. Women wear necklaces made of real or imitation turquoise (before 1947 turquoise was an important part of Balti–Ladakh trade). Every Balti decorates his or her hat with flowers, berries or leaves.

Although most Baltis can make or repair anything, the old tradition of an artisan class remains—blacksmiths and cabinetmakers travel from village to village and are paid for their work in butter and wheat.

The *maulvi* (religious leader) in most villages works his field and tends his flocks, in spite of his exceptionally high status in the community. While some of the smallest villages have a lower status religious leader (*ahon*), all villages of Baltistan apparently aspire to the honor of claiming within their village a *maulvi* descended from the Prophet. The Balti Sayyid lineage is an endogamous clerical group. They receive their religious training under local teachers. The mosque and the prestige of the *maulvi* or *ahon* are focal points for community activities. Only men, however, attend the mosque. It is expected that women will perform prayers at home or in the fields. One major event organized around the mosque is a "Feast of Merit" called *ol-chi-zan*. It is an occasion for participation by every member of the village. One of the kin groups will provide wood, water, wheat, butter and goat meat for a feast for the whole village. It is done for the oldest member of the clan so that he or she will attain merit in the eyes of Allah.

Village political authority resides with a hereditary headman who consults with an informal council of elders. Prior to the decline of the various Balti states, disputes which could not be settled locally were taken before the Cho. Today, such disputes are taken to the government-appointed district magistrates. Even today there is almost no personal crime in Baltistan. Disputes are almost entirely over property and water rights.

Balti society is patrilineal and patrilocal. However, since marriages are, for the most part, village and lineage endogamous, mother–daughter ties are very close. Although marriage preference is for paternal first cousins, most families are more concerned with contracting marriage for advantageous political and economic reasons, which frequently dictate marriage with other groups.

While the system is patrilineal, there are strong bilineal kinship ties. Marriages between lineages form networks called *phyoqs*, and *phyoq* partners are expected to provide political and economic support to each other.

A typical village is a highly factionalized collection of *phyoq* circles—individuals and lineages vying for prestige, which is for the most part based on economic status. Marriage and betrothal contracts are a central element in this competition. Perhaps for this reason, divorce is common with mate changes made for personal, factional or economic reasons or for barrenness.

There are several stages between betrothal and "full marriage," and at marriage the monetary portion of the dowry (*mahr*) is given with the bride. A marriage is considered truly "consummated" only when the first child is born. At that time, the rest of the woman's dowry in the form of household goods is transferred into her new household. However, birth of the child does not necessarily solidify the marriage. Children commonly stay with the father. Polygyny is accepted but rarely practiced.

Land is divided in accordance with Muslim inheritance law. Daughters inherit, though a lesser share than sons; and if there are no sons, then daughters inherit the whole. Her husband has control of, and a right to, the production of that property, but he does not own it. His children will inherit the land from their mother.

Before 1947, when Baltistan was cut off from the rest of Jammu and Kashmir, trade and travel between Baltistan, Ladakh and Srinagar was constant. Balti males traveled as far as Simla and even Calcutta to work as laborers. Since Partition in 1947, Baltistan has been more isolated. Because the disputed Kashmir cease-fire line forms the southeastern border of Baltistan, the whole region was closed to foreign travelers for 14 years.

When that restriction was eased in 1974, the region was flooded with Western mountaineering expeditions. For the first time in many years the Baltis had access to cash wages. The Balti has always been a load carrier, but during British colonial rule he was conscripted as corvee labor to carry loads to supply the British garrisons in Gilgit and Chitral. The Balti's reputation among mountaineering groups as a troublesome worker may stem from that early experience.

Change is rapid in Baltistan. Cash earned as a porter, for expeditions or on government development programs is replacing grain and butter as a medium of exchange, and consumer goods such as radios and plastic shoes are becoming more common. But more fundamental cultural change is accelerating. Two important features of Balti culture are the pre-Islam folk tradition on the one hand and Islam on the other. Recently, there has been increasing tension between the two traditions. A central piece of local folklore is the Balti version of the Gesar saga (Lepo Kesar), an epic poem which is found all over Central Asia and Tibet. The epic takes eight days to perform, but the songs and dances it contains are well known and are a source of great pleasure among the villages. Now, with the rise of Islamic fundamentalism, that tradition is coming into more intense conflict with Islam, the *maulvi* insisting that the old traditions are un-Islamic. Many villagers are now torn between the two major elements of their identity are Baltis.

BIBLIOGRAPHY

Books

Conway, W. M. *Climbing and Exploration in the Karakoram-Himalayas*. London: T. Fisher Unwin, 1894.
Cunningham, A. *Ladak: Physical, Statistical and Historical, with Notice on the Surrounding Countries*. London: Wm. H. Allen, 1854.
DeFelippi, Filippo. *The Italian Expedition to the Himalaya, Karakoram and Eastern Turkestan (1913–1914)*. London: Edward Arnold, 1932.
Emerson, Pat. "Ecology and Kinship in a Balti Village." In *Pakistan Society*, edited by Akbar Ahmed (in press).
Francke, A. H. *Antiquities of Indian Tibet*. Vol. 2. New Delhi: S. Chand, 1926.
———. *A History of Western Tibet*. London: S. W. Partridge, 1907.
Drew, Fredrick. *The Jammoo and Kashmir Territories*. London: Edward Stanford, 1875.
Duncan, J. E. *A Summer Ride Through Western Tibet*. London: Smith, Elder, 1906.
Hashmatulla Khan, Maulvi Al-Haq. *A History of Jammu*. Lahore: Hassan Publishing House, 1968.
Knight, E. F. *Where Three Empires Meet*. London: Longmans, Green, 1895.
Sufi, G.M.D. *Kashmir: Being a History of Kashmir*. New Delhi: Light and Life, 1974.
Thompson, Thomas. *Western Himalaya and Tibet*. London: Reeve, 1852.
Vigne, G. T. *Travels in Kashmir, Ladak, Iskardo*. 2 vols. London: Henry Colburn, 1842.

Article

Emerson, Richard M. "Charismatic Kingship: A Study of State-Formation and Authority in Baltistan." *Journal of Asian Studies* (in press).

Pat Emerson
Richard M. Emerson

BALUCH   Of the world's nearly 4.3 million Baluch, more than 2.5 million live in western Pakistan, about 1.5 million in southeastern Iran and some 238,000 in southwestern Afghanistan. The trans-border "heartland" of the Baluch is a close to 250,000-square-mile tract of desolate desert, mountains and seacoast known as "Baluchistan," or "place of the Baluch." However, substantial Baluch populations are found outside this area, notably in Pakistan's Sind and Punjab provinces and in the Persian Gulf emirates, where for centuries Baluch have gone to find their fortunes, originally as mercenary soldiers and slaves and more recently as workers in oil-related activities. Because much of the immigration to the Gulf is illegal, the exact number of Baluch there is hard to determine, but probably it is in excess of 200,000. There is even an isolated enclave of Baluch (less than 20,000) in Soviet Central Asia near Merv.

The Baluch language, Baluchi, belongs to the Iranic branch of Indo-Iranian and has affinities to tongues spoken in the northwest part of present-day Baluch territory. Baluch traditions trace the ancestry of many of the major tribal groups to the Middle East and the Caspian region; some native Baluch scholars even going so far as to suggest that the Baluch are descendants of Babylonian civilization. Others look to an Arabian or Syrian homeland with Hamza, the uncle of the Prophet, often cited as a key ancestor.

References in the tenth-century Persian *Book of Kings* suggest that, for several centuries earlier, Baluch had served prominently in the vanguards of Persian rulers, while Arab accounts from this period portray the Baluch as well established in the Kirman region of Iran, where they enjoyed a formidable reputation as brigands.

By the late fifteenth and sixteenth centuries a massive eastward thrust of Baluch, under their renowned folk hero, Mir Chakar Rind, carried them throughout most of Baluchistan and even into the Punjab. It was at this time that many of the existing Baluch clan and tribal groupings came into being, for the Baluch, as predatory nomads, absorbed into their society and polity many of the peoples in their path and acted as a magnet to others with freebooting inclinations. This ethnic heterogeneity is evident in the composition of those who call themselves Baluch today. Black slave groups of African origin, refugees from Pushtu-speaking regions and Brahuis of Dravidian language stock are some of the notable components in the contemporary Baluch population (see Brahui; Jat).

Outside the major cities like Quetta, Karachi and Zahidan, which contain substantial Baluch elements but which are also seats of government control, Baluch social organization remains traditional, although varied according to ecological adaptation. In easternmost and westernmost Baluchistan (in the Sulaiman Mountains of Pakistan and the Sarhad plateau of Iran, respectively) a way of life centered primarily on semi-nomadic sheep and goat pastoralism exists, augmented by dry-crop cereal farming, utilizing rainfall catchments (*band*) or date palm aboriculture. Here large segmentary tribal groups, such as the Marris and Bugtis of Pakistan's Sulaiman range and the Yarahmadzai of the Sarhad, give allegiance to paramount chiefs, or *sardars*, who are drawn from apical lineages.

In the central and southern Baluch regions a more ethnically diversified, caste-like social order persists, based on oases where date palms are the primary crop, irrigated by subterranean aqueducts (*karez*). At the apex of the oasis pecking order are families known as *hakim*, who are the traditional overlords, collecting tribute and leading their followers in internecine feuds with rival elites.

In the Makran region of Pakistani Baluchistan the most notable *hakim* are the Gitchkis, who trace descent from a Rajput soldier of fortune and who acted as largely autonomous delegates of the Khans of Kalat, a Brahui dynasty which ruled much of Baluchistan for several centuries prior to Partition of the subcontinent in 1947.

Below such power brokers are a large mass of freeborn farmers and nomads. The latter, often physically far removed from the seats of oasis power politics, have a social organization based on egalitarian relationships among members of the same camp or *halk*, which is often composed of bilateral kin. Nomads look to informal headmen (*komash*) to lead by example or persuasion rather than by coercion. Nomads engage in ongoing trade of wool and dairy products for the agricultural goods of the sedentaries. A particular occasion for such interaction is the autumn date harvest, or *hamen*, when nomads provide agricultural labor in return for a share of the harvest.

At the bottom of the oasis hierarchy in central and southern Baluchistan are menial groups, such as the Nakibs, who are often of markedly Negroid appearance. In the past such people might be outright slaves of higher-status Baluch, but they are now sharecroppers and servants and often among the most visible of the migrants from Baluchistan to the new job markets of the Middle East and the cities on the fringes of Baluchistan, notably Karachi.

Along Baluchistan's Arabian Sea shoreline and on the adjacent Sind coast are numerous small fishing communities, as well as a few sizable towns like Pasni and Ormara. Some of the inhabitants are people of ancient coastal lineage—the Meds, who may be the descendants of the lowly "Icthyophagoi" ("fish eaters") described in the chronicles of Alexander the Great, who traversed this coast in the fourth century B.C. Many of the latter came to the coast because of their allegiance to the Zikri sect, which worships a *mahdi* (Islamic messiah) called Nur Pak ("Pure Light"), whose dispensation is said to supersede that of Muhammad the Prophet. This belief makes them infidels in the eyes of the orthodox Muslims (such as the majority of Baluch, who are Sunnis of the Hanafi school). Historically, Nur Pak may be equated with the figure of Sayyid Mahmud Jaunpauri, an Indian Sufi who traveled widely on the frontiers of South Asia in the late fifteenth century. But whatever their actual origins, Zikri belief and practices (which do not include fasting on Ramadan, and a Haj not to Mecca but to a holy mountain in Makran said to be the throne of Nur Pak) have resulted in their past persecution at the hands of Sunni Baluch. Beginning in the mid-eighteenth century, many Zikris were harried from the desert to the even more inhospitable coast by Sunni chiefs, such as Nasir Khan of Kalat, who viewed his harassment of the Zikris as a *jihad*, or holy war. Along the coast, especially in the area of Karachi and points west to about 30 miles, such Zikri refugees came into the area of the Pax Brittanica, after the mid-nineteenth-century conquests of Sir Charles Napier. They remain in large numbers in this region today, comprising up to 15 percent of the total Baluch population.

Zikri Baluch villages (outside of major towns, which have their own municipal structures) are usually fairly egalitarian, headed by local leaders known as *wadera*, who govern through a combination of clout and consensus.

All Baluch often seem obsessed with suspicion of social "outsiders," who are seen as threats to female chastity (*lujj*) and hence male honor (*izzat*). This is reflected in fairly high rates of endogamy among the Baluch in comparison with other Muslim peoples. But for the Zikris, who feel themselves isolated even among other Baluch, such in-marriage reaches astronomical levels, with up to 64 percent of marriages being contracted between biological first cousins.

In addition to the secular forms of sociopolitical organization, many Baluch, being theologically unsophisticated, are less followers of *ulama* or "Great Tradition" Islamic leaders than of *pirs*, the idiosyncratic Sufi mystics, or "saints," who can be found throughout the hinterlands of the Muslim world as exemplars of the direct power of God in human affairs. Performers of miracles, curers of illness and seers of future events, Baluch *pirs* often enjoy high economic and political status among their *murid*, or disciples, and this is especially true among the Zikris, who derive from the spiritual repute of their *pirs* a sense of self-esteem denied them in the secular arena.

The Baluch and their territory have recently assumed special strategic significance on the global scene since they bestride access to critical warm water ports and oil-producing areas. During the heyday of the British Raj, the Baluch were allowed considerable regional autonomy as long as they served as a buffer to Russian ambitions on the Arabian Sea. Today this "Great Game" (as Kipling called it) of big power intrigue over the Baluch and their land continues in intensified form, especially since the Russian invasion of Afghanistan in 1979.

For the past several decades the Baluch, long accustomed to handling their own affairs, have been increasingly consolidated into the central governmental structures of Pakistan, Iran and Afghanistan. Resentments about contemptuous, heavy-handed and often corrupt administration by non-Baluch bureaucrats (such as the Punjabis, who dominate Pakistan's civil service and who often view the Baluch as near savages) have been rife among the honor-obsessed tribesmen. Regional autonomy and outright secessionist and irredentist movements have been the result, centered in Pakistan and headed by traditional elites, who resent usurpation of their accustomed powers by nation-states. In recent years Baluch insurgents have waged both guerrilla and propaganda wars against their various central governments, with the period 1973–1977 witnessing a large-scale insurrection in Pakistani Baluchistan spearheaded by the Marri tribe and its Sardar. The Baluch were abetted in this uprising by such outside forces as India, Iraq and Afghanistan, all of whom had vested interests in destabilizing Pakistan and/or Iran, the centers of Baluch population.

Open warfare had subsided by the summer of 1982, but the anti-Pakistani guerrillas known as Farari continued to receive safe haven in Marxist Afghanistan. This is particularly ironic because the Baluch share many cultural values with the Pushtun of Afghanistan, who comprise the bulk of the anti-Soviet Mujahidin insurgents based in Pakistan. Yet their differing ethnic-political interests often lead to armed conflict between Baluch and Pushtun "freedom fighters" when they meet on their respective cross-border forays (see Pushtun).

In Iran, the Sunni Baluch hold little brief for Khomeini-style Shia fundamentalism and were among the first of Iran's minority groups to protest openly the revolution's policies.

For Western strategists the ongoing "nightmare in Baluchistan" (to use the phrase of Selig Harrison, a canny observer of the current Baluch political scene) is that Baluch desire for regional independence will lead to an ever-increasing flirtation with the Soviets, who may agree to accede to Baluch political aspirations for a "cordon sanitaire" to the warm water ports and oil-producing areas of the Persian Gulf.

Undoubtedly the Baluch, long obscure in world affairs, will assume increasing importance and merit considerable attention in times to come.

BIBLIOGRAPHY

Books

Baloch, Mir Khuda Baksh Marri. *Searchlights on Balouches and Balochistan*. Karachi: Royal Book, 1974.
Coon, Carleton S. *Caravan: Story of the Middle East*. Rev. Ed. New York: Holt, Rinehart and Winston, 1958.
Harrison, Selig. *In Afghanistan's Shadow: Baluch Nationalism and Soviet Temptations*. New York: Carnegie Endowment, 1981.
Matheson, Sylvia. *The Tigers of Baluchistan*. London: Arthur Barker, 1967.
Pastner, Carroll. "Access to Property and the Status of Women in Islam." In *Women in Contemporary Muslim Societies*, edited by J. I. Smith. Lewisburg: Bucknell University Press, 1980.
———. "The Status of Women and Access to Property on a Baluchistan Oasis." In *Women in the Muslim World*, edited by Lois Beck and Nikki Keddie. Cambridge: Harvard University Press, 1978.
———. "Gradation of Purdah and the Creation of Social Boundaries on a Baluchistan Oasis." In *Separate Worlds: Studies of Purdah in South Asia*, edited by H. Papanek and G. Minault. St. Louis: South Asia Books, 1982.
Pastner, Stephen, and Pastner, Carroll McC. "Clients, Camps and Crews: Adaptational Variation in Baluch Social Organization." In *Anthropology in Pakistan*, edited by S. Pastner and L. Flam. Ithaca: Cornell University South Asia Program, 1982.
———. "Adaptation to State-Level Polities by the Southern Baluch." In *Pakistan: The Long View*, edited by L. Ziring, R. Braibanti, and H. Wriggens. Durham: Duke University Press, 1976.

Pehrson, Robert N. *The Social Organization of the Marri Baluch*. New York: Wenner-Gren Foundation. 1966.
Salzman, Philip C. "Multi-Resource Nomadism in Iranian Baluchi-stan." In *Perspectives on Nomadism*, edited by W. Irons and N. Dyson-Hudson. Leiden: Brill, 1972.
———. "Processes of Sedentarization Among the Nomads of Baluchistan." In *When Nomads Settle*, edited by P. C. Salzman. New York: Praeger, 1980.
Spooner, Brian. "The Iranian Deserts." In *Population Growth: Anthropological Implications*, edited by B. Spooner. Cambridge: MIT Press, 1972.
Wirsing, Robert. *The Baluchis and Pathans*. Report No. 48. London: Minority Rights Group, 1981.

Articles

Barth, Fredrick. "Competition and Symbiosis in North East Baluchistan." *Folk* 6:1 (1964): 15–22.
Harrison, Selig. "Nightmare in Baluchistan." *Foreign Policy* 32 (1978): 136–160.
Herring, Donald. "Zulfikar Ali Bhutto and the 'Eradication of Feudalism' in Pakistan." *Comparative Studies in Society and History* 21:4 (1979): 519–555.
Pastner, Carroll McC. "Accommodations to Purdah: The Female Perspective." *Journal of Marriage and the Family* 36:2 (1974): 408–414.
———. "Cousin Marriage Among the Zikri Baluchi of Coastal Pakistan." *Ethnology* 18:1 (1979): 31–48.
———. "The Negotiation of Bilateral Endogamy in the Middle East Context: The Zikri Baluch Example." *Journal of Anthropological Research* 37:4 (1981): 305–318.
———. "A Social Structural and Historical Analysis of Honor, Shame and Purdah." *Anthropological Quarterly* 45:4 (1972): 248–261.
Pastner, Stephen L. "Baluch Fishermen in Pakistan." *Asian Affairs* 9:2 (1978): 161–167.
———. "Cooperation in Crisis Among Baluch Nomads." *Asian Affairs* 62 (1975): 165–176.
———. "Ideological Aspects of Nomad-Sedentary Contact: A Case from Southern Baluchistan." *Anthropological Quarterly* 44:3 (1971): 173–184.
———. "Lords of the Desert Border: Frontier Feudalism in Southern Baluchistan and Eastern Ethiopia." *International Journal of Middle East Studies* 10 (1979): 93–106.
———. "The Man Who Would Be Anthropologist: Dilemmas in Fieldwork on the Baluchistan Frontier." *Journal of South Asian and Middle-East Studies* 3:2 (1979): 44–52.
———. "Pirs and Power Among the Pakistani Baluch." *Journal of Asian and African Studies* 8:34 (1978): 231–243.
———, and Pastner, Carroll McC. "Agriculture, Kinship and Politics in Southern Baluchistan." *Man* 7:1 (1972): 128–136.
———. "Aspects of Religion in Southern Baluchistan." *Anthropologica* 14:2 (1972): 231–241.
Salzman, Philip Carl. "Adaptation and Political Organization in Iranian Baluchistan." *Ethnology* 10:4 (1971): 433–444.

————. "Continuity and Change in Baluchi Tribal Leadership." *International Journal of Middle Eastern Studies* 4:4 (1973): 428–439.
————. "Islam and Authority in Tribal Iran: A Comparative Comment." *Muslim World* 65:3 (1975): 186–195.
————. "Movement and Resource Extraction Among Pastoral Nomads: The Case of the Shah Nawazi Baluch." *Anthropological Quarterly* 44:3 (1971): 185–197.
Spooner, Brian. "Kuch U Baluch and Ichthyophagi." *Iran* 2 (1964): 53–67.

Unpublished Manuscripts

Pastner, Carroll. "Sexual Dichotomization in Society and Culture: The Women of Panjgur, Baluchistan." Ph.D. dissertation, Brandeis University, 1971.
Pastner, Stephen. "Camp and Territory Among the Nomads of Northern Makran District, Baluchistan: The Role of Sedentary Communities in Pastoral Social Organization." Ph.D. dissertation, Brandeis University, 1971.
Salzman, Philip C. "Adaptation and Change Among the Yarahmadzai Baluch." Ph.D. dissertation, University of Chicago, 1972.
————. "Dates to Meet, Dates to Eat: Oasis Life in Tribal Baluchistan." Paper presented at the 72nd annual meeting of the American Anthropological Association, New Orleans, November 28–December 2, 1973.
Spooner, Brian. "Religious and Political Leadership in Persian Baluchistan." Ph.D. dissertation, Oxford University, 1967.

Stephen L. Pastner

BAMBARA   The Bambara form part of the large Manding language group and can communicate with Manding speakers as far west as Gambia (see Manding-speaking Peoples). They are found in all the regions of Mali and the northern Ivory Coast. Many thousands are scattered in Guinea and Gambia. Most are concentrated along both banks of the Niger River, from the interior delta to Bamako, and from the Bani River in the east to the plains of Kaarta to the west. In Mali they form 31 percent of the population and greatly influence the culture and politics of the nation.

The Bambara number close to 2.8 million people, of whom perhaps 70 percent, or 2 million, are Muslims, a figure that will vary by location and whether or not they are urban or rural. For instance, in Mali 80 percent of Bambara urban dwellers are Muslims, while only some 60 percent of rural Bambara are. These population statistics are rough estimations drawn from incomplete census data, but they show a great increase in Islamization in the past 10 years.

Rural Bambara live in patrilineal agricultural villages composed of extended, patrilocal, sometimes polygynous households comprising as many as 60 people. They are able farmers, and the very nature of their identity is based upon a specific form of cooperative village-based farming. Young men form an association called the *ton*, which provides crucial labor for the intensive periods of weeding and harvesting. This young men's association is an integral institution in Bambara patterns of socialization, which have roots in animist religious beliefs. The Bambara further divide their social universe into three strata: those of free birth; slaves; and endogamous castes, comprising ironworkers, leatherworkers and praise singers.

The Bambara refer to themselves as Bamanakan, speakers of Bamana. Language thus imparts identity, although the term ''bamana'' has shifted in meaning over many centuries. Bamana refers to a people with a distinctive social organization: hard-working farmers who usually cultivate the better yielding but more demanding clay soils of the savanna and who rely upon cooperative labor for harvesting and weeding. The mutual vulnerability of this form of farming established the need for a tight-knit community with equal regard for kin, offspring and neighbors. Everyone in Bamana villages thus has a claim on their neighbor's granaries, since each household participates in each other's farming. Bamana is also a generic term for pagan.

''Bamana'' translates as the ''rejection of the master,'' although the exact reference is no longer clear. One interpretation is based on Bambara legends of origin, which imply that they rejected and fled from their Malian overlords in the thirteenth century. The sixteenth- and seventeenth-century Arabic chronicles of the Niger Bend region use ''Bamana'' in a pagan, non-Muslim sense. Here the rejection implied is of Allah, the Master. In the period after World War II, when many Bambara became Muslims, Bamana has come to mean one whose ancestors were ''free,'' in the sense that they did not work for someone else.

From at least the beginning of the eighteenth century the Bambara formed part of a larger regional economy in which ethnic identity and occupations were closely identified. The Bambara were animist farmers who defined themselves in opposition to the Soninke (whom the Bambara called Maraka), who were cosmopolitan Muslim traders (see Soninké). The Bambara also defined themselves in opposition to the Somono, who were Muslim fishermen of diverse ethnic origins, and to the Fulbe (Fulani), who were herders. These social boundaries were not rigid, however. Instead, they were usually permeable, although crossing them often meant changing ethnic identity. Ethnic groups in the heartland of the Bambara, then, define themselves by their social boundaries, by their distinctive occupations and social organization and by their relationships to others.

In the course of the eighteenth century, the Bambara founded two kingdoms in the region where they presently predominate. The Segu and Kaarta kingdoms were fiercely traditionalist, and in the case of Segu, several idols formed part of the institutional apparatus of state. Although the Segu and Kaarta Bambara were pagans, they were not averse to using Islam when and where it suited them. Muslims thus came to have important roles within the administration as diplomats and councilors to the rulers and as representatives of other Muslims living in the kingdoms. Animist Bambara rulers often sought special prayers from famed Muslim clerics, and they rewarded such services with gifts of luxuries and slaves. Nonetheless, Islam existed in an uneasy balance with traditional religion until the conquest of the region by the French in the last two decades of the nineteenth century.

During the period of Bambara hegemony (ca. 1710–1861), Bambara identity began to devolve into two forms, although both were clearly defined in opposition to the Muslim Maraka traders. On the one hand, slave warriors came to dominate the Bambara states. These warriors were hard drinking, hard fighting and committed to immediate gratification. All these values were antagonistic to the pious, refrained and accumulative Muslim merchants. On the other hand, Bambara identity remained deeply imbedded in the organization of farming communities using collective labor practices. Bambara farmers still dependent upon the *ton* consider themselves to be the authentic Bamana.

Magic was the primary means through which Islam percolated into Bambara society. The Bambara are essentially pragmatic. They are not averse to adding new rituals to their established practices, especially when the efficacy thereof is proven. Amulets containing written verses from the Quran or prayers, known as *grisgris*, were common accoutrements to Bambara wardrobes. Indeed, illustrations of fiercely animist Bambara warriors show them bedecked with these amulets. The Somono and the Soninké followed a quieter path of conversion.

Beginning in 1852, Al Hajj Umar participated in a wave of militant Muslim revivals which overthrew the Bambara kingdoms of Segu and Kaarta. By 1861 Umar had established a theocratic state, albeit on rather slender foundations, stretching throughout the areas where the Bambara had ruled. The Umarian experience, however, was not conducive to conversion. Although the Umarians (whose leadership was largely dominated by the Tukulor but included a variety of other West African Muslim peoples) introduced the Tijaniyya brotherhood into the Bambara lands, they made few converts (see Tukulor). Indeed, the Umarian experience probably reinforced local animist religions longer than might otherwise have been the case. Anti-Muslim Bambara warlords led a 30-year resistance against the Umarians. Moreover, the Umarians did not fully reestablish a viable regional economy and a strong state in which Islam could have made progressive inroads. Although the French fought against Muslim states while conquering the western Sudan, their success paradoxically reestablished conditions favorable for the expansion of Islam.

By 1912, only a tiny fraction (about 3 percent) of the Bambara were Muslims. French pacification eroded the slave warrior tradition, although many Bambara served in the French colonial army. French conquest increased commercial opportunities throughout the western Sudan, and Islam once again spread on the heels of this commerce radiating outward from the cities, as it had done since the eleventh century. Trade and production for the market gnawed at the traditional forms of community solidarity and weakened them. As Islam seeped into these open cracks, it provided a new sense of community for those participating in a larger economic system. Islam also hastened the erosion of these communal bonds, which had rested upon both cooperation and young bachelors' labor. In a report written in 1909, a French administrator described how the penetration of Islam into a Bambara community had turned newly converted youth against their animist elders. The new opportunities for accumulation engendered by expanding markets stood in sharp opposition to the cooperative anti-accumulative strategy of the Bamana. Conversion also offered those of low social status an opportunity to escape from their place within Bambara society.

Bambara secret societies based on the age-grade system are on the wane among the Bambara, although from the perspective of the Bambara they are not necessarily incompatible with Islam. Bambara secret societies and Islam shared organizational similarities, and they appealed to a more universalist community than did the more strictly ancestral Bambara religion. Muslim Bambara now belong to one of several brotherhoods widespread in West Africa. The most popular is the Qadiriyya, established in West Africa from at least the fifteenth century. Tijaniyya has become more attractive with the demise of the Umarian state, and the Hamalist variation of Tijaniyya attracted a sizable following during and after World War II, much to the displeasure of the French, who saw this movement as anti-colonialist. In Bamako today, some Bambara belong to the Wahhabi denomination, popularized by the *imam* of the large city mosque donated by the Saudi Arabians.

Islam also expanded among the Bambara as a form of opposition to colonial rule. While the rebellions during the recruitment drive of World War I were organized along traditional animist lines, resistance after World War II was often articulated in an Islamic idiom. The most numerous conversions among the Bambara occurred after 1945. Most Bambara today admit to being Muslims and participate in Muslim celebrations and in Friday prayers. The adaptation of the Muslim lunar calendar to the Bambara agricultural cycle posed no serious hardships. For example, the fasting of Ramadan meshed naturally with the local "hungry" season. Islam continues to advance among the Bambara as the established forms of social organization and their cultural and political logic disappear.

BIBLIOGRAPHY

Books

Abun-Nasr, Jamil. *The Tijaniyya: A Sufi Order in the Modern World*. London: Oxford University Press, 1967.
Kaba, Lansine. *The Wahhabiyya: Islamic Reform and Politics in French West Africa*. Evanston: Northwestern University Press, 1974.
Meillassoux, Claude. *Urbanization of an African Community: Voluntary Associations in Bamako*. Seattle: University of Washington Press, 1968.
Monteil, Charles. *The Bambara*. New Haven: Human Relations Area Files, 1959.

Articles

Bazin, Jean. "War and Servitude at Segou." *Economy and Society* 2:2 (1974): 107–144.
Lewis, John. "Small Farmer Credit and the Village Production Unit in Rural Mali."
    African Studies Review 21:1 (1978): 29–48.
Roberts, Richard. "Production and Reproduction of Warrior States: Segu Bambara and
    Segu Tokolor." *International Journal of African Historical Studies* 13:3 (1980):
    389–419.

                                                              Richard Roberts

BANTU, CENTRAL TANZANIAN   Central Tanzania, a region of poor soils,
low rainfall and frequent famine, is the home of approximately 820,000 Bantu-
speaking people who have in common variants of the basic language family of
Central Bantu of the Niger-Congo. Perhaps half the people are Muslims, divided
unequally among the major ethnic groups of the Rangi, Turu and Iramba. While
their specific languages are Kirangi, Kinyaturu and Kinyiramba, Kiswahili is
widely known and used. Anthropologist George P. Murdock refers to them as
"Rift Cluster" (see Bantu-speaking Peoples).
    The Bantu of Central Tanzania generally are hoe agriculturalists, growing
sorghum, millet and maize and keeping cattle, sheep and goats. The poverty of
the environment precludes the growing of many cash crops except for some
peanuts and castor oil plants.
    Matrilineal descent is the rule. A man's heir is his sister's son, although it is
reported that around the town of Kondoa Islamic influence is resulting in a move
towards descent in the male line.
    The inhabitants claim to have migrated to the area from diverse directions but
seem to have links to the east and northeast. While small chiefdoms developed
among the Rangi, the Turu had only councils of elders in each small settlement.
Settlements were based on a segment of a lineage, and when land became scarce,
men moved away to found new communities by opening up fresh bush land.
Much of the area is covered by fairly dense *miyombo* bush. In the southern parts,
there is a particularly dense type of thorn scrub.
    Since 1974 most of the rural peoples of Tanzania have been compelled to
move into large village groupings under an official policy of villagization. These
groupings were originally called *ujamaa* villages. The word *ujamaa* means "familyness" and is used to translate the English term "African Socialism." However,
there has been little popular enthusiasm for the idea so that although all rural
Tanzanians are now required to live in "registered villages," only about a dozen
villages in the entire country are acknowledged to be of the *ujamaa* type. The
rationale for the policy was to make adult education easier, to increase access
to clean drinking water and other sanitation facilities and to improve communications and political control. Because most Tanzanians formerly lived in isolated homestead groupings, the new policy will probably have profound effects,

especially when coupled with a policy of universal primary education which seeks to provide all boys and girls, regardless of religious affiliation, at least six years of education in a secular school.

An unusual feature of Turu society is a powerful secret society of women called Imaa. One theory is that the society gained strength because of the absence of so many men on migrant labor. Some men view Imaa as a threat, and perhaps because of this there is a strongly held belief in *mbojo*, or were-lions. A part of the belief is that lion-men are employed and harbored by women. There are many lions in the area and frequent human casualties from their attacks, all of which tend to be blamed on *mbojo*.

Islam entered the area in the nineteenth century through slave trade, for which the town of Kondoa was a center. It subsequently became a center for Swahili culture, which is Islamic, and continues to hold this position today (see Swahili). One observer notes that 75 percent of the Rangi are Muslim; the census of 1957 put the figure at 90 percent. The Tanzanian government's *Statistical Abstract for 1963* gives an estimate of 24.3 percent Muslims for the entire central region, but this would include the Gogo, few of whom are Muslim. Most people in the small towns and trading centers throughout the region claim to be Muslim. Christian missions have been more active in the rural areas. Kondoa, where the mosque and Quranic school are active, is unusual in its degree of religious observance. All the Muslims are Sunni of the Shafi school.

Outside the urban centers, knowledge and observance of the tenets of Islam are, as elsewhere in Tanzania, minimal. Few people carry out daily prayers, Ramadan is not strictly observed, only a handful have made the Haj, and beer drinking is widespread.

Running parallel with Islamic beliefs are traditional ancestral rites and worship at important rain shrines. An account of a boy's circumcision ceremony among the Rangi relates that it was regarded by the participants as Islamic but that spirits of the ancestors were invoked and much beer was consumed.

Most rural people who migrate to the cities claim to be either Muslim or Christian, but the majority find it easier to become Muslim. The concentration of numbers of people into villages may well result in large-scale conversion to Islam. Discontent with existing economic and political realities might lead to the growth of fundamentalism.

BIBLIOGRAPHY

Books

Lewis, Ioan Myrddin. *Islam in Tropical Africa*. London: Oxford University Press, 1966.
Trimingham, J. Spencer. *Islam in East Africa*. Oxford: Clarendon Press, 1964.

Articles

Brain, James L. "More Modern Witch-Finding." *Tanganyika Notes and Records* 62 (1964): 44–48.

Danielson, E. R. "Brief History of the Waniramba People up to the Time of the German Occupation." *Tanganyika Notes and Records* 56 (1961): 67–68.

———. "Proverbs of the Waniramba Peoples of East Africa." *Tanganyika Notes and Records* 47, 48 (1957): 187–197.

Fosbrooke, H. A. "A Rangi Circumcision Ceremony: Blessing of a New Grove." *Tanganyika Notes and Records* 50 (1958): 30–38.

Gray, R. F. "The Mbugwe Tribe: Origin and Development." *Tanganyika Notes and Records* 38 (1955): 39–50.

———. "Positional Succession Among the Wambugwe." *Tanganyika Notes and Records* 36 (1954): 39–50.

Hunton, G. "Hidden Drums in Singida District." *Tanganyika Notes and Records* 34 (1953): 28–32.

Jellicoe, M. "The Turu Resistance Movement." *Tanganyika Notes and Records* 70 (1969): 1–12.

Nimtz, A. H., Jr. "Islam in Tanzania: An Annotated Bibliography." *Tanganyika Notes and Records* 72 (1973): 51–74.

Olson, H. "Rimi Proverbs." *Tanganyika Notes and Records* 62 (1964): 73–82.

Schneider, H. K. "The Lion-Men of Singida: A Reappraisal." *Tanganyika Notes and Records* 58–59 (1962): 123–127.

Wyatt, A.W.N. "The Lion-Men of Singida." *Tanganyika Notes and Records* 28 (1950): 124–128.

James L. Brain

BANTU, NORTHEAST The Northeast Bantu of East Africa, numbering nearly 5 million, perhaps 38 percent of whom are Muslims, include a variety of people with enough cultural and linguistic similarities to be grouped together. The term "Northeast Bantu" is mainly a linguistic one, indicating a degree of similarity greater than that which links them to other Bantu speakers (see Bantu-speaking Peoples).

The Northeast Bantu, who live primarily along the East African coast from southern Somalia through Tanzania, include some 32 separate peoples grouped into 6 major clusters: Ngindo, Zaramo, Pogoro, Shambaa, Taita and Mijikenda or "Nine Tribes" (sometimes derogatorily called "Nyika," meaning "bush"). While many are Muslims, some, such as the Matumbi (Ngindo cluster) are only nominally so, and the Kaguru (Zaramo cluster) are less than 50 percent Muslim.

One of the largest clusters is the Zaramo, its members variously classified by their language or by their matrilineal descent system, which distinguishes them from their neighbors. The Zaramo are located inland from the coast behind Tanzania's capital, Dar es Salaam. Many live in the city itself and have adopted an urban life-style modeled on that of the Swahili people of the coast (see Swahili). In rural areas, the Zaramo are similar to others of the cluster: the Kutu,

Kwere, Zigula, Kami and Sagara, who live in the lowland areas; the Luguru, Ngulu, Kaguru, and Vidunda, who live mostly in the mountains.

As a response to the slave trade, the Zaramo in the nineteenth century lived in fortified, stockaded villages, each with a headman. These disappeared in this century. Most of the slaving caravans centered on the port of Bagamoyo passed through the Zaramo area and into that of the Kami, Kutu and Sagara, causing great disruption and suffering. The Luguru, high in their mountain dwellings, were more secure and may have had slaves themselves; even today some people are said to have no clans because their mothers' mothers were slaves.

It is reported that some present-day Zaramo trace descent in the male line; this is also true of some of the Kutu. Others use whichever method is more advantageous. However, in the main, descent is still traced through the mother.

None of the Zaramo group traditionally had any form of centralized authority. Exogamous matriclans were dispersed throughout the area, and the local autonomous unit was a lineage or sub-clan presided over by an elder, who derived his authority from the ancestral spirits, to whom sacrifices are still made, even by those who are nominally Muslim. Among the Luguru, three such elders became important as rainmakers with special oracular powers, again, while professing Islam.

All the Zaramo group are hoe agriculturalists growing maize, sorghum and rice as their grain crops. All keep sheep, goats and fowl, but cattle are absent. The tsetse fly is widespread in the lowland areas, but the mountains are free from this pestilence and from the scourges of malaria and schistomiasis, which are prevalent in the plains.

The traditional Zaramo house is a large round structure of mud and wattle with a high, conical, thatched roof. Rectangular houses with corrugated metal roofs are becoming common.

The degree of Islamization varies greatly. Among the Zaramo, Kutu, Kwere, Kami, Luguru, Zigula and Sagara, the proportion of those calling themselves Muslim is probably between 80 and 100 percent. Christian missions have been active among the Nguru, Vindunda and Kaguru, thus the proportion of Muslims is perhaps no more than 30 to 50 percent. In trading centers and in the typical villages of the Kutu, a mosque and Quranic school are found, but religious practice is superficial. Praying on a regular basis is rare except during Ramadan.

The Ngindo cluster consists of a number of peoples tracing descent along male lines. They include the Pogoro, Ndamba, Mbunga, Ndengereko, Matumbi and Rufiji. These peoples inhabit the flood plains of two major confluent rivers, the Kilombero and the Rufiji. They grow rice as their staple crop since the area is well watered and fertile. They keep small stock and fowl but no cattle. The traditional land-holding unit was a segment of a patrilineage in a system of dispersed exogamous patricians.

Although many profess Islam, adherence to tenets of the religion outside the trading centers is minimal. To most, the wearing of a white skull cap and the adoption of an Arab name constitute the major requirements of being Muslim. In a few larger centers, Quranic schools teach something of the religion.

The other major cluster in Tanzania is the Shambaa (also Shambala and Sambaa). The Shambaa and Pare subgroups live in the high and healthy climate of the mountains. The Bondei live in the fertile plains area between the Usambara Mountains and the Indian Ocean. Unlike the Zaramo and Ngindo, the Shambaa once had a complex state system with a royal clan providing official rulers at all levels. Although the rulers professed Islam, rites to their ancestral spirits formed an important part of the general belief system. Today, as elsewhere in Tanzania, all traditional chiefships have been abolished, and elected or appointed members of the nationalist party, CCM (formerly TANU), are the rulers. There is little doubt, however, that ancestral rites continue.

The mountain areas are ideal for growing vegetables, and a large-scale trade has grown up over the past 30 years, with vegetables being trucked to the towns. Another valuable cash crop is cardamom. The main food crops are maize and beans, with cassava and bananas as important additions. The traditional houses were round and thatched all the way to the ground, but these have given way to rectangular plastered houses with thatched roofs.

Descent among the Shambaa is patrilineal; traditional dwelling groups were based on a segment of the patrilineage, themselves said to be part of dispersed patricians found throughout the area.

Christian missions have been active in the area, but the majority of the Shambaa are believed to be Muslim. Among the Bondei and Pare, the number is lower.

Since 1974 most of the rural people of Tanzania have been compelled to move into larger village groupings under an official policy of villagization. These groupings were originally called *ujamaa* villages. The word *ujamaa* means "familyness" and is used to translate the English term of "African Socialism." However, there has been little enthusiasm for the idea so that although all rural Tanzanians are now required to live in "registered villages," only about a dozen villages in the entire country are acknowledged to be of the *ujamaa* type. The rationale for the policy was to make adult education easier, to increase access to clean drinking water and other sanitary resources, and to improve communication and political control. Since most Tanzanians formerly lived in isolated homestead groupings, the new policy will probably have profound effect, especially when coupled with a policy of universal primary education which ensures that all boys and girls, regardless of religious affiliation, will receive at least six years of education in a secular school.

The other two clusters, the Mijikenda and Taita, are located in Kenya, although some Taita and Digo, a Mijikenda subgroup, live in Tanzania. The Taita live in a hilly area about 50 miles inland from the coast and have links with the non-Bantu Masai. All the other peoples are inhabitants of the coastal strip of Kenya who retain their separateness from and are regarded with some disparagement by the true Waswahili. Their major crops are rice, maize and cassava. Palms are an important part of their economy, not only for the coconuts but also for the lucrative palm wine business.

The proportion of Muslims is high, but the degree of religious observance varies widely. Some conversion takes place as a result of what some refer to as "Islamic spirit possession." Among the Giriyama (Mijikenda cluster), many Muslims observe the prohibition on drinking, and there is a considerable division between the Muslims and non-Muslims over questions of drink and diet.

Descent is patrilineal and dispersed patrilineages are common. Rather unusually for East Africa, a definable patrilineage is often the exogamous unit rather than the clan.

Throughout the entire Northeast Bantu ethnic group, the Muslims are Sunni of the Shafi school. In the main, conversion took place as a result of the slave trade, through contacts with Arabs and Swahili, or in imitation of those who were economically successful. Even so, apart from fasting during Ramadan, little observance of the faith is made other than in matters of dress, diet and the adoption of Arab names.

BIBLIOGRAPHY

Books

Adamson, Joy. *The Peoples of Kenya*. New York: Harcourt, Brace and World, 1967.
Barrett, D., et al. *Kenya Churches Handbook*. Kisumu, Kenya: Evangel Publishing House, 1975.
Bostock, P. G. *The Peoples of Kenya: The Taita*. London: Macmillan, 1950.
Brain, James L. "Less than Second-Class: Women in Rural Settlement Schemes in Tanzania." In *Women in Africa*, edited by Nancy J. Hafkin and Edna G. Bay. Stanford: Stanford University Press, 1976.
Bryan, M. A. *The Bantu Languages of Africa*. London: Oxford University Press, 1959.
Bunger, Robert, Jr. *Islamization Among the Upper Pomoko*. Syracuse: Syracuse University Program of Eastern African Studies, 1974.
Champion, A. M. *The Agiryama of Kenya*. London: Royal Anthropological Institute, 1967.
Feierman, S. *The Shambaa Kingdom*. Madison: University of Wisconsin Press, 1962.
Harris, G. "The Taita." In *Marriage in Tribal Societies*, edited by Meyer Fortes. Cambridge: Cambridge University Press, 1962.
Lewis, Ioan Myrddin, ed. *Islam in Tropical Africa*. London: Oxford University Press, 1966.
Murdock, George P. *Africa: Its Peoples and Their Culture History*. New York: McGraw-Hill, 1959.
Prins, A.H.J. *The Coastal Tribes of the North-Eastern Bantu: Pokomo, Nyika and Taita*. London: International African Institute, 1952.
Salim, A. L. *Swahili-Speaking Peoples of Kenya's Coast*. Nairobi: East African Publishing House, 1973.

Swantz, L. W. *Ritual and Symbol in Transitional Zaramo Society.* Uppsala: Gleerup, 1970.

Trimingham, J. S. *The Influence of Islam Upon Africa.* Oxford: Clarendon Press, 1964.

Winans, Edgar V. *Shambala: The Constitution of a Traditional State.* Berkeley: University of California Press, 1962.

Young, Roland, and Fosbrooke, Henry. *Land and Politics Among the Luguru of Tanganyika.* London: Routledge and Kegan Paul, 1960.

Zein, Abdul Hamid M. el. *The Sacred Meadows: A Structural Analysis of Religious Symbolism in an East African Town.* Evanston, Northwestern University Press, 1974.

Articles

Arens, W. "The Waswahili: The Social History of an Ethnic Group." *Africa* 45:4 (1975): 426–438.

Brain, J. L. "Ancestors as Elders: Further Thoughts." *Africa* 43:11 (1973): 122–133.

―――. "Kingalu: A Myth of Origin from Eastern Tanzania." *Anthropos* 66 (1971): 817–838.

―――. "The Kwere of the Eastern Province." *Tanganyika Notes and Records* 58–59 (1962): 231–241.

―――. "Matrilineal Descent and Marital Stability: A Tanzanian Case." *Journal of Asian and African Studies* 4:2 (1969): 122–131.

―――. "Symbolic Rebirth: The *Mwali* Rite Among the Luguru of E. Tanzania." *Africa* 48:2 (1978): 176–188.

Brantley, Cynthia. "An Historical Perspective of the Giriama and Witchcraft Control." *Africa* 49:1 (1979): 112–133.

Cashmore, T.H.R. "A Note on the Chronology of the Nyika of the Kenya Coast." *Tanganyika Notes and Records* 37 (1961): 153–174.

Christensen, J. B. "Utani Joking: Sexual License and Social Obligations Among the Luguru." *American Anthropologist* 65 (1963): 1314–1327.

Crosse-Upcott, A.R.W. "Male Circumcision Among the Ngindo." *Journal of the Royal Anthropological Institute* 89 (1959): 169–189.

Nimtz, A. H., Jr. "Islam in Tanzania: An Annotated Bibliography." *Tanzania Notes and Records* 72 (1973): 51–74.

Parkin, David. "Along the Line of Road." *Africa* 49:3 (1979): 272–282.

Townsend, H. "Age, Descent and Elders Among the Pokomo." *Africa* 47:4 (1977): 386–397.

James L. Brain

BANTU-SPEAKING PEOPLES   If one were to draw a line from Cameroon in West Africa to Kenya in East Africa, all peoples south of this line would be Bantu speakers except for a few thousand people speaking Nilotic, Cushitic or Khoisan (Click) languages. They comprise an enormous number of ethnic groups, frequently called tribes. In the country of Tanzania alone there are approximately 120 different groups.

All the millions of peoples in this vast area speak different languages classified as subgroups of Bantu, itself a subgroup of a still larger language family, Nilo-Congo. Few are mutually intelligible.

Bantu languages are characterized by a system of concords. An unchangeable stem has prefixes and suffixes attached to it to give singular and plural and to construct verbs. There is a complex system of noun classes requiring concordial agreement somewhat analogous to genders in Indo-European languages. Thus, the stem -ntu gives: muntu (a person) and Bantu (people). Variants on this can give: omuntu, abantu; umuntu, avantu; or, in its most simplified form in Swahili, mtu, watu. The range of prefixes attached to stems becomes clearer with an ethnic name like Ganda. In their own Bantu language, Ganda becomes: Buganda (the country of the Ganda), Luganda (the language), muganda (a person), Baganda (the people). However, because Swahili (Kiswahili—the language of Swahili) is widely used in East Africa, it is possible to hear the Swahili version of the same words, thus: Uganda (the country of the Ganda), Kiganda (the language), mganda (a person), Waganda (the people).

During the colonial period the Swahili version, Uganda, came to be applied to the entire country, while the vernacular version, Buganda, was used to denote the region inhabited by the Ganda people, and this usage continues.

It is safest and now customary when writing in English only to use the stem to avoid confusion inherent in the different possible forms. For example, Nyamwezi is now standard usage to write of the Nyamwezi people, a Nyamwezi person talking the Nyamwezi language and living in Nyamweziland.

The Bantu-speaking peoples probably originated in what today is eastern Nigeria. The migrations that led to their present wide distribution seem to have begun about 2,000 years ago. It is thought that they moved south through the rain forest, possibly using canoes, then settled in what is today the Luba area of Katanga in Zaire. From here they seem to have fanned out in a series of migrations until today they are found as far north as southern Somali (the North-east Bantu) and as far south as South Africa, a distance of more than 2,000 miles. Almost everywhere, the Bantu absorbed the pre-Bantu sedentary peoples they found before them. And almost everywhere they settled, their language developed distinctive characteristics of its own.

The secret of Bantu success was probably a knowledge of ironworking. This skill initially gave them an advantage as hunters and warriors and subsequently allowed farming groups to clear woodland more easily than with stone tools. In some areas the chief was referred to as the Feller (of trees) or the Ax-Holder, usages that probably reflect the use of iron.

Most Bantu peoples have retained their own traditional animistic religions steeped in the sacredness of ancestors and a multiplicity of gods and spirits related to forces and things of nature. Many millions (perhaps 20 million) have become Christians of various sects. In eastern Africa, a significant number are Muslims, the result of centuries of contact with Arabs and early converts along the coast, the most influential of these being the Swahili peoples. Among the major Bantu-speaking subgroups who have been most influenced by Islam are the Northeast Bantu, Interlacustrine Bantu and Central Bantu.

BIBLIOGRAPHY

Books

Greenberg, Joseph H. *The Languages of Africa*. Bloomington: Indiana University Research Center, 1970.
Johnston, Sir Harry. *A Comparative Study of the Bantu and Semi-Bantu Languages*. Oxford: Clarendon Press, 1919.
July, Robert. *A History of the African People*. London: Scribners, 1970.
Meinhof, Carl. *An Introduction to the Phonology of the Bantu Languages*. Translated by N. J. Warmelo. Berlin: Reimer Vohsen, 1932 (Orig. Leipzig, 1899.)
Murdock, George P. *Africa: Its Peoples and Their Culture History*. New York: McGraw-Hill, 1959.

Articles

Brain, J. L. "Eastern and Western Tanzania: A Comparison of Non-Culture Terms." *Ba Shiru* 6:2 (1975): 67–81.
Guthrie, M. "Some Developments in the Prehistory of the Bantu Languages." *Journal of African History* 3:2 (1962): 273–282.
Oliver, R. "The Problem of the Bantu Expansion." *Journal of African History* 8:3 (1966): 361–376.
Posnansky, M. "Bantu Genesis: Archeological Reflections." *Journal of African History* 9:1 (1951): 1–11.
Wrigley, C. "The Economic Prehistory of Africa." *Journal of African History* 1:2 (1960): 189–204.

James L. Brain

BARMA   The Barma, a small Muslim ethnic group living near the Chari and Bahr Erguig rivers between Bousso and N'Djamena in Chad, number only about 47,000. They speak a Central Sudanese dialect of the Chari-Nile language family. Despite their size, through their state of Bagirmi they have played a significant role in the politics of Chad. Today mainly poor peasant farmers, they have known greater power.

Bagirmi is not well known. The fleeting references to it in the *Cambridge History of Africa* contrast with the ampler coverage extended to other Sudanic kingdoms. This is because Bagirmi is located in Chad, which remains something of a *terra incognito*, some excellent French research notwithstanding.

The origin of Bagirmi is not clear. Tradition speaks of 12 brothers arriving from Yemen (ca. 1520) and creating an alliance with existing populations at Massenya, the future capital. A more likely origin would lie in the rise both of notions of political hierarchy and of the need for such a hierarchy among Central Sudanic speakers in response to the raiding activities of the Kanem-Bornu empire. The nascent polity expanded throughout the seventeenth century, reaching its apogee some time in the eighteenth century. During this time, according to tradition, its military forces roamed with success in the Kanem and Tebu territories and as far northwest as Bilma. To the east they were able to defeat the Sultan of Wadai. By the end of the eighteenth century, Bagirmi enjoyed hegemony over much of the area between Bornu and Darfur.

The early nineteenth century saw Islam used to challenge existing central Sudanic kingdoms. Wadai, employing the pretext that Bagirmi's ruler had contracted an incestuous marriage, attacked and devastated the kingdom in 1806. Thereafter, throughout the nineteenth century, Bagirmi strove diplomatically and militarily with indifferent success to reestablish its autonomy. To further this goal, in 1897 it signed a treaty of protection with France which culminated in its incorporation into French Equatorial Africa in 1910.

Two administrative zones can be distinguished in mid-nineteenth-century Bagirmi. Centered around Massenya were Barma horticulturalists, along with Chadian Arabs and Fulani semi-pastoralists. They were ruled directly by the hierarchy. Beyond this population concentration, largely to the south, were satellite ethnic groups (Ndam, Bua, Sonrai, Tomack and Sara), who were affiliated with Bagirmi by conquest but generally free to conduct their own affairs as long as they paid their annual tributes and aided raiding expeditions. In the core, walled Barma towns stretched along waterways at valuable defensive, agricultural or commercial sites. These often had something of a cosmopolitan character with officials, merchants and learned Muslim clerics present. Drawn around the towns were smaller villages, some of which were composed exclusively of slaves working for their absent owners. Finally, scattered throughout the countryside, were semi-permanent Arab or Fulani hamlets (see Arabs, Chadian; Fulani).

The stratification system in mid-nineteenth-century Bagirmi was complex. Barma distinguished two fundamental social categories—free persons (*kambege*), usually Barma, and slaves (*belge*), normally not Barma. These two categories provided individuals for the three major strata involved in Bagirmi life: officials, peasants and slaves. Bagirmi's political hierarchy appears to have been highly centralized during this period because the ruler (*mbang*) did not have to contend with numerous landed, hereditary nobles. Political offices were balanced between slaves and freemen and frequently allocated at the ruler's discretion. Offices bore with them the responsibility of administering villages and ethnic groups and provided rights to some of the wealth produced by these. Office also provided the privilege of raiding for slaves. Peasants were predominantly cereal producers who were required to yield a portion of their output as taxes to the official to whom they were responsible. Slaves, if they did not join the government, were either sold or settled in village plantations to produce for their owners, who were usually officials. Surplus products flowed from slaves and peasants to officials.

Islam probably came to Bagirmi towards the end of the sixteenth century. How it came is uncertain. The existence of an old Fulani Islamic center at the town of Bidiri only ten miles from Massenya, and the belief that the state was created as result of an alliance between Barma and Fulani does suggest that Islam may have diffused throughout Bagirmi from this center. In the mid-nineteenth century, Bagirmians are described as indifferent Muslims, probably due to their attachment to conceptions of the *mbang* (ruler) as a supernatural force. Such notions of "divine kingship," while helping to legitimize surplus extraction, conflicted with certain aspects of Islam.

Bagirmi experience with colonialism began in earnest in 1900, when the French defeated Rabah, their chief African competitor, for hegemony in the central Sudan. Colonialism in the first two decades meant the imposition of French taxes, forced labor and mandatory cash-cropping of cotton. The prohibition of raiding, combined with the abolition of slave village plantations, considerably reduced the flow of revenue to the pre-colonial state. Corvee labor and French taxes further diverted production inputs or their products from Bagirmi to French utilization. Such changes in the Bagirmi opportunity structure provoked considerable emigration from the old kingdom, or as one Barma phrased it: "Dono goto, debge goto" (Power gone, people gone).

Post-colonial Barma society exhibits low fertility, a tendency towards atomization of domestic units, a new stratification system and new Muslim piety. As opposed to many other populations in Africa, the Barma crude birth-rate was in the low thirties in the early 1970s. This has been argued to be the result of an interaction between brideprice, husband and wife age differentials and divorce—which contribute to a high incidence of sterility due to venereal disease. Contemporary Barma lack corporate descent groups. Villages contain wards composed, because of prevailing patrilocality, of patrilineally related households.

The normative household is a large, patrilateral, extended family with an elder directing his married sons' activities. In fact, household size appears to be relatively small (about five people), with extended families absent in three-fourths of the cases. Furthermore, in the past, village age-groups mobilized labor for households to deal with the most onerous farm chores. Such groups seem to be disappearing. Households, then, exhibit a dual atomization. First, they are starved for members, with their small numbers and low incidence of extended families probably attributable both to low fertility and to high emigration, and second, those few family members left are less able to count upon assistance from their neighbors.

Barma live in two types of houses: an older, circular adobe mud-brick house with thatched roof; and the more "modern" Sudanic rectangular adobe style. The latter is becoming more common, a reflection of the amalgamation of culture which is occurring in the Sudan, which tends to wipe out cultural uniqueness.

Contemporary Barma seem to take Islam seriously. Most Barma observe

Ramadan and other major Muslim ceremonies. They usually do not drink alcohol. Few can afford to make the Haj. Polygyny, a major way of gaining prestige for men, is generally restricted to wealthier, middle-aged gentlemen.

Quranic study is widespread. Conformity to Islamic precepts appears stricter than what was reported in the nineteenth century. At the same time many peasants, especially those with few official connections, simply do not know the old religion. This shift from a more particularistic to a universalistic theology may have come about because older notions justified a state which the French destroyed. A major syncretistic feature is the attempt to integrate Barma origin myths into Islamic cosmology and history. For example, Abd el Tukruru, ancestor of the first *mbang* (ruler), is supposedly connected with Hassan, son of Ali, which places the Barma in a Shia tradition, although today they are Sunni. Most villages are likely to have religious leaders (*mallamai*) to provide instruction and perform the various Muslim rituals.

Many Barma are members of the Tijaniyya *tariqa*, the most popular brotherhood in Chad. However, Sufi brotherhoods in Chad do not have the significance of those in West Africa or the Republic of Sudan.

Though relatively few in number (only about 1 percent in 1982 of the 4.6 million Chadians), Barma have played a significant role in the politics of independence and post-independence. Ahmed Koullamallah, descended on his mother's side from Bagirmi royalty, was the most prominent leader of Muslim political parties which at independence lost out to François Tombalbaye's southern-based PPT. A Barma, Mahamet Douba Alipha, served as Minister of the Interior throughout much of Tombalbaye's rule. Abdoulaye Lamana was Minister of Finance through much of the same reign. Small in numbers, and hence not threatening, poised geographically between a Muslim north and a non-Muslim south, and consequently with ties to both regions, it is possible that the Barma will continue to play a significant role in a future Chad.

BIBLIOGRAPHY

Books

Goody, J. *Technology, Tradition and the State in Africa.* London: Oxford University Press, 1977.

Greenberg, Joseph H. *The Languages of Africa.* Bloomington: Indiana University Research Center, 1970.

Oliver, R. *The Cambridge History of Africa.* Vols. 3 and 4. New York: Cambridge University Press, 1977.

Paques, Viviana. *Le Roi pecheur et le roi chasseur.* Strasbourg: Institut d'Anthropologie de Strasbourg, 1977.

Reyna, S. P. "Age Differential, Marital Instability, and Venereal Disease: Factors Affecting Fertility Among the Northwest Barma." In *Population and Social Organization*, edited by Moni Nag. Chicago: Aldine, 1975.

Articles

Devallee, M. "Le Baguirmi." *Bulletin de la Société de Recherches Congolaises* 7 (1925): 3–76.
Dubois, C. "Le Baguirmi en 1902." *Etudes et documents tchadiens. Série B* (1969): 1–3.
Lanier, J. "L'Ancien Royaume du Baguirmi. Histoire et coûtumes." *Renseignements coloniaux de l'Afrique française* 10 (1925): 457:474.
Paques, V. "Origine et caractères du pouvoir royal au Baguirmi." *Journal de la Société des Africanistes* 37 (1967): 83–214.
Lebeuf, A.M.D. "Boum Massenia, ancienne capitale du Baguirmi." *Journal de la Société des Africanistes* 37 (1967): 215–244.
Reyna, S. P. "The Extending Strategy: Regulation of Household Dependency Ratios." *Journal of Anthropological Research* 32 (1976): 182–198.

Unpublished Manuscripts

Reyna, S. P. "The Costs of Marriage: A Study of Some Factors Affecting Northwest Barma Fertility." Ph.D. dissertation, Columbia University, 1972.
———. "Metapower and Opportunity: A Multi-Level Analysis of Emigration in Colonial Bagirmi." Paper presented to the American Society for Ethnohistory, Albuquerque, New Mexico, October 1976.

S. P. Reyna

BASHKIR   The first recorded evidence of the existence of a people named Bashkir (Bashgird or Bashgurd) appears in the Arab chronicles of the ninth and tenth centuries A.D. Like the nearby Tatars, the Bashkir are a people of extremely mixed origins, related in part to the Oguz, Pechenegs, Volga-Kama Bulgars, Kipchak Turks and a variety of Mongol tribes (see Turkic-speaking Peoples). Although loosely organized even into the twentieth century, the Bashkir are believed to have experienced their ethnogenesis sometime in the sixteenth century.

Most Bashkir speak a variety of the northwest-Turkic (Kipchak) branch of the Altaic language family. Physically, they are among the most Mongoloid of the Middle-Volga cultures, having mixed with the same races who gave rise to the Kazakhs, Kirghiz and Karakalpak in Central Asia.

Bashkir is spoken by an estimated 1.5 million people, all of whom live in the U.S.S.R. There are two basic dialects: a southern or steppe dialect called Yurmatin, and a northern or forest dialect known as Kuvakan. The language itself is barely distinguishable from Tatar, being differentiated from the latter only on the basis of phonetics and grammatical characteristics (see Tatars).

More than 900,000 Bashkir live in the Bashkir Autonomous Soviet Socialist Republic (A.S.S.R.), with decreasingly fewer numbers dwelling in the neighboring provinces (*oblasts*) of Chelyabinsk, Perm', Orenburg, Sverdlovsk, Kurgan and Kuybyshev. More distant enclaves of Bashkir are found in Kemerovo

Oblast' and in the republics of Kazakhstan, Uzbekistan, Tadzhikistan, Kirghiza and the Ukraine. The Bashkir elements who are located more remotely from their homeland in the southern Ural Mountains tend to live in cities, varying from 61 percent urban in the Kazakh republic to 88 percent urban in Tadzhikistan. However, the overwhelming majority of Bashkir are rural collective farmers or sedentary pastoralists. This fact becomes quite evident within the Bashkir republic, where only a fifth of the almost 1 million Bashkir are townspeople.

Soviet journalists often portray the Bashkir as oil-field, refinery and petrochemical workers, who represent the principal industrial employees of the A.S.S.R. As the demographic statistics imply, this is only partially true. Bashkir in their own republic and adjacent provinces remain farmers and herdsmen just as their ancestors were.

Known to the Soviet people as the "Second Baku" after the famous oil field in Soviet Azerbaijan, Bashkiria had been the leading petroleum-producing region in the U.S.S.R. until the development of the oil deposits of Western Siberia in the 1970s. However, outnumbered by both the Russians and Tatar in the cities of the Bashkir republic, Bashkir themselves do not participate actively in the industries of their homeland.

Almost totally sedentary even before 1917, modern Bashkir live on over 600 collectives and more than 150 state farms. Within the A.S.S.R., there is a patent bias in favor of animal husbandry over crop production, although on most farms grain (spring wheat, rye, oats, buckwheat and millet), sugar beets and potatoes are grown. Legumes (peas, alfalfa etc.) and green (silage) corn are raised for animal feed.

Animal husbandry is practiced throughout the southern Ural region owing to a rich fodder base, massive common pastureland and an increasingly larger area sown to grasses. Bashkir horses long have been prized for their endurance. While horse herds elsewhere in the country have decreased considerably, those of the Bashkir appear to have flourished. Several breeds are raised for different purposes: draft horses are bred in northern Bashkiria; riding horses are trained in the southern steppe; pack horses are used in the Ural Mountains; and in the forests Bashkir horses are employed in hauling logs. Bashkir brood mares are milked at a rate of six times daily during the months of June and July. The milk product is made into the traditional Mongol beverage *kumyss*, which today is drunk both at ceremonies and for relaxation. Bashkir also tend growing herds of beef and dairy cattle, sheep and goats and poultry flocks. Animal herds of all types have increased steadily since the end of World War II.

Another traditional Bashkir occupation is beekeeping. Since 1917, this activity has spread even into the southeast steppes, where before the revolution it was a rarity. In the Ural forests, Bashkir still maintain "privately owned" hollow-tree apiaries, rich in legend and handed down from one generation to the next for centuries. Collective beekeepers not only keep commercial hives, they retain hollow logs for their own private purposes as well.

The Bashkir religious preference is Sunni Islam of the Hanafi school. Ufa, their capital, is one of four Muslim *muftiyats*, or spiritual directorates, in the Soviet Union. In fact, it is the only remaining pre-revolutionary synod. Three other directorates, including a Shia *muftiyat* in Baku, are in entirely different locations. A pre-revolutionary hearth of pan-Islamic fervor, Bashkiria (and Tatarstan) is virtually closed to visits by foreign Muslims. This probably reflects less on contemporary Bashkir religious behavior than it does on the apprehension of Soviet leaders.

As with all Central Asians, extended family relationships among the Bashkir persist under the heading of the collective farm. Traditionally exogamous, Bashkir men prefer to marry women from other farms or villages, although intrafarm marriages are increasing.

The family remains patriarchal, although less so than among other Muslim groups. Before the revolution, Bashkir women had more freedom than Muslim women in other parts of the Islamic world. For instance, they had the right to property beyond their dowries. They were almost never veiled except in the presence of their fathers-in-law, and divorce was relatively easy. Thus, when today Soviet officials boast about their liberating of Bashkir women from social and religious servitude, it is only a matter of degree. Still, in northeast Bashkiria, women dress in the old style even while going to mosque with the men.

Contemporary Bashkir dwellings consist of two halves: one for the older generation, and another for the younger adults. In general, the older folk still respect the old ways, preferring to sleep and eat on plank beds heaped with felt blankets, pillows and feather mattresses. The food they eat and the clothes they wear reflect earlier times. The younger generation conducts a more modern, Soviet life-style. The plank bed has been replaced with contemporary furniture. The handmade blankets and pillows have been superseded by ready-made materials. A Bashkir adult of 60 or younger typically dresses like a Russian. To his diet he has added more vegetables and potatoes. Like his Tatar brother, a Bashkir increasingly is observed to eat pork and to consume alcoholic beverages. (Although no official statistics exist, drunkenness and alcoholism are on the rise among Muslims of the Volga republics and also in more devout Central Asia. Drunkenness can be witnessed on the streets of Ufa and Tashkent, just as it can on those of Moscow and Leningrad.) Younger Bashkir most likely will use plates and utensils when they dine. Finally, the yurt is rarely seen, and the curtain which once divided the sexes within traditional residences is now a wall hanging, bedspread or drape.

The days of polygyny are gone, as they are supposed to be throughout the Soviet Union, forbidden by state law. No longer is the Bashkir widow obliged to marry her husband's younger brother. Child marriage is almost unheard of, and only a modified version of brideprice is lawful. While lavish brideprices are proscribed, dowries are yet permitted. At Muslim wedding receptions, money is pinned to the bride's gown.

Although many have forgotten their prayers, older Bashkir more often than not are true believers. It is through them that traditional ceremonies and rituals at marriage, childbirth, death and other events have been preserved. Soviet officials have encouraged the Bashkir to participate in the *sabantuy* festival of the Tatar. Otherwise, authorities have tried to eliminate most of the older customs, especially the longer holidays, which lower labor productivity. This even extends to the more secular of Muslim habits. Bazaar day, for example, has been shifted from Friday, a work day, to Sunday, the Soviet day of rest. Evidently, a few Bashkir and Tatars make pilgrimages to shrines in Central Asia.

A few western scholars believe the official Soviet dichotomy between Bashkir and Tatar is artificial, if not unjustified. They indicate that even today, more than 60 years after the creation of the Bashkir literary language (which is the approved administrative language of the Bashkir republic), only 67 percent of the Bashkir claim Bashkir as their native language, and 33 percent select Tatar. The Bashkir are a clear minority in their own republic, and granting them full nationality status shortly after the revolution was more a subterfuge for undermining Volga-Muslim unity than it was a recognition of real national consciousness.

Russianization, a process through which an ethnic minority adopts Russian as its second language, has been successful in Bashkiria. In 1970, just over half of the Bashkir people spoke Russian as a second language, but in 1979, almost 65 percent of them were able to speak it. This share was second only to the Tatars among major Muslim groups in the U.S.S.R., a fact no doubt related more to geography and practicality than to genuine preference. (Both the Bashkir and Tatar republics are minority enclaves located deep within the huge Russian republic, and politically both are patently subservient to the same.) Interestingly, though, the Bashkir are only weakly Russified. The share of the people who claim Russian as the native language equals only half the number of converts among the neighboring Tatars (5 percent versus 10 percent). There is some intermarriage with Russians.

BIBLIOGRAPHY

Books

Allworth, Edward, ed. *The Nationality Question in Soviet Central Asia*. New York: Praeger, 1973.
———. *Soviet Nationality Problems*. New York: Columbia University Press, 1971.
Katz, Zev; Rogers, Rosemarie; and Harned, Frederic, eds. *Handbook of Major Soviet Nationalities*. New York: Free Press, 1975.
Symmons-Symonolewicz, Konstantin. *The Non-Slavic Peoples of the Soviet Union*. Meadville, Pa.: Maplewood Press, 1972.

Articles

Dostal, Petr, and Knippenberg, Hans. "The Russification of Ethnic Minorities in the U.S.S.R." *Soviet Geography* 20:4 (1979): 197–218.

Jones, Ellen, and Grupp, Fred W. "Measuring Nationality Trends in the Soviet Union."
    Slavic Review 41:1 (1982): 112–122.
Marin, Yuri. "Central Asia Through Soviet Eyes." *Studies on the Soviet Union* 8:1
    (1968): 69:87.
Rorlich, A. A. "Acculturation in Tatarstan: The Case of the *Sabantui* Festival." *Slavic
    Review* 41:2 (1982): 316–321.
———. "Islam Under Communism: Volga-Ural Muslims." *Central Asian Survey* 1:1
    (1982): 5–42.
Shuiskii, S. A. "Muslims in the Soviet State: Islam a Privileged Religion?" *Oriente
    Moderno* 7–12 (1980): 383–402.
Wixman, Ronald. "Territorial Russification and Linguistic Russianization in Some Soviet
    Republics." *Soviet Geography* 22:10 (1981): 667–675.

Unpublished Manuscripts

Bennigsen, Alexandre. "Modernization and Conservatism in Soviet Islam." Paper pre-
    sented at the Conference on Religion and Modernization in the Soviet Union under
    the Auspices of the American Association for the Advancement of Slavic Studies,
    San Marcos, Texas, March 21–23, 1976.

                                                                    Victor L. Mote

BATAK   The several Batak peoples of highland north Sumatra, who number
perhaps 3.4 million, have remarkably complex religious lives, even in so syncretistic a nation as Indonesia, the world's most populous Muslim country. They
stand out as accepting congenially the religions of Islam, Christianity and animism. Perhaps 30 percent are Muslim.

There are roughly seven Batak groups, not including the Batak in the *rantau*
(the diaspora communities outside north Sumatra). They are:

1. The *Toba Batak* on the southeast shore of Lake Toba and on Samosir Island, acknowledged by many Batak to be the original Batak population. The Toba are certainly
   the group most Indonesians see as the prototypical Batak—brusque, hot-tempered but
   quick to cool off, true to their word and dependably plainspoken. In this, the Toba
   Batak are the antithesis of the stereotype of the Javanese—subtle, deferential, intriguing
   (see Javanese).
2. The *Simulungun Batak* to the northeast of the lake near Pematang Siantar, a group
   now sharing their homeland area with Muslim Javanese plantation workers. They are
   a mixed Christian/Muslim population.
3. The *Karo Batak* to the north bordering on Aceh, whose language is unintelligible to
   Toba speakers (who speak a dialect with the widest intelligibility among the other
   Batak groups). Karo Batak traditions derive from strong animism; Islam is making
   gains among the unconverted, but politically motivated conversions to Christianity
   since 1965 have increased that religion's membership as well.
4. The *Dairi* and *Pakpak* groups on the west coast of Lake Toba, who compose a united
   society identified by dialects.

5. The *Silindung* group near Taruntung south of the lake, often seeing itself as having a separate tradition and personality from the northerners. They are almost all Christian. Some ethnic classification schemes group these people as Toba.
6. The *Angkola Batak*, who are 10 percent Christian and 90 percent Muslim, with ceremonial traditions much closer to the uniformly Muslim Mandailing people than to the Christian Toba. Christian and Muslim Angkolans feel themselves ethnically closer to the Mandailing.
7. The *Mandailing*, bordering on Minangkabau society, historically reluctant to consider themselves as Batak. They frequently drop their Batak clan names in the move to the *rantau* cities.

The Batak area is ruggedly mountainous, broken occasionally by broad plains. Much of the Karo highlands and South Tapanuli is jungle. The soil, heavily volcanic, is fairly rich in some areas and supports two crops of paddy rice a year in a few plainlands. Karo Batak do considerable vegetable farming and truck their produce to Medan, but most commonly Batak agriculture is overwhelmingly wet rice cultivation. Most field work is done by hand, with some of the heavy plowing done by water buffalo in the more prosperous areas. Work groups are recruited on a kinship basis. Land is not to be sold to nonrelatives; clansmen left in the village work the rice lands of richer relatives who live in *rantau* cities. Despite the heavy migration to cities, Batak are loathe to sell their inherited rice land, as this is their measure of importance in village society and their assurance of continued participation in village councils. In times of national political turbulence, city Batak have often taken temporary refuge in their old villages, an option they are not likely to give up.

The southern Batak societies of Angkola and Mandailing and some of the Karo Batak north of Lake Toba are notably pious believers in Islam. Other Batak cultures, however, are overwhelmingly Protestant Christian, the result of German and Dutch missionary efforts starting in the 1850s. All Batak cultures, moreover, retain many beliefs and ritual practices from their indigenous religions that predated their conversion to monotheism. In some Batak homelands, Islam, Christianity and Batak ''animism'' stressing clan ancestral figures are practiced in the same communities. In religiously mixed areas, many Muslim families are linked to Christian ones through traditional bonds of marriage alliance, a prime social cement in Batak culture.

The main religious controversy in the Batak areas today concerns not Muslim–Christian relations but the degree to which each monotheistic religion can legitimately be ''blended'' with older Batak ritual practice. This is a particular concern of Muslims in the southern Batak societies of Angkola and Mandailing, where a strong if still minority Muslim modernist movement is insisting that Islam should be ''cleansed'' of compromises with the local *adat* (ethnic custom, including indigenous ritual, spirit beliefs, kinship and traditional politics).

The Batak societies, clustered around Lake Toba and extending on the west to the Indian Ocean, have been influenced from the north by the orthodox Muslim Acehnese (see Acehnese) and from the south by the equally pious Minangkabau

Muslims (see Minangkabau). In the early nineteenth century, Sunni Muslim (of the Shafi school) proselytizers forcibly converted the southern Batak in the areas of Angkola and Mandailing, while the Acehnese made converts among the Karo Batak of the north. First German, then Dutch missionaries, finding little success in these areas, concentrated their efforts among the animists of the central area around Lake Toba. Today the hegemony of the two religions is nearly complete.

The southern Angkola Batak demonstrate all the religious trends affecting Batak cultures in modernizing Indonesia. Relations between the 10 percent Christian minority and the Muslim majority are, for the most part, enviably harmonious. All homeland Batak societies are rent by numerous village and intravillage squabbles, but in Angkola these are largely kinship disputes over access to arable land or access to central government favors, not Muslim–Christian controversies. Often related to each other through a web of traditional kinship ties and united in a general feeling of common Angkola Batakness, Muslims and Christians in Angkola manage to be both fiercely pious and tactfully deferential of the other religion. Christians raise no pigs in the area, lest their Muslim clanmates refuse to eat in their homes. Muslims allow Christian grace to be said in their ceremonies. The village *hajjis* turn out to greet a new Protestant minister. Muslim children take great platefuls of holiday cakes to the homes of Christian families on Id al Fitr, gifts which Christian children return in kind on their major religious holiday in the area, New Year's Day. Mixed marriage is frowned upon by both sides, and the injunction to marry one's own faith has seriously reshaped the traditional Batak system of preferential cousin marriage. However, Christians and Muslims rather frequently do marry in Angkola, and such marriages are countenanced if one of the newlyweds changes to the partner's religion. Partly because of such Christian–Muslim marriages, partly because the Dutch favored Christians in choosing village headmen and partly because a lone Christian family in a Muslim village will often convert to Islam for lack of Christian friends, many Angkola families have a history of switching back and forth from one religion to the other. One sometimes finds a *hajji* and a Protestant minister descended from the same great grandfather, or a set of sons and daughters, some Christian, some Muslim. Importantly, their ties to each other in everyday village life and formal convocations generally override their religious differences.

Although to the people themselves sub-ethnic differences loom large, all Batak groups speak closely related dialects of Batak (a Western Austronesian language), share basically similar kinship systems of patrilineal clans and marriage alliances, celebrate births, deaths and marriages in similar ceremonies and share a common political heritage of small, kin-based village organization. Like many other highland Southeast Asian peoples, the Batak use kinship linkages to forge alliances between village chiefs and between local lineages.

One of the earliest Indonesian groups to invest heavily in modern education and to turn to city standards of social accomplishment, north and south Tapunuli Batak began moving out of their villages in small numbers in the early decades of this century. The men found work as schoolteachers or clerks in the Dutch colonial administration. Some Batak merely moved from one Batak area to another, in itself a revolutionary step at the time for a notoriously insular people. (Batak even today distrust the people over the next hill and believe that the farther one gets from home into "other people's territory," the more likely one is to fall victim to poisoners and spellcasters). Paradoxically, the Batak have developed into adept city migrants.

The organizational requirements of wet rice farming have shaped Batak village organization. In Toba, the traditional village or *huta* is no larger than 5 to 10 compound houses, divided into 30 or so households, clustered together behind a fence of pointed bamboo stakes in an expanse of rice paddies. This concealed and protective arrangement reflects a tradition, long since passed, of warfare among the villages. In Angkola, villages are larger, ranging from 20 households to several hundred, with occasional market centers having 1,000 or more households. There are no compound households and no Toba-type carved wooden houses. The normal Angkola *huta* contains both Muslims and Christians, although there seems to be a disproportionately large number of schoolteachers from Christian families.

Village organization is based upon the community of kinsmen and in-laws through marriage, all beholden to the dominant lineage of the *huta*. This dominant lineage is descendant from the family that first founded the village. The founder lineage owns the spot on which the village sits and owns access to the surrounding rice fields. An Angkola Batak's political relationship to his neighbors and to outside Batak groups depends on clan descent and marriage alliance. In the clan genealogies, the 100 or so named clans that make up the various Batak groups are seen as the descendants of a single founding ancestor.

At both society-wide and village levels, the basic political system of traditional society is *dalihan na tolu*, ideally, a generations-old debt relationship set up between three interdependent partners: 1) one's own immediate clansmen, 2) those men of another clan who have given their sisters and daughters to the first group as wives and 3) those men of another clan or at least another lineage who have received wives from the first group. Wife-giving groups are ritually superior, wife-receiving groups inferior. In ceremonial contexts, the wife-giving group is accorded great respect, while the wife-receiving group is put to work serving the dinner and cleaning the plates (they are, Batak say, the "daughter group" of the ones they serve).

This *dalihan na tolu* structure has left its imprint on Angkola Batak religious thought as well. Significantly, it is the superior wife-giving group that is called to intercede with a higher world of spirits on behalf of their daughter-taking groups, a primary axiom of Batak society that has been preserved in both Angkola Christianity and Islam. That is, it is just this superior group that petitions Allah on the taker groups's behalf if the latter's crops fail, if their clansman falls ill or if one of their number has no children or, almost as bad, no sons. Serious illnesses are also sometimes the occasion of combined religious and kinship efforts to better the situation. Angkola has both a scientifically trained government physician with a staff of nurses and numerous village *datu* folk healers, diagnosticians and sorcerers. The two sides coexist with fair equanimity; the physicians handle infectious diseases, most serious accidents, vaccinations, drug therapy of tuberculosis and hypertension, while the *datu* treat certain indigenous "mental illnesses" and certain chronic conditions and provide amulets for the protection of children. In unusually serious cases, the patient and his family may resort to some mixture of scientific medicine, *datu* treatment, petitions to wife-giving kinsmen and the ministrations of Islam or Christianity. The wife-givers can provide good luck, while the power of Allah or the Christian God can be mobilized to effect cures. In sorcery-caused ailments (quite common in the area), some Muslim or Christian victims will attempt to counter the powers of an evil *datu* with the "good powers" of their God.

Ritual life is another area where the religions have entered Angkola culture and worked significant change. Not surprisingly, the Angkola Batak have also domesticated Islamic ritual into line with their older religious system. For some, the traditions of Angkola have been particularly hospitable to certain aspects of Islamic thought and ceremonial practice. The Angkola emphasis on patrilineal clans and patrilineal inheritance coincides with the patrilineal stress of the Quran. In Minangkabau society, by contrast, tradition was based on matrilineal clans and on passing property from a man to his sister's son.

Ritual speech is another cultural sphere where Islam and indigenous Batak *adat* ritual have effected an intriguing synthesis. Angkola Batak society lays great emphasis on a person's rhetorical ability, on the aesthetics of speech and on the power of words themselves. Chants, riddles, magic formulas written on bamboo, proverb-filled eulogies of kinsfolk—verbal acrobatics of this sort—lie at the heart of Angkola custom. Islam's own deft use of verbal repetition and poetic plays on sound in the chanted prayers coincide with the Angkola Batak's well-developed sense of verbal beauty. The fact that Muslim prayers are in a foreign language in itself adds greatly to their power to work good or evil.

Not all Angkola Muslims agree with the harmonization of tradition and religion. The Muhammadiya movement is the main opponent of this conciliatory approach. Members, strict religious purists, see the verbal pyrotechnics of the Angkola ceremonies as blasphemous and refuse to attend them when such proverb-filled speeches will be delivered. Also blasphemous are the ritual dancing and ceremonial paraphernalia of weddings, funerals and housewarmings. Muhammadiya members will sometimes refuse to pay a large brideprice asked by the bride's non-Muhammadiya family, arguing that the cash payment will only be used to put on pagan rituals.

The controversy is a potentially explosive one in Indonesia and is a dialectic that affects other Indonesian ethnic groups trying to negotiate a blend of traditional religion and Islam.

BIBLIOGRAPHY

Books

Bruner, Edward M. "The Toba Batak Village." In *Local, Ethnic and National Loyalties in Village Indonesia: A Symposium*, edited by G. William Skinner. Southeast Asia Studies. New Haven: Yale University Press, 1959.

Castles, Lance. "Statelessness and Stateforming Tendencies Among the Colonial Batak." *Pre-Colonial State Systems in SE Asia Series.* Kuala Lumpur: Council of the Malayan Branch of the Royal Asiatic Society, 1975.

Kipp, Rita S., and Kipp, Richard, eds. *Beyond Samosir: Recent Studies of the Batak Peoples of Sumatra.* Southeast Asia Series, 62. Athens: Ohio University Center for International Studies, 1983.

LeBar, Frank M., ed. *Ethnic Groups of Insular Southeast Asia.* New Haven: Human Relations Area Files Press, 1972.

Liddle, R. William. "Ethnicity and Political Organization: Three Sumatran Cases." In *Culture and Politics in Indonesia*, edited by Clare Holt. Ithaca: Cornell University Press, 1972.

————. *Ethnicity, Party and National Integration: An Indonesian Case Study.* New Haven: Yale University Press, 1970.

Peacock, James L. *Indonesia: An Anthropological Perspective.* Pacific Palisades, Calif.: Goodyear, 1973.

Singarimbun, Masri. *Kinship, Descent and Alliance Among the Karo Batak.* Princeton: Princeton University Press, 1975.

————. "Kutagamber: A Village of Karo." In *Villages in Indonesia*, edited by R. M. Koentjaraningrat. Ithaca: Cornell University Press, 1967.

Siregar, Susan Rodgers. *Adat, Islam and Christianity in a Batak Homeland.* Southeast Asia Series, 57. Athens: Ohio University Center for International Studies, 1981.

Vergouwen, J. C. *The Social Organization and Customary Law of the Toba Batak of Northern Sumatra.* Translated by J. Jeune Scott-Kemball. The Hague: Nijhoff, 1964.

Articles

Bruner, Edward M. "Urbanization and Ethnic Identity in Northern Sumatra." *American Anthropologist* 63 (1967): 508–521.

Liddle, William. "Suku Simalungun: An Ethnic Group in Search of Representation." *Indonesia* 3 (1967): 1–30.

Siagian, Toenggoel P. "Bibliography on the Batak Peoples." *Indonesia* 2 (1966): 161–184.

Susan Rodgers Siregar

BATONUN   Early European explorers called the people who inhabit the north central-northeastern forest and savanna lands of the People's Republic of Benin, Bariba. They call themselves Batonu, Botombu or Batonun. The word "Bariba" is most frequently used by foreigners.

Legend proposes that the Batonun are descendants of Kisra, a seventh-century Persian warrior whose exploits in the Nile Valley were terminated by the Prophet Muhammad. Kisra refused to profess his faith in Islam and rode west to found a new kingdom in Busa, which is today a Batonun city in west central Nigeria. His military strength was seasoned with political expertise, and he acquired the homage, fealty—and daughters—of local land chiefs in exchange for his administrative, judicial and military talents.

Glimpses of Batonun are found in the journals of travelers, traders and would-be conquerors as early as the fifteenth century, but their ethnological origin remains elusive. Historians agree that they are a Sudanic people whose language stems from Voltaic and Manding substocks and whose culture emerged from a confluence of autochthonous as well as immigrant populations. Their political history shows the alliance of powerful landed families and clans with a group of equally powerful roving horsemen, the gradual extension of control over weaker agrarian and pastoral populations and, finally, the evolution of a social hierarchy responsive to the economic and military needs of the aristocratic group.

Today there are two Batonun polities: the Busa in the Kwara State of Nigeria claims a Batonun population estimated at 84,000 (perhaps half of whom are Muslim), and the Nikki in the Department of the Borghou, Benin, claims a population of approximately 508,000, of whom perhaps 161,000 are Muslim. Common socioreligious practices continue to manifest the cultural homogeneity of these groups; political organization has been dependent on the policies of respective national governments. Dialectical differences between eastern and western Batonun exist but do not inhibit communications; they appear to be related to older social and geographic influences rather than to political evolution.

While some Batonun earn their principal livelihood as traders, artisans or government servants, most are farmers. Batonun cultivate yams, sorghum, millet and corn, but rice, peanuts, cotton and beans are becoming important cash crops. Yams are planted in January as the harmattan gives way to the dry season, but all other crops are planted in May and June with the start of the rains. Hoeing and weeding are accomplished with locally forged hand tools, but many farmers, with the financial and technical assistance of the government, are introducing animal-drawn equipment into their operations. This latter practice has led the Batonun to transfer his bulls and yearling calves from the Fulani herd, where he traditionally maintains all of this stock, to the village, where he now manages them himself (see Fulani).

At present, a number of Batonun continue to live on isolated farms or in small villages accessible only by footpath or by unimproved roads. The extended family with its intrinsic social order and highly specialized division of labor can provide its own food, shelter, tools and clothing throughout the greater part of the year. According to age, rank, occupational heritage and aptitude, men share the duties of building houses, hoeing fields, forging tools, weaving mats, baskets and cloth, dyeing and sewing cloth, compounding medicines and hunting, fishing and trapping. Women raise children, cook, sweep, cut wood, draw water, coil and fire pottery, make soap and oil, spin cotton, pound grain, brew beer, distill alcohol, buy and sell market produce and assist men in the fields during planting and harvest operations.

Generally speaking, however, the variety and multiplicity of goods, services and opportunities in larger communities appeal to the Batonun, who often maintain a permanent household complex within the village and a smaller, semi-permanent "farm" complex a few miles away. Many villages offer the services of Batonun millers, carpenters, tailors, bicycle mechanics and agricultural extension agents. Many have mosques and youth centers; some hold regular public markets. A village designated as a "commune" has a locally elected mayor and advisory board and may have a number of national civil servants in its population, including a secretary, medic, veterinary practitioner, agricultural advisor and several primary schoolteachers. Towns or "district" centers add police, postal and forest services and have larger administrative, educational, medical and commercial facilities.

The Batonun family lives in a walled compound that typically houses several paternally related smaller families. In most cases the oldest man is the chieftain, or authoritative head of the household, and it is his duty to supervise its daily activities. Although age may eventually impair his ability to work in the fields, his importance as the primary link with the family's paternal ancestry elevates his status above that of his younger brothers who raise their individual families within the same compound and who share title to the land. Because he is the oldest living ascendant to the rights and lands of the lineage, the chieftain is the intermediary through whom the family solicits the aid of the ancestral spirits; the propriety with which he conducts ritual offerings and oversees larger funereal, marital and initiatory ceremonies will determine the health and prosperity conferred on the family during a given year.

Within the compound shared by the extended family, Batonun construct a number of buildings used and maintained by the larger family enterprise, as well as a number of buildings used as individual living quarters. Communal facilities include a traditional round entrance room, a large open court, a kitchen, a brewery, storage huts, silos, drying platforms, poultry houses and possibly a forge. Individual brothers' families maintain separate living quarters, baths and hearthstones. As family size increases, brothers may decide to enlarge the compound or to divide into new households. Construction and repair of buildings is done during the dry months of February, March and April, when materials are easily transported and agricultural activities are minimal. Round buildings have conical roofs; square or rectangular buildings have hip roofs. Roofs are of woven straw mats on bamboo and sorghum-stalk latticework or of corrugated tin on split black palm frames. Walls are of packed mud, mud-brick, woven grass or cement block. Plastered walls, improved floors and insulated mud ceilings are common. Doors and windows may be matted or made of tin and cut lumber. The increasing demand for tin and sawed lumber products has fostered the specialization of carpentry in urban and rural areas alike.

An extended period of traditional religious activity, which involves nearly all Batonun, traditionalist or Muslim, begins at harvest time (November, December) and continues until the start of the new year in April. Some ritual procedures originate at the family level and later require broader village or regional participation. Such large manifestations as funeral celebrations are sponsored by families who have enjoyed an especially productive year and who consequently invite hundreds of geographically—and by Western standards, genetically— distant relatives to join in honoring the long deceased founders of the lineage or clan. The event unites people who trace their origin to the same paternal ancestor—the land chief who succeeds in allying the natural spirits of the region, thus acquiring the original rights to the land. Cattle, sheep and goats are sacrificed, dances are performed, and gifts are exchanged.

Batonun society has a history of assimilating elements of other ethnic groups through the extension of political controls, but in the instances of the Fulani and the Hausa, the politically weaker group has remained independent and exclusive of Batonun culture. Fulani raise Batonun cattle in return for the right to graze their own stock on Batonun land. They are traditionally semi-nomadic peoples but increasingly prefer to establish permanent farm settlements outside Batonun villages, sending some of their families and herds on transhumance during the dry season. Like Fulani, Hausa people (see Hausa) limit most of their contacts with Batonun to economic spheres. They have long served the Batonun as merchants and traders, settling in larger towns and circulating to local markets. They usually live in separate quarters and respect the leadership of an *imam* but protect their commercial interests through measured concessions to Batonun politics.

The ability of these groups to preserve their separate identities within the larger complex of Batonun society is partly explained by their Islamic faith. In both legend and history, Batonun have sustained their traditional beliefs in the presence of Muslim influence, and in the early nineteenth century successfully defended their system during the Fulani *jihad*. However, economic interests had bred tolerance, and when a significant Muslim population was present in a Batonun village, the chief appointed a minister, a Batonun convert to Islam, to insure entente between the groups. The political position of the Muslim community improved as national governments weakened the authority of Batonun chiefs and, no less importantly, as the growing number of Batonun became adherents to Islam.

Batonun conversions to Islam were rare in pre-colonial times, but estimates suggest that one-quarter to one-third of their population now practices some form of the religion. Few Batonun acquire the status of *hajji*, and fewer still accept Quranic teaching so exclusively that they abandon all traditional practices. Many profess their faith, pray and fast according to Muslim doctrine but continue to offer libations to their ancestors, demonstrate forms of fealty to their own chiefs and seek the aid of traditional spiritual leaders in times of illness or need. The relatively new and self-styled interest that Batonun have shown in Islam must be interpreted within the larger context of twentieth-century urbanization and political reorganization—and in the subsequent mitigation of certain family and class institutions. But it is noteworthy that the Gani (Batonun New Year's Day) has long been celebrated on the day of the Maulud (Muhammad's birth), a tradition perhaps born of a conciliatory oath of Kisra's to bow twice yearly to Mecca.

BIBLIOGRAPHY

Books

Fage, J. D. *A History of West Africa: An Introductory Survey.* Cambridge: Cambridge University Press, 1969.
Labouret, Henri. *Africa Before the White Man.* New York: Walker, 1962.
Maquet, Jacques. *Civilizations of Black Africa.* Rev. and translated from the French by Joan Rayfield. New York: Oxford University Press, 1972.
Nelson, Harold D., et al. *Area Handbook for Nigeria.* Rev. ed. The American University FAS, DA Pam 550–157. Washington, D.C.: Government Printing Office, 1972.

Peter R. Watson
Population figures updated by Richard V. Weekes

BAWEANESE   The people of the Indonesian island of Bawean call themselves Orang Bawean. Outside their home country they sometimes refer to themselves (or are referred to) as Oran Boyan (Boyanese), the name under which they are registered in Singapore, the focus of their traditional migrations. Bawean is a small, rather out-of-the-way island in the Java Sea to the north of the town of Surabaya.

No exact population figures are available, but Baweanese may be estimated to number about 60,000. A strong migration ideal causes many Baweanese to leave. Conversely, people from Madura have migrated to Bawean. For this reason, Madurese numerically form a dominant group on Bawean (see Madurese). The Baweanese actually trace their descent from Madura, from which they migrated at the end of the fourteenth century.

Another population group is represented by a village in north Bawean, called Diponggo, whose inhabitants originated in Java. A third group is the Buginese from Sulawesi (see Bugis). Like the people from Diponggo, they have long since been fully integrated into Bawean sociey to the point of losing their original cultural identity. The fourth and most interesting subgroup is the Kemas, who originate from Palembang, Sumatra. Prior to World War II they dominated the economy of the island, but today they are economically no longer important. There are no exact population figures for these groups. The Madurese no doubt represent the largest group, estimated at about 20 percent. The others are much smaller, the Kemas only counting several hundred members.

The language spoken by the Baweanese is a rather course Madurese, much influenced by Malay as spoken in Singapore and Malaysia. The long tradition of migrations to these two countries is no doubt responsible for this phenomenon. The younger generation usually speaks the national language, Bahasa Indonesia. Roman script is now common, although the older generation prefers to write Malay/Indonesian with Arabic characters. Since part of the socialization process consists of mastering the Arabic script, the percentage of those able to write Arabic is considerable.

Geologically Bawean is an old volcanic island, the volcano being no longer active. The highest peak in central Bawean is 2,100 feet above sea level. It encloses a large lake, Telaga Kastoba. The climate is pleasant. Differences in temperature between the monsoons are small. A coral reef surrounding the island makes for rather dangerous sailing. The population inhabits the coastal areas with the exception of the village of Candi in central Bawean. A large part of the island is covered with forest. However, the influx of Madurese, who grow maize and sweet potatoes on the slopes of the mountains, has resulted in deforestation. Communication with the outside world is maintained by sailing boats (*prahu*) and a rather irregular motorboat service from Surabaya. Intra-island communication takes place on foot, horse, bicycle and motorcyle. A rather rudimentary road runs along the coast and encircles the island.

The most outstanding feature of Bawean culture concerns the complex of migration, *merantau*. It focuses on Singapore and the west coast of Malaya as popular *merantau* areas. Political developments after World War II resulted in cutting off the connection with these traditional areas, but new areas were soon found within the Indonesian archipelago with the Riau archipelago as the most popular substitute. The orientation towards *merantau* has influenced other aspects of Bawean life. According to an old migration tradition, only men *merantau*, the women remaining at Bawean. As a result, Bawean society is strongly matrifocal. Also, women outnumber men, which is why Javanese call Bawean *pulau wanita*, "island of women." Although the *merantau* pattern still holds and is indeed strong, postwar conditions have changed it so that more than ever Bawean men migrate together with their families.

Merantau, particularly to Singapore, has a firm root in Islam. The desire to make the pilgrimage to Mecca appears to have been a dominant motive for migrating. Baweanese worked in Singapore for a period of time to earn enough money to continue the journey to the Holy Land. On their way back, they returned to Singapore again to earn enough to continue home. Eventually, Singapore became the sole purpose of *merantau*, to work and settle there.

Because the Baweanese are staunch Muslims, most social institutions such as marriage and inheritance are regulated by the laws of Islam. In cases of disputes, decisions by the religious courts bind both parties. Polygyny occurs among the well-to-do, but it is not common. There is a preference for prearranged marriages with both parallel and cross cousins. Marriages are matrilocal. Today free choice marriages prevail, economic considerations being decisive for the choice of residence upon marriage. High divorce rates are due to several factors, such as the long absence of the men in one of the *merantau* areas and also the practice of marriage arrangement by the parents. Both factors appear to be less important today.

Two characteristics of the Baweanese personality affect their relationships with other people and relate to their life-style. They are staunchly independent, perhaps a reflection (or cause) of their practice of *merantau*, which requires independent action. While they do participate in some communal activity such as building a mosque or *madrasa*, cooperative action is not the norm. At the same time, they are not particularly enterprising and prefer a slower rather than faster pace of living.

Although originating in Madura, in the course of time the Baweanese developed a culture of their own, but influenced by Malay customs and values (see Malays). Baweanese feel themselves quite different from the Madurese, a feeling strengthened by economic rivalry. The Madurese attitude towards agriculture and life and leisure in general is more enterprising. The Madurese are more successful economically. They harvest better crops, live thriftily and spend their money buying new land. Another factor dividing the two is Islamic practice. The Baweanese generally are strict Muslims who take their daily ritual duties seriously, while Madurese immigrants, absorbed as they are with their agricultural pioneering, take a much looser view of religious practice.

There are mechanisms integrating the two groups, however. The Madurese migrate to Bawean either alone or in groups of men only. They marry Bawean women, of whom there is a surplus. As soon as they are settled, they tend to integrate themselves into Bawean culture.

Relations between the Baweanese and the once economically powerful Kemas are good. Since the Kemas settled on the island, they intermarried with the Baweanese. Nevertheless, the Kemas still live a rather separate life because of their former socially and economically higher status. Islam is an integrating agent as the Kemas participate in the religious life of the island.

Agriculture, fishing and mat-weaving are the most important aspects of economic life on Bawean. The income received from these activities is supplemented by money sent by the *merantau* to their families. About 60 percent of the island is used for growing rice and maize. The individualism of the islanders does not facilitate a well-arranged irrigation system, dependent as that is on cooperation. Both men and women take part in agriculture, but because of the absence of so many men, women often play a major role. Mechanization is nonexistent so the Baweanese use animals (buffalo and cattle, sometimes horses) and even manpower to plow the soil. The non-agricultural attitude of the Baweanese does not make them enthusiastic farmers, and the results are rather poor.

About 10 percent of the population is engaged in fishing or in related industries. The most important branch is *mayang* fishing, carried out most of the year. The fish, in this case, *ikan layang (decapterus kurra)* are caught with large nets from boats, some of them motorized. The fish is sometimes sold at sea to traders from

Java and Madura. The fish that is brought to the island is sold to local traders, and part of it is made into *ikan pindang* (salted fish), which is exported to Java.

The weaving of mats, once a famous product of Bawean Island, has deteriorated because it requires intensive labor, which today is not economical. It is exclusively women's work with the exception of the harvesting of the pandanus leaves, the raw materials, which is carried out by men.

The Baweanese are a truly Muslim people, no other religion being followed on the island. Nevertheless, a substratum of old influences can be observed everywhere, especially with regard to magic and related practices.

Not much is known concerning the history of the conversion of the Baweanese to Islam. It is accepted that Islam was brought to the island by Baweanese migrants themselves, who were converted to Islam in one of the *merantau* areas of Java. The population of the village of Candi was only recently converted. They were known as animists but because of political and social pressures became Muslims during the 1960s.

The Baweanese are Sunni Muslims and adhere to the Shafi school. The greater part of them are orthodox, as opposed to a small group of reformists who received their religious training at the well-known Islamic institute, Pondok Modern, in Gontor on the island of Java. Relations between the two groups are not cordial because of differences of opinion about such religious ceremonies as the *selamatan* (a communal feast symbolizing the mystic and social unity of the participants) held on the occasion of birth, circumcision, marriage and death. Other differences concern the way individuals ought to dress for Friday prayers at the mosque, the burning of incense, the use of "white" magic, the special prayers for death and the architecture of the mosque.

The power and influence of the local *kiai* (cleric) is great. In the stratification of prestige attached to professions, he occupies the highest position, surpassing the formal, wordly leaders. The influence of the *kiai* is felt everywhere, and when a Baweanese must make an important decision, he will always consult his *kiai* first.

While Baweanese observe all Muslim holy days—Id al Fitr, Kurban (Id al Adha), Isra Miradj (Lailat al Miraj)—two special festivals celebrate the birthday of the Prophet, Mawlid an-Nabi (Maulud). Maulud Masjid is organized by the *kiai*, who decides the material contributions to be made by the participating villagers. Sometimes his decisions place a heavy burden on the population. Maulud Lurah is organized by the village head and is celebrated two days before Maulud Masjid. For the village population, this commemoration provides a means to show off material wealth in the form of extravagant expenditures with the sole purpose of accentuating social status and rank. It has a typical potlatch character.

Two Sufi brotherhoods, Naqshbandiyya and Qadiriyya, are active on the island. Participants usually belong to both. They are a small minority since most Bawean *kiai* do not cooperate with the leader of both brotherhoods (who is the same person). The members of the brotherhoods are engaged in a rather "practical'' kind of mysticism, usually culminating in *dikhr* coupled with rhythmic movements of the body. Members are usually unsophisticated fishermen and peasants, and their activities often cause communication gaps and isolation from the rest of the population. Most feel they tend to neglect their "worldly duties."

Islamic values dominate the Baweanese code of behavior. They distinguish among allowed, encouraged, tolerated and forbidden behavior on the basis of the laws of the Quran.

According to the ultimate ideal, a Baweanese is to live a life as *merantau*, preferably in Singapore or Malaya, to obtain perfect knowledge of the Quran and *hadith*, make the Haj and at the end in old age to settle as a *kiai* in Bawean. Some of the younger generation might take a looser religious attitude, certainly outside the island, but will conform to the Islamic rules once he returns in fear of criticism and even ostracism by Bawean society. Extensive experience as a migrant considerably enhances one's prestige. However, boasting is abhorred. Unwillingness to participate in mutual cooperation (*gotong royong*) such as the building of mosques is criticized. Abhorred and feared are the activities of the *tokang seher*, the magician who uses magic for antisocial purposes. The society tolerates magic of minor importance, but in severe cases when the *tokang seher* is considered to be acting against the interests of society, they will not hesitate to liquidate him.

BIBLIOGRAPHY

Book

Vredenbregt, Jacob. *De Baweanners in hun moederland en Singapore een bijdrage tot de kulturele antropologie van zuidoost-Azie*. Leiden: Luctor et Emergo, 1968.

Articles

Alting, Siberg J. "Account of the Island Bawean." *Journal of the Indian Archipelago and Eastern Asia* 5 (1851): 383–393.
Jasper, J. E. "Het eiland Bawean en zijn bewoners." *Tijdschrift voor het Binnenlandsch Bestuur* (Batavia). 31 (1906): 231–280.
Lekkerkerker, C. "Sapoedi en Bawean, overbevolking en ontvolking." *Koloniaal Tijdschrift* 15 (1935): 459–476.
Vredenbregt, Jacob. "Bawean Migrations, Some Preliminary Notes." *Bijdragen van het Koninklijk Instituut voor Taal-, Land- en Volkenkunde* 120 (1964): 109–139.

Jacob Vredenbregt

BEJA   The Beja are a traditionally pastoral Muslim people whose territory covers some 110,000 square miles in the eastern part of Sudan plus around 20,000 or so additional square miles in adjacent parts of Eritrea. Beja also range into southern Egypt. Numbering more than 1.5 million, they are 6 percent of Sudan's population. Thousands of the Beja who traditionally have lived in Eritrea in the last decade have been driven into Sudan by the ravages of the wars.

The language of the Beja (To Bedawie) is Northern Cushitic. Some Beja, in southern Egypt and along the Nile in Sudan, are bilingual or monolingual in Arabic. One group usually classified with the Beja, the Beni Amer in Eritrea and the adjacent Sudan, speak the Ethio-Semitic language Tigre as well as To Bedawie (see Beni Amer; Tigre).

The Beja nation may be classified into five principal divisions of "true," or native, peoples: Bisharin, Hadendowa/Hadendiwa, Amarar, Beni Amer/Amir and Ababda. At least seven lesser divisions of those acculturated to Beja language and culture but who are former non-Beja are the Halanga, Hassanab, Artiqa, Kumailab, Shaiab, Ashraf and Hamran. Five main dialects are reported for the Beja: Hadendowa, Bisharin, Amarar, Ababda and Halanqa, of which the last two have nearly disappeared.

Bisharin live in a great arc of some 48,000 square miles, from the Red Sea coast (Mohammed Ghol northward to the Egyptian border area), westward to the Nile Valley, and then west of the Amarar and Hadendowa regions, southward along the plain of the Atbara River. The two great subdivisions of the Bisharin are the Um Ali and the Um Nagi. Four clans of the Um Nagi and all of the Um Ali live in the Atbai subregion of the Bisharin, consisting of steppe and desert which supports camel herding. The remainder of the Um Nagi are herders and cultivators living in the somewhat more verdant Atbara subregion, south of Sidon.

Hadendowa live north of Eritrea between the Atbara River and the Red Sea "hill" country. They are by far the most populous of the Beja divisions and are absorbing some of the lesser divisions. They are largely nomadic cattle herders but cultivate as well.

Amarar live in a 25,000-square-mile territory along the Red Sea coast from Port Sudan northward to Mohammed Ghol and extend westward to Bisharin territory, about halfway to the Nile. Two subdivisions exist, the Amarar proper and the Otman. Both groups are camel and sheep herders and cultivators. Today, many Amarar and Hadendowa are sedentary cultivators of cotton and other commercial crops in areas of modern irrigation projects.

Ababda are the northernmost of the Beja nation and are now largely acculturated into Egyptian Arabic society. However, ethnographic data from the nineteenth century on the Ababda generally accord with current information on the Beja of the Sudan. They live in southern Egypt and northern Sudan from the Nile to the Red Sea. Ababda were used by the Funj kings and later by the Turks to safeguard trade routes south of Aswan. The Qireijab, an Arabicized group of coastal Beja fishermen, are associated with the Ababda.

Gabail Ukhra ("other groups") is the collective term for the lesser divisions of the Beja nation. Most are found along the Red Sea coastal plain and hills from the Tokar delta area northwards to Port Sudan. Others are in the Kassala area. The Hamran, a small remnant of a once larger division, are on the north bank of the Setit River, well south of Kassala, and are the southernmost of the Beja.

In socioeconomic terms four kinds of Beja are found, the last not being traditional. One are the camel and sheep herders of the north, who also conduct some horticulture of grain. Two are the cattle, sheep and camel herders of the south, who are also either rain-horticulturalists or riverine cultivators. Those along rivers may live part of the year in permanent villages of mud-walled houses. Three are those in temporary or permanent commercial and subsistence cultivation of crops, principally cotton and grain, but who also have flocks of animals. Such cultivation is mainly in the Gash (Qash) delta and the Barka River's Tokar delta. The two are flush-irrigated inland deltas some 200 miles apart. Four are townsmen and modern urbanites in the greater Khartoum area and in various towns such as Kassala and Port Sudan.

Bejaland is largely of dry tropical continental climate, but having the influence of Mediterranean climate in the north. Climate is dominated much of the year by hot, dry air from the Sahara/Arabian desert system, into which northern Bejaland grades. Rainfall ranges from unknown in the extreme northeast to as much as 10 to 15 inches in the southern riverine extensions of the Beja. Vegetation varies from sparse shrubs, light seasonal grass, dotted thorn brush, and occasional acacias to increasing amounts of these, with heavier grass after rains, especially along the wadis. Some steppe is being transformed into true desert owing to overgrazing and intensive shifting horticulture.

The Beja have been in Bejaland at least since sometime between 4000 and 2500 B.C. They are an indigenous African people who were noticed by the Egyptians of the Sixth Dynasty. Bejaland was of interest to outsiders as a source of gold and as a transit area for caravans along the Nile and from the Nile to the Red Sea. Thus, contact was made with the Beja by Hellenistic Egyptians and Greeks, Romans, Meroetic peoples of Sudan, Axumites of Ethiopia and expanding Muslim Arabs. Bejaland was part of a weak Ottoman Turkish sphere of influence exerted from coastal ports in the sixteenth through the early nineteenth centuries. In the sixteenth century, the Bisharin, Hadendowa, Amarar and Ababda were in a process of emergence and consolidation as major Beja divisions. In 1821, Egypt's Mohammed Ali began his conquest of what is now Sudan. He also destroyed the Funj kingdom and ended its slight control of the Beja (see Funj). At various times in the past, some of the more accessible Beja clans were under allegiance to the Turks and then to the Egyptians and paid tribute to them occasionally.

Muhammad Ahmad el Mahdi began his mission of nativist revitalization in Sudan in 1881. By 1883 he had won significant battles against Egyptian forces. Some Beja clans, especially Hadendowa, took part in the revolt against Egyptian domination. Osman Digna, a Beja *emir* of the Mahdi, led largely Hadendowa forces with modest success against British and Egyptian regulars having British officers. A near defeat of 4,000 well-trained British troops took place outside of Suakin on the coast. There, courageous Beja men and boys armed with spears and sticks took heavy casualties and broke infantry square (military combat formation). This action may have been the only time native forces broke a British army square equipped with modern ordnance. The event gave rise to Rudyard Kipling's famous and laudatory "Fuzzy Wuzzy" verses, which included:

> 'E's the on'y thing that doesn't give a damn
> For a Regiment o' British Infantree!

The Beja have a characteristically fashioned huge crown of fuzzy hair (*tiffa*), first recorded in Egyptian rock paintings ca. 2000 B.C. Long greased ringlets hang down from the head, which has a fluffed crown of looser hair on top.

Only rarely was a Beja division or major subdivision unified under the leadership of one *nazir* or *shaikh*. Unity was achieved at times because of an outside, non-Beja, threat. In recent years in much of Bejaland, a government administrative unity has been achieved under a Pax Sudanica. Divisions and major subdivisions consist of a number of patrilineally organized clans, each named after an eponymous ancestor. Clans in turn consist of segmentary patrilineages (*bedana*) and sublineages (*hissa*). A *bedana* or more than one such unit has a *shaikh* whose authority is modest, resting upon consent of those led and growing to its greatest in time of war. The *shaikh* does not settle all disputes in his unit(s); any outsider of some prestige would do. Disputes are often settled by discussions under pre-Islamic Beja law.

Each *bedana* has its own grazing territory and water sites, used by others with permission. However, the arid ecology and limited carrying capacity of much of Bejaland means that for all or most of the year *bedana* ordinarily fission into groups of 1 to 12 houses (families) in search of sustenance for the herds. Such migratory groups might wander far across territories of other *bedana* and even settle for a season or two of commercial crop cultivation in the Gash or Tokar areas. Because of the customary dispersal of a *bedana* in the steppes of Bejaland, much day-to-day authority is wielded by the patriarch of a family.

No patron-client (master-serf) relationships exist for the Egyptian and Sudanese Beja as they do for the Beni Amer. Instead, the non-Beni Amer divisions are generally egalitarian in social relations. Despite the marked patrilineality of the Beja, medieval Arabic writings and contemporary ethnographic traits demonstrate a matrilineality and matrilocality. Some Hadendowa display a matri-patrilocality for a newly married couple in which the groom lives with his wife's family in order to render bride service. Traces of an avunculate are found throughout Bejaland. An avunculate is a social relationship of superior authority of a maternal uncle towards his nephew (sister's son).

Habitation for pastoral Beja consists of a rectangular, portable dwelling, erected and dismantled by women. A framework of poles is roofed by a fine-weave matting on the interior and a heavier coarse-weave one for the exterior. Woven walls of black or gray goat hair complete the dwelling, which is open on one side. A house is occupied by one nuclear family. Interior furnishings include a bed made of split date palm fronds and other materials, camel hide containers for milk and water, coffee and other cookware and baskets of a superfine weave allowing the holding of liquids. Sedentary Beja live in mud-walled houses having heavier and more numerous interior furnishings. Traditional animal skin clothing has now been almost entirely replaced with commercial clothing.

The diet of nomads is high in animal protein and low in carbohydrates. North and central region nomads live on dairy products, especially camel's milk, some slaughtered stock, and a little grain. Southern Beja consume more cultivated food. Camels, sheep, goats and, in the south, cattle are milked by men. Some ritual is associated with this male task. Praise of livestock is sung, often accompanied by a lute (*basonkw*). Beja have an expert technical knowledge of the needs and care of animals plus a great amount of associated lore. Beja are highly skilled at camelmanship.

Virtually all Beja practice some horticulture, with sorghum the principle crop. For northern and central Beja, this means broadcasting of seed in wadi beds during the rains, but not tending the growing crop. Harvest is often diminished because of grazing on the crop by the stock of passing families. Many hold an animal sacrifice and feast (*karama*) before sowing of seeds. Northern Beja must purchase at least a part of the grain they consume.

As with other Cushitic-speaking peoples, Beja are not supposed to eat fish. However, a significant exception is found among some Red Sea Beja, who are few in number and specialize in fishing.

Rites of passage having pre-Islamic Beja and also Muslim elements are at birth, circumcision (of males), betrothal, marriage, death and remembrance or second funeral. The rites are especially followed by pastoral or recently pastoral Beja. After the birth of a child, a fire or lamp is kept burning for 40 days. This keeps malevolent spirits (*jinn*) away from the mother. As with other Cushitic-speaking peoples, the mother is thought to be ritually polluted with the blood of childbirth. Beja mothers are believed to be particularly vulnerable to local spirits at this time. The afterbirth of the newborn infant is magically secured from harm. For most, the birth of a boy is greeted with the trill of exaltation, "l-l-l-l-l-l," or by chanting. A newborn girl is greeted with silence.

The father is not permitted to see the infant for a month and not allowed contact with his wife for 40 days. In a rite in which a sheep is slaughtered, the child is named and admitted to the Muslim religion. Clitoridectomy of a minor or major removal of tissue and infibulation are practiced upon females, the former operation taking place in infancy. Males may be circumcised just after birth or later in boyhood, when they are segregated in a special house with the performer of the operation. Around the age of 14 to 15 a boy is given a steel sword and circular leather shield, the emblems of manhood. Stout sticks are also weapons wielded with skill, as against British forces in the last century. Younger boys are armed with knives.

Following Muslim Arab custom, preferential marriage is between a young man and his father's brother's daughter. Polygyny is rare but is practiced by wealthier men. After the marriage contract is made between the concerned families, substantial bridewealth (*sadag*) passes from the groom's family to the bride's father, mother and oldest maternal uncle, in the form of livestock, clothing and other goods, especially weapons. A house is constructed for the bridal pair by kinswomen and female neighbors. When matri-patrilocal residence is followed, instead of straight patrilocal residence, the construction is done near the residence of the bride's father. The couple resides there for a period of one to three years while the groom renders herding bride service to his father-in-law.

The newly married couple desires male children and female camels during their life together. Hospitality to all, including strangers, is important, but does not necessarily extend to friendliness to aliens. A very strict mother-in-law avoidance is maintained by a married man. A heinous insult is to accuse a man of sexual familiarity with his wife's mother. A good man must be courageous when it comes time to fight, but also patient during legal negotiations and deliberations.

At death, the deceased is washed, wrapped in a shroud and buried in a grave, usually marked with stones in a Muslim rite. Three post-funeral remembrances of the deceased are held: 7 to 9 days later, 40 days later, and one year later. More important people have a great feast at the 40–day remembrance. Women may own some livestock but, contrary to Islamic law, they do not inherit livestock, other important portable property or rights to use land. Such practice secures wealth in the hands of the males of a family.

Shariah law is present and interpreted by uneducated *qadis*. Muslim religious orders are of some importance for settled Beja but of little importance to nomads. *Salif*, customary Beja law, is still more important than either Shariah or modern Sudan code law. *Salif* emphasizes the mandate of hospitality and provides for rates and modes of compensation for all manner of physical injury, ranging from a blow through death at the hands of another. Protracted *salif* proceedings by elders invariably maintain peace between individuals. Women do not take part in the *salif* proceedings.

Islam in its religious aspect is not deep-rooted or well understood by Beja. Their strong support for Mahdism was largely politically rather than religiously motivated and a reaction against the Turks and Egyptians. Rural pastoralists do not drink alcohol. Prayers are perfunctory, and pilgrimage is not practiced even though pilgrims pass through Bejaland. Witchcraft in the form of evil eye and evil thought is believed. Malevolent *jinn* and other invisible spirits abound and can take animal form. Spirits cause illness, madness and accidents in humans. They can be warded off with fire, yet they frequent hearths and rubbish heaps (sites of spontaneous combustion showing the presence of spirits). Other spirits have abodes in bodies of water. Black, contagious magic is practiced, for example, to improve the efficiency of a sword upon one's foe. Sacred pagan rites for ceremonies with animal sacrifice are used. Ceremonial drum beating (*nahas*) is an important socially unifying element. *Nahas* takes place upon the death of a member of a leader's family, as a summons to war (now rare) and as a call to a festive occasion.

Today, the Beja are partially dependent upon cash, with which they buy clothing and many necessary and desired artifacts. Their view of the good life is one of numerous livestock and green, well-watered pastures. Money is a means to the animals of the pastoral or cultivator-herder ways. Accordingly, it is with reluctance that Beja settle to earn wages in the older Tokar and Gash irrigation schemes or in newer ones such as in Butana on the Atbara. Non-agricultural jobs in the modern Sudan economy attract them even less. Fewer than 5 percent of the Beja are town dwellers, even when one considers the employment of Beja stevedores and railway laborers in Port Sudan.

Government plans for settling pastoralists, recent droughts killing domesticated animals and the need for cash to pay taxes are reducing pastoralism among the Beja. Increased settlement of Beja will lead to their greater participation in the Sudan political process and their increased demand for the regional autonomy of Bejaland. Such participation and demand was begun in 1965, when the Beja Congress won ten seats in the Sudan parliament and began to work for Beja autonomy. The concomitant of the ending of traditional socioeconomic isolation of the Beja is the beginning of their political involvement in a multinational state created by Britain and Egypt.

BIBLIOGRAPHY

Books

Beshir, Mohamed O. *Revolution and Nationalism in the Sudan*. New York: Barnes & Noble, 1974.
Kipling, Rudyard. "Fuzzy-Wuzzy. Soudan Expeditionary Force. Early Campaigns." In *Rudyard Kipling's Verse: Definitive Edition*. Garden City, N.Y.: Doubleday, 1940.
Murdock, George P. *Africa: Its Peoples and Their Culture History*. New York: McGraw-Hill, 1959.
Paul, Andrew. *A History of the Beja Tribes of the Sudan*. Cambridge: The University Press, 1954.
Sorbo, Gunnar M. "Nomads of the Scheme—A Study of Irrigation Agriculture and Pastoralism in Eastern Sudan." In *Land Use and Management*, edited by P. O'Keefe and B. Wisner. London: International African Institute, 1977.
Trimingham, John Spencer. *Islam in Sudan*. London: Oxford University Press, 1949.

Articles

el-Arifi, S. A. "Pastoral Nomadism in the Sudan." *East African Geographical Review* 13 (1975): 89–103.
Hair, P.E.H. "A Laymen's Guide to the Languages of the Sudan Republic." *Sudan Notes and Records* 47 (1966): 65–78.

Henin, Roushdi A. "Economic Development and Internal Migrations in the Sudan."
    Sudan Notes and Records 44 (1963): 100–119.
Lewis, B. A. "Deim El Arab and the Beja Stevedores of Port Sudan." *Sudan Notes and
    Records* 43 (1962): 16–49.
McLoughlin, Peter F. M. "The Gash-Tokar Economic Region: Some Aspects of Its
    Labour Force and Income." *Sudan Notes and Records* 46 (1965): 67–83.
Milne, J.C.M. "The Impact of Labour Migration on the Amarar in Port Sudan." *Sudan
    Notes and Records* 55 (1974): 70–87.
Reed, William. "A Study of Marine Fisheries in the Sudan." *Sudan Notes and Records*
    43 (1962): 1–15.
Rodin, David. "The Twentieth Century Decline of Suakin." *Sudan Notes and Records*
    51 (1970): 1–22.

Frederick C. Gamst

BENGALIS   Among the Bengali peoples of the South Asian subcontinent is
to be found the world's second largest Muslim ethnic group, after the Arabs.
The Bengalis number nearly 152 million altogether, and about 61 percent, or
93 million of them, are Muslims. They share with Bengali Hindus, Buddhists
and Christians the acceptance of the diverse complex of symbols and social
interaction patterns which, in their entirety, comprise a distinct culture, most
saliently marked by common usage of the Bengali (*bangla*) language and inheritance of its various literatures and traditions.

   The historic homeland of the Bengalis is the Bengal region of pre-modern
India, which all Bengali refer to as *bangla deş*, the "territorial homeland of the
Bengali peoples." The heart of the Bengal region is its 80,000 square miles of
delta, the product of millennial effluvia of the great Ganges-Brahmaputra-Meghna
river system which still today traverses it, and mention of which as a distinct
region is found in Vedic literature. By the first millennium B.C. a complex
civilization had begun to develop in the region.

   Politically, the Bengal region today covers more than 110,000 square miles,
incorporating the Indian state of West Bengal and the nation of Bangladesh.
This politico-geographic division corresponds largely to the population majority
areas of the two largest religious communities which crosscut Bengali ethnolinguistic identity: Hindu and Muslim. By the terms of the 1947 Partition carving
Pakistan out of the British Indian empire, the Muslim-majority districts of East
Bengal became the eastern half of that "two-winged" Islamic nation. In an
especially bloody revolution supported by India, it became independent Bangladesh in 1971.

   The population of Bangladesh is presently estimated at 96.5 million, about
83 percent of whom are Muslim. The remainder are Hindu and a few non-
Bengali Buddhists. About 21 percent or 12 million of the population of India's
West Bengal Province (pop. 58 million) are Muslim Bengalis. Over a period of
more than 50 years, but particularly in the past two decades, several million
have migrated to Assam Province in India. The earliest migrants assimilated into

the Assamese population; later migrants settled in the area of Nowgong in the Brahmaputra Valley, where they occupied poor farmland and made it productive, largely in rice. These Bengali Muslims did not integrate with surrounding peoples and today live in a state of antagonism with non-Muslims, who resent their large numbers, especially when elections are called (see Assamese). Other Bengali Muslims live in the Indian states of Bihar, Orissa and Tripura, where their presence sometimes leads to violence with non-Muslim populations. Still other Bengalis live in Burma's Arakan Province, especially Akyab District (see Burmese).

Bengali is a Sanskrit-related, Indo-Aryan language which emerged in its modern form by at least A.D. 1000. Its literary tradition, recorded in a variant of the Sanskrit script, dates from around the fourteenth century.

The vast majority of Bengalis, Hindu and Muslim alike, are classic peasant wet rice cultivators of the Bengal Delta. Theirs is an economy adapted to both the blessings and the vicissitudes of monsoon agriculture, grounded on an endlessly fertile terrain but forever buffeted by a fickle climate, bearing storms one year, drought the next. The region has traditionally had three rice crop seasons, one of them, the monsoonless winter, relatively unproductive until the recent advent of mechanized irrigation. Rice, in myriad varieties, is the staple food, served at every meal, supplemented by vegetables, spices and fish when available. Muslims also eat fowl, goat and beef when they can afford it. Bengali cultivators grow jute throughout much of the region, in addition to other cash crops, such as sugar cane, betel nut and betel leaf. The peasant economy is also served by a variety of artisan craftsmen, most of whom, even in Muslim-majority areas, are members of the relevant Hindu caste groups.

Across the massively populated delta, with its typical human densities of more than 1,500 per square mile, the primary physical expression of community is the settled village, usually composed of two or more neighborhoods or hamlets, called *para*. From Moghul times onward, the countryside has been divided for revenue and, since British days, census purposes into officially designated village units, called *mauja*. But the groupings which peasants themselves socially recognize as villages may or may not reflect these administrative boundaries and are the product of the proximity of peasant homesteads and the intimate social relations such closeness facilitates among the locally resident kin groups.

Among Bengalis, there is a form of social organization denoted by the word *samaj*, which implies a cultural concept of community. Etymologically, *samaj* is rooted in the notion of "going together," although in its modern usage it is rightly translated as "society" in general or, in more limited context, "association." For Bengali Muslims *samaj* is both a symbolic and an organizational referent for the political and religious community. Its leadership consists of a sort of council of elders, a group of men from differing homesteads, perhaps even different villages, under whom a subgroup of other homesteads is at least nominally united in loyalty and under whose sponsorship various religious activities take place.

Bengalis reckon kinship in complex ways, ingeniously expanding and contracting the number and types of their relatives with reference to an intricate symbolic system. Although Bengali kinship may be considered patrilineal, the entire body of one's kinsmen, designated as *atmiyasvajan*, or "one's own people," includes the widest possible range of persons to whom one is related by blood or marriage and also those with whom one has established a solidary social relationship in some extrafamiliar context. For both Hindu and Muslim individuals a particular line of succession is also sorted out. This patrilineage is referred to as one's *bamsa*, a word whose original literal meaning and continued metaphoric allusion suggests the continuous linkage of nodes in a bamboo tree. The specific lineage segment of the larger agnatic group with which one resides in a single peasant homestead is referred to as one's *gosthi*, a localized patrilineage. Finally, that subset of kinsmen taking a living male as the source of dependence, whether one actually resides with him or not, is called a *paribar*. Within the homestead, each such *paribar*, headed by a married man, lives in its separate household, which may be composed of a nuclear, joint or extended family. Commonly called *cula* (hearth) or *khana* (eating group), these households at once contain and separate out from the larger residential agnatic group each subgroup whose members collectively depend for livelihood on some form of income-producing activities and/or property. One's family membership and place of residence are thus both starting point and metaphor for all one's activities in the world, as the Bengali expression for "family life" (*sangsar*), meaning first "the home" and second "the world," suggests.

Bengali Muslims place importance on patrilocal post-marital residence. Although they are guided by Shariah with respect to inheritance, their actual practice appears to result in circumvention of the law in regard to bequeathal of immovable property to women. It is infrequent to find Muslim women inheriting cultivable land.

A number of expectable Muslim family and marriage practices are present. Men are allowed polygynous marriages, but studies show no more than 5 or 6 percent actually have more than one wife at a time. The Muslim Family Laws Ordinance, promulgated in Pakistan in 1961 and still in force in Bangladesh, requires, among other things, that a married man seeking to take an additional wife must, before doing so, justify his decision in terms consistent with Hanafi law to a locally constituted arbitration council and receive its permission. *Purdah*, the seclusion of women, is strongly enforced, particularly in rural areas.

In contrast to Hindus, Muslims allow cousin marriage on both parental sides. They do not, however, evince the preference for mates within the descent group. Cousin marriage occurs in seemingly random fashion in either parental line, match choices being governed by other criteria. Bengalis seem, in fact, to prefer with each new marital alliance to develop ties with hitherto unrelated kin groups. One detailed study of cousin marriage reports its incidence at only 11 percent of over 460 marriages recorded over five generations. The divorce rate in Bangladesh appears to be about 15 percent.

While among the Muslim minority in Hindu-dominated West Bengal there is a higher degree of caste-like organizations, in Muslim-majority Bangladesh a comparative egalitarianism exists among the broad mass of cultivating peasantry. Significant differences in wealth do exist in the countryside, but more often than not these are correlated with distinctions of social rank and prestige. Such distinctions are, moreover, often marked by the distribution of eponymic, sometimes patronymic, titles, variously associated with high religious status or historical roles. Many are Islamic in reference. That accorded highest respect, Sayyid, proclaims putative descent from the Prophet; Shaikh from his tribe; and Mullah and Khandakar, classes of clerics. Title-bearing or not, Muslim cultivating families impose relatively few status barriers to intermarriage among themselves, the mate-choice criteria of respectability (economic wherewithal, education and reputation for righteous conduct) applied in each match being considered.

Ranked below the ''respectable'' cultivators, however, there exist occupationally marked, endogamous status groups. These, depending on the region, may include circumcisors (*hajjam*), butchers (*khasai*), oil pressers (*khulu*) and weavers (*jola*), among others. Of particular interest is a class of itinerant traders of different sorts, collectively known as *bediya* or *bede*, including a broad range of petty commercial specialists, from bangle sellers to snake catchers who sell venom to traditional healers. ''Respectable'' cultivators avoid marriage into these groups.

Islam came to Bengal at the end of the thirteenth century with Turkish expansion across eastern India. Subsequent Muslim conquest and gradual political hegemony over the region, culminating in Moghul rule after 1576, set the stage for massive conversion. Chief agents of Islamization were Sufi missionaries. Numerous Sufi *shaikhs* are known to have spread the seeds of Islam on an unusually fertile soil in rural East Bengal, which, being the last outpost of a syncretic popular Buddhism in India at that late date, was ripe for a religiously mystical and social egalitarian appeal. To this day several Sufi orders flourish in Muslim Bengal, notably the Chistiyya and the Qadiriyya. Bengalis practice saint worship despite nineteenth-century revivalist efforts to purge it, as witnessed by the widespread participation in *urus*, or commemorative gatherings at saints' tombs.

Muslim ''fundamentalist'' revivalism—most notably in the form of the Fara'idi Movement, unique to Bengal—was an important nineteenth-century force in promoting the widespread Sunni orthodoxy present among the Muslims today, as well as in fomenting their sense of ethnic and communal identity. Revivalism undoubtedly played a role in Bengali Muslim separatism, leading to their mass participation in the Pakistan movement (and, in an ironic post-Partition reversal, the ethnic Bengali quotient of their collective identity came to the fore, leading in turn to the creation of Bangladesh).

For all its syncretism, Bengali Islam displays many of the religion's classic features. Bengali Muslims are largely Sunni and for the most part observe the Hanafi school of law. Shafi, Hanbali and one other school peculiar to northern

Bangladesh known as Ahle Hadith may be found, but they are decidedly in the minority. The Five Pillars of the Faith are deeply embedded in Bengali soil. Daily individual and weekly congregational prayer are practiced; the Ramadan fast is undertaken dutifully by most and virtually forced upon the reluctant; pilgrimage to Mecca is a widely hoped for accomplishment, conferring prestige on those who manage it. Similarly, the traditional Muslim festivals are celebrated, the two Ids particularly. Although they are Sunnis, Bengali Muslims nonetheless have a long tradition of celebrating Muharram, mourning the martydom of Hasan and Hussain, Shia martyrs, by erecting symbolic representation of their tombs and engaging in mock enactments of the Battle of Karbala. Finally, side by side with orthodoxy, belief in *jinn* and their magical efficacy or harmful potency is common to Muslim peasant conceptions of suprahuman forces in the world.

Modern urbanization has been developing steadily in Bengal over the past century and a half, but its sociocultural impact has been relatively little studied. Much of the region still consists of peasant villages and provincial towns, which scarcely qualify as more complex localities in terms of social relations. Moreover, the Bengali metropolitan industrial and professional middle classes, whether in Calcutta or Dakha, the capital of Bangladesh, are of recent origin, and their members for the most part are no more than one generation at best removed from the hinterlands. The extent of secularization, Westernization or cultural modernization is difficult to ascertain. Rural-urban differences are present in many respects, and the essentially rural expression of Bengali Muslim culture finds many departures among urbanites, both in degree and kind. The basic structure of social relations or its symbolic underpinnings, however, do not follow any wide divergence between country and city life. Moreover, in Bangladesh especially, Islam remains a bedrock of primordial sentiment and national identity, while in West Bengal the Muslim minority strives to maintain allegiance to "the Faith," working out the necessary compromises that continued existence as a minority may require.

BIBLIOGRAPHY

Books

Aziz, K. M. Ashraful. *Kinship in Bangladesh*. Dacca: International Centre for Diarrhoeal Disease Research, 1979.

Basu, Tara Krishna. *The Bengal Peasant from Time to Time*. London: Asia Publishing House, 1962.

Beech, Mary Jane, et al. "Introducing the East Bengali Village." In *Inside the East Pakistan Village: Six Articles*. Reprint Series, 2. East Lansing: Michigan State University Asian Studies Center, 1965.

Bertocci, Peter J. "Bangladesh: Composite Cultural Identity in a Muslim-Majority Nation State." In *Change in the Muslim World*, edited by Philip H. Stoddard, David C. Cuthell, and Margaret W. Sullivan. Syracuse: Syracuse University Press, 1981.

———. *Bangladesh History, Society and Culture: An Introductory Bibliography of Secondary Source Materials.* South Asia Series, 22. East Lansing: Michigan State University Asian Studies Center, 1973.

———. "Models of Solidarity, Structures of Power: The Politics of Community in Rural Bangladesh." In *Political Anthropology Yearbook I: Ideology and Interest: The Dialectics of Politics,* edited by Myron J. Aronoff. New Brunswick, N.J.: Transaction Press, 1980.

———. "Patterns of Social Organization in Rural East Bengal." In *Bengal East and West,* edited by Alexander Lipski. South Asian Series, 13. East Lansing: Michigan State University Asian Studies Center, 1970.

———. "Rural Communities in Bangladesh: Hajipur and Tinpara." In *South Asia: Seven Community Profiles,* edited by Clarence Maloney. New York: Holt, Rinehart and Winston, 1974.

———. "Toward a Social Anthropology of Bangladesh: A Bibliographic Essay." In *Pakistan-Bangladesh: Bibliographic Essays in the Social Sciences,* edited by Eric Gustafson. New York: Columbia University Southern Asia Institute, 1976.

Bhattacharya, Ranjit K. "The Concept and Ideology of Caste Among the Muslims of Rural West Bengal." In *Caste and Social Stratification Among the Muslims,* edited by Imtiaz Ahmad. Delhi: Manohar Book Service, 1973.

Ellickson, Jean. "Symbols in Muslim Bengali Family Rituals." In *Prelude to Crisis: Bengal and Bengal Studies in 1970,* edited by Peter J. Bertocci. South Asia Series, 18. East Lansing: Michigan State University Asian Studies Center, 1972.

Fruzzetti-Ostor, Lina. "The Idea of Community Among West Bengal Muslims." In *Prelude to Crisis: Bengal and Bengal Studies in 1970,* edited by Peter J. Bertocci. South Asia Series, 18. East Lansing: Michigan State University Asian Studies Center, 1972.

Inden, Ronald B. *Marriage and Rank in Bengali Culture.* Berkeley: University of California Press, 1976.

———, and Nicholas, Ralph W. *Kinship in Bengali Culture.* Chicago: University of Chicago Press, 1976.

Islam, A.K.M. Aminul. *A Bangladesh Village: Conflict and Cohesion.* Cambridge, Mass.: Schenkman, 1974.

Jahangir, B. K. *Differentiation, Polarisation, and Confrontation in Rural Bangladesh.* Dacca: Centre for Social Studies, 1979.

Karim, A. K. Nazmul. "Changing Patterns of an East Pakistani Family." In *Women in New Asia,* edited by Barbara Ward. New York: UNESCO, 1963.

Maloney, Clarence; Aziz, Ashraful; and Sarkar, P. C., eds. *Beliefs and Fertility in Bangladesh.* Dacca: International Centre for Diarrhoeal Disease Research, 1981.

Owen, John E., ed. *Sociology in East Pakistan.* Dacca: Asiatic Society of Bangladesh, 1962.

Roy, Manisha. *Bengali Women.* Chicago: University of Chicago Press, 1975.

Sobhan, Salma. *The Legal Status of Women in Bangladesh.* Dacca: Institute for Law and International Affairs, 1978.

Thorp, John P. *Power Among the Farmers of Daripalla: A Bangladesh Village Study.* Dacca: Caritas Bangladesh, 1978.

Van Schendel, Willem. *Peasant Mobility: The Odds of Life in Rural Bangladesh.* Assen, Netherlands: Van Gorcam, 1981.

Zaidi, S. M. Hafeez. *The Village Culture in Transition: A Study of East Pakistan Rural Society.* Honolulu: East-West Press, 1971.

Articles

Bertocci, Peter J. "Community Structure and Social Rank in Two Villages in Bangladesh." *Contributions to Indian Sociology* n.s. 6 (1972): 28–52.

———. "Marriage Alliance and Dyadic Solidarity in Rural Bangladesh." *Asian Thought and Society* 6 (1981): 104–121.

———. "Microregion, Market Area and Muslim Community in Rural Bangladesh." *Bangladesh Development Studies* 6 (1975): 348–356.

Corwin, Lauren A. "Caste and Class in a Rural Town." *Man in India* 55 (1975): 159–169.

Ellickson, Jean. "Islamic Institutions: Perception and Practice in a Village in Bangladesh." *Contributions to Indian Sociology* n.s. 6 (1972): 53–65.

Khan, Fazlur Rashid. "District Town Elites in Bangladesh." *Asian Survey* 19 (1979): 469–484.

Lindenbaum, Shirley. "Implications for Women of Changing Marriage Transactions in Bangladesh." *Studies in Family Planning* 12 (1981): 394–401.

O'Connell, Joseph T. "Dilemmas of Secularism in Bangladesh." *Journal of Asian and African Studies* 11 (1976): 64–81.

Zaman, M. Q. "Conflict Resolution in a Bangladesh Village: Some Cases and Two Models." *Eastern Anthropologist* 34 (1981): 173–197.

Unpublished Manuscripts

Bertocci, Peter J. "Elusive Villages: Social Structure and Community Organization in Rural East Pakistan." Ph.D. dissertation, Michigan State University, 1970.

Corwin, Lauren A. "Urban Life in a Rural Town: The Role of Provincial Elites in Bengali Society." Ph.D. dissertation, Michigan State University, 1974.

Ellickson, Jean. "A Believer Among Believers: The Religious Beliefs, Practices and Meanings in a Village in Bangladesh." Ph.D. dissertation, Michigan State University, 1972.

Khan, Fazlur Rashid. "A Sociological Study of the Elite in a Town of Bangladesh." Ph.D. dissertation, University of Edinburgh, 1977.

Thorp, John P. "Masters of Earth: Conceptions of Power Among Muslims of Rural Bengal." Ph.D. dissertation, University of Chicago, 1978.

Peter J. Bertocci

BENI AMER   The pastoral Beni Amer of eastern Sudan and northwestern Ethiopia are one of the five groups recognized as Beja, the others being the Hadendowa, Bisharin, Ammarar and Ababda (see Beja). Unlike the others, however, the Beni Amer are not so much a tribe in the ethnic sense as a confederation of various groups that have formed a single political unit. They number perhaps 266,000.

Traditional social organization among the Beni Amer features an unusual (for the Beja) characteristic, that of a marked social stratification resembling a caste structure. This structure is a carefully detailed system of mutual rights, privileges and duties under which a majority of the population endures a status comparable to serfdom. According to the Beni Amer themselves, only a small minority— roughly one-eighth to one-tenth of the population—are actually Beni Amer, and are known as Nabtab. The remaining majority are people who ''belong'' to them, and are called Tigre, or Hedareb (see Tigre). Although this system was officially abolished by the British colonial government in Sudan in 1948, and during a comparable period was being discouraged in Eritrea by the Ethiopian government, some of the stronger social characteristics, such as the ban on intermarriage, have been slow to disappear.

The office of chief or Diglel of the Beni Amer, and with it the political formation of the tribe, emerged in the sixteenth century under the Funj confederation of Sennar, when a Beja dynasty became a dominant power in the eastern Sudan around 1725 (see Funj). It received quasi-recognition as one of the provincial lordships of Sennar and encouraged local representation of the Beni Amer as a group for purposes of taxation or tribute. The office of the Diglel (in Sudan called the Nazir) survived into the Turkish and Egyptian regimes of the Sudan and western Ethiopia but was broken by the Mahdists. It was during the Mahdist period, when the Beni Amer were without a leader and scattered, that they seemed on the point of political disintegration. In 1980, following the death of their Diglel in Eritrea, his successor took office under the new Italian administration. Seven years later the Beni Amer in Sudan were given a Diglel of their own under the Anglo-Egyptian Condominium. They were divided for administrative purposes, with about two-thirds of the population being in Eritrea and the remaining third in Sudan. The two Diglels, however, were sons of the last Diglel to govern the united tribe, and the present two are their sons (first cousins). Today, under these two heads, the Beni Amer are organized into more than 40 sections. These sections vary widely in size, and whereas some are centuries-old, based on lineage, others are of recent political invention. There are no rigid and uniform criteria from which they have been derived.

The common traits which the Beni Amer share are several: religion (Sunni Islam), language, common social customs and, to an extent, common descent. But with the exception of religion none of these traits coincides uniformly over the tribe, but rather they overlap the various sections somewhat irregularly. The bond of common descent is the strongest one which they share, but even this is limited to the upper group, the Nabtab. The remaining peoples derive from a number of backgrounds, including various known tribes which have become Beni Amer subjects, either through conquest or voluntary submission.

Beni Amer society in the past clearly operated on two levels, each with its own mechanism. For the Nabtab political unity has reflected common descent. But the Nabtab-Tigre relationship has been one of rulers and ruled. The old feudal-like system did not so much prevent the Tigre from accumulating material wealth through land and livestock as it assured the material ascendancy of the Nabtab, however marginal. This system of economic and social interdependence was closely tied with the Tigre need for political and physical protection by the Nabtab. With the pacification that has taken place in this century, this need has disappeared and slowly so have the incentives for the social observance of the old system.

Although exposed to Islam since the Funj period, the Beni Amer have been Muslim only since the last century. The renaissance of Sufism that took place in nineteenth-century Arabia under Sayyid Ahmed Idris led one of his disciples, Sayyid Muhammad Uthman al-Mirghani, to proselytize successfully in the Sudan. It was under Muhammad Uthman's son, al-Hassan, that the Mirghaniyya (better known as the Khatmiyya) became, and remains today, the dominant Muslim Sufi order in eastern Sudan and Eritrea. The Beni Amer as a group give complete religious allegiance to the Khatmiyya. This allegiance has been further cemented by marriages between the family of the Diglel and leading families of the Khatmiyya.

Beni Amer traditions of marriage, kinship and inheritance are similar to those of the other Beja groups, enjoying some diversity only in detail. The Beni Amer, themselves representing a number of ethnic groups, have no one uniform practice exclusive to themselves. But for all of the Beja and the Beni Amer, aspects of social and ritual life are increasingly reflecting orthodox Muslim practice.

The Beni Amer, on the whole, are bilingual. Some sections speak To Bedawie, a Cushitic language, and some Tigre, an Ethio-Semitic language. The more northern Beni Amer, around the Tokar area in Sudan, speak To Bedawie, whereas the more southern ones, in the vicinity of Kassala and in Eritrea, are Tigre speakers. This situation partially reflects the original formation of the Beni Amer, where the dominant To Bedawie speakers in the north conquered the numerically larger Tigre-speaking peoples, although some of these people, ethnically from the Beja Hadendowa, also speak To Bedawie. While Arabic is considered the lingua franca of the area and for religious reasons is highly prestigious, many of the elderly and a majoriy of women do not know the language. Both Tigre and To Bedawie tend to be relegated to oral use today, although To Bedawie can be written in the Arabic script and Tigre in both Arabic and Ethiopian (Gez) scripts.

The Tokar Beni Amer were traditionally camel pastoralists; the southern and eastern ones largely cattle pastoralists, a fact which reflects the greater amount of rainfall as well as the several river systems and natural reservoirs located in the southern range. With the political upheavals in Ethiopia over the past 20 years they have tended to shift westward gradually so that their populations are approximately reversed, with many Beni Amer living in the Sudan and only occasionally, if at all, venturing into Eritrea for grazing.

The Beni Amer are today a group in political as well as economic transition. Their gradual integration into the larger national polities of the Sudan and Ethiopia is restructuring their society in a direction which has not yet crystallized into another system. Although today many Beni Amer are cattle and camel pastoralists, they include semi-sedentary pastoralists who practice limited cultivation, sedentarized subsistence agriculturists and cash-crop agriculturists, as well as urban and peri-urban wage earners.

BIBLIOGRAPHY

Books

Hudson, Richard A. "Beja." In *The Non-Semitic Languages of Ethiopia*, edited by M. Lionel Bender. East Lansing: Michigan State University Press, 1976.
Paul, Andrew. *A History of the Beja Tribes of the Sudan*. London: Frank Cass, 1971.
Trimingham, J. Spencer. *Islam in Ethiopia*. London: Oxford University Press, 1952.
———. *Islam in the Sudan*. London: Oxford University Press, 1949. Reprint. London: Frank Cass, 1965.

Articles

Lewis, B. A. "Deim el Arab and the Beja Stevadores of Port Sudan." *Sudan Notes and Records* 43 (1962): 16–49.
Nadel, S. F. "Land Tenure on the Eritrean Plateau." *Africa* 16 (1946): 1–22, 99–109.
———. "Notes on Beni Amer Society." *Sudan Notes and Records* 26:2 (1945): 51–94.
Paul, Andrew. "Notes on the Beni Amer."*Sudan Notes and Records* 31:1 (1950): 223–245.
Seligmann, C. G. "Notes on the History and Present Condition of the Beni Amer." *Sudan Notes and Records* 13:2 (1930): 83–97.

Deborah L. Mack

BERBERS   Berbers are a widely dispersed Muslim ethnic group of more than 14 million people living in North Africa, the Sahara Desert and Sahelian West Africa. Aside from other identifying factors which apply unevenly to them, the unit of identification is that of the tribe. Other common group indicators, such as social behavior, life-style, occupations, language and forms of communication, differ widely from tribe to tribe and within tribes as well. There is no common Berber language, for example, and tribal dialects tend towards mutual unintelligibility even within the same country or region. The only dialect which exists in written form is the incomplete Tifinagh script of Saharan and Sahelian Tuareg.

As an identifiable people, Berbers existed in a state of tribal self-government long before the Arab conquest in the seventh century. The name probably comes from *barbari*, the word meaning "barbarians" applied to them by the Romans and from which comes the English designation for that area, the Barbary Coast. Some linguists classify the Berber languages as Hamitic; ethnolinguist Joseph Greenberg classifies them as a group within the Afro-Asian family.

The Berbers do not use the name to describe themselves as a people or ethnic group. The name most commonly used, in slightly different dialectal forms, is Imazighen—"Free Men." Beyond this generic appellation they identify themselves in order of family and clan membership, and ultimately as members of a particular tribe, such as Ait 'atta or Ait Waryaghar ("Ait" meaning "sons of"). The nomenclature consists of a linked series of names in order, first the given name, then the father's name, then the name of a recent ancestor. The larger, tribal designation came to be applied during periods of foreign conquest, most recently by the French in their administration of North and West Africa. With the advent of nation-states in this region and the effort to impose a system of nationalism and Arabized education on the population, particularly in the "Berber strongholds" of Morocco and Algeria, Berber particularism has been greatly reduced.

The largest number of Berber groups is found in Morocco, where they form about 34 percent of the population (7.8 million). The Berber proportion in Algeria is about 21.5 percent (4.5 million). Elsewhere the percentages are: Mauritania 20 percent, Niger 8 percent, Mali 6 percent, Libya 5 percent. There are a few villages inhabited by Arabic-speaking Berber groups in southern Tunisia, while tribes descended from the early Islamic Sanhaja confederacy predominate in Mauritania. Berbers also form the majority of the population in the Western Sahara (ex-Spanish Sahara), where they number approximately 90,000. The Berber tribes, which form the great majority in this disputed territory, are divided into 8 major tribal groups and 45 factions. The major tribes, in order of numerical importance, are the Reguibat Sahel (located near the Mauritanian border), Reguibat Lgouacem (Saqiet al-Hamra), Izarguin Tekna (Al Ayoun), Oulad Delim (Tiris al-Gharbiya), Bou Sba (Tiris al-Gharbiya), Tidrarin, Assoussiyine, Filala and Ait Lahsen (all along the north coast).

As the earliest identifiable, indigenous ethnic stock in North Africa, the Berbers have common cultural traditions, beliefs and legends that set them apart from other peoples, including their various conquerors. However, the tradition of independence inherent in the Imazighen appellation, as well as the tribal organization, has always worked against the development of a Berber political entity. The only example of a Berber "state" in recent history was the Republic of the Rif created by the Ait Waryaghar leader, Abd al-Karim al-Khattabii (Abdel Krim), in the 1920s as a resistance movement against Spanish (and later French) colonization. Berber history had its periods of greatness, however. Early in the Arab/Islamic invasions of North Africa a Berber tribal chief from the Moroccan Rif was converted to Islam, taking the Arab name Tariq ibn Ziyad. He recruited an army of tribesmen on behalf of the Arab governor of the province and led the successful Muslim invasion of Spain. In the eleventh to thirteenth centuries two Berber tribal confederations established successive Islamic territorial "empires" independent of the eastern Caliphs. The first al-Murabitun (Almoravids) built a dynasty in Morocco that brought Islam deep into sub-Sahara Africa. The second al-Muwannidun (Almohads) established formal political control over the area of modern Morocco, Algeria and Tunisia, plus Spain.

Berbers are Sunni Muslims subscribing in general to the Maliki school of Islamic law, with the exception of the Mzab people, who are Hanafites. However, the Berber observance of Islamic belief and ritual reflects to a considerable extent pre-Islamic traditions and a sense of distinctiveness. The practice of saint worship is highly developed among them. Local saints (*igurramen*) play prominent roles in the prevailing balance of powers that characterizes the Berber tribal political order. *Igurramen* possess both charismatic and healing powers along with the supposed ability (*baraka*) to intercede on behalf of a supplicant. These powers are inherited at birth, as the *igurramen* belong to saintly lineages that are separate from the normal family-clan-tribe linkages. In addition to these religious and intercessory responsibilities, the saints are called upon to supervise local elections, arbitrate disputes, mediate clan rivalries and assess penalties or collective punishments. Many *igurramen* live in sacred enclosures around shrines containing the bones of their distinguished ancestors. The majority are local, but in some cases a saint's *baraka* is powerful enough to attract disciples, and over time his following establishes a sort of religious order (*tariqa*) at a particular location (*zawiya*).

Berber distinctiveness is highly visible in Morocco due to compartmentalization of the country and the traditional balance between central government (*makhzan*) and dissident tribes (*siba*). The Rifians occupy most of northwestern Morocco, the Jbala-Ghmara (Ghomara) Rif region of 6,000 peaks, narrow valleys and an extremely rugged coast. There are some 30 Berber tribes in this region. Their life is based mainly on the cultivation of cereal crops—barley, wheat, rye and maize. Until recently the Rif was the most neglected part of Morocco and the scene of the only mass revolts against the Moroccan central government.

The most powerful Rifian tribe is the Ait Waryaghar, sedentary agriculturists in the Al-Hmam district. The tribe figured prominently in Moroccan history through the Abdel Krim revolt of 1920–1926.

The second large Berber group in Morocco is the Berraber. All speak the Taberberit dialect of Tamazight. Berraber life is characterized by transhumance— the practice of pasturing livestock according to fixed patterns of movement. Some Berraber tribes practice summer transhumance, others move only in winter, while a third group maintains intermediate permanent residences between summer and winter pastures.

The Berraber, regardless of transhumant practice, inhabit permanent villages with fortified communal granaries, where they spend at least a part of each year. The villages have adjacent farmlands where a variety of cereals and other vegetable crops are cultivated, with one segment of each tribe detailed to guard and cultivate the fields while the majority are away. The granary, with its quadrangular stone watchtower, is a characteristic sight in Berber Morocco. Houses are flat-roofed, of dried mud reinforced with stone. On transhumance, however, the tribesmen live in tents of black or grey striped goat hair, often designed in striking patterns.

The Shluh of the western High Atlas and the Sous region are the southernmost of the Moroccan Berber groups. Their spoken language, Tashilhait, has three mutually intelligible dialects, Shilha, Susi and Drawa. The Shluh, like the Rifians, engage in mixed farming with considerable variation in residence patterns due to different environmental conditions. At lower mountain levels they practice intensive agriculture. There is a limited amount of transhumance, with herds left in the care of hired shepherds. In the Sous valley and areas west and south of the mountains along the Atlantic coast, subsistence agriculture is the rule, managed with difficulty by a combination of dry farming and elaborate irrigation networks.

Farther east is a transitional zone of steppe and pre-Saharan territory with agriculture confined to oases and the valleys of intermittent watercourses. Here live black Berber-speaking groups called *haratin* (probably from Tashilhait *ahardan*, meaning "black"). Considered by the Shluh—if not throughout Morocco— as inferior, they are nevertheless essential to Berber society as cultivators of the oasis palm groves and as tanners, well-diggers and builders.

In Algeria the Kabyles form the major Berber subgroup. Their homeland, Kabylia, is a massive mountain block, the Djurdjura, which is difficult to penetrate. Until the French arrived in the nineteenth century, Kabylia had never been ruled directly by any central power.

Kabyles, like Rifians, are sedentary mountain farmers. Because of the extreme ruggedness of the terrain, they have developed extensive terracing for maximum use of limited land. The Kabyle villages of stone houses with red tile roofs balance like eagle nests on the ridges with the farmland spread below. Rainfall is adequate, but overpopulation and limited arable land have forced thousands of Kabyle males to emigrate to either Algerian cities or metropolitan areas of Europe.

Kabyle social structure is village-oriented. Each Kabyle village has its assembly, composed of males elected by age and seniority. Islam among the Kabyles is circumscribed by unwritten or customary laws (*qanuns*) which govern personal behavior and relationships. Great stress is placed on honor, humility, virility, male guardianship and superiority over women, the value of challenge and response in ensuring the dignity of individuals and the preservation of group identity.

The Mzabites in Algeria hold themselves separate from both Arabs and other Berbers in religious practice and life style. The community dates from the eleventh century, when a group of Ibadi Kharijites, persecuted for their religious extremism, emigrated from northern Algeria to a desolate region in the Sahara about 330 miles south of Algiers. Here they established five cities: Ghardaya, Beni Isguen, Melika, Bou Noura and El-Ateuf. The five have a total population estimated at 80,000. They observe the Hanafi school of Islam in contrast to the Maliki majority. They are also an urban society.

These Mzab cities are built along the slopes of the intermittent Wadi Mzab, which is dry except for a flow about once every 12 years. Subsurface water, existing at depths of 30 to 200 feet, has been drawn from wells to nourish an elaborate network of palm groves and gardens maintained by constant labor on the part of the Mzabites. It is this determined agricultural effort plus rigorous observance of fundamental Islamic doctrine that has given the Mzabite community its separate identity from surrounding Arab and Berber communities.

Berber social and political organization is relatively uncomplicated. The two basic elements of the political system are segmentation and marginalism. In the former, a tribe tracing descent from a common agnatic ancestor in the male line will nonetheless be segmented into a number of clans, then into a sub-clan and finally into nuclear family units. The relationships between these segments at each level are characterized by balance and opposition. Political authority in the system is diffused; clan chiefs, or, for that matter, heads of an entire tribe, serve on a temporary basis after election and can easily be removed. The very flexibility and diffusion of the system has given rise to the distinctive balance of opposing forces called *leffs*, which are more or less permanent divisions, or moieties. In the past, *leffs* functioned for mutual defense in time of war, as promoters of the blood feuds, or simply as an extension of imagined brotherhood between extended clan groups.

With the institution of centralized authority, first by the French and subsequently by the independent governments of Morocco and Algeria, the defensive element in the *leff* system gradually declined, as did its purpose of balancing opposition in the pattern of interclan, intertribal warfare characteristic of Berber society. Today, its chief function is that of reinforcing group loyalty.

Marginalism refers to the partial but voluntary opting out of the wider political system by the group. Tribal dissidence in the past concerned refusal to pay taxes to any ruler or to accept any authority as above that of the tribe. Numbers and accessibility were the key features to successful (or unsuccessful) marginalism. The Kabyles remained beyond the reach of successive Algerian urban-based rulers until the French ''pacification'' of the 1880s. Three-fourths of Morocco was dissident country prior to the French protectorate. The Mzab voluntarily accepted French supervisory rule in return for recognition of its theocratic organization and Ibadi religious doctrines.

Modernization has affected the Berbers in a number of ways and at various levels, although, in general, the group has strongly resisted incorporation into contemporary technological society. The growth of urbanization in North Africa, along with diminution of agricultural resources in Berber areas, has produced extensive rural-to-urban migration with a resultant large Berber population in the cities. A large part of Europe's unskilled labor force is composed of economically disadvantaged Berbers.

Of all Berber subgroups, the Tuareg is the only one still largely transnational in habitat, unique in customs and social organization, resistant to supratribal pressures, and marginal in its position in national society in those countries where its people live.

A now poor but proud people, they have retained a distinctiveness often romanticized in film and novel. Sometimes called the People of the Veil, the men wear an indigo headdress which covers their faces from puberty to death, while their leaders also wear splendid blue robes indicating their noble status.

There are seven Tuareg groups found in southern Algeria, Niger, Mali and southwestern Libya. Their main areas of concentration are the Tassili 'n Ajjer and Ahaggar mountains of Algeria, the Air Mountains of Niger, and the Adrar 'n Iforas straddling the Algerian-Malian border. Until the advent of massive Saharan oil development and the opening up of the desert, the Tuareg were isolated from technological change. They existed as camel-breeding nomads, constantly on the move between water holes and grazing grounds. They were also traditionally "guardians of the Sahara," furnishing guides and protection to caravans transiting the desert between western and northern Africa. With French pacification of the area ending in 1902, the Tuareg no longer functioned as the desert policemen. The Saharan oil boom, the attractions of urban life and the terrible droughts of the early 1970s have seriously reduced Tuareg freedom of movement and restricted their way of life. At least in Algeria, and probably elsewhere, more Tuareg have abandoned their nomadic existence than still follow it.

Like "Berber," the name "Tuareg," meaning "forsaken ones," is foreign and was probably given to them by the Arabs. Even more than other Berbers, who tend to overlay Islam with extensive saint worship and membership in Sufi brotherhoods and who supplement Shariah with customary laws, the Tuareg have retained a way of life and sociopolitical organization only incidentally Islamic.

The Tuareg language is both oral (Tamarshak) and written (Tifinagh), pictographic in nature but using lines, circles and dots rather than pictures as with Egyptian hieroglyphic. Tamarshak, common to all groups, is rich in imagery but limited to the Tuareg experience.

Social divisions among the Tuareg are complex and have tended to break down in recent years with the struggle to survive in the face of natural disasters, such as the 1967–1974 drought in the Sahel, and government pressures to conform. An example is the Ahaggar Tuareg, among whom there has been a division into three noble and several vassal tribes.

Unlike other Berber communities, the Tuareg balance the responsibilities of the men and women. The women are the guardians of the language. The Tuareg child inherits its mother's social status, and women carry their status with them when they marry, including any property owned by them before marriage. Some Tuareg recognize matrilineal descent. Another departure from common Muslim practice is that Tuareg first cousins never marry. Male-female relationships are described by the proverb: "Men and women towards each other are for the eyes and for the heart, not only for the bed."

It appears that Berbers as a separate Muslim group will be absorbed eventually into the larger Muslim social entity represented by African nation-states, not through any one factor but rather as a consequence of the universal conformity imposed by technology. However, the general rejection among Islamic peoples of the values accompanying this technology wherever it is perceived as "Western" finds in certain cases an answering echo among the Berber minorities in the North African states. A debate over the Arabization of the educational curriculum in Algeria provoked violent reactions among the predominantly Berber population of the Kabyle region, where Arabization, promoted for nation-building purposes by the government in its ongoing effort to break away from the French influence, was perceived by the Kabyles as aimed at destroying their traditional Berber values, language and cultural traditions. At one point, army units sealed off the entire region to prevent an anticipated outbreak of Kabyle violence.

With the exception of those in Morocco, no other Berber population group possesses either the political cohesion or the ability to influence decision making as an elite that would enable the group to play an ongoing role in national development. Moroccan Berbers are highly visible, and this fact plus their traditional importance to the monarchy, through the army and the continued access to the ruler of certain senior tribal *shaikhs*, suggests that the "Berber factor" in internal Moroccan policies is likely to retain its importance until such time as a major change occurs in that nation's political structure.

BIBLIOGRAPHY

Books

Abu-Lughod, Janet. *Rabat: Urban Apartheid in Morocco*. Princeton: Princeton University Press, 1980.
Alport, E. A.. "The Mzab (Algeria)." In *Peoples and Cultures of the Middle East*, edited by Louise E. Sweet. Vol. 2. New York: Natural History Press, 1970.
Bourdieu, Pierre. *The Algerians*. Boston: Beacon Press, 1962.
Briggs, Lloyd Cabot. *Tribes of the Sahara*. Cambridge: Harvard University Press, 1960.
Coon, Carleton S. *Caravan: Story of the Middle East*. New York: Rinehart & Winston, 1958.
———. *Tribes of the Rif*. Harvard African Studies, 9 (1931). Reprint ed. New York: Kraus Reprint, 1970.
Crapanzano, Vincent. *The Hamadsha: A Study in Moroccan Ethno-psychiatry*. Berkeley: University of California Press, 1973.
Eickelman, Dale F. *Moroccan Islam: Tradition and Society in a Pilgrimage Center*. Austin: University of Texas Press, 1976.
Fathaly, Omar, and Palmer, Monte. *Political Development and Social Change in Libya*. Lexington, Mass.: Lexington Books, 1980.
Geertz, Clifford. *Islam Observed: Religious Development in Morocco and Indonesia*. New Haven: Yale University Press, 1968.
Gellner, Ernest. *Saints of the Atlas*. Chicago: University of Chicago Press, 1969.

————, and Micaud, Charles, eds. *Arabs and Berbers: From Tribe to Nation in North Africa*. Lexington, Mass.: Lexington Books, 1973.

Hart, David. *The Aith Waryaghar of the Moroccan Rif: An Ethnography and History*. Tucson: University of Arizona Press, 1976.

————. *Dadda 'Atta and His Forty Grandsons: The Sociopolitical Organization of the 'Ait Atta of Southern Morocco*. Cambridge: MENAS Press, 1981.

Hoffman, Bernard G. *The Structure of Traditional Moroccan Society*. The Hague: Mouton, 1967.

Le Tourneau, Roger. "North Africa: Rigorism and Bewilderment." In *Unity and Variety in Muslim Civilization*, edited by E. von Grunebaum. Chicago: University of Chicago Press, 1955.

Montage, Robert. *The Berbers: Their Political and Social Life*. London: Frank Cass, 1972.

Nicolaisen, Johannes. *Ecology and Culture of the Pastoral Tuareg of Ahaggar and Air*. Copenhagen: The National Museum, 1963.

Quandt, William B. "Berbers in the Algerian Elite." In *Foreign Affairs Research Series*, 12707. Santa Monica, Cal.: Rand, 1970.

Rennell, Francis J., Baron. *Peoples of the Veil*. Oosterhout, Holland: Anthropological Publications, 1970.

Shinar, Pessah. "Notes on the Socio-economic and Cultural Roots of Sufi Brotherhoods and Maraboutism in the Northern Mahgrib." In *Proceedings of the First International Congress of Africanists*, edited by Lalage Brown and Michael Crowder. Evanston: Northwestern University Press, 1964.

Slavin, Kenneth, and Slavin, Julie. *The Tuareg*. London: Bentry Books, 1973.

Spencer, William. *Algiers in the Age of the Corsairs*. Norman: University of Oklahoma Press, 1976.

————. *Historical Dictionary of Morocco*. Metuchen, N.J.: Scarecrow Press, 1980.

Thompson, Virginia. *The Western Saharans: Background to Conflict*. New York: Barnes & Noble, 1980.

Trimingham, J. Spencer. *The Influence of Islam Upon Africa*. New York: Praeger, 1968.

Vinogradov, Amal R. *The Aith Ndhir of the Middle Atlas: A Study in Moroccan Tribalism*. Ann Arbor: University of Michigan Press, 1974.

Waterbury, John. "The Maghreb." In *The Middle East in the Coming Decade: From Wellhead to Wellbeing*, edited by John Waterbury and Ragaei El Mallakh. New York: McGraw-Hill, 1978.

Westermarck, Edward A. *Marriage Ceremonies in Morocco*. London: Curzon Press, 1972.

————. *Ritual and Belief in Morocco*. 2 vols. Hyde Park, N.Y.: University Books, 1968.

Woolman, David S. *Rebels in the Rif*. Stanford: Stanford University Press, 1968.

Wysner, Glora. *The Kabyle People*. New York: n.p., 1945.

Zartman, I. William, ed. *Political Elites in Arab North Africa*. New York: Longman, 1982.

Articles

Berque, Jacques. "Tradition and Innovation in the Maghrib." *Daedalus* 102 (1973): 239–250.

Clarke, Thurston. "Land of Free Men." *Geo* 4 (1982): 66–77.

Farrag, Amina. "Social Control Amongst the Mzabite Women of Beni-Isguen." *Middle Eastern Studies* 8:3 (1971): 317–328.

Hart, David M. "Morocco's Saints and Jinns." *Tomorrow* 7:1 (1959): 153–162.

Lewis, William H. "Feuding and Social Change in Morocco." *African Studies Review* 20:13 (1977): 65–78.

Sutton, Keith. "Population Resettlement—Traumatic Upheavals and the Algerian Experience." *Journal of Modern African Studies* 15:2 (1977): 279–300.

Wall, Ernest. "Folklore of the Berbers." *Religion in Life* 23:1 (1954): 114–124.

William Spencer

BERI   The Arabs distinguish two ethnic groups on the border of Chad and Sudan, the Zaghawa and Bideyat, the former a more settled group of cattle raisers, the latter a more nomadic group of camel breeders. Both Zaghawa and Bideyat in their own language call themselves Beri and know that they belong to one ethnic group. (Phonetically, the "r" in Beri is flapped, or retroflexed, as in the Spanish *pero*, "but.")

Together the Bideyat and Zaghawa number close to 313,000 with the Bideyat population the smaller at about 25,000 (based on census figures of more than ten years ago). In the Republic of Chad, 40,000 or so Zaghawa live in the northeastern area of Wadai Province. From west to east, their clans include the Guruf, Dirong, Kabka, Kigé and Kobé. East of the international boundary, in the northwest of Darfur Province, the Zaghawa are represented by a tiny group of Kabka clans that migrated from their home in the Kabka hills and now live around the Tundabay pool. Kobé clans live around the village of Tine. Other clans in the Sudan belong to the Gala, the Tuèr and the Artaj or Unay. Some other clans of various origins live farther east, outside Dar Zaghawa, in Dar Sueni, and in Dar Beri among the Fur and Tunjur peoples (see Fur; Tunjur).

The Bideyat of Chad live in the Ennedi hills, north of the Zaghawa. Again, Arabs distinguish among them the Borogat, living in the west and influenced by the neighboring Gurean, and the Bilia, living east, a less nomadic group whose contacts are limited to the Borogat and the Zaghawa.

Zaghawa and Bideyat speak the same language which they call Bèrí-á, here spelled Beri, characterized by the presence of tones. It is a dialect cluster of four groups of dialects: Tuèr-Gala, Kobé-Kabka, Dirong-Guruf and Bideyat. The language spoken by the Berti is probably a Beri dialect and apparently developed separately (see Berti). Beri belongs to the Saharan branch of the Nilo-Saharan language family and includes the languages of the Kanuri, Kanembu and Tebu. However, it has been recently suggested that Beri belongs to the Chadic languages. More evidence is needed to make a decision. Beri dialects are rarely written; the Chadian national radio has broadcast news and commentaries in Beri since August 1982.

Beri territory is surrounded by desert in the north, east and west, but there is considerable variation in Beri homelands. South of the desert, the Ennedi Mountains are a group of ravine-cut tablelands with altitudes varying from 3,000 to 5,000 feet. Abundant precipitation (4 to 6 inches in July) and impermeable soil produces dense vegetation, grass and trees where wildlife abounds. In rainy season wadis can run for several hours and then disappear north into the Murdi depression, west in the Jurab basin and east in the valley of Wadi Howar. In the hills, underground water maintains permanent springs and pools.

South of the Ennedi hills, where the tableland averages from 2,300 to 3,000 feet, rain is even more abundant (more than 14 inches annually) but irregular. Water rapidly soaks away in the vast sandy expanses or forms only pools in clay basins. Animal life is less visible, but meadows are more extensive and garden cultivation in the wadis more reliable. This area is more densely inhabited.

The problem of water is a major preoccupation of the Beri, who must, in normal times, wait nine dry months for a short rainy season between the end of June and the end of August. Some years, rain is insufficient, others it is abundant but concentrated; there have been some years without rain, as during the great drought and famine of 1969–1970.

To survive, the Beri, who depend largely on animal husbandry, often practice transhumance, driving some of their animals (mainly camels and sheep) north to graze during dry season, returning south when it rains. Cattle are driven along specific circuits, not too far from the villages or settlements.

In addition to raising and marketing animals, Beri also gather wild grasses and tubers, as well as gum, which they sell in the markets. Those Beri remaining sedentary cultivate millet on cleared fields fenced with thorny plants. If rain is sufficient, there will be a crop. Women grow vegetables in small gardens in wadi beds.

Many Beri are merchants who travel south and east from their territory to look for food supplements; in the north they seek salt, sal soda (*natron*) and dates, which they consume, sell or trade. They export their cattle, camels and sheep, selling them as far away as Omdurman, Egypt and Libya. In return they buy sugar, tea and manufactured goods such as fabrics, plastics, blankets, cookwear and soap. While camels provide most of the transport, trucks are coming into frequent use despite the absence of good roads. Where once barter was the method of buying and selling, today nearly all transactions are carried out in local currency.

Blacksmiths (*haddad*) live among the Beri and manufacture the tools necessary for agriculture, as well as weapons and jewelry. Blacksmiths also work with wood and leather, making mortars and pestles, boxes, saddles. They hunt and make nets from gazelle tendons; on their own looms, they weave wild cotton. Their wives make pottery and frequently are hairdressers. The *haddad* are remarkable well diggers (see Haddad).

Trade, the development of small businesses, wages from work for hire and salaries from government employment have created a strong monetary element in Beri economic life. As expected, this aspect also affects Beri society, which must adapt itself to change.

Before the arrival of French and British colonialism at the beginning of the twentieth century, Beri society was formed into a loose confederation of tribes, groups of numerous clans of unequal importance and highly individualized. For each tribe there was a dominant clan. The clan was concentrated around a mountain where its village was located or to where it looked for refuge when under attack. The name of the clan was often that of the mountain; other names derived from the name of an important wadi or an animal which was important to the founder of the clan.

Exogamous marriage created allies of clans and prevented total isolation. This rule was not equally respected by all clans at all times. Until recently, for instance, the Kobé were always exogamous, while the Gala and Tuèr clans sometimes were endogamous. Members of a given clan followed the same rules concerning such items as forbidden foods and cattle brands. When a clan member committed a crime, the entire clan was responsible for paying the penalty.

Prior to the coming of Islam, Beri believed in a god, Iru, whom they approached through their founding ancestors and to whom they made sacrifices in order to assure rain or prosperity generally. The ancestor usually would be present in the form of a large snake, or as a *manda* or genie residing in a mountain or tree. If his intercession was not effective, worshippers addressed Iru directly.

The conversion of the Beri to Islam took place gradually; among the Zaghawa of Sudan it took place earlier and was established more deeply than among the Zaghawa and Bideyat of Chad. Tradition says that Abdullay Boru introduced Islam to the Kobé clan in the seventeenth century. At the end of the nineteenth century and the beginning of the twentieth, Mahdist and Senussi movements did not succeed in securing support among the Zaghawa. In the Ennedi hills, around Beskere and Baki, the Senussi success was short-lived. In 1957, one could find in Hiri-ba (a small village shown on French maps as ''Iriba''), the residence of the Sultan of the Zaghawa in Chad, one mosque, two *fuqura* (jurisconsultants) and some learned members of the royal house. The fast of Ramadan was strictly observed; some of the villagers (mainly from among the royal family) had made the Haj, and the Friday prayer was well attended.

Islam has weakened the clan system. Villages have become more hospitable to outsiders. Ancestor cults have been abandoned as well as most of the sacrifices—or they have been reinterpreted in order to be acceptable to Islam. Taboos, however, continue to be respected, and some pre-Islamic shrines are still visited. Marriage is still exogamous, at least among the clans that made it a rule, but marriage to the father's brother's daughter is gaining ground in acceptance, if not in practice.

Marriage alliances are tied with compensation in cattle (brideprice). In spite of efforts by the governments to reduce payment to 10 to 20 cattle, sometimes the price is as high as 60, usually about 40, making marriage expensive. Other animals can be substituted, particularly camels and horses (sheep are not very popular), and in the past few years cash has become acceptable.

The Beri practice polygyny if they can afford it. Clan chiefs, however, often exceed the limit of four, especially sultans, who have been known to have more than a dozen wives. Male circumcision is practiced; female circumcision is practiced only among daughters of royal clans.

Justice is rendered in compliance with Maliki jurisprudence when disputes are brought to official courts. However, customary law is still observed, and the practice of vendetta is current. Stealing camels from neighbors' herds, while declining, is prevalent.

Inheritance laws have been modified by Islam. Females no longer are excluded and receive half of what males inherit. The custom of levirate, which provides for the oldest son to inherit the wife or wives of his deceased father, is still in force.

Women have a more conservative attitude than men in regard to traditional religious practices. They visit shrines, respect taboos, resort to geomancy and magic. Yet they are ready to accept change if innovation is likely to improve their working conditions.

One special benefit brought to the Beri by Islam has been the introduction of writing. Learning, piety and the study of Islamic law are highly respected. Trade has become a more prestigious occupation.

In colonial times, Beri political life was controlled by a supreme chief who collected taxes and administered justice, enforcing law and order with the support of the colonial authorities, a system imposed more completely in Chad than Sudan. The Beri in Chad had a single sultan who was originally the Kobé headman; under his authority were three other chiefdoms, each headed by a man appointed by the sultan. Among the Bideyat, the French reinforced the authority of two chiefs loyal to the colonial government.

Independent Chad has not eliminated the traditional chiefdomship system, but it has tried to reduce the role of the chiefs and to increase government surveillance of their activities.

In Sudan, the system was looser. The Zaghawa were divided into seven chiefdoms with only three being important. The British authorities relied upon the hereditary chiefs and never tried to bring them all under one of them. Since independence, the Sudan government has considerably reduced the power of the chiefs, meeting with no small amount of resistance.

In both Chad and Sudan, attempts to create a "national community" by reducing the particularities of the various ethnic groups have not reached their goal, more so in Chad, which has for so long been close to chaos. There is still a deep Beri nationalist feeling alive in both countries for the Beri are concerned about their economic welfare, their political independence and the preservation of their personality.

BIBLIOGRAPHY

Books

Fuchs, P. *Die Völker der Südost-Sahara (Tibesti-Borku-Ennedi)*. Vienna: Braumüller, 1961.
MacMichael, H. A. *A History of the Arabs in the Sudan and Some Account of the People Who Preceded Them and of the Tribes Inhabiting Darfur*. 2 vols. Cambridge: Cambridge University Press, 1922.
Tubiana, Marie-José. *Survivances préislamiques en pays zaghawa*. Paris: Institut d'Ethnologie, 1964.
———, and Tubiana, Joseph. *Contes zaghawa*. Paris: Quartre-Jeudis, 1962.
———. *The Zaghawa from an Ecological Perspective*. Rotterdam: Balkema, 1977.

Articles

Balfour-Paul, H. G. "A Prehistoric Cult Still Practised in Muslim Darfur." *Journal of the Royal Anthropological Institute of Great Britain and Ireland* 86:1 (1956): 77–86.
MacMichael, H. A. "Notes on the Zaghawa and the People of Jebel Midob." *Journal of the Royal Anthropological Institute of Great Britain and Ireland* 42 (1912): 288–335.
Spence, B. "Stone Worship Among the Zaghawa." *Sudan Notes and Records* 1:3 (1918): 197–199.

Marie-José Tubiana

BERTI   According to their own tradition, the original homeland of the Berti is the Tagabo Hills region in northern Darfur Province of the Republic of Sudan. About 30,000 Berti inhabit this original tribal area. Another, probably larger, group of Berti live near Um Keddada and Taweisha in eastern Darfur, where they migrated during the second half of the eighteenth century, when the neighboring Meidob began to penetrate into the original Berti territory (see Meidob). A number of Berti, intermingled with the Fur, live around and partly in El Fasher, the capital of northern Darfur, and small Berti colonies dating back to the Mahdist period exist elsewhere in the Sudan, particularly in Gedaref and near Um Ruwaba in Kordofan. A number of Berti live with other ethnic groups in Jazira.

Originally, the Berti spoke their own language, which belonged to the Middle Sahara language group and was close to the Zaghawa language, but for several generations now they have spoken only their own dialect of Arabic.

The Berti area of northern Darfur is an upland plateau lying from 2,200 to 3,300 feet above sea level and consisting mostly of stable old sand dunes. The vegetation varies from an open grassland of the dry savannah in the north, where the annual rainfall averages 8 inches, to a light woodland savanna in the south with an average rainfall of 20 inches.

Unlike most of their neighbors, the Berti are fully sedentary in small villages, often consisting of less than 100 people. The village is organized as a cluster of individual homesteads. The core of each village is formed by men who are members of the same patrilineage and are usually genealogically close. Most married couples reside patrilocally, but the incidence of uxorilocal residence is high (21.8 percent). If husband and wife are of different lineages, a uxorilocal marriage is the starting point of the growth of a new lineage within the village, which eventually leads to the fission of the village along lineage lines. The fission of villages is a perpetual process which is usually triggered by disputes among the inhabitants about following a particular *shaikh* or over land near the larger villages.

Individual homesteads in the village consist of a circular or nearly square yard enclosed by a millet-stalk fence about six feet high. In this enclosure are one to four conical roofed houses of millet stalk and grass and approximately the same number of flat-roofed, rectangular shelters of the same material.

Each homestead is inhabited by an individual family or by its fragment resulting from either divorce or death. The composition of the homestead is affected by the fact that the couple do not establish their own homestead immediately after they marry and start to cohabit as husband and wife. First the husband must complete the transfer of bridewealth to his wife's parents, and the latter must agree to their daughter's establishing her own independent household. It is their duty to furnish the money received as bridewealth. This generally takes several years to pay, and the average time between the wedding and setting up house is four years. During this time, both husband and wife live with their natal families and the husband regularly visits his wife at her natal home. One or more children are born to most couples before they establish their own homestead, and a typical Berti household at the time of its inception consists of a married couple and their children. Later it grows to include the elementary families of the parents and those of their daughter or daughters. In the final stage, after the married children leave the household of their parents and set up their own home, the homestead is typically inhabited by an elderly married couple or a widow living on her own. It happens only rarely that the elderly widowed father of either the husband or wife lives with them, and even rarer are the cases of some other of their kinsmen residing permanently with them.

Boys usually marry between the ages of 20 and 24, girls between 18 and 22. The Berti express a strong preference for marriages between closely related kin. The marriage between the children of two brothers is considered the best, followed by the marriage between the children of a brother and a sister and between children of two sisters. If no close cousin is available, a marriage within the lineage is usually sought, and a considerable preference is also expressed for marriages within the same village or cluster of villages. Intermarriage between the Beri and neighboring tribes rarely occurs. The girl's marriage and the boy's first marriage are always arranged by the parents, and the boy's father is responsible for the payment of bridewealth.

Some men, as they grow older, marry additional wives according to their own wishes, the bridewealth being their own responsibility. But the polygyny rate is not high; only 20 percent of all married men have two or occasionally three wives. The husband does not have his own homestead but dwells alternately in those of his wives.

Each homestead, irrespective of its composition, constitutes a household and a basic unit of production. The Berti have a mixed economy, the main element of which is hoe cultivation practiced on rain-fed fields. The rainy season in the north starts in July and lasts through September; in the south, it spreads from June through October. The most important crops are millet and sorghum. The Berti around Taweisha in eastern Darfur also grow peanuts, partly for their own consumption, but mainly as a cash crop. Other cultivated plants are okra, sesame, watermelons, roselle, cucumbers, pumpkins and occasionally tomatoes.

The second component of Berti economy is animal husbandry, more important in arid northern areas than in the woodland savanna around Taweisha. Farmers keep cattle, goats and sheep, donkeys, less frequently horses and, in the north, camels, which are used for riding and transport.

The third important sphere traditionally has been the collecting of wild-growing gum arabic, which was the only real cash crop in the arid northern areas. Most of the gum-yielding trees died in the severe drought of the early 1970s; this, together with the drop in the price of gum arabic at international markets, has drastically reduced its production in northern Berti areas, where it is no longer profitable. Gum arabic still continues to be collected in the woodland savannah.

Berti are not self-sufficient in their production; they depend heavily on the local markets, and cash plays an important role in their economy. It is needed for payments of bridewealth, damages and government taxes as well as to secure the immediate material existence. Berti have to buy many products which form the basis of daily nutrition, such as red peppers, dried tomatoes, oil, salt, sugar and tea, plus manufactured products.

As gum arabic alone has never been sufficient to produce cash, all surplus cultivated crops are marketed. Cattle merchants visit the Berti regularly every year to buy sheep and cattle. In recent years, an increasing number of young Berti men have been leaving for Libya to work as labor migrants for several years in order to increase the cash supply.

If a household is short of labor due to the absence of some of its members, illness or a woman's pregnancy, it mobilizes a work party of kin and neighbors who are provided with a supply of millet beer. Rich households regularly employ poor Berti or Meidob for weeding their fields or herding their animals.

The traditional political system of the Berti was centralized and pyramidal with the paramount chief occupying the apex. Subordinated to him were the *omdas* standing at the head of *omodiyas*—lower-level political subdivisions. The office of paramount chief has been abolished by the Sudanese government, and the Berti are now administered through the hierarchy of village, divisional and regional councils within the provincial council of Northern Darfur. The system of *omodiyas* has been maintained, and for the Berti, the *omdas* still represent important authorities wielding a certain amount of judicial power. Subordinated to each *omda* are individual *shaikhs*, whose own following ranges widely from a few to several hundred men. Most *shaikhs* are "masters" of lineage territories responsible for the collection of tithe, part of which is given to the *omda*, but some *shaikhs* have no authority in the distribution of land because they do not live in their own lineage territory.

The main duty of the *shaikh* is to collect the annual cattle tax from his followers. He also accompanies his followers to the local court and settles minor disputes in informal moots together with village elders—all married men who have their own homesteads. A certain political role is played by lineages, which are responsible for the payment of blood money in case of homicide, injury or damage inflicted by a member of one lineage on the property of another.

Like all Sudanese, the Berti follow the Maliki law school. Only a few belong to the only existing Sufi brotherhood, Tijaniyya, which recruits its members mostly from among merchants and remains fully restricted to towns and market centers.

A number of men who attended Quranic schools and reputedly have learned the Quran by heart are recognized as *fuqura* (sing. *faqi*), the only title by which Berti denote all religious leaders and officials. In each village, there is usually one *faqi* (sometimes distinguished from other *fuqura* by being called *faqi-l-hilla*—the *faqi* of the village) who leads prayers, officiates at weddings and funerals, performs prayers for rain on behalf of the community and advises on division of inheritance, which, however, never proceeds according to Quranic injunctions and more often than not totally excludes daughters. There are other *fuqura* who are not recognized as religious leaders of their respective communities but specialize in making amulets or are diviners or healers. Some of the *fuqura* are of non-Berti origin; the Fur enjoy the reputation of producing the best *fuqura*, and a number of them have settled permanently among the Berti (see Fur).

An outstanding feature of Berti religious ritual is the communal offering (*karama*) to God, jointly organized by the inhabitants of the village. The sacrificial animal is usually a young bull, but sometimes only goats or sheep are sacrificed. Any misfortune is taken as a sign that God is angry with the people and must be reconciled by an offering. *Karamas* are made in order to bring rain, to ensure a good harvest or simply to secure the health of all members. Communal *karamas* are also arranged by the village at Maulud and Id al Fitr. Apart from communal sacrifices, *karamas* in which all neighbors participate are organized by individual men when there is an illness in the family, in case of a difficult childbirth, after the death of a kinsman, after the birth of twins and at Id al Adha.

Although all Berti consider themselves to be Muslims, Ramadan is the only month when most men, not only the *fuqura* and a few older men, pray regularly five times a day. Some men do not pray at all during the rest of the year, and most pray only on Friday at noon. The Ramadan fast, however, is kept by all men, although by far not by all women. Ramadan is also the only month when the consumption of millet beer is significantly reduced; during the rest of the year it is widely consumed by both men and women, including a number of *fuqura*.

Not surprisingly, Berti are not considered particularly good Muslims by most of their Arab neighbors; they themselves, however, tend to stress their religiosity and take pride in speaking Arabic. They look down upon their non-Arabic-speaking neighbors, particularly the Meidob and the Zaghawa (see Beri). They consider them to be impure, and the very fact that they speak their own languages which Berti are not able to understand is taken as a clear sign of their lack of Muslim faith.

BIBLIOGRAPHY

Books

Holy, L. *Neighbours and Kinsmen: A Study of the Berti Peoples of Darfur*. London: C. Hurst, 1974.

Ladislav Holy

BILIN   Until recently perhaps 50,000 Bilin Agaw lived in the Keren region of western Eritrea Province in Ethiopia. Many are now dispersed across Eritrea and in refugee camps in Sudan. They call themselves and their language Bilin, some of their neighbors call them Bogos and they are listed as Bilen and Belen in the literature. They also call themselves Gabra Tarqwe Qur (*qur* means "sons of").

The Bilin are the northernmost of seven or so extant divisions of the Agaw, an Ethiopian people speaking one of a number of unwritten Central Cushitic (or Agaw) tongues ranging in degree of mutual intelligibility from dialect to language. George P. Murdock, in his *Africa: Its People and Their Culture History*, said of the Agaw: "All indications point to the Agaw as one of the culturally most creative peoples on the entire continent."

Bilin habitat is one of moderately high plateau ranging from 3,000 to 6,600 feet above sea level. Most live along the seasonally flowing Barka and Anseb rivers and their tributaries as well as on higher dissected remnants of tableland. Bilinland covers some 2,000 square miles and is generally a steppe dotted with trees and shrubs having continuous grass cover only after the rains. Small sods of perennial and the widespread seasonal grass provide forage for livestock.

According to evidence from oral traditions and linguistic affiliations, the ancestral Bilin migrated out of the Agaw heartland of central Abyssinia, in Lasta, perhaps as early as the tenth century. There were probably a number of successive migrations of Agaw into Bilinland. It appears the Bilin conquered and subjugated the native people of the Keren region, who were Tigre-speaking herders and cultivators. These "serfs" now speak Bilin Agaw.

The Bilin are composed of two major and one minor tribes. The Bet ("house of") Gabra Tarqwe is said to be founded by a patriarch of that name who migrated from Lasta. The people of Bet Tarqwe, the second major tribe, followed into the Keren region sometime later. The former tribe dwells in the south, the latter in the north of Bilinland. A third minor tribe, the Bab Janjeren, has become acculturated to Bilin ways. They now speak Agaw. They have been joined administratively with the Bet Taqwe and live in the northeast of the Bilin region.

The Bilin live at a focal point of world conflict and not on a timeless, changeless aboriginal reservation. From earliest, pre-Bilin times to the recent past, Keren has been on the caravan route between the Red Sea and the Nile Valley in Sudan. Ottoman Turkish occupation of the Eritrean seaport of Massawa in 1557 marked the beginning of three centuries of its sphere of influence in northern Ethiopia. Bilin were slaved by the Turks as late as the mid-nineteenth century. Egypt began to replace the Turks by the 1830s and controlled Bilinland by 1850.

Bilin history is a microcosm of the changes of the past 150 years in Eritrea. The global importance of this region, and the Keren-Bilin area central to it, was radically and almost instantly transformed when the Suez Canal was opened in 1869 by the British. The Red Sea was changed from a remote cul-de-sac of the Indian Ocean into *the* artery of commercial and military navigation between Europe and the Indo-Pacific region. The great geopolitical importance of the Red Sea and its coastal lands such as Eritrea (which means "land of the Red Sea") continues into the present with contests in the area between the United States and the Soviet Union.

In the late nineteenth century, Britain tried to diminish growing French power in the Red Sea-Sudan zone by encouraging its satellite state, Egypt, and then the new but weak European state, Italy, to control strategic Eritrea. The Egyptian consolidation of its movement into Eritrea was under the leadership of Werner Munzinger Pasha, a Swiss soldier-scholar-adventurer. Munzinger made himself the protector of the Bilin and occupied the Keren-Bilin region in 1872–1874. While among the Bilin in 1859, Munzinger wrote the sole principal work to date about the people, *On the Customs and Law of the Bogos*, now out of print. A number of Egyptian defeats by Ethiopian armies in 1875–1876 left only Keren-Bilinland in Egyptian hands.

To gain support in its fight against Mahdist revolts in Sudan, Britain signed the Anglo-Ethiopian Treaty in 1884, with Egyptian buildings and stores in the stronghold of Keren in Bilinland going to Ethiopia along with the rest of Eritrea. Despite the treaty, Britain allowed Italy to occupy Massawa in 1885 and use this port as a base to conquer all of Eritrea in 1889, with Keren-Bilinland falling in June.

Italian Eritrea was used as the staging ground for the debacle of an Italian invasion of Ethiopia in 1896 and the more successful, mechanized invasion in

1935–1936. Bilin troops were used by the Italians in both invasions. British and Ethiopian armies drove the Italian forces out of all of northeast Africa in 1941 with a major three-and-one-half-month battle taking place in Bilinland around Keren. Under a United Nations directive, Eritrea was federated with Ethiopia in 1952. But in 1962 Ethiopia annexed the province.

With Eritrean separatist movements contending against Ethiopia, increasingly heavy fighting has taken place between the two sides since 1961. Ethiopia was first aided by the West, then by the Soviet bloc. The war has resulted in tens of thousands of local casualties and has caused perhaps 1 million of the 3 million Eritreans to be displaced from their homes, mostly as refugees in Sudan. Successful guerrilla warfare of 1974–1977 by the militant and well-organized Eritrean Peoples Liberation Front (EPLF), allied with the Eritrean Liberation Front (ELF), led to conventional open warfare against Ethiopian government forces trained and equipped by the United States and Israel. The taking of Keren from bastions in surrounding Bilinland by the EPLF was the capstone to effective control of most of their province by Eritreans. Wracked by war, the Kerenites and the Bilin chaffed under the rigid militant control of young, super-dedicated EPLF cadres. In the countryside Bilin were caught between EPLF units and Ethiopian aerial attacks with modern ordnance.

In 1977 the new revolutionary government of Ethiopia began to receive large-scale military aid from the Soviet bloc. Orchestrated by the Soviets, a lethal juggernaut of armor, heavy artillery, rockets, helicopters and jet fighter-bombers, aided by reconnaissance satellites and backed by trained infantry, knocked holes at strategic places in the Eritrean lines. In the final pitched battle in Bilinland, about 100 T–54 tanks and other armor, supported by MIG 21 and 23 jets, were stopped for days in the narrow verdant Elabaret Valley outside of Keren. Perhaps one-third of Ethio-Soviet armor was lost, as were much of the valuable commercial citrus and tomato plantations of the valley. After several days of fighting, the EPLF pulled back from the Keren vicinity into the Bilin hinterland. In all, during recent years, by force of arms, much of the Bilin cultural tradition has been uprooted and the people displaced from their homeland.

About 68 percent of the Bilin are Muslim. The rest are Christian, largely Roman Catholic, but also Protestant and Ethiopian Orthodox. In the first half of the nineteenth century all Bilin were nominally Ethiopian Orthodox with traces of older pagan Agaw rites still prevalent. Sabbath rest was observed on Saturday and Sunday. Priests knew almost nothing about Christian practices and holidays and may not even have been baptized. Egyptian and Beni Amer slaving led many Bilin to accept Islam in the 1860s to 1880s in order to escape captivity. The occupation of Bilinland by Munzinger aided the Islamization, which provided a means to control the Bilin. Roman Catholicism was introduced in the 1850s by French Lazarist missionaries and continued by Italian Catholic orders when the Italians expelled the French in 1896. Muslim Bilin follow the Sunni branch of Islam.

Aside from a few thousand townsmen in Keren, where they are a small minority, most Bilin live in country hamlets of four to six houses plus ancillary structures. The houses are beehive shaped with domed, thatched roofs coming either all or most of the way down to the ground, in the latter case exposing a dry stone wall. Wattle poles hold the thatch, which smells of smoke from the hearth, in the one-door, no-window building. The three-stone cooking hearth and main bed are hidden behind a fiber mat, which hangs from the roof and partitions the house. A visitor remains in the partitioned half nearest the door, where he is offered strong coffee and, perhaps, some of the rich Bilin tobacco.

The fields around the hamlet reflect the fact that the Bilin are sedentary, subsistence agriculturalists. However, traditions and survivals of customs indicate a much greater dependence upon cattle in the distant past. The grains cultivated are sorghum, mainly, but also barley, maize and wheat; the legumes are peas, lentils, chickpeas and horse beans; oil seeds are flax and sesame. A largely cereal diet is consumed in the form of flat bread, parched grain and native beer. Numerous goats plus lesser numbers of cattle and some sheep are kept as a medium of wealth, for dairy food and for meat, which is eaten ordinarily only on ceremonial occasions. Until several decades ago, all milking and herding was done by serfs and not by members of the Bilin elite. Camels and donkeys are used for transport, often in caravans, and oxen for plowing. Periodic major droughts and overwhelming cloud-like swarms of locusts have devastated the Bilin area recently and in the more distant past. Additionally, much of the livestock has been killed in the current fighting.

The most striking feature of Bilin society, and one shared with neighboring peoples, is the cleavage into two social strata of elite and serfs, or bondsmen. The former group is called *adara* (master, lord) and the latter, *gulfare* (bondsman). About one-quarter are *adara* and three-quarters *gulfare*.

Two kinds of bondsmen exist: hereditary, with a client status fixed at birth; and contract, with a client status entered into because of debt, need for protection or some other reason. Although a contract bondsman could purchase freedom from his contract, he or she could never become a member of the elite.

The elite are descendants of the original conquering Agaw migrants, and the client-bondsmen are descendants of the Tigre-speaking peoples already in the area. A male of the elite can take a bondswoman as a wife, but a bondsman cannot marry a female of the elite. No matter how wealthy a client may become, he is never considered either a member of the elite or superior to a poor "master."

An unbalanced reciprocity of obligations existed between elite and bondsmen in the past, with rigidly specified rights and duties. The client had many fixed payments at specified times or during particular ceremonial occasions, mostly in service, livestock and dairy products, but also in crops and booty. The patron provided protection and legal assistance and occasional small gifts. Cropland was originally controlled by kinship groups of elite. Presently, the reciprocal obligations are largely gone, and many bondsmen control arable land. In the past few years, the EPLF has undertaken more uniformly equitable redistribution of the land.

Each of the two major tribes of the Bilin nation is united by links of patrilineal kinship and organized into segmentary lineages and sublineages, both of which are called *hissat*. A lineage has its own territory. Traditionally, each lineage had a hereditary, somewhat sacred, but politically weak chief. Descent and inheritance is reckoned patrilineally within the *hissat*. Most local political power is in the hands of a council of elders covering a number of related hamlets. At the council, the well-developed law of the Bilin (Fetech Magarech) is invoked in interminable proceedings.

Customary law and kinship organization are intertwined in three levels of society. The widest level is all of the Bilin elite and encompasses their native bondsmen. The middle level is one of all elite kinsmen who can reckon kin ties to the seventh degree. These ''masters'' have blood revenge and other legal responsibilities to one another, obligations not found on the wider level. The lowest level is that of the nuclear and extended patrilocal family. Both forms of this level are developmental manifestations for any particular family during different phases of its growth. The traditional law has been followed less in modern times, especially with the development of the Islamic legal system, Shariah, among the Bilin.

Family life is male dominant. At the birth of a child, women assisting the mother give a cry of joy for a boy and are silent for a girl. The father may not enter his house for several weeks after the birth. At around 18 years of age, a young man becomes an adult male after a seven-day rite of passage focusing on himself and his mother's brother, an anomalous matrilineal practice among the Bilin.

Bilin marriage is the giving of a young woman by her family to a man by means of a contract. Bridewealth in cattle or other goods is given by the groom's family to the bride's family. The bride brings a modest dowry of necessary household items to her groom. Polygynous marriages are rare and found only among a few rich men. Generally, a Muslim Bilin woman is as free to move about in public and express her views before those outside of the family as are non-Muslim women of Eritrea.

Currently Eritrea, including Bilinland, suffers through one of the longest and severest of armed conflicts in modern African history. Bilin peasants have moved or been forced from most of their hamlets, now largely abandoned and in ruins. The future of Bilin society depends upon the outcome of the Eritrean war, which in turn depends upon global strategic considerations beyond the ken of the average Bilin.

BIBLIOGRAPHY

Books

Davidson, Basil; Cliffe, Lionell; and Bereket Habte Selassie. *Behind the War in Eritrea.* Nottingham: Spokesman, 1980.

Murdock, George P. *Africa: Its Peoples and Their Culture History*. New York: McGraw-Hill, 1959.
Nadel, Siegfried F. *Races and Tribes of Eritrea*. Asmara, Ethiopia: British Military Administration, 1944.
Pankhurst, Richard. *Economic History of Ethiopia, 1800–1935*. Addis Ababa: Haile Sellassie I University Press, 1968.
Trimingham, J. Spencer. *Islam in Ethiopia*. London: Frank Cass, 1965.

Articles

Bender, M. L. "The Languages of Ethiopia." *Anthropological Linguistics* 13 (1971): 165–288.
Jordan, Gebre-Medhin. "Eritrea: Pre-Capitalist Social Formations." *Horn of Africa* 3 (1981): 20–33.
Hertzon, Robert. "The Agaw Languages." *Afroasiatic Linguistics* 3 (1976): 31–45.
Nadel, Siegfried F. "Land Tenure on the Eritrean Plateau." *Africa* 16 (1946): 1–21.

Frederick C. Gamst

BONANS   The Bonans, among China's smaller minority nationalities, number only about 9,000. Most Bonans (Baoans, Paoans) live in the north central province of Gansu, but a few may still live in Qinghai Province, their former homeland. Those in Gansu live in the villages of Dadun, Ganmei and Gaoli, located in the foothills of Jishi Mountain, near Linxia, Dahejia and Liuji. The Qinghai Bonans live in Tongren County, specifically in three villages on both banks of the Longwu River. Dahejia is on the Huang (Yellow) River just inside Gansu and only a short distance downstream from Xunhua, home of the Salars (see Salars). Muslim Dongxiang live in the same general area (see Dongxiang).

Nothing concrete is known about the Bonans' origin. The relatively few samples of Bonan oral literature recorded so far strongly suggest that they had originally been Mongol soldiers who during either Genghis Khan's time or the subsequent Mongol world empire were sent to the area around present-day Tongren County. After the fall of the Mongol Yuan state in China in 1368, most Mongols retreated to Mongolia, but a few, including the later Bonans, stayed behind. After many generations of mingling with neighboring Tibetans, Hui, Han and Tu, a distinct nationality emerged whose members began calling themselves Bonans.

It is not known exactly when the Bonans were called that name by others, but records of the Wanli reign (1573–1620) report the existence of a Bonan camp in what is now Tongren County. Later this camp became a town which still exists on the banks of the Longwu River under the Chinese transliteration "Baoan." Sometime in the early nineteenth century a portion of the Bonans converted to Islam, a factor which caused friction to develop with the surrounding Buddhist Tibetans and Tu. Finally in 1962, this conflict reached a point where the Islamized Bonans decided to move. First they lived in Xunhua, home of the fellow Salars, for several years, and then they followed the Huang River downstream to the Dahejia area, where they still live. Those Bonans who retained their Buddhist faith stayed in Tongren but became strongly acculturated to their neighbors, especially the Tibetans. Only a small but unknown number of persons remain in Tongren who from an ethnolinguistic point of view can still be considered Bonan.

Bonan belongs to the Mongolian group of the Altaic family of languages. It is relatively close to Tu (Monguor) and Dongxiang. The Bonans do not have their own script but use Chinese in their written communications. There are two major dialects, Dahejia and Tongren. A language similar to the latter is spoken by some Han and Hui.

The Bonan consonants differ little from those of other Mongolian languages. It has no strict vowel harmony. Like Mongolian, Bonan maintains a qualitative difference between its five short and four long vowels, except that long vowels appear in monosyllabic words and in the initial syllable of polysyllabic words. Examples are *u-*, "to drink"; *ābe*, "father"; *ōle*, "mountain."

Like Tu, Dongxiang, Daur and Moghul, the Bonan language has preserved the initial consonants *f-* and *h-* of Middle Mongolian which are no longer found in Modern Mongolian. For example, *felan*, "red" (cf. Dongxiang *hulan*, Tu *fulān*, and Daur *hulān*), but Mongolian *ulagan*. In addition Bonan retains other initial consonants which no other Mongolian languages retain. For example *na-*, "to fall," but Mongolian *una-*.

The Bonans living in Gansu belong either to the Old Teaching or the New Teaching sects. Old Teaching refers to adherents of practices strongly influenced by Chinese cultural elements; New Teaching followers seek to purge Islam of its Sinitic deviations (see Hui). During the republican period, the warlord Ma Bufang sent the head of the New Teaching Sect from Qinghai to strengthen the sect's control over the Bonans living around Dahejia. In 1958 the Bonans, in concert with the Hui, Salars and Dongxiang living nearby, "abolished the feudal powers and system of oppression in Islam." They accused *mullahs* of "trying to smash social reforms, poisoning the relations among nationalities, and arbitrarily interfering with the freedom of marriage."

The Bonans' main economic activity is farming, with wheat and rye being the two most important staple crops. By 1978, food production had increased some 160 percent over that of the early 1950s. Major sideline activities are logging, silversmithing and charcoal making. The best known product of the Bonans is the Bonan knife, which enjoys considerable popularity in wide parts of Gansu and Qinghai provinces. It is made of either brass or copper, with artistically carved bone handles. In 1949 there were 100 persons in the three Bonan villages making this knife; by 1973 more than 500 artisans were producing some 30 different varieties.

Starting in the 1950s, the Bonans have cooperated with the Salars of Xunhua in planting trees on the slopes of Jishi Mountain that separates these two nationalities. Industry is relatively little developed in the Bonan villages, the most notable evidence being repair shops for farm implements. A 60-mile all-weather highway connects Dahejia with Linxia.

BIBLIOGRAPHY

Books

"Bonan zu." In *Zhongguo shaoshu minzu*. Beijing: Renmin chubanshe, 1981.
Bonan zu jianshi jianzhi hebian. Beijing: Renmin chubanshe, 1963.
Todaeva, Bulyash Khoichievna. *Baoan'skii yazyk*. Moscow: Nauka, 1964.

Articles

Todaeva, Bulyash Khoichievna. "Einige Besonderheiten der Paoan-Sprache." *Acta Orientalia Hungaricae* 16 (1963): 175–197.

Henry G. Schwarz

BONERATE   Egalitarianism between sexes, particularly husband and wife, is a striking feature of the Muslim peoples of Bonerate, a small island in the Sea of Flores, Indonesia. Neither sex is confined to the household; both participate generally in the same economic and family tasks; inheritance is equal between sons and daughters; divorce is rare.

Bonerate belongs to the Kabupaten ("district") Selayer in the province of South Sulawesi. Its total population is approximately 5,400, which includes people of various origins and affiliations. The largest ethnic group is the Bonerate, who are regarded as the descendants of the original population and early Butonese immigrants (see Butonese). They call themselves Orang Bonerate and are referred to by the same term by their neighbors. Other ethnic groups represented on the island are Bajau, Bugis, Butonese and Selayarese. Religions other than Islam are not found on Bonerate. Ethnic relations are marked by the absence of firm boundaries and show a high level of integration.

The Bonerate language is spoken in all villages and is the language of local market communication. All over South Sulawesi, different languages have been in prolonged and often intimate contact with each other. This makes the decision as to what is a dialect and what is a language difficult. Detailed linguistic research or classifications of the variations in verbal communicative systems in this part of Indonesia have not been carried out. The reference to a Bonerate "language" is based on the knowledge that the tongues spoken on the neighboring islands and Bonerate are not mutually understandable. This does not mean, however, that the inhabitants of the different islands always are unable to communicate verbally. First, Bonerate individuals master more than the local "language," being bi- and even trilingual. Second, a significant number of the islanders have some knowledge of Bahasa Indonesia (the national language). Generally, more men than women understand and are able to speak Bahasa Indonesia, largely due to the greater mobility of men, who often visit distant islands and harbors, mostly as sailors. Intermarriage between inhabitants of the different islands is common, exposing women as well as men to languages other than their mother tongue. Also schools are gradually being established in the smaller villages on Bonerate; because most teaching is in Bahasa Indonesia, this language will probably take over as the lingua franca, and more women will master it. According to Bonerate people, their language shares many similarities both Butonese, while several of their neighboring islanders speak a Makassarese/Bugis language which locally is called the Selayar language. Bonerate language has been included with the Muna-Butung group (see Butonese).

Bonerate, meaning "Flat Sands," has two minor hills, the highest of which reaches less than 600 feet above sea level. The island, formed from corals, is almost circular in shape, fringed by extensive reefs, and is approximately 27 square miles. The soils are of poor quality, in most places no more than 12 inches deep. Where fields are cleared, seeds are sown between coral-limestones, which pierce the soil everywhere and cannot be removed. There are no rivers or creeks, and water is a scarce resource during the dry season. Due to ocean breezes and the shallow soils, the island is soon arid in the dry season. Water for human consumption is fetched from village wells. During the dry season, the water is often of poor quality and brackish.

Bonerate has nine villages (*kampung*); six of them are located close to the shore, three are inland. Most houses have bamboo walls and thatched roofs and are built on piles. The size is highly variable from small, one-room all-thatch huts to houses with a veranda, bedrooms and a separate firehouse/kitchen. Formerly, Bonerate economy was based on trading, slaving and piracy. There are indices pointing to the probability that the island was never able to feed a large population solely from domestic resources. Today, most men of the age group 16–30 years are absent from 6 to 10 months yearly while they are involved as *prahu* crews in the trade between the Moluccas and Java. To their neighbors Bonerate men are noted sailors and *prahu* builders. Because of the lack of suitable wood on Bonerate, material for shipbuilding is brought from the neighboring island of Lambego.

Bonerate islanders regard themselves first of all as agriculturalists. They practice a system of slash and burn agriculture. Due to the lack of water, only one crop per year is possible. Primary forest is absent from Bonerate; secondary forest, in some instances, and bushland, in most cases, are cleared in the preparation of swiddens. Fields are usually cultivated for up to three years and then lie fallow from six to ten years. The technological level is low; a *parang* (long-bladed knife) and a digging/weeding iron rod are the only agricultural implements in use. Corn is the staple crop, backed by cassava, which is exported. In addition pumpkins, watermelons and such vegetables as peas and beans are grown. Some fruits, such as bananas, papaya, breadfruit, lemons and coconuts, are grown for local consumption. Domesticated animals are few but include some goats, ducks, hens, dogs and cats. Most animal proteins in the diet derive from fishing and the gathering of other marine animals such as worms and mollusks. In spite of the richness of sea fauna, fishing is clearly second to agriculture in importance. The gathering of marine resources is carried out in what spare time is left after agricultural labor is completed. That is during nights or during the hottest hours of the day, when the villagers find it too exhausting to work in the fields. This holds true also for the people dwelling in the coastal villages. Thus, fish as food is a scarce item.

The Bonerate kinship system is clearly bilateral. Kin terms are the same whether the linking relative is one's mother or father. It is a generational system; all members of each generation are grouped terminologically. In the generation of ego, relative age and a distinction between siblings and cousins is emphasized. Thus, elder siblings are referred to as *ikaka* and younger as *yaisu*. Gender is marked by adding the suffix *moane* (male) or *vovine* (female). Parallel and cross cousins are named *sapisa*. In the parent generation *ina* (mother) and *ama* father are identified; all other members of that generation are *tuha*, with the exception of the in-laws, who are *davo*. Grandparents and grandchildren are named *ompu*. One's children are *anak*. In everyday encounters, however, parents are referred to with teknonymic terms by the name of the eldest son.

Bonerate culture can be described as matrifocal. In everyday life, the relative egalitarianism between the sexes is striking, and this is particularly visible in the husband-wife relationship. Children are tended to by both father and mother, or by brothers and sisters and by more distant relatives and neighbors. Husband and wife cooperate in most agricultural work. The gathering of seashore animals for consumption is also an activity in which all members of the household participate. Fishing, however, is generally an all-male occupation.

In case of inheritance, Bonerate sons and daughters receive equal shares; the only exception is that the youngest daughter (or the youngest son in case there is no daughter) inherits the house and all household equipment. Social rank is traced through women; a man cannot marry a woman of significantly higher socioeconomic status than himself. Polygyny is a restricted possibility by local cultural standards. There is very little divorce.

According to official records, Bonerate is all Sunni Muslim, and the islanders confirm this verbally. Four islanders were *hajjis* in 1978. All villages have a mosque, but with the exception of the month of Ramadan, these are poorly frequented. Islam touches individuals in many aspects of life. Life-cycle rituals such as the first haircutting, circumcision of both girls and boys, marriage and death are not complete without Quranic readings. *Imams* are, however, only present in the largest village. In the other villages, it is the privilege of elder men to read from the Quran. Most of them are not able to understand Arabic and thus do not know the meaning of the text they read.

Traditional beliefs are also an integral part of the religion of most Bonerate villagers. Offerings are presented at irregular intervals at small altars to provide good crops and good health and to thank spirits for good fortune. The altars are built of bamboo to form a simple grate which is hung in a tiny rope from a twig stuck into the ground. Altars are usually placed below large trees or facing the sea on the beach. The offerings are called *pakande*, which is the Bonerate term for food or a small meal. *Pakande* in this context consist of some boiled rice, one or two cigarettes, and water placed in a small bamboo tube attached to the grate. When offerings are made, a small fire is lit under the grate to make smoke sift through it. Beliefs in spirits are also demonstrated at various life crisis such as at birth and when people are severely sick. On special occasions, a possession ritual is arranged. Today this ritual has many characteristics of being public entertainment.

War dances and *joget* (a dance where women and men dance together without touching each other) are popular entertainments in the largest villages. These dances are, however, only for the descendants of nobles and other high-ranking people such as civil servants and military personnel. In earlier times, Bonerate had a stratified society with sharply defined classes: kings, queens and their descendants; nobility; commoners; and slaves. Today, this social division is of almost no importance in everyday interaction.

Village life is usually monotonous, with hard work and very little festivity. The villagers do know about the outside world. Several of the men have visited distant ports as sailors. In spite of this, Bonerate is a relatively backward island, even on an Indonesian scale. The villagers have little interest in what happens at other places, and communications are poor. Bonerate is in many ways a forgotten island; that is a feeling many of the islanders share. They know about artificial fertilizers and insecticides. Some have seen modern fishing technology in use; they know it is possible to provide adequate drinking water, and they long for better health services. But they have little faith in the prospects of a better livelihood. An island so poor in resources would probably never be chosen for development. Agricultural potentials seem indeed limited. The ocean is rich in fish, but the neighboring Bajau people are more experienced fishermen (see Bajau). Sea trade is being modernized in Indonesia, but Bonerate is too isolated; there are no decent harbors. The people lack the capital needed to build motor vessels in order to replace their *prahus*, which are powered by wind alone.

Harald Beyer Broch

BOSNIANS   "Bosnian (or Bosnian-Hercegovinian) Muslim" is synonymous with "Serbo-Croatian-speaking Muslim," the former term giving emphasis to the area where most live and the latter to the language that distinguishes them from all other Muslims. Colloquially, they refer to themselves simply as Muslim (Muslimani), and in the Yugoslav census they are categorized as "Muslims in the ethnic sense" (*Muslimani u smislu narodnosti*). Some Christian Yugoslavs, particularly in the villages and small towns of ethnically mixed regions, will refer to them incorrectly and pejoratively as Turks (Turci), but they should not be confused with the ethnic Turkish minority also living in Yugoslavia (see Turks, Rumelian).

According to the 1971 census, there were 1.7 million Serbo-Croatian-speaking Muslims in Yugoslavia, or some 8 percent of the total Yugoslav population (in 1983, this percentage would give 1.8 million). These live mostly (86 percent) in Bosnia-Hercegovina, one of the six republics of post-World War II Yugoslavia. Serbo-Croatian-speaking Muslims comprise 40 percent of the population within Bosnia-Hercegovina, with a mixture of Serbs (37 percent) and Croats (21 percent) constituting nearly all of the remainder. All three groups speak Serbo-Croatian (albeit distinct dialects), and the primary criterion of ethnic differentiation is religion, the Croats being Catholic and the Serbs Orthodox. Nearly all of the remaining Serbo-Croatian-speaking Muslims live in adjacent republics of Serbia (9 percent of all Serbo-Croatian-speaking Muslims in Yugoslavia) or Montenegro (4 percent). In addition to those still residing in Yugoslavia, there is also a large number, estimated at several hundred thousand, who emigrated to Turkey in successive waves as Bosnia-Hercegovina was occupied (1878), then annexed (1908) by the Austro-Hungarian Empire, again when it became part of the newly formed Yugoslavia following World War I, and still again when the Communist regime came to power after World War II. In the modern Turkish context they are known, as they were in the Ottoman Empire, as Boşnak. Another smaller immigrant community resides in the United States, chiefly in the Chicago area, where they maintain their own mosque. Of an estimated 4.4 million Bosnians in the world, perhaps 2.2 million are Muslims.

The ethnogenesis of the Bosnian Muslims took place after first the Bosnian Kingdom (1463) and then the Hercegovinian Duchy (1483) fell to the Ottoman Empire. Over the following 400-year period that the Ottomans ruled Bosnia and Hercegovina, there were wholesale conversions to Islam, unlike any other area of Ottoman Europe except Albania (see Albanians). The origin of these converts is still subject to debate. The traditional view is that the aristocracy of the medieval Bosnian and Hercegovinian states converted in order to preserve its economic and political superiority under the new regime and that the Bogomils, a heretical sect once important in the area, converted en masse in reaction to previous excesses of Catholicism. These views have now been seriously questioned, including whether the heretical sect present in Bosnia-Hercegovina even was the Bogomils. Nor is there conclusive evidence that the converts were predominantly either Serb or Croat. The Bosnian Muslims had their origins in a combination of all these groups, plus smaller numbers of Slavicized Muslim immigrants from elsewhere in the Ottoman Empire.

It is clear that Bosnian Muslim ethnogenesis was both a complex and a gradual process. There was no forcible conversion (except for the child levy, or *devširme*), but a variety of factors created a situation favorable to conversion. Chief among these were the various advantages afforded Muslims within the Ottoman Empire and a tradition of shifting religious allegiances in pre-Ottoman Bosnia-Hercegovina. The development of Bosnian towns as Ottoman centers and the influence of these on the adjacent peasantry created points from which Islam, as well as other Middle Eastern culture traits, could effectively be diffused.

The situation which developed in Bosnia-Hercegovina as a result of the Turkish conquest was unique in the Balkans. The ruling landowners were indigenous but Islamized Slavic speakers, known as begs and agas. This class tended to be even more conservative than the Turks themselves and were frequently in contest with the centralized power at Constantinople. Beneath the wealthy landowning class were serfs who were predominantly Christian, although they included some Muslims as well. The free peasantry that existed alongside the serfs was predominantly Muslim, most having been given this status at the price of conversion. Reliable figures are unknown for the Turkish period itself, but at the time of the Austrian annexation in 1878, there were in Bosnia-Hercegovina 6,000–7,000 begs and agas in control of some 85,000 serfs. Of the latter, 60,000 were Serbs, 23,000 were Croats, and about 2,000 were Muslim. In addition, there were nearly 77,000 free peasants, nearly all of whom were Muslim.

The demographic patterns established during the Ottoman period persist today in their essential features. Throughout the period, cities and towns were overwhelmingly Muslim. Although much less true than formerly, urban and regional centers of Bosnia-Hercegovina are still disproportionately Muslim. The countryside is populated by all of the three major ethnic groups. Although some regions are largely Muslim and Serb or Muslim and Croat, the pattern is highly irregular, and in many parts of Bosnia-Hercegovina the population includes all three of the major ethnic groups. Villages are most often ethnically homogeneous, although mixed villages are not uncommon. In the latter case, ethnic groups are usually segregated into distinct neighborhoods or hamlets. Ethnic segregation is also characteristic of traditional areas in cities and towns.

In the rural sector, there is little economic differentiation between Muslims and Serbs or Croats. Apart from eschewing pigs and plum brandy (the national drink of Yugoslav Christians), Muslim peasants tend to gain their subsistence in the same manner, from the same crops and livestock, using the same tools and methods, as Christian peasants in nearby villages. The most characteristic pattern is a combination of grain agriculture and livestock herding, especially sheep, with the latter growing in relative importance in higher and less fertile regions. In western and southern portions of Bosnia-Hercegovina, some Muslims are totally engaged in the transhumant herding of sheep. Serbo-Croatian-speaking Muslims constitute a large proportion of urban and market town craftsmen. Locally, particular traditional crafts (e.g., ceramics, woodworking, barrelmaking, wool fulling, milling, sandal making) may be exclusively in their hands, although this ethnic dominance does not necessarily extend to other regions. The descendants of the landowning Muslim aristocracy, because of their greater access to education in the recent past, are today often found among the professions or governmental bureaucracies.

Serbo-Croatian-speaking Muslims are universally Sunni. Religious doctrine and practice are closely patterned after the Turkish model. Mosques and other

Islamic institutions, excluding the Islamic legal system, are tolerated by the post-World War II Communist government. Islamic schools are permitted but may not substitute for compulsory secular education.

Although religious affiliation defines the ethnic boundary between Bosnian Muslims, Serbs and Croats, each group is also set off by a distinct subculture unrelated to its religious beliefs and practices. This differentiation is especially pronounced in the expressive dimensions of culture such as costume, home furnishings, folk song and dance, cuisine and dialect. Some Islamic traits have persisted longer in Bosnia-Hercegovina than in Anatolia whence they were derived. Thus, Bosnian Muslim women wore the veil until it was banned in 1950, and traditional Bosnian Muslim men still wear the fez, both of which were prohibited in Turkey in 1922. Many of the cultural differences between ethnic groups in Bosnia-Hercegovina consist of relatively minor variants of a general regional subculture. In a different valley or another sector of the province, the set of ethnic variants may vary considerably. Although such differences between ethnic groups may be objectively small, they are highly significant socially, both as focal points of ingroup identity and criteria of outgroup identification.

Forms of social organization among the Bosnian Muslims are in many respects a combination of traits found among Bosnian Christians and among Muslims of the Middle Eastern core area. Thus, Muslim women traditionally enjoyed a status somewhat below women in Bosnian Christian communities but still decidedly better than women of many Middle Eastern Muslim communities. This has improved even further under the post-World War II government. Polygyny, now forbidden by law, was always extremely rare among Muslim peasants of Bosnia-Hercegovina, although a few cases (established prior to the law prohibiting them) still remain in the more heavily Islamized regions. Like other ethnic groups of the central Balkans, the traditional peasant household was of the patrilocally extended type known in the ethnographic literature as the *zadruga*. Often these spanned several different generations, including all patrilineal collaterals, and could range in size up to 90 or 100 members.

The Bosnian Muslim peasantry is strictly endogamous. Those few marriages contracted outside the group are nearly always to other Muslim Yugoslavs, usually Albanians or Gypsies (see Gypsies). Marriage to other than Muslims is slightly more common in the urban sector, especially in the period immediately following World War II (a time of strong pan-Yugoslav sentiment) and among intellectuals and the politically active. Muslim emphasis on patrilineal affiliation and genealogy is much less pronounced than among Bosnian Christians, especially Serbs. Similarly, fictive kinship is much less prevalent and has considerably less importance among Bosnian Muslims. The only socially significant form is based on sponsorship of the first haircut of a male child. This is used primarily to establish relations across ethnic lines. Christians almost never practice this other than with Muslims, although other forms based on sponsorship of baptisms and weddings are highly significant. Affinal relations establish the primary social links between members of different Muslim communities, achieving even greater significance (in lieu of emphasis on patrilineal and fictive kinship) than among Bosnian Christians. Preferred marriage of one's father's brother's daughter was never practiced, except in the past among some of the land-owning aristocracy.

In ideological culture, as in social organization and material culture, Bosnian Muslims exhibit a combination of Middle East Islamic and European Christian traits. As in other aspects of Bosnian Muslim culture, this is not so much intermediate to the two as a fusion, drawing freely on both but creating a new and unique Bosnian Muslim pattern. Two themes of particular significance are *sudbina* (fate, often interpreted as submission to the will of God) and *sevdah* (romantic or melancholy love). These are readily seen in both the fine arts, especially literature, and folk creation. They are particularly typical of the *sevdalinka*, an urban folk song form that is uniquely Bosnian Muslim. Bosnian Serbs and Croats exhibit these same values, less so than Bosnian Muslims but more so than Serbs and Croats outside Bosnia.

BIBLIOGRAPHY

Books

Bresloff, Leon M. "Economic Adaptation and Development of Family Types in a Bosnian Town." In *Essays in Balkan Ethnology*, edited by William G. Lockwood. Berkeley: Kroeber Anthropological Society, 1967.

Djurdjev, Branislav. "Bosna." In *Encyclopedia of Islam*, edited by H.A.R. Gibb, et al. Vol. 1. London: Luzac, 1960.

Donia, Robert. *Islam Under the Double Eagle*. New York: Columbia University Press, 1981.

Donia, Robert, and Lockwood, William. "The Bosnian Muslims: Class, Ethnicity, and Political Behavior in an European State." In *Muslim-Christian Conflict: Economic, Political and Social Origins*, edited by Suad Joseph and Barbara L. K. Pillsbury. Boulder, Colo.: Westview Press, 1978.

Erlich, Vera. *Family in Transition: A Study of 300 Yugoslav Villages*. Princeton: Princeton University Press, 1966.

Lockwood, William G. "Bosnian Muslims." In *Harvard Encyclopedia of American Ethnic Groups*, edited by Stephen Thernstrom. Cambridge: Harvard University Press, 1980.

————. *European Moslems: Economy and Ethnicity in Western Bosnia*. New York: Academic Press, 1975.

————. "Living Legacy of the Ottoman Empire: Serbo-Croatian Speaking Moslems of Bosnia-Hercegovina. In *Mutual Effects of the Islamic and Judeo-Christian Worlds: The East European Pattern*, edited by A. Ascher; F. Halasi-Kun; and B. K. Kiraly. New York: Burt Franklin Press, 1979.

————. "Religion and Language as Criteria of Ethnic Identity: An Exploratory Comparison." In *Ethnicity and Nationality in Eastern Europe*, edited by John W. Cole and Sam Beck. Amsterdam: University of Amsterdam, 1981.

Lockwood, Yvonne R. *Text and Context: Folksong in a Bosnian Muslim Village*. Co-
    lumbus, Ohio: Slavica, 1983.
Vucinich, Wayne S. "Yugoslavs of the Moslem Faith." In *Yugoslavia*, edited by Robert
    J. Kerner. Berkeley: University of California Press, 1949.

Articles

Balić, Smail. "Eastern Europe: The Islamic Dimensions." *Journal of the Institute of
    Muslim Minority Affairs* 1:1 (1979): 29–37.
Lockwood, William G. "Bride Theft and Social Maneuverability in Western Bosnia."
    Anthropological Quarterly 47 (1974): 253–261.
————. "Converts and Consanguinity: The Social Organization of Moslem Slavs in
    Western Bosnia." *Ethnology* 11 (1972): 55–79.
————. "The Peasant Worker in Yugoslavia." *Studies in European Society* 1 (1973):
    91–110.
————. "Social Status and Cultural Change in a Bosnian Moslem Village." *Eastern
    European Quarterly* 9 (1975): 123–134.
Matley, Ian M. "Transhumance in Bosnia and Herzegovina." *Geographical Review* 58:2
    (1968): 231–261.
Smajlović, Ahmed. "Muslims in Yugoslavia." *Journal of the Institute of Muslim Minority
    Affairs* 2:1 (1980): 132–144.

William G. Lockwood

BRAHUI   The Brahui are a group of tribes distinguished linguistically from
neighboring Indo-Iranian-speaking Pushtun and Baluch by their Dravidian language. Their presence in South Asia, separated by more than 1,000 miles from
the Dravidian tongues of south India, has long been a puzzle to linguists. The
Brahui homeland is Kalat, a district of Pakistan, where 861,000 persons claim
Brahui as their mother tongue. An additional 18,000 Brahui speakers reside in
Afghanistan. Brahuis are overwhelmingly Sunni Muslims, but sectarianism is
not emphasized.

Kalat, an area of some 30,000 square miles, is divided into the highlands of
Sarawan and Jhalawan and the lowland plain of Kachhi. There are two distinct
ecological zones based on altitude, and Brahui settlement types range from fully
settled villages dependent on *qanat* underground waterway irrigation, through
transhumant villages pursuing a mixed economy based on cultivation and animal
husbandry, to pastoral nomadic camps. For the past 100 years or so the numbers
of Brahui engaged in pastoral nomadism have consistently declined. In Sarawan
especially, the majority of tribesmen have shifted to a transhumant economy, a
pattern in which highland cultivating villages are occupied for nine months of
the year. During the winter, transhumants migrate with their animals to Kachhi,
where they live in tent camps. With the recent introduction of machines for
irrigation, many transhumant villages are abandoning the winter migration, and
animal holdings are declining.

The Muslim preference for endogamous marriage, especially with father's brother's daughter, is found among the Brahui. Marriages are arranged, but the preferences of the couple are taken into consideration. Men can take multiple wives, but the expenses attendant on marriage tend to limit this practice. Divorce is rare. The ideal family form is the patrilineal extended household, married sons remaining with the parents. At the father's death, brothers should continue to live together, maintaining the undivided family estate under the direction of the eldest son. In fact, extended families based on the sibling link are rare. The desire of younger sons to head households, retaining their own sons after marriage, leads to division of the estate. Extended families are more common among transhumants and fully settled villagers. Elementary families consisting of parents and their offspring predominate among nomadic Brahui.

The basic unit of Brahui political organization is the tribe, membership in which is based on patrilineal descent and political allegiance. The two criteria of membership need not coincide. There is no Brahui tribe with a unified, coherent genealogy. Each tribe is conceived of as having been founded by a man, often an emigrant to Kalat, who gave his name to the group. The tribal unit is divided into a varying number of primary, secondary and tertiary sections, down to the lineage. Although the tribal charter is presented in a genealogical idiom, the primary sections often retain beliefs of separate origin. Groups of Pushtun and Baluch have been absorbed into Brahui tribal units, and sections have shifted from one tribe to another. The alignment of the political bond with genealogical ideology is expressed in the concept of *shad-i-gham* (joy and sorrow). The term is used to indicate the obligation to share joy and sorrow at all levels of society from the life crises of the family to the collective defense of tribal honor.

Each tribal unit has a hereditary authoritarian chief (*sardar*), who, prior to the national state, had the right to collect taxes and to make binding decisions when mediating disputes. Leadership at lower levels is relatively underdeveloped. Each primary section has a hereditary leader (*takkri*). Local communities have prominent men, many of whom have a favored relationship with the *sardar*. These individuals cannot issue authoritative commands or initiate binding mediation.

Until the independence of Pakistan in 1947, Brahui tribes were loosely united in a confederacy under the Ahmadzais, a ruling dynasty which established itself in the late seventeenth or early eighteenth century. The origins of the Brahui confederacy were obscure, but evidence suggests that the need for stable access to winter grazing areas in Kachhi was a precipitating factor, the Brahui being largely nomadic at that time. The confederacy was essentially limited to military activities. It never succeeded in suppressing conflicts among the tribes, nor did it collect taxes from them.

In the nineteenth century the British, concerned about Russian expansion in Central Asia, established a formal relationship with the Khan of the Ahmadzais.

In return for the right to a permanent military presence in Kalat and to control foreign relations, the British paid annual subsidies to the Khan and the chiefs. A railway, telegraph and roads were constructed, linking Kalat with the empire. Internally, however, the khanate continued to function in traditional ways.

The Brahui were isolated from the independence movement, and the Khan evidenced considerable reluctance to join the new nation of Pakistan. Party politics, weakly developed in all Pakistan, were virtually nonexistent in Kalat. The Khan finally signed the Instruments of Accession in 1948, and the period since then has been one of increasing national integration, although the process has been slow and is by no means complete.

The problem of national penetration and replacement of tribal governance is exacerbated by the fact that there are no cities in Kalat. There are several towns which serve as administrative and commercial centers, but very few Brahui are town dwellers. During the period from 1950 to 1970, the national government concentrated on establishing a network of services based on the towns; these had a minimal effect on the rural and nomadic population. Tribesmen continued to depend on their *sardars*. The *sardars*, in turn, became middlemen, holding appointed or elected government offices at the national and local levels. They continued to collect traditional taxes and to provide administrative and mediation functions for their tribesmen.

Since 1970 the government has begun to extend services, such as primary schools and electrification, into the countryside. Increased literacy and more productive agricultural practices are likely to contribute to greater national integration.

BIBLIOGRAPHY

Books

Swidler, Nina. "Brahui Political Organization and the National State." In *Pakistan's Western Borderlands*, edited by Ainslie T. Embree. Durham: Carolina Academic Press, 1977.
———. "The Development of the Kalat Khanate." In *Perspectives on Nomadism*, edited by William Irons and Neville Dyson-Hudson. Leiden: Brill, 1972.
———. "Sedentarization and Modes of Economic Integration in the Middle East." In *When Nomads Settle*, edited by Philip Carl Salzman. New York: Praeger, 1980.
Swidler, Warren W. "Adaptive Processes Regulating Nomad-Sedentary Interaction in the Middle East." In *The Desert and the Sown*, edited by Cynthia Nelson. Berkeley: Institute of International Studies, University of California, 1973.
———. "Some Demographic Factors Regulating the Formation of Flock and Camps Among the Brahui of Baluchistan." In *Perspectives on Nomadism*, edited by William Irons and Neville Dyson-Hudson. Leiden: Brill, 1972.

Articles

Swidler, Nina. "The Political Context of Brahui Sedentarization." *Ethnology* 5:12 (1973): 299–315.

Unpublished Manuscripts

Swidler, Nina. "The Political Structure of a Tribal Federation: The Brahui of Baluchistan." Ph.D. dissertation, Columbia University, 1969.
Swidler, Warren W. "Changes in the Relationship Between Men and Herd Animals with Increasing Sedentarization in Baluchistan." Paper presented at the 8th annual meeting of the American Association for the Advancement of Science, Washington, D.C., December 26–30, 1966.
————. "Technology and Social Structure in Baluchistan, West Pakistan." Ph.D. dissertation, Columbia University, 1968.

Nina Swidler
Population figures updated by Richard V. Weekes

BUDUMA   One of the oldest and traditionally the most warlike group of inhabitants around the islands of Lake Chad are the Buduma, who call themselves and their language Yedina. Some of these islands they share with the Kuri (see Kuri). The word "Buduma" is of Kanembu origin and means either "grass" or "free." If the former, it describes the environment in which the people live—aquatic reeds and grasses, papyrus and floating islands. If the latter, it describes their independence from formal government to the extent of freedom to raid their neighbors for cattle, the basis of Buduma economy.

The Buduma call themselves Yedina because they believe they are descendants of Yed (or Yad), whose origin is unclear; Yed's ancestors were either Sao or Fulani. The Fulani hypothesis derives from the Buduma's concentration on stockbreeding and herding, the traditional occupation of the Fulani (see Fulani). One legend states that a son of a Fulani leader was black (Fulani have a reddish skin color) and was exiled to Sao country and put on a deserted island in Lake Chad. Buduma have never been known to enslave a Fulani.

The Sao hypothesis of Buduma origins, and the one most accepted, states that Ngaltekkeh, son of a slave (pre-Islamic) settled on a sand dune around Baga-Sola with his two sons, Nganai and Yed (sometimes called Bulu). Nganai left to visit Yemen. A few years later, thinking that Nganai was dead, Yed married his brother's wife, who soon produced a baby. Nganai returned and Yed fled to Tagel (Tigal) Island. One day he saw a gourd full of grass floating by; he jumped into it and was pushed by eastern winds until he ran aground in the country of the Sao, a physically enormous people. They welcomed him, he married a local girl, then left in a pirogue (boat), this time carried by a westerly wind. He and his wife disembarked on the island of Kuma, not far from the island of his brother, Nganai. Forgiving Yed, Nganai shared his herd and offered him four craftsmen; a potter, a blacksmith, a weaver and a hairdresser in order to help him begin life anew. From Yed thus came the Yedinas, or today's Buduma.

The Buduma carry forward a tradition of being a fiercely independent, insular people resistant to outside influence. They resisted incorporation into the Kanem-Bornu empire; indeed, they were a menace to the empire, carrying out violent raids on the cattle herds of the Kanembu, their neighbors in the north and west, the Kotoko to the south and the Arabs in the east. Always feared, the Buduma were considered villainous.

The Buduma today number approximately 49,000, nearly all of whom live in Chad. About 4,000 live in Niger and 3,000 in Nigeria. There are some 600 permanent villages with an average size of 60 families. Only the original villages on the highest islands contain solid houses similar to those of the Kanembu. Most Buduma live in temporary camps or settlements, where they build shelters out of branches on small permanent or floating islands. Because of the swarms of mosquitoes at night and prior to the introduction of mosquito nets, the Buduma slept in holes dug in the sand and covered with matting.

The Buduma are divided into four major and three minor lineages: the Guria (37 percent of the Buduma population), the Maibuloa (23 percent), the Budjia (22 percent) and the Madjigodjia (14 percent), plus the Ursawa, Siginda and Media. They live in six lake districts and along the rivers of Bornu. The Guria, the most important group, is headed by the Mehul clan in Yakua in the district of Bol. The Madjigodjia, strongly competitive with the Guria, live on the western islands of Bol and in the district of Tataverom. The Budjia hold the leadership of Tataverom but are also settled in Boso and Ngigmi. The Maibuloa are apparently the only legitimate descendants of the mythical ancestor, Yed or Bulu; one of the Maibuloa clans, the Riga, claims nobility since its members say they are descendants of the founding ancestor of the Buduma. Among all families and clans, there is a deep awareness of social structure of clan membership, which gives individuals higher or lower status.

For centuries the Buduma have lived outside the control of established government, ruling themselves through their chosen chiefs, the *katchella*, also called *kella* on the islands. The area was the scene of incessant tribal warfare, most notably between the Guri and the Madjigodjia, with the hegemony of the Guria eventually imposed on the rest.

Islam became the religion of the Buduma only after 1910, when French colonialism subdued their warlike behavior. Previously, the Buduma worshiped the god Kumani, founder of the world. He first created trees, then grass, then man, the only being in possession of reason, which, in some way, has led the Buduma to consider the eldest of the family stupid. Kumani lived only a few feet above the ground, so that it was forbidden to pound grain into flour with the usual long pestle for fear of striking him (Buduma use millstones to grind grain in contrast to the more common mortar-pestle pounding technique). Associated with the god Kumani were spirit cults with priests whose function was to keep the many spirits contented. Vestiges of spirit worship continues within the Islam practiced by the Buduma today.

The isolation of the Buduma from other major ethnic groups is apparent in their language, classified among the Chadian group of the Nilo-Saharan family, which includes Kotoko and Kanembu. The language has a limited vocabulary, especially among the central islands, and contains many loan words from Kanembu and Kanuri, particularly the names of domestic animals (except cattle), colors, locations and the numerals six and nine.

One of the most distinguishing characteristics of the Buduma is their facility to adapt themselves to the smallest variations of the level of Lake Chad. Their land territory, for grazing cattle and growing millet or corn, can vary by about 8,000 square miles in a few seasons as the lake rises and subsides. When it subsides, younger Buduma leave their protected highland villages and swim their cattle to new grazing grounds. Fishing is secondary at these times, being left to the lower economic and social status groups (who once were the slaves brought back from raiding expeditions). The older generations remain in the permanent villages, where they constitute the spiritual point of reference for the Buduma population and the sanctuary of traditions.

An example of this mobility was the drought of 1973, when the level of Lake Chad fell. The number of settlements in the district of Bol almost tripled as Buduma moved to new islands on which to graze their cattle.

When Lake Chad rises and grazing land diminishes, fishing becomes more important. By the time the lake rose significantly in 1956, Nigeria had become a lucrative market for smoked fish, *banda*, and Buduma took their papyrus pirogues and traded fish to earn money with which to purchase more cattle for the next lake subsidence, which indeed came in 1973.

Perhaps more than any other ethnic group in the region, the Buduma are the best-equipped people to adapt to natural disaster. Even in the worst of times, they are enterprising enough to exploit their advantages.

BIBLIOGRAPHY

Books

Bouquet, Christian, and Cabot, J. *Atlas pratique du Tchad*. Paris: I.G.N., 1971.
———. *Le Tchad*. Paris: P.U.F., 1973.
Carbou, H. *La Region du Tchad et du Ouaddai*. Paris: Leroux, 1912.
Chapelle, J. *Le Peuple tchadien*. Paris: L'Harmattan, 1981.
LeBeuf, A. *Les Populations du Tchad au nord du 10ème parallele*. Paris: P.U.F., 1959.
Le Rouvreur, A. *Saheliens et sahariens du Tchad*. Paris: Berger-Levrault, 1962.
Tilho, J. *Documents scientifiques de la mission Tilho*. 3 vols. Paris: Imprimerie Nationale, 1914.
Urvoy, Y. *Histoire de l'empire du Bornou*. Paris: Larose, 1949.

Zeltner, J.-C. *Pages d'histoire du Kanem*. Paris, L'Harmattan, 1980.

Christian Bouquet

BUGIS   One of the largest and best-known societies in Indonesia, the Bugis number more than 4 million and live in South Sulawesi Province. They share the area with some 2 million others, including, in descending order of size, the Makassarese (Muslims), Toraja (half Christian, half traditionalist) and the Mandar (Muslim). Bugis predominate in the center of the province and are a majority of the inhabitants of Pare-Pare, the second largest city and a major port. Ujung Pandang, the largest city and provincial capital, has a mixed Bugis and Makassarese population, and the regencies to the south are composed largely of the latter group (see Makassarese). While the northeast section of the province is the site of the oldest Bugis kingdom, Luwu, the rest of the northern regencies are inhabited by Sa'dan Toraja and Mandar peoples.

All Bugis speak a single language, Basa Ugi or Ogi, which has its own script. Bugis written works, called *lontara'*, number in the hundreds, making Bugis a significant world literary tradition. Historical treatments, didactic treatises, astrological calendars and personal diaries have been composed in the script, and most children continue to study the Bugis writing system from printed pamphlets in primary school. Command of the national language, Bahasa Indonesia, varies by age, status and degree of outside experience; older villagers are often unable to speak Indonesian fluently.

Certain aspects of Bugis society (rank, migration, historical *lontara'*) have been extensively studied by Dutch, French and American scholars, while other, less immediately striking aspects (kinship, ritual, esoteric *lontara'*) have received less attention.

Three salient features of Bugis society are its system of rank, organization by kingdom and prevalence of circular migration. These features together form a society which is both highly structured internally and extensively linked to surrounding areas.

Informants give several versions of the system of social rank, the versions reflecting the informants' own perspectives. Nobles will generally present rank as a list of titles, each defined by a subject's parents' ranks, using a patrilineally based logic of marriage combinations. One such list ranks *datu* as the highest possible rank, which can only be preserved through marriage with other persons of the same rank. The next title is that of *petta* (the highest rank now living in the Rappang district); such persons are often addressed with the title *andi'*. *Cera'* designates members of the next lower class, but the accompanying address term is *andi'*. *Puang* is both the name of and the address form for the next class. *Uwa* is a lower, less often found title. All other Bugis are, in this view, commoners (*tau sama*) and without a title.

Commoners, on the other hand, will tend to present rank not as a list of titles but as a set of classes, with the *tau sama* on the bottom. *Tau deceng* (or decent people) are the next highest class, including the descendants from noble-commoner mixed marriages. *Arung* designates the descendants of rulers (including anyone who could legitimately be addressed as *andi'*). The use of a particular title, in this view, is more the outcome of a successfully claimed close kin tie to a ruler's descent line than the result of a precise logic of hypergamous marriage.

In one noble's account of Bugis society, rank marks the directness of descent from the god Batara Guru, who descended to earth, and the correctness of the marriages that were contracted in each subsequent generation. In another such account, the present nobles descend from a later group of rulers, "the people who came down" (*tau manurung*) from the upperworld. In both accounts, rank is conceived of as Bugis-wide. Thus, an *arung* in one kingdom could be, and was, called to rule over another kingdom. Rank is still a salient social category for Bugis and underlies address forms, deference behavior and assignment of leadership roles and governmental positions.

Buginese polity before independence consisted of a number of villages and districts (*wanua*) grouped into kingdoms ruled by a Matoa or Arung. The largest kingdoms of Luwu', Wajo' and Bone entered in shifting alliances with each other, with smaller kingdoms (Soppeng, Sidenreng, Tanete and others) and with non-Buginese polities (primarily the Makassarese kingdom of Gowa and the Dutch). This political fluidity was made possible in part by a stratum of potential rulers held in common by all kingdoms.

Out of the political structure that developed in each of these kingdoms has come a particular political theory. Wajo' and Rappang nobles will describe the local polity as built "from the bottom up" through an association of *wanua*. Elsewhere (Sidenreng, for example), the right to rule derived from direct descent in a kingly *addatueng* line. Each of these theories about earlier political structure continues to be used as the basis for commentary on current political activity in the respective districts: people are more independent in one district, more likely to listen to powers-that-be in another. The tone of current political life varies from one district to the next along these axes.

The third salient feature of social life is the continual movement of individuals and families between their Bugis homeland and work sites in Sumatra, Kalimantan and Malaysia. At least from the late seventeenth century (and occasioned by both growing Dutch monopoly pressure and the Dutch-fueled, prolonged Gowa-Bone war) Bugis sailors roamed the seas. Less spectacularly, Bugis families began to migrate to other spots in the Malay world. Growing demands in the archipelago for Western goods led to a remarkable increase in the volume of Bugis ship (*prahu*) trade in the eighteenth century, and internal political squabbles in foreign states (notably Johor) were seized on by Bugis leaders, who subsequently became kingmakers to the Malay sultanates. As large rubber- and copra-producing estates increased their demand for cheap labor in the early 1900s, these *prahu* links to the outside world were used by land-poor Bugis (particularly of the Wajo' district) to begin cycles of circular migration to Borneo and the Malay peninsula. The Islamic rebellion of the 1950s drove additional numbers of Bugis out of the homeland, with many choosing to open up new rice-farming areas in southern Sumatra.

The pattern of both emigration and circular migration (leaving and returning again after several years' time) is itself shaped by the structure of Bugis society. First, Bugis of lower rank can obtain higher status (but not rank) within their community by gaining wealth and experience abroad. Second, migration prior to this century was often by high-ranking local leaders and large numbers of followers. Such migrants of high rank could both establish effective power bases elsewhere (as in Riau) and call for others to follow them from the homeland. In this century many middle-rank (*tau deceng*) people count among the emigrants, men who thereby hope to pull up their status in the community. These two features of migration—increased status and high-ranking overseas leaders—thus promote the reproduction of the cycle.

A Bugis village may consist of several discrete bilateral descent categories or of several kindred nodes, focused on a prominent member of the community and consisting of his kinsmen and affines. Marriages are often arranged by parents or grandparents of a couple with an eye to seeking a partner of equal rank and economic status for their child or grandchild. Marriages between close bilaterally reckoned cousins (ideally first cousins) are preferred in order to preserve the purity of blood, keep wealth within the descent line and minimize friction between the future in-laws.

A couple lives with the wife's parents immediately after marriage and usually for several years thereafter. Houses are usually inherited by daughters; land and other wealth is divided either following Islamic principles or equally among sons and daughters.

Rice is both the main subsistence crop and an important export from the Bugis districts. The central plains of Sidenreng-Rappang, Soppeng and Bone produce yields of two to four tons per acre, often for two seasons a year. Rice improvement programs have been relatively successful there. According to the 1980 census, 66 percent of South Sulawesi households engage in farming; among Bugis the percentage would probably be somewhat higher. Other major occupations are animal husbandry, trade and fishing. Bugis often work as day laborers in cities of Sulawesi and elsewhere in the archipelago.

Preparing wet rice land for planting is increasingly done with tractors, although some farmers use oxen. The timing of planting is (at least in theory) regulated by district-wide councils, which draw on the predictions of local calendrical/ agronomic authorities (*palontara'*) as well as the records of the farm bureau. Men and women work together to plant fields in rotating labor exchange groups. At harvest time workers travel from district to district, timing their arrival to the local agricultural cycle, and harvest fields for a fixed share of the yield. Men and women harvest together.

About one-third of farming households in South Sulawesi do not own sufficient land and must sharecrop on the fields of wealthier farmers, generally for one-half of the crop. This dependency, combined with irregular rainfall and a shortage of long-term alternative occupations, has contributed to out-migration.

Unlike the rather hazy histories of Islam elsewhere in Indonesia, in South Sulawesi Islamic conversion can be said to have begun with the official adoption of the religion by the king of Makassarese Gowa in 1605. Gowa proceeded to establish Islam by force over most of the Bugis area so that by 1611 the majority of Bugis were under the rule of a professed Muslim.

The characteristics of religion in the Bugis area can be grouped under three institutions: the village-based ritual complex, the *pesantren* (religious school) and the modernist Muhammadiya organization.

Village rituals range from small family meals held to commemorate a life-crisis point of transition to village-wide agricultural and thanksgiving rites. Many involve the offering of blood to guardian spirits or the making of vows to placate spirits who live in sacred village spots. A major rice ritual includes the reading of the Bugis origin story, La Galligo, the night before sowing seed. In this story, and in other accompanying rituals, various gods (*dewata*) are invoked. For some Muslim Bugis these *dewata* are integrated into a spiritual pantheon with Allah at its summit; this view is opposed by other *pesantren*-oriented commentators.

One small but well-known group of Bugis has retained what they call "the Bugis religion," called *toanni*. These people live primarily in Sidenreng-Rappang; some are registered as Muslims, the rest (more than 17,000) as "Hindu." This latter classification is an artifact of Indonesia's laws of religious classification, and this group in fact considers itself outside any of the world religions. Toanni beliefs focus on Batara Guru (the ancestor of the kings of Luwu'), Sangiassri (the rice deity) and Patotoe (God).

Pesantren schools in the Bugis area have been linked informally to the Nahdatul Ulama (NU) and the Darul Dakwah Wal-Israd, a Pare-Pare-based missionary organization that has built two universities in South Sulawesi. The *pesantren* preserve and propagate a traditional set of religious practices (longer *tarawih* prayer sessions, the *talqin* at death) which NU-leaning villagers follow. Instruction at some *pesantrens* now includes many secular topics and minimizes the use of Arabic explanatory texts.

Muhammadiya social and missionary activities in the Bugis area are concentrated on constructing hospitals and all levels of schools, including a university and several teacher training colleges. Its base is in the towns and cities and has stressed a purist reform (or rejection) of older, traditional practices. In particular, Muhammadiya teachers have sought to reduce the length of worship sessions, the size and number of rituals and the complexity of regulations regarding religious purity.

In the interstices of these organizations are several Sufi orders, notably Chalwatiyya and WAKTU, based on recitation of a *ratib* (the confession of faith).

In villages and cities alike, Bugis are known for their concern for *siri'*, a word which can mean both honor and shame. The greatest feelings of shame come from sexual transgressions (or even remarriage), and honor can be restored only by a violent retributive act. So central is this value to Bugis thought and conduct that a campaign was recently launched (perhaps in vain) on provincial television to convince listeners that *siri'* should be rethought as "human value" rather than "getting even." However, such retributions are still tightly bound with ideas of status, rank and honor/shame and together give shape to Bugis identity.

BIBLIOGRAPHY

Books

Andaya, Leonard Y. "The Nature of Kingship in Bone." In *Pre-Colonial State Systems in Southeast Asia*, edited by Anthony Reid and Lance Castle. Kuala Lumpur: Monographs of the Malaysian Branch of the Royal Asiatic Society, 1975.
Chabot, H. Th. "Bontoramba, A Village in Goa, Makassar." In *Villages in Indonesia*, edited by R. M. Koentjaraningrat. Ithaca: Cornell University Press, 1967.
Mattulada. "Pre-Islamic South Sulawesi." In *Dynamics of Indonesia History*, edited by H. Soebadio. Amsterdam: North-Holland, 1978.

Articles

Lineton, Jacqueline. "'Pasompe' Ugi': Bugis Migrants and Wanderers." *Archipel* 10 (1975): 173–201.
Makaliwe, W. H. "An Economic Survey of South Sulawesi." *Bulletin of Indonesian Economic Studies* 5:2 (1969): 17–36.

Unpublished Manuscript

Millar, Susan. "Bugis Society: Given by the Wedding Guest." Ph.D. dissertation, Cornell University, 1981.

John Bowen

BURMESE   Of the 1.4 million Muslims in Burma, about 36.5 percent, or 512,000, are essentially Burmese. The rest are, or are the descendants of, Indians, Arabs and Persians who formed the original nucleus of Muslims and came to Burma early in the history of Islam or who arrived during the British conquest, which sparked waves of Indian Muslim and Hindu immigration. A few are Chinese Muslims called Panthay or Huizui (see Hui).

Many Burmese Muslims are not pure Burmese, although they all speak Burmese. For no known etymological reason, they are called Zerbadees. They are sons or descendants of a variety of combinations of people: 1) Indian Muslim fathers and Burmese Buddhist mothers, whether or not they converted to Islam, 2) Indian Muslim fathers and Burmese Muslim mothers, 3) Burmese Muslim fathers and Burmese mothers who then converted to Islam, 4) Burmese Muslim mothers and Burmese fathers who converted to Islam (very rare), 5) Burmese Muslim fathers and mothers.

The term "Zerbadee" is not popular with the Muslims of Burma who are caught between their desire to preserve their separateness as Muslims, on the one hand, and their tendency to assimilate into Burmese society, on the other. "Burmese Muslims" is more acceptable to most Muslims in Burma. The governments of Burma have, at different times, variously classified the Muslims as Zerbadees, Arakan Muslims, Kamans and Myedu, all part of the "Burman-Indian races" or as "Burman Muslins," which includes all the Zerbadees plus Indian and native Burmese Muslims.

There are two groups of Burmese Muslims who are native to Burma. One is the native Burmese, who speak Burmese and reflect Burmese culture. The other is the Muslims of Arakan.

Arakan District, extending some 350 miles along the eastern shores of the Bay of Bengal, is cut off from Burma by a range of nearly impassable mountains which were an obstacle against permanent Muslim conquests but permitted occasional inroads and contacts between Bengal and Burma. The northern part of Arakan, the Mayu District, was the point of contact with East Bengal, the extreme eastern limit of Islamic overland expansion. As in Burma, so, too, in Arakan there is a long tradition of Indian settlement.

Among the Arakanese Muslims today are distinct groups, including the Myedu Kala or Kulabyo (*kala, kla, klu* being the Burmese term originally denoting Indians and, eventually, all Westerners; the term "Panthee" is usually used to denote all Muslims) and the Kamans, among others. Arakanese Muslims are Sunni despite the preponderance of some Shia traditions among them. They call themselves Rohinga or Roewengyah. In dress and, today, language they are undifferentiated from their Buddhist neighbors, although Arab, Indian, Bengali and even Persian cultural influence are still apparent in their art and music. The language once commonly spoken by the Arakanese Muslims, Rohinga, a mixture of Bengali, Urdu and native Arakanese elements, has been largely displaced by Burmese and Arakanese, a dialect of Burmese.

The Mayu district in northern Arakan, overwhelmingly Muslim, has been under separate frontier administration distinct from the rest of Arakan since 1961. This special status in deference to the Muslim character of the population came in the wake of the Mujahid rebellion, which raged sporadically and violently in Arakan between 1948 and 1961, on a background of social and economic tensions between Arakanese Muslims and Buddhists, reciprocal killings and population displacements.

Burmese Muslims, in contrast to Arakanese and Indian Muslims (who are concentrated in Rangoon and the center of the country), live in far-flung districts of Burma. They are rural, living mostly in villages, although a few Burmese Muslim communities are found in some towns and cities. Their main source of livelihood is agriculture.

The Islam of the Burmese Muslims is Sunni, which they practice in a lax rather than an orthodox manner. While some low-level religious leaders, like village *imams*, may be Burmese Muslims, usually Indian Muslims occupy religious leadership roles. Their juridical rite is Shafi.

The family system of the Burmese Muslims is patriarchal. They are generally monogamous and practice circumcision. Burmese Muslim women do not cover their faces with veils.

Generally speaking, Burmese Muslims enjoy cordial relations with the majority community of Burmese Buddhists, mainly because their way of life in all its aspects, including home customs, food, language, dress and appearance, is not distinct. However, in the years preceding Burmese independence in 1948, the leadership of the Burmese National Movement rejected the pleas of the Burmese Muslims for recognition as a distinct ethnic minority, similar to the status that was granted to other ethnic groups such as the Shans, Karens, Kachins and Chins.

Unlike Indian Muslims in Burma, Burmese Muslims have been slow to organize. Indian Muslims were organized as long ago as 1922, when they created a branch of the Indian Congress Party in Burma. Not until 1946 did Burmese Muslims in upper Burma organize by founding the Jamiyyat al-Ulama, Burma; two years later, the Indian and Burmese Muslims joined to form a single organization by the same name. Unity between the two groups was short-lived. They split in 1958 over personal rivalries as well as disagreements on matters of pro-Indian or pro-Burmese orientation.

Antagonisms between Indian and Burmese Muslims have prevented them from uniting into a single organization. However, they do cooperate in promoting celebrations of the Prophet's birthday (Maulud), which include mass rallies, essay contests, lectures and sermons in the mosques and other competitions, plus processions. They also cooperate in supporting the Dar al-Muin (Society for Welfare), which today confines itself to the problems of burial rites for Muslims, caring for the mausoleum of the last Moghul emperor, Saraj al-Din Bahadur Shah, and lobbying against Prime Minister U Nu's declaration making Buddhism the state religion, prior to General Ne-Win's military coup in 1962.

While personal relations between Muslims and Buddhist Burmese have generally been amicable, there have been times of strife. Tensions flared into violence in 1938 incited by economic disparities as well as religious contentions. Buddhists resented the increasing prominence of Indian Muslims in the British-controlled government and in business. They resented Muslim intermarriage with Burmese women because of the temporary nature of such marriages in which Indian Muslims returning to India abandoned their native wives. Not until 1953 did Burma pass a law which, over Muslim objections, gave women the right to divorce in the event they were abandoned. Since the 1962 revolution, after which all Muslim political activity was halted and emigration of Indians encouraged by the nationalization of all branches of the country's commerce, did overt rivalry between Muslims and Buddhists diminish.

BIBLIOGRAPHY

Books

Harvey, G. E. *British Rule in Burma: 1842–1942*. London: Faber and Faber, 1946.
Yegar, Moshe. *The Muslims of Burma. A Study of a Minority Group*. Wiesbaden: Harrassowitz, 1972.
———. "The Muslims of Burma." in *Crescent in the East: Islam in Asia Minor*, edited by Raphael Israeli. London: Curzon Press, 1982.

Articles

Collis, M. S., and Bu, San Shwe. "Arakan's Place in the Civilization of the Bay: A Study of Coinage and Foreign Relations." *Journal of the Burma Research Society* 15:1 (1925): 39–43.
Harvey, G. E. "The Fate of Shah Shuja, 1661." *Journal of the Burma Research Society* 12 (1922): 107–112.
Khin Khin U. "Marriage in the Burmese Muslim Community." *Journal of the Burma Research Society* 36 (1954): 24–33.
Khin Maung Kyi. "The Mujahid Story." *Guardian Monthly* (Rangoon) 2 (1955): 38–40.
Gaffari, Maung Ko. "The First Muslim Community of Rangoon: Arakanese Muslims' Part in Defence of British Invasion." *Guardian Monthly* 7 (1960): 45.
Thaung, Dr. "Panthay Interlude in Yunnan: A Study in Vicissitudes Through the Burmese Kaleidoscope." *Burma Research Society, Fiftieth Anniversary Publication* (Rangoon) 1 (1961): 473–478.
Yegar, Moshe. "The Muslims of Burma Since Independence." *Asian and African Studies, Annual of the Israel Oriental Society* (Jerusalem) 2 (1966): 159–205.
———. "The 'Panthay' of Burma and Yunnan." *Journal of Southeast Asian History* (Singapore) 7 (1966): 73–85.

Moshe Yegar

BURUSHO   The towering, silver-gray peaks of the Karakorum and Hindu Kush ranges dominate the arid highland of northeastern Pakistan. Here, in a sharply cleft valley that skirts the base of the 25,550-foot Mount Rakaposhi, reside the Burusho, a Muslim people of distinct language and culture. Their oasis-like settlements spread along the slopes overlooking the mid-section of the Hunza River and the southern banks of the tributary Nagar River at altitudes of 6,500 to 10,500 feet. In this, their home country, the Burusho number approximately 60,000; perhaps 10,000 more have moved south to Gilgit, the administrative and marketing center of the northern mountain region, and to its nearby agricultural colonies established since the 1930s.

The neighbors of the Burusho on one side, occupying the upper or northern reaches of the Hunza River valley, are the agro-pastoral Wakhi, speakers of an Iranian language of the same name. On the other side, occupying the lower reaches of the valley, are the predominantly agricultural Shin, speakers of Shina, one of the so-called Dardic group of Indic languages (see Shina-speaking Peoples). Living amidst the Burusho in separate, endogamous communities are small numbers of the low-status Dom—musicians, artisans and small farmers—who speak Dumaki, a little-known Indic language (see Baltis).

Burushaski, the language of the Burusho, exhibits Iranian influences but as yet remains unclassified and is, like the other languages of the area, unwritten. Formerly, the Burusho were the dominant groupings in the twin kingdoms of Hunza and Nagar, which controlled the right and left banks of the Hunza and Nagar rivers, respectively, with Hunza encompassing all Wakhi lands to the north. While the Burusho are often referred to as the Hunzakuts or Nagarkuts, these terms, meaning the "people of Hunza" and the "people of Nagar," are applicable to the Shin, Wakhi and Dom populations of these kingdoms as well.

For most of their recorded past, Hunza and Nagar paid token allegiance to the ruling powers of Chinese Turkestan and Kahmir, while retaining effective political autonomy and independent military capabilities. The two states intermittently engaged in warfare over territory and raided the caravans travelling the Silk Route along their northern frontiers. In 1891, they were defeated and occupied by a British-led expeditionary force in a move designed to preempt Russian and Chinese expansion. Subsequently, under the dominion of the colonial government, Hunza and Nagar enjoyed much the same status as did the other princely states of the subcontinent. Both states were abolished and their *mirs* (rulers) retired on pensions by 1974. Today, they form separate administrative subdivisions of Gilgit, one of three districts in the federally governed Northern Areas Province.

Severe ecological constraints impinge upon Burusho social and economic organization. The Hunza and Nagar valleys, and adjoining regions, are a barren, dessicated environment. Precipitation averages about six inches per year. The terrain is extremely rugged, steeply inclined and, for the most part, devoid of all vegetation save low desert scrub. Settlements are found on spurs and ridges, wherever land can be levelled or terraced. Because the two rivers run far below, little if any use is made of them. Instead, habituation depends on water borne to each settlement on winding aqueducts from springs and melting glaciers often located several miles away. The major canals of Hunza and Nagar represent monumental feats of engineering, and the construction of each marks an epoch in local social history.

The Burusho are primarily subsistence farmers specializing in the cultivation of wheat and also barley, buckwheat, millet, potatoes (a post-conquest introduction) and a variety of vegetables. Apricots, prepared in diverse ways, are another staple of their low protein diet. In addition, they keep some livestock, mainly sheep, goats and small-sized cattle, primarily for milk products, wool and traction. On the edges of their fields and irrigable slopes they grow trees for fruit, wood, nuts and leaf fodder. Viticulture for wine making, until recently considered a prestige avocation, remains an important sideline, despite new official prohibitions.

Among readers of popular "health food" literature in the West and Japan, the Burusho are famous for their supposed vegetarianism, extraordinary good health and long age spans. In fact, most Burusho relish meat and strive to achieve living standards at which they can consume more of it. They are no less subject than are other local peoples to diseases common to the region, and they suffer an especially high incidence of tuberculosis, staph infections, cataracts and various types of dysentery. Rates of infant mortality and survival to old age are comparable to those of populations found in similar economic-ecological circumstances. Indeed, the rate of female infant mortality is thought to be higher than most, due to differentials in care and nutrition.

The economic ideal is to be self-sufficient through farming and the occasional sale of fruit, wood and livestock for cash. Virtually all households attempt to meet their basic needs in this way, working their own holdings. However, acute shortages of arable land per capita have pressed many Burusho men to seek salaried jobs in government or military service and wage employment in the bazaars of Gilgit and the cities of the plains beyond. Those better off invest in small businesses throughout the Northern Areas, principally general merchandise stores, restaurants, jeep transport and construction contracting partnerships, and send their sons to Gilgit for secondary school or apprenticeships with skilled craftsmen. Burusho entrepreneurs are reputed for their thrift, industry and organizational capabilities. These trends have been greatly accelerated in recent years by the completion of the Karakorum Highway, which links China with Pakistan and traverses the length of the Hunza River valley. Buses and taxi vans now regularly make the 60-mile trip to Gilgit in two or three hours.

About two-thirds of the Burusho of Hunza term themselves Ismaili or Maulai; they belong to the Nizari sect headed by the Aga Khan. The remaining one-third and all of the Burusho of Nagar are described simply as Shia. According to local tradition, Islam was carried to Hunza by Shias from Kashmir via the court of the Balti king, Abda Khan III, who was converted during a period of exile in Badakhshan sometime about the year 1800. The two sects maintain separate local religious facilities, mosques and *matam sarai* ("mourning places") for the former, *jamaat khana* ("followers' houses") for the latter. The Aga Khan's appointed regional council for the Northern Areas oversees the Ismaili community. Under its direction, a yearly tithe is collected and various charitable enterprises including a school, scholarship program and visits by physicians are administered. The Shia lack a comparable centralized organization. While neither sect supports full-time clergymen or ritual specialists, there are among the Shia a few men, titled *shaikh*, who have earned wide reknown and religious authority for having attended seminaries in the Punjab and in Iran and Iraq. Among the Ismailis, there are a few men respected for their learning in the Kalaam-ey-Peer and other important texts of the Nizaris. The Ismaili subcouncil for Hunza appoints a pious local householder as *khalifa* to officiate at life crises and relay the word of the Imam. Shia congregations similarly choose an *akhund* for themselves. Sect membership in Hunza entails neither residential segregation nor political alignment, and Shia and Ismaili alike regularly join in common neighborhood- and village-based thanksgiving and merit-making rites and in organizing elaborate ceremonial observances at the time of a local resident's death. The absence of sectarian conflict and the willing tolerance of doctrinal differences is a matter of considerable pride for the Burusho. Marriages, friendships and business partnerships frequently cut across sect membership. Furthermore, inside the local community (but not vis-à-vis outsiders) the seclusion or veiling of women is not practiced, although many aspects of social organization involve the religiously sanctioned separation of males and females.

Within each former kingdom, the Burusho were subdivided into moieties with analogous infrastructures. The moiety of the Burusho of Hunza comprised three major divisions, or phratries, identified with the three ancient residential centers of Ganesh, Altit and Baltit which ring the royal compound of Karimabad. In turn, phratries included patriclans grouped by location of their respective historical residential centers. Patriclans are broken down further into lineages focused on proximate, well-remembered founding ancestors. Each patriclan possesses high altitude grazing grounds and exclusive territories of original settlement but otherwise now lacks significant corporate functions. Lineages, consisting of the patrilineal descendants of ancestors two to four generations removed from the eldest living member, constitute the largest effective kin-based political units today.

The stated ideal is for the households of a lineage to stay spatially and morally close and engage in constant mutual aid and association. Following tradition lineage seniors act as leaders, representatives and spokesmen for their group in public disputes and in the political and administrative councils of their localities.

Women are in their mid-teens and men in their late teens when they first marry. The woman goes to live with her husband, who himself resides in his father's or grandfather's household for as long as the latter actively acts as a household head. The vast majority of marriages are monogamous; polygyny is accepted but generally deemed unfeasible if two childbearing and socially active women must cohabit. Women at the time of marriage receive a dowry consisting of personal apparel, jewelry, bedding, and housekeeping equipment, goods which they are entitled to keep if they are divorced (as usually happens if they are believed infertile) or widowed without children and must move to live with their nearest male agnate. In addition, when they visit their natal home following the birth of their first child, it is their right to take back with them something of substantial value, such as a calf, a load of grain, fruit, cloth or a sewing machine. Males inherit the bulk of the familial estate, including the land, house, sheds, livestock and implements, divided in equal shares between the sons of one man irrespective of maternity. Partition among married brothers whose father is deceased or retired usually is delayed at least until one brother has a child. Currently, in a significant number of cases, when one or more brother remits earnings from distant jobs, all choose to stay united in joint households for pragmatic reasons. Subsequent to partition moral impulses justify close collaboration in household management, and until their sons are grown up and married, brothers often claim that they keep a single account of major assets and expenditures.

Inside the village community, the household is the basic unit in terms of which routine activities of production, consumption, socialization, care and hospitality are handled. Household personnel are classified for task roles by age and gender, regardless of generational standing and relation to household head. All have equal entitlement to support, food, space and provisions qualified by these criteria and differences in physical capabilities.

The household is counted as a single unit represented by its head in the councils of its village and neighborhood. Formerly, the *mir*'s grain and fodder taxes and labor service were imposed per household, and, additionally, each household owed the *mir* and/or his local administrative appointees various special payments in kind when it held marriages, circumcision ceremonies or other major rites. Today, village and neighborhood councils supervise household contributions of labor and material to communal work gangs, ceremonies and building projects. Each village, for instance, has its own reservoir dug originally and periodically dredged by general call-up of village labor. In these and related matters of civic government, in the use of communal facilities, in the distribution of food shares from public rites and in the allocation of the vital water supply, equality of right and obligation is vigorously asserted.

Previously, too, the royal polity provided a framework for public rites, festivals and sports. Elaborate dance ceremonies held under the aegis of the *mir*, in his courtyard and in village centers, aroused great public fervor and excitement. Nowadays young men and boys will get together for a game of volleyball or meet in a friend's home to feast and listen to a performance of the hereditary Dom dance musicians, often recorded on cassette tapes.

BIBLIOGRAPHY

Books

Ali, Tahir. "Ceremonial and Social Structure Among the Burusho of Hunza." In *Asian Highland Societies in Anthropological Perspective*, edited by C. von Furer-Maimendorf. New Delhi: Sterling, 1981.
Biddulph, John. *Tribes of the Hindoo Kush*. Reprint ed. Graz, Austria: Akademische Druck-u., 1971. (Originally published 1880.)
Lorimer, David L. R. *The Burushaski Language*. 3 vols. Oslo: Aschehoug, 1935–1938.
Muller-Stellrecht, Irmtraud. *Hunza und China (1761–1891)*. Wiesbaden: Franz Steiner, 1978.

Articles

Huttenback, Robert A. "The 'Great Game' in the Pamirs and the Hindu Kush: The British Conquest of Hunza and Nagar." *Modern Asian Studies* 9:1 (1975): 1–19.

Lorimer, Emily O. "The Burusho of Hunza." *Antiquity* 12 (1938): 5–15.

Staley, John. "Economy and Society in the High Mountains of Northern Pakistan." *Modern Asian Studies* 3:3 (1969): 225–243.

Unpublished Manuscript

Ali, Tahir. "Social Structure and Household Viability in a Mountain Desert Kingdom." Ph.D. dissertation, University of Rochester, 1982.

Tahir Ali

BUTONESE   The islands of Buton and Muna lie to the southeast of Sulawesi, one of the Greater Sunda Islands of Indonesia. The name "Butonese" is often used for the inhabitants of both islands and also for those of the smaller islands of the same area, like the Tukang Besi Islands, east of Buton. For many centuries, all of these islands, plus part of the Sulawesi mainland, constituted a single political unit, the Sultanate of Buton.

The population of this area is far from homogeneous. There are considerable differences in physical type and in local cultural traditions. The people speak several languages, the most important being Wuna, spoken in the greater part of Muna Island, and Wolio, spoken in Buton's capital, Bau-Bau and surroundings, including the old fortified residential town of the sultans, commonly known as the Kraton Wolio. All languages of the area belong to the Malayo-Polynesian group of the Austronesian language family (see Malayo-Polynesian-speaking Peoples). The total population is about 622,000, half of which speaks Wolio.

Most of the islands are mountainous, like Buton, but some are not, like Muna, which is partly hilly, partly flat. The soil is not very fertile. There is not enough rice grown in the islands to satisfy the local needs, but there is a relatively important harvest of corn and cassava. Many Butonese make a living as fishermen. There is a tradition of sailing to faraway islands to earn money in commercial enterprise or labor—either temporarily or permanently—as blacksmiths or tinkers. Since the independence of Indonesia, strict regulation of imports and exports has cut off Butonese traffic with the southern Phillippines. On the other hand, the incorporation of Irian Jaya has meant new opportunity for migration. People of Butonese origin live throughout eastern Indonesia.

Nearly all Butonese are Sunni Muslims. Inhabitants of the area professing another religion are usually of outside origin. However, the Islam observed by the Butonese reflects their unique past.

Little is known of the history of Buton before the coming of Islam. Some historical sources say the people of Ternate brought Islam to the Butonese after having defeated them in a war. It is known that by the end of the sixteenth century Buton was a Muslim country ruled by a sultan. As the sultanate was enlarged with the addition of conquered and allied areas, an adapted organization of the state had to be established in which the rights and duties of all citizens and authorities were laid down. Such a regulation was installed in the beginning of the sixteenth century and was maintained until the beginning of the twentieth century, when it was rendered inoperative by the Dutch colonial government. It became ceremonial until it was officially abolished after the independence of Indonesia.

The organization of the Buton sultanate was closely connected with religion and, at least in theory, was based on Islamic principles. In fact, however, it was based on a principle of inequality. Differences between rulers, allies and tributaries were reflected in a kind of caste system based on class. The highest class was the nobility, whose titles *laode* (men) and *waode* (women) preceded their names. The middle class was the *walaka* or free citizens, having "La" or "Wa" before their names. The third class was the *papara*, the villains. Marrying out of one's class, although not completely impossible, was regarded as a serious offense.

Each class had its own task in public life. The *papara* were excluded from official ranks but supplied the military service which made the executive power of the government a reality. There were special tasks and titles for the *walaka*. But the highest places were reserved for the nobility. And the Sultan, although officially chosen for his office by the Council of Wolio, the assembly of the highest officials of the country, always had to be a member of the most noble family of all. A number of rules secured personal ties between members of different classes, like the special relationship between a member of the noble class and the *papara* women who wet-nursed him during his babyhood and her husband. The result was that everyone felt himself a member of a coherent society which was dependent upon his or her contribution. This social order was connected with religious principles, emphasizing the responsibility and duties attached to offices and ranks, not only towards fellowmen and state but also towards God. This was summed up in the national motto: "Give up possession to secure life, give up life to secure the country, give up the country to secure religion."

A sharp line was never drawn between religious and state occasions or public and religious leaders. The head of the state, the Sultan, although limited in his power to the execution of the decisions of the Council of Wolio, nevertheless was regarded as the highest religious leader, the Khalifa.

The discontinuance of the sultanate meant breaking with tradition. The new government sought to obliterate all remnants of the aristocratic past. The festive celebration of the end of the Ramadan fast, Lebaran (Id al Fitr), held in the Kraton, was replaced by a service held in Bau-Bau. The celebration of Id al Adha, formerly connected with elaborate Kraton ceremony, was changed completely. All religious ceremonies seemed less meaningful in the eyes of the

Butonese, who cherish their traditions. And the people of rank who used to attend the Friday services in the great mosque of the Kraton, fully dressed in their uniforms, refrained from attending, as the wearing of these insignia of office was abolished.

Despite the changes which modernization of the Butonese society brought, the position of Islam among the people has not weakened. The explanation lies, again, in the history of Buton.

The aristocracy used to have many prerogatives, among them the opportunity for education. Butonese nobility not only built a tradition of good education for both boys and girls but also cultivated literary art. Knowledge of foreign languages, especially Malay and Arabic, was encouraged. Many loan words from these languages bear witness to Butonese knowledge of them. The phonology of the Wolio language indicates that exact pronunciation of Arabic words was more pursued here than in other parts of Indonesia. Arabic characters were used for a Wolio writing system, and writing books and long poems became an integrating part of Butonese culture.

Closely connected with this Arabic-based and Malay-tinted literary tradition was the influence of Islamic mysticism. This mysticism, more eclectic than bound to one of the traditional orders, shows two main directions. One is the road which leads to meditation and contemplation aiming at the vision of God; the other is directed towards the recognition of what is essential in religion, trying to look through the outward forms and find the hidden meanings. The outcome of the latter might take the shape of contempt or at least neglect of prescribed performances, like the daily prayers, as being good for the simple-minded but not necessary for those who have developed a sense for higher religious experience. On the other hand, the search for the hidden meaning of religious practice might lead to looking for consistent principles of behavior in all circumstances of everyday life. This practical application of religious principles is the subject matter of many poetic works of didactic and moralistic character. One example is a moralistic poem which explains that marriage can only be of real value if it is based on mutual love of husband and wife. Taking a second wife is so offensive and vexatious to the first one that it cannot be excused by referring to the acceptability of polygyny. Polygyny is at best a forgivable weakness of the husband.

Another feature of the Butonese approach to religion is love of nature. Nature is seen as the material form of God's creation and therefore is best praised by glorifying everything around. This thought is found in classical poetry as well as in the background of the texts of many popular songs, even love songs. Modern, pop songs with Wolio texts are not regarded as conflicting with the also popular *qasidah* songs, sung in Indonesian or Arabic, and are seldom frowned upon by people of strict religious views.

For Butonese, the disappearance of traditional rituals and their replacement by official government religious ceremonies is not a significant loss. Butonese find the essence of their religion elsewhere, beneath the surface of the forms.

BIBLIOGRAPHY

Books

Anceaux, J. C. *The Wolio Language*. The Hague: Martinus Nijhoff, 1952.
Facts about the Province of South East Sulawesi. Kendari, Indonesia: Provincial Government, 1973.

Articles

Berg, E. J. van den. ''Adatgebruiken in verband met de Sultans-installatie in Boeton.'' *Tijdschrift voor Indische Taal-, Land- en Volkenkunde* 79 (1939): 496–528.
————. ''De viering van den raraja hadji in de Kota Wolio (Boeton).'' *Tijdschrift voor Indische Taal-, Land- en Volkenkunde* 77 (1937): 650–660.
Cense, A. A. ''Mededelingen uit de verslagen van Dr. E. J. van den Berg.'' *Bijdragen tot de Taal-, Land- en Volkenkunde* 110 (1954): 154–184.
Ligtvoet, A. ''Beschrijving en geschiedenis van Boeton.'' *Bijdragen tot de Taal-, Land- en Volkenkunde* 26 (1878): 1–112.

J. C. Anceaux

C

CHAM Very little is known of the fate of the approximately 175,000 or so Muslim Cham of Vietnam and Kampuchea following the tumultuous revolutionary events in the area since the 1970s. A few hundred made their way by boat to the northeastern coast of pensinsular Malalysia, and perhaps a similar number made their way to Indonesia. There is virtually no record of Cham in the refugee camps of Thailand. It seems probable that their number may have been greatly reduced by war, disease, starvation and enforced cultural assimilation during the past four decades. It is known that they have undergone a prolonged period of hardship.

The Cham and their close relatives are remnant populations of the ancient kingdom of Champa, which is usually said to have been destroyed by the Vietnamese in A.D. 1471. At that time most of the Cham fled to Angkor (a predecessor state of Kampuchea), where they were well received by the Khmer king. The remainder sought refuge along the least agriculturally attractive portions of the central and southern Vietnamese coast or in the highlands of the Darlac plateau.

Before the fall of Champa, the Cham had been very active in the long-distance sea trade between India and China and were allied to the Malays of Melaka both economically and politically. After defeat, the Cham who fled to Angkor reestablished their ties with the Malays and other Islamic peoples, but those who remained in Vietnam became increasingly isolated and less orthodox, some even losing most if not all of their Islamic traditions.

The language of the Cham and the closely related dialects of the Rhade, Jarai, Raglai, Rai and Churu are isolated geographically among languages of other families. According to most authorities, Acehnese, in northern Sumatra, is the closest relative of the Cham language and its related dialects (see Acehnese). However, recent research suggests that early Malay was very close to both early Cham and early Acehnese. Some of the greater present similarity between Cham and Acehnese is related to processes of linguistic change (different from those in Malay) in which unstressed initial syllables of words were eventually lost and to a greater linguistic acculturation between Cham and Acehnese for several centuries following the fall of Malacca to the Portuguese in 1511. In any case, modern Cham and modern Malay, which is sometimes employed in ritual contexts among the Cham of Kampuchea, are distinct.

The Cham of Vietnam are divided between Muslims and Brahmanists. Brahmanists, whose practice of Hinduism is apparently no more orthodox than the Islamic practices of the Muslims, call themselves Cham *jat* or Cham *harat*, meaning Cham of "pure race." The Muslims call themselves Cham *pak* or Cham *muk* ("southern" or "community" Cham), and others refer to them as Cham *bani* (the latter word referring to their use of the equivalent of *bin* or *binti* to mean "son of" or "daughter of" in their Islamic names).

Recent ethnographic data on the Cham are scarce because of the warfare in the Cham area during the past 40 years and because of their status as a relatively unimportant minority in Vietnam and Kampuchea. Apparently their material lifestyle differs little from that of very poor Vietnamese or very poor Khmer peasants. They are somewhat less inclined to grow wet rice than their neighbors and more inclined to grow cash crops such as cotton, indigo, sesame and market vegetables. They tend cattle and work as fishermen and boatmen. Some are small-scale traders.

In the past, Cham society was dominated by a few powerful matrilineal clans (*kut*) which were joined to each other and to a royal patrilineage through marriages. Minor lineages (*prok*) were localized and had 40 to 50 members divided into 6 to 10 households. The more powerful matricilans included lineages in many villages. Matriliny was strong. Even recently, real property was inherited through women, and men resided in or near the household of the wife's parents (matrilocal residence). In this respect the Cham are more similar to the Minangkabau and the Kerinci than to the Acehnese, whom they most closely resemble in matters of language (see Minangkabau).

The strength of matrilineal institutions is clear in the common distinction between people who are members of one's own matrilineage (*gap batian*), paternal relatives (*gap gan*) and others (*urang lingiu*). Marriage to anyone belonging to the same matrilineage is prohibited, but marriage with paternal relatives is allowed and, in case of Muslims, even preferred, especially between the children of brothers. The sororate, marriage to a sister of a deceased wife, was widely practiced in the past. Kinship terminology is basically generational (Hawaiian), with seniority modifiers distinguishing relative ages of siblings (Yuman) much like Malay kinship terms. However, the seniority modifier terms for elder and younger aunts and uncles differ according to whether these relatives are maternal or paternal.

Brahmanist communities in Vietnam were divided into two very distinct classes, nobles and laborers. Marriages within the same class were strongly preferred. Marriage of a prince to a common woman was allowed, but marriage of a princess to a common man was not.

Muslim communities of Vietnam and of Kampuchea were essentially classless except for the distinction between rulers and others. In the period from the fall of Champa in the fifteenth century to the end of the eighteenth century, during which Cham royalty continued to exist, the religion of the king seems to have been a personal matter, varying between Muslim and Brahmanist. In the traditional world of the villages, leaders of the Cham Muslims were religious teachers (*gru*) and religious leaders (*katip, imam*).

BIBLIOGRAPHY

Books

Aymoniers, Etienne. *Les Tchames et leurs religions*. Paris: Leroux, 1891.
Maspero, Georges. *Le Royaume de Champa*. Paris: G. Van Oest, 1928.

Articles

Benedict, Paul K. "Thai, Kadai, and Indonesian: A New Alignment in Southeastern Asia." *American Anthropologist* 44 (1942): 576–601.
Blagden, C. O. "A Malayan Element in Some of the Languages of Southern Indochina." *Journal of the Straits Branch of the Royal Asiatic Society* 38 (1902): 1–27.
Coedes, G. "La Plus Ancienne Inscription en langue chame." *New Indian Antiquary*, extra series 1 (1939): 46–49.
Durand, E. M. "Notes sur les Chams." *Bulletin de l'Ecole Française d'Extrème Orient* 7 (1907): 313–355.
Jaspan, M. A. "Recent Developments Among the Cham of Indo-China: The Revival of Champa." *Asian Affairs* 57:2 (1970): 170–176.
Lafont, P. B. "Contributions à l'étude des structures sociales des Chams du Vietnam." *Bulletin de l'Ecole Française d'Extrème Orient* 52 (1964): 157–171.
Manguin, Pierre-Yves. "L'Introduction de l'Islam au Camps." *Bulletin de l'Ecole Française d'Extréme Orient* 66 (1979): 255–287.
Morrison, G. E. "The Chams of Malacca." *Journal of the Malayan Branch of the Royal Asiatic Society* 22:1 (1949): 90–98.
———. "The Early Cham Language and Its Relationship to Malay." *Journal of the Malayan Branch of the Royal Asiatic Society* 48:2 (1975): 52–59.
Mus, P. "Cultes indiens et indigènes au Champa (conference faite au Musée Louis Finot)." *Bulletin de l'Ecole Française d'Extrème Orient* 33 (1933): 367–410.
Ner, M. "Les Musulmans de l'Indochine française." *Bulletin de l'Ecole Française d'Extrème Orient* 41 (1941): 151–200.
Nguyen, Thieu Lau. "La Population cham du Sud-Annam s'accroit-elle?" *Institut Indochinois pour l'Etude de l'Homme, bulletin et travaux* 6 (1944): 213–223.

Ronald Provencher

CHECHEN-INGUSH   The Chechen and Ingush have lived for centuries in the remote mountain valleys of the northern Caucasus. Their rugged homeland today is known as the Chechen-Ingush Autonomous Soviet Socialist Republic.

Their languages are almost identical and belong to the Veinakh group of northeast Caucasian language family in the Ibero-Caucasian classification.

A fiercely independent peoples, both groups have a bewildering list of other names. The Chechen call themselves Nakhchuo or Kokhchi, while others call them variously Sheshen, Tsatsan and Mizholzhegi. The Ingush call themselves Galgai, but they are also known as Lamur and Kist'i.

The valley of the Fortanga River has traditionally divided the two groups. Before 1917, it was not unusual to see the Ingush considered simply a Chechen tribe; subsequently, they have been considered separate but closely related groups. The area of their greatest concentration has long been referred to as Chechnia. Both groups have increased in population through this century. The Chechen now number about 815,000 and the Ingush some 200,000. One-half of the population of their republic consists of Russians and Ukrainians who live in the larger cities such as the capital, Grozny, a petroleum and petrochemical center.

Islam has been present among the Chechen at least since the first Cossack settlements were founded along the Terek River after the sixteenth century; perhaps Islam even predated the Golden Horde in the thirteenth and fourteenth centuries. Many of the Ingush were still Christian in the early nineteenth century; today they are all Muslim or descendants of Muslims.

The central fact of Chechen history which still dominates legend and national identity is the Shamil revolt of the nineteenth century. Led by the Imam Shamil, the revolt against Russian encroachment (1834–1858) was only one of a number led by *imams*, but the Shamilist came to stand for Muslim nationalist fervor against Russian occupation. The revolt ended in defeat for most of the peoples of the Caucasus and the flight of some, such as the Chechen Karabulak, to Turkey. Those who remained in Chechnia were only lightly touched by Russian culture, although some of the Chechen-Ingush fought on the side of the Bolsheviks in the Russian Civil War (1918–1921). Despite early indications that the Chechen-Ingush would be allowed to live in their traditional fashion, they came under the brunt of Stalin's nationality purges (1930–1941). Most of the Chechen-Ingush leadership had been eliminated prior to 1941. Even though Chechen-Ingush units served in the Red Army and partisans fought against the Germans as they entered Chechnia, the Chechen-Ingush were chosen for deportation after the German retreat. In 1944, all were deported to the east, their republic was abolished and their literary language proscribed.

As with other deported groups, the Chechen-Ingush were rehabilitated after the Twentieth Party Congress, and on January 9, 1957, the Presidium of the U.S.S.R. restored them as a people and provided for their return to Chechnia. Some have returned to their restored autonomous republic, and Chechen is once again a literary language. It is impossible to state with certainty how many remain in their Central Asian exile.

The Chechens and the Ingush, in contrast to the Circassians, Kumyks and others of Caucasia, have tended to favor a relatively more democratic system of social relations between heads of households. While their clans are led by patriarchs, they do not have a system of hereditary leaders and classes endowed with specific obligations and prerogatives. Class distinctions have been based more on material wealth (with large landowners at the top and landless serfs at the bottom) than on birth. This feudal system has been greatly altered by the imposition of communism and the institution of collectives.

Traditionally, the Chechen and Ingush have been fervent Sunni Muslims—as recently as 1940 there were more than 2,600 mosques in Chechnia and a variety of sects and orders. Polygyny was rarely practiced. Infant betrothal was a common practice, as was marriage by abduction and the institution of *siga*, temporary marriage.

Chechen and Ingush have generally been exogamous, in contrast to the Daghestanis and Circassians, who share their mountains. For instance, marriage between blood relations is forbidden within a span of three generations. At marriage, Chechens recognize the *kebin*, a dowry paid by family of the bridegroom to the bride or her family as a guarantee against divorce.

The position of women among the Chechen-Ingush has been one of subordination to the males, as is characteristic throughout the Caucasus. Traditionally, the wife has not been permitted to eat with her husband or to speak with his relatives. Among the Chechens, husbands and wives never addressed one another by name in the presence of others. While the Communist social system undoubtedly asserts pressures on the Chechen-Ingush to modify their traditions, it is probable that among these independent mountain people these traditions die hard.

BIBLIOGRAPHY

Books

Allen, William Edward, and Muratoff, Paul. *Caucasian Battlefields*. Cambridge: The University Press, 1953.
Baddeley, John F. *The Russian Conquest of the Caucasus*. New York: Longmans, Green, 1908.
Bennigsen, Alexandre. *The Evolution of the Muslim Nationalities of the U.S.S.R. and Their Linguistic Problems*. Oxford: Central Asian Research Centre, 1961.
Geiger, Bernhard, et al. *Peoples and Languages of the Caucasus*. The Hague: Mouton, 1959.
Nekrich, Aleksandre M. *The Punished Peoples*. New York: Norton, 1978.
Smirnov, N. A. *Islam and Russia*. Oxford: Central Asian Research Centre, 1956.

Larry W. Moses

CIRCASSIANS   The Circassian population of the Soviet Union represents a relatively small remnant of a once large and important group of people. As a result of a series of bloody wars, starting in the beginning of the nineteenth century and ending in the mid-1860s, roughly 90 percent of the Circassian population was either killed or forced to flee to various parts of the Ottoman Empire. Today they number about 880,000 in the Soviet Union, 1.2 million worldwide.

The Circassians once dominated the entire fertile steppe area of the western North Caucasus between the Baltic Sea on the west, the Stavropol Plateau on the east, the lower Don River to the north and the Caucasus Mountains to the south. In its more restrictive and more precise meaning, the ethnonym "Circassian" designates the tribes of northwest Caucasic speakers who called themselves Adyge. Adyge is still the self-designation of the Circassian nation. In the pre-revolutionary period they were also referred to in Tatar, Turkish and Russian as Cherkess (from whence came the English—Circassian). In ancient times they were known as Kerkete.

Closely related to the Circassians and often considered subgroups of them are the Abkhaz, Abaza and Ubykh peoples. The Abkhaz and Abaza are basically one ethnic group, sharing the common self-designation Apswa. Some of the dialects spoken by both are mutually intelligible. The Abkhaz are a group of Apswa that crossed the Caucasus Mountain range in the distant past and settled in the northwestern corner of Georgia among the Mingrelians and Georgians. The establishment of two distinct (Abkhaz and Abaza) peoples out of the Apswa is a relatively modern development. Up until the early part of the twentieth century the Abaza were still referred to as Kuban Abkhaz, and the languages of these two groups were considered dialects of one language. The Ubykh are a relatively small group who formerly inhabited the Black Sea coast area. The Circassians, Apswa (or Abazgi) and Ubykh peoples together comprise the northwestern (Abazgo-Kerketian or Abkhazo-Circassian) branch of the Caucasic peoples and languages.

The Circassians were formerly divided into a number of tribal groups, each maintaining a distinct territory. These tribes were comprised of a number of patriarchal clans, each of which being further divided into extended families. Although tribally endogamous, these patriarchal clans were strictly clan exogamous in their marriage pattern. The majority of Circassians maintained these tribal divisions into the twentieth century. Those who maintained these divisions were also basically democratic in their social structure and lacked a hereditary hierarchy. The eastern Circassians, the Kabard or Kabartai, on the other hand developed a strongly feudal social division. They lost, for the most part, their tribal divisions and became more organized into a "nation" than did their western relatives. The development of this feudal structure was the result of the strong influence of the Nogai Tatars (the Golden Horde) on the eastern Circassian tribes between the fifteenth and sixteenth centuries (see Nogai).

Kabard society was divided into basically five distinct social groups. At the top was the highest ruling class. Under them was the nobility, which was further divided into four classes. They were followed by the free peasants, who owned their own lands. Beneath this group came the serfs, and at the very bottom were slaves. The second wife of Ivan IV (Ivan the Terrible) was a Kabard princess.

Regardless of class, all Circassians maintained a common, unwritten code of behavior called the Adyge Khabz. This "judicial system" governed virtually all aspects of life. Vendetta was required, as was the purchasing of brides. The Circassians also maintained strict laws of hospitality and practiced the custom of *atalikat*, the exchanging of male children between families. In addition to the Adyge Khabz, the Circassians followed the Shariah.

Christianity was introduced among the Circassians between the sixth and twelfth centuries by Byzantine missionaries. The Circassian religion, however, was more of a blending of the pre-Christian religion with Eastern Orthodox elements. Sunni Islam (Hanafi school) was first introduced in the sixteenth century by the Golden Horde. At first Islam was accepted only by the nobility among the eastern Kabard Circassians, and only slowly did it penetrate the lower classes. Islam was introduced among the western Circassian tribes, as well as among the Abkhaz, Abaza and Ubykh, only in the eighteenth century from the Ottoman Turkish town of Anapa on the Black Sea coast. By the late eighteenth century Islam was well established among all of these peoples, although many Christian and traditional survivals remained. In the nineteenth century Sufi orders attempted to "purify" Islam in this region. They were popular and widespread in influence in the eastern North Caucasus, but they met with far less success among the Circassians.

The traditional economy of the Circassians, the Ubykh and the Abaza was based primarily on animal husbandry. They were famed throughout the Caucasus for the breeding of fine horses as well as cattle and sheep. Circassian stallions were prized throughout the Middle East and the Russian Empire as well. The fine racehorses known in the Middle East as "Kabartai" were later sold to Europeans. The term "Arabian stallion" was adopted for the Kabartai horse. The Circassians were also famed for their horsemanship and marksmanship. Their craftsmen were also reknowned for the making of high quality Caucasian tunics, tight-waisted black jackets that flare at the bottom with pockets for bullets across the front. In Russian this tunic is called a *cherkeska*. Circassians were equally well known for the making of black sheepskin hats (*papakh* or *kalpak*) and black soft leather boots. These three elements formed the traditional costume of all Caucasian males, regardless of racial, ethnic, linguistic or religious background.

The lands occupied by the Circassians are among the most productive in the U.S.S.R. today and rival the Ukraine in crop yields. As such, they were very attractive to the Slavs (Russians and Ukrainians) as well. Starting in the sixteenth and seventeenth centuries, Cossacks (basically runaway serfs who organized themselves into military bands, based on the Tatar model) began moving into the Circassian lands. In the eighteenth century Catherine the Great transferred a large number of Ukrainian Cossacks into these lands. Although relations between these Slavs and the Circassians were never good, and there were constant

skirmishes, a modus vivendi had developed by the early nineteenth century. By
in large, these Cossacks adopted the way of life of the Circassians, including
their folk traditions, such as horsemanship, horse breeding, marksmanship, the
traditional male costume and the squatting dances performed by the Circassians.
Although these Slavs basically maintained the Slavic languages and Christian
religion, they adopted the Tatar language as a second tongue, which permitted
easy communications with the Tatars and the North Caucasians who also spoke
it.

The Russo–Turkish wars of the nineteenth century broke this modus vivendi.
These wars were fought on three fronts: the Balkans, the Crimea and the Caucasus. The Christian Cossacks were called upon to fight the infidel Muslim
Caucasians, and, conversely, the Circassians joined the other Muslim Caucasians
against the Russians and their empire. These wars were disastrous to the Circassians, as well as to many other North Caucasians and the Crimean Tatars
(see Tatars). The Circassian population was decimated. Unlike the Daghestanis,
Chechens, Karachai, Balkars and others who could retreat into their isolated and
easily defensible mountain valleys and gorges, the Circassians lived in the open
steppes. A policy of virtual genocide was carried out against them. Only among
the Kabards, who generally did not take part in these wars, was a significant
population left after the 1860s. It has been estimated that approximately 500,000
Circassians emigrated to Turkey between 1861 and 1864. In addition to the
Circassians, the majority of the Crimean Tatars, Nogai, Karachai, Balkars and
Abkhaz also emigrated. The entire surviving Ubykh population emigrated.

In the 1830s the Abkhaz population was estimated at approximately 130,000.
By 1866 it had been reduced to 65,000, and by 1881 to a mere 20,000. Only
the Muslims emigrated. By the late nineteenth century what was once a relatively
small Christian minority became the majority, and the Abkhaz of the Soviet
Union today are primarily Eastern Orthodox in religion. What remains of the
Circassian, Abaza, Abkhaz, Crimean Tatar, Nogai, Karachai and Balkar populations today are only small remnants of once far more numerous peoples.

The actual number of Circassians in Turkey and other Middle Eastern countries
is not known. It is estimated that there are approximately 2 million people of
Circassian background living in the Middle East today, although many have
been linguistically and ethnically assimilated, especially in Turkey. So many
lived in Turkey in the 1920s that Soviet nationality policy among the remaining
Soviet Circassians was to make the Soviet Union appear as a great and benevolent
state, one that openly supported the Circassian people. The Circassians received
three separate autonomies, and after a number of reorganizations, the Adygi
Autonomous Oblast' (A.O.), the Karachai-Cherkess A.O. and the Kabardino-
Balkar Autonomous Soviet Socialist Republic (A.S.S.R.) emerged. It is not by
accident that the names of these autonomies correspond to important Circassian
ethnic identities.

Soviet nationality and language policy among the Circassians has been particularly complex. Prior to the revolution the Circassians were all considered by

the Russians to be a single Cherkess people. After the revolution, and much against the wishes of the Circassians themselves, two Circassian "nationalities" were created. The eastern Circassians (i.e. the feudally structured groups) were designated as Kabards and the western groups as Cherkess. The Circassian literary language, which had been established in the late nineteenth century (on the basis of one of the major Kabard dialects) and employed the Arabic script, became the official literary language of all Circassians after the revolution.

In 1922 all Quranic schools were closed, and a major effort was waged by the Soviets against Islam. In 1923–1924 the Circassian literary language was changed to the Latin script. To further complicate matters the Soviets decided (against the will of the Circassian leaders) to create another Circassian literary language. In 1927 a separate Adygei literary language was established on the basis of one of the western Kyakh dialects. The Kyakh dialects are the dominant ones used by the Circassians in Turkey, although relatively few use it in the U.S.S.R.

In the 1930s the Circassians were again reorganized. They were now divided on a territorial rather than social (or dialectic) basis. The western tribes were designated as Adygei, the central ones as Cherkess and the eastern Circassians as Kabards. Thus many who were Kabards in the 1920s became Cherkess if they lived in what became the Karachai-Cherkess A.O. In addition to this, the Abaza, who numbered a mere 13,826 and who were on the verge of total assimilation by the central Circassians, were given a distinct literary language of their own, one which used the Latin script. In 1938, both Circassian literary languages and Abaza were changed to the Cyrillic script. At the same time Arabic, Turkic and Persian words and expressions were purged from the languages and replaced by Russian ones. It was also decreed that any further language borrowing must come from Russian itself. Russian was made a mandatory language of study, and the Circassian languages were used in the schools only through the fifth grade, after which all education was in Russian only. In the early 1960s Circassian and Abaza were eliminated completely as languages of instruction in the schools.

The history of Abkhaz is somewhat different. The Soviets wanted to maintain them as a separate group, and they have received an inordinate amount of support as an ethnic group. Abkhaz was originally written in the mid-nineteenth century in the Cyrillic script. It was changed to the Latin in 1928, to the Georgian in 1938 and finally back to the Cyrillic in 1954. Little is printed in any of these languages anyway, and that which is tends to be translations from other languages, most notably Russian. Few books are available in them, and when they are printed few copies are issued. In the Circassian languages (in 1979) only four-tenths of one book were available per person. The same is true of Abaza. In addition, few newspapers are available in them. The bulk of the material in the "native language" newspapers are written in Russian, with only a few columns printed in the native language itself.

The Circassians remain predominantly rural in their settlement patterns. In

1970 (the latest available figures) 76.9 percent of the Circassians, 82.4 percent of the Abaza and 65.5 percent of the Abkhaz lived in rural areas. During the Soviet period the economy of the Circassians has changed little and is still based on raising cattle, sheep and horses, as well as the growing of cereals, fruits and other agricultural products, although agriculture is now mechanized and collectivized. There has been little industrialization in the Circassian lands. In Abkhazia, more of a change has come about. Since Abkhazia is mountainous and subtropical in climate, it has become a major area of tourism. Tea, citrus and other important specialized crops are grown there.

Gerontologists have given considerable attention to the Abkhaz because of the purported inordinate proportion of Abkhazis claiming to be centenarians. This assertion is questioned by many scientists, and its veracity remains to be proved. Nonetheless, a large proportion do live to old ages, and those that do seem to be in excellent physical and mental health.

Although the Circassians of the U.S.S.R. are a relatively small remnant population, they have been able to retain their language and culture to a high degree. In spite of the fact that the Adygei live in scattered villages in a veritable "sea of Russians," over 97 percent still claim Adygei as their native language. The Circassians look with pride not only on their own historical past but also on the fact that much of what is considered the epitome of Russian folk culture (e.g., the costume, dances and horsemanship of the Cossacks) was borrowed by the Slavs from them. There is nary a Russian that does not associate the squatting dance of the Cossacks as an important part of contemporary Russian culture, thanks to the Circassians.

BIBLIOGRAPHY

Books

Bennigsen, Alexandre. "Muslim Conservative Opposition to the Soviet Regime: The Sufi Brotherhoods in the North Caucasus." In *Soviet Nationality Policies and Practices*, edited by Jeremy R. Azrael. New York: Praeger, 1978.
———. "The Muslims of European Russia and the Caucasus." In *Russia and Asia: Essays on the Influence of Russia on the Asian Peoples*, edited by Wayne Vucinich. Stanford: Stanford University Press, 1972.
———, and Lemercier-Qaulquejay, Chantal. *Islam in the Soviet Union*. Translated by Geoffrey E. Wheeler. London: Pall Mall Press, 1967.
Blanch, Lesley. *The Sabres of Paradise*. New York: Viking Press, 1960.
Geiger, B., et al. *Peoples and Languages of the Caucasus*. The Hague: Mouton, 1959.
Kim, Maxim. *The Soviet Peoples: A New Historical Community*. Moscow: Progress, 1974.
Luzbetak, Louis J. *Marriage and the Family in Caucasia*. New York: Johnson Reprint, 1966.
Moser, Louis. *The Caucasus and Its People*. London: n.p. 1856.

Wixman, Ronald. *Language Aspects of Ethnic Patterns and Processes in the North Caucasus*. Department of Geography Research Paper, 191. Chicago: University of Chicago Press, 1980.

Articles

Abaza, R. "The Abazinians." *Caucasian Review* 18 (1959): 34–40.
Abkhazian, T. "Literature on Abkhazia and the Abkhazian-Abazinian." *Caucasian Review* 7 (1958): 125–143.
Adighe, R. "Cherkess Cultural Life." *Caucasian Review* 2 (1956): 85–104.
Bennigsen, Alexandre. "Mixed Marriages in the Caucasus: The Problem as Observed in the Karachay-Cherkess Autonomous Region." *Central Asian Review* 16:3 (1968): 217–222.
————. "The Problem of Bilingualism and Assimilation in the North Caucasus." *Central Asian Review* 15:3 (1967): 205–211.
Bouda, K. "Language Problems in the Caucasus." *Caucasian Review* 1 (1955): 122–127.
Feizullin, G. "The Persecution of National-Religious Traditions of the Moslems of the USSR." *Caucasian Review* 3 (1956): 69–76.
Halasi-Kun, T. "The Caucasus: An Ethno-Historical Survey." *Studia Caucasica* 1 (1963): 1–47.
Kandelaki, K. "Soviet Nationality Policy in the Caucasus." *Caucasian Review* 2 (1956): 7–16.
Karcha, R. "The Status of Popular Education in the Northern Caucasus." *Caucasian Review* 7 (1958): 110–124.
————. "The Struggle Against Nationalism in the Northern Caucasus." *Caucasian Review* 9 (1959): 25–38.
Kobychev, V. A., and Robakidze, A. T. "Basic Typology and Mapping of Dwellings of the Caucasian Peoples." *Soviet Anthropology and Archaeology* 7:4 (1969): 13–28.
Krupnov, E. I. "The Most Archaic Culture of the Caucasus and Caucasian Ethnic Community." *Soviet Anthropology and Archaeology* 3:3 (1964): 31–45.
Silver, Brian. "The Status of National Minority Languages in Soviet Education: An Assessment of Recent Changes." *Soviet Studies* 26:1 (1974): 28–40.
Smirnova, I. S. "Some Religious Survivals Among the Black Sea Adygei." *Soviet Anthropology and Archaeology* 3:1 (1964): 3–8.
Tatlok, T. "The Ubykhs." *Caucasian Review* 7 (1958): 100–109.
Trakho, R. "Literature on Circassia and the Circassians." *Caucasian Review* 1 (1955): 145–162.
Weightman, G. H. "The Circassians." *Middle East Forum* 37:10 (1961): 26.
Wixman, Ronald. "Ethnic Nationalism in the Caucasus." *Nationalities Papers* 10:2 (1982): 137–156.

Ronald Wixman

D

DAGHESTANIS Daghestan (literally, "Land of Mountains"), located in the far eastern reaches of the Great Caucasian Chain in the Soviet Union, is one of, if not the most, ethnically heterogeneous regions on earth. The 1.4 million inhabitants are known collectively as Daghestanis. They are considered to be among the most conservative Muslim, anti-Russian and anti-Soviet peoples in the U.S.S.R. They remain, along with the ethnically, culturally and linguistically related Chechens, among the least modernized, Sovietized, educated and Russified peoples of the entire Soviet Union (see Chechen-Ingush).

Although all of the mountain Daghestanis speak languages that belong to the northeastern branch of the Ibero-Caucasian language family, linguistically they are extremely diverse. The term "Daghestani" includes the following ethnic groups: Avars, Dargins, Lezgins, Laks, Tabasarans, Rutuls, Tsakhurs and Aguls. They are all Caucasic speakers and inhabitants of the highland regions of the Daghestan Autonomous Soviet Socialist Republic. They share the area with the Kumyk and Nogai, who are Turkic speakers and inhabit the lowlands of northern and northeastern Daghestan (see Kumyk; Nogai).

Avars

The Avars are the most numerous of the Daghestani peoples, with a population of 544,000. The contemporary term "Avar" covers 15 distinct ethnic groups: the Avars proper; the eight Andi peoples (Akhwakh, Andi, Bagulal, Botlikh, Chamalal, Gogoberi, Karata and Tindi); the five Dido (Tsez) peoples (Bezheta, Dido, Ginukh, Khunzal and Khwarshi); and the Archi (who linguistically form a transitional group between the Avaric and Lak peoples). The Avars themselves inhabit the plateau area of central and western Daghestan, extending into the highlands of southern Daghestan and contiguous areas in northern Azerbaijan and southeastern Chechnia. Their control of the important river valleys (which were the main routes of communication and trade for highland Daghestan) and central plateau areas (in which many trading and artisan centers were located) gave them dominance over the highland Andi-Dido and Archi peoples. The dialect of Khunzakh became the lingua franca of all of western and central Daghestan.

The Andi peoples inhabit the westernmost part of the Avar territory in Daghestan. The Dido peoples live in the highest and most inaccessible part of the Avar territory, near the border of the Georgian S.S.R. The Archi inhabit the single mountain village (*aul*) Ruch Archi, in the southeastern part of the Avar territory, near the lands inhabited by the Laks. By the turn of the twentieth century all of these peoples were being consolidated around the numerically more numerous and culturally dominant Avars. Up until the 1930s they were all considered officially distinct ethnic groups with distinct languages. Since that time they have been officially classified as Avars and their languages as dialects of Avar (although none of these languages is mutually intelligible with Avar). The Avar language itself is comprised of five dialects (Khunzak, Gidatl-Andalay, Karakh, Antsukh and Charoda) which are not mutually intelligible. In fact, they are five distinct languages.

Dargins

The contemporary term "Dargin" includes a diverse group of peoples: the Dargins proper, the Kaitak and the Kubachi. They number approximately 250,000. The Dargins inhabit east-central Daghestan; the Kaitaks live in the southeastern corner of the Dargin territory; and the Kubachi inhabit the single *aul* Kubachi, in the south-central part of the Dargin territory. By 1900 these three peoples were being consolidated around the Dargins, who, like the Avars, were numerically and culturally dominant in this region. The Dargin language itself is comprised of three mutually unintelligible dialects (Akusha, Khurkili or Urakhi and Tsudakhar). The dialect of the *aul* Akusha became the dominant one over time, as it was the most important artisan, trading, cultural and religious center in the Dargin territory. Since the 1930s the Kubachi and Kaitaks have been officially classified as Dargins and their languages as dialects of Dargin, even though they are not mutually intelligible with any of the Dargin dialects.

Laks

The 110,000 Laks inhabit the area of south-central Daghestan between the territories of the Avars and Dargins. They are ethnically less complex than either of the other groups, and all of the dialects of Lak are mutually intelligible. Although the Lak language has been classified as being related (albeit distantly) to Dargin, it is not mutually intelligible with any of the Dargin languages or dialects.

Sumurian Group

In the high mountainous area to the south of the Avars, Laks and Dargins live a group of peoples who for purpose of convenience are grouped linguistically into what is called the Sumurian group. This group is comprised of the Tsakhurs (15,000), Rutuls (16,000), Aguls (10,000), Tabasarans (80,000) and Lezgins (420,000). The Tsakhur territory straddles the border of Daghestan and Azerbaijan, as does that of the Lezgins, who live to the east of them. North of the Lezgins and south of the Dargins, from west to east, live the numerically small Rutuls, Aguls and Tabasarans. The languages of these peoples are radically different from one another. In addition, the Tabasaran language is comprised of two non-mutually intelligible dialects. At times the numerically small Shahdagh peoples who live in northern Azerbaijan near the border of Daghestan (Budukh, Dzhek and Khinalug) are also classified as peoples in the Sumurian group or as southern Daghestanis. These peoples have all but been totally assimilated by the Azeri (see Azeri).

Until the Soviet period these ethnonyms were not used by the Daghestani peoples themselves. Prior to the Russian Revolution the various Caucasic Daghestani peoples lacked distinct ethnic identities. They identified on a variety of levels, however: as Muslims (which they also applied to the other Islamic peoples of the Russian Empire and the world); as Daghestanis (which they also applied to the Turkic Kumyk and Nogai and the Mountain Jews); as Mountaineers (which they also applied to all the mountain peoples of the North Caucasus); as Caucasians (in which group they also included the other North Caucasian peoples, the Azeri, Georgians, Abkhaz, Mingrelians and Svanetians); by clan or clan federation (which were, at times, multi-ethnic in composition); and by village or valley of habitation.

Not only did the various peoples of Daghestan lack distinct ethnonyms, they lacked terms in their own languages for their languages. There was no word in Avar for the Avar people or language, nor was there a word in Dargin for the Dargins as a distinct ethnic group or for the Dargin language. All of these ethnic designations were created during the Soviet period, or earlier, by outsiders. To this day, these ethnonyms are not widely used by the Daghestanis themselves. The Avar self-designation, for example, is Maarulal, which means "mountaineer."

A number of social and economic factors also hindered the formation of distinct ethnic identities in the pre-Soviet period. These peoples (with the sole exceptions of some of the Lezgin and Tabasaran clans) were socially divided into strictly endogamous patriarchal clans (marriage between first or second cousin being the preferred marriage pattern). This social system greatly hampered the consolidation of clans into ethnic units. The clans were comprised of extended families recognizing common ancestry. They were also basically democratic (i.e. lacking a hereditary hierarchy), and lands and property were owned communally by the clan. Such socioeconomic organization led to a strong sense of clan cohesion and family loyalty. In addition, the clans often formed voluntary unions called "free societies" or "federations" (Avar-Bo; Dargin-Darqwa; Lezgin-Para), many of which were multi-ethnic.

The Akusha Darqwa, for example, included not only the important Dargin *auls* of Akusha (the largest and most important of all Dargin villages) and Tsudakhar, and the Dargins in them, but also a number of Avar and Lak *auls*. The Utsmi Darqwa included Dargin, Kubachi and Kaitak *auls*, and the Burkun Darqwa included Dargin and Lezgin *auls*.

The contemporary Dargin nation, in essence, was formed by the unification during the Soviet period of all of the Dargin (and Kubachi and Katiak) free societies around the Akusha Darqwa. The ethnonym "Dargin" is basically a Russian form of the Dargin term for free societies, *darqwa*. Similarly, the contemporary Avar nation was formed by the unification of the Maarulal Bo (Mountaineer Federation), which included most of the northern Avar clans, with the Baqaulal Bo (Rugged Men Federation), which included most of the southern Avar clans, as well as those of the Andi and Dido peoples. The contemporary self-designation of Avars (Maarulal) derives from the Maarulal Bo. The Lezgin nation was formed by the union of the three major Lezgin federations, the Akhty, Alty and Dokuz Para. Some Lezgin clans, however, had been part of the Rutul Magal (the free society that included all of the Rutal clans).

This sociopolitical system, while hampering the formation of distinct ethnic groups, acted as a unifying factor among the Daghestanis. The traditional economy of the Daghestanis was based on animal husbandry (transhumance sheep- and goatherding in the higher mountain areas and cattle breeding in the foothills, lower plateaus and lowlands), home or cottage industries and artisanry (gold and silver smithing, rug and textile weaving, leather working, pottery and the making of weapons). As opposed to living in the lowlands and taking their herds to summer mountain pastures, which is the more common form of transhumance pastoralism, the Daghestanis (like other Caucasian mountaineer peoples) had their permanent dwellings in the highlands and brought their animals into the lowlands (to northern Daghestan or Azerbaijan) in winter. Women rarely accompanied the men on these journeys. Agriculture was relatively less important than animal husbandry, artisanry or cottage industries among the Daghestanis. Much of the agricultural produce was purchased in trading towns or in the lowlands.

Many Daghestani *auls* were famed throughout the Caucasus, the Russian Empire and at times even the Middle East for their fine artisanry. The most famous of these *auls* is Kubachi, which was reknowned for the making of high quality gold and silver jewelry and filigree, daggers and swords and chain mail. The Kubachi were so famous for their making of chain mail that they were often called Zerekhgeran (Persian for "makers of chain mail") as an ethnonym by the neighboring and Middle Eastern peoples. This *aul* is still famous throughout the Soviet Union for gold and silver smithing, filigree and jewelry, although the motifs have changed. Many Avar *auls* were well known for the making of fine *kilims* (woven rugs) and textiles, and many Dargin *auls* were reknowned for fine leatherworking, jewelry and pottery.

As a result of this economic pattern, the languages of the artisan and trading centers became important lingua francas for the people who used them. Thus the Khunzakh dialect of Avar, the Akusha dialect of Dargin and the Kumukh dialect of Lak became important languages among the highlanders (and others) who used these important trading centers for their economic activities. In addition, a vertical zone principle developed, whereby peoples living at higher elevations learned the languages of the villages and towns below them. Similarly, Daghestanis who lived north of the Great Caucasus Chain (most Avars, Andi-Dido peoples, Laks and Dargins) took their flocks and herds into the lowlands of northern Daghestan, areas dominated by the Turkic Kumyks. Many also found part-time employment in the Kumyk towns of Buinaksk, Khasavyurt and Temir Khan Shura (Makhchakala). As a result, Kumyk became the most important lingua franca among these peoples, and virtually all males were at least bilingual (their own language and Kumyk). Many highland Andi-Dido peoples were often multilingual, knowing their own language, that of the village or valley below them, Khunzakh, Avar and Kumyk. The southern Daghestanis (Tabasarans, Aguls, Rutuls, Tsakhurs, Lezgins and the southern Avars and Dargins) took their flocks southward into northern Azerbaijan. Many also found part-time employment in the Azeri towns of Shemakha, Kuba and Nukha in northern Azerbaijan, Baku (capital of Azerbaijan) and Derbent (an Azeri town in coastal southern Daghestan). Among these peoples, Azeri was the lingua franca.

Since Kumyk is easily mutually intelligible with the other Kipchak Turkic languages (Crimean Tatar, Nogai, Tatar, Bashkir, Kazakh and Kirghiz) and to a lesser extent with the other Turkic languages (Turkish, Azeri, Turkmen and Uzbek), the knowledge of this language was advantageous to the Daghestanis, whose own languages were spoken in only a limited area. The same can be said of Azeri. The knowledge of Turkic languages gave the Daghestanis access to communications with the various Islamic (and Turkic) peoples of the Russian Empire and the Middle East. Although classical Arabic served as the important literary language of the Daghestani mountaineers, Kumyk and Azeri served as the lingua franca. By the early twentieth century a major process of unification of the Daghestanis (assimilation) by the Kumyk in the north and the Azeri in the south was underway.

Another important unifying factor was religion. With only a few minor exceptions, all of the Daghestani peoples were Sunni Muslims of the Shafi school. The spread of Islam into Daghestan, however, had been a slow and arduous process. It was first introduced by Arab conquerors between the eighth and thirteenth centuries. At that time the traditionalist religion of the Daghestanis was still entrenched, and Zoroastianism, Judaism and Christianity had already been spreading. In the fifteenth century Islam was reintroduced from the south by the Persians (mainly among the Lezgins and southern Daghestanis), and in the sixteenth and seventeenth centuries from the north by the Golden Horde.

Many pre-Islamic beliefs and traditions, however, persisted. Among the more important of these were the worship of local and clan deities, pilgrimages to holy sites and the important local system of governance, the common law, *adat*. The final Islamization of Daghestan came in the nineteenth century.

At the beginning of the nineteenth century, as a result of the growing hostility between the Caucasian mountaineers and the Russians and of the alliances formed between the rulers of the local khanates with the Russian government, the Daghestani mountaineers became fertile ground for the spread of Sufism, primarily the Naqshbandiyya order. The *tariqa* opposed Russian-infidel rule and the perceived corruption of the local feudal lords. Although feudalism had taken hold in highland Daghestan (being introduced by the Kumyk and Azeri in the lowlands) it had only limited power in the highlands, and these feudal khanates never succeeded in subduing the majority of the mountaineers. Sufism reached its peak in the mid-nineteenth century under the leadership of Imam Shamil, an Avar who declared Daghestan an independent country in 1834. Conservative Islam and the Shariah (Quranic law) were further instituted, and a major campaign was mounted to eliminate the pre-Islamic holdovers. The movement succeeded in making Sufism an important element in Daghestan, whose basis was to shield the local Muslims from infidel influence. For 25 years, Shamil fought the Russians and their allies. He surrendered in 1858 and later died in Mecca.

After the defeat of Shamil, the majority of Circassians, Abaza, Abkhaz, Karachai and Nogai, as well as the surviving members of the Ubykh nationality, emigrated to the Ottoman Empire. Few Daghestanis or Chechens, on the other hand, emigrated. They remained and continued a long struggle against the Russians, and later the Soviets. Among the Daghestanis and the Chechens the Sufi orders became active in these resistance movements. Hostility continues today as these peoples view the officially sanctioned leaders of Islam in the U.S.S.R. as stooges of the regime. Anti-religious education has not lessened the Sufi movement among the Daghestanis, especially among the Avars, Dargins and other highland peoples, less so among the Laks and Lezgins. Soviet sociologists and ethnographers confirm that Islam is still a major force among the Daghestani mountaineers. Religious institutions abound (circumcision of male children, religious marriages and burials, family mosques). Intermarriage between Daghestani Muslims and non-Muslims is rare, female children are often taken out of school at an early age and the *kalim* (brideprice) is still widely practiced, as is arrangement of marriages by parents. Traditional patriarchal clan values survive. The Sufi orders, organized along traditional patriarchal clan lines, tend to reinforce local customs and traditions and are in turn reinforced by family loyalties.

The conservative Islamic nature of the Daghestanis, their violent anti-Russian attitudes and their great ethnic and linguistic heterogeneity created for the Soviets a difficult task in organizing and Sovietizing this region. At the time of the Russian Revolution the majority of Daghestanis demanded the unification not only of Daghestan but of the entire Muslim North Caucasus region into one Islamic state with Arabic as the official language. The modernists (educated merchants and modernizers), who were relatively weak (they were few in number and viewed as traitors to Islam by the majority), pushed for the unification of Daghestan around Turkic languages, Kumyk and/or Azeri. Both groups supported the unification of the Daghestanis into one people and opposed the development of local literary languages based on the spoken tongues of highland Daghestan.

In an attempt to win over the Muslim North Caucasians, the Soviets established the United Mountaineer Republic in 1918. This territory was formally incorporated into the Soviet Union in 1920 as the Mountain Autonomous Republic. Arabic was the official language. The move was opposed by the majority of the North Caucasians, and they continued to revolt well into the late 1920s.

Once Soviet power was established, the republic was divided into numerous "ethnic" territories. In 1921, the Daghestan A.S.S.R. was formed. Arabic remained the official language until 1925–1926, at which time all Quranic schools were closed and Arabic was removed as the language of education, publication and communication. This was accompanied by a major anti-Islamic campaign, and many of the local religious leaders were executed.

There followed a short-lived pro-Turkic policy, and Azeri became the official language of Daghestan. The writing script was changed, and all the languages of Muslims in the U.S.S.R. were put into a modified Arabic script called New Adzham. By 1928 this "pro-Turkic" policy was cancelled as it was no longer considered necessary to appease the local population. Avar became the official language of all Avars, Andi-Dido and Archi peoples. Dargin became the official language of the Dargins, Kaitaks, and Kubachi. The Aguls were to merge officially with the Lezgins, and the Tsakhurs and Rutuls with the Azeri. Between 1928 and 1929, these languages were given new forms and put into the Latin alphabet. In 1938–1939, the written forms were again changed, this time to Cyrillic. This was accompanied by a linguistic "purge" of Arabic, Persian and Turkic elements and replacement by Russian ones. Russian was made a mandatory language of study. In the early 1960s, all education in the languages of Daghestan was eliminated, and Russian became the only language of instruction.

In spite of an overt policy of Russianization, few Daghestanis have abandoned their native tongues. According to the 1979 census, only 1 percent of the Avar, Dargin, Tabasaran, Rutul and Agul populations considered Russian their native language; comparable figures for the Lezgins and Laks were 5 percent and 4 percent, respectively, and that of the Tsakhurs was below 1 percent.

The Soviets have also followed a policy of relocation of the Daghestani mountaineers into the lowlands of northern and eastern Daghestan. While this policy has met with limited success, the vast majority of Daghestanis still choose to live in the mountains and in rural areas. There are no major cities in the mountainous areas of Daghestan; therefore, a Daghestani who wishes to move to a city must move into Kumyk, Azeri or Russian areas within Daghestan or leave Daghestan itself. As late as 1970, a survey showed the percentage of Daghestanis living in rural areas ranged from 52 percent for the Laks to 99 percent for the Aguls. As rural dwellers, the Daghestanis display the lowest levels of education in the U.S.S.R. Recent Soviet emigrés who had lived in Daghestan report that it is one of the most underdeveloped regions in the Soviet Union.

Cottage industries, artisanry and animal husbandry remain the predominant economic activities among the Daghestanis. Now, however, goods are sold through government collectives, the lands (including pasture) are owned by the state and herds have been collectivized, all to the disgruntlement of the Daghestanis. While they had lived in clan collectives and their lands were communally owned, Soviet control was not welcomed. Daghestan remains not only the poorest, least modernized and least industrialized region of the Soviet Union, its people stand out as the most anti-Soviet.

BIBLIOGRAPHY

Books

Bennigsen, Alexandre. "Islamic, or Local Consciousness Among Soviet Nationalities." In *Soviet Nationality Problems*, edited by Edward Allworth. New York: Columbia University Press, 1971.
———. "Muslim Conservative Opposition to the Soviet Regime: The Sufi Brotherhoods in the North Caucasus." In *Soviet Nationality Policies and Practices*, edited by Jeremy R. Azrael. New York: Praeger, 1978.
———, and Lemercier-Quelquejay, Chantal. *Islam in the Soviet Union*. Translated by G. E. Wheeler. London: Pall Mall Press, 1967.
Blanch, Lesley. *The Sabres of Paradise*. New York: Viking Press, 1960.
Conquest, Robert. *The Nation Killers*. London: Macmillan, 1970.
Geiger, B., et al. *Peoples and Languages of the Caucasus*. The Hague: Mouton, 1959.
Human Relations Area Files. *The Caucasus*. Subcontractors Monograph HRAF-35, Columbia-1. New Haven: HRAF, 1956.
Kim, Maxim. *The Soviet People: A New Historical Community*. Moscow: Progress, 1974.
Moser, Louis. *The Caucasus and Its Peoples*. London: n.p., 1856.
Rogov, Vladimir. *Languages and Peoples of the USSR*. Moscow: Novosti Press Agency Publishing House, 1966.
Silver, Brian. "Language Policy and the Linguistic Russification of Soviet Nationalities." In *Soviet Nationality Policies and Practices*, edited by Jeremy R. Azrael. New York: Praeger, 1978.
Wixman, Ronald. *Language Aspects of Ethnic Patterns and Processes in the North Caucasus*. Department of Geography Research Paper, 191. Chicago: University of Chicago Press, 1980.

Articles

Adighe, R. "Literature on Daghestan and Its People." *Caucasian Review* 4 (1957): 101–108.
Bennigsen, Alexandre. "The Problem of Bilingualism and Assimilation in the North Caucasus." *Central Asian Review* 15:3 (1967): 205–211.

Bouda, K. "Language Problems in the Caucasus." *Caucasian Review* 1 (1955): 122–127.

Feizuillin, G. "The Persecution of National-Religious Traditions of the Moslems of the USSR." *Caucasian Review* 3 (1956): 69–76.

Gardanov, V. K.; Dolgikh, B. O.; and Zhdanko, T. A. "Major Trends in Ethnic Processes Among the Peoples of the USSR." *Soviet Anthropology and Archaeology* 1:1 (1962): 3–18.

Halasi-Kun, T. "The Caucasus: An Ethno-Historical Survey." *Studia Caucasia* 1 (1963): 1–47.

Kandelaki, K. "Soviet Nationality Policy in the Caucasus." *Caucasian Review* 2 (1956): 7–16.

Karcha, R. "The Status of Popular Education in the Northern Caucasus." *Caucasian Review* 7 (1958): 110–124.

———. "The Struggle Against Nationalism in the Northern Caucasus." *Caucasian Review* 9 (1959): 25–38.

Kobychev, V. A., and Robakidze, A. I. "Basic Typology and Mapping of Dwellings of the Caucasian Peoples." *Soviet Anthropology and Archaeology* 7:4 (1969): 13–28.

Krupnov, E. I. "The Most Archaic Culture of the Caucasus and the Caucasian Ethnic Community." *Soviet Anthropology and Archaeology* 3:3 (1964): 31–45.

Sergeeva, G. A. "Field Work in Daghestan in 1959." *Soviet Anthropology and Archaeology* 1:2 (1962): 57–63.

Silver, Brian. "The Status of National Minority Languages in Soviet Education: An Assessment of Recent Changes." *Soviet Studies* 26:1 (1974): 28–40.

Ronald Wixman

DAJU   According to the oral traditions of the Daju, they appear to be one of the oldest communities of western Sudan and eastern Chad, their story beginning at least in the thirteenth century. Accounts of their origins are many and diverse, but through all runs a common theme showing Daju to have traditions of independent rule, warfare with neighbors and syncretistic Islam.

The Daju live in three general areas. In Chad, they live in the province of Sila (where in 1970 their population was estimated at 52,000) and in Wadai and Guerra (1970, 30,000 population). They pay allegiance to the Daju sultan in Goz-Beida, the capital of Sila. Another group lives in Darfur Province in Sudan with a concentration—and sultan—in Nyala. A third group whose leader is a sultan in Dar El Kabira lives in southern Kordofan. In 1970, perhaps 30,000 Daju lived in Sudan. (See appendix 2 for estimated 1983 population.)

In their own language the Daju in Chad call themselves Daju Sila, while those in Sudan call themselves Daju Ferne or Fininga. In Arabic, they call themselves Beke. Controversy surrounds the origin of this word. In Sudan a well-known group, the Bego or the Beyko, is said to bear close resemblance to the Daju in terms of language, traditions and physical appearance; some believe they were once the same as the Daju but separated at some time in the past. A Bego sultan once declared: "Our tribe goes back to Ahmed el Dagj, but we reject all connection with the Daju now.'' Ahmed el Dagj is believed to be the founder of the Daju. As with all groups in this part of Africa, the Daju claim to have originated in Yemen in Arabia, but there is no hard evidence of this.

There is no universally accepted classification of the Daju language. Joseph Greenberg calls it one of the Eastern Sudanese group of the Nilo-Saharan family. This would place it in the family of the Tama, Beri, Kanembu and Kanuri. This theory is backed by Marie-José Tubiana, who related the Daju to the Tama (see Tama-speaking Peoples). Robin Thelwall links it to the Nubian languages, also Nilo-Saharan. Others reject Greenberg and place Daju in a separate category altogether. The language is spoken by older Daju and a few young people. Most speak Arabic, the children being introduced to it while learning to chant the Quran in classes run by the village *faqi* (cleric).

Nearly 90 percent of the Daju are sedentary cultivators living in small villages in dry, hilly country where farming requires hard work and ingenuity. The basis of their economy is grain production—millet, sorghum, corn. They gather cereal grasses, berries and wild fruit. They are not deeply involved with animal husbandry; they have donkeys for transport, a horse if they can afford it and a few goats. If they own cattle, they entrust these to Arabs, whose stock they allow to graze on harvested millet straw and thus fertilize the fields. Their relationship with nomadic Arabs is generally good except when herds stray; then the Daju's reputation for belligerence becomes apparent.

Daju villages are composed of houses that are round with conical shaped roofs. In towns their houses are rectangular, made of mud-brick and terraced, flat roofs.

Traditionally, the Daju have been divided into tribes and subdivided into patrilineal clans, such divisions being recognized today. Each tribe was ruled by a sultan, the clans by chiefs giving allegiance to the sultan. While once possessing almost total authority over the tribes, sultans today have only nominal authority; they do possess war drums, the symbols of primacy, and preside over religious ceremonies. The sultanship is passed down from father to son. Royal clans (*leoge*) enjoy preeminence. Their children, nephews, uncles and wives receive special privileges and are deferred to by others.

The *letuge* are clan leaders who assist the sultan in carrying out religious rites and governing the tribe. They also assist in directing warfare and nominating a new sovereign if there is any question as to who succeeds a deceased sultan.

Another important element in the social structure of the Daju is the clerics, *togonye*, who in pre-Islamic times led the various cults, the rain cult being the most important since the Daju subsist on agriculture. Other elements of traditional religion included fire, which was used in the induction of a new sultan, harvest festivals and launching of war expeditions.

Daju were Muslims by the fifteenth century, probably much earlier. They are Sunni and follow the Maliki school, as do most Muslims in central Africa. They quote one noted Maliki scholar, Sidi Khalil, with reverence, although they use as juridical guidance Ibn Abi Zayd Al-Qayrawani's *Risala*, a compendium of dogma and Islamic law according to Maliki rite.

Their practice of Islam reflects their pagan past. When Ahmed el Dagj crossed the Darfur border into Chad in the fifteenth century, he noted that the Guadiens (Daju) were still fetishists. While the Daju today are Muslims and accept the "Five Pillars of the Faith," they are somewhat slack in observance. There are few mosques in Daju country; Friday prayer is not attended by everyone, and Daju make various accommodations to fasting and giving alms. Few have been to Mecca, and above all, the Daju daily ignore the prohibition against fermented beverages; *merisa* (millet beer) is their national drink.

The Daju are active in the Tijaniyya Sufi brotherhood, and their sultans maintain a close relationship with the Grand Master of the Order. They do not reject the Quran on which they make their oaths and base their commitments. Indeed, oaths are important and are usually made before pages of the Quran which are enfolded by wicker matting, wrapped in a scarf and suspended far from any wall or fence which would diminish the free will of the person swearing the oath. Swearers must be in a state of purity, having gone through ritualistic ablutions (menstruating women are not allowed to swear as they are considered unclean). "Whoever swears must do so by Allah or remain silent," according to Khalil.

The influence of Islam is visible in the unfolding of the life cycle from birth to death. A newborn baby, on its first day of life, is given water which has washed a wooden board on which were written verses of the Quran. On the seventh day, the newborn's head is shaved except for a tuft on top of the skull. This tuft becomes a "lock of Allah's" and will be seized by the Archangel Gabriel to help the child "at the last day" over the bridge of Cirath, which, according to Islamic tradition, "is thinner than a hair and sharper than a saber."

To find a name for the child, a *faqi* hides behind his back two rosaries on which the father has written two names. The mother then chooses one of the hands, usually the right hand, but it is assumed that the selection is made by Allah.

Boys are circumcised around the age of eight, usually by a blacksmith (*haddad*) pronouncing "Bismillahi" in a vibrating voice. A woman will circumcise girls at a younger age.

In each village, young boys and girls become members of social and work groups which perform community chores, such as keeping the village clean and organizing dances. They are under constant scrutiny of a leader, who sees that they do their *shahada* and *fatiha* chants.

Male dominance is characteristic of Daju family life. From the start, parents express their wish for a male heir. The family coddles the young boy; when he is an adolescent his representative makes a proposal of marriage to the parents of a young girl. He will decide about building the house, preparing the fields, planting, buying of stock, going to market. It will be his or his father's decision that he goes to advanced religious training to become a *faqi* or *imam* or leader of a village. There are ten categories of male heirs and only seven for female heirs; and a boy inherits twice that of a girl.

The role of women is subservient. She must please her husband; otherwise he will marry a second wife who would live in another village. She raises the children alone, goes for water twice a day, sows millet, grinds the grain, prepares the meals, buys dry meat in the market along with salt, pepper and other ingredients of meals. She sells chicken and eggs, but not livestock such as goats; this is the job of the husband. And she must produce as many children as possible, preferably boys.

Daju women do not wear veils and often go bare-breasted while among their kinsmen. They prolong their beauty by whitening their teeth with a stick and tatooing their eyelids, gums and lips with acacia thorns dipped in antimony powder.

The Daju have singular pride in their past glories in warfare. Their oral traditions remind them that they once ruled central Darfur before the Tunjur in the sixteenth century. Quarrelsome and adventurous, the Daju, if one is to believe a legend, largely spread by themselves, took part in all the conquests and battles in Syria, Iraq, Armenia and Asia Minor. They helped invade Egypt and Nubia, all stories that have never been proved.

What has been established, however, is that the Daju, Fur, Wadaians and Arabs were constantly at war with each other. Records show that the Daju-Sila fought in Dar Sinyar, Dar Fongoro and against the Arabs in Darfur, that they joined their neighbors in opposing the Mahdi, that they fought the Masalit and confronted the French. Following a period of peace after the "entente cordial" between the French and the British, the Daju again went to battle between 1939 and 1945. The Sultan of Sila, Brahim ould Mustafa, served in a marching battalion in Chad against the Germans and Italians.

Wrote one French colonel to his successor on his departure from duty in Goz-Beida in 1962: "The independent mood of the Daju, the mountainous nature of their country, their great aptitude to overcome difficult terrain and natural obstacles which they developed through their national sport of hunting and their search for honey, seem to be the principal reasons which saved the independence of Sila."

Since independence, the Daju have remained involved in conflict. It was at Nyala, Sudan, in the heart of Daju country, on June 6, 1966, that the National Liberation Front (for Chad) was formed. The Daju were there and participated in battles fought for control of the country.

BIBLIOGRAPHY

Books

Barth, H. *Voyages et découvertes dans l'Afrique Septentrionale et Centrale pendant les années 1849 à 1855*. Translated by Paul Ithier. 4 vols. Paris: A. Bohne, 1860–1861.

Brown, W. G. *Nouveau Voyage dans la Haute et Basse Egypte, la Syrie, la Dar-Four*. Translated by J. Castera. 2 vols. Paris: Dentu, 1800.

Carbou, H. *La Région du Tchad et du Ouadaï*. 2 vols. Paris: Leroux, 1912.

El Tounsy, Mohamed Ibn Omar. *Voyage au Darfour*. Translated by Dr. Perron. Paris: B. Duprat, 1845.

———. *Voyage au Ouaddai*. Translated by Dr. Perron. Paris: B. Duprat, 1851.

Greenberg, Joseph H. *The Languages of Africa*. Bloomington: Indiana University Press, 1966.

Grossard, Lieut. Col. *Mission de délimitation de l'Afrique Equatoriale Française et du Soudan Anglo-Egyptien*. Paris: Larose, 1913.

MacMichael, H. A. *A History of the Arabs in the Sudan and Some Account of the People Who Preceded Them and of the Tribes Inhabiting Darfur*. 2 vols. Cambridge: Cambridge University Press, 1922.

Nachtigal, G. *Sahara and Sudan*. 3 vols. (Vol. 3: *Ouaddaï et Dar-Four*, edited by E. Croddek.) Leipzig: Brockhause, 1889.

Thelwall, R.E.W. *Aspects of Language in the Sudan*. Coleraine, Northern Ireland: New University of Ulster, 1978.

Tubiana, Marie-José. *Survivances preislamiques en pays Zaghawa*. Paris: Institute d'Ethnologie, 1964.

Tubiana, Marie-José, and Tubiana, Joseph, eds. *Contes Zaghawa*. Paris: Les Quatre Jeudis, 1961.

Articles

Hillelson, E. H. "Note on the Dago with Special Reference to the Dago Settlement in Western Kordofan." *Sudan Notes and Records* 8:1 (1925): 59–73.

Macintosh, E. H. "A Note on the Dago Tribe." *Sudan Notes and Records* 14 (1931): 171–178.

Thelwall, R. "Lexico Statistical Relations between Nubian, Daju and Dinka," pp. 265–286 in *Etudes nubiennes*. Cairo: Institut Français d'Archéology Orientale (IFAO), 1978.

Unpublished Manuscripts

Berre, Henri. "Essay sur les dadjo." Archives de Fort-Lamy, 1946.

Giovansily, Lieut. "Eléments de monographie du district de Biltine." Archives de Biltine, 1936.

Largeau, Col. "Instructions au commandant de la 12e compagnie et du poste de Goz-Beida." Archives de Goz-Beida, 1912.

Henri Berre

DECCANI   The Deccan Plateau in south central India coincides with what used to be the princely state of Hyderabad, until 1948 ruled by the Sunni Muslim dynasty of Asaf Jahs (the *nizams* of Hyderabad). Its Muslim inhabitants, now citizens of the states of Andhra Pradesh, Mysore and Maharashtra, number over 8.9 million and share to a great extent a common and distinctive heritage and culture.

Muslims have always been a small minority of the population—never more than 12 percent—yet, from the fourteenth century until 1948 they ruled the Deccan. Since its very beginning, Muslim rule in the Deccan largely depended on the immigration of Muslims from other Islamic countries. Local converts as well as settlers from north India, who called themselves Deccanis, competed with foreigners, soldiers, learned men and adventurers from Central Asia, Iran and the Hadramaut coast for royal patronage at the courts of the Bahmani sultans and their successors at Bijapur, Bidar, Berar, Ahmadnagar and Golconda. The more recent Muslim immigrants from north India are called ''Hindustanis.'' Large groups of Pushtun served in the *nizam's* army and police force. The Deccan also has its share of Gujarati Memons, Khojas and Bohras as well as Ahmadis and Wahhabis.

Those Arabs who first arrived in the eighteenth century to act as bodyguards for local rulers constituted a unique settlement. Their *jemadars* (military chiefs) were not only formidable soldiers but also prosperous moneylenders who maintained their own courts of justice and jails for defaulting debtors. Today pure Arabs (*usul*) are rare. Their descendants, offsprings of mixed marriage, termed *mawalud*, form a community which maintains its identity in dress, customs and language (now a corrupted form of Arabic). These Muslim groups have generally become an integral part of the region's Muslim urban communities in such cities as Gulbarga, Nizamabad and Hyderabad, where they constitute almost 37 percent of the cities' populations.

As a predominantly urban community, the Muslims constituted the ruling class and dominated government and military services. They were also found in trade and commerce. The lower Muslim class was employed by the wealthy landlords (*jagirdar*) in Hyderabad. Under the last resident *nizam*, Osman Ali Khan (1911–1948), Muslim dominance in the services and the army increased dramatically.

In 1948 the newly independent government of India forcibly removed the Muslim dynasty of Asaf Jahs. This event had a significant effect on the political, cultural and socioeconomic condition of the Deccani Muslims. A considerable number of civil servants, politicians, landlords and members of the commercial class emigrated to Pakistan. Those who stayed faced the necessity of adjusting to radically changed circumstances. The Muslims, used to thinking of themselves as rulers of the state, now had to learn how to be a minority under a Hindu majority government.

The political revolution that followed the invasion of Hyderabad by Indian troops greatly deprived the middle- and lower-class Muslims of their sources of patronage and power. The abolition of the *jagirdars* by the Hyderabad Military Government in 1949 eliminated the landlords. Many of these families, totally unprepared for this development, were plunged into destitution and despair.

The change in the Deccani Muslim community is most evident in the walled or old city of Hyderabad, where three-fourths of the city's Muslim population resides. The vast compounds of the various *nizams*' palaces—Purani Haveli, Chow Mahalla, King Koti—are deserted and barricaded. The *deorhis*, or city palaces of the noble families and landlords, are crumbling or have been razed to make room for public buildings or roads. The once elegant mirror hall of Salar Jung's palace now contains a cooperative store selling flour and soap. Its garden has become a repair shop for cars. In the shadow of these relics live the former servants of the big establishments of Muslim government and nobility, subsisting on small pensions or meager incomes of family members. A traditional *hakim* (doctor) wearing his purple fez squats all day on a sidewalk offering potions for sale. Another, who invented a type of ink, now advertises his product by submitting old and stained references from Muhammad Ali Jinnah, Jawaharlal Nehru and Mahatma Gandhi.

The mass of Muslims in the Deccan now earn their living in small trade, as laborers in industry, as carpenters, blacksmiths, tanners, shopkeepers and rickshaw drivers. The high birthrate (there is strong opposition to family planning) and the low literacy rate of this group stand in the way of economic improvement.

Muslim professionals have adjusted more easily to the new situation, entering banking, business, central government service or employment as scientists or teachers. This group has contributed to the Indian nation one president (Zakir Husain) and a number of ambassadors, governors and scientists.

The majority of Deccani Muslims speak Dakhni, an archaic variation of Urdu, which is an Indo-Iranian language developed in north India (see Urdu-speaking Peoples). Around 1885 Urdu replaced Persian as the administrative language of the state. It also was made the medium of instruction in Hyderabad's Osmania University. Following the overthrow of the *nizam*, Urdu, the language of the minority, was replaced as an official language by Telegu in Andhra Pradesh, Kannada in Mysore and Marathi in Maharashtra. The government refused to grant Urdu even the status of a secondary language. This complete withdrawal of state government patronage left the Deccani Muslims with a strong feeling of cultural loss. Dakhni had only recently attracted the attention of such linguistic scholars as Abdul Haq and S. M. Qadri Zor, professors of Urdu at Osmania University and founders of societies for the propagation of Urdu language and literature.

Political leaders and intellectuals take a keen interest in the community's political standing on the Indian subcontinent. They organize seminars and lectures to discuss the Indian Muslims' present condition and future. Middle-class educated Muslims, who support a more secular outlook and modern attitude towards personal law, Muslim education and minority status, often find it hard to bridge social and educational gaps in communicating with the more conservative Muslim community and religious leaders. The political party, Majlis Ittihad-ul-Muslimin, originally a cultural-religious association of the middle class and nobility founded in 1926, developed into an aggressive communal party during the independence movement. It was banned in 1948, but was revived in 1959. It has been successful in municipal and general elections, although it is strongly opposed by educated Muslims and others seeking social and cultural advancement.

Deccani Muslim culture is distinct from north Indian Muslim culture in that it has harmonized Hindu and Muslim elements to a large degree. In rural areas,

Muslims are closer to Hindu society culturally and socially than in the cities. Many local Hindu castes have Muslim branches, e.g., the Banjaras, whose Muslim counterpart is called Mukeri, are traders in cattle and are butchers. They practice endogamy and do not accept food from lower Hindu castes. They speak the local language, Kannada or Telegu, as well as Dakhni.

The social life of the Deccani Muslims focuses, as elsewhere in India, on the immediate family and religious community. Traditional settlement patterns are often maintained, particularly in the older parts of the cities. The Shia community in Hyderabad still clusters around the Salar Jung Palace; the Bohras live near their mosque, as do the Arabs and other Muslim groups.

The Shia, although probably forming less than 5 percent of the Muslim community, have played an important part in the cultural life of the Deccan because early Deccani sultans were Shia and attracted many followers to their courts and cities. After the conquest of the Deccan by the Moghuls in the late seventeenth century, their importance declined. Yet even under the Asaf Jahs a considerable proportion of the *jagirdar*, nobility and official class, was Shia, the most eminent of them being the family of Mir Alam and Salar Jung. The last *nizam* had strong leanings towards Shiism.

The Shia commemoration of the martyrdom of Hussain in the month of Muharram has special significance in Hyderabad and in some of the larger cities of the region. The old city of Hyderabad abounds in small and spacious *ashurkhanas*, which serve as meeting halls for the Shia community and storage places for the standards (*alam*) of the Muharram processions. The oldest and most remarkable is the Badshahi Ashurkhana, constructed by the Qutb Shahi dynasty in the late sixteenth century. It is accessible only during the first ten days of the month of Muharram.

The religious center of the Sunni community in Hyderabad is Mecca Masjid, next to the lofty structure of Char Minar (four minarets), which also contains a mosque above its high arches. The graves of Hyderabad's Asafi Muslim rulers line the main entrance.

Worship of saints is common among Deccani Muslims. One of the oldest centers of pilgrimage is Gulbarga, where the Chisti Pir Hazrat Syed Mohammad Gesu Daraz, popularly known as Khwaja Banda Nawaz (d. 1422), is venerated by Hindus and Muslims alike. The most popular saints in Hyderabad are the brothers Hazrat Yusuf and Hazrat Shareef, who accompanied the army of the Moghul ruler, Aurangzeb, to the Deccan and were famed for their extreme piety. On Thursday nights, music sessions draw large crowds to the graves. Every street and lane in Hyderabad seems to possess its own saint, whose grave, sometimes located in the middle of the road, is carefully attended. Graves are usually decorated with flags and fresh flowers and sometimes with bright paintings of tigers. The administration of the larger tombs has traditionally been in the hands of families who exert a strong material as well as spiritual influence on the Muslim community.

The center of Deccani Muslim culture, Hyderabad, bears all the characteristics of a transitional and changing society. Like no other Indian city it has, though, preserved a measure of Oriental charm and communal harmony as well as a variety of language, dress, and customs. Having lost its economic and political privileges, the Muslim community as a whole lacks vitality and initiative. Although its memories of bygone days form an important part of its consciousness, almost nothing is being done to preserve this recent heritage for future generations, neither by the Muslim community itself nor by the government of the state.

BIBLIOGRAPHY

Books

Ali, Mir Laik. *Tragedy of Hyderabad.* Karachi: Pakistan Co-operative Book Society, 1962.
Dube, S. C. "A Deccan Village." In *India's Villages*, edited by M. N. Srinivas. 2nd ed. London: Asia Publishing House, 1960.
————. *Indian Village.* Ithaca: Cornell University Press, 1955.
Khusro, A. M. *Economic and Social Effects of Jagirdari Abolition and Land Reforms in Hyderabad.* Hyderabad, India: Osmania University Press, 1958.
Lynton, H. R., and Rajan, Mohini. *The Days of the Beloved.* Berkeley: University of California Press, 1974.

Articles

Rashiduddin Khan. "Muslim Leadership and Electoral Politics in Hyderabad: A Pattern of Minority Articulation." *Economic and Political Weekly* 6:15 (1971): 783–794, and 6:16 (1971): 833–840.
Smith, W. C. "Hyderabad, Muslim Tragedy." *Middle East Journal* 4 (1950): 25–51.
Wright, Theodore P., Jr. "Revival of the Majlis Ittihad-ul-Muslimin of Hyderabad." *Moslem World* 53:3 (1963): 234–243.

Unpublished Manuscripts

Jacobson, Doranne. "Hidden Faces: Hindu and Muslim Purdah in a Central Indian Village." Ph.D. dissertation, Columbia University, 1970.
————. "Purdah in Central India." Paper presented at the 68th annual meeting of the American Anthropological Association, New Orleans, November 20–23, 1969.
Mines, Mattison. "The Muslim Merchants of Pallavarus, Madras: The Human Factor in Economic Behavior." Ph.D. dissertation, Cornell University, 1970.

Kerrin Gräfin Schwerin
Population figures updated by Richard V. Weekes

DIOLA   The Diola constitute the major ethnic group in the Lower Casamance region of southwestern Senegal. Numbering about 100,000 persons there, 450,000 elsewhere in Senegal, plus some 63,000 in Guinea Bissau and the Gambia, the Diola comprise several subgroups which are distinguished from one another by linguistic and cultural variations.

The isolation of these subgroups is reflected in the fact that, until the mid-nineteenth century, the Diola had no single word to identify themselves. From the late fifteenth century, the term "Floups" or "Felupes" was used by European travelers to refer to them. The term "Diola," apparently of Wolof origin, came into common usage during the mid-1800s. Some nineteenth-century sources spell the term, Yola. The Senegalese government has adopted the simplified spelling, Jola.

The several dialects of the Diola language, or dialect clusters, belong to the Bak subgroup of the West Atlantic language group. Diola is related closely to Manjak and Balant and more distantly to Wolof and Serer.

Although the Diola have been described as comprising as many as 15 subgroups, an underlying cultural unity is manifested in a common social organization, in the structure of indigenous religious beliefs and rituals and, above all, in their traditional wet rice agriculture.

Today, the Diola form three main cultural groups. South of the Casamance River among the Diola of Kasa, greater isolation has facilitated the retention of local customs and religious practices. Muslim *marabouts* never penetrated into Kasa, and, although many of the Diola-Kasa are now Catholic, traditional beliefs remain strong. North of the river in Fogny and Combo and in Boulouf, most of the Diola (approximately 150,000) have become Muslim, without, however, sacrificing their social and cultural identity. In the extreme eastern part of the Lower Casamance along the Soungrougrou River the Diola have adopted Manding agricultural techniques, and some have even abandoned their own language. Outside of this small Mandingized area, however, the Diola language together with the important men's initiation ritual and traditional rice farming have been retained.

The distinctively Diola rice crop is grown on wetlands bordering the *marigots*, or tidal streams, which crisscross much of the Basse Casamance. Some of the most fertile land is actually reclaimed from the mangrove thickets which proliferate along the *marigots*. Using the *kajando*, a long-handled hoeing and digging tool, the Diola construct low earthen dikes around their fields to keep out the salt water and to retain rain water during the growing season. As early as the seventeenth century, European observers noted the existence of these farming methods. Archeological evidence suggests that wet rice farming is far older still and may date to the middle of the first millennium A.D.

Men and women share the exacting labor of rice cultivation. With the arrival of the rainy season in late June or July the men prepare the fields, using the *kajando*. Once the heavier August torrents have inundated the fields, the women transplant the seedlings from nurseries, a task which entails working all day long in water frequently above the knee. Rice, depending on the variety, matures in 90 to 120 days, during which period the men, too, are at work caring for the fields. The rains end in late October, and from late November to January the women harvest the new crop. The dry season is then devoted to other activities including fishing, hunting, building houses or seeking seasonal employment in the cities. This traditional division of agricultural activity is followed by all the Diola south of the Casamance River and by the inhabitants of Fogny-Combo and Boulouf.

During the 1920s and 1930s the Diola of Fogny-Combo and Boulouf, encouraged by the colonial administration, began to cultivate peanuts on a large scale as a cash crop. Peanuts grow in the higher and drier soils of cutover forest land. The crop, which is raised by the men, does not require continuous care. Hence, the Diola have been able to establish a dual agriculture: rice for local consumption and peanuts as a source of income.

Diola society is patrifilial and totally lacking in political centralization. Before the colonial period, all subgroups apparently shared a common social organization. The basic residential unit, the extended family compound, or *fankafu*, usually comprised three generations of male descendants of an elder, together with their in-married wives and the unmarried female descendants of the elder. Related family groups lived together in a ward (*kalolaku*), and wards were loosely joined into a village (*esukay*). The component wards were frequently widely dispersed and, on occasion, might come into conflict with one another over ownership of rice fields; the appellation ''village cluster'' is thus as apt as ''village.'' Most Diola village clusters number several hundred to 2,000 inhabitants (although a few are as large as 5,000). This is the highest level of social organization in Diola society. Centralized political authority is nonexistent. Indeed, until French colonial administrators began to appoint village chiefs early in the twentieth century, the only form of village-wide authority was informal councils of elders.

Today, among the Muslim Diola of Fogny-Combo and especially of Boulouf, widespread urban migration of young people and the growing individualism which has accompanied the spread of the cash economy have led to the gradual breakup of the *fankafu*. Many younger men now inhabit nuclear family dwellings near the parental compound.

Traditional Diola religion centers on the *sinaati*, shrines which are the abodes of spiritual forces. Many shrines take the form of a forked stake set in the ground and perhaps covered by a small hut. A large proportion of them are associated either with a particular extended family group or with a ward. Most shrines are entrusted to the care of an elder male in the lineage. In pre-Islamic society, men approached the *sinaati* to fulfill their ritual obligations, to insure success in war and cultivation and to seek relief from illness. The *sinaati* were thought to visit specific ailments upon individuals who transgressed rules of social or ritual conduct. Contact with the *sinaati* was, and still is, accompanied by libations of palm wine or by animal sacrifices. While indigenous religion remains a dominant force south of the Casamance River, it occupies only a subsidiary role among the Muslim northern Diola.

Islam attracted its first Diola converts during the 1890s. The early Muslims were men who had traveled to the Gambia to trade rubber and palm produce. Within a few years several northwestern Diola communities, which maintained the closest commercial contact with the Manding, were predominantly Muslim (see Manding-speaking Peoples). Also beginning in the 1890s the establishment of French colonial administration over the Diola fostered increased communications between local populations and the outside world. Dyula (Manding) traders, some of whom served as *marabouts*, now circulated through the region. In addition, about 1900, the Mauritanian *marabout* Sharif Mahfuz established himself among the Diola. All of these factors fostered conversion.

During the 1920s, roads were constructed throughout the Lower Casamance, encouraging continued urban migration. The resulting partial integration into colonial society stimulated the rapid spread of Islam. By the end of the 1930s a majority of the northern Diola were converted. Today nearly 95 percent of the 110,000 inhabitants of Fogny-Combo and the 44,000 people of Boulouf are Muslim. Among all 613,000 Diola, perhaps 53.5 percent, or 328,000, are Muslim.

Diola Muslims, like their coreligionists in the rest of Senegal, belong to a Sufi *tariqa*. The Diola, however, attach less importance to *marabouts* than do the Wolof, Serer and Tukolor. Indeed, many Casamance Muslims do not even follow a particular *marabout*. Diola independence and egalitarian spirit are further reflected in the complete rejection of the Mourid brotherhood.

A majority, and perhaps as many as three-quarters of Diola Muslims, are associated with the Qadiriyya, which was originally brought to the Lower Casamance by Dyula traders and Manding *marabouts*, and by Sharif Mahfuz. In their choice of a *tariqa* the Diola are less exclusivist than their northern Senegalese counterparts. Some Diola have even gone so far as to take both the Tijaniyya and the Qadiriyya, a situation which is regarded as anathema by the Tivaouane school of the Tijaniyya. The Diola attitude reflects the fact that Islam did not reach them until after the period of nineteenth-century militant Tijaniyya reform. Both the Qadiriyya and the Tijaniyya were spread through the Lower Casamance only by peaceful means.

Most Diola Muslims, at least in Boulouf, are largely unlettered in Arabic. Many *marabouts*, however, as well as most *imams*, are local Diola who have achieved varying degrees of literacy in Arabic. In Muslim communities in Boulouf, important Islamic holidays assume the aspect of community-wide celebrations, with the entire village gathering to pray at the central mosque. The Friday prayer, too, draws all the men together, while daily prayers are observed at the mosques of each ward.

In Boulouf and in Fogny-Combo the village-wide initiation ceremony, or *bukut*, which is held every 15 or 20 years, continues. This ceremony and the attendant initiation retreat are central to Diola cultural identity and to the transmission of traditional knowledge. Many pre-Muslim sacrifices and libations, however, have been removed from the *bukut* as a result of the Islamization of the population.

Most Muslims accept the *bukut* initiation as congruent with their new religion. In recent ceremonies in Boulouf, however, a small Tijaniyya minority assumed a more orthodox position and refused to allow their sons to participate in the initiation retreat. This group has served, in communities where it is strong, to promote more complete Islamization through the abandonment of traditional religious practices.

In Muslim Diola communities today, many of the traditional religious shrines have disappeared, and the remainder are in the care of a few non-Muslim elders. Although regular sacrifices to the *sinaati* are rare, particularly in Boulouf, many Muslims do continue to consult the *sinaati* in time of illness.

BIBLIOGRAPHY

Books

Diarra, Fatoumata-Agnes, and Fougeyrollas, Pierre. "Ethnic Group Relations in Senegal." In *Two Studies on Group Relations in Africa: Senegal and the United Republic of Tanzania*. Paris: UNESCO, 1974.
Linares de Sapir, Olga. "Agriculture and Diola Society." In *African Food Production Systems*, edited by P. F. McLoughlin. Baltimore: Johns Hopkins Press, 1970.
Murdock, George P. *Africa: Its People and Their Culture History*. New York: McGraw-Hill, 1959.
Nelson, Harold D., et al. *Area Handbook for Senegal*. 2nd ed. The American University FAS, DA Pam 550–70. Washington, D.C.: Government Printing Office, 1974.
Sapir, J. David. *A Grammar of Diola-Fogny*. Cambridge: Cambridge University Press, 1969.
———. "West Atlantic: An Inventory of the Languages, the Noun Class Systems, and Consonant Alteration." In *Current Trends in Linguistics*, edited by Thomas Sebeok. Vol. 7. The Hague: Mouton, 1971.
Thomas, Louis V. "The Cosmology of the Diola." In *African Systems of Thought*, edited by Meyer Fortes and G. Dieterlen. London: Oxford University Press, 1965.
Trimingham, J. Spencer. *The Influence of Islam Upon Africa*. New York: Praeger, 1968.

Articles

Linares de Sapir, Olga. "Shell Middens of Lower Casamance and Problems of Diola Protohistory." *West African Journal of Archaeology* 1 (1971): 23–54.
Sapir, J. David. "Kujaama: Symbolic Separation Among the Diola-Fogny." *American Anthropologist* 72:6 (1970): 1330–1348.

Unpublished Manuscripts

Leary, Frances Anne. "Islam, Politics, and Colonialism: A Political History of Islam in the Casamance Region of Southwestern Senegal, 1850–1914." Ph.D. dissertation, Northwestern University, 1970.

Mark, Peter. "Economic and Religious Change Among the Diola of Boulouf (Casamance), 1890–1940: Trade, Cash Cropping, and Islam in Southwestern Senegal." Ph.D. dissertation, Yale University, 1976.

Snyder, Francis. "Land Transfers and Land Reform in Senegal." Paper presented at the 16th annual meeting of the African Studies Association, Syracuse, N.Y., November 3, 1973.

———. "A Problem of Ritual Symbolism and Social Organization Among the Diola-Bandial." Yale Law School Program in Law and Modernization, Working Paper No. 2, 1972.

Peter Mark
Population figures updated by Richard V. Weekes

DIVEHI   The Divehi people, or Maldivians, occupy the whole of the Maldive Islands, an archipelago of coral atolls in the Indian Ocean about 400 miles west of Sri Lanka. There are some 1,000 little islands and islets, stretching for 475 miles and grouped into a score of atolls. Most islands have fresh water because rainfall is abundant, and vegetation is lush on islands where enough humus is mixed with the coral sand. Coconut palms predominate.

The people refer to themselves and their language as Divehi (islander) and their country as Divehi Rajje (Republic of Maldives). They number around 200,000 and live on 200 of the country's islands. Divehi (sometimes spelled "Divessi") are not found elsewhere except on the island of Maliku (Minicoy on the maps) to the north, which was once part of Divehi Rajje but now belongs to India. To the south of the Maldives lies Chagos Archipelago, containing Diego Garcia, but it was uninhabited until modern times. The Divehi people are conscious of their ethnic identity, and their country has almost always been politically independent or autonomous. The Maldive Republic has been a member of the United Nations since 1965.

The capital of Divehi Rajje is Malé, an island city in the center of the country, from which Indian traders came to call the country "Maldiv." Malé is one mile long and has a population of 40,000. It is the only town in the Maldives, with houses of coral stone and many mosques that give it a pious air, the tranquility of which is shattered nowadays by cars and motorcycles. Nowhere else on the islands are there high schools, banks and shops. It also has the only government hospital.

Divehis began settling in the Maldives probably as early as the fifth century B.C. for the islands are alluded to in the early legends of Sri Lanka. There is no doubt that most of the Divehi people came from Sri Lanka, but there was an early substratum of Tamil-Malayalam population, apparent in the old kinship system and faintly reflected in the language. A tribe-like group from Giravar Island in the North Malé Atoll, which once ruled Malé and claimed descent from Tamils, until recently lived in Hulule, the airport island near Malé, and is largely acculturated by Divehis. There is no other aboriginal population in the Maldives.

Pre-Muslim civilization reached its height in the tenth to twelfth centuries, as the whole country was welded together by a highly centralized political system derived from Sri Lanka, perhaps brought by political exiles. From Sri Lanka came Theravada Buddhism as the official religion, *stupa* architecture and sculpture motifs (reproduced in coral stone), a script similar to that of medieval Sinhala, a calendar and an astrological system, magic and exorcism and elements of caste and language, much of which still exists. The people's appearance, mannerisms and food habits betray their derivation from Sri Lanka and south India.

The Divehi language is Indo-Aryan resembling an early form of Sinhala called Elu, although it also contains some earlier Prakrit elements. In recent centuries, it has borrowed words from Arabic, Hindi, Tamil and Gujarati, but sparingly. The language is written in a unique script invented about three centuries ago, consisting of nine Arabic numerals and nine old Sinhala numerals used for consonants, plus a complement of ten vowel marks placed over and under the consonants. It is easily learned and suits the language well. It reads from right to left and combines elements of both the Arabic and South Asian script systems, but Arabic words, such as personal names and greetings, are inserted in the script in Arabic.

The Divehis are 100 percent Muslim. It is believed that in 1154 a saint from Morocco dispelled an apparition in Malé harbor, converted the king and designated him sultan. Thereafter, all his subjects were compelled to accept Islam. The *Tarikh*, a chronicle in Arabic, records the reigns of 92 sultans (and a few sultanas). Ibn Batuta, the famed Arab traveler and chronicler, appeared in Malé in 1343 and stayed for a year and a half as *qadi* (*qazi*), as there was no judge there trained in Islamic law.

The Portuguese ruled the Maldives for 15 years in the mid-sixteenth century but were overthrown by a hero, Muhammad Takurufan, whose epic deeds as narrated today show the antipathy of the Divehis to outsiders and to Christians in particular. The British signed an agreement to "protect" the Maldives in 1887, but did not administer it internally and left no colonial stamp. They withdrew in 1965, and in 1968 a republic was proclaimed and the sultanate abolished. The government today, however, is still highly centralized.

The country is divided into 19 administrative atolls, each having an appointed atoll chief and a staff of officers. Each inhabited island has an appointed island chief and an assistant. Citizens of each island are listed in local census records. No one can get lost in the Maldives, and no one exiled to another atoll can run away, since all boat movements are known to the island chief. Moving from one island to another is difficult, as the law requires 12 years of residence before citizenship can be transferred; marriage is preferentially within the island.

Almost all land is owned by the state. The Island Office can allot house sites to certified citizens of the island. The government leases "uninhabited" islands to individuals, who often sublease them and live in Malé. If a family lives on such an island to collect coconuts and product, its members must still belong to one of the 200 "inhabited" islands. In Divehi there is no word for "city," "town" or even "village." All are just "island," the basic administrative unit.

The economy rests on fishing, mostly of bonito and tuna, by line and hook. Most men are fishermen, but on each island there are only a few men who own boats. The boats are wooden craft of exceedingly fine workmanship, 30 to 40 feet long, fitted with lateen sails. Among the 6 or 10 men of a boat crew, there is a clearly defined hierarchy, each grade getting a certain percentage of the fish catch. A boat owner wields political power and may become an island chief. Surplus fish is dried and smoked and exported to Indian Ocean countries. Boats taking dried fish to Malé return to their home islands with manufactured or processed items such as flour, rice, sugar, kerosene and cloth. All fish exports and most imports to the Maldives are monopolized by the government.

Agriculture is not highly regarded. Three kinds of millets are grown, and yams and tapioca in the south. Some houses have a breadfruit, banana or papaya tree, but few have vegetable gardens. Rice and Sri Lanka curry condiments are relished, but not many can afford these, for the per capita income is not much more than $100 a year. The most common diet consists of millets or yams, fish broth and coconut.

There are now two other sources of income for the Maldives: the tourist business (there are hotels on many otherwise uninhabited islands, patronized by Europeans) and the Maldive Shipping Lines, but most of the income from these sources goes to a few favored families in Malé, where it supports a standard of living far above the rest of the country.

The ethos of Islam is very strong. Each island has at least one mosque whose functionary, *mudim*, is paid by the government in Malé. The island chief, *katib*, must also be a religious leader qualified to preach Friday sermons. There is a system of atoll courts having *qadis* as judges, and the Shariah is interpreted and enforced by the attorney general. Cases involving inheritance, divorce and sexual offenses, for example, are tried under religious law. All citizens are also required to observe the fast of Ramadan and the two Id festivals and to give to religious charity. No marriage of non-Muslims is possible, and all children are christened with an Arab name. Shafi law has been official since the sixteenth century, and rules of ablutions and prayer times are rigidly enforced.

The Divehi also follow a parallel religious system called *fandita* (from *pandit*, an Indian "learned person"). Through its rituals, people seek healing, solution to problems and success. *Fandita* men are found on all the islands, and Malé has 200 of them. They validate their occupation in terms of Islam by intoning Arabic-sounding incantations, writing Arabic-looking marks on white flags to fly over fields or boats or scratching words from the Quran on the corners of magic diagrams inserted into cylindrical charms to be worn on the person. These charms are strung with a black string as in India and Sri Lanka. In the south, Sinhala *fandita* mantras induce black magic, love or prosperity. In payment for his services, a *fandita* man traditionally receives 2 percent of the fish catch.

Divehi people are exceedingly fearful. Women and children often run at the sight of a stranger, and there is general fear of the evil eye and of *jinns*, particularly the latter. (Names of some *jinns* are derived from Buddhist deities.) Nearly every household keeps a lamp burning all night. Houses seldom have windows—except in Malé—to reduce the risk of *jinns* entering from outside. This fear is well enough known to be the point of derisive humor elsewhere. To illustrate: a Divehi young man who went to Cairo to study religion was asked by his professor where he came from. When he mentioned the Maldives, the professor responded, "Ah! That is where Allah exiled the *jinns* from the whole world."

The life cycle consists of birth followed by a honey-feeding ceremony, the naming ceremony on the seventh day, circumcision (for girls, this is carried out by puncturing the vulva with a sharp instrument until a little blood appears), a puberty ceremony for girls at the time they don women's dress, marriage, divorce and death. The corpse is buried in the mosque yard facing Mecca, with sculptured head and foot stones. Education is not provided by the state in most islands, but the mosque schools teach some reading and religion. Most Divehis are literate because their parents teach them, and they also learn to pronounce the Arabic letters so they can intone the Quran. The high literacy rate, until recently, has not been a modernizing factor, as there has been little to read in most islands except a few religious pamphlets mimeographed in Malé.

The traditional society had a clear gradation of ranks, especially in Malé and in atoll headquarters. Nobility has now been abolished. Caste never became elaborate as in the rest of South Asia, but the major occupation and artisan groups, especially in the southern islands, remained virtually hereditary well into this century. And everywhere today the palm tree climbers, known as *raveri*, are in some respects a low caste.

The Maldive divorce rate is the highest among countries in the United Nations. In 1974, for each 100 marriages there were 85 divorces (87 in Malé). One can meet numerous people who have married 10 or more spouses. This is not inconsistent with the whole cultural pattern. The family is loosely structured. Marriage is not usually arranged and is without ceremony. A man can repudiate his wife according to Islamic law and report it to the *qadi*. A divorced woman can always return to the home of her official guardian and after three menstrual periods can remarry. Children are usually raised by the mother, but the father gives child support. Divorce is seldom traumatic for children as it is casual, not often attended by acrimony. The divorced parent may be seen by his children every day on the island and may even join the family again by remarriage.

The game of marriage and divorce may be important to the mental health of Divehis, because in those small isolated islands interpersonal relations are often the only source of excitement. It is principally in marriage, divorce and politics that personality finds expression.

The greatest problem in the Maldives is population growth, now about 3.3 percent a year. Copra, once exported, is now all locally consumed, and the fish catch cannot feet more people in addition to providing more exports. The population density is 1,600 per square mile. People accept, and until recently the government enforced, the attitude that family planning is un-Muslim. There is no recognition in the country of the prospects of doubled and quadrupled population. Given the divorce and remarriage pattern, the birthrate is likely to remain high. If this growth cannot be accommodated, perhaps many of the mentioned cultural features will become obsolete in the process of adaptation to the resource base. The stream of tourists, foreign aid (especially from Arab countries) and United Nations development agencies has set in motion a new phase in the history of the Divehis.

BIBLIOGRAPHY

Books

Bell, H.C.P. *The Maldive Islands: Monograph on the History, Archaeology and Epigraphy*. Colombo, Ceylon: n.p., 1940.
Hockley, T. W. *The Two Thousand Islands*. London: n.p., 1935.
Maloney, Clarence. *People of the Maldive Islands*. Madras: Orient Longman, 1980.

Article

Maloney, Clarence. "The Maldives: New Stresses in an Old Nation." *Asian Survey* 16:7 (1976): 654–671.

Clarence Maloney

DONGXIANG   Three Muslim ethnic groups live in the villages and towns along the rivers flowing out of the Qilian and other mountains in north central China. The largest is the Dongxiang (the others, the Bonans and Salars), numbering approximately 307,000, most of whom live in the Dongxiang Autonomous County in Gansu Province. This county, established in 1950, is in Linxia Hui Autonomous Prefecture and borders on the Tao River in the east, the Daxia River in the west and the Huang (Yellow) River in the north. Smaller groups form compact communities in Hezheng County and Linxia City, both also in Gansu Province. Still smaller groups live in the provincial capital of Lanzhou and are scattered throughout Dingxi District as well as the Ningxia Hui Autonomous Region.

The seat of Dongxiang County is Sonoba, 8,600 feet high in a dry mountain area from which radiate 19 mountain ranges, from 10 to 20 miles in length.

Before 1950, the Dongxiang were known as Dongxiang Hui or Mongolian Huihui, but the Dongxiang referred to themselves simply by what is now the official designation. The word is Chinese and means "the eastern village," that is, a village located east of Linxia, the nearest major city. Some foreign observers have called the Dongxiang "Santa," but in its present usage this word refers only to a Dongxiang who is a practicing Muslim, and it is thus strictly a religious term.

Dongxiang is one of several Mongolian languages, which, in turn, belong to the Altaic language family. Quite a few words in its lexicon resemble words of the same meaning in Modern Mongolian, and some are even identical to words presently used in Inner Mongolia. Many other words are close to Middle Mongolian spoken in the thirteenth and fourteenth centuries. This is, of course, not surprising because at that time the Dongxiang were cut off from the mainstream of Mongolian life and from later changes in the Mongolian language.

A remnant of Middle Mongolian in Dongxiang is the intervocalic -g- and -d-, as in *nogosun* (wool) and *shidun* (tooth). Both words are still written this way in the traditional script used in Inner Mongolia but are pronounced *noos* and *shüd* respectively.

Certain grammatical features, such as declension and adverbial use, are also similar to Modern Mongolian. On the other hand, Dongxiang contains features not found in Modern Mongolian. For example, it has neither long vowels nor vowel harmony. Also, in some words, final -r and -g are absent, e.g., *kha* (hand), which in Modern Mongolian is *gar*.

The Dongxiang never had their own writing script. In the past, the relative handful of literates used the Arabic script for religious purposes and Chinese for secular transactions. At present, a script based on the Latin alphabet is being introduced in Dongxiang County on an experimental basis.

The Dongxiang's origin is still a matter of debate because relevant documents shed little light on their past. One oral tradition describes them as descendants of Mongol soldiers who during Genghis Khan's campaigns settled in the Hezhou region (now Dongxiang County), where they gradually became citizens. Some place names tend to support this theory; for example, "Dazidi" (the Place of the Dazi) refers to "Dazi," an old Chinese epithet for the Mongols. Similarly, "Zhayingtan" (Encampment Beach) is said to be the site of an old Mongol garrison, and "Mading" suggests a place where the Mongol army grazed its horses.

Historical records reveal that when in 1226 Genghis Khan attacked the Tangut state of Xixia for a second time, the Hezhou area became an important staging area where a military farm (*tuntian*) was established. During Monghe's reign Hezhou was used as a major strongpoint in the campaign against the Tibetans. After Kublai Khan conquered the Tangzang area of northern Tibet, he established in Hezhou three different kinds of offices. The incumbent of one of these, Ananda, one of Kublai's many grandsons, adopted Islam during Timur's reign (1295–1307), and most of his 150,000 troops followed suit.

Another theory sees the Dongxiang as part of the Chagatai khanate, which flourished during the Yuan period in what is now Chinese (Xinjiang) and Soviet Central Asia. There they converted to Islam but were promptly discriminated against by other Mongols who resisted conversion. To avoid further friction, the Islamized Mongols moved eastward by way of Xingxingxia. When they reached

Zhenfan (today's Minqin County in Gansu) they split into two routes. One group crossed the Helan Mountains and went to Hetao, where their descendants are today Muslim Mongols of the Alashan Left Banner in Inner Mongolia. The other group turned south, crossed the Huang River and settled in the Hezhou area.

A third notion, held by only a few persons, claims that the Dongxiang were originally Hui living in the present Dongxiang area who over the centuries mingled with Han and Mongols. Judging by linguistic and other evidence, this theory is probably incorrect. There is a general consensus that the main stock of the original Dongxiang was Mongol, not Hui (see Hui). Later, during the Ming and Qing dynasties, these Mongols began to intermarry with Hui, Han and Tibetans living in the area. Surnames among the present Dongxiang are reminders of this intermingling. Surnames like Ma and Mu are clearly of Hui origin. Dongxiang families with names like Wang, Kang, Zhang, Gao and Huang say they descended from old Han families. Place names like Tangwangchuan, Wangjiaji, Zhangjiacun, Gaojiazhuang and Miaoerling also reflect old Han residences. The least numerous surnames are of Tibetan origin; in fact, only the Yang clan from Yangzhijia claims descent from Tibetans.

The mainstay of the Dongxiang economy is farming, the major crops being potatoes, wheat, highland barley, millet and corn. Of these, potatoes take up some 66,880 acres. The Dongxiang's potato mash, grainy and sweet, is used in making various snacks, liquor, vinegar noodles and many other food items which have found wide acceptance among members of other ethnic groups in Gansu and Qinghai provinces. Economic crops are broad bean, hemp, sesame seeds and rape seeds. Along the banks of the Tao and Daxia rivers grow large quantities of melons and fruit, and in the mountainous areas are many kinds of wild medicinal plants.

Some 90 percent of the Dongxiang area has suffered from severe soil erosion. This problem has been somewhat alleviated in recent years through massive reforestation. As a result, over one-third of the steep slopes are now cultivated. Food production in 1978 was 70 percent higher than the record crop of 1949.

In recent years a few industrial plants have been erected in the Dongxiang area. They are mostly factories for making generators, farm implements, cement, flour and bricks. All-weather roads connect Sonoba with Lanzhou and Linxia and within the county; unimproved roads connect Sonoba with every commune seat.

Before the Communist takeover, there were three Muslim sects among the Dongxiang. Sixty-eight percent belonged to the Old Teaching (*lao jiao*), which was introduced in the late eighteenth century and included many practices of pre-Islamic Chinese culture. The New Teaching (*zin jiao*), introduced around the turn of this century, was numerically much smaller but politically ambitious and sought a purer observance of Islamic law and practices. Numerous clashes broke out between the two sects, to a large extent because of the support given to the New Teaching by the Ma clan, which dominated Gansu and Qinghai provinces during much of the republican period. There was also a third sect, called the Newly Awakened Teaching (*xin sing jiao*), but it had very few adherents and practically nothing is known about it.

As late as the 1940s the Dongxiang area had 595 mosques, 9 religious schools, 12 major religious leaders such as *ahongs* and *mullahs* and more than 2,000 religious personnel. This averaged out to 1 mosque for every 30 households and 1 religious professional for every 9 households. The status of religion and its observance by the Dongxiang today await the enterprise of researchers and the permission of the government of the Peoples Republic of China.

BIBLIOGRAPHY

Books

"Dongxiang zu." In *Zhongguo shaoshu minzu*. Beijing: Renmin chubanshe, 1981.
Todaeva, Bulyash Khoichievna. *Dunsyanskii yazyk*. Moscow: Nauka, 1961.

Articles

Nasunbayar. "Düngsiyang helen-ü temdeglel." *Mongolyn sudlalyn zarim asuudal, Studia Mongolica* (Ulaanbaatar) 3:1–5 (1961): 53–106.
———. "Düngsiyang helen-ü tuhai tobqi temdglel." *Monggol helen-ü shinjilchen-ü ügülel-üd* (1976): 300–384.
Schwarz, Henry G. "A Script for the Dongxiang." *Zentralasiatische Studien* 16 (1982): 153–164.

Henry G. Schwarz

DUNGANS (SOVIET UNION) The Dungans are a small Chinese Muslim population living in the Soviet Union. They have lived there for about 100 years and number some 50,000, a number which is increasing rapidly; the average Dungan family has eight children.

The Dungans originally lived mainly in Gansu and Shaanxi provinces in northwest China, although some also came from Xinjiang in the far west near the Soviet border. The question of their precise origin has never been settled satisfactorily. According to various Western, Chinese, Dungan and Soviet scholars, the ancestors of the Chinese-speaking Muslims of China could have come from one or two or a mixture of several of the following groups: Persians, Arabs, Mongols, Manchus, Turks, Tanguts, Kitans, Uygurs or Tibetans (see Hui).

The Dungans migrated to Soviet Central Asia in two movements. The first was the gradual emigration from the Ili River valley in Xinjiang, where they had been settled by Emperor Zianlong in the eighteenth century. In this movement there were two major migrations: that of 1867, after an outburst of racial conflict between Dungans and the Taranchi (Turks); and that of 1881, when part of the Ili River valley was returned by Russia to the Chinese government. The second movement was the headlong flight in 1877 of those who had supported the autonomous state of Kashgaria.

The Dungans do not call themselves "Dungans" unless they are speaking or writing in Russian. In the past, they called themselves *Zhongyuan-ren* (in Chinese; Zhongyuan is the common name for Henan province). Since about 1960, however, the Dungans have tried, with reasonable success, to change this term to Huizu, a name by which the Hui, or Chinese-speaking Muslims, are commonly known throughout China. Russians use the term "Dungane."

The Dungans are divided into two groups: the Gansu Dungans who live in the Kirghiz S.S.R.; and the Shaanxi Dungans who live in the Kazakh S.S.R. They may also be divided into a small group of city dwellers and a larger group of collective farmers. Urban Dungans live mainly in Frunze and Alma-Ata, while farmers live in Kazakh S.S.R., Kirghiz S.S.R. and Uzbek S.S.R. In cities there are Dungan poets, writers, linguists, academicians, historians and newspaper editors. Some well-educated Dungans work in the Dungan section of the Academy of Sciences. On the collective farms, besides the farmers, there are Dungan chairmen, teachers and doctors.

With the exception of the *mullahs*, most Dungans arrived in Russia 100 years ago as poor illiterate peasants. At first those who could write used the Arabic script, familiar to them from the Quran. Later, various versions of the Latin alphabet were adopted and discarded, having proved unsuitable. During this time they wrote a number of books in the Latin alphabet. The present alphabet was adopted at a series of conferences in Frunze from 1953 to 1955. This alphabet was based on the Cyrillic script with five additional letters. An extensive literature, including a newspaper, textbooks, collections of poetry and short stories, novels, dictionaries and works on linguistics, history and phonetics now is published in this alphabet.

Dungans speak two similar dialects, Ganzu and Shaanxi. The Ganzu dialect is the official language used in all publications, schools and radio broadcasts.

There is controversy about the Dungan language. Strong evidence indicates that it is Chinese, with three tones. However, Dungans themselves insist that their language is not Chinese but an independent language with Chinese roots, shaped by ethnic, economic and other factors and influenced by Turkic and Russian languages. Dungan scholars stress that the two Dungan dialects are quite different both phonetically and syntactically from the Ganzu and Shaanxi dialects of Chinese.

Most Dungans speak Dungan, Russian and either Kirghiz or Kazakh. Many claim to know Tatar, Uzbek or Uygur. Among themselves, they speak Dungan, however their speech is sprinkled with Russian—single Russian nouns (mainly domestic, agricultural or Communist terms), Russian exclamations and Russian set phrases and common expressions. Urban Dungans speak fluent Russian; some old and even middle-aged men and some of the young and older Dungan women in the collective farms speak only Dungan.

Dungans are proud to be Dungans and regard themselves as an independent community speaking an independent language. They have cut their ties with China and have isolated themselves from their country of origin by indifference on the part of most of farmers and hostility on the part of many Dungan scholars. Hostility between China and the Soviet Union may also be a factor, but there appear to be other likely reasons for Dungan rejection of China. One is their lengthy residence in the Soviet Union, where they live quite well (they appear to be happy and have no nostalgia for the past). Another is their knowledge that the Muslims were suppressed and massacred by the non-Muslim Chinese during the Ching dynasty. As an immigrant community from China attempting to preserve their identity, the Dungans are conservative and nationalistic. As a small ethnic minority they wish to be regarded as an independent community, speaking their own language—they use such terms as "Dungan language," "Dungan dialects," "Dungan people," "Dungan food" and even "Dungan vinegar" when speaking in Russian.

Farmers live on "Dungan" collective farms (*kolkhoz*) or villages (*selo*), "Dungan" because 75 to 90 percent of the people are Dungans, the rest being from a large variety of ethnic groups.

Collective farms have a population of from 6,000 to 11,000, with 750 to 1,300 households and 1,200 to 2,600 workers. These farms have electricity, running water and gas for cooking. Each has a village council (*soviet*) which deals with the management of the farm. In each collective there are one or two schools, all subjects being taught in Russian. Dungan children already speak Dungan so in addition they have instruction in reading and writing Dungan for two hours a week.

Each farm has one or two day nurseries, one hospital with an outpatient clinic and a separate maternity clinic. There is also a palace of culture, which often has a large auditorium and a small library attached. Most farms also have general stores and a post office, plus such additional facilities as a bathhouse, machine repair shops, motor depots, greenhouses, tobacco factories, dairies, dining halls, bookshops, barbers and evening schools.

Most Dungans live in comfortable, well-built and spacious houses, many with an enclosed courtyard. The main gates are often decorated, carved and painted blue. There is a summer kitchen and a vegetable garden. Most have a private plot of land, usually about half an acre, adjacent to the courtyard or outside the courtyard walls. While once they produced rice, Dungan farmers now raise sugar beets and some vegetables, milk and cattle. In their private plots they grow vegetables for their own use and other crops such as garlic and tobacco for private sale.

Most Dungans wear Western clothes. Dungan brides, however, still wear the bridal costumes of 100 years ago. Shaanxi women still wear Chinese trousers underneath their dresses. The trousers are always tied tightly around the ankles (Shaanxi are regarded as more conservative than Gansu). The women were binding their feet until as recently as 1948. Most middle-aged and old Dungan men wear either a skull cap or a felt hat, and most married women of all ages wear a kerchief on their heads tied at the nape. Dungan women have never worn veils. They were always allowed to appear in public with uncovered heads. Elaborate coiffures decorated with jewelry were worn by Dungan women in the past, and this seems to be the explanation. The modern bride still follows this custom but always holds one or two large red kerchiefs.

Dungans living in the Soviet Union among the Kirghiz, Kazakhs, Uzbek and Russians have adapted their way of life to the local customs and climate. The gradual change in their material culture is probably also a result of the availability of, or perhaps more importantly the lack of, appropriate materials in the shops and factories and the different skills of the local craftsmen.

Dungan food, despite some small changes and the influence of neighbors, is similar to the cooking of north China. Dungans still eat with chopsticks, and the names of their national dishes, seasonings and cooking terms are Chinese. Dungan food is lavishly seasoned with garlic and vinegar. Fried vegetables are a favorite dish. They eat mutton, lamb and chicken but, as Muslims, they do not eat pork. Fish dishes are rare. They still follow the north Chinese habit of preferring noodles to rice and enjoy various dishes made from wheat flour. Normally, rice is not served to guests. Tea, served in wide-rimmed bowls with no milk or sugar, and many plates of all kinds of sweets (chocolates, candies, dried fruits, biscuits) are served before and after every meal.

Dungans are a hospitable people. Though occasionally they serve the traditional "four-dish" meal to guests, they favor a festive banquet with dishes arranged in three rows extending the length of a long table. These can consist of 9, 18, 24, 36 or 48 dishes. Dungan women cook and serve all the meals but rarely sit down to eat with guests.

There exists an unwritten Dungan tradition about mixed marriages. All Dungan girls should marry Dungan men. Gansu Dungan girls may marry Shaanxi Dungan men, but Shaanxi prefer their daughters to marry only Shaanxi men. Kazakhs and Kirghiz, being Muslim, are acceptable for husbands, but not Russians. Similar but less strict rules apply in the case of Dungan men. Dungans have Kirghiz or Kazakh wives, and some city Dungans have been known to marry Russian women, all of whom must learn Dungan and cook Dungan food.

Dungans belong to the Sunni sect of Islam and observe Hanafi law in personal matters. They are proud of being more devout and more strict than their non-Dungan Muslim neighbors. One explanation for this strictness is that the Kazakh and Kirghiz are pastoral nomads while Dungans are settled farmers. Dungan *mullahs* (*ahong*) pay periodic visits to the collective farms, giving names to newborn babies, although most young parents today do not ask for this help and rely on their mothers and grandmothers to choose a name. Common Dungan names include Fatima, Khazan, Mahmud and Abdurakhman. As for surnames, Ma—one of the most common surnames among Chinese Muslims—in Russian has become Makeev or Makeeva. (The most prominent Dungan woman scholar is Fatima Makeeva.) The surname "Sushanlo" comes from the Chinese, "a village head by the surname of Su." The surname "Shivaza" comes from the Chinese, "the tenth child."

Dungans of the older generation still fast for 30 days during the month of Ramadan. The fast is not observed by the younger generation. They give the excuse that they work hard all day in the fields and need proper nourishment to maintain their strength.

In general, young Dungans are either actively against or indifferent to Islam, but they turn to religion after about the age of 40. Some sources place the "critical age" at 55. This change has nothing to do with poverty or ignorance. Some pious Dungans in well-to-do families, whose sons may be studying at universities in Frunze or Moscow, pray in the courtyard and go to the mosque.

Both young farmers on the collectives and older Dungans from the cities usually show respect for the elders and the clergy. Most Dungan scholars, however, write rather critically about Islam. They claim that some Dungans still have a strong religious-feudal mentality, which the *mullahs* constantly seek to arouse. The *mullahs*, it is said, often try to force Dungans not to allow their children to attend school or college. Dungan girls sometimes do leave school because of this pressure.

Dungans have preserved not only their speech and food but many other aspects of Chinese and Muslim culture that they brought with them to Russia—religion, songs, poems, stories, legends, banquets, love for the land and wedding and funeral customs. Dungan wedding celebrations last for up to 10 days and include elaborate banquets. Much of the tradition brought from China is no longer practiced there.

The Dungans do well. What with large families, quite often several members bring in wages. They are self-sufficient in meat and vegetables; their collectives provide all they need. They are all related to one another, not only in the same collective but throughout the whole of Soviet Central Asia. As a closely knit community they look after and visit each other. They come from a long line of farmers, and their love for the land can be seen not only in the well-tended and neat rows of vegetables in their private plots and by the abundance of flowers in their courtyards but also in their enthusiasm and pride in their farms.

BIBLIOGRAPHY

Books

Dragunov, A. A. *Issledovaniia v oblasti dunganskoi grammatiki, I. kategoriia vida i vremeni v dunganskom iazyke (dialekt gan'su)*. Trudy instituta, Moscow: 1940.
Dyer, Svetlana Rimsky-Korsakoff. *Soviet Dungan Kolkhozes in the Kirghiz SSR and the Kazakh SSR*. Oriental Monograph Series, 25. Canberra: Faculty of Asian Studies, Australian National University Press, 1979.
Iusupov, Il'ia, I. *Dungane v period oktiabria*. Frunze, U.S.S.R.: Kirgizgosizdat, 1958.
———. *Kolkhoznoe selo Masanchin*. Frunze, U.S.S.R.: Ilim, 1967.

Shinlo, L. T. *Kul'tura i byt sovetskikh dungan.* Frunze, U.S.S.R: Ilim, 1978.
Sushanlo, M. *Dungane (istoriko-etnograficheskii ocherk).* Frunze, U.S.S.R.: Ilim, 1971.
———. *Sem'ia i semeinyi byt dungan.* Frunze, U.S.S.R.: Ilim, 1979.

Articles

Dragunov, E. and A. "Dunganskii iazyk." *Zapiski Instituta vostokovedeniia* 61 (1938): 117–131.
Dyer, Svetlana Rimsky-Korsakoff. "Muslim Life in Soviet Russia: The Case of the Dungans." *Journal of the Institute of Muslim Minority Affairs* 3 (1981): 42–54.
———. "Soviet Dungan: The Chinese Language of Central Asia; Alphabet, Phonology, Morphology." *Monumenta Serica* 26 (1967): 352–421.
———. "Soviet Dungan Nationalism: A Few Comments on Their Origin and Language." *Monumenta Serica* 33 (1977–1978): 363–378.
———. "Soviet Dungan Weddings: Symbolism and Traditions." *Monumenta Serica* 33 (1977–1978): 363–378.
Wexler, Paul. "Zhunyanese (Dungan) as an Islamic and Soviet Language." *Journal of Chinese Linguistics* 8:2 (1980): 294–304.

Unpublished Manuscripts

Dyer, Svetlana Rimsky-Korsakoff. "The Dungan Dialect: An Introduction and Morphology." M.S. thesis, Georgetown University, 1965.
———. "Dungan Nationalism." Paper presented at the Second National Conference of the Asian Studies Association of Australia, Sydney, May 14–18, 1978.
———. "The Soviet Dungans: Chinese Muslims in the Soviet Union." Paper presented at the 24th annual meeting of the Permanent International Altaistic Conference, Jerusalem, August 16–21, 1981.
Iusurov, Kh. "Vosstanie dungan v Severo-Zapadnom Kitae i pereselenie ikh v Semirech'e (1860–1890 gg.)." M. A. thesis, Frunze University, 1948.

Svetlana Rimsky-Korsakoff Dyer

DYULA Of the three main groups of Manding speakers in West Africa, the Dyula are the most difficult to define and locate because the meaning of the term "Dyula" (pronounced "joola") has changed throughout history. With the Mandinka and Bambara they form a linguistic and cultural population of more than 11.5 million (see Manding-speaking Peoples).

The word *dyula* means "trader" in Manding. *Dyula* can also refer to a Muslim trader who can speak a Manding language (though not necessarily as his first language), or it can refer to a specific ethnic group which differentiates itself from other Manding groups. Here, "Dyula" refers to the ethnic group of Manding speakers situated in northeastern and north central Ivory Coast, southwestern Upper Volta and contiguous areas of Ghana (where they are often called Wangara) and Mali.

The population size of the ethnic Dyula can only be guessed. Not only are census data outdated and unreliable, but the term, for instance, in the Ivory Coast (where they are most numerous) means an occupation category of people speaking a Manding dialect who are not ethnic Dyula. Certainly there are at least 1 million ethnic Manding-speaking Dyula in West Africa, of whom close to 98 percent are Muslim.

Historically the ethnic Dyula community has maintained two distinct subgroups: the warriors, called *tuntigi* or *sonanqui*; and the traders and Islamic scholars, called *dyula*. Though these distinctions are still remembered and maintained in village residence patterns, the occupational obsolescence of the warriors in modern society along with their conversion to an Islam untainted by traditional practices has made the differences in life-style and values between the two groups progressively disappear.

The Manding languages belong to the large Niger-Congo family of languages. The Dyula language or dialect is very closely related to Bambara, another Manding dialect (see Bambara). It is uncertain when dialect differentiation took place, but Dyula settlements began in the area by the fifteenth or possibly fourteenth century. Unlike other Manding groups, the Dyula have not developed or maintained a "caste" of *griots*, or praise-singers, concerned with keeping oral histories.

Dyula are literate, in varying degrees, in Arabic, which they use primarily for textual studies of the Quran and religious treatises. Some historical texts were written in the past, and traditions are still committed in writing in Arabic today. In a very few cases texts were written in Dyula in Arabic script. Except among reformist Muslims, Arabic maintains its place as the language of the sacred realm, and French and English are used for secular writings. Although Dyula are a small minority of the population of the Ivory Coast, the commercial Dyula language is becoming the second spoken language of a majority of the population.

The Dyula developed out of a migration of Manding-speaking traders from the ancient Mali empire in areas where they remained ethnic minorities. Trading clans spread throughout West Africa. Through the succeeding centuries many of these groups were amalgamated into the societies in which they settled, as for example in Nigeria and in the Mossi empire of central and eastern Upper Volta. In the west (Guinea and western Ivory Coast), the traders accompanied other Manding groups—warriors, blacksmiths and peasants. Although the traders were Muslims, they lived among traditionalists who spoke the same language and had the same cultural heritage. The ethnic Dyula however, settled in communities in which they were strangers. They maintained their separate identity and formed their sense of "Dyulahood." They became a distinct ethnic group, adopting some of the customs of surrounding groups but maintaining their Manding culture.

Dyula spread Manding influence, technology and culture throughout many areas of West Africa during their trading voyages and settlements. They introduced Islam, Arabic literacy and a particular mosque architectural style, characterized by sun-dried mud-bricks and numerous projecting supporting timbers.

The Dyula also became known for their work in weaving. They developed the long-distance salt–kola exchange trade, carrying Saharan rock salt from Niger River entrepôts south to exchange it for kola nuts grown in the forest areas of Ivory Coast and Ghana. They also provided the horses and guns used by many of the empire builders of the western Sudan.

In the late seventeenth or early eighteenth century, Manding-speaking warriors conquered the non-Muslim, non-Manding groups ruling these Dyula and created a loose empire around the village of Kong in northeastern Ivory Coast. Related warriors created smaller offshoot "kingdoms" in the Korhogo area of modern Ivory Coast, in southern Mali and in southwestern Upper Volta. The pagan groups acted as food providers, foot soldiers and even slaves for their Manding-speaking conquerors in the Kong empire.

The warriors were different in many ways from the Dyula. They had a warrior ethic and strove for political control, while the Dyula theoretically believed in nonviolence and abstained from political involvement. Though the warriors considered themselves Muslims, they participated in pagan initiation ceremonies while the Dyula did not. Because the warriors were Manding-speaking, they were called "Dyula" in this area. Even so, within Dyula society the two groups were kept distinct. The *sonanqui* maintained a loose control over their empire until the arrival of Samory Touré, a Manding-speaking conqueror from Guinea, just prior to French occupation.

While Manding society is traditionally divided into freeborn, slave and endogamous artisan castes, Dyula society in Ivory Coast did not maintain clear divisions between the freeborn and the artisans, probably because as a minority group the Dyula could not create a traditional Manding society out of their small numbers. When the Kong empire developed and Dyula numbers increased, Dyula had already lived for some time, possibly centuries, in a society without Manding caste divisions and so were not uncomfortable in maintaining a non-casted society. Some Dyula villages do have a few artisan groups, such as blacksmiths, but endogamy is not as strictly held as in other Manding-speaking societies. Slavery was important in precolonial Dyula society as it freed Muslim scholars from producing food, thus allowing them to devote their time to study. It also allowed traders to devote full time to commercial pursuits.

As with other Manding speakers, the Dyula are divided into patrilineal clans, or *jamu*. Each *jamu* carries a particular surname, such as Touré, Traore or Coulibaly. Reinforcing the unity of the Manding, these clan names are often found in all three of the main Manding-speaking ethnic divisions. Patrilineages with a recognized common ancestor are smaller divisions within each *jamu*. In a Dyula village the members of a patrilineage live in the same quarter and have a quarter head who watches over the harmony of the group. The quarters of a village contain one predominant lineage which founded the quarter. Associated stranger groups of the same or different *jamu*, who arrived after the founding lineage, may also live in this quarter. A village council consists of the heads of the different quarters who regulate village affairs. The head of the village is usually a descendant of the founder of the village. Although every Dyula village has an *imam* who is respected and consulted in religious and moral decisions, he does not usually become involved in day-to-day decisions. The Dyula have historically had an aversion to political involvement. Thus most political leaders are members of the warrior subdivision. There have even been instances when Dyula lineages have given up their position as village heads when a warrior lineage settled in the village.

Marriage among the Dyula remains polygynous, even though the 1965 Civil Code of the Ivory Coast has outlawed polygamy. The Dyula continue to contract polygynous marriages without officially registering them with the government. Parents or lineage heads generally arrange the marriages of the young. The Dyula follow Islamic marriage restrictions, although Dyula men do marry pagan women. They assume that the wife will convert to the husband's religion. For the same reason, Dyula women are not permitted to marry pagan men. Dyula marriages seem to take place most frequently between kin members, though not necessarily close kin. Some scholars have suggested that the Dyula, as traders, prefer to keep marriages within the family so that the family can maintain control over the assets of the heirs on the death of the parents. The warrior lineages follow these marriage patterns more closely now than they did in the past.

Women in Dyula society are not veiled or secluded, but they are restricted and controlled by the male family members. Dyula girls do not usually have any choice in their first marriage partners. The new Civil Code prohibits forced marriages, but they do still occur in villages not under direct government supervision. The marriage ceremony incorporates Manding customs, such as the exchange and sharing of kola nuts between the two families.

Dyula society places great emphasis on marriage, and women are generally urged to contract another marriage if divorced or widowed. Divorce is usually easier for the man to obtain, but in any case the families of the two disputants are always involved in trying to settle the affair short of divorce. Dyula women are considered financially independent of their husbands, although in recent years the women have less and less of an opportunity to gain a living on their own. The traditional areas of female labor and trade, such as the spinning of locally grown cotton or the selling of condiments in the markets, no longer provide them with sufficient income to meet their basic needs. Thus they are becoming more dependent on their husbands.

For centuries the Dyula education system has been based on a study of the Quran under masters who have achieved various levels of scholarship. Most young boys and many young girls spend a few years under the tutorship of a village master learning prayers, the rudiments of Arabic and portions of the Quran. The particularly gifted student may continue his studies through a commentary on the Quran, a basic text of Maliki law and a work on ethical conduct. Upon completion of these three works he may be awarded a white turban, a symbol of his religious knowledge and a source of prestige in the Dyula community.

The Dyula give respect to their Islamic scholars and go to them for help with everyday problems or if they are in ill health. Non-Muslims also consult them for the same services. The scholars earn money by writing charms to bring good luck. Quranic verses are enclosed in leather pouches and worn around the neck or somewhere on the person. People suffering from various illnesses also pay the holy men to pray for them or to prescribe certain herbal medicines. Also considered to be particularly efficacious is for the scholar to write a Quranic verse in charcoal on a wooden tablet. The verse is then washed off and the patient then drinks this water or rubs it on his body in order to achieve a cure.

Warrior lineages have traditionally had initiation societies which educate and prepare the young for their place in society. These Dyula initiation societies borrowed heavily from surrounding pagan peoples, particularly from the Senufo (see Senufo). These are secret societies and involve non-Islamic rites which prepare the initiate for entrance into adulthood. Dyula lineages, as opposed to warrior lineages, did not usually participate in these rites. In recent years, many villages have discontinued the initiations.

The Dyula have been slow to send their children to Western-style schools. Children in traditional Dyula lineages are often denied a Western education in the government village schools because their relatives fear that it may turn the young away from Islam. Due to this attitude the Dyula have been underrepresented in clerical and administrative white collar jobs in the independent governments of West Africa, particularly in Ivory Coast.

The Dyula are strongly Muslim. In the area of the Kong empire, Dyula is synonymous with Muslim. Converted pagans, in certain contexts, relate that they have become "Dyula." The Dyula take pride in their venerable Islamic heritage. Some Dyula clans have traditions of origin relating them to the Islamic holy city of Mecca. As with most Muslims in West Africa, the Dyula are Sunni and follow the Maliki juridical school. It is doubtful, however, that Islamic tribunals were ever used in Dyula society.

Where Dyula have lived closely with pagan groups, they have borrowed extensively for certain rituals. Masquerades continue to be a vital part of village ritual life. During the month of Ramadan, the women have two special celebrations called *kurubi*. On the fifteenth night they wear special costumes and dance to drum music until dawn. The second *kurubi* celebration starts on the twenty-seventh or twenty-eighth night. The women again dance until dawn and continue this each night until the new moon appears. The noise and revelry during these celebrations are said to keep away the *jinn* or evil spirits, who are believed to be particularly threatening at this time. Other traditions relate that the good luck for the year is given out by angels during the night, and one should not go to sleep for fear of missing them. Educated Muslims relate these celebrations to the Islamic Lailat al Qadr, or "Night of Power," when Muhammad is said to have received the revelation from the Angel Gabriel, related in *sura* 97 of the Quran. The Id al Kabir or Tabaski and the Prophet's birthday are also celebrated in most Dyula villages.

Many Dyula claim to belong to one of two Sufi orders, but few actually follow the rites. The majority of Dyula of the interior villages are Qadiriyya, a conservative order, while the majority of the Dyula Sufis in Abidjan are Tijaniyya. Dyula are not attracted to Wahhabi fundamentalism. However, the Association of Orthodox Muslims, recognized by the Ivorian government in 1976, holds many Wahhabi views. The association is less dogmatic and less puritanic in its desire to return to strict Islam. The Dyula are heavily represented in this fundamentalist organization.

Dyula society has always been essentially town-oriented. It places a high value on the Friday communal prayer, which is best accomplished in a town setting with an established mosque. Dyula society has also traditionally placed a high value on mobility and commercial competition and a low value on agriculture, in which they engage when circumstances force them to. After the emancipation of slaves in the early twentieth century, Dyula village economy became based on subsistence agriculture and weaving in the off season. Islamic scholars still attract students for traditional Quranic schools and can thus earn a meager living through the gifts from their pupils.

The chances for developing the agricultural sector of the Dyula areas are not very good. If the older generation of some areas continues to bar school entrance to many of the children, their futures will not be bright. Unable to read or even speak the official language of the country (French or English), they have only meager chances for lucrative employment. The upgrading of the political and economic position of the Dyula in contemporary society will depend on their ability to trust in the strength of their culture and religion while playing a full role in the development of the independent nation-states of West Africa.

BIBLIOGRAPHY

Books

Bird, Charles S., ed. *The Dialects of Mandekan*. Bloomington: African Studies Program, Indiana University, 1982.

Bravmann, Rene A. "Making Tradition and Figurative Art Among the Islamized Mande." In *African Images: Essays in African Iconology*, edited by Daniel F. McCall and Edna G. Bay. New York: Africana, 1975.

Delval, Raymond. *Les Musulmans d'Abidjan*. Paris: CHEAM, 1980.

Gingiss, Peter. "Dyula." In *Muslim Peoples: A World Ethnographic Survey*, edited by Richard V. Weekes. Westport: Greenwood Press, 1978.

Griffeth, Robert. "The Dyula Impact on the Peoples of the West Volta Region." In *Papers on the Manding*, edited by Carleton T. Hodge. Bloomington: Indiana University, 1971.

Levtzion, Nehemia. *Muslims and Chiefs in West Africa*. Oxford: Clarendon Press, 1968.

Lewis, Barbara Caroline. "The Dioula in the Ivory Coast." In *Papers on the Manding*, edited by Carleton T. Hodge. Bloomington: Indiana University, 1971.

Marty, Paul. *Etudes sur l'Islam en Côte d'Ivoire*. Paris: Ernest Leroux, 1922.

Perinbam, B. Marie. "The Julas in Western Sudanese History: Long-Distance Traders and Developers of Resources." In *West African Culture Dynamics*. The Hague: Mouton, 1980.

Person, Yves. *Samori: Une Revolution dyula*. 3 vols. Dakar: IFAN, 1968–1975.

Stevens, Phyllis Ferguson. *Aspects of Muslim Architecture in the Dyula Region of the Western Sudan*. Legon, Ghana: Institute of African Studies, 1968.

Articles

Bravmann, Rene A. "Gur and Manding Masquerades in Ghana." *African Arts* 13:1 (1979): 44–51.

Derive, Jean. "Le Chant de kurubi à Kong." *Annales de l'Université d'Abidjan*, series J (Traditions orales), 2 (1978): 85–114.

Green, Kathryn L. "Kong: Lost City of the Ivory Coast." *Craft International* (Summer 1982): 33–35.

Launay, Robert. "Joking Slavery." *Africa* 47:4 (1977): 413–422.

Partmann, Gayle. "Quelques Remarques sur le dioula véhiculaire en Côte d'Ivoire." *Annales de l'Université d'Abidjan*, series H, 18:1 (1975): 241–259.

Perinbam, B. Marie. "Notes on Dyula Origins and Nomenclature." *Bulletin de L'IFAN1*, series B, 35:4 (1974): 676–689.

Prussin, Labelle. "Sudanese Architecture and the Manding." *African Arts* 3:4 (1970): 12–19, 64–67.

Unpublished Manuscripts

Gingiss, Peter. "Dyula: A Sociological Perspective." Paper presented at the Conference on Manding Studies, School of Oriental and African Studies, London, 1972.

Green, Kathryn L. "The Sonangui and Dyula in Kong (Ivory Coast)." Paper presented at the African Studies Association annual conference, Bloomington, Indiana, 1981.

Launay, Robert. "Manding 'Clans' and 'Castes.' " Paper presented at the Conference on Manding Studies, School of Oriental and African Studies, London, 1972.

―――. "Tying the Cola: Dyula Marriage and Social Change." Ph.D. dissertation, King's College, Cambridge, 1975.

Lewis, Barbara Caroline. "The Transporters' Association of the Ivory Coast: Ethnicity, Occupational Specialization, and National Integration." Ph.D. dissertation, Northwestern University, 1970.

Person, Yves. "The Dyula and the Manding World." Paper presented at the Conference on Manding Studies, School of Oriental and African Studies, London, 1972.

Prussin, Labelle. "The Architecture of Djenne: African Synthesis and Transformation." Ph.D. dissertation, Yale University, 1973.

Kathryn Green

E

ENDENESE   The Endenese live in central Flores, one of the larger islands, of the Lesser Sunda in eastern Indonesia. Their political/administrative area, or regency, is called Kabupaten Ende, with the city of Ende its capital. They share the regency with half of another ethnic group, the Lionese, who speak a dialect of Endenese, a Malayo-Polynesian language. The population of the regency is 202,000, of which 25.9 percent, or 52,318, are Muslim. The rest are Roman Catholic or traditionalist. Many Endenese live in other parts of Flores and throughout Indonesia. In such places as Manggarai (western Flores) and on the north coast of Sumba, entire villages are occupied totally by Muslim Endenese. A rough estimate without justifying data might place the Endenese population at 86,000, with perhaps 38,000 of them Muslim.

There are three levels at which the word "Endenese" is used. First, the word can be applied to all the inhabitants of the regency. This term is rarely employed except in terms of government administration.

"Endenese" or "Ata ('people') Ende" is also used to distinguish the people from the Lionese, or Ata Lio, and it is in this sense that the word is used here. The Endenese are also sometimes called Ata Ja'o, after the first person singular pronoun. The Sikkanese, a neighboring people to the east, refer to them as Ata Soge. Finally, Endenese can also refer to the inhabitants of the town of Ende, including the population of a small island nearby, Pulau Ende.

The Endenese are divided into two cultural groups: coastal and mountain Endenese. The mountain Endenese, although almost all nominally Catholic, still retain their traditional religion, whereas the coastal Endenese long have been Muslim. Both groups enjoy this cultural distinction; the coastal Endenese are named Ata Ende; the mountain people are termed Ata Ndu'a, or "Mountain People," as illustrated by the following chant collected in a mountain village:

Ata Ende//Ata Ndu'a   The Endenese//the Mountaineers
ata surha//ata kafi   The Muslims//the "kafirs"
mai mbeja//sa'a sawe   Come, all of you//here, every one of you
kaa hara//minu imu   To eat together//to drink with us

Islam came to Ende during the sixteenth and seventeenth centuries. Unlike in other parts of Indonesia, it came to Ende not from the west but from the east, namely, the island of Solor (see Lamaholot). The influence of the Bugis is also discernible in their present culture. There seems to have occurred a good deal of migration from Sulawesi. Muslim Endenese has a script similar to that of Buginese, called *lota*, probably from the Indonesian word for lontar palm, on whose leaves the script is scratched (see Bugis).

The arrival of Islam and the Portuguese may have occurred virtually at the same time. The struggle between Muslims and the Christian Portuguese took place on the small island of Pulau Ende. In 1570, the Portuguese mission built a fortress there called "Fortaleza do Ende Minor," to prevent attacks by Javanese pirates. The Muslim inhabitants in 1605 drove the Portuguese from the island, and by 1772 the last Portuguese had been driven from the area.

After the Portuguese came the Dutch. In 1839 the first contact was made between the Dutch and the Raja of Ende. By this time, the people of Ende had become almost completely Muslim.

According to the founding myth of the rajadom of Ende, a man from overseas (Jawa), who married a daughter of the native lord of the land of Ende, was given power and rights over the land by his father-in-law and became the founder of the Endenese dynasty. The first raja is usually named Jari Jawa (probably derived from an Indonesian expression of *dari* Jawa—"from Java"), but sometimes called Raden Husen, a typical Muslim name.

The Raja of Ende was one of the two Muslim rajas in Flores (Ende and Solor). Under the Dutch colonial administration, all the Endenese were under the Muslim rajas, although some, especially the mountain Endenese, retained their traditional culture.

After the Indonesian government dissolved the rajadom and replaced it by the regency, the Muslim raja still exercised great influence because he was elected the first regent.

The coastal Muslim Endenese are more involved in cash economy than the mountain people because they live near the main road which leads to the town of Ende and also because they are not self-sufficient in agricultural production. The soil is unsuitable for crops except cassava, which was introduced recently. Mountain Endenese are essentially agricultural.

The coastal Muslims live by fishing, by growing cassava and by small-scale trading. The fish can be sold quickly because of the main road. Cassava is grown only for family consumption.

Most coastal people have experience in trading or business outside Flores in their youth. They have much higher social mobility than the mountaineers. Accordingly, the coastal people, despite their unfavorable natural circumstances, have greater cash income than those of the mountains. The relative wealth of the Muslims can be seen by the fact that there can always be found some *hajjis* in every complex of villages, individuals who could afford the pilgrimage to Mecca.

In the traditional political order, the Endenese are divided into a number of ritual domains, called *tana*. Usually, one *tana* contains both Muslim coastal and non-Muslim mountain Endenese. There is a complementary relationship between the two groups in various aspects of their culture. In verbal expression, they are sometimes compared to the "house" and the "verandah." Although there is no institutionalized ceremonial exchange between them, there is constant contact, either social or economic. At the time of Id al Fitr, the mountain people prepare a special kind of cooked rice wrapped in leaves, which they take down to their friends or relatives on the coast. In matters of trade, textiles from the coast are exchanged for agricultural products from the mountain.

Yet the relationship between the two is not always harmonious. Because Endenese traditional culture revolves around agricultural rituals, the coastal Muslims, who live mainly from fishing, tend to be organized separately from the *tana*. Instead of following traditional *adat* law, Islamic law and the modern concept of "development" introduced by the Indonesian government are the main organizing principles for the Muslims. When asked their identity, they more often mention their *desa* (Indonesian administrative units, "villages") rather than their *tana*. Most of the village heads are Muslims. Whereas the coastal people sometimes accuse the mountain people of not following the principles of "development," the mountaineers, in turn, suspect that witches, who are considered incarnations of "evil," obtain their knowledge from the Muslims. This tension between them has rarely emerged except under the guise of situations such as disputes over land boundaries.

Kin relationships, whether real or fictional, extend throughout the domain, both coastal and mountains. Most of the coastal people have close or distant relatives among the mountain folk.

Marriage sometimes takes place between a Muslim woman and a Catholic mountain man. In this case the husband is converted to Islam and goes to the coast to settle. Marriage between Muslim men and Catholic women is rare.

BIBLIOGRAPHY

Articles

Needham, R. "Endeh: Terminology, Alliance and Analysis." *Bijdragen tot de Taal-, Land- en Volkenkunde* 124 (1968): 305–335.
———. "Endeh II: Test and Confirmation." *Bijdragen tot de Taal-, Land- en Volkenkunde* 126 (1970): 246–258.
Nooteboom, C. "Vaartuigen van Endeh." *Tijdschrift voor Indisch Taal-, Land- en Volkenkunde* 76 (1936): 97–126.
Roos, S. "Iets over Endeh." *Tijdschrift voor Indisch Taal-, Land- en Volkenkunde* 24 (1877): 481–580.

Satoshi Nakagawa

F

FONGORO The Fongoro call themselves Gelege, but no one else does. The Fur call them Kole, the rest of the world, Fongoro. They are a disappearing Muslim ethnic group inhabiting a vast hilly territory along the Chadian–Sudanese frontier. The area commonly known as Dar (home of) Fongoro hosts small colonies of Fongoro/Gelege, Sinyar, Formono, Fur-Dalinga, Daju-Galfige and families of larger ethnic groups such as the Masalit and Kajakse. The Chadian half of Dar Fongoro is especially inhospitable as a result of the tsetse fly, the lack of water and an almost complete absence of services (medical, police, health, trade). The area is wooded and very rich in small and large game. As a result of its topography and its surfeit of wildlife, agriculture is limited to fermentation in pits of the fruits of the doleib-palm (*Borassus flabellifer*) and the cultivation of early maturing sorghum. Animal husbandry not being feasible, the inhabitants rely to a large extent on hunting and gathering. The main products of the area are honey, dried fish and meat, a little elephant ivory and the leaves of the palm, which are used for weaving mats.

The only road in the area runs in a north–south direction along the eastern fringes and is closed to trucks for six months every year. During and after the rainy season transportation by donkey or on foot is extremely difficult owing to the numerous streams. The area traditionally has been a refuge for individuals of many ethnic groups who had and still have pressing reasons to cherish the region's isolated and inhospitable nature.

Settlement of immigrants, individuals and families, still takes place, generally in the southern part of Dar Fongoro. Others go still farther south to Am Dukhn, a market center near the spot where the international frontiers of Sudan, Chad and Central African Republic (C.A.R.) meet. Settled and nomadic nationals of three countries visit this seasonal market, which is supplied by trucks from the main towns of Sudan's Darfur Province. The recent establishment in the market town of a police post, a law court and an army post has prompted certain newcomers to settle far away from Am Dukhn. On the other hand, the majority of recent settlers are traders and land-hungry subsistence farmers from areas to the north. Apart from Am Dukhn the only centers of importance are Kabar in Sudan and Gabassour in Chad, both seats of traditional chiefs.

The Fongoro are of Gula origins, the Gula being an enslavable (*fertit*) group of the past. (Today there are Gula communities scattered in the southeast of Chad and the northeast of C.A.R. speaking widely divergent languages. The so-called Gula-Mamoun, who live in the C.A.R. near Lake Mamoun, are the possible ancestors/brothers of the Fongoro/Gelege.) Historically the Fongoro/Gelege lived on the fringes of the Keira sultanate of Dar Fur. In R. S. O'Fahey's words, Dar Fongoro "was the critical frontier between Fur and Arab, who between them transformed the region into a slaving cockpit" (see Fur).

Fur infiltration is held to have begun in the eighteenth century, resulting in the indigenous pagan populations being pushed to the less fertile western part of Dar Fongoro. In the nineteenth century pastoral nomadic Arabs made incursions into the region from the southeast. The Fur sultans countered these, dismissed the still functioning Fongoro chief and parcelled part of Dar Fongoro estates, to be administered by their agents. Five of these estates were the domain of the sultans, and they supplied the court with game, fish and honey. In the late nineteenth century Dar Fongoro and Dar Sinyar were given as a present to the Daju Sultan of Dar Sila (see Daju; Sinyar). Throughout the reign of the Daju the inhabitants of Dar Fongoro suffered greatly from raids by various neighboring groups. The area was divided into French and Anglo-Egyptian parts during the 1923 settlement of the international frontier between the two powers. The leader of the French delegation, Lieutenant Colonel Grossard, later commented in his book that the Fongoro had withstood the onslaughts of their neighbors less well than the Sinyar.

Their historically inferior status and their loss of social organization as a result of the many incursions from the outside, resulting in the destruction of the Fongoro ruling dynasty, has prompted the Fongoro to assimilate into the larger Fur group. This process, which has been going on for at least a century, involves Islamization and the adoption of Fur culture in all its aspects. Today it is an insult to call someone Fongoro or to assume on good grounds that someone belongs to this group. It is difficult to find a person who can still speak the nearly extinct Fongoro/Gelege language, which is Central Sudanic, Sara-Bongo-Bagirmi Branch. This language is closely related to that of the Kara and Gula-Mamoun in C.A.R. Therre is also some similarity with Sinyar, but a number of consonants in Fongoro which are also found in languages from southern Chad and C.A.R. are not found in Sinyar.

Over the years innumerable Fur-ized Fongoro have migrated to Fur towns and are by now indistinguishable from the Fur in terms of education or profession. Those who have remained behind are still largely engaged in traditional economic activities and speak Fur rather than Arabic as their lingua franca. It is impossible to estimate the number of Fongoro; if the language criterion is used, they would number several hundred at the most.

BIBLIOGRAPHY

Books

Grossard, Lieutenant Colonel. *Mission de délimitation de l'Afrique Equatorial Française
    et du Soudan Anglo-Egyptien.* Paris: Larose, 1913.
O'Fahey, R. S. *State and Society in Dār Fūr.* London: C. Hurst, 1980.
                                                                Paul Doornbos

FULANI   The Fulani of West Africa form the largest nomadic society in the
world. Their herds of cattle and sheep are the major single source of meat for
hundreds of villages, towns and cities from Wadai, beyond the eastern shore of
Lake Chad, to the Atlantic coast of Senegal. The fact that they live in many
countries, occupy rugged countryside and are highly mobile means that their
numbers are not precisely known, but it is reasonable to estimate that the Fulani
nomads number between 7 and 8 million. Along with those who are settled, the
Fulani may number as many as 16 million, 93 percent of them Muslim.

The Fulani call themselves Fulbe. English and Hausa speakers call them
Fulani. Hausa may also refer to them as Filani and Hilani. They are called Peul
by French speakers, Fula by the Manding, and Fulata by the Kanuri. Their
language is Pular in Senegal and Fulfulde in Nigeria and most areas; it is of the
West Atlantic subfamily of the Niger-Congo group, which also includes Wolof,
Serer and Temne. A rich and flexible language which lends itself to literature,
it is usually written in Roman script, although Arabic was used in the past.

While a detailed survey of the Fulani across West Africa remains to be compiled, a generalized description would begin with the division of them between
the nomadic and sedentary.

The Bororo'en are fully nomadic Fulani with large cattle herds. They have
adapted ecologically to great tracts of open grassland and orchard bush. They
inhabit areas of low peasant farmer density and have weak Islamic affiliation
and knowledge.

The Fulbe Ladde (Bush Fulani), also called Fulbe Na'i, or Cattle Fulani, are
semi-sedentary, for they often rely upon various crops to round out their subsistence. They live in a symbiotic relationship with peasant farmers and seasonally camp in or close to towns and villages. They claim to be Muslims and
adhere more closely to the tenets of Islam than do the Bororo'en.

The Fulbe Mbalu (Sheep Fulani) are a relatively small group of Fulani scattered
in assorted enclaves who gain their total subsistence from herding sheep.

The Toroobe are the aristocrats of the Fulani, schooled in Sunni Islam and
prominent in politics, law, religion and letters. For many years, they have married
and intermingled freely among the Hausa and other local non-Fulani peoples
(see Hausa). Many belong to the Qadiriyya *tariqa.* Generally, they do not speak
Fulfulde.

The Fulbe Siire (Town Fulani) are largely Fulani who for one reason or other have lost their cattle. The group also includes former Fulani slaves, Fulfulde-speaking tradesmen and other blacks who aspire to higher status by calling themselves Fulani. (This prestige stems from the Fulani-led *jihad* of 1804, which began in what is now northwestern Nigeria.)

Nomadic Fulani, who are lighter in skin color than the local black peasantry, call the latter "Haabe" and are strongly averse to intermarriage with the darker peasants. The degree of Haabe and Fulani Islamization is varied, as is their retention of pre-Islamic cultural elements. The embracing of Islam over the centuries has not led to the breakdown of ethnic boundaries through intermarriage. Therefore, the cultural homogeneity, as viewed by the casual observer in the western Sudan, is more apparent than real. While diversity in cultural and social affairs persists, Islam has provided an atmosphere in which life-style differences are tolerated.

The subcultures of both Fulani and Haabe vary greatly throughout the western Sudan, although all of them fall within the title of "Western Sudanese Islam." The following is a description of one such subculture, that of the Fulbe Ladde or Fulbe Na'i (Bush or Cattle Fulani). It begins with the life cycle of a Fulani boy.

At two years of age the boy is weaned. He will have had several months of pillowing his head on the abdomen of a calf as he sleeps. He will have seen little of his father, his needs having been attended by his mother and his older sisters. As he grows older, he is introduced to the set of values expected of him. He must love his mother, and he must show respect for his seniors, particularly males. He will understand the importance of cattle in Fulani society. He will develop faith in Islam, know that he must be circumcised and that obedience to Allah's laws will bring rewards in the afterlife. Rewards for his secular actions are of uncertain outcome. He may attend his cattle well, yet they may die. He may have a healthy body, yet he may be impotent or infertile. Whatever the uncertainty of the mundane world, Fulani believe in their social system; theirs is a steady-state theory of culture. They believe that their ancestors understood the nature of the ideal society and that it is the duty of "modern" Fulani to live according to the code, or unwritten charter, handed down by their ancestors. The only way in which they should compete with their forebears is in having more children and more cattle.

To a Fulani, self-awareness and role consciousness begin at an early age. A Fulani of four or five years of age will proudly proclaim that he or she is a Fulani, not a *kaado*, or black person. Boys and girls of six have already begun to identify with their adult roles as they serve in an apprentice capacity in the camp, corral and pasture.

After learning from older mentors the expectations of their own sex, children soon yearn for more responsibility and status. The Fulani ideal is to marry and to beget and bear children. Marriage occurs at an early age, and the female anxiously awaits pregnancy. Birth control is unthinkable, since through her fecundity the woman gains status in the eyes of her husband and his family, provides workers for the household and guarantees security for her senior years.

The woman also works with her husband in the processing of the commercially valuable dairy products and the preparation of other foods. In her later years, she enjoys the respect and devotion of her children while gaining assistance from her daughters-in-law.

When a boy is seven, he has already accumulated enough skills to tend a herd full time. At this age, he begins through his daily labor to build equity in his father's herd, and if his father has a sufficient number of cattle, the son will be given enough of a herd to support a bride when he reaches 20 or 25. As he grows old, he in turn must surrender his cattle to his sons. The reduction of his herd reflects the dimunition of his status. The father may withhold cattle in order to obtain a plurality of wives (to the Islamic legal limit of four) and thus sustain his prestige further into his senior years.

Although pastoral Fulani are largely illiterate, they are sophisticated social analysts. The culture abounds in rich proverbs, fables, myths and riddles which subtly embed the basic views and precepts of their value system. Such oral literary forms entertain and stimulate thinking. Examples include the following:

"If your brother's beard catches fire, go home and put water on your own" (the dominance of self-interest over cooperation). "Tight pants are no cure for diarrhea" (if there is a problem, its fundamental cause must be attacked). "If a woman has cattle, whether she be black or a leper, marry her" (their strongest statement on the value of cattle). "If a man marries a woman with wealth he carries his staff in vain" (he cannot use a stick to beat her).

Like that of nomads elsewhere, the pastoral Fulani's future is bleak, for nomadism is a cultural and ecological heritage from past ages when human populations were limited and the demand for food was correspondingly less. Land now must be used through a more economical system to get the most yield from the least acreage. Comparative studies of nomadic societies show that nomads have built social systems especially resistant to change, but they cannot withstand inroads made by organized modern society. As Fulani turn more and more to ranching and farming, their children, with or without formal education, will join the urban proletariat. In recent years, pregnant cattle have appeared on the butcher's block, a phenomenon that bodes ill for Fulani traditionalism. Nomadism is moving toward its demise.

BIBLIOGRAPHY

Books

Bello, Ahmadu. *My Life*. Cambridge: Cambridge University Press, 1962.
Botting, Douglas. *The Knights of Bornu*. London: Hodder and Stoughton, 1961.
Brelvi, Mehmud. *The Fulani of Northern Nigeria*. Lagos: Government Printing Office, 1945.

Derman, William. *Serfs, Peasants, and Socialists: A Former Serf Village in the Republic of Guinea*. Berkeley: University of California Press, 1973.

Diarra, Fatoumata-Agnes, and Fougeyrollas, Pierre. "Ethnic Group Relations in Senegal." In *Two Studies on Ethnic Group Relations in Africa: Senegal; The United Republic of Tanzania*. Paris: UNESCO, 1974.

Dieterlen, Germaine. "Initiation Among Peul Pastoral Tribes." In *African Systems of Thought*, edited by Meyer Fortes and Germaine Dieterlen. London: Oxford University Press, 1965.

Dupire, Marguerite. "The Place of Markets in the Economy of the Bororo (Fulbe)." In *Markets in Africa*, edited by Paul Bohannan and George Dalton. Evanston: Northwestern University Press, 1962.

———. "The Position of Women in a Pastoral Society." In *Women in Tropical Africa*, edited by Denise Paulme. Berkeley: University of California Press, 1963.

Ekwensi, C. *Burning Grass: A Story of the Fulani of Northern Nigeria*. New York: Humanities Press, 1962.

Hill, Polly. *Studies in Rural Capitalism in West Africa*. Cambridge: Cambridge University Press, 1970.

Hopen, C. Edward. *The Pastoral Fulbe Family in Gwandu*. London: Oxford University Press, 1958.

Johnson, H.A.S. *The Fulani Empire of Sokoto*. London: Oxford University Press, 1967.

Kirke-Greene, A.H.M. *Adamawa, Past and Present*. London: Oxford University Press, 1958.

Last, Murray. *The Sokoto Caliphate*. New York: Humanities Press, 1967.

Murdock, George P. *Africa: Its People and Their Culture History*. New York: McGraw-Hill, 1959.

Nelson, Harold D., et al. *Area Handbook for Chad*. The American University FAS, DA Pam 550–159. Washington, D.C.: Government Printing Office, 1972.

———. *Area Handbook for Guinea*. The American University FAS, DA Pam 550–174. 2nd ed. Washington, D.C.: Government Printing Office, 1975.

———. *Area Handbook for Nigeria*. The American University FAS, DA Pam 550–157. Washington, D.C.: Government Printing Office, 1972.

———. *Area Handbook for Senegal*. The American University FAS, DA Pam 550–70. 2nd ed. Washington, D.C.: Government Printing Office, 1974.

———. *Area Handbook for the United Republic of Cameroon*. The American University FAS, DA Pam 550–166. Washington, D.C.: Government Printing Office, 1974.

Paden, John N. *Religion and Political Culture in Kano*. Berkeley: University of California Press, 1973.

Stenning, Derrick J. "Cattle Values and Islamic Values in a Pastoral Population." In *Islam in Tropical Africa*, edited by I. M. Lewis. London: Oxford University Press, 1966.

———. *Family in Gwandu*. London: Oxford University Press, 1958.

———. "Household Viability Among the Pastoral Fulani." In *Peoples of Africa*, edited by James L. Gibbs. New York: Holt, Rinehart and Winston, 1965.

———. *Savannah Nomads: A Study of the Wodaabe Pastoral of Western Bornu Province, Northern Region of Nigeria*. London: Oxford University Press, 1959.

———. "Transhumance, Migrating Drift, Migration: Patterns of Pastoral Fulani Nomadism.'' In *Cultures and Societies of Africa*, edited by Simon Ottenberg and Phoebe Ottenberg. New York: Random House, 1960.

Trimingham, J. Spencer. *The Influence of Islam Upon Africa*. New York: Praeger, 1968.

————. *Islam in West Africa*. London: Oxford University Press, 1959.

Articles

Ba Amadou, Hampate. ''The Fulbe or Fulani of Mali and Their Culture.'' *Abbia* 14–15 (1966): 55–87.

Dalton, K. G. ''A Fulla Settlement in Mende-land.'' *The Bulletin of the Sierra Leone Geographical Association* 6 (1962): 4–5.

————. ''Life of the Fullas in Northern Province, Sierra Leone.'' *The Bulletin of the Sierra Leone Geographical Association* 6 (1962): 11–13.

De Leeuw, P. N. ''The Role of Savanna in Nomadic Pastoralism: Some Observations from Western Bornu, Nigeria.'' *Netherlands Journal of Economic and Social Sciences* 13 (1965): 178–189.

Goddard, A. D. ''Are Hausa-Fulani Family Structures Breaking Up?'' *Samaru Agricultural Newsletter* 11 (1969): 34–47.

Greenberg, J. H. ''Studies in African Linguistic Classifications: Fulani.'' *Southwest Journal of Anthropology* 5 (1949): 190.

Ibrahim, Mustafa B. ''The Fulani: A Nomadic Tribe in Northern Nigeria.'' *African Affairs* 65 (1966): 171–177.

C. Edward Hopen
Population figures updated by Richard V. Weekes

FUNJ   The Islamic Nubian kingdom of Sinnār dominated the Nile Valley between Egypt and Ethiopia from about 1500 to 1821; today some people who pride themselves on a historical association with this state identify themselves as Funj, but the terms of their association have been diverse.

Recent archaeological work has exposed some elements of the material culture of the early Funj, whom the modern Shilluk remember as the previous inhabitants of the homeland along the White Nile, which they presently occupy. It is possible that these early Funj were also a linguistic group, for several of the court titles of Sinnār (*mānjil, manfōna, mankarūkān, manamalecna, karalrau, mānīk*) would seem to derive from a language otherwise unknown; as early as the sixteenth century, however, Arabic served as the lingua franca of the northern Sudan, and no language known as Funj survives today.

Modern Funj identity has been mediated by the historical experience of Sinnār. During the sixteenth and seventeenth centuries people from lands adjacent to Sinnār often called the land Funjistan, or the ''Kingdom of the Funj.'' At this time the term ''Funj'' applied to the hereditary nobility of Sinnār as a whole and distinguished this group both from the ethnically diverse subject class of commoners and from members of the elite of slave status. This hereditary nobility possessed a corporate identity defined by an intricate and highly disciplined system of compulsory matrilateral parallel cousin marriage. Inheritance was through the female line, by which the right to rule the kingdom itself and each of its constituent territorial parts was distributed over space and through time among appropriate members of the royal clan, the Unsab, and its subordinate lineages.

During the eighteenth century Sinnār gradually disintegrated in civil strife, and its nobility fractured into territorial patrilineages who claimed Arab descent, usually Abbasid, but occasionally Sharifian. Only two groups are known to have continued to identify themselves as Funj throughout the eighteenth century; the immediate royal family itself and the community of Northern Funj resident along the Nile in and around Karamakol, between Dongola and the Shaiqiya country. Both groups have adopted Umayyad Arab identity and patrilineal descent.

The Turkish government of Egypt conquered Sinnār in 1821. The Turks pensioned off the old royal family and gave them estates in and around al Mayna on the Blue Nile opposite Sinja. A community comprised largely of members of the former sultan's family reside in this area today, and they are known as Funj and Umayyads—as are those individual descendants of the former kings who live elsewhere.

The Turks governed substantial parts of southern Sinnār indirectly via members of the family of the former *wazirs*. These leaders identified themselves as Hamaj rather than Funj, but the Turks nevertheless designated the area they administered the Funj Mountains. With the exception of the family of the former sultans and the Northern Funj, modern Funj are most likely to have their place of origin within this nineteenth-century colonial jurisdiction. The Funj Mountains included the diverse sedentary peoples who lived on either side of a belt of more important and therefore directly administered Turkish districts which lined the banks of the Blue Nile and extended southward to embrace the gold-bearing region of Bela Shangul in western Wallagga. Within the Funj Mountains the designation "Funj" was employed as a term of self-identification not only by some surviving members of the hereditary nobility of Sinnār (excluding the Hamaj) but also by many ordinary Muslim individuals who looked back with affection to the pre-colonial period. In most cases these Funj were native speakers of Berta, Gumuz or one of the other languages of the Funj Mountains whose lack of literacy in Arabic and formal education in the Islamic sciences precluded their fabrication of a more sophisticated Arab pedigree.

Nineteenth-century travelers were wont to call the indigenous (and now apparently extinct) language of Jebel Ghule, the seat of Hamaj government over the Funj Mountains, by the name of "Funj." There is no indication, however, that this nineteenth-century Funj language of Jebel Ghule bears any relationship to the putative earlier Funj language from which were derived the non-Arabic titles in eighteenth-century documents from Sinnār.

The Anglo-Egyptian government of the Sudan (1898–1956) preserved a truncated portion of the Turkish Funj Mountains as an administrative district called Southern Funj, towards whose diverse populations, including the Funj, a considerable measure of anthropological attention has been directed. It was found that while many individuals might indeed identify themselves as Funj in some special contexts—or be so designated by those around them—in other situations the same individuals would be known as Arabs, Umayyads, Berta, Gumuz, men of a particular geographical community or followers of a specific religious or political leader or, in recent times, citizens of the Sudan or Ethiopia. Given the near-universality of plural cultural identities among these Funj, it would have been pointless, if not actually impossible, to enumerate the group. They did not constitute a "tribe," or speak the same native tongue or share a set of similar roles in the social structure. Nor did their customs, life-style or beliefs distinguish them in any consistent fashion from those of their neighbors who did not bear any form of claim to Funj identity. In short, the concept of Funj was found not to be a meaningful category of contemporary social analysis in the Southern Funj district; rather, its significance is almost exclusively historical.

BIBLIOGRAPHY

Books

James, Wendy R. "The Funj Mystique: Approaches to a Problem of Sudan History." In *Text and Context: The Social Anthropology of Tradition*, edited by Ravindra K. Jain. Philadelphia: Institute for the Study of Human Issues, 1977.
———. "Social Assimilation and Changing Identity in the Southern Fung." In *Sudan in Africa*, edited by Yusuf Faḍl Ḥasan. Khartoum: Khartoum University Press, 1971.
O'Fahey, R. S., and Spaulding, J. L. *Kingdoms of the Sudan*. London: Methuen, 1974.
Triulzi, Alessandro. *Salt, Gold and Legitimacy*. Naples: Instituto Universitario Orientale, 1981.

Articles

Kleppe, Else J. "Research on Debbas, Upper Nile Province." *Azania* (1981): 1–21.
Spaulding, Jay. "The Funj: A Reconsideration." *Journal of African History* 13:1 (1972): 39–54.
———. "A Test in an Unidentified Language of Seventeenth-Century Sinnar." *Bulletin d'informations méroïtiques* 12 (1973): 30–34.
———. "Three Court Titles from an Extinct Language of the Northern Sudan." *Bulletin d'informations méroïtiques* 12 (1972): 35–36.
———. "Toward a Demystification of the Funj: Some Perspectives on Society in Southern Sinnar." *Northeast African Studies* 11:1 (1980): 1–18.

Ḥasan, Yusuf Faḍl. "The Umayyad Genealogy of the Funj." *Sudan Notes and Records*
46 (1965): 27–32.

Jay Spaulding

FUR   The Fur is the largest ethnic group in the Darfur region of western Sudan
Republic, numbering some 720,000 people. Their language, Fur, is the most
obvious feature distinguishing them from surrounding groups. It is the only
member of a major subfamily of the large Nilo-Saharan language family. The
Fur are nominally Sunni Muslims following the Maliki juridical school.
   The Fur were once rulers of the greatest empire of western Sudan. Succeeding
the Tunjur empire in the seventeenth century, the Keira clan of the Fur gained
control of vassal states and trade with Cairo—and brought Islam to the western
mountains. In 1874, Sultan Ibrahim b. Muhammad al Husayn and his forces fell
to an army of the Khedive of Egypt. Although nominally under the suzerainty
of Egyptian Sudan, Fur leaders continued resistance. Not until 1916, when the
British invaded Darfur and defeated Sultan Ali Dinar (1898–1916), did the area
become politically integrated into Sudan. Dar Fur became Darfur Province.
Integration of the people into Sudan Arab society remains an uncompleted and
contentious problem.
   The area inhabited by the Fur is made up of two main elements: the plains
and the volcanic ranges of Jebel Marra and Jebel Si. The general elevation of
the plains is about 3,000 feet above sea level, while Jebel Marra rises to nearly
10,000 feet. In the plains the rainfall varies between 11.81 inches in the north
and 23.62 inches in the south. The soil is generally infertile except in the alluvial
beds of the wadis which drain the ranges of Jebel Marra. The groundwater is
usually close to the surface in the wadis and supplies drinking water not only
to the local Fur farmers but also to animals of nomadic groups (mostly Baggara
Arabs and Fulani) which migrate into the lowlands from the south and north in
the dry season (see Fulani). By a simple hoe technology the soil in the wadis
beds is cultivated for long periods (10–15 years) before it is left fallow for a
few years.
   In Jebel Marra the rainfall is higher; the southwestern foothills contain fertile
soils. The main crop is millet, with tomatoes and chili peppers as major cash
crops. Terracing is generally constructed on the steeper slopes in order to prevent
erosion.
   The Jebel Marra and Jebel Si ranges constitute the heartland of the Fur, and
it is from this area that they have expanded to the surrounding lowlands; in the
west almost to the border of Chad where they confront the Masalit, towards the
southeast into Dar Fongoro, towards the south into the Baggara Arab area south
of Nyala and in the east into the Arabized Birgid area. From El Fasher in the
northeast they extend to Dar Furnung on the Zaghawa boundary in the north
(see Beri; Fongoro; Masalit; Tama-speaking Peoples).
   There is little information about the processes through which Fur expansion

came about centuries ago. Fortress-like ruins (unfortunately not dated) from Jebel Marra to Dar Furnung indicate that the mountains provided the base for the growth of political power centers. The presence of terraces, especially on the southwestern slopes of Jebel Marra, in large areas which today are deserted, also indicate that the mountains in earlier times carried a higher population density, probably because the mountains could be defended more easily. Both the population build-up and competition might have stimulated political centralization.

In Fur oral tradition, the builders of the massive stone constructions are said to be a mysterious people called the Torra, although political centralization is not associated with the Torra but with three successive dynasties: the Daju, based south of Jebel Marra; the Tunjur, based in Dar Furnung; and the Keira, based in Turra on the western foothills of Jebel Marra. Growth of centralization was stimulated by control over trade. On the plains and in the areas farther south have been found evidence of goods which were in high demand in the civilizations along the Nile for thousands of years: ivory, ostrich feathers, slaves. Eighteenth-century historical records show that there was extensive trade in these and other goods from Darfur to Egypt via the so-called 40 days road (Darb al Arbain) and that direct and indirect control over this trade was an important source of power for the Fur sultans of the Keira dynasty. At that time the lowlands were incorporated in the administrative structure of the Fur sultanate (see Tunjur).

Despite cultural variations among the local communities, which are scattered over a large (probably more than 43,500 square miles) and ecologically varied area, there is a set of symbols so widespread that they can be seen as a basic theme in Fur culture. This theme deals with the problem of establishing fundamental qualities like solidarity, trust and support in basic social relations. These qualities contrast with two other types of qualities: hidden unsociability or betrayal, and open competition or conflict. A set of symbols expresses these universal problems in Fur culture. The phrase *bora fatta* ("milk white") is the basic symbolic expression of the quality of solidarity. The primary reference of *bora fatta* is mother's milk. *Bora fatta* also refers to a mixture of millet/flour and water, when the mixture is used in ceremonies. On these occasions the millet mixture is considered analogous to mother's milk, and it expresses a quality of unconditional support and solidarity.

When a woman is giving birth the child should be delivered into a wooden dish while "*bora fatta, bora fatta*" is uttered repeatedly by the women present. At circumcision the boy is seated on the same kind of dish turned upside down, and during the ceremony millet mixture (*bora*) is thrown on the participants with the exclamation "*bora fatta!*" A broken dish is also used at funerals to move earth over the grave, while the rest of the ritual is performed according to Islamic conventions.

The *bora fatta* symbolic complex is also used in such other critical events as rain ritual, war ritual and curing rituals for certain diseases like dysentery and smallpox. The color white (*fatta*) is associated with solidarity. Negation of solidarity—betrayal—is associated with the color black and most explicitly expressed in witchcraft beliefs and accusations. Witchcraft is a force which operates unconsciously when the witch is asleep. It is believed that a black bird flies out from the heart of the sleeping witch to suck blood from its victims who get sick and die. Open witchcraft accusations are rare, but a person who is less active in his participation in such social occasions as the communal consumption of the two regular daily meals or work parties is exposed to suspicion of witchcraft. The conceptual contrast between a mother's milk and witchcraft, and its symbolic expressions, white and black, is the Fur way of dealing with establishing solidarity and serves as a mechanism for maintaining this quality among community members.

The *bora fatta* complex also contrasts with another set of symbols expressing competition. Competition in its extreme is killing, and the relation between killer and the victim's relatives is described by the term *kewa* (''blood''). *Kewa* also means leprosy, and occurrence of this disease is explained as the consequence of the leper having eaten with a killer of one of his relatives. Envy of other's property or position is a less extreme form of competition. Loss of objects and sickness is frequently explained as caused by the envy of a rival, the envy operating through conscious power of the rival's evil eye (*nungi toké*—''hot eyes'').

The mystical sanction, leprosy, which is believed to occur if behavior associated with relations of solidarity is extended to people with whom there may be a relation of blood, serves as a constraint on including strangers in the community.

In traditional Fur society, marriage does not establish a joint household; the spouses are essentially two separate management units although connected with some reciprocal obligations. Husband and wife have their own plots of land, and they decide independently what they want to cultivate and how much labor they put into cultivation. They keep the yield in separate granaries, which are individually controlled.

The first consideration in traditional Fur cultivation is production of sufficient grain (millet or sorghum) for home consumption. Since responsibility for feeding the children lies with the mother, women have to commit more of their time to millet cultivation than do men. The husbands are, however, responsible for supplying their wives and children with a certain amount of market goods such as cloth, shoes, sugar and tea and consequently must cultivate more cash crops. It is part of the wife's obligation to prepare food (porridge and beer) for the husband, but she gets the grain for this food from his granary. To sell millet products—porridge and beer—is considered as shameful (*ora*) as prostitution. This can be seen as another expression of the *bora fatta* complex.

The institutionalized weekly markets in different villages regulate the trade in cash crops and manufactured goods. In the marketplace a man can thus get a cash income by selling his crops to the petty traders.

Cash can, however, be converted into rights in human beings, through the marriage institution. Marriage requires payment of bridewealth, traditionally specified as a cow to the bride, a cow to the girl's mother, a cow to the girl's father, two rolls of cotton cloth to the mother's sister, two rolls to the mother's brother, and two rolls to the father's sister. Actual bridewealth may vary substantially from this ideal and is today usually paid in money. For the bridewealth to a man's first marriage he will usually be helped by his father and other relatives on both parents' sides. Later marriages he will finance himself. The polygyny rate is low, but the frequency of divorce is high. A survey of post-menopause women's marital careers indicated that on average they had two to three husbands.

The choice of marriage partners differs between the Fur of the mountains and those of the lowlands. In the mountains, a mother's sister's daughters (*kalankwe*) are said to be the preferred choice for males, but other cousins are also recommended. In the lowlands, however, *kalankwe* is not allowed. The reason given for this is that sisters tend to help each other giving milk to their children and that children who have had milk from the same breasts may not marry each other, an Islamic proscription.

After marriage the groom is expected to move to the village of his wife and help her parents in cultivation for about a year. This may lead to permanent settlement in the wife's community, although ideally the couple after the bride-service should move to the husband's community. Avoidance behavior (*bagi*) is practiced between a person and his or her mother-in-law/father-in-law and, for a man, his wife's elder sister and, for a woman, her husband's elder brother. A person's relation to the junior siblings of his or her spouse is much more relaxed, and he or she may even marry such siblings in case the spouse dies. (It is strictly prohibited to marry the spouse's elder siblings.)

Except for relations prohibited by incest regulations (linear descendants, siblings, half siblings, linear ascendants, parent's siblings), marriage is not regulated with reference to exogamous or endogamous groups like clans or lineages.

It was through the policies of the sultanate that Islam first gained influence among the Fur. The Islamization process was promoted by the sultan's policies of granting privileges to Muslim immigrants, especially those from West Africa, to build mosques and establish Islamic education for boys. At the age of about 8 to 10 years, every boy (except those who go through the government's formal school system) will go to Quran school for about four years. During this time the boys will leave their family and move to a *faqi* (cleric-teacher) in another village and help cultivate his fields.

Islamic elements have penetrated traditional rituals such as the substitution of Allah for *wuonga* (forefathers) in verbal utterance during rain rituals and association of sacred trees and stones with Islamic saints. At life-cycle events the *faqi* participates. Only recently have Sufi orders been established, the most important being the Tijaniyya. With expansion of the education system, there has been a trend towards more orthodox Islam, and the brotherhoods seem to have attracted wide interest among teachers and secondary school pupils.

After Darfur was conquered and incorporated in the Anglo-Egyptian administration of Sudan in 1916, the cash needs of the cultivators increased, as a consequence of both the introduction of regular taxation and the increase in imported consumer goods. These cash needs are being met in two ways: through the increased production of cash crops and through labor migration. In the late 1960s about 25 percent of the male inhabitants of lowland villages were away as migrants, mostly in the Nile Valley.

The emphasis on cash cropping has forced a change in family organization. No longer can husband and wife operate independently because cash crops (peanuts, chili peppers, onions, wheat, mangos, sugar cane, oranges, okra, sesame, Virginia tobacco) require irrigation and intensive labor. Cooperating husband and wife today are producing joint family households.

The result also is a trend to identify with the values of the larger Sudanese Arab society, exemplified by greater seclusion of women. Assumption of Arab identity has long been used by the elite to enter the professions on a more equal basis with Arabs, whose own elite has been unwilling to treat an educated Fur as an equal. A major problem is that very few of the young educated Fur have the economic resources or the political influence necessary to participate as equals with the Arabs. Although the factors underlying the Arab elite's unwillingness to treat an educated Fur as an equal may be based just as much on social class as on ethnic identity, the important fact is that the young Fur elite interprets this rejection in ethnic terms. Their alternative strategy has been to base their political support on the identification with, and articulation of, Fur identity. At present this policy has not developed into irredentism. It could, however, change rapidly if the economic situation of the Fur cultivators changed in such a way that they could be made to believe that Arabs were responsible for their difficulties. Already there is antagonism because trade to a large extent is in the hands of Arab traders. There is a danger that the antagonism may be aggravated if Arabs are able to exploit the economic potentials in commercial farming better than the Fur because of Arab access to investment capital.

BIBLIOGRAPHY

Books

Balfour-Paul, H. G. *History and Antiquities of Darfur*. Museum Pamphlets, 3. Khartoum: Sudan Antiquities Service, 1955.
Barth, F. *The Fur of Jebel Marra*. Khartoum: Department of Social Anthropology, University of Khartoum, n.d.
————. *Human Resources: Social and Cultural Features of the Jebel Marra Project Area*. Bergen Occupational Paper in Social Anthropology, 1. Bergen, Norway: Studia University Bookstore, n.d.
Haaland, G. "Beer, Blood and Mother's Milk." In *Signs and Scarcities*, edited by R. Grønhaug. Oslo: Universitetsforlaget, 1982.

————. "Economic Determinants in Ethnic Processes." In *Ethnic Groups and Boundaries*, edited by F. Barth. Boston: Little, Brown, 1969.

————. "Language Use and Ethnic Identity." In *Aspects of Learning in the Sudan*, edited by R. Thelwall. Londonderry: The New University of Ulster, 1978.

————. "Nomadism as an Economic Career Among the Sedentaries of the Sudan Savannah Belt." In *Essays in Sudan Ethnography*, edited by I. Cunnison and W. James. London: C. Hurst, 1972.

Jernudd, B. "Linguistic Integration and National Development: A Case Study of the Jebel Marra Area, Sudan." In *Language Problems in Developing Nations*, edited by J. A. Fishman. New York: Wiley, 1968.

O'Fahey, R. S. *State and Society in Dār Fūr*. London: C. Hurst, 1980.

————. "Saints and Sultans: The Role of Muslim Holy Men in the Keira Sultanate of Dār Fūr." In *Northern Africa: Islamization and Modernization*, edited by M. Brett. London: Frank Cass, 1973.

————, and Spaulding, J. L. *Kingdoms of the Sudan*. London: Methuen, 1974.

Theobald, A. B. *Ali Dinar: Last Sultan of Darfur: 1898–1916*. London: Longman, 1965.

al-Tunisi, Muhammed b. Umar. *Voyage au Darfur*. Translated by N. Perron. Paris: Benjamin Duprat, 1945.

Articles

Arkell, A. J. "Darfur Antiquities—II. The Tora Palaces in Turra." *Sudan Notes and Records* 20:1 (1937): 91–105.

Beaton, A. C. "The Fur." *Sudan Notes and Records* 29 (1948): 1–39.

————. "Fur Dance Songs." *Sudan Notes and Records* 24 (1940): 305–329.

————. "Youth Organization Among the Fur." *Sudan Notes and Records* 24 (1941): 181–188.

Cooke, R. C., and Beaton, A. C. "Bari and Fur Rain Cults and Ceremonies." *Sudan Notes and Records* 22:2 (1939): 186–203.

Felkin, R. W. "Notes on the For Tribe of Central Africa." *Proceedings of the Royal Society of Edinburgh* 13 (1884–85): 205–265.

Lampen, G. C. "History of Darfur." *Sudan Notes and Records* 31 (1950): 177–209.

O'Fahey, F. S. "Slavery and the Slave Trade in Dar Fur." *Journal of African History* 14:1 (1973): 29–43.

Unpublished Manuscript

Beaton, A. C. "A Grammar of the Fur Language." Mimeograph. Institute of African and Asian Studies, University of Khartoum, 1968.

Gunnar Haaland

G

GANDA   The Ganda belong to the Bantu-speaking people of Africa and live in Uganda. Ganda is the root of their tribal name, and to this, several prefixes are added to form related concept words: *mu*ganda—a member of the tribe; *ba*ganda—the plural; *Lu*ganda—the language; *Ki*ganda—the religion and tradition; *Bu*ganda—the land of the Baganda. Uganda is the name given to the entire country as formed by colonial British rule (see Bantu-speaking Peoples).

Buganda was one of the African kingdoms which developed in the interlacustrine region around lakes Victoria, Edward, Albert and Kygoa and included in addition to Buganda the kingdoms of Bunyoro, Ankole, Karagwe, Koki, Buziba, Toro and Soga states. The kingdom of Buganda was established in about A.D. 1300 northwest of Lake Victoria, a region of fertile soil, pleasant climate, adequate rainfall and lush natural growth; all in all a favorable environment for human development. At the beginning of the nineteenth century Buganda became the strongest kingdom in the area. It had a well-organized and centralized government under the absolute rule of the *kabaka* (king). According to local traditions a dynasty of about 35 kings ruled over it.

The Ganda had their own indigenous religion with its gods (*balubale*), fetishes, ghosts, priests and rituals, which were well known and established. "The Baganda," remarked John Roscoe, one of the leading scholars who lived in Buganda for many years, "have always been a religious nation and zealous in their observance of the rites and ceremonies connected with their religion." Some aspects in their religion were helpful to the diffusion of Islam and Christianity. The Ganda, for example, already believed in a supreme being, the god Katonda, creator and ruler of the universe. Nevertheless, in daily life his influence was not felt in the same way as that of other national gods or local clan gods.

When the first Europeans reached Buganda (I. H. Speke and J. A. Grant in 1862 and H. M. Stanley in 1875), they were impressed with the well-organized kingdom and indicated that the Ganda were far more advanced and cultured than any of their neighbors. They were also surprised by their tidy dress and the advanced structure of their clean homes, which were much superior to those of any of the surrounding peoples.

During the British rule (1894–1962) the Kingdom of Buganda constituted one of the four provinces of Uganda, and it enjoyed extensive autonomy. It was officially abolished in 1967 by President A. M. Obote.

The Ganda constitute the biggest of some 40 ethnic groups which comprise the population of Uganda. They are about 18 percent of the total population of 13.8 million, or 2.5 million. Of these approximately 503,000 are Muslims, half the Muslims in Uganda. For the nation, 70 percent of the people are Christian, 6.6 percent are Muslim and the remainder keep their traditional religion. In Buganda, Muslims constitute 20 percent of the population.

The Ganda are mostly small farmers growing their staple food, bananas, and such cash crops as coffee, cotton and tea. Kampala, the capital of Uganda, is within their area, and because of the higher level of education among urban Ganda, they are the main manpower source of civil servants, administrators and professionals. Ganda farmers do not live in villages but on scattered *shambas*, or plots of land. Their houses are normally constructed of earth-covered wooden frames. Rooms are plastered inside, and the roof is usually corrugated metal sheets.

Socially, the Ganda are divided into a number of kinship divisions or clans (*kiko*), and each clan is a family which traces its origin to one ancestor and has a common totem. The Ganda family is patriarchal, and the status of women is inferior to that of men. Women, for instance, may not sit on stools, and they must eat apart from men. Polygyny is practiced among all non-Christians. Marriage is exogamous in the sense that a man may not marry a woman of the same clan.

Ganda women, however, contribute considerably to the family's economy. In urban centers they engage in petty trade as shopkeepers. On farms, they work in the fields and sell agricultural products. In the 1960s, the first women graduated from Makerere University of Kampala; women are active in public and political affairs. Among Muslims, education for girls lags behind that of the Christians.

Islam was the first monotheistic religion to enter Buganda. Its initial diffusion occurred in the middle of the nineteenth century during the reign of Kabaka Suna II (ca. 1832–1856) when Arab and Swahili traders arrived from Zanzibar and the coast of East Africa. Suna treated the Muslim traders favorably, and Buganda witnessed the first stages of Islamization. The king and some of his relatives were influenced by several Muslim religious ideas and even studied a few short chapters of the Quran, particularly those considered to be formulas for protection against magic and spirits. Nevertheless, because of the relatively long journey from the coast, the small demand for cloth and other merchandise, along with the limited number of Muslim traders who arrived in the kingdom, the impact of Islam was meager.

The process of Islamization in Buganda reached its climax during the reign of Kabaka Mutesa I (1856–1884). Mutesa was a clever, pragmatic and shrewd king, and he encouraged Muslim traders to come to his country mainly to get from them material benefits and especially guns and gunpowder to strengthen his position among his neighbors.

His approach to religion was utilitarian. Nonetheless his unusual curiosity, wit and intelligence led to his being genuinely impressed by certain Muslim religious ideas. Besides, the Kabaka was a secular monarch who, although carrying out some important religious duties, was not considered a god or a priest.

The kings of Buganda were often in conflict with the traditional religious establishment of gods, mediums and priests. Therefore, Mutesa tried to use the new religion, Islam, to weaken the influence of the traditional priests. In 1865, Mutesa declared Islam the official religion of Buganda and imposed it on all his subjects, a situation that lasted ten years. A royal decree was issued that the three rituals of regular prayers, fasting during Ramadan and eating lawful meat must be considered obligatory and the transgressor would be convicted and might even be put to death.

Coercion and threats were used to enforce the new religion among the people, thus assuring the superficial character of Islam in the country. For example, a custom connected with the Muslim pre-prayer ablutions was to clean and dry the feet by rubbing them on a big stone placed before the mosque. When the Kabaka wished to know if his subjects were performing the prayers regularly, he would send his inspectors to see if they had stones in front of their courtyards. Said one observer, "Therefore all the people from chief to peasant brought large stones and placed them before their homes. Every morning, noon and evening, they just wetted them with water . . . even those who did not know how to pray did the same to save their lives." (Even today there will be stones at entrances to some mosques and courtyards on which Muslims rub and clean their feet before entering the place of prayer.)

The impact of the Muslim traders during Mutesa's period was reflected in both religious and secular areas and contributed greatly to the country's progress. Among the most important skills introduced by the Arabs in Buganda were those of reading and writing in the Arabic script, the use of cloth and garments, the use of the calendar, the cultivation of such new agricultural products as wheat, rice and various fruits and vegetables, as well as mat making, soap manufacturing and various other crafts. The supply of guns and gunpowder by the Arabs was greatly increased.

The arrival of Christianity in Buganda in the 1870s brought a change in the position of Islam. The first Protestant missionaries arrived in 1877; in 1879 the Catholics followed and Islam's position was challenged. The Kabaka was given to understand that the Christian world possessed technical superiority, greater force, wider resources and more wealth than the Arabs and that he could utilize these advantages for the advancement of his interests. Mutesa's attitude towards Islam was shaken, and he allowed the missionaries to teach him and his subjects the precepts of Christianity. However, the rivalry between Catholics and Protestants weakened the Christian influence, and in the competition between Christians and Muslims, the Muslims' influence was usually more successful. Although Mutesa was, during most of his reign, nearer to Islam, he shrewdly realized that a greater advantage might be gained by avoiding clear identification with any religion, and from time to time he consulted the traditional gods and mediums.

The history of Buganda after Mutesa reflects the vitality of the Islamic nucleus established during his regime, and when his successor, Mwanga, assumed the throne in 1884, the Muslim position was generally strong. When war broke out between Muslims and Christians towards the end of the 1880s, the Muslims won. With European help, the Christians reversed the victory and crushed the Muslims by 1884, when Buganda became a part of the British protectorate of Uganda. Since then, Christianity has been the dominant religion of the country.

The position of Muslims in the colonial period was weak. While Christians, with foreign help, developed schools and health facilities, Muslims languished. They lacked foreign assistance and objected not only to secular education but to sending their children to schools run by Christians. Quranic schools did not prepare their young people for government positions.

Personal rivalries and religious conflicts among the Muslims were additional negative influences on the development of Islam in Buganda. Prince Nuhu Mbogo, the Muslim brother of Kabaka Mutesa I, was officially recognized by the British in 1892 as the leader of the Muslim community. The fact that Mbogo came from the royal family strengthened his leadership. Mbogo was a moderate and accepted by all Muslims as their sole leader. This situation changed drastically after his death in 1921, and his successor Prince Badru Kakungulu became involved in Muslim internal rivalries. One of the conflicts which left a crucial and still visible mark on the Muslim community was the Juma-Zukuli dispute. The point of issue was whether the ordinary noonday prayer (Zukuli) might be omitted on Fridays or should be prayed in addition to the Juma, which is recited on Fridays. In Buganda, under the influence of the Swahili teachers, the Juma prayer was recited in conjunction with Zukuli. The issue arose in a severe form after Nuhu Mbogo's death when Abdullah Sekimwanyi, one of the most learned Muslim *shaikhs* and one of the first of the Baganda to make the pilgrimage to Mecca (in 1920), started to pray the Juma alone. He was followed by others. His opponents were led by Prince Badru Kakungulu, the son of Mbogo, who was under the influence of a Swahili *shaikh*, Khalfan ibn Mubaraka. The Kakungulu faction was called the Juma-Zukuli and was the more popular and influential group. This ostensibly religious aspect was inextricably involved with political and personal jealousy.

The two factions differed also on other religious issues. The Juma faction objected to the use of *matali* (drums) at religious ceremonies and insisted on the use of the calendar to determine the timing of Ramadan, while the Juma-Zukuli allowed the use of drums and determined the start of Ramadan by the sight of the moon. These differences among the Baganda Muslims still exist.

Despite its competitive disadvantages Islam expanded in the colonial period due to improved communications and security. Baganda Muslim traders, shop-keepers, watchmen, cooks and interpreters (Muslims generally knew Kiswahili better than the Christians and therefore were recruited by British administrators as interpreters) penetrated from their center in Buganda into other areas and spread Islam there (see Nyankole; Soga). Muslim population growth was proportionately higher than that of any other religion in Uganda.

In the first five years of Uganda independence, when the ruling party of Prime Minister Obote, the Uganda Peoples Congress, was allied with the Kabaka of Buganda, the Baganda Muslims exerted increasing influence through their leader, Prince Kakungulu, who was a close relative of the Kabaka. The government recognized Id al Fitr as a national holiday. The right to slaughter animals for public consumption was granted exclusively to the Muslim community. But in 1965, when the cracks in the coalition between Obote and the Kabaka became wider, a new split, mainly political in character, occurred. Obote established a new Muslim organization called the National Association for the Advancement of Muslims (N.A.A.M.). Its main aim was to recruit the support of Muslims of Uganda, including Buganda, for government policies and to oppose Prince Kakungulu, who supported his uncle, the Kabaka, and whose center was in the Kibuli hills of Kampala. After the abolishment of Buganda kingdom by Obote in 1966, the activities of the Kibuli groups were severely limited, and its leaders, among them Prince Kakungulu, were arrested.

General Idi Amin's coup in January 1971 reversed the situation entirely. N.A.A.M. was outlawed. Kibuli followers took revenge upon their rivals. Idi Amin, a Muslim, tried to recruit support of Muslims both within and outside Uganda by emphasizing his devoutness. Islamic activities and construction of new mosques occupied a prominent place. Although more than two-thirds of the population in Uganda were Christians, Idi Amin convinced the Arab and Muslim world that the majority were Muslims and declared Uganda a Muslim country. Uganda was admitted as a member of the Islamic Conference Organization and became a beneficiary of Arab financial aid. The Islamic Development Bank in Jeddah in 1978 pledged $60 million for building an Islamic university in Kampala "in appreciation of Idi Amin's untiring effort in the Islamization of Uganda." This Muslim preeminence ended with the fall of Idi Amin in 1979.

During Idi Amin's rule the main motives for conversion to Islam were fear or desire for benefits. When Amin was toppled, Christians in various parts of the country, especially in the town of Masaka, took revenge, killing Muslims and burning houses and shops. In April 1982 Obote promised an Arab delegation that he would re-open the Islamic University and "build a united nation without any tribal or religious discrimination.

The majority of Muslims in Buganda are Sunnis, following the Shafi school. Shia are found among those few Asian Muslims who remained in Uganda following Idi Amin's efforts to expel them. Ahmadiya missionaries are active and have been responsible for translating chapters of the Quran into Luganda, building mosques (the largest in Wandageya near the center of Kampala), establishing primary schools and spreading religious propaganda. Their success has been small, and Sunnis regard them as infidels.

Muslim Baganda observe the basic tenants of Islam, although few pray five times daily. They observe Ramadan and Id al Fitr and follow dietary laws. The most popular ceremony is Maulud, which is celebrated all year round in prayers, food and dancing. Maulud gatherings are frequently used for political purposes, and because of their appeal, numbers of converts join Islam. Muslims have adopted some Arab ways of life in food and dress; men usually wear the Arab *kanzu* and cover their heads with white caps and turbans.

In the villages Islamic rites are mixed with Kiganda traditional religious superstitions. Some witch doctors are Muslim and continue to use charms and drugs; many Muslims retain their spirit huts and conduct ceremonies on such occasions as expectant births, before planting and harvesting and on the death of a family member.

BIBLIOGRAPHY

Books

Coupland, R. *East Africa and Its Invaders from the Earliest Times to the Death of Seyyid Said in 1856.* Oxford: Clarendon Press, 1956.
Fallers, L. A., ed. *The Kings Men.* London: Oxford University Press, 1964.
Faupel, J. F. *African Holocaust: The Story of the Uganda Martyrs.* London: Geoffrey Chapman, 1962.
Irstem, T. *The King of Uganda.* Stockholm: Ethnographical Museum of Sweden, 1944.
Kiwanuka, M.S.M. *A History of Buganda from the Foundation of the Kingdom to 1900.* London: Longman, 1971.
Karugire, S. R. *A Political History of Uganda.* London: Heinemann, 1980.
King, N.; Kasazi, A.; and Oded, A. *Islam and the Confluence of Religions in Uganda 1840–1966.* Tallahassee, Fla.: American Academy of Religion, 1973.
———. *Muteesa of Uganda.* Kampala: East African Literature Bureau, 1967.
———. *The Kings of Buganda.* Kampala: East African Publishing House, 1971.
Kritzeck, J., and Lewis, W. H., eds. *Islam in Africa.* New York: Van Nostrand-Reinhold, 1969.
Lewis, I. M., ed. *Islam in Tropical Africa.* London: Oxford University Press, 1966.
Low, D. A. *Buganda in Modern History.* London: Weidenfeld and Nicolson, 1971.
Martin, D. *General Amin.* London: Faber and Faber, 1974.
Oded, A. *Islam in Uganda.* Jerusalem: Israel Universities Press, 1974.
Oliver, R. *The Missionary Factor in East Africa.* London: Longmans, Green, 1952.
Roscoe, J. *The Buganda.* Oxford: Clarendon Press, 1964.
Welbourn, F. B. *Religion and Politics in Uganda, 1952–1962.* Nairobi: East African Publishing House, 1965.
Wright, Michael. *Buganda in the Heroic Age.* London: Oxford University Press, 1971.

Articles

Allen, J. "Muslims in East Africa." *African Ecclesiastical Review* (Uganda) 7 (1963): 255–262.

Bamumoba, Jerome. "Islam in Ankobe." *Dini na Milal* (Kampala) 2 (1965): 5–17.

Brunchvig, R., and Schacht, J. "Notes on Islam in East Africa." *Studia Islamica* 28 (1965): 91–136.

Carter, F. "The Education of African Muslims in Uganda." *Uganda Journal* 29 (1963): 193–199.

Gale, H. P. "Mutesa, Was He a God?" *Uganda Journal* 20 (1956): 72–87.

Gee, T. W. "A Century of Muhammadan Influence in Buganda." *Uganda Journal* 11 (1958): 139–150.

Katumba, A., and Welbourn, F. G. "Muslim Martyrs of Buganda." *Uganda Journal* 28 (1964): 151–163.

Nsimbi, M. B. "The Clan System in Buganda." *The Uganda Journal* 28: 1 (1964): 25–30.

Oded, A. "A Bibliographic Essay on the History of Islam in Uganda." *A Current Bibliography on African Affairs* 8:1 (1975): 54–63.

Pirouet, M. L. "Religion in Uganda Under Amin." *Journal of Religion in Africa* 11:1 (1980): 13–29.

Twaddle, M. "Muslim Revolution in Buganda." *African Affairs* 71:282 (1972): 54–72.

Watt, W. M. "The Political Relevance of Islam in East Africa." *International Affairs* 42 (1966): 36–44.

Welbourn, F. B. "Some Aspects of Kiganda Religion." *Uganda Journal* 26 (1962): 171–182.

Unpublished Manuscripts

Kiwanuka, M.S.A. "The Traditional History of the Buganda Kingdom." Ph.D. dissertation, University of London, 1965.

Nsambo, A. "Islam in Buganda." English translation from Luganda. Makerere University, Kampala, 1967.

Arye Oded

GAYO   The approximately 202,000 Gayo live primarily in the highland areas of the province of Aceh, Indonesia. From 60 to 70 percent live near the town of Takengon in the regency of Central Aceh. Increasingly large numbers have moved to cities elsewhere in Indonesia, principally Banda Aceh, Medan and Jakarta. They are totally Sunni Muslim.

The term "Gayo" is used by Gayo and others to refer both to a people and to their language, Bahasa Gayo of the Western Malayo-Polynesian group (see Malayo-Polynesian-speaking Peoples). Acehnese sources indicate that Gayo was already a distinct ethnic term by the sixteenth century, and an ethnohistorical perusal of Gayo and Acehnese traditions suggests that Islamization of the area was well under way by the seventeenth century. Although certain Gayo political categories were adopted from the Acehnese and the area was under a nominal Acehnese suzerainty in language and culture, the Gayo are closer to the Karo Batak than to the Acehnese (see Acehnese; Batak). It appears likely that the Gayo were one of several distinct peoples living along the northern coast of

Sumatra who later moved inland under pressure from expanding Islamic kingdoms in Pasai and Perlak.

Gayo speak of four geographical subdivisions. Gayo Lut is the area around
Lake Tawar and Takengon, while Gayo Deret is the adjacent district to the south.
Gayo Lues consists of the northern part of southeastern Aceh, and Gayo Serbojadi
is a small highland district in east Aceh. Residents of all four subdivisions agree
that the origin point for the Gayo lies in Gayo Deret; the other three subdivisions
were settled during subsequent migrations. Gayo speech differs slightly among
districts, primarily in lexicon and in nasality. Gayo grammar is constant across
these divisions and is very similar to Malay grammar.

The principal unit in Gayo society is the *belah* (division, side), a localized
descent line. In certain districts a village consists of several such *belah*, each
providing one of three village officers (*reje, imem* and *petue*). This is the case
in Gayo Lues, for example. Elsewhere, the *belah* will overlap village boundaries,
as is the case with the Ciq clan in Gayo Lut, so that the ultimate integration of
the *belah* is at the level of the clan rather than the village. In a third variation
on Gayo social structure, the village itself is one of several *belah* in a larger
village complex and is further divided into named lineage segments (*kuru*).

Whereas Dutch law studies portrayed the Gayo *belah* as an extreme case of
a non-territorial-based social unit, in fact each of three *belah* forms is at once a
territorial and a social unit. This double articulation of land and society regulates
access to farmland, incorporates newcomers as co-*belah* members and strictly
delimits the boundaries of *kuru, belah* and village (*kampung*). Furthermore,
lineage and clan ties, which are rarely remembered beyond the fourth generation,
are focused upwards towards a founding ancestor whose grave serves as a focal
sign for a *belah* or *belah* grouping.

A Gayo village, regardless of its precise articulation with the *belah* structure,
was traditionally governed by a *reje*. A *petue* was his assistant, while an *imem*
(*imam*) was charged with collecting the *zakat* and *fitrah* (religious taxes), ensuring
that collective prayers and religious feasts were properly observed and officiating
at marriages. Succession to all three offices was in each case patrilineal (from
father to son or to brother's son).

The *belah* (less often, the *belah* grouping) is exogamous. Two forms of
marriage serve to articulate inter-*belah* relations. In the ideologically primary
marriage form, a couple will live in the man's village after marriage and all
children from the marriage are affiliated to his lineage. A perduring relation of
exchange, visiting and observance of appropriate norms of conduct is thereby
established between the wife-giving or "source" line and the wife-takers or "the
sold one." As the Gayo terminology suggests, this marriage form involves a
bridewealth payment from the man's to the woman's family.

In the second marriage form, the man is taken into the woman's family and
becomes "like a son" to her parents. Rather than based on an idea of exchange,
this marriage form is thought of as a "picking up" (*angkap*) of a man, a term
which is also the name of the marriage type. In certain Gayo districts (particularly

Gayo Lues) an *angkap* marriage is a response to certain specific conditions (a household with only daughters, men with no bridewealth to offer) and is relatively rare. In the district of Serbojadi this form of marriage is the statistically prevalent one. When an *angkap* marriage has been made, children remain affiliated to the woman's lineage.

Division of estates and succession to office in Gayo traditionally followed lineage lines, with all children remaining in the lineage after marriage receiving equal shares. In Gayo Lues, however, a strong patrilineal ideology has led to a bias in estate division towards virilocally married couples. Children and inherited property also remain in the lineage upon divorce; the spouse who originally married into the lineage returns to his or her natal lineage, taking only that property that had been brought to the marriage.

These *adat* rules of marriage, inheritance and divorce have undergone substantial changes since the beginning of Dutch rule in 1904. The two major sources of change were Dutch administrative regulation and modernist Islamic campaigns to reform *adat*. Dutch contractually based legal philosophy was applied by local administrators in such a way that marriage was redefined as a contract between two individuals. These persons then produced children and wealth and retained individual property claims to both. Wealth earned together was to be divided equally between divorcing spouses or relatives of the deceased. Children tended to remain in natal lineages, but in villages closer to Takengon, a divorced and departing mother took half of the children with her.

Modernist Islam entered Gayo in the late 1920s through west Sumatran traders, but several Gayo *ulama* soon thereafter attended reformist-leaning schools in Aceh and Surabaya. Takengon soon became the center for the reformist group (*kaum muda*) which sought to change traditional practices deemed to be contrary to the tenets of Islam, including the traditions and legal norms governing marriage, inheritance and divorce. Whereas the Dutch administration has sought to remake Gayo *adat* in accord with its legal views, the reformists argued that Islamic law should be applied to Gayo society through a judicial body independent of *adat* specialists and traditional rulers.

Shortly after independence (1945), a separate Islamic court, the Mahkamah Syariah, was established in Takengon and began to hear inheritance and divorce cases. The impact of the court was most felt in its strict application of Islamic inheritance law, which allots shares to both sons and daughters at a ratio of two to one. An opportunity was thus created for descendants of married-out children to sue for a redistribution of ancestral wealth. Villagers did begin to bring such suits to the court and consistently won their cases. The result has been an increasing tendency both to divide property roughly along Islamic lines in order to prevent the possibility of future lawsuits and to give away property before death. Moreover, since a child is now virtually guaranteed a share of the parental estate regardless of the marriage form followed, a secondary result has been to downplay the formal post-marital alliance to either the man's or woman's lineage.

Instead, an alternative marriage form has become common in Takengon and in nearby villages whereby residence is left undetermined by the marriage.

Gayo conceptions of male–female role relations contain a relatively fluid idea of sexual division of labor. Although a man will refer to his wife as "owner of the house," women engage in peddling trade, management of small enterprises and extra-village social activities as often as do men, who are more often occupied tending livestock, working in rice fields or hunting. Men and women work together in the rice fields, and men are often occupied with the care of the younger children. Rural Gayo rarely engage in the circular migration character-istic of the Acehnese and Minangkabau, nor do Gayo men spend long periods away from home.

Parents hold four major debts to their children: the initial ritual bathing of the child at which the child is introduced to the natural and social worlds; circum-cision or incision; education (primarily in Quran reading); and marriage. The child is then a full person in the society, and undertakes care in old age, burial at death and aid through prayer for his or her parents.

Although there are no written sources for the history of Islam in Gayo, in-digenous traditions and the long-term Acehnese suzerainty indicate that the Gayo have been Muslims for at least three centuries. Although one Acehnese account claims that the Gayo fled upriver from the coast to avoid becoming Muslims, this refusal to become Muslim, were it to have occurred, would have been in the early fourteenth century, at the time of the conversion of the northern coastal city-states. The story is therefore consistent with an eventual conversion of the Gayo to Islam by the time of Sultan Iskandar Muda's reign in the early seven-teenth century, when the Gayo appear to have been included in the Acehnese realm.

The entire corpus of Gayo origin myths is structured around Islamic (often originally Judeo-Christian) tales, beginning with a sea voyage by the son of the King of Rum (Constantinople), whose boat lodges on the Gayo origin mountain, to a version of Joseph and his brothers (the origin myth for Isaq) and the story of Cain and Abel, which serves as the charter for man's relation to hunting spirits. Gayo attribute their early conversion to Islam to the missionary work of Abdurrauf, the early seventeenth-century west Aceh *ulama* whose commentary on the Quran was disputably the central religious text in early Aceh. Moreover, there are no Gayo traditions or tales in which Gayo are represented as non- or pre-Islamic. Ethnohistorically Gayo conversion took place in the distant, murky past; mythically, Islam is represented as present at the beginning.

Ritual practice in Gayo appears to rest on a basis of Sufi ontology, with frequent references to the Light of Muhammad (Nur Muhammad) and the power to be derived from gnosis. Creation is by progressive concrete manifestation of inner being along a chain from God to man, and man's soul is a pre-existent concretization of the Light of Muhammad, the archetype of all souls, just as Muhammad is the archetype of all being.

These Sufi ideas provide exegeses for rituals structured around communication with spiritual beings through a combination of spells, concentrated gnosis and ritual objects. Incense, a certain citrus and uncooked rice of four colors (representing the four constituents of all matter: earth, air, fire and water) are combined with various cooked foods at ritual meals (*kenduri*). The *kenduri* are held for major life crises (name giving, circumcision, birth, death), for points in the agricultural cycle, or for any significant change in a person's condition, such as curing an illness, changing a name, departing on a journey. The Islamic festivals are also primarily kinds of *kenduri* in the traditional Gayo view. Three major festivals are widely and enthusiastically observed throughout Gayo: Id al Fitr (as a *kenduri* ending the fasting month), Id al Adha, the *kenduri* celebrating Ismael's sacrifice by proxy, and Maulud, the Prophet's birthday, a day of exchanging meals between households or between villages, the only such day in the Gayo feast calendar.

In every Gayo village, the five-times-daily prayer is regularly carried out by at least a certain number of the adult men. The *maghrib* prayer is often conducted at a mosque or prayer house; the other four prayers, when observed at all, are usually conducted at home. Friday prayers in the mosque are a regular feature of life in all villages, with the sermon given in a mixture of Indonesian and Gayo.

Gayo verbal art is also infused with Islamic topics. The *saman* is a series of songs and chants performed by boys (in rare instances girls) who kneel in a row, swaying from side to side, accompanying their song with unison slapping of hands to knee, chest and one's neighbor's hands. The *saman* closely resembles the *ratib*, chanting "la ilaha illallah" (there is no God but Allah) until a trance-like state is produced. Religious songs (including songs commemorating the war with the Dutch in Gayo Lues) are part of the *saman* repertoire.

A style of conduct based on avoiding shame or embarrassment colors Gayo social interactions with a tone of reticence and reserve, and an investment of feeling in kin ties turns the Gayo community outside the homeland in upon itself. Gayo are thus considered to be close-knit and lacking the aggressive desire for advancement of the Batak or the trading spirit of the Acehnese. However, an attitude of silent watching has been of aid to the Gayo in their recent gradual advancement within the national bureaucracy. A fluent command of Indonesian has also helped them in these endeavors. More important, perhaps, Gayo have been successful in preserving a texture of social discourse and artistic production that remains uniquely Gayo.

John Bowen

GBAGYI   The Gbagyi, a subgroup of the Gbari, live in four Nigerian states: Niger, Plateau, Kaduna and Kwara. These states form the heartland of Nigeria and constitute an area of great ethnic heterogeneity. Gbagyi come into contact with numerous peoples, ranging from centralized Town Fulani and culturally similar Kamberi (see Fulani; Kamberi).

Although there are linguistic and cultural similarities from one Gbagyi group to another, there is no single Gbagyi society or culture. Indeed, there is no Gbagyi language. There are related Gbagyi languages, forming a language chain; that is, adjacent languages are mutually intelligible, but those at one or more steps removed are not. All Gbagyi languages, however, belong to the Benue-Plateau branch of the Niger-Congo language family.

All Gbagyi claim to come from Bornu and to have split into their two main sections after emigrating from there. The Gbagyi Ngenge ("True Gbagyi") live in Plateau State near Abuja (soon to be Nigeria's new capital). They number about 200,000, of whom perhaps 10 percent are Muslim. The Gbagyi Yamma ("Western Gbagyi") are centered in Niger and Kwara states. About half of the 100,000 Gbagyi Yamma are Muslim.

Despite their large numbers, however, Gbagyi find their power and solidarity threatened through their division among four states, a division reflecting historical realities. The Gbagyi have constantly struggled to forge and maintain an identity against the hostile pressures of the Hausa-Fulani and other unsympathetic neighbors.

The Gbagyi are related to the Bassa, Kamuku and Kamberi peoples and share a number of customs with them. Like the Kamberi, for example, their women carry loads on their shoulders rather than their heads, for "just as women have vaginas and men penises, men carry loads on their heads and women on their shoulders."

The Gbagyi have seen themselves pushed from one settlement to another. They perceive themselves as peaceful agents of civilization who have founded cities only to see their enemies, often the Hausa or Hausa-Fulani, drive them to marginal lands, a process continuing in their forced resettlement to make way for the building of Nigeria's new capital of Abuja. In addition, their conquerors refuse to refer to them by their own name, Gbagyi (singular, Gbagyiza), but instead call them "Gwari," which in Hausa means "slave" or "barbarian." That feeling of being discriminated against as much as pride in their heritage has helped form a common Gbagyi consciousness, transcending Christian/Muslim/traditionalist and Ngengi/Yamma differences.

Gbagyi marriages require a nine-year brideservice on a man's future father-in-law's farm. It is performed with a man's age-mates, and increased conjugal rights are accrued. The young man must give his future mother-in-law presents each year of his brideservice. Typically the presents consist of *ucha* (a grain) and guinea corn. On the wedding day he gives the final presents to his mother-in-law.

At that time the typical bride is about thirteen and the groom in his early twenties. Betrothal is common between children of men who have worked on a *gormu* or brideservice team. It is traditional for such teams to go from farm to farm to fulfill brideservice. Betrothals cement alliances among team members which are necessary for Gbagyi families tend to segment upon the death of elders.

Therefore, although the ideal family consists of an extended patrilateral group of father and mother, married sons and their conjugal families, plus unmarried children, the father's death leads to fissioning. Within the family, the relationship between husband and wife is formal; the Gbagyi practice husband avoidance by the wife.

Among traditional Gbagyi, divorce is possible but limited to two major causes: for men, infertility; for women, a lover. If a woman has no children, her husband is free to set her aside. In fact, he will do so only after all else fails if she is acceptable in other ways. If she is good sexually, hard-working, gentle in de-meanor, a man will urge her to consult various doctors. He will seek to discover whether jealous relatives or rivals have bewitched her. Only reluctantly will he end an otherwise happy union.

If a husband does end a union through divorce because of infertility, any future children she might have would belong to him. Never, among traditional Gbagyi, is a man considered to be the infertile partner. Since no one will marry an infertile woman knowingly, a woman divorced for that reason will sleep with men in other villages. Any children conceived in those unions will belong to her ex-husband; in fact even after his death any children she bears will be his and she is expected to marry his brother—even if for only a ritual three days.

A woman's lover must exercise caution, for if he were ever foolish enough to enter her husband's compound, he could be killed with no crime connected. The need to choose a lover who will not cross a husband's path is an attempt to preserve the integrity of marriage.

Marriage integrity is safeguarded beyond the grave, for the Gbagyi have the custom of the junior levirate. A widow has the duty to marry her dead husband's younger brother. If he has no younger brother, then she should marry a functional equivalent. Such a marriage preserves the alliance formed by the marriage and ensures that children will be raised in her dead husband's name.

The Gbagyi need to establish permanent relationships is seen in their regulation of land. All Gbagyi land is communal. No one owns land, but each Gbagyi has the right to land sufficient for his or her needs. Grants once made cannot be revoked unless the tenant fails to give yearly gifts to the chief. The tenant, in turn, cannot alienate land, although he may lease it to another.

Trees in open land are communal, and the village head manages them for everyone's benefit. Shade and economic trees on a person's land are his to manage. Water, however, belongs to everyone. Streams and the fish in them, nonetheless, belong to those who occupy the land. Under normal circumstances, permission for strangers is not refused but must be obtained nevertheless to use these resources.

Similarly, Cattle Fulani must obtain leave to graze their animals on communal land. Such permission is usually given if the Fulani promise to pay for any damages their herding may cause and to submit disputed cases to arbitration. The Gbagyi have learned from experience the need to obtain advance assurances.

Traditionally, land occupancy is inherited patrilaterally from a man to his eldest son, brother or father, in that order. If, however, all are dead, then the value of the crops goes to a man's mother or elderly widow, depending on the particular Gbagyi group. If a minor inherits, then his mother holds property in trust for him, for a man's mother is seen as always having his best interests uppermost.

Inheritance, especially among the Gbagyi Yamma, has been heavily influenced by Islamic practice. Sons receive twice as much as daughters. Widows are cared for by their offspring. If there is none, then the *alkali* (judge) among Muslims, chief among non-Muslims, administers the estate and gives one-eighth of its value to the widow. He gives some money to *mallamai* (clerics) for their aid, if it is a Muslim area. Otherwise, the elders receive the payment for administrative duties.

Women cannot inherit anything directly. Their brothers or a male guardian must care for the property for them. In that regard, they are treated as legal minors. In actual practice, Gbagyi brothers and sisters are quite close, and rarely is there conflict over the use of real or other property. Gbagyi families are close and cooperate in economic matters. Indeed, since there are no lineages among the Gbagyi, the patrilateral extended family forms the basis of continued economic cooperation, supplemented by members of the brideservice work team.

The Gbagyi have been noted for their farming skill for centuries. They are hoe farmers who also cultivate economically useful trees and practice a number of craft specialities.

Gbagyi witchcraft reflects many of the people's values. There are three general principles operating in all cases of traditional Gbagyi witchcraft: 1) All things have a cause, 2) All witchcraft attempts to right a wrong, in which "wrong" is defined as non-Gbagyi behavior and 3) The witch is but a means for expressing aggression and righting wrongs which cannot be openly manifested by a people who pride themselves on being peaceful, gentle and non-aggressive. Two of the three ways in which witches are recruited are connected explicitly with women: inheritance and through drinking mother's milk or others feeding from one's mother. The third way of "inheriting" witchcraft, via apprenticeship, does not exclude women's roles.

Anti-witchcraft procedures includes the cooperation of Muslim clerics. *Mallamai* often practice "medicine" and magic to help cure people, including those suffering from witchcraft. Moreover, they often cooperate with Gbagyi chiefs in identifying and rooting out witches. Indeed, Hausa belief that the witch is often also an unwitting victim may ameliorate treatment at the hands of outraged victims.

Traditional Gbagyi believe in reincarnation and the efficacy of the dead. Children are reincarnated ancestors. Perhaps that belief is explanation for Gbagyi joy in the birth of twins, for the Gbagyi consider twins a great blessing. Infants are named after ancestors, again affirming the belief that they are indeed ancestors. Nevertheless, as with the Hausa, the Gbagyi practice first child avoidance so that a first child's warmest relations are with its kinsmen.

Treatment of the dead is another significant feature of Gbagyi life. The dead are buried on the day of death except in the case of an old man. There is much rejoicing when an elder dies, for he is seen to have special power that will be used to aid those left behind. For that reason, the Gbagyi do not destroy the homes of the dead or move. To do so angers the dead and causes them to bring hardship on those left behind.

The dead, including Muslims, are buried diagonally in a grave at least five feet deep in the compound. Two stones are placed on the grave at head and feet. At the first stone, rooster's blood mixed with honey and millet flour is placed. Drummers play at the grave. A hut, as a memorial, is built for a chief. After eight days, a party is held in his honor.

All Gbagyi believe in a supreme creator god, who is easily viewed as Allah. Their personal gods, nature gods and various other spirits can be subsumed under the Islamic rubric of *jinn*. Indeed, social forces had been at work before the colonial period to pull Gbagyi into Islam. The colonial period only accelerated those forces, and the post-independence vortex has but logically continued that movement.

The construction of Abuja for Nigeria's new capital has affected the Gbagyi. Covering 365,000 square miles, the development has meant resettlement of the Gbagyi and related ethnic groups, but not the Hausa.

Predictably, Gbagyi and other ethnic groups are suspicious of resettlement. Gbagyi students and intellectuals have attempted to monitor the planning, but there are no plans to halt the resettlement.

Christian, Muslim and traditional Gbagyi are united in opposing what they deem as Hausa-Fulani oppression. While Gbagyi Muslims use their conversion to enhance and protect their ethnic identity (and thereby incur the wrath of their fellow non-Muslim Gbagyi), they remain loyal to the Hausa ideal, but they resent being sloughed off as "Gwari," "barbarians." They object to every ethnic slight, every joke that portrays them as dim-witted, every popular song that ridicules them, to every attack on their ethnic pride.

BIBLIOGRAPHY

Books

Gunn, Harold. *Pagan Peoples of the Central Area of Northern Nigeria*. London: International African Institute, 1956.
———. *Peoples of the Plateau Area of Northern Nigeria*. London: International African Institute, 1953.
———, and Conant, Francis. *Peoples of the Middle Niger Region, Northern Nigeria*. London: International African Institute, 1960.
Kirk-Greene, A.H.M., ed. *Gazetteers of the Northern Provinces of Nigeria. The Central Kingdoms*. Vol. 3. London: Frank Cass, 1972.
Meek, Charles K. *The Northern Tribes of Nigeria*. London: Frank Cass, 1971.

Na'ibi, Malam Shuaibu, and Hassan, Alhaji. *Gwari, Gade and Koro Tribes*. Ibadan: Ibadan University Press, 1969.

Temple, C. L., ed. *Notes on the Tribes, Provinces, Emirates and States of the Northern Provinces of Nigeria, Compiled from Official Reports by O. Temple*. London: Frank Cass, 1965.

Articles

Nadel, S. F. "Witchcraft in Four African Societies." *American Anthropologist* 54 (1952): 18–29.

Salamone, Frank A. "Continuity, Change and Conflict in Gbagyi Law." *Research in Law and Sociology* 3 (1980): 221–253.

———. "Gbagyi Witchcraft: A Reconsideration of S. F. Nadel's Theory of African Witchcraft." *Afrika und Ubersee* 63 (1981): 1–20.

Unpublished Manuscript

Yusuf, A. B. "Legal Pluralism in the Northern States of Nigeria: Conflict of Laws in a Multi-Ethnic Environment." Ph.D. dissertation, State University of New York, Buffalo, 1976.

Frank A. Salamone

GBAYA   The Gbaya-speaking peoples (often referred to as the Baya), who number in excess of 1 million, are the largest ethnic grouping of east-central Cameroon and the western Central African Republic. The various Gbaya dialects have been classified in the Eastern (sometimes called Ubangian) branch of Greenberg's Adamawa-Eastern language subfamily, which in turn is a part of the broad Niger-Congo language grouping.

In pre-colonial times (prior to the 1890s), Gbaya political formations seldom encompassed more than a few local patrilineal clan units. However, in cultural and linguistic terms, the Gbaya are subdivided into more than a dozen regional sub-cultural groupings on the basis of variations in dialect and custom. Of these subgroups, only the Gbaya Yaiyuwe of Meiganga Sub-prefecture in Cameroon, along with a minority of the closely related Gbaya Lai of Betare Oya (Cameroon), Gbaya Dooka of Garoua Boulai (Cameroon) and Baboua (Central African Republic) and Gbaya Kara of Bouar (Central African Republic) and Bozoum (Central African Republic) have been significantly influenced by Islam. The discussion which follows focuses on the Gbaya Yaiyuwe, who numbered some 50,000 to 60,000 people in 1980. (Estimates of Islamization indicate Gbaya Muslims may exceed 200,000 in both countries. *Ed.*)

The Gbaya first came into contact with Islam in the early 1800s as a result of the Adamawa *jihad* of the Fulani from northern Cameroon and northern Nigeria. In particular, the founding of the Fulani city-state of Ngaoundere in the 1830s marked the start of significant Muslim influence on the Gbaya when regular slave raids on Gbaya groups began to be launched from Ngaoundere. The Gbaya also first came into contact with Muslim Hausa and Kanuri traders at this time, as long-distance caravans penetrated the Gbaya area in search of slaves, ivory and kola nuts. Some of these Muslim traders settled down in the larger Gbaya villages, and in continuing their commercial activities, they were active in disseminating Islam.

By the 1850s, a number of Gbaya leaders had established regular tribute and trade relations with the Fulani and Hausa and used these links to increase their power within their local communities. A condition of the establishment of friendly relations between Ngaoundere and these Gbaya groups was that the Gbaya chiefs espouse Islam. Mosques or prayer grounds were established in the larger Gbaya villages, but the influence of Islam at this period was restricted to the immediate followings of chiefs. This process of political centralization continued throughout the latter half of the nineteenth century, and in the 1890s when French and German explorers first entered this region, several relatively strong Gbaya chieftaincies had developed at towns such as Bertoua, Baboua, Lokoti (near Meiganga) and Betare Oya.

Thus, from the very outset of Gbaya contact with Islam, there has been a close association between this religion and centralized political power in Gbaya society. The association continues today in that Gbaya canton chiefs are all Muslim and mount a court display of titled officials and retainers, musicians and *imams* which is closely modelled on Fulani Muslim patterns. Moreover, the present-day government of the province of northern Cameroon is dominated by Muslim Fulani, and the sub-prefects appointed in Meiganga, as well as the prefects at Ngaoundere, have virtually all been Muslim (see Fulani).

Islam remained the only world religion in contact with the Gbaya for almost a century until the late 1920s, when the first Christian missionaries began work in the Meiganga region. Despite the veneer of Islam in Gbaya political circles during this period, traditional Gbaya religion remained strong in other spheres of everyday life. The traditional religion combined a belief in a distant high god with a large number of rituals and sacrifices to recently dead ancestors and to various nature spirits. Witchcraft beliefs were also prominent and focused on sources of social tension in intra-village life. Gbaya religion had no full-time ritual specialists and no collective organization above the village level. Gbaya religious practice was therefore very much in the hands of individuals and/or local kin group heads and was largely oriented towards the assurance of health, security and success in economic ventures over the near term.

Gbaya traditional religion has declined substantially in influence in recent years, and although an undercurrent of traditional belief remains strong, most Gbaya today overtly claim affiliation either to Islam or to Christianity. The most recent census survey on religion, dating to 1960, indicated that the Gbaya of Meiganga were evenly divided between Christianity and Islam, but in all likelihood Christianity is gradually gaining an upper hand since it is more popular among the growing proportion of Western-educated Gbaya, as well as among women. Islam retains a strong influence on Gbaya involved in commerce, in cattle husbandry and the cattle trade and in traditional and modern political activities. Conversely, Islamic influence is little in evidence in Gbaya domestic life or in other facets of day-to-day existence. As such, Islam among the Gbaya is primarily a "public" religion of adult men.

There are few Quranic schools in the Meiganga region, and most of those available are run by non-Gbaya Muslims in the larger, multi-ethnic villages and towns. Consequently, few Gbaya Muslims have formal religious training, and only a handful are literate in Arabic. Among the Gbaya affiliation to Islam occurs either at birth in Muslim families or, frequently, as a result of conversion in adulthood, when the man concerned begins to participate in commercial or political contexts associated with this religion. In many such cases, these conversions are not ritually formalized but take place on an ad hoc basis when the individual begins to perform the required prayers and to observe the fast. Other markers of Islamic conversion are few among the Gbaya. All male children, whether from Muslim families or not, have already been circumcised as a matter of routine at about the age of five. The Haj is only rarely made by Gbaya, and other "pillars" of the faith are not normally observed. Traditional Gbaya religion already possessed a belief in a distant high god, which Gbaya Muslims tend to conflate with Allah. The categories of Islamic belief are sufficiently malleable to accommodate many of the Gbaya beliefs concerning the spirit world. And many Gbaya, whether Muslim or not, have recourse to *mallamai* from non-Gbaya ethnic groups for purposes of curing and charm preparation. Islamic brotherhoods such as the Tijaniyya, although present in neighboring Fulani and Hausa communities, have not diffused to the Gbaya.

The basis of Gbaya social organization remains the patrilineal clan, clan affiliation being determined by the transmission of the clan name from one's father rather than by tracing extensive genealogical interconnections. Small groups of clansmen and their families reside together in village residential quarters of several dozen people, under the leadership of the eldest male inhabitant, but the total membership of a Gbaya clan never acts together as an organized unit.

Gbaya domestic groups consist of nuclear or extended family households inhabiting one or more mud-walled houses surrounded by an enclosing fence or wall. First marriage occurs at about age 15 for women and 18 for men, and about 20 percent of currently married men practice polygyny. Gbaya marriage rules forbid a man to marry consanguineal kin as well as members of the clans of grandparents even though no explicit genealogical links may be traceable. Bridewealth payments remain moderate compared with those of neighboring ethnic groups in Cameroon, amounting to 50 percent or less of a man's average annual income. Wife seclusion is not practiced. Indeed, Gbaya marriage customs, partitive inheritance rules and other aspects of family life have remained essentially unaffected by Islam, although Muslim Gbaya normally call upon a *mallam* to officiate at marriage, naming and death ceremonies.

The Gbaya region of Cameroon is effectively a rural area with the population of the largest town of Meiganga scarcely attaining 10,000 people and the next

largest towns about 2,000. Gbaya villages normally average less than 200 inhabitants, with from one to as many as a dozen clan quarters, and are sited along
the few motor roads. Villages are under the authority of a village headman, who
is drawn from the clan which is presumed to have founded the village. Next in
the local administrative hierarchy comes the canton chief with responsibility for
a series of villages. Above the canton chief, the Cameroon administrative hierarchy of sub-prefect, prefect, and up takes over. The settlement of local disputes
is normally the responsibility of village headmen and canton chiefs. However,
in the absence of effective sanctions, village headmen find dispute management
difficult, and intra-village conflicts often lead to village fission and relocation.
Islamic law normally plays no role in the adjudication of disputes, although
according to Cameroonian legal codes, the parties to a dispute may opt for
judgment according to the principles of Maliki law current among northern
Cameroonian Muslims.

The Gbaya economy is based principally on slash and burn agriculture, with
maize and cassava the main subsistence and cash crops. Both men and women
actively participate in farming activities, the men undertaking the initial heavy
labor of clearing new fields and the women doing most of the hoeing. Both men
and women are involved in harvesting and share in the cash proceeds from the
sale of crops according to their labor inputs. Most Gbaya families spend much
of the period from January to August living in encampments in the bush near
their maize fields, which may be located as near as 300 feet or as far as a half
dozen or more miles from the village. During this time, collective village life
and the weekly markets dwindle to a minimum. In these conditions of dispersed
settlement and a low population density, hunting and the gathering of wild plant
foods still make significant contributions to the Gbaya diet in combination with
the staple crops. The diversity of the Gbaya diet, combined with the predictability
of Gbaya agriculture, make for a stable subsistence economy with little risk of
serious famine.

Within the last several decades, Gbaya farmers have also become involved in
cattle ownership, following the lead of the pastoral Fulani people, who share
the humid Meiganga savannas with them. Gbaya farmers today own about one
cow per capita, and several cattle owners normally pool their cattle and hire a
herdsman to care for them on a full-time basis. These paid herdsmen are usually
drawn from adjacent Muslim peoples. Alternatively, Gbaya farmers may enter
into a bond friendship relationship with a pastoral Fulani who is pasturing his
herd nearby. The Gbaya will entrust his holdings to the pastoral Fulani, who
looks after them as part of his herd. Gbaya and pastoral Fulani who establish
such relations also engage in the exchange of agricultural and cattle products.
Gbaya sell their mature cattle to Muslim butchers and cattle brokers for transport
to the urban markets of Cameroon. Cattle ownership can be highly lucrative
and, at present, constitutes the main Gbaya investment strategy, although Gbaya
participation in this economic activity is limited by lack of capital.

Although the Gbaya enjoy a stable subsistence economy, they are often frustrated in their attempts to involve themselves in commercial and wage-earning activities, which are dominated by Hausa, Fulani and Kanuri (see Kanuri). Their cash crop income is also limited by marketing difficulties due to their distance from the more populous regions of Cameroon. Broadly speaking, Gbaya see themselves as being presented with two alternative models for economic success. On the one hand, they can attempt to penetrate the Western-oriented economic sector, which is closely associated with the life-style of southern Cameroonian peoples. This alternative is linked with cultural attributes such as European-style education, the use of French and/or English languages, Western dress and the practice of Christianity. On the other hand, Gbaya may seek to model their lives after those of the urban Muslims of northern Cameroon, a mode of livelihood associated with trading and cattle, with Islam and the use of Fulani and/or Hausa languages and with ample robes and embroidered skull caps. At the present time, the balance of choice between these radically different alternatives is a fine one, and it is difficult to predict the direction of future social change for the Gbaya people of Cameroon.

BIBLIOGRAPHY

Books

Burnham, Philip. *Opportunity and Constraint in a Savanna Society*. London: Academic Press, 1980.
————. "Racial Classification and Identity in the Meiganga Region: North Cameroon." In *Race and Social Difference*, edited by P. Baxter and B. Sansom. Harmondsworth: Penguin Books, 1972.
————. "Raiders and Traders in Adamawa." In *Asian and African Systems of Slavery*, edited by J. Watson. Oxford: Basil Blackwell and Mott, 1980.

Article

Burnham, Philip. "*Regroupement* and Mobile Societies: Two Cameroon Cases." *The Journal of African History* 16:4 (1975): 577–594.

Philip Burnham

GORONTALESE   The Gorontalese occupy nearly half of the northern peninsula of Sulawesi, officially known as the Province of North Sulawesi in the Republic of Indonesia. The area's main city is Gorontalo (pop. 90,000) on the Gulf of Tomini, 0° north latitude, 123° 3' east longitude.

The Gorontalese are divided into six subgroups, each with a history of its own. They include the Gorontalo, Suwawa, Limbotto (Limuwu), Bolango, Atinggola (Andagile) and Boelemo. Together they number slightly more than 500,000, at least 98 percent of them being Sunni Muslim.

There are several opinions regarding the origins of the people of Gorontalo.

One is that they were an indigenous tribe located around Lake Limbotto. Another is that the Suwawa and Boelemo originated in South Sulawesi and migrated north. There are records to show that the Suwawa kingdom was founded in the eighth century and had trading relations with the Lusu kingdom in South Sulawesi. The kingdoms of Gorontalo and Limbotto came into existence in the fourteenth century and gained influence around the Gulf of Tomini. They conducted trade with peoples throughout the Molucca Sea, including the Ternate (see Ternatan–Tidorese). In 1673 all the groups created a federation which later became the Kingdom of Lima Pohalaa. In 1889 the Dutch gave the kingdom the name "Gorontalo."

While each group at one time had its own language, today only two are in local use, Gorontalese and Suwawa. During the past few decades, the use of these local languages has declined with the advancement of the government-sponsored use of Bahasa Indonesia, the national language.

Most Gorontalese are rice farmers (dry and wet rice fields). In the mountainous hinterland villages, agriculture is the main economic activity. The population along the northern and southern coasts and along Lake Limbotto also fish, while those living around the harbors of Gorontalo, Kuandang, Tilamuta and Bumbulan frequently become seasonal harbor laborers.

Islam apparently came to Gorontalo in the early sixteenth century. In 1563 King Matolodulakiki declared it the official state religion. In 1677, the Dutch Governor Padtbrugge of the Moluccas advocated Christianity and required observance of the religion in formal Dutch–local agreements. This policy was opposed by a number of local maharajas, two of whom were banished to Ceylon. By the end of the century, religious conflicts had become widespread, Muslims and Christians both considering the other *kafir*, non-believers. A Muslim who became a Christian could be thrown out of his community, deprived of his hereditary rights and even exiled. If he were a descendant of the aristocracy he might lose his right to succeed to higher positions. On the other hand, non-Muslims, especially Chinese or Dutch, who accepted Islam were received with many honors.

Time, education and the efforts of both Muslim and Christian organizations such as the moderate Muhammadiya and missionaries have quelled the conflicts between the religious groups. A recent survey by the Higher State Institute of Islamic Education of Ujung Pandang at Gorontalo indicated that about 97 percent of the respondents considered themselves tolerant towards other religious groups (in addition to some 10,000 Christians of various sects, there are also Hindus and Buddhists in Gorontalo). Evidence of this attitude is the custom of mutual assistance and support during religious celebrations. Another example is the frequent occurrence of marriages between people with different religious backgrounds. Within one family there might be members professing different beliefs. If a Christian celebration is conducted in front of a Muslim home, Muslims will often light candles either because there are Christians among the members of the household or simply for the sake of tolerance. Even in more difficult and complicated situations, such as a change of religion by a family member, the conflicts are usually settled calmly.

The people of Gorontalo call themselves Waü, or Watia in the refined language (Gorontalese has two language types: elite and common). Brothers and sisters are both called *wutato*, the older is then called *wutata mohuhula*, the younger one *wutata yaliyali*. The mother is called *tiilo*, and the father *tiamo*.

Although family relationships among Gorontalese are as a rule not based on the patrilineal system, in former times the position of the son was high. Quite often a man was urged by his relatives to take another wife if his marriage did not produce a son. This custom is now gradually disappearing, especially since there are more employment opportunities for daughters.

Ceremonies recognizing birth, marriage and death are common. Although the public health service is now actively engaged in the *desa* (village), many births are still attended to by the *dukun*, or healer. For this reason, the public health service is currently attempting to provide training and extension services to the *dukun* in the *desa* in order to improve their skills as midwives.

The *dukun* is generally considered to be capable of predicting the newborn baby's future. If its umbilical cord is long, the child will have a high intellect. A birthmark on the sole of the foot indicates a strong character. A common ceremony in this context is the planting of the *yiliyala* (placenta) under the house (see Arabs).

The ideal marriage is by way of proposal, which is a usual procedure regardless of the actual situation. A marriage in secret (*mopoteteä*) through elopement, once fairly common, today occurs only rarely.

Although Islamic marriage law in principle applies fully, Gorontalese still maintain the custom of *tonelo*. In the past *tonelo* required a wedding gift from the bridegroom to the bride in the form of slaves, the number reflecting the bride's status. For members of high nobility (maharaja) this meant four to eight slaves; three slaves were required for middle-class nobility (*wali wali mowali*), and two slaves for the common people (*tau daata*). For the slaves, *tonelo* was not required. Today, the whole affair is carried out in terms of money, slavery being forbidden.

More common today is the orthodox Islamic *mahr* system of marriage, whereby the wedding gift of the bridegroom-to-be is based upon his wealth or earning power. Usually the bridal gift consists of a copy of the Quran and praying equipment. In addition he pays an amount of money for administrative wedding expenses to the Office of Religious Affairs. Interwoven in all the stages of weddings and marriages are traditional custom, Islamic practice and government laws.

Ceremonies for the dead generally follow the Shariah, such as washing the body, wrapping it in *kafan* cloth and placing it properly in the burial ground. However, traditional customs have not been eliminated. Some wealthy families still organize social gatherings on the first, third, fifth, seventh, fortieth and thousandth day after death. Frequently, a family finds itself deeply in debt after these successive commemorations.

Prior to adopting Islam, Gorontalese had a general belief in an absolute almighty power (La). Kings and other leaders were thought to have mystic and supernatural powers. Ancestor worship was common and still survives in various forms. All material things were thought to contain a spirit which should not be disturbed and, if treated well, could be beneficial. Today, ceremonies can be observed among Muslims which incorporate dances of worship (*dayango*) and sacrifices (*mopoaa*) to these spirits.

The meeting of Islam and traditional religion was usually harmonious. The spirits who inhabited the forests, plains, valleys and rivers became the *jinn* of Islam; the demons became the Islamic Devil. Amai, the Maharaja of Gorontalo in 1523, accepted the Shariah based on *adat* (custom), saying that Shariah did not contradict *adat*. In the case of conflict, *adat* would prevail. *Adat* received further support in 1550, when Maharaja Motalodula Kiki ruled that local custom was based on Shariah and Shariah was based on *adat*. Magical practices were not eliminated. As late as the mid-seventeenth century, *adat* was supreme. Any maharajah who decreed that *adat* should be based on the Shariah and the Shariah was based on the Quran had to abdicate.

Gorontalo was ripe for the introduction of Sufi teachings. Various mystic brotherhoods established themselves, including the Naqshbandiyya and Chalwatiyya. In Limbotto so many people withdrew from society to meditate that their reluctance to work, combined with long, nighttime ceremonies requiring the participants to sleep all day, severely affected the economy of the community. One traveler to Gorontalo in those days reported that the only thing Islamic about the people was their abstinence from eating pork.

By the beginning of the twentieth century, political, social, cultural and youth organizations founded in Java were having an impact on the Muslims of the outlying provinces. Among these were such Islamic groups as the Diniya Islamiya, whose purpose was, and is, to promote the true meanings and practices of Islam. Community improvement became a popular goal. The Syafii school in Gorontalo preaches: "Labor with science for the sake of mankind is more useful than only worshipping for your own sake." The Muhammadiya organization, with branches throughout Indonesia, works under the slogan: "Let us compete for the welfare of the public." Muhammadiya has penetrated into the smallest and most isolated valleys and villages of Gorontalo.

BIBLIOGRAPHY

Books

Kuno, Kaluku. *Lukisan Segi Kebudayaan Dari Limo lo Pohalaa (Gorontalo)*. Vol. 1. Gorontalo, Indonesia: Penerbit Rumah Sangkar Gelatik Telaga, n.d.

Lipoeto, M. *Sedjarah Gorontalo (Oedeoloewo looe limo lo pohalaa)*. Vols. 1–4 (1943); 5–6 (1945); 7–11 (1949); 12–13 (1950). Gorontalo, Indonesia: Pertjetakan Rakyat.

Nur, S. R. *Beberapa aspek hukum adat tatenegara kerajaan Gorontalo pada masa pemerintahan "Eato" (1673–1679)*. N.p., 1979.

Usman, A. J. *Sedjarah kerajaan Suwawa dan kerajaan di Sulawesi Utara*. Jakarta: n.p., 1972.

S. R. Nur

GUJARATIS Located in the westernmost portion of central India, Gujarat includes the region of Kutch, Kathiawar and Surastra and the territories between the rivers Banas and Damanganga. The state encompasses great contrasts from wet fertile rice-growing plains in the southern tip to the almost rainless salt deserts of Kutch. To the west lies the Indian Ocean with two major gulfs, Kutch and Cambay, exposing the major commercial seaports of Surat, Broach and Cambay, to which Gujarat owes much of its historical importance.

The cultural diversity in Gujarat is directly related to the varied physical features of the land. However, the unifying force in this diversity is the Gujarati language spoken by approximately 36 million persons. Gujarati is an Indo-Iranian language with a number of dialects and class variations and is one of the 14 regional languages specified in the Indian constitution. Gujarati possesses a long literary tradition, well represented in the arts and literature of Gujarat.

Between the fourth and the eighth centuries, Gujarat was ruled successively by the Mauryas, the Sakas, the Guptas and the Balabhis, who were later conquered by the Chalukyas and the Vaghelas. In the late thirteenth century, Gujarat fell to the Muslims in one decisive battle when Karna, the last Vaghela ruler, was defeated by the armies of Turkish Sultan Ala al-Din Khaldji of Delhi. The Moghuls under Akbar again conquered Gujarat in 1593. The Marathas succeeded the Moghuls in 1758 and subsequently turned the area over to the British.

In 1947 the Gujarat States Agency was formed, incorporating Rewa Kantha, Surat, Kaira, Nasik and Thana with Bombay. Later, all component states joined the union of India and were incorporated into the state of Bombay. Further reorganization led to the state of Gujarat in 1960 as the fifteenth state of the Indian republic.

Gujarat experienced numerous unsuccessful land-based raids by the Arabs through the eighth century. Concurrently, immigrant Arab trading communities settled on the western Indian seacoast, from where they conducted the Indian Ocean trade. They were later joined by Persian traders. The ultimate expansion and subsequent extension inland of these Muslim trading communities was directly related to the flourishing trade across the ocean. And wherever the communities settled, the Muslims built mosques.

For the Muslims in Gujarat, the late eleventh century, during the reign of Siddharaj Jayasingha, proved to be their most glorious period. The alien Muslim population experienced exceptional generosity and fairness from the Hindu ruler. Moreover, this period witnessed considerable Muslim proselytization, which resulted in the establishment of Muslim communities of all sects. Muslim missionaries of the Shia sect, who came to Gujarat to find converts, used Hindu beliefs of incarnation and declared Hazarat Ali as the tenth avatar of Vishnu. The missionaries simplified their teachings and used the language which those in the lower stratum of the society could at once follow. Thus religious songs (*bajans*), a common form of poetry, were also used to reach the masses.

The Turkish invasion of Gujarat further opened the way to a large influx of Muslims from the north and the conversion of numerous Rajputs to Islam.

The Muslim population of Gujarat is 2.3 million, divided into 130 subgroups or communities, with memberships ranging from 65,000 to as low as 100 individuals. Among the largest Muslim communities are the Shaikhs, Sunni Vohras, Pathans, Momins and Daudi Bohras.

Although Gujaratis are primarily farmers producing cotton, rice, wheat, jowar, bajri and pulses, commerce is the major occupation of Gujarati Muslims. The contour of the area with its open seacoast and ports has lent itself to the needs of the trader. Besides the sea routes, numerous land routes connect the coast and the interior. The important Muslim trading communities are the Khoja, Sunni Vohra, Sulaimani, Daudi Bohra and Memon. These communities, on the whole, have prospered economically and consequently have achieved a higher index of education compared to other Muslim communities.

Members of trading communities who are not engaged in mercantile ventures usually are agrarian. Among them are the Fakir and Kasbati, which, while traditionally not engaged in agriculture, now pursue this occupation. They are poor, with a very low level of literacy.

The traditional Muslim artisan is rapidly losing importance, and communities which were previously engaged in crafts, such as blacksmithing, carpentry, pottery and roof building, are now changing over to labor and service-oriented occupations. Because of the transition, these communities are rather poor and have a low index of education. Some communities not adversely affected, such as those of goldsmiths, have a better index of education. Khumbhar, Tai, Soni and Suthar are included in this group.

Muslim communities which have retained their service-oriented occupations, as well as those which have recently shifted to this occupation, have a low index of education. These communities include Behlim, Bhand, Dhobi, Hajam, Mochi and Bhatiara. Besides the barber, washerman, shoemaker, mimic and musician, this group also includes domestic servants.

Many Muslims work as farmhands or industrial laborers. Those who are shifting from traditional occupations usually opt for labor where the income is steady. Ramna, Kasai, Malek, Nagori and Chakda are a few of the communities included in this group. On the whole, this group is economically and educationally poor.

A number of Muslims are engaged in government or private services, many working as policemen. Most of the communities have held the same occupations since the inception of Muslim rule in Gujarat. Sayyids, Moghuls, Pathans and

Shaikhs are in this group. Most of them are fairly well off economically and show a high standard of education.

Muslims in Gujarat are very much a part of the larger Indian society, and as a result, Muslim social organization is greatly influenced by the Hindu social structure. Muslim society is theoretically opposed to the caste system, yet there is considerable evidence to suggest that in practice Muslims maintain the caste system as much as their Hindu counterparts.

However, there are some basic differences in the manner in which the Hindus and the Muslims view the caste system. For the Muslims the system is not religiously ordained but is a social fact. Secondly, there is no Muslim substitution for the Brahmin or the priest class, which not only occupies the highest stratum but also controls the rigidity of the system. Further, Islam is a proselytizing faith aimed towards converts and thus includes various members of lower and poorer castes whose caste status is unclear. Finally, the Muslim system does not allocate occupations in a hierarchy, so there is no pollution index.

The strongest similarity in the Hindu and Muslim caste systems is the endogamous pattern of marriage and a keen sense of birth and lineage. Thus Sayyids, the descendants of Muhammad, rank highest in the Muslim hierarchy, with Shaikhs, by virtue of their proximity to the Prophet, close behind. The literate and landed castes come next in line with agrarian, craft and service communities following.

The communal organization of the Gujarati Muslims is commonly referred to as Jama'tbandi. This system is the traditional expression of communal solidarity in a concrete form. It is designed to regulate the affairs of the community and apply sanctions against infractions of the communal code. Several measures are adhered to in order to assure this solidarity, among which marriage and kinship regulations play a major role. These include joint family living and a patrilineal descent system. Secondly, customary Indian law, which denies females the right to inherit, is followed rather than Islamic law. This ensures the agrarian communities' retention of ancestral land. Further, solidarity is encouraged through cousin marriages. Cross-cousin marriages outnumber parallel-cousin marriages, both of which maintain endogamous relations and preserve the wealth within the extended family. The endogamous pattern is often carried to the extent that members of a dispersed caste tend to marry members from the same locale, thus leading to fragmentation into even smaller groups, which in turn leads to strong in-group bonds and eventually to a tightly knit Jama'tbandi system.

Social organization at the Jama'tbandi level varies from community to community. A lower-class community in a small area is able to run a mosque and the attached rest house, maintain cohesion and pacify quarrels. Some larger communities, such as the Bohra and Khoja, which have religious leaders, have developed elaborate and highly formalized systems with written and registered constitutions. Their organizations, which resemble bureaucracies, own large properties, undertake housing projects and run schools, dispensaries and weekly or monthly newspapers. They are two of the most cohesive and prosperous communities in Gujarat.

Muslim households consist of extended families with several married and unmarried brothers, unmarried sisters and other relatives, with the father at its head. Kinship terminology is classed according to crucial links to the ascending generation and one's own generation. Children are brought up with affection and care within the extended family. Children from well-to-do households are sent to both religious and secular schools at an early age.

Marriage patterns vary. Some communities have a closed, endogamous pattern where deviations are not easily tolerated (Bohra, Khoja, Memon, Tai, Dudhwalla and Dhobi). Others are endogamous but tolerate marriage with those who are their equals. A few very loosely organized communities permit intermarriage freely among themselves and with others (Kasbati and Siphai).

Gujarati Muslims have also been subject to modernization from within India and from the outside world. On the social level, modernization has come directly from educational institutions, particularly the universities and governmental and industrial spheres. Stringent caste rules and regulations often go unheeded by university-educated people. There is more emphasis on economic gain than on occupational caste in acquiring status. Marriage across caste lines is on the rise. And there is a shift from the community to the individual, often resulting in disintegration of the traditional communities.

Modernization often has taken the form of absorbing and sometimes merely imitating Western values and culture, which sometimes is in opposition to Islam. Yet, in cases where modernization and Islam have been combined, as in the case of the Khoja Ismailis, the communities have reaped benefits from the traditional organizations.

BIBLIOGRAPHY

Books

Ahmad, Imtiaz, ed. *Caste and Social Stratification Among the Muslims.* 2nd ed., Delhi: Manohar Book Service, 1979.
———. *Ritual and Religion Among Muslims in India.* Delhi: Manohar Book Service, 1980.
Hollister, J. N. *The Shi'a of India.* London: Luzac, 1953.
Majmudar, M. R. *Cultural History of Gujarat.* New York: Humanities Press, 1964.
Misra, Satish C. *Muslim Communities in Gujarat.* New York: Asia Publishing House, 1964.
Morris, H. S. *The Indians in Uganda.* Chicago: University of Chicago Press, 1968.
Sharib, Zahurul Hassan. *Indian Village in Transition.* Bombay: All India Institute of Local Self-Government, 1967.
Srinivas, M. N. *Social Change in Modern India.* Berkeley: University of California Press, 1966.

Articles

Khan, Zilhur, "Caste and Muslim Peasantry in Gujarat." *Man in India* 48 (1968): 133–148.

Patel, S. D. "Navsari Town and Its People." *Gujarat Research Society Journal* 33:3 (1971): 194–200.

Pocock, D. "The Bases of Factions in Gujerat." *British Journal of Sociology* 8 (1957): 295–306.

Merun H. Nasser-Bush
Population figures updated by Richard V. Weekes

GUJARS   Muslim Gujars, unlike other Muslims in India, are an unenviable people for they have not been able to attain the same socioeconomic and religious status as their co-religionists. Being converts, they have neither been accepted fully into the Muslim fold, nor have they been able to break away completely from their early Hindu moorings. Whether the latter situation has contributed to the former or vice versa, or whether it is their nomadic way of life which has kept them out of the mainstream of the Muslim community is difficult to say. Perhaps all these factors have contributed, together with the fact that they are despised by other Muslims for their life-style, which is viewed as full of intrigue and corruption.

There are numerous opinions as to the origins of the Gujars. General A. Cunningham, who wrote *Ancient Geography of India* in 1924, places them among the Scythian tribes who conquered Kabul about 100 B.C. and marched into India. They established themselves in Kashmir and northwestern India, where such place names as Gujranwala and Gujarat (now in Pakistan) are testimony to their early settlements. By the middle of the fifth century they had built a Gujar kingdom, Gujradesa. V. A. Smith, author of *The Early History of India* in 1924, traces their origin to the White Huns, who in about A.D. 465 poured into India as nomadic hordes. D. Ibbetson in 1883 said they came after the Huns, became Hindu and eventually founded the kingdom of Rajasthan. He suggests that Gujars, Jats and perhaps Ahirs are of one ethnic stock who entered India at different times and settled in different places, this opinion being supported by the fact that these groups eat and smoke together today.

Most likely, Gujars are the products of intermixture between early Indo-Aryans and later tribal immigrants, possibly Scythians and Huns. This theory may account for the considerable linguistic affinity of the Gujar language with the Indo-Aryan (Indo-Iranian) languages, together with certain socioreligious practices and *gotra* (clan) names which are common among Gujars, Jat and Rajputs (see Jat). However, Gujars do not enjoy the same social status vis-à-vis the Jat and Rajputs but are considered inferior because of their racial and cultural intermixtures.

Gujars were converted to Islam in different localities at different times. In all probability this process started with the attack of Mahmud of Gazni and the plundering of Somnath in Gujarat in 1024, when Gujars and Jat fought valiantly to defend their kingdom. The Gujars of Oudh and Meerut attribute their conversion to Timur, when he attacked Delhi in 1398 and forcibly converted the people. Successive invasions of Muslims from the northwest quickened this process. When Babur invaded India in 1525, he found that in northern Punjab, Gujars and Jat had already adopted Islam. The process continued through the seventeenth century under the Moghul rule of Aurangzeb, who forcibly converted the Gujars of Himachal Pradesh.

Pushtun and Baluch Muslims of northwestern India were contemptuous of these Gujar and Jat Muslim converts, seized their lands and drove them from their homeland to seek a nomadic life. Since then, the Gujars have been wandering in jungles and hills with their herds of buffalo in search of grazing land.

Today Muslim Gujars are found in greatest numbers in every part of northwestern India and Pakistan from the Indus River to the Ganges, from the Hazara Mountains to peninsular Gujarat. They are especially numerous along the banks of the upper Jumuna River near Jagadhri and Buria and in the Saharanpur District in Uttar Pradesh. They are also present in small pockets in and around Delhi, Rewari and Gwalior. In the northern hill regions of India Muslim Gujars are mostly confined to the states of Jammu and Kashmir and Himachal Pradesh. In Pakistan Punjab they are numerous in such places are Gujranwala, Gujarat and Gujarkhan.

There are both Hindu and Muslim Gujars. The former live in the foothills and adjoining plains, practicing agriculture and leading sedentary lives. The Muslim Gujars live in the hills and lead a pastoral, semi-nomadic life with seasonal migrations between low and high mountains in search of more congenial climate and pastures for their buffalo.

Hindu and Muslim Gujars live in complete social and geographical isolation from each other. A recent morphometric and serogenetic study conducted by the author revealed significant differences between the two groups. However, common sociocultural practices together with linguistic affinity attest to their common origin. Muslim Gujars manifest considerable Turkish and Afghan physical features due, most probably, to intermarriage with Muslim invaders from western Asia.

Gujars have well-built bodies, tall statures, dolichocephalic (long) heads, long noses with convex nasal bridge, long narrow faces, light eyes and light brown skin with large prominent teeth. The men sport a characteristic beard which is usually well trimmed. They frequently dye their beard and hair with a thin paste of myrtle (*mehndi*), a practice particularly of the elderly who wish to hide their gray hair.

Males wear a long shirt, a *tehmad* (lungi) and a white turban similar to those worn in Rajasthan. Women also wear a long shirt and a *churidar* pajama. They do not observe *purdah* or wear a veil. They are usually bedecked with fine and intricate silver jewelry.

Muslim Gujars have recently started building semi-permanent settlements. They live in a single-room house with no windows and a single entrance, along with their cattle. Their kitchen is in one corner on a slightly raised platform. Inside, the house is dark, stuffy and smoky from constant fires. Because they are disliked by their neighbors as menials, they lead an isolated life.

Gujars speak Gujari, considered to be a dialect of Rajasthani, an Indic language (of the Indo-Iranian sector of the Indo-European family) similar to most languages of northern India. In Himachal Pradesh the language is mixed with Western Pahari. Literate Gujars write in the Urdu script which they learn from *mullahs*.

Muslim Gujars are Sunni and observe Muslim customs mixed with Hindu practices. They keep a copy of the Quran in their homes and hang wall calendars with photos of Mecca and Medina. A devout Gujar prays five times a day. Id al Zuha (Id al Adha) and Id al Fitr are their main festivals. Some still conduct their marriages in Hindu fashion. Like Hindus, they worship a family deity. When a baby is born, a pandit (Brahmin priest) is asked to fix a lucky time for the first bath for the mother. When a boy is four or five years of age he is circumcised. A pandit is consulted to fix a lucky day for betrothal, but the *mullah* reads the *nikah* (marriage ceremony). They bury their dead in the Muslim way but make fire offerings (*agyari*) and upset a pitcher of water near the grave as do Hindus before cremating their dead. Gujars also offer food to their dead ancestors on Fridays, the way Hindus observe *shrads*, but instead of feeding the Brahmins, Muslims feed the beggars in hopes that through the beggars food will reach their dead ancestors. Gujar Muslims also observe some of the Hindu festivals such as Holi and Nag Panchmi.

Gujars are divided into hundreds of exogamous *gotras*, clans derived from the names of founders or from places of their early settlement. Their main function is to regulate marriage to the benefit of the clan. Among prominent *gotras* are the Chandel, Bhatti, Banja, Lodha, Gorsia, Dedhar, Jinar, Bhumbla, Katarya, Poswal, Kasave, Rawal and Tomar.

Among Muslim Gujars, descent is patrilineal, marriage is patrilocal with consanguine marriages preferred. Child marriage is common, the average age of girls being 15 to 18 years and of boys 20 to 25. Marriages are usually arranged by parents in various ways. The most usual is through payment of brideprice by the groom's family in the form of cash or buffalo. A less expensive arrangement is by exchange whereby families supply each other with daughters for their sons to wed. When a father has only a daughter, he may practice *gharjawain* and bring the son-in-law into his home.

Divorce and remarriage are permissible, divorce being easy. The woman simply leaves her husband and starts living with another man, who, in turn, pays compensation to the former husband. Children born of a previous marriage remain with their father unless they are small; they then stay with the mother until old enough to return. Most divorces are caused by barrenness of the wife, incompatibility and adultery. While monogamy is most common, sometimes a man will contract a second marriage with permission of the first wife, who not only continues to live with her husband but also enjoys a privileged position.

Gujars favor the joint or extended family system, although there is an increasing demand by newlyweds for nuclear family life. As soon as a son is married, he is given his share of the property and a few buffalo. Females are not entitled to a share of their father's property on his death as long as there is a son to inherit. But the debts of the father must be repaid equally by all the married sons (unmarried sons are exempt).

The economy of the Muslim Gujars revolves around raising buffalo so there is a constant search for unrestricted pasture lands. There is little interest in sending children to school, and the fast-changing world around them appears to have little impact. Few have shown interest in economic development plans of their semi-sedentary communities. The Muslim Gujars are economically static and vulnerable to exploitation by the trading and commercial community. Their illiteracy, poverty and low social status make them an unenviable group of people.

BIBLIOGRAPHY

Books

Baden-Powell, B. H. *The Indian Community*. Delhi: Cosmo, 1972.
Cunningham, A. *Ancient Geography of India*. Calcutta: Chuckervertty, Chatterjee, 1924.
Ibbetson, D. *A Glossary of the Tribes and Castes of the Punjab and North-West Frontier Provinces*. Reprint ed. Patiala (Punjab): Punjabi University Languages Department, 1970. (Originally published 1883).
Munshi, K. M. *Glory That Was Gujaradesa (A.D. 550–1300)*. Bombay: Bharatya Vidya Bhavan, 1954.
Russel, R. V., and Lal, Hira. *The Tribes and Castes of the Central Provinces of India*. Vol. 3. Delhi: Cosmo, 1975.
Singh, Pal R. C., ed. "Himachal Pradesh." In *Census of India*. Vol. 20. Simla, India: Government of India Press, 1961.
Smith, V. A. *The Early History of India*. Oxford: Oxford University Press, 1924.
Thakur, Upendra. *Some Aspects of Ancient Indian History and Culture*. New Delhi: Abhinar, 1974.

J. C. Sharma

GURAGE   An Ethiopian chronicle of the fourteenth century contains the earliest known reference to the Muslim Gurage of Ethiopia. Their traditional homeland in southwestern Shoa Province lies roughly between Lake Zway on the east and the Awash River on the west. Bordered on all sides by groups who speak Cushitic languages, the Gurage represent the southernmost extension of North Ethiopic Semitic. No reliable figures exist on the number of speakers of Guragina, which is spoken only by the Gurage, but they are estimated to exceed 2.3 million, of whom one-third are Muslim.

Islam is the predominant religion practiced by the Selti, Walane, Ulbareg and Innekor Gurage in the "eastern" language (or dialect) cluster, and by the Gogot in the "western" grouping. Among the latter, some adherents to Islam are found in Chaha, Enor and Masqan. Linguistic distinctions, as between the Chaha and Enor, correspond to territorial-political divisions demarcating the small, autonomous, internal governing clan chieftaincies. Clan chiefs are the highest political officers. At no time in Gurage history has there been a supreme political officeholder who exercised rule over all the Gurage. The authority of Muslim clan chiefs is recognized equally by non-Muslim and Muslim subjects.

No conspicuous differences in the cultural ways of life distinguish Muslim Gurage from Gurage who practice other religious customs. In districts inhabited by Gurage having different religious habits, Muslims live side by side with Christians and families which still adhere to traditional religious beliefs and rituals. All are settled agriculturalists who depend upon *Ensete ventricosum* (the "false banana" plant) as a food staple and keep small herds of cattle. *Ensete* is not only the mainstay of the Gurage diet, but its by-products serve a variety of utilitarian purposes, including use as fuel and for insulation in house construction. The cultural complex which has developed around the digging-stick horticulture of *ensete* dominates less the mode of life of the eastern Gurage than that of the western grouping. Poor soil conditions unsuitable for the growing of grains and a wide variety of root crops have conditioned the almost total dependency on *ensete* of the western Gurage. Their eastern neighbors have adapted to the techniques of plow cultivation, and their surpluses of grains and other crops are sold and exchanged in markets in the western region. *Ensete* horticulture permits high population density, and in districts where arable land is scarce, the Gurage often exceed 240 persons per square mile.

Gurage villages are compact and separated from one another by open fields used for communal grazing of livestock and small forests of eucalyptus trees. Sacred forests in which good and evil spirits are believed to dwell are found in predominantly Muslim districts, often alongside dwellings in which Muslims gather to recite prayers. Ideally, villages are composed of families related through the eldest males, married sons and their wives and children living on their father's land. Muslims cooperate in common economic pursuits, such as *ensete* horticulture, tending cattle and house construction, with villagers of other religious persuasions. They also participate in each other's birth, marriage and death ceremonies. Food, other than meat, is shared without concern for particular religious preference. At rural markets, or in towns and cities, Muslims purchase meat from animals slaughtered only by other Muslims. Children accept the father's religious calling. Today, they attend Ethiopian government schools, which, although officially Christian, make allowances for Muslim children to receive Islamic instruction, to participate in daily prayers and to observe holy days. The absence of the practice of *purdah* among Muslim Gurage facilitates the participation of women in market activities, both in the rural areas and in the towns.

The principal center of Islamic worship for Muslim Gurage is the shrine of Shaikh Said Budella, which is located in the western district of Gyeto. Near the Shaikh's shrine is the sacred forest of the Gurage Thunder God. Two generations ago the guardian priest of the sacred forest, the grandfather of Shaikh Budella, became a convert to Islam during the campaigns launched against the Gurage by Emperor Menilek II at the close of the last century. Stories of miracles attributed to Shaikh Budella, a follower of the Tijaniyya order, have spread his religious influence and spiritual power beyond the confines of Gurage territory. Muslims making the annual pilgrimage to his shrine travel distances from as far away as Jimma, Sidamo and Harar. Both the Qadiriyya and Tijaniyya orders are represented among Muslim Gurage, but the distribution of adherents between these two orders is not known.

No formal centers of Islamic education exist in Gurageland, nor is the region a major center of religious propagation. The vast majority of Muslim Gurage are not lettered, having learned by rote their prayers recited in Arabic, a religious duty performed with considerable display of devotion. Quranic teaching is confined primarily to the homestead, which may be visited occasionally by Muslim holy men who offer religious instruction in prayer recitation and interpret local disputes according to Islamic law. Mosques are inconspicuous even in districts predominantly inhabited by Muslims. Where they have been built, the style of construction is identical to the ordinary domestic dwelling, which is round, with an angled thatched roof supported by a large center post.

Islam was introduced among the Gurage perhaps as early as the thirteenth century. In this era of Islamic expansion in Ethiopia, several Muslim sultanates flourished in Shoa Province. A Muslim invasion of Christian Ethiopia in the sixteenth century left behind in Gurage territory contingents of Muslim soldiers who established a foothold for the later expansion of Islam. Thus, Islam became a thin veneer over traditional religious rites.

Pre-Islamic beliefs and rituals remain entrenched among some Muslim Gurage who worship nature spirits, believe in the supernatural power of celestial beings and wear amulets to ward off evil spirits. Muslim Gurage merchants and traders in regions outside their homeland, especially in Addis Ababa, Jimma and Harar, maintain active religious ties with other Muslim Ethiopians. Together with migrant laborers, they are the principal agents of cultural change in Gurageland. Muslim Gurage, whose economic way of life brings them into constant contact with devout believers in other regions of Ethiopia, are the principal proselytizers of Islam among Gurage of different religious faiths.

William A. Shack

BIBLIOGRAPHY

Books

Cerulli, Enrico. *L'Islam di Ieri e di Oggi*. Rome: Instituto per L'Orient, 1971.
Hetzron, Robert. *The Gunnan-Gurage Languages*. Naples: Instituto Orientale di Napoli, 1977.
Leslau, Wolf. *Ethiopians Speak: Studies in Cultural Background, II. Chaha*. Berkeley: University of California Press, 1966.

————. *Ethiopians Speak: Studies in Cultural Background, III. Soddo*. Berkeley: University of California Press, 1968.

Murdock, George P. *Africa: Its People and Their Culture History*. New York: McGraw-Hill, 1959.

Shack, William A. *The Central Ethiopians: Amhara, Tigrina and Related Peoples*. Ethnographic Survey of Northeast Africa, part 4. London: International African Institute, 1974.

————. *The Gurage: A People of the Ensete Culture*. London: Oxford University Press, 1966.

Shack, William A., and Cohen, Percy. *Politics in Leadership: A Comparative Perspective*. Oxford: Clarendon Press, 1979.

Shack William A., and Habte-Miriam, Marcos. *Gods and Heroes: Oral Traditions of the Gurage of Ethiopia*. Oxford: Clarendon Press, 1974.

Shack, William A., and Skinner, Elliott P. *Strangers in African Societies*. Berkeley: University of California Press, 1979.

Trimingham, J. Spencer. *Islam in Ethiopia*. London: Frank Cass, 1965.

Articles

Bender, M. Lionel. "Languages of Ethiopia." *Anthropological Linguistics* 13 (1971): 165–288.

Fleming, Harold C. "Sociology, Ethnology and History of Ethiopia." *International Journal of African Historical Studies* 9:2 (1976): 248–278.

Leslau, Wolf. "Asat, the Soul of the Gurage." *Africa* 10:3 (1969): 281–290.

Needham, Rodney. "Gurage Social Classification: Formal Notes on an Unusual System." *Africa* 39:2 (1969): 153–166.

Shack, William A. "Notes on Occupational Castes Among the Gurage of Southwest Ethiopia." *Man* 54 (1964): 50–52.

————. "Religious Ideas and Social Action in the Gurage Bond-Friendship." *Africa* 33:3 (1963): 198–206.

————. "Some Aspects of Ecology and Social Structure in Ensete Complex in Southwest Ethiopia." *Journal of the Royal Anthropological Institute* 93:1 (1963): 72–79.

GYPSIES Gypsies profess, in nearly all cases, the religion dominant in their area of residence. Thus, there are Catholic Gypsies, various types of Protestant and Orthodox Gypsies and, throughout the Islamic world and those portions of southeastern Europe where the Ottomans most recently ruled, large numbers of Muslim Gypsies. The particular sect of Islam which they profess varies with the area. Everywhere they are accused by non-Gypsies of being only superficially Muslim and of lacking true piety. While this alleged indifference in religious matters is frequently overstressed, there often is a fusion of Islamic and traditional Gypsy religious belief and practice, particularly among those Gypsies still nomadic.

Ethnographic information concerning Muslim Gypsies (with the exception of those in Yugoslavia) is both meager in quantity and poor in quality. The general literature on Gypsies often does not even mention those in the Middle East, although their number there is probably even greater than in Europe. Very little has been written specifically of Gypsies in the Islamic world, and nearly all of that which exists is extremely unreliable. Furthermore, generalizations are difficult. Muslim Gypsies, even within a single state, do not constitute a unified group either culturally or socially. A great amount of differentiation has occurred between different groups of Gypsies, and, everywhere, specifically Gypsy custom has been mixed with that of the various peoples among whom they have travelled.

It is impossible even to estimate the total number of Muslim Gypsies. The population is considerable and is spread over every nation of the Middle East, Central Asia, the Caucasus, North Africa, the southern Balkans and the northwestern portion of the Indian subcontinent. Factors contributing to this lacuna include the general inadequacies of census data in most of the area, the special difficulties of counting nomads, the fact that Gypsies have been overlooked by most social scientists working in the Islamic world, the existence in some regions of Gypsy-like groups that are difficult to distinguish from them, the ongoing process of Gypsy assimilation and, especially, the attempt by many Gypsies to avoid their pariah status by hiding their ethnic identity. The difficulties of an estimate in the face of such problems is illustrated by the example of Yugoslavia, where both census data and knowledge of Gypsies are better than anywhere else in this part of the world. The 1971 census reports 78,485 Gypsies in Yugoslavia, but both official sources and reliable scholars consider the true figure to be much higher, probably around 20 times as many. The issue is confounded further by not knowing what proportion of these are Muslim (although one can assume that roughly one-half are).

The Gypsy mother tongue is Romany, an Indic branch of Indo-European closely related to Sanskrit. With the exception of very young children, however, no Gypsy anywhere is a Romany monolingual. The nature of their occupational status and their relationship to non-Gypsies require them to speak at least one other language, and often several. Muslim Gypsies speak a number of different dialects of Romany, while others have evolved an argot (in the manner of English Gypsies) which is partially derived from Romany. Many others have lost their distinctive language. This is especially true of sedentarized Gypsies, except where their settlements are recent or especially large.

Muslim Gypsies are known by a very wide variety of names, of which the most common are Čingāne (Turkish), Nawar (Arabic), and Qorbati or Kowli (Persian). Their own name for themselves in Romany is Rom or Dom, although this is said to be less widely known in the Islamic world than in Europe and the Americas. There is also a great number of local names, some derived from certain Gypsy occupations and some from the names of particular Gypsy tribes. Others result from use by non-Gypsies of certain derogatory terms as generic names.

Gypsy ethnogenesis apparently took place in northwestern India, where there still live Gypsy-like peoples thought to be derived from the same stock as Gypsies elsewhere (see Gujars; Jat). They are believed to have entered Persia by the ninth century, whence they spread across the Middle East, arriving in the Balkans in the early fourteenth century. They comprise a number of different ''tribes,'' each identified with a particular sub-culture, often including a distinct dialect of Romany and a particular occupation or set of occupations traditional to the group. In theory, each tribe or group of Gypsies is endogamous (although marriage with other types of Gypsies and non-Gypsies is not uncommon in practice). In many respects, Gypsies can be considered a caste, or group of closely related castes, intruded into a society that is generally non-caste in structure.

There are large numbers of Gypsies in the Islamic world who are nomadic. Most, like Gypsies elsewhere, differ from all other types of nomads in that they move from settlement to settlement rather than pursuing a life in less inhabited areas. Each tribe, composed of various camping groups, has its own political structure. Some are attached to and migrate with tribes of pastoral nomads (e.g., the Basseri in Iran), serving as their blacksmiths. Such groups have their own internal structure which is subservient to the pastoral nomadic chief. Many other Gypsies have been sedentarized in either villages or urban areas, some very early after their arrival in the area. The largest Gypsy settlement in the world is thought to be Šuto Orizare, a suburb of Skopje, Yugoslavia, with a population of 32,000, nearly all of whom are Muslim Gypsies.

Gypsy occupations in the Islamic world have much in common with those in Europe and the Americas. Especially common are various types of smithery and metal working (particularly iron and copper), entertainment (as musicians, dancers, animal trainers and performing dervishes), trading in livestock (particularly draft animals), fortune telling, petty trade, manufacturing of certain crafts for which the raw materials are available free or very cheaply (bricks, sieves, tambourines, brooms, baskets, rush mats, turned wood artifacts, etc.) and as agricultural laborers. Begging is also common. Urban Gypsies are frequently employed in those occupations of lowest esteem—as garbage collectors, porters, shoeblacks, street sweepers, carriers, cleaning women and, during the Ottoman period, executioners. In the modern period, there are some sedentarized Gypsies who have found employment in factories and shops and even a few who have surmounted the discrimination to which they are everywhere subjected to become doctors, teachers, engineers and other professionals. This is especially true in the Socialist nations of the Balkans, where special opportunities have been made available to Gypsies but where, on the other hand, they have not (with the exception of Yugoslavia) been allowed the option of a traditional Gypsy lifestyle.

BIBLIOGRAPHY

Books

Barth, Fredrik. *Nomads of South Persia: The Basseri Tribe of the Khamseh Confederacy.* New York: Humanities Press, 1961.

Clébert, Jean-Paul. *The Gypsies*. London: Vista Books, 1963.

McDougall, Bart. *Gypsies: Wanderers of the World*. Washington, D.C.: National Geographic Society, 1970.

Quelquejay, Chantal Lemercier-. "Čingāne." In *Encyclopedia of Islam*, edited by H.A.R. Gibb et al. London: Luzac, 1960.

Vukanović, T. P. "The Killing of Old People Among Gypsies on the Balkan Peninsula." In *VIe Congrès des sciences anthropologiques et ethnologiques, Paris*, Vol. 2, Paris: Musée de l'Homme, 1960.

Articles

Arnold, Hermann. "Some Observations on Turkish and Persian Gypsies." *Journal of the Gypsy Lore Society*, 3rd series 46 (1967): 105–122.

Dunin, Elsie. "Čoček as a Ritual Dance Among Gypsy Women." *Makedonski folklor* 6 (1973): 193–198.

———. "Gypsy Wedding: Dance and Customs." *Makedonski folklor* 7–8 (1971): 317–326.

Francis, H. J. "Gypsies in Afghanistan." *Journal of the Gypsy Lore Society*, 3rd series 41 (1962): 158–159.

Kendrick, D. "Notes on the Gypsies in Bulgaria." *Journal of the Gypsy Lore Society*, 3rd series 45 (1966): 77–84.

———. "Three Gypsy Tales from the Balkans." *Folklore* 78 (1967): 59–60.

Levy, Juliette de Bairacli. "The Gypsies of Turkey." *Journal of the Gypsy Lore Society*, 3rd series 31 (1952): 5–13.

Rajab, Katani, J. "Jottings on Gypsies in the Middle East." *Journal of the Gypsy Lore Society*, 3rd series 41 (1962): 150–153.

Rajput, A. B. "Reshman: The Elusive Gypsy Singer of Pakistan." *Journal of the Gypsy Lore Society*, 3rd series 47 (1968): 47–49.

Regensburger, Reinhold. "Gypsies in the Land of Israel." *Journal of the Gypsy Lore Society*, 3rd series 37 (1958): 69–70.

Sykes, Percy M. "Gypsies of Persia." *Journal of the Gypsy Lore Society*, 3rd series 32 (1953): 344–345.

Uhlik, Rade. "Serbo-Bosnian Gypsy Folk Tales." *Journal of the Gypsy Lore Society*, 3rd series 31 (1952): 90–100; 33 (1954): 54–65; 35 (1956): 62–76; 37 (1958): 4–20; 38 (1959): 134–143.

Vukanović, T. P. "Gypsy Bear-Leaders in the Balkan Peninsula." *Journal of the Gypsy Lore Society*, 3rd series 38 (1959): 106–127.

———. "Gypsy Pilgrimages to the Monastery of Gracanica in Serbia." *Journal of the Gypsy Lore Society*, 3rd series 45 (1966): 17–26.

———. "The Gypsy Population in Yugoslavia." *Journal of the Gypsy Lore Society* 3rd series 42 (1963): 10–27.

———. "The Manufacture of Pots and Pans Among the Gypsies in the Region of Kosovo and Metohija." *Journal of the Gypsy Lore Society*, 3rd series 40 (1961): 35–44.

———. "Musical Culture Among the Gypsies of Yugoslavia." *Journal of the Gypsy Lore Society*, 3rd series, 41 (1962): 41–61.

———. "The Position of Women Among Gypsies in the Kosovo-Metohija Region." *Journal of the Gypsy Lore Society*, 3rd series 40 (1961): 81–100.

———. "The Vampire." *Journal of the Gypsy Lore Society*, 3rd series 36 (1957): 125–143; 37 (1958): 21–31, 111–118; 38 (1959): 44–55.

Walton, James. "The Gypsy Bender Tent and Its Derivatives." *Man* 58 (1958): 89–90.

Wilkinson, M. A. "A Note on Gypsies in Southern Yugoslavia Today." *Journal of the Gypsy Lore Society*, 3rd series 32 (1953): 39–41.

Windfuhr, Gernor L. "European Gypsies in Iran: A First Report." *Anthropological Linguistics* 12 (1970): 271–292.

Winstedt, E. O. "Palestinian Gypsies." *Journal of the Gypsy Lore Society*, 3rd series 31 (1952): 77–78.

———. "Syrian Gypsies." *Journal of the Gypsy Lore Society*, 3rd series 30 (1951): 78–79.

Yates, D. E. "The *Nuars* in Jordan." *Journal of the Gypsy Lore Society,* 3rd series 36 (1957): 145–147.

William G. Lockwood

H

HADDAD The most despised, subjugated and socially inferior peoples of the African Sahel are the Haddad, the blacksmiths, a most puzzling Muslim ethnic group. Numbering perhaps 230,000, they subsist as clients to patrons in a relationship of mutual contempt, scorn and a dependency which guarantees service to the patrons and security for the client.

"Haddad" is derived from *haddad*, which is Arabic for "iron." Wherever Arabic is the lingua franca, *haddad* is the generic name for blacksmiths. A more polite name in Arabic is *usta*, which means "craftsman." Every non-Arabic-speaking ethnic group has its own name for them: Teda, Duude; Daza, Aza; Kanembu, Nogoa; Zaghawa, May; Fur, Miro; Maba, Kolek; Masalit, Kule; Sinyar, Kodro; Daju-Sila, Dagince; plus many more.

The Haddad have no language of their own. They speak the tongue of their patrons, with whom they live, whether pastoral or sedentary. When their patrons prosper, they do; when their patrons fail, the Haddad seek better luck elsewhere.

Whether they serve agricultural or pastoral nomadic populations, a large number of similarities can be noted with regard to Haddad social organization and means of subsistence and of attitudes pertaining to their association with host populations. They live outside the societies they serve and whose values therefore do not apply to them. The most basic factor for their being placed outside society is that collectively they can hold no property rights to animals or usufruct rights to land. Similarly, they are not allowed to use wells, except for themselves individually and their riding animals. Being unable to engage in either agriculture or animal husbandry on their own (although occasionally they do farm small plots), they can only forge iron, hunt and gather and perform various special tasks for their patrons.

Haddad marginality is expressed in many different ways. They are despised to such an extent that ritually, socially and spatially they are forced to live apart from their hosts. Money is thrown in front of them, not handed to them, although the more enlightened will place the money in a Haddad's breast pocket. Wandering Haddad minstrels play the drum and sing from inside a makeshift hut so that neither performer nor audience sees the other. Touching, such as in shaking hands, let alone eating with a Haddad, is considered repulsive and taboo. If a Haddad's private grain crop looks promising, it is not unusual for the local chief to have the plants pulled for fear the Haddad will become self-sufficient and thus independent. Masalit women have been known to tickle their babies so they would laugh at a Haddad passing by.

Intermarriage with a Haddad is forbidden, of course, by most ethnic groups. Should a Masalit become a blacksmith, he could not marry any but a Haddad, the occupational support for this caste-like behavior being so strong. Nevertheless, Haddad who no longer work as hunters or blacksmiths, but as traders or officials, are still forcibly endogamous. It is noteworthy that within this extreme division of labor (especially among the Zaghawa of Chad and western Sudan) many tasks involve pounding (see Beri).

The origin of the widespread attitudes of contempt for Haddad are difficult to reconstruct because of several layers of ideological justification. Among these are religious, i.e., "Islamicly sanctioned"; supernatural beliefs concerning their incomprehensible magical powers in forging and knowledge of magic and medicine; reprehensible hunting techniques involving the use of nets.

Subjugated, relegated to a subservient and inferior status, the Haddad have developed an attitude of scorn and superiority themselves. They despise society as much as society despises them, and they exemplify this with their Quranicly sanctioned claim to be descendents of David to whom God taught ironworking. From hindsight, the social inferiority of the Haddad is the result of an intricate dialectic fed by repulsion on the part of pastoral immigrants for indigenous hunting techniques and skills in ironworking and magic and an urge to survive collectively on the part of the Haddad. This is exemplified by their propensity to inspire fear, initially in all innocence, by living according to their own customs, later on actively catering to special demands which were abhorrent to their hosts' sense of morality. Thus the Haddad who never formed part of society had little feelings of solidarity or responsibility towards it.

As P. Fuchs explained in his 1961 study of the Sahelian people: "The fact that especially the highest ranking personalities (kings and chiefs) preferred to have a smith as counsellor can be explained by the fact that these 'people without conscience,' as they were often called, are prepared to commit the biggest crimes and vileness for their masters, who would never dare entrust those acts to other subjects" (author's translation).

So a Haddad who is ordered to kill or injure a member of "society" by his pastoralist patron feels no moral qualms whatsoever for his act. Both parties considering themselves superior to the other, the Haddad transform their weakness into physical immunity. In theory and practice it has become a social error to scold, abuse, beat or kill a Haddad. They are precluded from waging war alongside their patrons. Murder of a Haddad or theft of his property must be avenged by his patron.

Historically the Haddad of the sultanates of Wadai, Darfur and Dar Masalit were governed, judged and taxed by a special Haddad "sultan," who, moreover, held an important position in the real courts of the sultanates. In Wadai, the "sultan" of the Haddad was the physician for the royal family and as such was permitted to enter the harem. Also it was his duty, at the beginning of a new reign, to blind the sultan's brothers, nephews and cousins. He also had the tasks of shaving the sultan's head weekly and preparing the body of a dead sultan for burial.

Prior to and during the Islamization of the Sahel and the Sudan, states were often headed by sacred kings whose subjects believed that it was they who brought life and death, sickness and health. Frequently the king remained in seclusion, veiled from the view of his people and outsiders. He conversed with visitors and petitioners through intermediaries or from behind a curtain. It was forbidden to see the king eat or in other ways note his "humanness." If he became ill, he was likely to be killed by family insiders lest the mortality of the king be exposed. The introduction of Islam did not immediately disturb the mythic basis of royal authority; as recently as the 1870s, the sacrality of the king still largely existed, even though the kings had been Muslims for 200 years. Only when rulers turned Islam from an imperial cult into a state religion and thus brought it to the masses did their sacrality break down.

Throughout this experience, Haddad, being outside the society, did not have to recognize the sacrality of the rulers. They could converse directly with the king and do many things that no other mortal would contemplate doing.

The tasks which Haddad perform across the Sahel vary considerably. In northern Chad they are engaged in ironworking, woodworking and leatherworking. They play the drum and harp and sing praise songs and songs of mockery in return for money. They are also carriers of secrets of a political and magico-religious nature and serve as confidants to high-ranking personalities, who use them as spies, purveyors, matchmakers and go-betweens. As magicians, they produce amulets and question the sand oracle. The Duude of the Teda also serve as *griots*, reciting genealogies; the Aza of the Daza of Borku are also hunters and gatherers, tanners and maintainers of wells. The Danoa of the Kanembu are weavers, fishermen, farmers, dyers of textiles and rope makers.

All pastoral groups speaking an eastern Saharan language—the Kanuri, Kanembu, Teda, Daza, Zaghawa, Bideyat—which form an uninterrupted population from northeastern Nigeria to northwestern Sudan, have roughly similar attitudes towards their Haddad clients. The Zaghawa treat their Haddad as despicable subhumans, to be held at a distance. In Dar Zaghawa only Haddad ride donkeys. In many contexts, the color black is associated with the Haddad, because it is the color of their heart and soul as well as their past. Crippled, misformed and black animals are given to the Haddad along with any animal that is hermaphroditic.

Apart from being poor, Haddad are poorly educated. Teachers estimate that Haddad children are no more than 1 percent of the enrollments in Quranic and government primary schools.

Traditionally, Haddad have lived in separate quarters in towns, but as in many other ways, the modernizing world is changing some of Haddad's circumstances.

In many towns in western Sudan, they live intermingled with other ethnic groups. Some are reputed to own herds of cattle; some have become shopowners on the profits reaped from wholesale trading of scrap iron to other Haddad. The sharper edges of their universally inferior status have been blunted somewhat although its material and ideological bases remain intact. In a sedentary and urban, market-oriented context, many of the alleged initial reasons for contempt, fear and discrimination have disappeared to a great extent. Net-hunters have become very few, and employment of fire in manufacturing has lost much of its former magic now that baker and brickmaker have become common occupations.

Yet it is the memory of past inferiority coupled with an immense corpus of myths and anecdotes which has prevented the few Haddad who have made careers outside their "proper" domain from being treated as equals. The majority of the Haddad, however, do not strive for equality.

Haddad occupational monopolies and reputation enable them to remain aloof from the ideological changes which have accompanied the spread of trade and services. The wave of "Sudanization," which stresses the virtues of literacy, abstention from alcohol and tobacco, seclusion of women and religious ortho-doxy, has barely touched the Haddad. But the Haddad face a predicament. Their primary occupation, ironworking, is being threatened by the import of relatively cheap and durable agricultural tools, knives and spears, the products on which they live. The end of their monopoly might signal the end of their socially inferior status, a prospect not welcomed by most Haddad.

BIBLIOGRAPHY

Books

Chapelle, Jean. *Nomades noirs du Sahara*. Paris: L'Harmattan, 1957.

El-Tounsy, Muhammad b. Umar. *Voyage au Ouaday*. Translated by Dr. Perron. Paris: Benjamin Duprat, 1945.

Forbes, R. J. *Studies in Ancient Technology*. Vol. 8. Leiden: Brill, 1963.

Fuchs, P. *Die Völker der Südöstlichen Sahara, Tibesti, Borku, Ennedi*. Vienna: n.p. 1961.

Lebeuf, Annie M.-D. *Les Populations du Tchad (nord du 10° parallèle)*. Paris: P.U.F., 1959.

Le Rouvreur, Albert. *Sahariens et sahéliens du Tchad*. Paris: Berger-Levrault, 1962.

MacMichael, H. A. *A History of the Arabs of the Sudan*. London: Frank Cass, 1967. (Originally published 1922.)

Nachtigal, Gustav. *Sahara und Sudan*. Vol. 1 (1879), Vol. 21 (1881). Berlin: Weid-mannsche Buchhandlung, Verlagshandlung Paul Parey. Vol. 3 (1889). Leipzig: F. A. Brockhaus.

O'Fahey, R. S. *State and Society in Dār Fūr*. London: C. Hurst, 1980.

Articles

Huard, P. "Introduction et diffusion du fer au Tchad." *Journal of African History* 7:3
    (1966): 377–404.
Nicolaisen, Johannes. "The Haddad—A Hunting People in Chad." *Folk* 10 (1968): 91–
    100.

Paul Doornbos

HARARI Inside the walls of the old Muslim city of Harar in Ethiopia, its inhabitants evolved a unique preindustrial urban culture which persisted from the 1500s to recent decades. Although political and economic changes have dispersed the Harari from their old city, the ethnic group, which numbers no more than 30,000, persists in mercantile centers in the region and has representatives in other urban centers throughout much of the world.

Until the last generation, almost all Harari were born, raised, married and died inside Harar, which is located on a highland ridge approximately midway between the Red Sea and the Ethiopian highlands. Over the centuries Harar has served as the dominant center of Islam within the Horn of Africa, acting as a center for scholarship and Sunni orthodoxy.

Although they are termed Harari in Arabic and European literature and are called Adere by their ethnic neighbors, the Somali, Oromo, Argobba and Amhara, they refer to themselves by terms which reflect the extent to which their identity is based upon their old city. They call Harar Ge, "the place, the city," and they call themselves Ge Usu', "the people of the city." Their customary way of life is Ge 'ada, which might be translated either as "the Harari way," or "the etiquette of the city."

The Harari language also indicates the degree to which the people of the city have encapsulated themselves through the years. The Harari call their language Ge Sinan, "the city language," and it was spoken only within the city until the Harari diaspora of recent years. Harari is a distinct Ethiopian Semitic language. It is related to Amharic, the Ethiopian national language, but the two are as mutually unintelligible as are Spanish and French. Its closest surviving cognate is Selti Gurage, probably implying a distinct historical connection with the Eastern Gurage cultures (see Gurage).

The Harari have preserved the identity of the unique city culture despite the pressure of daily contacts with the four ethnic groups which frequent the markets of the city. Linguistically, the Harari are polyglots. Harari is the language of the home and the in-group language of the city, but almost all are fluent in the Oromo language (see Oromo). Many merchants speak Somali (see Somalis). Most boys and some girls memorize the Quran, and many men speak Arabic with fluency. Amharic has been a significant presence since the conquest in 1887 of the formerly independent emirate of Harar by the army of the Ethiopian Empire. Amharic is now taught in the city's *madrasa* and in the national secondary schools located in the growing city outside the wall. Thus many Harari are conversant with four or more languages. But, significantly for the stability of Harari culture, no one but the Harari speak the city's language.

The Harari also retain their cultural exclusivity by strongly discouraging marriages with non-Harari. Most Harari are monogamous. In 1975, only two instances of dual marriage were recorded, and these were considered curiosities. Occasionally, in times past, secondary marriages were arranged by Harari men with women from outside Muslim groups as a means of establishing political and economic alliances. However, these wives and their children were seldom brought back to the city. Marriage with a non-Muslim, even today, results in ostracism from the group.

Harari society is characterized by an intricate mosaic of ties and obligations which provide a very high degree of social solidarity and which further exclude ethnic outsiders. Three social institutions provide the core of Harari society: kinship, friendship and *afocha* community organizations. Kinship emphasizes connections bilaterally between living relatives, utilizing a terminology of the Sudanese or bifurcate-collateral type. In contrast to many Arabic-speaking and East African societies, the Harari do not emphasize patrilineal kinship reckoning, and the corporate lineages which play such an important role in the inner workings of other preindustrial Muslim cities do not exist in Harar. Rather, the Harari trace relationship through both parents and their mothers' and fathers' brothers and sisters. The households of each of these relatives has a specific status for the Harari doing the reckoning and provides a network of obligations and expectations which guides behavior. Harari society as a whole, can be pictured in the kinship dimension as a spiderweb-like system of overlapping and interconnecting networks which ultimately interrelates all Harari.

Friendship provides another dimension of Harari society and is strongly defined in mutually exclusive groups for each Harari man and woman. Characteristically, in the old city a boy forms a core of close friends from his age-mates (not his brothers), usually from the same neighborhood, and a girl finds friends among the daughters of women who visit her mother at home. Later these friendships are organized in closed groups each numbering about five to eight persons. One belongs to one and only one such group, and one's friends are one's equals and confidants. Friends are particularly important in negotiating the trials of adolescence, spending so much time together that, in effect, they grow up together and condition the development of each other's personality. If kinship in Harar provides a network which links all Harari in a system of differentiated statuses, friendship provides Harari with a small group of trusted equals who retain their association throughout life.

Cross-cutting both kinship and friendship is the *afocha*, or community organization. The *afocha* is formally concerned with weddings and funerals and provides each Harari with social, ceremonial and economic support for these rites of passage. They convene as the occasion demands, with weddings clustered in the seventh and eight months of the Muslim calender. Since *afochas* range in size from 50 to 75 members, and since one's *afocha* is mobilized for the rites of what English speakers would call uncles, aunts and cousins, as well as closer relatives, these functions are frequent. Since each wedding or funeral is attended by the *afochas* of all the close relatives of the person concerned, each ceremony convenes a significant segment of Harari society, often involving several hundred persons. Although formal rites dominate the *afocha* activities, gossip and news of the city pass along between participants in the lulls. Thus *afocha* meetings are important if informal forums which efficiently communicate strategic information to the participants.

Afochas are sex-distinct. In 1975 there were 24 men's *afochas* in the old city and 14 women's *afochas*, although the number of each was greater a decade earlier. A young man usually chooses to join his father's *afocha*, and a young woman typically belongs to her mother-in-law's group, but there are many exceptions to these generalizations. The spatial distribution of membership in *afochas* is significant to the city's social solidarity. A particular *afocha* draws most of its members from a single locale in the city, but there are always some members in other sections. Thus a community representation is assured, but there are always those who can bring in news from other areas of the city. Usually a neighborhood has members of several *afochas* in residence, so these are by no means separate social blocs within the city's society.

In the traditional society of the old city of Harar, the interlocking relationships provide a coherent encompassing system of social ties which, in effect, defines the role of every Harari to each of his or her fellow citizens and brings them together in a kaleidoscopic array of occasions. Within a single neighborhood or in the markets, a Harari might encounter relatives, friends and *afocha*-mates and persons connected through combinations of these ties. As long as a person is a Harari, however, that person is never a stranger. Conformity to the internalized sanctions of the ways of life of the city and the ethic of Islam is strongly reinforced by constant social visibility and the pressure of efficiently circulating public opinion. The changes of recent years have greatly affected the structure and function of this carefully balanced system.

Women in the old city lead a vigorous and visible, if somewhat separate, social life which provides a solid and conservative force in Harari culture. Harari women do not wear the veil, nor are they secluded within their compounds, although much of their time is spent in their homes and those of their friends, kin and *afocha*-mates.

Women's *afocha* events are formal, requiring the wearing of elaborately embroidered black robes and the fulfillment of dozens of prescribed duties, ranging from preparation of special meals through prayers. A single traditional wedding involves ten days of designated preparations. The drumming, singing and enthusiastic conversation of a women's *afocha* announces a wedding far beyond its compound wall. The end result is fatigue, if not exhaustion, among the participants. Some old ladies sleep for two days after the event.

Many Harari women contribute to their household economy by selling produce from their husbands' farms in the open-air stalls of the city's markets. Market women often belong to one of several rotating credit associations, called *baha*. The capital thus accumulated is utilized by the recipient with or without the advice of her husband. Women are able to further supplement their independent incomes by raising small quantities of tobacco and retailing it. The elaborate basketry of Harar, for which the city is famed, is a women's industry, from the preparation of the component grasses through the weaving (often done by young women working in friendship groups) and merchandising.

Traditionally Harari girls underwent clitoridectomy at the age of 10 or 12 years in the ceremony of *absuma gar*. Unlike the neighboring Somali and Oromo, who rigorously maintain this practice as ensuring female purity, the Harari seem to be relaxing this part of female initiation.

The traditional social life of the Harari required considerable time for full participation, and the economy of the city was rich enough to afford it. Besides having productive farmlands which extended some 30 miles from the city, many Harari were merchants. The wealth of the Harari derived from their occupancy of a superior position in a system of ethnic stratification, wherein the Oromo, who are the vast majority in the region, occupied an inferior economic situation. Harari absentee landlords collected upwards of 70 percent of the product of their Oromo tenant farmers and sharecroppers, and Harari monopolized the markets at which the Oromo purchased imported cloth and manufactured items and sold their agricultural commodities for cash. Recent rural and urban property reforms have radically altered the city's economy.

Harar's site is ideal for supporting a preindustrial city. The region surrounding the city receives upwards of 40 inches of rainfall a year and produces enough sorghum in most years for export as well as satisfying the city's needs. Limited irrigation is practiced, particularly in the area near the city, and here numerous species of citrus, mangos, papayas, bananas and other fruits are raised. Cash crops are coffee and, especially important in the ceremonial life of the Harari, kat (*Catha edulis*), a stimulant plant. Somali, inhabiting the lower and drier regions outside the agricultural zone, bring cattle, sheep, goats and camels to the city's butcher shops. The Harari staple dish, a spicy meat, potato and vegetable stew eaten with a sorghum sourdough bread, epitomizes the nutritional variety which the Harari can afford.

The spatial arrangement of the old city of Harar sets the scene for the enactment of its society. The mud and stone wall, built in the sixteenth century, provides the physical manifestation of its social boundaries. Its five gates link Harar with the outside world and, in the days of the emirate, facilitated regulation of those who entered for purposes of trade. Conceptually the city is divided into five quarters, and each of these is subdivided into many smaller neighborhoods, whose names derive from such local landmarks as saints' shrines and mosques.

The Harari are Sunni Muslims who practice the Shafi legal convention. The city is famed as a center of Islamic learning throughout the Horn of Africa and despite many pressures of change the practice of Islam by Harari retains its strength. The twin-towered Jami mosque is the religious focus of the community, although nearly every neighborhood has its own small mosque. Harari tradition insists there are 333 mosques in the city. At least 50 were functioning in 1975. Attendance at the mosque is socially significant. In earlier days if a Harari were absent from his neighborhood mosque for three consecutive days men from his prayer group (*jama's*) would inquire at his home concerning his health.

Ramadan fasting is almost universally practiced by adults in the old city, and drinking of alcoholic beverages is minimal and considered reprehensible.

Harar is noteworthy for its remarkable proliferation of Muslim saints' shrines, called *awach* ("fathers") by the Harari. It has been called *madinat al-auliya'*, "the city of saints," in Arabic literature. There are over 150 shrines in and around Harar. Although their celebration is considered unorthodox by the strictest Muslims of the city, most Harari take part in *awach* celebrations at some time, and there seems to be no conflict in practice between these celebrations and orthodox Islam. By no means are the celebrations surreptitious or underground, although most of them are held at night.

As an integrated system, the traditional way of Harari life is a thing of the past. A series of economic and political events, having roots in the late nineteenth century, but culminating in the 1970s, has radically altered Harari society.

Harar had been an independent emirate since 1551, but it underwent a series of conquests beginning with the Ottoman Egyptian occupation from 1876 to 1885. A brief restoration of the emirate was followed by the defeat of the city's forces by Ras Makonnen in 1887 and the consequent incorporation of Harar in the expanding empire of Ethiopia. During the early period of Ethiopian rule, Harar's taxation and political affairs were managed by the occupiers, but its internal society and economy continued to function. The erosion of Harari economy began at this time with the confiscation of lands by Ras Makonnen as rewards for his troops. A much more long-lasting blow was dealt by the opening of the Djibouti–Addis Ababa railway in 1913, which bypassed Harar. The rise of Addis Ababa and the opening of the interior of Ethiopia during the first half of the twentieth century was a period of increasing stagnation for the old city of Harar.

Harari, who had maintained trading posts on the caravan routes for centuries, began to leave the old city in significant numbers in 1948. At that time, the newly restored Ethiopian rule of the city (following the Italian Occupation, 1936–1941) was perceived as hopelessly oppressive. The richer markets of Addis Ababa and Dire Dawa provided sufficient impetus to break the rule that all Harari should raise their families in Harar. As Harari of means shifted from agriculture to merchandising during the next two decades, this movement of population out of the city slowly gained momentum. It became a virtual diaspora after the Ethiopian Revolution of 1974. The already weakened economy of the Harari still residing in the old city, their number now reduced to about 8,000, was vitiated by two major reforms of the revolutionary government. The Rural Property Act of 1975, which proclaimed a maximum individual landholding of 10 hectares (about 25 acres) and which affected a much needed land redistribution throughout Ethiopia, eradicated the extensive Harari holdings of farms which had been tilled by Oromo tenants.

Also, in 1975, the Urban Property Act restricted the ownership of the number of homes and rooms by individual landlords. This was designed to eliminate exploitative landlordism, particularly in Addis Ababa. Its effect in Harar, however, was perceived as a cultural disaster. The reform mandated a redistribution of occupancy without regard to ethnic affiliation. The Harari found themselves sharing their compounds and sometimes their homes with outsiders, most of them Christian Amharas. The city had ceased to be either the locale of a comfortable way of life or the sanctuary of Harari culture.

Despite the dispersal of Harari, the ethnic group continues to thrive, albeit under altered conditions. Between 20,000 and 25,000 Harari are estimated to reside in Addis Ababa, most of them living in three organized communities. Although they are one of Ethiopia's smallest ethnic groups, they have contributed significantly to the country's managerial and executive (although not its military) ranks. In the 1980s, there were several Harari M.D.'s and Ph.D.'s in Ethiopia and elsewhere. An Ethiopian ambassador and a cabinet minister are Harari, as is the president of Addis Ababa University.

Wherever they are, Harari maintain the basic institutions which held them together in the old city. Friendship has been altered to take on more important roles in community organization. *Afocha* responsibilities have been retained for weddings and funerals but have lessened in intensity. Kin ties, diligently as ever recounted and discussed by Harari women, continue to interconnect the community, and the Harari language, although losing ground to Amharic, is still the language of the home. In Djibouti, Jeddah, Sana's and Mogadishu there are Harari *afochas* which preserve the solidarity of the ethnic group, and, despite the losses and changes of recent times, there are still a few thousand Harari in the old city, their cultural home.

BIBLIOGRAPHY

Books

Burton, Richard. *First Footsteps in East Africa*. London: Routledge & Kegan Paul, 1966.
Cerulli, Enrico. *Studi etiopici I: La lingua e la storia di Harar*. Rome: Instituto per L'Oriente, 1936.
Koehn, Peter, and Waldron, Sidney R. *Afocha: A Link Between Community and Administration in Harar, Ethiopia*. Syracuse: Syracuse University Foreign and Comparative Studies, 1978.
Leslau, Wolf. *Ethiopians Speak: Studies in Cultural Background I. Harari*. Berkeley: University of California Press, 1965.
———. *Etymological Dictionary of Harari*. Berkeley: University of California Press, 1963.

Paulitschke, Phillipe. *Harar: Forschungsreise nach den Somal-und Gala-ländern Ostafrikas*. Leipzig: F. A. Brockhaus, 1888.

Trimingham, J. Spencer. *Islam in Ethiopia*. London: Frank Cass, 1965.

Wagner, Ewald. *Legende Und Geschichte: Der Fath Madinat Harar von Yahya Nasrallah*. Wiesbaden: Kommissionsverlag Franz Steiner GMBH, 1978.

Waldron, Sidney R. "A Farewell to Bab Haji: City Symbolism and Harari Identity, 1887–1897." In *Working Papers on Society and History in Imperial Ethiopia: The Southern Periphery from the 1880's to 1974*, edited by D. L. Donham and Wendy James. Cambridge: African Studies Centre, 1979.

———. "Harar: The Muslim City in Ethiopia." In *Proceedings of the Fifth International Conference on Ethiopian Studies*, edited by Robert L. Hess. Chicago: University of Illinois Press, 1979.

———. "Within the Wall and Beyond: Harari Ethnic Identity and Its Future." In *Urban Life: Readings in Urban Anthropology*, edited by George Gmelch and Walter P. Zenner. New York: St. Martin's Press, 1980.

Articles

Ahmed, Yusuf. "An Inquiry Into Some Aspects of the Economy of Harar and the Records of the Household Economy of the Amirs of Harar (1825–1875)." *Ethnological Society Bulletin* (University College of Addis Ababa) 7 (1961): 125–132.

Caulk, Richard. "Harar Town and Its Neighbors." *Journal of African History* 18:3 (1977): 39–380.

———. "The Occupation of Harar: January 1887." *Journal of Ethiopian Studies* 3 (1971): 1–19.

Wagner, Ewald. "Eine Liste der Heiligen von Harar." *Zeitschrift der Deutschen Morgenlandischen Gesellschaft* 123:2 (1973): 269–292.

Unpublished Manuscript

Waldron, Sidney R. "Social Organization and Social Control in the Walled City of Harar." Ph.D. dissertation, Columbia University, 1974.

Sidney R. Waldron

HAUSA   The Hausa are a large and diverse West African group, collectively the most numerous Muslim people south of the Sahara.[1] Although Hausa speakers are to be found throughout West Africa, most Hausa live in the northern states of Nigeria and, to a lesser extent, in the southern parts of the Niger republic. Their language is a lingua franca spoken by perhaps 38 million people, 32 million in northern Nigeria alone.[2]

It would be misleading to speak of the Hausa as a tribe or ethnic group. These terms suggest a cultural homogeneity which Hausa-speaking groups lack. There is more cultural difference between some Hausa groups than there is between some Hausa and non-Hausa peoples.[3] A stereotype of the Hausa man in the minds of many Nigerians is that of a pious Muslim and a sharp trader, kind and hospitable to others and dressed in a distinctive gown and embroidered cap.

Although Hausa speakers actually come from a variety of subcultures (considerable cultural variation exists among rural Hausa but much less among city Hausa), any Hausa man, regardless of his original sub-culture, is likely to adopt the stereotyped image as soon as he travels from home. Thus, being Hausa can often provide a useful social identity which, however, gives the mistaken impression that there is a uniform Hausa culture. However, modern mobility and communication are making the Hausa a less varied group; simultaneously, the tendency for politicians to utilize at times the Hausa identity as a basis for political mobilization can serve to create a self-consciousness about being Hausa. The Hausa may therefore eventually *become* an ethnic group.[4]

A large part of the Hausa identity involves being Muslim. Nowhere in Hausaland is the impress of Islam absent. Prior to European conquest, the Hausa lived in walled city-states with a sharply hierarchical social organization reminiscent of the European feudal era. Sunni Islam first came to the region in the fourteenth century, brought by western Sudanic and Arab merchants. The Maliki school of law, still followed by the Hausa, dates from this early period. Almost as old is the Ajemic script—a form of medieval Arabic writing—which made the Hausa a literate people long before Europeans arrived. Thus, Islamic influence has a long history among the Hausa, particularly in the cities and among the ruling aristocracy.

The purity of that Islam, however, was questioned by a Fulani-speaking scholar and religious leader, Uthman dan Fodio, who in 1802 declared *jihad* against the traditional Hausa rulers. Ultimately, most of the Hausa artistocracy were replaced by followers of Uthman, and Islam was extended far to the south. The old Hausa states became emirates linked to a central caliphate in the new city of Sokoto, which today remains a center of Muslim learning and orthodoxy. The extent to which the *jihad* was a religious war rather than a Hausa–Fulani conflict remains controversial—members of both groups fought on both sides. When the British conquered northern Nigeria at the turn of the century, they found it more practical to retain the Fulani system of government, giving rise to a policy of indirect rule. As a result, they shored up the power of the Sokoto Caliphate so that Islam spread with renewed strength.

In many areas the *jihad* left Fulani ruling Hausa. Soon, however, these Fulani intermarried with Hausa and for the most part lost their distinctive language and customs (see Fulani). Other Fulani became "Hausa-ized" as drought and epidemic destroyed their herds and forced them to become cultivators. The influx of Fulani has caused some scholars to term the composite group the Hausa-Fulani, but this label is misleading. Many Fulani remain pastoral nomads, culturally distinct from Hausa, while many Hausa trace their origins to other, non-Fulani groups. Hausa-Fulani places undue emphasis on a single one of the streams whose modern confluence has created the Hausa. Actually, Hausa often have the same sort of hyphenated ethnic identity common in North America. Just as there are Italian-Americans and Irish-Canadians, so are there Fulani-Hausa, Gbari-Hausa and Kanuri-Hausa. At times, entire communities have, for various reasons, become Hausa (e.g., Gbari, Koro), adopting Hausa language and dress and certain of the most widespread Hausa customs, as well as the Muslim religion. Some Hausa like to distinguish between the seven traditional city-states of the Hausa—the Hausa Seven or Hausa Bakwai—and all other Hausa, termed the "useless Hausa" or Hausa Banza. The historical truthfulness of this distinction is unclear (see Gbagyi).

Given the cultural differences of the Hausa, ethnographic generalizations are hazardous. Most Hausa are farmers, using the hoe (not plow or draft animals) to till land. The land itself ranges from the parched southern fringe of the Sahara to well-watered areas in the lower half of Nigeria's Kaduna State. Depending on climate, subsistence crops may include millet, guinea corn, rice and yams; cash crops may include peanuts, cotton and tobacco. Wherever cattle-herding Fulani pass through Hausa regions, milk and beef are part of the normal diet for those who can afford them.

It is common for Hausa to engage in some kind of craft or trade during the long dry season. During this time, they turn to commercial activities and such semi-hereditary crafts as smithery or butchering. They also repair bicycles, make rope, weave, work leather, make pottery, embroider caps and gather firewood for sale. Many men leave their homes during the dry season to seek work in wealthier areas.

Hausa kinship systems vary. Sometimes they are based on loosely organized clans which trace descent through the male line; sometimes there are no clans and with nearly equal stress on the mother's descent line. Individuals are expected to show their parents and older in-laws great respect, while grandparents may be joked with, along with mother's brothers' and father's sisters' children (cross-cousins). Parents often feel shame of their firstborn, mothers at times requiring encouragement to nurse them. Children, firstborn in particular, are often given to relatives to raise. Divorce is not uncommon, and any children of the marriage are considered to belong to the husband's family and usually remain with them, in accordance with Maliki law. Circumcision is universally practiced, although the age at which it takes place varies. Children usually spend some years studying with a *mallam*, or Quranic scholar, girls generally receiving less such education than boys.

The Hausa *mallam* has great moral authority, stemming from Islam's prestige. It is common, during the dry season, to see even men of advanced years studying with a *mallam*. *Mallamai* are also the chief supernatural practitioners of the Hausa dispensing all kinds of protective talismans and medicines. One of these (*rubutu*) is the water used to wash the ink from a prayer board on which has been written a *sura* of the Quran. *Mallamai* are supported by charity, but they are likely to farm as well. Children studying with *mallamai* are given food by the entire community, each woman who cooks reserving a portion for students or at least donating any remaining food to them. Many men, particularly in the urban areas, belong to one of the Muslim brotherhoods or *tariqas*, the most powerful of which is the Tijaniyya. Thousands of Hausa perform the Haj to

Mecca and Medina each year, most of them flying from Kano on flights organized by the federal government.

Hausa traditional religions linger on chiefly among groups resistant to Islam, such as the Maguzawa, and, to a lesser extent, groups in the Niger republic (where the *jihad* was less successful than farther south). The traditional religions are usually tied to particular clans and involve specific gods or spirits associated with each clan, each god having his or her special rituals. For example, a god may require a sacrifice at a particular spot and of a particular animal—usually a chicken or a goat—with specific markings. Possibly related to Hausa traditional religion is the spirit possession or *bori* association. *Bori* (similar to the Ethiopian Zar cult) involves women far more than it does men. Initiates of the association are believed to be possessed by particular spirits in response to the drumming of the praise-songs of these beings. Initiation into an association is often related to barrenness or having had a series of children who died in infancy.

The Hausa version of Islam includes seclusion of women. This seclusion is not total, since women are generally free to visit each other in the evening and to go on extended visits to relatives. Hausa men consider wife-seclusion to be prestigious. Hausa women sometimes say that they prefer to be secluded because this practice releases them from arduous labor in the fields and permits them to spend their energies on their personal economic pursuits. Most women either engage in some form of trading (through intermediaries) or make some item or foodstuff for sale.

The Hausa language is today spoken in cities of at least 18 different nations including not only Nigeria and Niger but also Ghana, the Ivory Coast, the Sudan, Upper Volta, Benin and Togo. Hausa belongs to the Chadic branch of the Afro-Asiatic family and derives a substantial portion of its vocabulary from Arabic. It is the dominant and still-spreading language of the northern half of Nigeria and is taught in universities in Nigeria, the United States, Great Britain and France.

The best sources of current Hausa research and bibliography are the periodicals *Kano Chronicles* (published by Abdullahi Bayero College, Kano, Nigeria) and *Savanna* (published by Ahmadu Bello University Press, Zaria, Nigeria).

NOTES

1. I would like to thank Ralph Faulkingham and Harold Olofson for their aid in preparing this entry. All errors remain my own responsibility.

2. I am here indebted to Kirk-Greene (1967) for the information that the BBC lists the Hausa as being spoken in over 18 different nations. The figure of 31 million Hausa speakers also derives from Kirk-Greene, who in 1967 estimated that there were perhaps 20 million Hausa in Nigeria and a total of 25 million in West Africa as a whole. Assuming a 25 percent increase in population between 1967 and 1976, we arrive at the figures of 25 million Hausa speakers in Nigeria and 31 million for all of West Africa. (Updated on the same basis to 1983. *Ed.*)

3. For example, there appears to be more cultural difference between the Hausa studied

by Faulkingham (1975) and the Hausa described by Smith (1955) than there is between the latter and the Kanuri (as discussed by Cohen, 1967).

4. This discussion owes much to Monsieur Guy Nicolas, both to his published work (1975) and to personal communications. Needless to say, Monsieur Nicolas bears no responsibility for my interpretations, the errors of which are entirely my own.

Jerome H. Barkow
Population figures updated by Richard V. Weekes

BIBLIOGRAPHY

Books

Barkow, Jerome H. ''Operationalizing the Concept Ethos.'' In *Survey Research in Africa: Its Applications and Limits*, edited by William M. O'Barr, David H. Spain, and Mark A. Tessler. Evanston: Northwestern University Press, 1973.
———. ''Strategies for Self-Esteem and Prestige in Maradi, Niger Republic.'' In *Psychological Anthropology,* edited by Thomas R. Williams. The Hague: Mouton, 1975.
Buntjer, B. J. ''The Changing Structure of the Gandu.'' In *Zaria and Its Region: A West African Savanna City and Its Environs.* Zaria, Nigeria: Ahmadu Bello University, 1970.
Charlick, R. *Induced Participation in Nigerian Modernization: The Case of Matameye County.* Rural Africana, 18. East Lansing: Michigan State University African Studies Center, 1972.
Cohen, Abner. ''Cultural Strategies in the Organization of Trading Diasporas.'' In *The Development of Indigenous Trade and Markets in West Africa*, edited by Claude Meillassoux. London: International African Institute. 1971.
———. ''Politics of the Kola Trade.'' In *Nigeria: Modernization and the Politics of Communalism,* edited by Robert Melson and Howard Wolpe. East Lansing: Michigan State University Press, 1971.
———. ''The Social Organization of Credit in a West African Cattle Market.'' In *Nigeria: Modernization and the Politics of Communalism,* edited by Robert Melson and Howard Wolpe, East Lansing: Michigan State University Press, 1971.
———. ''Stranger Communities: The Hausa.'' In *The City of Ibadan*, edited by P. Lloyd, A. Mabogunje, and B. Awe. London: Cambridge University Press, 1967.
Didhoff, Gretchen *Katsina: Profile of a Nigerian City.* New York: Praeger. 1970.
Faulkingham, Ralph Harold. *The Spirits and Their Cousins: Some Aspects of Belief, Ritual, and Social Organization in a Rural Hausa Village in Niger.* Research Report No. 15. Amherst: University of Massachusetts Department of Anthropology, 1975.
Goddard, A. D.; Fine, J. C.; and Norman, D. W. *A Socio-Economic Study of Three Villages in the Sokoto Close-Settled Zone.* Institute for Agricultural Research Paper No. 33. Zaria, Nigeria: Ahmadu Bello University, 1971.
Greenberg, Joseph H. *The Influence of Islam on a Sudanese Religion.* Reprint ed. Seattle: University of Washington Press, 1969. (Originally published 1947.)
———. ''Some Aspects of Negro-Mohammedan Culture Contact Among the Hausa.'' In *Cultures and Societies of Africa*, edited by Simon Ottenberg and Phoebe Ottenberg.

New York: Random House, 1960. (Reprinted from *American Anthropologist* 43 [1941]: 51–61.)

Hake, James M. *Child-Rearing Practices in Northern Nigeria*. New York: Africana, 1972.

——. *Parental Attitudes Toward Education in Northern Nigeria*, Kano, Nigeria: Government Printer, 1970.

Hill, Polly. *Rural Hausa: A Village and a Setting*. London: Cambridge University Press, 1972.

——. *Studies in Rural Capitalism in West Africa*. Cambridge: The University Press, 1970.

——. "Two Types of West African House Trade." In *The Development of Indigenous Trade and Markets in West Africa*, edited by Claude Meillassoux, London: International African Institute, 1971.

Ibrahim, Madauci; Isa, Yahaya; and Daura, Bello. *Hausa Customs*. Zaria, Nigeria: Northern Nigeria, 1968.

Kirk-Greene, Anthony A. M. *A Modern Hausa Reader*. New York: McKay, 1967.

Lewis, I. M., ed. *Islam in Tropical Africa*. London: Oxford University Press, 1966.

Miner, Horace. "Culture Change Under Pressure: A Hausa Case." In *Africa: Social Problems of Change and Conflict*, edited by Pierre L. Van Den Berghe, San Francisco: Chandler, 1965.

——. "Urban Influence on the Rural Hausa." In *Urbanization and Migration in West Africa*, edited by Hilda Kuper. Berkeley: University of California Press, 1965.

Mortimore, Michael J. "Land and Population Pressure in the Kano Close-Settled Zone, Northern Nigeria." In *People and Land in Africa South of the Sahara*, edited by R. Mansell Prothero. New York: Oxford University Press, 1972.

——. "Some Aspects of Rural-Urban Relations in Kano, Nigeria." In *La Croissance urbaine en Afrique noire et à Madagascar*. Colloques Internationaux, 539. Vol. 2. Paris: C.N.R.S., 1972.

Murdock, George P. *Africa: Its People and Their Culture History*. New York: McGraw-Hill, 1959.

Nicolas, Guy. *Dynamique sociale et appréhension du monde au sein d'une société Hausa*. Paris: Institut d'Ethnologie, 1975.

Olofson, Harold. "Playing a Kingdom: A Hausa Meta-Society in the Walled City of Zaria, Nigeria." In *The Anthropological Study of Play: Problems and Prospects*, edited by David F. Lancy and B. Allan Tindall. Proceedings of the first annual meeting for the Anthropological Study of Play. Cornwall, N.Y.: Leisure Press, 1976.

Onwuejeogwu, Michael. "The Cult of the Bori Spirits Among the Hausa." In *Man in Africa*, edited by Mary Douglas and Phyllis M. Kabery. New York: Doubleday-Anchor, 1969.

Paden, John N. "Aspects of Emirship in Kano." In *West African Chiefs: Their Changing Status Under Colonial Rule and Independence*, edited by Michael Crowder and Obaro Ikime. New York: Africana, 1970.

——. "Communal Conflict and Violence in Kano, Nigeria." In *Nigeria: Modernization and the Politics of Communalism*, edited by Robert Melson and Howard Wolpe. East Lansing: Michigan State University Press, 1971.

————. *Religion and Political Culture in Kano*. Berkeley: University of California Press, 1973.

————. "Urban Pluralism, Integration, and Adaptation of Communal Identity in Kano, Nigeria." In *From Tribe to Nation in Africa*, edited by Ronald Cohen and John Middleton. San Francisco: Chandler, 1970.

Plotnicov, Leonard. "The Modern African Elite of Jos, Nigeria." In *Social Stratification in Africa*, edited by A. Tuden and Leonard Plotnicov. New York: Free Press, 1970.

Rehfisch, F. *The Social Structure of a Mambila Village*. Reprint ed. Zaria, Nigeria: Ahmadu Bello University Department of Sociology, 1972. (Originally published 1955.)

Schwartz, Frederick A. O., Jr. *Nigeria: The Tribes, the Nation, or the Race*. Cambridge: MIT Press, 1965.

Schwerdtferger, Friedrich. "Housing in Zaria." In *Shelter in Africa*, edited by Paul Oliver. New York: Praeger, 1971.

Smith, Mary Felice. *Baba of Karo: A Woman of the Muslim Hausa*. London: Faber & Faber, 1954.

Smith, Michael G. *The Economy of Hausa Communities of Zaria*. London: H. M. Stationery Office for the Colonial Office, 1955.

————. "The Hausa of Northern Nigeria." In *Peoples of Africa*, edited by James Gibbs, Jr. New York: Holt, Rinehart and Winston, 1965.

————. The Jihad of Shehu Dan Fodio." In *Islam in Tropical Africa*, edited by I. M. Lewis. London: Oxford University Press, 1966.

————. "Pluralism in Precolonial African Societies." In *Pluralism in Africa*, edited by Leo Kuper and M. G. Smith. Berkeley: University of California Press, 1971.

————. "The Social Functions and Meaning of Hausa Praise-Singing." In *Peoples and Cultures of Africa*, edited by Elliot P. Skinner. Garden City, N.Y.: Doubleday, 1972.

Trimingham, J. Spencer. *The Influence of Islam Upon Africa*. New York: Praeger, 1968.

————. *Islam in West Africa*. London: Oxford University Press, 1959.

Articles

Barkow, Jerome H. "Evaluation of Character and Social Control Among the Hausa." *Ethos* 2 (1974): 1–14.

————. "Hausa Women and Islam." *Canadian Journal of African Studies* 6:2 (1972): 317–329.

————. "The Institution of Courtesanship in the Northern States of Nigeria." *Africa* (Geneva) 10 (1971): 58–73.

————. "Muslims and Maguzawa in North Central State, Nigeria: An Ethnographic Comparison." *Canadian Journal of African Studies* 7 (1973): 59–76.

Charlick, R. B. "Participatory Development and Rural Modernization in Hausa Niger." *African Review* 2 (1972): 499–524.

————, and Thorbahn, Peter. "Population Dynamics and Drought: A Village in Niger." *Population Studies* 24:3 (1975).

Goddard, A. D. "Changing Family Structures Among the Rural Hausa." *Africa* 43 (1973): 207–218.

Greenberg, Joseph H. "Islam and Clan Organization Among the Hausa." *Southwestern Journal of Anthropology* 3 (1947): 193–211.

Hill, Polly. "Hidden Trade in Hausaland." *Man* 4:3 (1969): 392–410.

———. "Landlords and Brokers: A West African Trading System (with a Note on Kumasi Butchers)." *Cahiers d'études africaines* (France) 6:23 (1966): 349–366.

LeVine, Robert A., and Price-Williams, Douglass R. "Children's Kinship Concepts: Cognitive Development and Early Experience Among the Hausa." *Ethnology* 13:1 (1974): 25–44.

Olofson, Harold. "Hausa Language About Gesture." *Anthropological Linguistics* 16:1 (1974): 25–39.

———. "Yawon Dandi: A Hausa Category of Migration." *Africa* 46:1 (1976): 66–79.

Salmone, Frank A. "Becoming Hausa: Ethnic Identity Change and Its Implications for the Study of Ethnic Pluralism and Stratification." *Africa* 45 (1975): 410–424.

———. "The Serkawa of Yauri: Class, Status, or Party?" *African Studies Review* 18:1 (1975): 88–101.

———. "Some Aspects of Social Stratification Among the Hausa." *International Journal of Group Tensions* 1 (1971): 335–339.

———. "Toward an Understanding of the Traditional City: A Nigerian Example." *International Journal of Group Tensions* 2:3 (1972).

Scott, Earl P. "The Spatial Structure of Rural Northern Nigeria: Farmers, Periodic Markets, and Villages." *Economic Geography* 48:3 (1972).

Smith, Michael G. "Co-operation in Hausa Society." *Information* 11 (1957): 2–20.

———. "The Hausa System of Social Status." *Africa* 29:3 (1959): 239–252.

———. "Historical and Cultural Conditions of Political Corruption Among the Hausa." *Comparative Studies in Society and History* 6:2 (1964): 164–198.

———. "The Social Functions and Meaning of Hausa Praise-Singing." *Africa* 27 (1957): 26–44.

Thom, Derrick J. "The City of Maradi: French Influence upon a Hausa Urban Center." *Journal of Geography* 70 (1971): 472–482.

Yahaya, Ibrahim Yaro. "Kishi Feeling Among Hausa Co-Wives." *Kano Studies*, n.s. 1 (1973): 83–98.

Yusuf, Ahmed Beitallah. "Capital Formation and Management Among the Muslim Hausa Trades of Kano, Nigeria." *Africa* 45:2 (1975): 167–182.

———. "Hausa Verbal Honorifics: A Case Study in Socio-linguistics." *Savanna* 2 (1973): 227–230.

———. "A Reconsideration of Urban Conceptions: Hausa Urbanization and the Hausa Rural-Urban Continuum." *Urban Anthropology* 3:2 (1974): 200–221.

Unpublished Manuscripts

Barkow, Jerome H. "Hausa and Maguzawa: Processes of Group Differentiation in a Rural Area of North Central State, Nigeria." Ph.D. dissertation, University of Chicago, 1970.

Dry, D.P.L. "The Place of Islam in Hausa Society," Ph.D. dissertation. Oxford University, 1952.

Fahrmeier, E. "Cognitive Development Among the Hausa: A Psychometric Study." Ph.D. dissertation, University of Chicago, 1971.

Faulkingham, Ralph Harold. "Political Support in a Hausa Village." Ph.D. dissertation, Michigan State University, 1970.

————. "The Politics of Descent in a Rural Hausa Village in Niger." Paper presented at the fifteenth annual meeting of the Africa Studies Association, Philadelphia, November 1972.

Kirk-Greene, Anthony H. M. " 'Mutumin Kirki': The Concept of the Good Man in Hausa." Hans Wolff Memorial Lecture, Indiana University, April 11, 1973.

Miner, Horace. "The Zaria Hausa in Rural Ecosystem," Paper presented at the fifteenth annual meeting of the African Studies Association, Philadelphia, November 1972.

Paden, John N. "The Influence of Religious Elites on Political Culture and Community Integration in Kano, Nigeria." Ph.D. dissertation, Harvard University, 1968.

Schildkrout, Enid. "Islam and Political Incorporation Among Urban Immigrants in Ghana." Paper presented at the fifteenth annual meeting of the African Studies Association, Philadelphia, November 1972.

Thom, Derrick J. "The Niger-Nigeria Borderlands: A Politico-Geographical Analysis of Boundary Influence on Hausa." Ph.D. dissertation, Michigan State University, 1970.

Works, John A., Jr. "Pilgrims in a Strange Land: The Hausa Communities in Chad, 1890–1970." Ph.D. dissertation, University of Wisconsin, 1972.

HAZARAS   One of Afghanistan's most impoverished ethnic groups, yet most resistant to central government domination, is the Hazaras. After the Soviet invasion of Afghanistan in 1979, they became virtually independent of government control.

Most of the Hazaras live in central Afghanistan in an area known as the Hazarajat, which extends south of the Kho-i-Baba Mountains to somewhere north of Kandahar and west of Ghazni to beyond Dai Kundi and Yak Awlang. Others live in regions north of the Hindu Kush—in Baghlan, Samangan, Balkh and Jawzjan. Some, most of them dislocated from the Hazarajat after the Hazara–Afghan war in the last century, live in Qala-Nau, in Mashad, Iran (where they are known as Berberis) and in Quetta, Pakistan. There has been no census, but preliminary data from an unfinished census suggests that the Hazaras may number more than the 1 million formerly estimated by scholars.

Other groups are sometimes classified as Hazaras or Hazara-related. The Taimanis on the eastern and western extremities of the Hazarajat are probably Hazara-related, even though the groups in the west are associated with the ethnically composite Aimaq (see Aimaq). A group physically and culturally similar to the Hazaras occupy the western plateaus of Kahmard and Sayghan; these were once called Hazara Tatars, but now they call themselves simply Tatars, sometimes even Tajiks. The Moghols (Mongols) of Ghor may be related but are considered ethnically distinct (see Moghols).

The Mongol affinities of the Hazaras are evident in their physical appearance, their language and their kinship system. Most Hazaras clearly look Mongoloid, but a few of them, mostly those of higher status, have heavy beards and lack the characteristic epicanthic eyefolds. Hazaragi, an Indo-Iranian language having a large admixture of Mongol words, is the traditional language of the Hazaras. It is still the dialect of the home and of public affairs in isolated districts. Hazaras who have regular contact with the towns and markets have adjusted to Dari, the standard Afghan Farsi dialect. Further evidence of the Hazaras' Mongol affinities exist in the Hazara kinship system. Like the Mongols, Hazaras distinguish older and younger siblings by different terms.

Apparently for some centuries the Hazaras have been Persianizing, as their language suggests. Evidence of this also exists in their religious affiliation. Almost all are Shias like the Persians (see Persians). Most are Ithna Ashari ("Twelvers"), but an undetermined number (they say around 20,000) are Ismailis ("Seveners"). The Ismailis live on the eastern fringe of the Hazarajat; they maintain social ties with the Ismailis of Badakhshan and Qataghan, most of whom are Tajik. Strong negative feeling prevails between the two Shia sects. Ithna Ashari Hazaras often deny having any ethnic affinity with Ismaili Hazaras, even when they are neighbors and appear in other respects to be related. Not all Hazaras are Shia. The Hazaras of Qala-Nau are Sunni. The Hazara Tatars of the past probably called themselves Tajik to indicate a sectarian difference, for they are now Sunnis, like the other "Tajiks" of the area (see Tajik).

Hazara origins are obscure. They appear to be descendants of two types of people: the "original" Indo-Iranian inhabitants of the Hindu Kush region, and the Mongol and Turkic groups who came to dominate it in the thirteenth and fourteenth centuries. The term *hazara* itself suggests a Mongol-Persian blend. It means "thousand" in Farsi, but it is believed to be a Persianized equivalent for the Mongol word for "thousand," *minggan*. The Mongols at one time designated a fighting unit by this term; as this unit consisted of a kinship unit providing a thousand horsemen, it meant, in fact, "tribe." Presumably as the Hindu Kush Mongols acquired Farsi, the Farsi equivalent replaced the Mongol word. By the fifteenth century, *hazara* meant "mountain tribe," and somewhat later on it came to mean specifically the group now called Hazara.

This shift in meaning corresponded with a retreat of the Mongol tribes into the mountainous area now known as the Hazarajat. They were gradually pushed out of the more desirable lowlands neighboring the Hindu Kush by competing tribal groups. From the south and west they were pressed by the Pushtun tribes; from the north by Turkmen tribes who liked to raid them for slaves (see Turkmen). Eventually, the Hazaras retreated into the territories they now occupy. In the nineteenth century the government of Afghanistan gained control over the whole area. But the Hazaras rebelled in 1891; after two years of war they were totally crushed. Many were forced out of their homelands; most fled to Mashad and Quetta. Later the expatriate Hazaras were offered amnesty to return and were given land.

An important consequence of the war was the opening of the Hazarajat to Pushtun nomads, who grazed their flocks there during the summer. By loaning money and selling products from India, the nomads gained economic advantage over many Hazaras and acquired ownership of some of their lands. Impoverished

Hazaras migrated to the cities, mainly Ghazni, Kabul and Mazar-i-Sharif, to work as hired laborers in winter, returning in spring to farm their lands.

Today, the Hazaras are generally poor. Recent famines in the Hazarajat have exacerbated their poverty, and more Hazaras have migrated to the cities permanently. During the 1970s, in Kabul especially, large numbers of them tried to survive as day laborers. The Hazaras are Afghanistan's underprivileged ethnic minority.

The Hazarajat and other Hazara territories are mountainous. The climate is severe in winter; because of heavy snowfalls many people are isolated in their homes for several weeks every year. Summers are mild, but in the highest cultivated valleys, which reach up to 10,500 feet, they are short. Considering the harshness of the terrain the Hazarajat is densely populated. Every tract of cultivable soil is used. Each year in almost every valley a few more square yards are cleared for cultivation. Population pressure, despite the heavy migration, has remained intense.

In the past the Hazaras were nomads, subsisting mainly on the herding of sheep and goats and raising horses for fighting in their perpetual internecine feuds. Today they survive by mixed grain farming. They cultivate the alluvial floors of the valleys and exploit the rugged higher ground above them in different ways, as conditions allow. The most important yields come from irrigated plots, but wherever possible they also cultivate dry tracts of land beyond the reach of surface water. They also keep small numbers of sheep and goats, which they pasture on the mountains in summer. Their most important products are wheat and barley; where necessary, fava beans are rotated with the grains. Milk products are the main source of protein. Wool is a source of fiber, although used clothing was until recently so cheaply available that the Hazara women were weaving less cloth—they have continued to make woolen rugs of the Gilam type. In summer, where feasible, the women and children take the flocks into the mountains for several weeks. The men, who cannot leave their fields for long periods, visit the pasturage areas periodically.

Traditionally the Hazaras were organized in lineages which reckoned their relationship through males; males of a given area counted themselves descendants of a common ancestor. Lineage memory apparently varied. Sheikh Ali Hazaras, for example, appear to have retained a shorter lineage memory than many other Hazaras. In the 1970s memory of the tribal lineages generally seemed to be declining. Where elderly people remembered male ancestry back to seven or eight generations, younger people would remember only half that number. Internal village structure, however, probably changed little. Social affairs within the village were resolved, as before, by the consensus of the leading men.

Hazara marriage patterns follow the Muslim practice; they prefer to marry first cousins on their father's side, and there is a high incidence of intra-village marriage. Hazaras seldom marry outsiders. When they do, it is their women who are given to men of other ethnic groups. In such cases, the children are not usually considered Hazara.

Hazara leaders, known as *mirs* or *khans*, used to be powerful, and their elder sons usually succeeded them in office. After the Hazara-Afghan war the tribal system and the power of their leaders was weakened by political controls imposed by the government. Two kinds of political leaders are now distinguishable: the *khanawada* (or *khan*), whose influence is based on personal wealth, kinship and other social connections; and the *araab* (or *malek*), who is an appointed representative, usually upon the suggestion of the people he represents. Normally *araabs* and *khanawadas* are relatives and allies.

Another kind of influential person among the Shia Hazaras is the Islamic authority, the most prominent always being a Sayyid. A group of Sayyids (who claim descent from Muhammad) are interspersed among the Hazaras and are highly venerated. They seldom give their daughters in marriage to non-Sayyids, but because the Hazarajat Sayyids take wives from the Hazaras, they have become so much like the Hazaras in culture and physical appearance that some authors call them Hazara-Sayyids. These authorities use their "sacred" qualities to serve the religious needs of the common people. The most prominent of them have studied Islam formally and are known for personal piety. Their prayers and good favor are believed to bring blessings, and the charms they prepare (if they are willing to do so) are considered especially efficacious. Sayyids are part of large informal networks that have at times been mobilized to exert influence on public affairs.

After 1978, when the Khalq Party took over the Afghanistan government, the Hazaras in diverse areas, without coordination, revolted, the earliest to revolt being those in the northern and eastern provinces. Since the Soviet invasion in December 1979, the entire Hazarajat with the exception of a landing strip in Bamian, has remained virtually independent of government control. Interest in tribal ties based on patrilineal descent appears to have been rekindled in this context. Subgroups within the Hazarajat, however, have remained autonomous, each managing its own judicial and administrative affairs. An attempt in 1979 to unite the Hazaras, in which a prominent Sayyid was elected to be first of several rotating supreme commanders, failed.

The active resistance units among the Hazaras are called "fronts." Those fronts that have seen the most military action against Afghan and Soviet military forces, because they lie along the routes of access into the Hazarajat, are Behsud (which controls the Unai Pass) and Sheikh Ali, Turkmen and Surkh-o-Parsa (because they control access to the Shibar Pass) and the Hazara communities of Turkestan, especially Chararkint and Dare-Suf.

BIBLIOGRAPHY

Books

Adamec, Ludwig W., ed. *Historical and Political Gazettes of Afghanistan.* "Sheikh Ali," in Vol. 1, *Badakshaw*; "Kala Nao Hazaras," and "Taimanis," in Vol. 3,

Herat; "Orozqan," in Vol. 4, *Kandahar*; "Dara-i-Suf," in Vol. 5, *Mazar-i-Sharif*; "Hazara," in Vol. 6, *Kabul*. Graz: Akademische Druck-u. Verlagsanstalb, 1972–in press.

Aslanov, M. G., et al. "Ethnography of Afghanistan." Translated by Mark and Gretta Slobin. In *Afghanistan: Some New Approaches*, edited by G. Grassmuck, L. W. Ademec, and F. H. Irwin. Ann Arbor: University of Michigan Press, 1969.

Bacon, Elizabeth E. *Obok: A Study of Social Structure in Eurasia*. New York: Wenner-Gren Foundation for Anthropological Research, 1958.

Canfield, Robert L. *Faction and Conversion in a Plural Society: Religious Alignments in the Hindu Kush*. Museum of Anthropology, Anthropological Paper No. 50. Ann Arbor: University of Michigan, 1973.

———. *Hazara Integration into the Afghan Nation: Some Relations Between the Hazaras and Afghan Officials*. New York: Afghanistan Council of the Asia Society, 1972.

———. "Suffering as a Religious Imperative in Afghanistan." In *Psychological Anthropology*, edited by Thomas Williams. The Hague: Mouton, 1975.

Dupree, Louis. *Afghanistan*. Princeton: Princeton University Press, 1973.

Ferdinand, Klaus. *Preliminary Notes on Hazara Culture*. Historiskfilosofiske Meddelelser: Det Kongelige Danske Videnskabernes Selskab. 37:5 Copenhagen, 1959.

Jung, Chris J. *Some Observations on Patterns and Processes of Rural-Urban Migrations to Kabul*. New York: The Afghanistan Council of the Asia Society, 1972.

Kakar, M. Hasan. *Afghanistan: A Study in Internal Political Developments, 1880–1896*. Kabul: Privately published, 1971.

———. *Government and Society in Afghanistan: The Reign of Amir Abd al-Rahman Khan*. Austin: University of Texas Press, 1979.

———. *Pacification of the Hazaras of Afghanistan*. New York: The Afghanistan Council of the Asia Society, 1973.

Schurmann, H. F. *The Mongols of Afghanistan: An Ethnography of the Mongols and Related Peoples of Afghanistan*. The Hague: Mouton, 1962.

Articles

Bacon, Elizabeth E. "An Inquiry Into the History of the Hazara Mongols of Afghanistan." *Southwestern Journal of Anthropology* 7 (1951): 230–247.

Canfield, Robert L. "The Ecology of Rural Ethnic Groups and Spatial Dimensions of Power." *American Anthropologist* 75:5 (1973): 1529–1541.

Cervin, Vladimir. "Problems in the Integration of the Afghan Nation." *Middle East Journal* 6 (1952): 400–416.

Davydov. A. D. "Rural Community of the Hazaras of Central Afghanistan." *Central Asian Review* 14:1 (1965): 32–44.

Dianous, H. J. de. "Hazaras et mongols en Afghanistan." *Orient* 19 (1961): 71–98.

Dupree, L. "Further Notes on Taqiyya: Afghanistan." *Journal of American Oriental Society* 99:4 (1979): 680–682.

Ferdinand, Klaus. "Ethnographical Notes on Chahar Aimak, Hazara, and Moghol." *Acta Orientalia* 28:3–4 (1965): 175–204

———. "Nomad Expansion and Commerce in Central Afghanistan." *Folk* 4 (1962): 123–159.

Tapper, Nancy. "The Advent of Pashtun *Maldors* in Northwestern Afghanistan." *Bulletin*

of the School of Oriental and African Studies (University of London) 36 (1973):
55–79.

Thesinger, Wilfred. "The Hazaras of Central Afghanistan." *Geographic Journal* 121
(1955): 312–319.

Unpublished Manuscripts

Bacon, Elizabeth E. "The Hazara Mongols of Afghanistan." Ph.D. dissertation, University of California, Berkeley, 1951.
Canfield, Robert L. "Islamic Coalitions in Bamian and the Translation of Afghan Political
Culture." Paper presented at the Meetings of the American Anthropological Association, Washington, D.C., December 5, 1980.

Robert L. Canfield

HUI   The Hui (pronounced "whey") are the most widely distributed and the
second largest of all ethnic minorities in China. They are Muslims, or atheists
of Muslim parentage, who speak Chinese as their native language and who trace
their descent to Arabs and Persians who began settling in China during the
seventh century A.D. Among China's ten Muslim minorities, the Hui are the
most numerous, having the longest history in China, and are the most acculturated
to the Han Chinese majority. They are the only Muslims in China who speak
Chinese as a mother tongue and live dispersed through all provinces of the
country.

According to the 1982 census of the People's Republic of China, Hui on the
mainland total 7.2 million. There are also thousands of Hui on Taiwan as well
as in Hong Kong, Macao and countries of Southeast Asia and elsewhere to which
Chinese have migrated. All Hui are Sunni Muslims of the Hanafi school of
Islamic jurisprudence, a fact that means little, however, in their everyday lives.

In Chinese, Hui are known as Huihui, Huihui *minzu* ("Huihui people" or
"Huihui nationality") and Huizu (a contraction of Huihui *minzu*). Traditionally
they have also called themselves Huijiaoren ("Hui-religion—Islam—people"),
Mumin (from the Arabic *mu'min*) and Jiaomen (a term meaning something like
"people of the Teaching"). Today the Chinese government promotes the use
of "Musilin" ("Muslim") to denote Hui (and others) who actively believe in
Islam as distinct from Hui in general, a portion of whom no longer practice the
religion. In other countries Hui are called by such names as Panthay and Dungan
(see Dungans [Soviet Union]). In English the Hui have often been referred to
simply as Chinese Muslims, a term that has caused much confusion because it
also rightly includes the nine other Muslim ethnic groups in China (see Bonans;
Dongxiang; Kazakhs; Kirghiz; Salars; Tajik; Tatars; Uygur; Uzbek).

Islam was introduced to China during the flourishing Tang dynasty (A.D. 618–
906). Arab and Persian merchants and mariners sailed to and settled in Canton
and other southeastern Chinese port cities, bringing the religion just after it was
founded. Muslim soldiers, brought across Central Asia to help China's emperor
quell a rebellion in A.D. 757, introduced Islam to the interior. Many of these

Arabs, Persians and Central Asians, nearly all men, married local Han Chinese women and remained in China, speaking Persian and Arabic as their lingua francas. They lived in special districts (called "barbarian settlements"), where they were held responsible for maintaining law and order according to the customs of their homelands. The Muslims increased in numbers as the children of mixed Muslim and Han marriages were raised as Muslims and as foreign Muslims continued to settle in China for several more centuries. Another major Muslim influx came with the Mongols, who conquered China in the thirteenth century and imported thousands of Central and West Asian artisans, scholars and administrators to help them rule China. Muslims directed the financial administration of the empire and were appointed to other high positions in the central and provincial governments.

While the Muslims remained a distinctly foreign minority during their first seven centuries in China, during the next five centuries they had relatively little contact with the rest of the Muslim world. When Han Chinese overthrew the Mongols in 1368, they sought to wipe out the much-resented foreign influence and thus prohibited the use of foreign languages, foreign names and foreign clothing and restricted foreign travel. European capture of the Asian sea trade from the Arabs also contributed to halting Muslim migration to China. It was during this period (the Ming dynasty, 1368–1644) that the Muslims in China became sinicized, acculturating to Han Chinese ways through the adoption of Han surnames, clothing and food habits and through speaking Chinese as their everyday language. The continued in-marriage of Han women, as well as the adoption of Han children and occasional conversion of Han adults, further contributed to the increase in the number of Muslims and, at the same time, to their becoming increasingly similar, physically as well as culturally, to the Han. Muslims ceased being referred to as Arabs, barbarians and foreigners and came to be known instead by a new name, Huihui.

The next phase of Muslim history in China was one of violent ethnic conflict between the Han and the Hui. From the sixteenth to early twentieth century, Muslims of northwest China (Hui, Salars and others) and Hui in Yunnan in southwest China rose against both local Han and the government in a series of rebellions said to have claimed as many as 10 million lives. Exacerbating the ethnic conflict were intense factional cleavages within the Muslim communities themselves, notably that between the so-called New Teaching adherents inspired by Naqshbandi fundamentalism and ideas of reform and Old Teaching adherents who clung to established practices of Chinese Islam (see Dongxiang).

With the founding of the Republic of China in 1912, the Hui were formally recognized as one of China's "five great peoples" (usually translated "races" in English), part of the new Western-inspired government's attempt to win over the independent-minded minorities who dominated more than half of China's territory. Many Hui, following trends among the Han, became actively engaged in reform movements. During the civil war between the Chinese Communists and Nationalists, both sides actively sought to win Hui loyalties. After the

Communist victory and establishment of the People's Republic of China (PRC) in 1949, several thousand Hui fled with the Nationalists to Taiwan, while the majority remained on the mainland. There the Communist leaders developed a Soviet-inspired minority policy that formally identified major ethnic groups as "minority nationalities" (*shaoshu minzu*) and promised them rights of autonomy and self-government in exchange for their support. The Communist party has now recognized 55 ethnic groups as minority nationalities and established 107 so-called autonomous governments at three levels—5 at the provincial level, 30 at a middle (prefectural) level and 72 at the county level. Twelve of these bear the name "Hui."

By objective criteria, Hui are more similar to Han than they are distinctive. In most regards, in fact, they are clearly more similar to the Han than to China's other Muslim minorities. Many Hui insist there are clear physical differences between themselves and the Han (primarily that they have larger noses, more facial and body hair and deeper-set eyes), but such differences are not easily observed. Similarities between the Hui and Han are so great that many observers have concluded the Hui to be "not a separate race from the Han" but only "Han who believe in Islam." This is incorrect. Hui agree they are Chinese (*Zhongyuan-ren*) by citizenship but insist they are not Han (*Han-ren* or *Han-min*). Many Hui explain that Hui are not Han who converted to Islam but that Hui have "foreign blood," and specifically "Arab blood," which Han do not. Hui identity is thus not just a matter of one's present-day religious belief but of an inherited legacy acquired at birth (with the exception of those who convert to Islam in order to marry a Hui) and symbolized as being Hui "by blood." Thus Hui who never pray or go to a mosque, or who describe themselves as "not religious," can still be regarded as Hui.

What distinguishes Hui from Han in everyday life are primarily the facts that Hui generally do not eat pork (the favorite meat of the Han) and often avoid all "Han food" on the grounds that it has been contaminated by pork, that Hui usually marry other Hui, and that they tend to maintain a certain social distance (relating in large part to Hui tradition forbidding them to eat Han food). Another major distinction and barrier to interaction traditionally was Hui refusal to partake in what Hui call "Han religion" (or "Han-people superstition"), meaning the amalgam of Buddhism, Taoism, Confucianism, folk religion and ancestor worship that was fundamental to Han culture and social organization before 1949. Thus, traditionally Hui were stigmatized as deviant, if not amoral, for failing to adhere to hallowed Han norms and were characterized by Han as peculiar for aspects of their own culture, such as the ritual use of a "secret" language (Arabic) and the "peculiar" habit of avoiding pork. Hui distinctiveness has diminished since 1949 because of the government's view that most Han popular religion is essentially superstition and, as such, is to be abolished. At the same time, government policy has added to Hui distinctiveness by permitting Hui to continue to bury their dead in Muslim cemeteries while all Han must now be cremated, and by exempting Hui from some aspects of China's controlled birth program.

Results of China's 1982 national census show a Hui population of 7.2 million out of a total 14.6 million people belonging to the 10 traditional Muslim ethnic groups (and out of a total mainland Chinese population of slightly over 1 billion). This may be quite accurate although many knowledgeable persons believe that the total Muslim figure is much higher. According to 1982 figures, the Hui population has grown more rapidly in recent years than any other major ethnic group in China, including the Han. At the same time, despite the lack of statistics, it appears that Hui-Han intermarriage is increasing and that some children of such mixed marriages are being declared Han.

Hui live in all provinces and major cities of China (including Tibet). In some communities Hui are the majority, while in others, they live scattered among the Han or other minorities. Their rural–urban balance is probably similar to that of China as a whole, however; about 80 percent rural. Generally speaking, Hui are most numerous proportionately in the northwest and fewest in the southeast, with the distinctiveness of Hui ranging accordingly along this continuum.

Perhaps 40 to 60 percent of all Hui live in the northwest provinces (or autonomous regions) of Gansu, Ningxia, Shaanxi, Qinghai and Xinjiang, a relatively poor and backward zone of China. Hui do not constitute a province-wide majority in any of these provinces but have nevertheless been culturally and, formerly, politically dominant in many districts, causing much of the northwest to be traditionally regarded as Muslim territory.

Economic patterns among the Hui are today largely the same as among the Han. Most are sedentary peasants who raise rice and other grains for sale to the state, engage in collective small-scale "sideline" industries and may additionally raise vegetables and small livestock for private gain. Hui are characterized as more engaged in raising cattle and sheep than the Han.

In urban areas, most Hui, like most Chinese in general, are employed, housed, educated, and provided medical care by the state. Most work for government-owned factories and workshops. The only occupational specializations distinguishing Hui from Han are the *ahongs* (Hui religious leaders) and those supplying "pure and true" (i.e., *halal* or Islamic) food.

Until 1949, Hui family structure followed quite closely the Confucian-inspired Han pattern, with early marriage arranged by parents, patrilocal residence after marriage, demand for sons to carry on the male line, a large joint family ideal, subordination of young to old and female to male and great emphasis on filiality (*xiao*) towards parents and ancestors. A dramatic difference, however, was that Hui family structure was not reinforced by the daily, monthly and annual rites of ancestor worship so central to Han households and ideology. Instead Hui tended to impute a sense of kinship to the Hui community at large, referring to each other as "faith kin," talking about "all Hui under heaven being one family" and using their local mosque for many ritual functions that Han performed in their homes or in lineage halls and temples. Whereas Han rituals related to marriage, childbirth and death occurred chiefly in the context of the family and its home or ceremonial hall with family elders playing leading roles, major portions of Hui rituals took place at the mosque, where the *ahong* and mosque elders assumed major roles. For Hui traveling outside their home communities, being Hui was a major basis for establishing new "connections" and ensured temporary hospitality and assistance.

New marriage laws, economic organization and population control policies enacted since 1949 have significantly modified traditional patterns. Strict patrilocality has given way to frequent neolocality and matrilocality, with much more moving about as family members are assigned to work in other parts of the country. National policies now outlaw arranged marriage and polygyny, give women equal divorce and inheritance rights, specify late marriage (deferring to middle or late twenties) and reward those who adhere to the family planning norm of only one child per couple. Many decisions traditionally made within the family have been made the official responsibility of the administrative "unit" to which each individual belongs, usually one's place of work. Decisions made by the unit include such personal matters as when and whom the individual may marry, when the couple may have a child and where one may travel away from his or her place of residence. *Purdah* does not exist among the Hui, and, even before 1949, except in some parts of northwest China, Hui women did not wear veils.

The government extends special considerations to Islam, all the while taking measures to ensure that all Islamic activity is consistent with official policies and under the control of the Muslim leaders loyal to the government. The Chinese Islamic Association, founded in Beijing in 1953 and reporting to the Religious Affairs Bureau of the State Council, is central in this regard. Mosques are exempt from property and housing taxes, and government funds have been provided for renovation of several famous old mosques. Government funds are also provided for the official pilgrimage delegation sent each year to Mecca with goodwill stops in other Muslim countries.

A major area of official consideration concerns the provision of Muslim food. In work units (including the military) where Muslim employees are numerous, special dining facilities are provided. In units employing only a few Muslims the government instead provides for a food subsidy to enable them to eat at one of the "Huimin" (or "pure and true") restaurants that are ubiquitous throughout China, or to compensate them for bringing food from home. The government supports the three annual Muslim festivals traditionally celebrated by Hui (Id al Fitr, Id al Adha and the birthday of the Prophet Muhammad) by making extra food supplies available, by exempting from slaughter taxes the cattle and sheep killed for the festivals and by giving the day off to Muslims working in government enterprises.

The greatest resentment expressed by Hui today is over incidents during the Cultural Revolution, when Red Guards in many parts of China forced Muslims to eat pork and cremate their dead, defiled their mosques and humiliated *ahongs* (for example, by forcing them to tend pigs or parade down the street wearing a pig part). Yet Muslims survived the Cultural Revolution better than other religious groups, and at almost all times some mosques remained open where at least foreign Muslims were permitted to observe Friday prayer and the major festivals.

Hui spokesmen are quite positive about the more liberal religious policies since 1979. Many Muslim leaders have resumed leadership roles, and a few have even traveled abroad to participate in international conferences. In 1980 the Chinese Islamic Association convened a national conference, its first in 17 years, and several regional and provincial Islamic associations now meet annually. Government supported training of new *ahongs* has also begun.

Taiwan has twice provided a new home for Chinese emigrating from the mainland. Both times Hui were among them. The first migration, during the mid-seventeenth century, was from the southeast coastal province of Fujian. With few exceptions, Hui descended from this migration have now been assimilated by their Han neighbors. The second migration occurred when Chinese loyal to the Nationalists fled the Communists in 1949. Muslims among them are usually said to number 20,000. Nearly all are Hui and nearly all are city dwellers.

Although the Hui are few in number on Taiwan, they enjoy considerable visibility and support from the government. This is due in large part to foreign policy considerations (especially much-valued connections with Saudi Arabia) and to the Nationalist government's policy of maintaining that Taiwan's Muslims represent all the Muslims of mainland China. In contrast to PRC policy, Nationalist policy is to treat the Hui as only a religious group and to downplay all ethnic differences.

BIBLIOGRAPHY

Books

Broomhall, Marshall. *Islam in China: A Neglected Problem*. Reprint ed. New York: Paragon, 1966. (Originally published 1910).

Bush, Richard C., Jr. *Religion in Communist China*. Nashville: Abingdon Press, 1970.

China Islamic Association. *Chinese Moslems*. Beijing: Foreign Languages Press, 1955.

————. *Chinese Moslems in Progress*. Beijing: Nationalities Publishing House, 1957.

————. *Moslems in China*. Beijing: Foreign Languages Press, 1953.

————. *The Religious Life of Chinese Muslims*. Beijing: Foreign Languages Printing House, 1981.

Dreyer, June Teufel. *China's Forty Millions: Minority Nationalities and National Integration in the People's Republic of China*. Cambridge: Harvard University Press, 1976.

Eberhard, Wolfram. *China's Minorities: Yesterday and Today*. Belmont, Cal.: Wadsworth Press, 1982.

Fei Hsiao Tung. *Toward a People's Anthropology*. Beijing: New World Press, 1981.

Gowing, Peter. "Islam on Taiwan." In *Handbuch der Orientalistik*. Vol. 3. Leiden: Brill, 1975.

Israeli, Raphael. *Muslims in China: A Study in Cultural Confrontation*. London: Curzon Press, 1980.

Kao Hao-jan. *The Imam's Story*. Hong Kong: Green Pagoda Press, 1960.

Ma, Ibrahim T. Y. *Muslims in China*. Kuala Lumpur: Utusan Melayu Berhad, 1975.

MacInnis, Donald E. *Religious Policy and Practice in Communist China: A Documentary History*. New York: Macmillan, 1972.

Pillsbury, Barbara L. K. "Being Female in a Muslim Minority." In *Women in the Muslim World*, edited by Lois G. Beck and Nikki Keddie. Cambridge: Harvard University Press, 1978.

———. "Islam: Even unto China." In *Change and the Muslim World*, edited by Philip H. Stoddard et al. Syracuse: Syracuse University Press, 1981.

———. "Pig and Policy: Maintenance of Boundaries between Han and Muslim Chinese." In *Minorities: A Text with Readings in Intergroup Relations*, edited by B. Eugene Griessman. Hinsdale, Ill.: Holt, Rinehart and Winston, Dryden, 1975. (Also published in *Ethnic Groups* 1:2 [1976]: 151–162.)

Pong, Raymond, and Caldarola, Carlo. "China: Religion in a Revolutionary Society." In *Religion and Societies: Asia and the Middle East*. Berlin: Mouton, 1982.

Yin Ming. *United and Equal: The Progress of China's Minority Nationalities*. Beijing: Foreign Language Press, 1977.

Articles

Chang, Hajji Yusuf (Chang Chao-li). "Muslim Minorities in China." *Journal of the Institute of Muslim Minority Affairs* 3:2 (1981): 30–34, 66–69.

Forbes, Andrew. "The Muslim National Minorities of China." *Religion* 6 (1976): 67–87.

Joyaux, François. "The Muslim Minorities of the Chinese People's Republic." *Islamic Review* 56 (1968): 23–26, 40.

Ma Yu-huai. "Twenty Years of the Ningsia Hui Autonomous Region." *China Reconstructs* 28:2 (1979): 34–43.

Pai Shou-i. "Historical Heritage of Chinese Muslims." *China Reconstructs* 13:7 (1964): 37–40.

Pillsbury, Barbara L. K. "Factionalism Observed: Behind the Face of Harmony in a Chinese Community." *The China Quarterly* 74 (1978): 241–272.

———. "The Muslim Population of China: Clarifying the Questions of Size and Ethnicity." *Journal of the Institute of Muslim Minority Affairs* 3:2 (1981): 35–58; and 4:1–2 (1982): 188.

———. "Muslims on Taiwan." *Journal of the Institute of Muslim Minority Affairs*, in press.

———. "The 1300-Year Chronology of Muslim History in China." *Journal of the Institute of Muslim Minority Affairs* 3:2 (1981): 10–29.

"Vignettes of Hui Life." *China Reconstructs* 28:2 (1979): 44–46; and 28:3 (1979): 75–77.

Zhou Qing, and Xiong Yu. "Some Perceptions Concerning Minority Population Developments in China." *Renkou Yanjiu* (Population Research) 3 (1982): 33–37. (In Chinese. Translated by Joint Publications Research Service, No. 81460, pp. 75–83.)

Unpublished Manuscripts

Hunsberger, Merrill. "Ma Pu-Fang in Chinghai Province, 1931–1949." Ph.D. dissertation, Temple University, 1978.

Lipman, Jonathan H. "The Border Worlds of Gansu, 1895–1935." Ph.D. dissertation, Stanford University, 1981.

Pillsbury, Barbara L. K. "Cohesion and Cleavage in a Chinese Muslim Minority." Ph.D. dissertation, Columbia University, 1973.

Barbara L. K. Pillsbury

I

INDO-MAURITIANS   The island of Mauritius lies in the western Indian Ocean, some 500 miles east of Madagascar and 20 degrees south of the equator. On its 720 square miles are nearly 1 million people, all descendants of immigrants who arrived, voluntarily or involuntarily, in the eighteenth and nineteenth centuries. An independent country within the British Commonwealth since 1968, Mauritius is almost totally dependent on the production of sugar.

Mauritius is an ethnically plural society consisting of Indo-Mauritians, both Hindu and Muslim, from five linguistic groups (68 percent), Europeans, mostly of French descent and Creoles of mixed African and European descent (29 percent); and Chinese from two linguistic groups (3 percent). The 170,000 Muslims of Mauritius came from the Indian subcontinent and make up about 17 percent of the total population, or 24 percent of the Indo-Mauritian population. By origin, they can be divided into two major groups: those whose ancestors came as indentured laborers between 1834 and 1907 from India's United Provinces, Bihar, Orissa, Bengal and the Tamil- and Telegu-speaking areas of southern India, and a smaller group of traders from the Gujarati-speaking areas of west India, notably Kutch and Surat, most of whom arrived after World War I.

In the 1972 census 73 percent of Muslims returned themselves as Sunni Hanafi, 5 percent as Sunni Shafi, 3 percent as Ahmadiyas, and 2 percent as followers of Shaikh Momine and other Muslim sects. Only 15 percent claimed adherence to Islam without specifying a sect, indicating a high degree of sectarianism among Mauritian Muslims.

There are 65 mosques in Mauritius, the largest and most important of which is the Jumma mosque founded in 1852 in Port Louis, the capital. All mosques but one have been constituted as *waqfs*, or charitable organizations, as defined by the laws of Islam. A *waqf* board created in 1941 supervises their finances and administration. Each mosque is administered by a *mutawali*, or manager, who is usually elected by the congregation. The *jammat*, or religious association, forms around the mosque and helps members with marriages and funerals and runs a *madrasa* (religious school) for children. Villages which cannot afford a mosque still have a *jammat*.

The most striking Muslim ceremony in Mauritius is the Yamsé (Ashura) held during the month of Muharram, commemorating the martyrdom of Hussain, one of the sons of Ali. A Shia ceremony, it is performed without reference to sect in Mauritius. Large floats are constructed of papier-mâché in the form of onion-domed tombs, drawn by horses with human faces, accompanied by musicians and groups of Muslims bearing green and red flags. Some frenzied participants thrust long, pointed skewers into their scalps, faces, chests and backs. The floats are sponsored by *dagras* associations. The *dagras* is the tomb of a *pir*, or saint. Its custodian is often the patrilineal descendant of the *pir*. Participants make vows to the *pir*, promising in return for a benefit to donate money for the procession or to thrust skewers into themselves.

The Yamsé and the worship of *pirs* are condemned by orthodox Muslims and are dying out in Mauritius. On a popular level, there is some syncretism in the island, and some Muslims make offerings to local Hindu deities and Catholic saints.

Virtually all the Gujarati Muslims (see Gujaratis) have their businesses in Port Louis. The Kutchi Memons are chiefly importers of rice, the staple food of the island, while the Sunni Surtis have become dealers in cloth. Nearly all trade in these commodities is in their hands, but many also run large wholesale and retail shops. Both these communities are endogamous, importing spouses from their villages of origin in India. The Kutchi Memons are particularly strict in this matter. The children of a Memon who marries outside the community are known as half-Memons and are not considered eligible to marry pure Memons, hold office in the mosque or join the Kutchi Memon Society. Both Memons and Surtis retain certain customs and ceremonies, especially surrounding marriage, which derive from Hinduism. There are small numbers of other Gujarati Muslims in Mauritius, notably the Halai Memons, the Orah Surtis (from Ahmedabad), the Miabhais or Maliks, the Patni Borahs (from Patna), and the Daudi Borahs, who are Shia. The wealth of the Gujarati Muslims has enabled them to found many charities, orphanages and schools, which are open to all Muslims.

About 43 percent of the Muslim population lives in the five towns of Mauritius. Some 30 percent of the population of Port Louis is Muslim and includes a few small distinctive groups, such as the "Cocknies," from Cochin on the southwest coast of India; the Khojas, an Ismaili group, but not followers of the Aga Khan; the Comorian or Anjouan from the Comoro Islands off Madagascar; and the offspring of Muslim–Creole unions known popularly as Creole Lascars. Fifty-seven percent of Muslims live in villages scattered throughout the island. These same villages are inhabited by Hindus, Creoles and Chinese. Most rural Muslims are agricultural laborers, although some are small planters of sugar cane. There are a number of Muslim butchers and shoemakers, as these occupations are shunned by Hindus. Muslim dock workers, laborers and small shopkeepers can be found in Port Louis.

The patrilineal joint family household is the ideal among Muslims, but it is achieved only by the relatively wealthy. Polygyny is rare. Most Muslims also speak Creole, a French patois which is the lingua franca of the island. The more educated speak English and French. Some 84 percent of Muslims claim Urdu as their mother tongue, but this probably records a political rather than a linguistic fact, as only 37 percent cite it as the language spoken in the home. Parents can opt to have Urdu taught to their children in school.

Although there is a Muslim political party, the Muslim Committee of Action, it does not command the adherence of all Muslims. Some belong and have stood as candidates for election to the majority, Hindu-dominated Labour Party, the Independent Forward Bloc, also a Hindu party, and the Parti Mauricien, composed largely of Creoles and Franco-Mauricians. In the 1982 elections many young Muslims appear to have supported the victorious Mouvement Militant Mauricien party.

Burton Benedict
Population figures updated by Richard V. Weekes

BIBLIOGRAPHY

Books

Benedict, Burton. *Indians in a Plural Society*. London: HMSO, 1961.
———. *Mauritius: Problems of a Plural Society*. New York: Praeger, 1965.
———. "Pluralism and Stratification." In *Essays in Comparative Social Stratification*, edited by L. Plotnicov and A. Tuden. Pittsburgh: University of Pittsburgh, 1970.
Critchfield, Richard. *The Golden Bowl Be Broken: Peasant Life in Four Cultures*. Bloomington: Indiana University Press, 1973.
Emrith, Moomtaz. *The Muslims in Mauritius*. Port Louis, Mauritius: Paul Machay, 1967.
Hahn, Lorna, and Edison, Robert. *Mauritius: A Study and Annotated Bibliography*. Washington, D.C.: The American University, 1969.
Malim, Michael. *The Island of the Swan: Mauritius*. London: Longmans, 1962.
Meade, James E., et al. *The Economy and Social Structure of Mauritius*. London: Methuen, 1961.
Ommanney, F. D. *The Shoals of Capricorn*. London: Longmans, 1952.
Simmons, Adele Smith. *Modern Mauritius: The Politics of Decolonialization*. Bloomington: Indiana University Press, 1982.
Titmuss, Richard M., and Abel-Smith, Brian. *Social Policies and Population Growth in Mauritius*. London: Frank Cass, 1961.
Toussaint, A., and Adolphe, H. *Bibliography of Mauritius: (1502–1954)*. Port Louis, Mauritius: Esclapon, 1956.
Villiers, Alan. *The Indian Ocean*. London: Museum Press, 1952.

Articles

Benedict, Burton. "Factionalism in Mauritian Villages." *British Journal of Sociology* 8:4 (1957): 328–342.
———. "Stratification in Plural Societies." *American Anthropologist* 64:6 (1962): 1235–1246.

.

J

JABARTI   The Tigrinya-speaking Muslims of Ethiopia call themselves Jabarti, a name which they consider pejorative if used by Tigrinya-speaking Christians. There is no ethnic group called Tigrinya, which is strictly a language spoken by some 2 million Ethiopians who live mostly in Tigre Province, although most Jabarti, who number perhaps 200,000, live in Eritrea Province and its capital, Asmara. (In central Ethiopia, Amharic-speaking people who are Muslim are also called Jabarti. *Ed.*)

The languages of most Ethiopians are Afro-Asiatic with two subclassifications: Semitic and Cushitic. Tigrinya, unlike the other languages of the Horn of Africa (Afar, Somali, Oromo), is Semitic, called Ethio-Semitic. It does not have a script of its own. Gez, the language for ritual of the Ethiopian Church (Monophysite or Coptic), to which most Tigrinya belong, is also the script that has been used in the long tradition of literacy among Tigrinya speakers. Gez (or Ge'ez or Guz) is sometimes called Ethiopic. The name probably is derived from the name and language of one of the southern Arabian Semitic tribes, the Agazi (or Ag'azyan) that migrated to Africa about 25 centuries ago. Jabarti write in Gez, although some also write in Arabic.

Tigrinya speakers believe that they are descendants of the early migrations from southern Arabia. The name "Abyssinia," which is used by some to describe Ethiopia or the Tigrinya-Amhara parts of it, is probably derived from another southern Arabian tribe, the Habeshat (or Habasat). Tigrinya speakers, along with the Amhara and other highland Ethiopians, sometimes call themselves Habesh.

Tigre Province, where most Tigrinya speakers live, is the heartland of the great empires that have ruled this part of Africa. It was Axum that succeeded earlier societies such as Cush or Punt where Semitic immigrants gained their independence from southern Arabia. It was a king of Axum who converted to Christianity and brought his country into the Christian fold. It was from here that through conquest the kingdom grew to include parts of southern Arabia and over towards the Nile Valley. It was through the Axumite kings that the succession passed which is alleged to have begun with Solomon and Sheba and continued "without interruption" through the late Haile Selassie.

Tigrinya speakers are aware of this history. They view their language as being closer to Gez and therefore to the true language of Monophysite Christian literature. They view themselves as a purer stock than even their Semitic, Amharan neighbors to the south and certainly purer than the Cushitic peoples bordering them, the Oromo, Afar and Somali.

The highlands area occupied by Tigrinya speakers generally consists of plateaus roughly 5,000 to 7,500 feet or higher in altitude, crossed by rivers that may cut 1,000 or more feet below the level of the plateaus. The people prefer to inhabit the high elevations, where they engage in agriculture supplemented by some animal husbandry. Being near the equator, the temperature on the plateau is moderate with a small variance of from 60°F to 70°F throughout the year. Rainfall is heaviest during the summer months, June to September, but as recent years have proved, the area is subject to periodic drought.

The list of crops cultivated by Tigrinya speakers includes *tef* (*Eragrostos abyssinia*), a small grain, maize, wheat, millet and barley as staples and a wide variety of other plants as supplementary staples such as chili peppers, various beans, cabbage, peas and onion. Animal husbandry is secondary and includes cattle, sheep, goats, horses, donkeys, dogs, cats, chickens, bees and camels. Some observers have argued that Abyssinia was one of the major centers of the domestication of plants, a contention that has some adherents and is generally noted by writers on the subject, but not widely accepted by specialists.

Land rights are intricately intertwined with kinship or heredity. S. F. Nadel was one of the first to describe the relationship between land rights and social structure among the Tigrinya speakers. In his *Races and Tribes of Eritrea* he describes the *enda* as follows:

It is composed of a greatly varying number of individual families all claiming descent from a common ancestor whose name the *enda* bears. An *enda* which grows very large splits into two or more sections, which in the course of time acquire a name and social identity of their own. The *enda* is, in a sense, a territorial unit, for the most important form of land tenure in the country, the hereditary, absolute land rights of *resti* is bound up with the *enda* group. Land of the *resti* type can also be owned by the individual family within the *enda*; but these individual land rights are conceived of as being derived from the land rights vested in the *enda* itself, in virtue of the ancient first occupation of the land. This corporate conception of land ownership is revived in every dispute over land, and indeed constitutes the strongest bond of cohesion in the *enda*.

More recent micro-studies of land tenure among the Tigrinya speakers find the land tenure system to have a dynamic element to it. In the traditionally settled areas the *resti* system is still based upon descent. However, in some newly settled areas there was an incipient *resti* system that is not yet based upon descent, real or purported. As in any land tenure, there are disputes that must be resolved through legal systems or through some other collective structure. Power, economic or other, plays a role in the settlement of these disputes as it does in any other system.

While many Jabarti live in the highlands, most live in lower villages in Eritrea. Here there are not the scattered homesteads characteristic of the Christian-dominated areas. Jabarti live in tightly packed villages and go daily to their fields, returning home at night. The family-owned land and house remains with the family; even when sons move away to Asmara or to other countries, they remain forever welcome to their villages and expect a share of the land when the head of the family dies. Land passes from generation to generation patrilineally.

Jabarti are patrilocal. When a son marries, he brings his bride to his father's home after a wedding ceremony which takes place in both bride's and groom's parents' home. While first cousin marriage is accepted, it is not common. Selection of the bride is the responsibility first of the son's mother, who makes arrangements with the prospective bride's mother. At the time of the wedding, gifts are exchanged with careful notation of which family gives what. Generally, the bride's family pays a sum of money or makes a gift in kind to the groom's family to help the groom support the bride.

The birth of sons is expected and particularly welcomed, as evidenced by the fact that traditional Jabarti bury the placenta of a boy baby inside the hut and the placenta of a girl baby outside the hut, signifying that the adult male remains while the adult female will reside elsewhere with her husband. A popular jest among Jabarti when referring to a person who has lived in one place for a long time (whether in his native home or in the city or overseas) is that his placenta must be buried there.

Newborn children are given amulets to wear around their necks which contain miniature Qurans. On the seventh day after birth, boys are circumcised in the home in the presence of the *shaikh*.

Jabarti are Sunnis of the Hanafi juridical school, an exception in an area where the Shafi predominates, but common where Ottoman Turks have had influence. A pious people, the Jabarti are resolutely Muslim. It is expected that a person will pray five times a day, observe Ramadan scrupulously and abstain from pork and alcohol. In Asmara, Muslims do not visit Christian homes, nor do they eat off of dishes that Christians have used. Each goes to his own restaurant, although Christians will patronize Muslim establishments. Intermarriage between Muslims and Christians is rare indeed.

Women are not veiled or secluded among Jabarti. When they do go out in public, they wear a shawl in such a way that no hair appears, nor any skin except face, wrists or ankles. When male visitors who are not kin dine in a Jabarti home, the wife does not join the meal; the men eat together, waited upon by a daughter. Women do not go to the mosque except on Ramadan and then only through a separate entrance and never when men are present. Jabarti accept polygyny, but this is only practiced by the wealthy, who are relatively few.

Jabarti recognize saints and celebrate their anniversaries with festivities which usually involve sumptuous meals, to the extent that these can be afforded. Care of saints' tombs and concern for commemorations is largely the province of women.

Urban Jabarti are among the poorest of the population. Business, the trades, government are largely in the hands of Christian Tigrinya, who employ Muslims (Muslims seldom employ Christians). Where Muslims are in business, it is usually in the manufacture of clothing—essentially sewing—and managing small shops.

The poor state of the Muslims reflects not only old traditions but also their lack of education. For most, schooling stops at an early age so that children can assist in the family enterprise, whether farming or petty business in the city. Christians continue their education and are able to maintain and even improve their economic conditions.

A good Jabarti is one who is pious. He attains status in his community if he has been able to obtain material possessions, but even more if he is able to take care of his family well, raise sons who are respectful and marry off his daughters to worthy families.

Currently there is political ferment in Ethiopia and Eritrea Province. Emperor Haile Selassie was toppled from power by a military coup in 1975, an event that did not greatly displease the Tigrinya speakers. There had long been lingering resentment among them dating from the nineteenth century, when the Amhara kings were willing to abandon them to Italian control. After the conquest of Ethiopia in 1936, the Italians created a province which included all the Tigrinya speakers. The Ethiopian reconquest (with British and Sudanese help) and sub-sequent reintegration of Eritrea into Ethiopia has left a legacy of discontent that has contributed to the Eritrean liberation struggle. However, whatever their historic differences with the Ethiopian governments, it is extremely unlikely that there is any support for separatist movements from Christians of Tigre Province.

Eritrea, which was turned over to Ethiopian control by the British in 1952, has been a continuing source of unrest and rebellion. The Ethiopian government has tended to characterize the rebels as being mainly Muslims who wish to gain independence in Eritrea for primarily ethnic and religious reasons. The Eritrean Liberation Front claims to have the support of both Jabarti and Christians in Eritrea. The economic neglect of Eritrea by the central government for the past 20 or 30 years lends credence to the ELF's claim.

BIBLIOGRAPHY

Books

Bauer, Dan F. *Household and Society in Ethiopia: An Economic and Social Analysis of Tigray*. Occasional Papers Series, Committee on Ethiopian Studies, African Studies Center, Monograph No. 6. East Lansing: Michigan State University, 1977.
Bender, Marvin L., et al. *Language in Ethiopia*. London: Oxford University Press, 1976.
Grove, A. T. *African South of the Sahara*. London: Oxford University Press, 1967.
Levine, Donald N. *Wax and Gold*. Chicago: University of Chicago Press, 1965.

Lipsky, George. *Ethiopia: Its People, Its Society, Its Culture*. New Haven: Human Relations Area Files, 1962.

Longrigg, Stephen H. *A Short History of Eritrea*. Oxford: Clarendon Press, 1945.

Marcus, Harold, ed. *Proceedings of the First U.S. Conference on Ethiopian Studies 1973*. Occasional Papers Series, Committee of Ethnic Studies, African Studies Center. East Lansing: Michigan State University, 1975.

Murdock, George Peter. *Africa: Its People and Their Culture History*. New York, McGraw-Hill, 1957.

Nadel, S. F. *Races and Tribes of Eritrea*. Asmara, Eritrea: British Military Administration, 1944.

Paul, A. *A History of the Beja Tribes of the Sudan*. London: Frank Cass, 1971.

Shack, William A. *The Central Ethiopians: Amhara, Tigrina, and Related Peoples*. Ethnographic Survey of Africa, Northeast Africa. Part 4. London: International African Institute, 1974.

Simmoons, Frederick. *Northwest Ethiopia: Peoples and Economy*. Madison: University of Wisconsin Press, 1960.

Trimingham, J. Spencer. *Islam in Ethiopia*. Reprint ed. London: Frank Cass, 1965. (Originally published 1952.)

Ullendorf, E. *The Ethiopians: An Introduction to the Country and People*. London: Oxford University Press, 1960.

————. *The Semitic Languages of Ethiopia: A Comparative Phonology*. London: Taylor's Foreign Language Press, 1955.

Articles

Greenberg, Joseph H. "The Languages of Africa." *International Journal of American Linguistics* 20:1 (pt. 2)(1963).

Leslau, Wolf. "The Languages of Ethiopia and Their Geographic Distribution." *Ethiopian Observer* 2:3 (1958): 116–121.

Nadel, S. F. "Land Tenure on the Eritrean Plateau." *Africa* 16 (1946): 1–22, 99–109.

Thomas R. DeGregori
Richard V. Weekes

JAHANKA   In the purest sense of the word, the Jahanka (Jahanke, Jahaanké, Diakhanké) are not an ethnic group. They do not speak a language widely considered as their own, nor do they inhabit a particular area thought clearly to be "Jahanka territory." The Jahanka are a group of clans, originally Soninké (see Soninké), who over a period of several centuries have come to recognize their unique identity. This identity is based in part on a common heritage, in part on close lineage relationships and in part on the strongest Muslim clerical, educational and magical tradition in all of West Africa.

    The sedentary Jahanka occupy distinctive "Jahanka villages" in Senegal and The Gambia (Senegambia) south of an imaginary line drawn from the mouth of the Gambia River to the confluence of the Senegal and Faleme rivers. A few Jahanka villages stretch southward into Guinea towards the edge of the Futa

Jalon highlands. This area is typical of West Africa's drier savannas. Brush and trees grow lush in the summer rainy season and then turn crisp and dry during seven or eight months without rain. Temperatures in these areas can range as high as 108° F, and they seldom drop below 54° F at night.

Because they live interspersed with a much larger Mandinka population, the Jahanka practice many Mandinka social customs. Mandinka is almost universally their common, everyday language (see Mandinka). However, because of their Soninké roots, many Jahanka still speak and use the language of the Soninké— Azer. Much of the language of Jahanka religious functions is Azer with a large influence of Arabic loan words. It is this "Arabized" language that some refer to when speaking of a Jahanka language. Their emphasis on Muslim education and their clerical calling lead a high percentage of Jahanka males to become literate in Arabic and in their languages of common use, the latter written with Arabic script. Unlike the Mandinka and many others in Senegambia, few Jahanka attend non-Islamic schools. Consequently, few are literate in French or English, the official languages of Senegal and The Gambia.

Understanding the nature of Jahanka ethnicity requires knowledge of their history and of their long tradition of Islamic scholarship, education and magical activity. The Jahanka claim their place of origin to have been Ja (Dia), in Masina on the Niger River in modern Mali, but they uniformly look to a period of residence in Jahaba ("Great Jaha"), on the Bafing River east of the modern Mali–Senegal border as the formative period of their ethnicity. It was in Jahaba, living together, that four major Soninké lineages came under the religious influence of one of West Africa's greatest clerics of all time, al-Hajj Salim Suwari. The most persuasive evidence suggests that this influential residence took place late in the fifteenth or early in the sixteenth century.

Carrying with them the prestige of Suwari's teachings, the Jahanka (which means "the people of Jaha") spread from Jahaba south towards Futa Jalon and west towards the mouth of the Gambia River. In these regions, they established their own villages and took on the status of being the region's most specialized clerical elite. Jahanka clericalism was not like any other, however. It was based upon Suwari's esoteric interpretation of Muslim scriptures and upon his staunchly held principles of avoidance of political affiliation and pacifism. In a region that witnessed widespread Muslim militancy, the Jahanka disdained *jihad*, and they never felt driven to proselytize. Their specialty became what might loosely be called "Suwarian magic," which includes divination, offering prayers, making charms and practicing medicine for others—all grounded in Suwari's symbolic interpretation of scriptures and his special ways of construing charms and healing.

Jahanka clerics have always been careful in teaching their knowledge of Suwarian magic. They conduct large, prestigious schools in their villages, where students from all over Senegambia learn the Quran and the great books of Islamic sciences. However, it is but one or two select students, nearly always of the most notable Jahanka lineages, who are taken aside to become practitioners of Suwarian magic.

The Jahanka have been careful, too, about ties of marriage in their polygynous society. They are not totally endogamous, but they make sure their daughters marry only into other Jahanka lineages, regardless of distances separating the families. Some lineages have exchanged daughters for generations. Sons can marry non-Jahanka women as a way of increasing Jahanka numbers in their patrilineal and patrilocal society, but this is not a frequent occurrence. Few Jahanka men who have the maximum number of four wives have more than one from a non-Janhanka family. Jahanka lineages of the same village thus are reliant upon one another, and beyond the village, Jahanka clans that sometimes are separated by hundreds of miles maintain a common identity and close ties of dependence through obligations inherent in the marriage relationship.

Over the years, these close family relationships, in combination with their unique Suwarian heritage, the care with which they guard and transmit their knowledge and their reputation as being Senegambia's most prestigious Muslim clerical elite, have led to their being identified separately as Jahanka. It is an identity they carry proudly into the present.

There are more than 60 Jahanka villages in Senegambia and Guinea, their populations ranging from a few hundred to 2,000. Altogether, perhaps as many as 50,000 people consider themselves to be Jahanka. Each Jahanka village is more or less independent of other villages in their neighborhoods, and each is something of a self-sufficient theocratic community. A typical village is divided into several large wards inhabited by members of the same clan—that is, persons sharing the same patronymic. Within each ward are several sublineages called *so*, which consist of persons who trace their ancestry back several generations to a single relative. A major function of the *so* is to redistribute income gained from clerical activities or trade throughout the entire sublineage. Within each *so* are up to a score of basic household work units, called *lu*. A typical *lu* contains a married father, his sons (married or not), their sons and all their wives and unmarried daughters. Each *lu* inhabits its own fenced-off area, farms its own fields and keeps its own supplies of food. Usually the eldest living head of a *lu* in a given *so* is regarded as head of the sublineage, though younger men can supersede their elders if they are of outstanding ability and have considerable personal authority. When the head of a *lu* dies, each married son having enough dependents to make a reasonable work force forms his own *lu* and becomes its head.

Most Jahanka villages have a single lineage of prime prestige, which is the major clerical lineage; a number of other lineages of less highly regarded clerics; a few lineages of merchants; a few of endogamous artisans; a few of slaves, or people who are descended of former slaves and who definitely are of low status; and a large population of students drawn from the village's hinterland to attend its Islamic schools. The village center is invariably the school of the great clerical lineage, the master of this school being the village's unnamed leader. His seniority, his ancestry and his level of education in more orthodox Islamic studies as well as in magic make him the effective decision maker of the village. The other clerical lineages have Quranic schools of their own, but only at the school of the major lineage can one study the most advanced Islamic texts.

It is a rare male Jahanka child who does not attend one of the village schools. Male children are considered as students, with less regard for their personal qualities until they have achieved a minimal level of Islamic education. For children of the major clerical lineages, completion of advanced studies taking 20 years or more is almost compulsory. Students, including non-Jahanka, come from long distances to attend the most noted schools. They are lodged among the various households in the village. Students pay for their education by giving gifts regularly to the master through their host. Most important for the village economy, students spend considerable time working for the schoolmaster. In the agricultural season, this involves intensive farm labor.

Only the best students study advanced Islamic texts and entertain hopes of becoming what Senegambians call a *fudi (fode)*, a person of considerable learning. Of these only a select few, usually including the master's most gifted children and nephews and a few others, are taken off secretly and instructed for two or three years in Suwarian magic. Non-family members selected for instruction in magic pay dearly for it, not only as they are receiving instruction, but subsequently, as they are practicing the magical arts and giving gifts to the man who made it possible for them to do so.

Females do not attend schools as do males. They are expected merely to learn how to pray and how to obey. Their importance to the Jahanka community derives from their being marriageable daughters, wives who are liable to bear many children, laborers in rice fields and persons who will perform domestic chores.

Every Jahanka village has one or two lineages whose members specialize in commerce. Some years back, commerce seems to have been of even greater importance to certain Jahanka families than it is today. There was a time when Jahanka merchants brought slaves to work on Jahanka farms. Also, Jahanka merchants were important itinerant Senegambian traders during the several centuries when that area participated heavily in the Atlantic slave trade. Today, Jahanka merchants trade more in such basic commodities as paper, soap, coffee, printed cloth and batteries—some of the few items not produced by the Jahanka community.

The artisans of a Jahanka village have their own special tasks. Blacksmiths are most frequently engaged in manufacturing and repairing tools used on farms. Leatherworkers tan hides that are used to cover the amulets and charms made by magical practitioners. Members of these artisanal groups serve as messengers for lineage heads, and they act as unbiased councils when disputes take place or when goods are to be divided among lineages. Though endogamous, the artisan lineages are in no way despised. Children of these lineages may attend Jahanka schools to the highest levels save for magical instruction.

As with many West African groups, slavery among the Jahanka is an institution that was once widely recognized but is now not so openly discussed. Large

Jahanka families sometimes measured their wealth and status by the numbers of slaves they possessed. For these reasons the Jahanka clung to the institution long after colonial governments made slavery illegal. In fact, according to a man who lived and studied among the Jahanka in the 1970s, "For many purposes the institution of slavery (among the Jahanka) continues to exist today and slave families remain distinctly separate from the free-born."

Yet in spite of their educational institutions and their often exceptional agricultural production, Jahanka villages are best known for being places to visit for magical services. Divination is probably the most common of these services. Many Senegambians wish to know what the future holds for them, and Jahanka diviners are reputed to be the best in West Africa. Others come to Jahanka magical practitioners to be prayed for. Important Jahanka *shaikhs* spend whole days or several days secluded in prayer for clients. Persons obtain charms from Jahanka clerics for all sorts of reasons. Some make a person intelligent, some ward off dangers, including illness and the malice of enemies, and some work more specifically, to absolve one of guilt in a court case, for example, or to protect one from accident on a long trip. Few Senegambians fail to have such charms on their bodies or about their houses.

Jahanka medical practitioners tend to specialize—some treat ear problems best, some deal best with stomach disorders, some are best at treating mental illness. Throughout much of Senegambia, there is a referral system where sick clients are referred to the Jahanka specialist who can best serve them. Much Jahanka medical practice is based upon use of medicines derived from flora and fauna of Senegambia, some of it of proven medicinal value. Jahanka villages are often purposefully located near forests where certain plants or trees grow, so the villages' medical practitioners can make easy use of their leaves, bark or roots.

Because their religion is one of the cornerstones of their ethnic identity, virtually all Jahanka are Muslims—Sunnis following loosely the Maliki rite. Over the last 150 years or more, they have incorporated the teachings of the Qadiriyya Sufi order with their unique, Suwarian form of Islam. For some Jahanka, possession of knowledge of the Qadiriyya litany is an indicator that an individual has attained the highest levels of magical training from a Jahanka expert.

The depth of their religious feelings are manifest in Jahanka personal values. While respect is accorded with increasing age, greater respect is associated with levels of learning and with those who give outward evidence of being particularly blessed by God. A Jahanka attains such blessedness through regular prayer and recitation and through leading a life of piety. Thus, Jahanka who are most admired are those who are sober, contemplative, lacking in concern for worldly affairs and possessions, generous and even-tempered. Loud, boastful, irresponsible people, or those who are negligent towards either their family duties or educational pursuits do not earn respect. Jahanka consider a person to be succeeding in life if through his activities he has enabled his lineage to achieve considerable economic gain. However, it is important to consider how the individual obtains economic success. Wealthy schoolmasters and magical practitioners are more highly regarded than wealthy merchants. Persons who leave the village and become wealthy in non-traditional ways are not regarded with favor. Respect for Jahanka women is related to the number of children they bear and to the general support they give to their husbands and their lineages. Artisans' status is related to their abilities to perform their crafts.

Jahanka celebrate passage through normal stages of life much like the Mandinka. There is a naming ceremony when a newborn child reaches one week in age; a ceremony following circumcision, which takes place early in age; and an elaborate ceremony at marriage. The marriage rite is filled with much symbolism relating to the Jahanka heritage and the continued unity of the Jahanka lineages. Besides celebrating the usual Islamic holy days of Id al Kabir (Adha), Id al Fitr and the Prophet's birthday, Jahanka celebrate as major rites of passage successful completion of various stages in the curriculum of the Islamic school.

In recent decades changes normally associated with "modernization" have been having serious effects on Jahanka communities. The move towards urbanization has had the most serious impact. Jahanka clerics need large student populations (for their farm labor) and wealthy people requiring their services to remain economically viable. Because much wealth is increasingly found in urban areas, Jahanka clerics have been moving to cities. There, where school buildings are difficult to secure and where they face competition from the growing secular opportunities, the clerics have difficulty operating schools on their usual large scale. Even when they do operate large urban schools, land is scarce and the students cannot be used to work on their teachers' fields as was done in the rural community.

Recent events have been causing the pool of good, serious students to shrink, too. Many first sons of magical practitioners—the ones who traditionally would have unchallenged opportunity to study Jahanka teachings through the highest and most secret levels—are now availing themselves of scholarships from Islamic countries of North Africa. Other capable Jahanka young men are finding new ways of attaining wealth and prestige without studying for 25 years.

The result is the alteration of the centuries-old Suwarian chain of Islamic education and the serious erosion of the prestige associated with being a learned Jahanka. In a group where this chain of teaching and the status associated with it is fundamental to the Jahanka sense of identity and ethnicity, one has to question what the distant future may hold for the continued existence of this unique group of West African clerics.

BIBLIOGRAPHY

Books

Curtin, Philip D. *Economic Change in Precolonial Africa: Senegambia in the Era of the Slave Trade*. Madison: University of Wisconsin Press, 1975.

————. "Pre-Colonial Trading Networks and Traders: The Diakhanke." In *The Development of Indigenous Trade and Markets in West Africa*, edited by Claude Meillassoux. London: Oxford University Press, 1971.

Fisher, Humphrey J., and Fisher, Allen G. B. *Slavery and Muslim Society in Africa.* Garden City, N.Y.: Doubleday, 1971.

Sanneh, Lamin O. *The Jahanke: The History of an Islamic Clerical People of the Senegambia.* London: International African Institute, 1979.

Suret-Canale, Jean. "Touba in Guinea—Holy Place of Islam." In *African Perspectives: Papers in the History, Politics and Economics of Africa Presented to Thomas Hodgkin*, edited by Christopher Allen and R. W. Johnson. Cambridge: Cambridge University Press, 1970.

Wilks, Ivor. "The Transmission of Islamic Learning in the Western Sudan." In *Literacy in Traditional Societies*, edited by Jack Goody. Cambridge: Cambridge University Press, 1968.

Articles

Hunter, Thomas C. "The Jabi Ta'rikhs: Their Significance in West African Islam." *The International Journal of African Historical Studies* 9 (1976): 435–457.

Sanneh, Lamin O. "The Origins of Clericalism in West African Islam." *Journal of African History* 17 (1976): 49–72.

————. "Slavery, Islam and the Jahanke People of West Africa." *Africa* 46 (1976): 80–95.

Unpublished Manuscript

Hunter, Thomas C. "The Development of an Islamic Tradition of Learning among the Jahanka of West Africa." Ph.D. dissertation, University of Chicago, 1977.

Donald R. Wright

JAT Probably more than 30 million Jat live in the Indian subcontinent. They are not a homogeneous ethno-linguistic group; rather, they are immersed in several ethnic groups in which they retain an identity, often based upon occupation and heritage. They speak the language and usually share the religion of the people among whom they live. They will not be found in any modern census; the last census report on them, in 1931, showed about 6 million in the Punjab.

Most Jat are Hindu and Sikh and live in India, concentrated in Punjab Province, where they are mainly hardworking farmers. Perhaps 10 million are Muslim, nearly all of whom live in the various provinces of Pakistan. Others live in small communities in Indian Kutch, Saurashtra, Rajasthan and such large cities as Delhi, Ahmedabad, Jaipur and Bombay, where they are mostly traders, laborers and, to a small extent, minstrels. Indeed, as some of the Jat may be the precursors of Gypsies, they may well live throughout the world (see Gypsies).

Most historians agree that the Jat arrived in the subcontinent as invaders and migrants from Central Asia during the great migrations two or three thousand years ago. But unlike other invaders such as the Rajput, the Jat did not establish ruling dynasties. By language and appearance they were presumably Indo-Iranian who in the course of time mixed with other waves of invaders and older Indian inhabitants, especially in the Punjab and Sind. And while the word "Jat" lives on today, it no longer means what it did in the past.

Early historical records indicate that while the ancient Indians and Persians called the people Jat, the Arabs called them Zutt. In Persia and the Arab world, "Jat" and "Zutt" became synonymous with "Indian," regardless of the ethnic origin of the Indians involved.

The Persian poet Ferdowsi reports that the Sasanian king, Bahram Gur (A.D. 420–438) invited 10,000 musicians from India to embellish one of the national festivities. The Arab historian, Hamza al Isfahani, called them Zutt. Bahram was so pleased with their musical performances that he wanted them to stay on. He granted them land, oxen and grain. But as they were minstrels and not peasants, they ate the oxen and grain and let the land lie barren. The enraged Bahram Gur expelled them from his country. They turned west and south and remained what they had been, minstrels. These are said to be the first known ancestors of the European Gypsies.

At the same time Bahram Gur was being entertained by the Zutt minstrels, Jat divisions were fighting in the Persian army. They were much valued for their fighting qualities and were accepted without regard to their caste or ethnic origin.

As long as a strong Persian empire defended its northern and eastern boundaries, invaders from Central Asia were forced to press wave after wave into northwestern India. The inhabitants, including the Jat, gave way to them, some retiring westward into southern Persia and Mesopotamia, some southward. In regions along the Indus River that were not irrigated by its canal systems, only cattle breeders could exist, and among these were the Jat. Buffalo breeders were the most successful emigrants from Sind to the west. Their animals, although slow in walking, were excellent swimmers. They could keep swimming for days, forming themselves into a kind of raft by placing the head of one on the neck of the next animal. The exact route of migration is not known, but somehow they went along the Arabian seacoast. Arab historians, who called them "Zutt," report that they and their buffalo reached Mesopotamia in the first centuries A.D. That they came from Sind and not from the Punjab can be proved by the races of their domesticated buffalo. They are the same in Iraq and Sind, whereas Punjabi buffalo have different characteristics.

The Zutt of Iraq, who lived in the marshes for the benefit of their animals, made trouble for the pre- and post-Islamic Arabs. Reports exist of fights and deportations, of revolts and emigrations. It is likely that they reached Egypt, the lands around the Black Sea, and in the end, Europe. To all these countries they introduced the water buffalo directly or indirectly.

With the spreading of Islam the westward movement of the Zutt or Jat came to an end. The soldierly Jat, who were still defending the Persian kingdom, were the first to encounter the Arabian armies. In a second line stood those Jat who were guarding the border of the Indian kingdoms. In Sind, kings Rai and Chach, with the help of Jat, were reconverting the population to Brahmanism. They were opposed by the then ruling Buddhist chiefs, who were also helped by the Jat. But Brahmans and Buddhists alike had to give way to the Islamic Arabs. In A.D. 711 Arab armies invaded and conquered Sind. Arab and Persian historians report about the first encounters between conquerors and Jat. The Jat who were followers of the Brahmans, who had come to an agreement with the Arabs, were treated benevolently. But if they were followers of Buddhists who were fighting the Arabs as allies of the Brahmans, they were treated severely and degraded in every possible way. Still the inhabitants of Sind and India were called indiscriminately Zutt or Jat in the generic sense of "Indian."

The inter-Islamic controversies during the first centuries after Muhammad had as one consequence the settling down of a group of temporarily powerful heretics, the Qarmatians, in Sind from the Indus delta up to Multan. They came mainly by sea from Bahrain, where a colony of seafaring Sindhis or Jat had made a good living as traders. (Colonies of such Sindhi traders were plentiful along the coast of the Persian Gulf and of East Africa.) It seems that the whole population of Sind became confessors of the Qarmatian creed, following the example of the then ruling Sumra. Later on the Kalhoras (1736–1778) revived some of their heretic thoughts and practices. It is said that even today Sindhi *pirs* show lingerings of the Qarmatian doctrines (see Sindhis).

It was to convert the Qarmatians that the Ghaznavids and Ghorids invaded India. Under the pretext of having orders from the caliph to reconvert the people to the true faith, they conquered part of the Punjab and Sind down to Multan. Again the inhabitants of the Punjab and Multan were called generically Jat, and very soon they were displaying their fighting spirit. Mahmud of Ghazni incorporated Jat into his army and sent them west to fight against his enemies, who were partly Turkish extraction, as was he himself.

From this time onward the main historical events did not happen in the west–east direction but in the north–south. The Jat outside the Indian subcontinent lost their importance. After the twelfth century their name is mentioned only occasionally.

The last invasion of special importance to the Jat were the Baluch, who descended from the mountains west of Sind. They were slowly driven from their old habitats near Kerman to the east and southeast. In the eleventh centuries they began their descent into the Kachhi plain in small unobtrusive groups. In the following centuries their number increased. They had first no intention of conquering Sind, although their social organization, the *tuman*, was a fighting confederation. They gained political importance when Sindhi rulers asked for their military help. In this respect they were first mentioned in the fifteenth century as auxiliary forces to the Langah ruler of Multan. When in the seventeenth century the dynasty of the Kalhora declined, the Talpur-Baluch came to political power, and Baluch, after 1786, were the domineering group of Lower and Upper Sind (see Baluch).

In the *tuman* confederations of the Baluch were strong elements of Jat who had emigrated from the Indus plain to the region of Kalat and the Sulaiman range to avoid the raiding groups of the Ghaznavids, Ghorids and Moghuls. Like the Baluch themselves they had a preference for raising camels. They became the "Jatt," the camel drivers of the Baluch. This is the reason why "Jatt" in Lower Sind is synonymous with "camel driver." Such a Jatt could be anything but birth, such as Jokhia, a Sumra or a Samma (ethnic groups). At the same time the peasants of Sind were still to a great part Jat by birth. To a Baluch, who despised all sedentary people tilling the land, Jat became a generic name for all small farmers and tenants, which they used contemptuously. To distinguish themselves from these suppressed and despised Jat, the camel-rearing and camel-driving Jat called themselves Jat-Baluch or Mir-Jat, the camel drivers of the Baluchi Mirs.

These differences in the meaning of the name "Jat" according to time, place and people give the background to an understanding of the use of this name at present. The majority of linguists are of the opinion that "Jat" in the Punjab, "Jat" in Upper Sind and "Jatt" in Lower Sind designate one and the same people, the differences in pronunciation being only dialectical. Nevertheless, now as in former times, "Jat" has a different meaning for whoever uses the name. In Lower Sind the occupational meaning has superseded the ethnic one. Every camel driver is called Jat, may he be even a Baluch by birth. As "Jatt" also means "stupid" in Sindhi, every man called Jat is tinged by this word similarly. The land-tilling Jat of Upper Sind are to the Baluch the prototype of the submissive, hardworking peasant. Contemptuously he calls all landworking classes Jat, giving thus the ethnic name an occupational meaning. A special case is the tribe of Jat-Baluch in the Indus delta, formed by many groups of cattle-breeding and landworking Jat under the rule or the guidance of a Baluch family.

Fate has been most kind to the Jat of the Punjab. There they are the husbandmen par excellence, and their social standing is one of the highest. So "Jat" as a husbandman became again known as a generic term in the Punjab. Uncertain is the meaning of "Jat" in the western Punjab. If a man is looked upon as a husbandman like the eastern Punjabi Jat his status is high. If somebody compares him to the domineering Rajput, his status is relatively low. This explains why some Jat groups are esteemed husbandmen, others indifferent peasants, still others despised working classes in the Baluch sense.

There have been Jat in Afghanistan since pre-Islamic times, when they were inhabitants of the eastern Iranian mountains and plains. There they received land from Hindu rulers, who used them as guardians of their borderlands. English travellers and officials reported them to be numerous (perhaps 600,000) even in the eighteenth century. They were landowners, camel drivers and enterprising members of trading caravans. In the nineteenth century it was said, "Everywhere you meet a Jat and a Kirar [Sindhi trader]." At the same time there were other

Jat, wandering minstrels, thieves and robbers. They roamed from Kandahar and Kabul in the east, to Herat and Mashad in the west. They seem to have been of the same strain that enraged Bahram Gur.

The landowning, camel-driving Jat are no longer mentioned in twentieth-century Afghanistan. In 1964 it was difficult to find a descendant of the Jat in Kabul, where it is known they are still occupied as their ancestors were with transport by caravans. As nothing is known about a massacre of Jat by the Soviet armies since 1981, it is to be supposed that they are now incorporated into other groups, most probably the Baluch in a generic sense, as these people now stand in the same landowning and camel-rearing position as once the Jat did.

The minstrel Jat exist today in Afghanistan. Their number is small, about 13,000 persons, but their reputation is as bad as ever. They are said to kidnap children, to prostitute their women, to steal wherever possible. They live by smithery, selling wicker baskets, playing the tambourin harmonium, singing and dancing and trading horses. This could be a description of the former European Gypsies. Aparna Rao characterizes them as people of the white tents, similar to those in Pakistan, where they are called ''Nath.'' To look into the origin of white tents, in marked contrast to the black tents of the cattle breeders, may be a rewarding task.

Thus it is that the word ''Jat,'' as a name, has been in use for more than 1,500 years. At least in India there have been groups called Jat throughout this period. Continuing integration and disintegration has transformed these ancient groups in a process of adaptation to changing historical and geographical conditions. Other groups repeatedly used the name ''Jat'' in a different generic sense, further confusing its ethnic meaning in a given context. Nevertheless, the name ''Jat'' somehow has been preserved. The task remains to determine the ethnic meaning of this word with respect to time, locality and people.

BIBLIOGRAPHY

Books

Baines, Sir Athelstane. *Grundriss der Indo-Arischen Philologie und Altertumskunde.* Vol. 2, no. 5. *Ethnography, Castes and Tribes.* Strassburg: J. Trübner, 1912.
Bray, Denys. *Census of India, 1911.* Vol. 4. *Baluchistan.* Calcutta: Superintendent, Government Printing, 1913.
Burton, Sir Richard F. *Sindh and the Races that Inhabit the Valley of the Indus, with Notices of Topography and History of the Province.* Karachi: Oxford University Press, 1851.
Cunningham, Joseph Davey. *A History of the Sikhs from the Origin of the Nation to the Battle of the Sutlej.* Reprint ed. Oxford: Oxford University Press, 1955.
''Djat.'' In *Encyclopaedia of Islam.* Vol. 2. Leiden: Brill; London: Luzac, 1965.
Ibbetson, Sir Denzil. *Punjab Castes, Being a reprint of the Chapter ''The Races, Castes and Tribes of the People.''* In the *Report on the Census of the Punjab.* Reprint

ed. Lahore: Superintendent, Government Printing, 1916. (Originally published 1883.)

Lambrick, H. T. *Sind, A General Introduction.* History of Sind Series, 1. Hyderabad (Sind), India: Sindhi Adabi Board, 1964.

Articles

Rao, Aparna. "Qui sont les Jats d'Afghanistan?" *Afghanistan Journal* 8:2 (1981): 55–64.

Westphal-Hellbusch, S. and Westphal, H. "Zur Geschichte und Kultur der Jat." *Forschungen zur Ethnologie und Sozialpsychologie.* Vol. 7. Edited by Hilde Thurnwald. Berlin: Duncker and Humblot, 1968.

Sigrid Westphal-Hellbusch

JAVANESE   The Javanese, the world's third largest Muslim ethnic group (after Arabs and Bengalis), occupy the central and eastern part of the island of Java, the fifth largest island of the island nation of Indonesia. They call themselves Weng Jawa or Tiyang Jawi in polite speech. The Indonesian term is Orang Jawa. They form the largest ethnic group (58 million) of the extremely plural population of the Indonesian republic, itself the nation with the world's largest Muslim population.

There are also Javanese on other islands of Indonesia, such as South Kalimantan (South Borneo) and North Sulawesi (North Celebes). Additional large Javanese groups are to be found in south and east Sumatra. Because Dutch colonialists had for two centuries moved Javanese laborers overseas, there are also Javanese communities in South Africa, Surinam in South America and New Caledonia in Melanesia.

As citizens of a modern unitary nation, the Javanese recognize the Bahasa Indonesia, the Indonesian national language, and they communicate in that language during their work or in conversations with persons from other Indonesian ethnic groups. At home, however, they speak their own native language, Javanese, which is different and mutually unintelligible in relation to Bahasa Indonesia.

The Javanese language has a long literary history which goes back to the eighth century, its own script deriving from the fourth-century south Indian Pallawa script. Today's Javanese is characterized by an elaborate system of styles. There are nine styles of speech that incorporate obligatory distinctions according to differences in status, rank, age and degree of acquaintance between addressee and addresser. In the Javanese conception, these styles constitute language levels, the one more formal and polite and therefore ranking higher than the other. The drastic changes which have occurred in Javanese society, especially after World War II, have had a considerable impact upon the system. After the war, many Javanese did not attempt to master the speech levels adequately, and the current process of change from traditional agrarian and feudalistic society to a modern industrial and democratic one will no doubt simplify the system in a not too distant future. Moreover, the use of Bahasa Indonesia has now become an easy way out for a Javanese who is uncertain about the accurate use of the correct style of speech in addressing another Javanese, due to uncertainty about the latter's status in relation to his own.

Nearly all Javanese, about 90 percent, are Muslim. The remaining 10 percent are Roman Catholic, Protestant Christians, Buddhists or recent converts in south central Java to Hinduism.

In the earliest stages of conversion to Islam in the thirteenth century, the commercial aristocracy in the port towns of northern Java had also adopted many elements of mysticism that seem to have characterized south Indian Islam. As mysticism had long played an important role in the Hindu-Buddhist Javanese religion during the pre-Islamic period, it stimulated the easy acceptance of Islam among the Javanese. More orthodox Sunni teachings of the Shafi school of law were acquired at a later period of Javanese pilgrims on their return from Mecca.

During the fifteenth century, Islam penetrated into the interior regions of east and central Java through the zealous activities of Muslim missionaries who became holy men (*wali*) in Javanese folklore. In the inland regions, where pre-Islamic Hindu and Buddhist Javanese cultural and religious traditions were strongest, the influence of Islam was less strong, and the religion was modified into a typically Javanese kind of Islam, combining Hindu-Buddhist Javanese religious concepts with Muslim beliefs. The Javanese themselves continued to call this Javanese version of Islam the Agami Jawi or Kejawen, or sometimes in a degrading manner, Islam Abangan (Red Muslims). They make a clear distinction between people who adhere to the Kejawen religion and those who practice the more puritan kind of Islam, who are called Santri Muslims.

There is no way of estimating the proportion of the Javanese population who adhere to Kejawen and the proportion to Santri within the total Javanese population. Although the former seems to be more dominant in the interior regions and the latter more in the coastal regions, there are no two geographically distinct areas which both categories of Javanese Muslims can consider to be their homeland.

The Kejawen Muslims do not strictly follow Islamic principles. They do not, for example, perform the daily or weekly prayers, nor do they fast during the month of Ramadan. They do not seriously observe the strong Muslim taboo against eating pork. However, like any other Muslim, they firmly believe and have solemnly declared that "there is no God but Allah, and Muhammad is His Prophet."

The Kejawen peasants live in overcrowded village communities and are primarily engaged in subsistence wet rice agriculture on miniscule plots of irrigated fields or, in particular areas, cultivate sugar and tobacco for large government or semi-government estates. They consider important the rice goddess Dewi Sri (the Javanese version of Shri, Vishnu's wife in Hindu mythology) in fertility rites which are connected with agricultural production. Just as important in the everyday peasant life of the Kejawen Muslims are the numerous malevolent and benevolent spirits that inhabit the countryside in wells, at crossroads, in big banyan trees and in numerous other places. These spirits figure prominently not only in ceremonies at significant points in the life cycle of the Javanese individual but also in magic, curing and sorcery.

In the towns and cities of Java which still have, with one or two exceptions, a largely preindustrial character (being mainly administrative centers rather than centers of industry and commerce), living patterns are dominated by the culture and life-style of the gentry or civil servant class called *priyayi*. Some of these people, who subscribe to the Kejawen Muslim world view, basically follow the same belief system as the peasants, although in a more sophisticated way. Javanese *priyayi* philosophers, for example, have developed elaborate teachings on the Javanese concept of fate, on the correct attitude towards fate, death and calamity and on the most adequate way of dealing with supernatural beings. In addition, the *priyayi* style of life places great value on mysticism. In order to attain the mystical state and to come to an experience of God within the self, one must concentrate one's entire mental capacity towards that end, deny as far as possible one's physical needs and practice meditation. Various religious movements and organizations (*kebatinan*) that offer mystical and other kinds of spiritual enlightment to their members under leadership of a teacher (*guru*) flourish in *priyayi* society today.

In contrast to both Kejawen peasants and *priyayi*, the Santri are very concerned with formal Islamic doctrine and look down on the Kejawen concepts and beliefs of the supernatural world. Santri Muslims are present at all social levels of Javanese society, among the peasantry in rural areas, among the lower levels of urban population who are engaged in manual labor, among the urban commercial class and even among the white collar *priyayi*. They are predominant, however, in the commercial class.

In some areas of central and east Java, Santri Muslim mystical or Sufi *tariqa* movements are prevalent. A number of Santri, but also Kejawen religious movements, carry the messiah (Ratu Adil) idea.

The central ritual in Kejawen religion is the *selamatan*. This involves a communal sacred meal, either very simple or very elaborate, depending on the importance of the occasion and the financial resources of the host. It has the function of promoting *selamat* (emotional calm) and is conducted in association with life-cycle ceremonies, with the Muslim calendar, with agricultural production and fertility rites and with the social integration of the village. *Selamatan* ceremonies are also performed at special occasions, such as before leaving on a long trip, on changing residence, on taking a new personal name, after recovering from an illness or upon fulfillment of vows.

Although the *selamatan* is mainly connected with the Kejawen Muslims, the Santri sometimes participate in *selamatan* meals and even perform *selamatan* rituals themselves, but less frequently and restricted generally to burial and mortuary ceremonies.

The Javanese household usually consists of one nuclear family, although in a number of areas the uxorilocal extended family has become the statistical pattern. Polygyny is rare. Among the peasants only slightly more than 1 percent practice polygyny, and among the lower-class non-white collar town and city population, the percentage is slightly higher, whereas among the *priyayi* it is also rare, due probably to the influence of secular education. Beyond the nuclear family, no significant kin group exists except for a small occasional bilateral kindred who gather at celebrations and a limited ambilineal kin group to care for the ancestral graves.

In the early twentieth century a Javanese, K.H.A. Dahlan (b. 1868), brought Islamic reformist ideas to Indonesia. Under the influence of the Islamic modernist, Muhammad Abduh of Al Azhar University in Cairo, Dahlan founded the Indonesian reform movement, the Muhammadiya, in 1912 in central Java. This later became a nationwide movement working actively in education, social welfare and religious reform. Attacking not only Kejawen syncretism but also Santri scholasticism and mysticism, the Muhammadiya became a threat to rural religious leaders who consequently reacted by forming a counter-organization, the Nahdatul Ulema (Union of Muslim Scholars) in 1926 in east Java. This organization also developed into an Indonesian nationwide organization, especially after independence in 1950, when it became a strong Indonesian political party which represented orthodox Islamic ideology.

Education in postwar Indonesia experienced a tremendous explosion. During the pre-war colonial period in 1940, there were only 105 public and private secondary schools (including those exclusively for the Dutch), providing education to about 22,400 students. By 1968 there were 4,515 secondary schools providing education to some 1.2 million students. In 1940 Indonesia had three colleges and not a single university; 28 years later the nation had 363 institutions of higher education, divided into 40 state universities, 87 colleges of Islamic theology, 236 registered private universities and over 200 vocational colleges. About one-fourth of all these institutions were located in Java, and roughly one-third of the 118,000 students were Javanese.

Cultural values and ideals which came from the West through formal education, the revolution, the disruption of tradition and political upheavals during Indonesia's decolonization have all had great impact on Javanese orientation. Many Javanese now accept life with grace rather than as a necessary evil where endeavor is restricted by fate. Many are now much more achievement-oriented and find satisfaction and pride in the endeavor towards achievement itself, rather than considering endeavor as merely a means to subsist. Many are also more future-oriented now.

In cities such as Surabaya, where banking systems, life insurance companies and the total monetary structure are beginning to stabilize and to stimulate confidence among the public, many Javanese are beginning to save for their future. The increasing use of the democratic Indonesian language and the development of a more democratic Indonesian social etiquette diminish the traditional hierarchic character of the *priyayi* value orientation.

While these new values are emerging in cities among the educated Javanese, the countryside, of course, moves more slowly. There, the traditional and conservative value systems prevail.

R. M. Koentjaraningrat
Population figures updated by Richard V. Weekes

BIBLIOGRAPHY

Books

Anderson, Benedict R. *Mythology and the Tolerance of the Javanese*. Ithaca: Cornell University Press, 1965.

Burger, D. H. *Structural Changes in Javanese Society: The Supra-Village Sphere*. Ithaca: Cornell University Press, 1956.

Cooley, Frank L. *Indonesia: Church and Society*. New York: Friendship Press, 1968.

Critchfield, Richard. *The Golden Bowl Be Broken: Peasant Life in Four Cultures*. Bloomington: Indiana University Press, 1973.

Dewey, Alice. *Peasant Marketing in Java*. New York: Free Press of Glencoe, 1962.

Drewes, G.W.J. "Indonesia: Mysticism and Activism." In *Unity and Variety in Muslim Civilization*, edited by G. D. von Grunebaum. Chicago: University of Chicago, 1955.

Geertz, Clifford. *Islam Observed*. Chicago: University of Chicago Press, 1968.

————. "The Javanese Village." In *Local, Ethnic, and National Loyalties in Village Indonesia: A Symposium*, edited by G. William Skinner. South East Asia Studies. New Haven: Yale University Press, 1959.

————. *Modjokuto: Religion in Java*. Cambridge: MIT Center for International Studies, 1958.

————. *Peddlers and Princes*. Chicago: University of Chicago Press, 1963.

————. *The Religion of Java*. New York: Free Press, 1960.

————. *The Social History of an Indonesian Town*. Cambridge: MIT Center for International Studies, 1965.

Geertz, Hildred. *The Javanese Family: A Study of Kinship and Socialization*. New York: Free Press of Glencoe, 1961.

Gille, Halvor, and Pardoko, R. H. "A Family Life Study in East Java." In *Family Planning and Population Programs*, edited by B. Berelson, et al. Chicago: University of Chicago Press, 1966.

Holt, Claire, ed. *Culture and Politics in Indonesia*. Ithaca: Cornell University Press, 1972.

Jay, Robert R. *Javanese Villagers*. Cambridge: MIT Center for International Studies, 1969.

Koentjaraningrat, R. N. "The Javanese of South Central Java." In *Social Structure in Southeast Asia*, edited by George P. Murdock. Chicago: Quadrangle Press, 1960.

————. *Some Socio-Anthropological Observations on Gotong-Rojong Practices in Two Villages in Central Java*. Ithaca: Cornell University Press, 1961.

————. *Villages in Indonesia*. Ithaca: Cornell University Press, 1967.

LeBar, Frank M., ed. *Ethnic Groups of Insular Southeast Asia*. New Haven: Human Relations Area Files Press, 1972.

Liddle, R. William. *Ethnicity, Party, and National Integration: An Indonesian Case Study*. New Haven: Yale University Press, 1970.
Lyon, Margo L. *Bases of Conflict in Rural Java*. Berkeley: University of California Center for South and Southeast Asia Studies, 1970.
Nieuwenhuijze, Christoffel A. O. van. *Aspects of Islam in Post-Colonial Indonesia: Five Essays*. The Hague: W. van Hoeve, 1958.
Peacock, James L. *Indonesia: An Anthropological Perspective*. Pacific Palisades, Cal.: Goodyear, 1973.
———. *Javanese Folkdrama and Social Change*. Cambridge: Harvard University Press, 1965.
———. *Muslim Puritans*. Berkeley: University of California Press, 1978.
Vreede-de-Stuers, Cora. "Indonesia." In *Women in the Modern World*, edited by Raphael Patai. London: Free Press, 1967.
Vreeland, Nina, et al. *Area Handbook for Indonesia*. 3rd ed. The American University FAS, DA Pam 550-39. Washington, D.C.: Government Printing Office, 1975.
Wallace, Ben J. *Village Life in Insular Southeast Asia*. Boston: Little, Brown, 1971.

Articles

Geertz, Clifford. "The Javanese Kikaji: The Changing Role of a Cultural Broker." *Comparative Studies in Society and History* 2 (1960): 228–249.
Geertz, Hildred. "Latah in Java: A Theoretical Paradox." *Indonesia* 5 (1968): 93–104.
Peacock, James L. "Ritual, Entertainment, and Modernization: A Javanese Case." *Comparative Studies in Society and History* 10:3 (1968): 328–334.
Soepomo, Poedjosoedarmo. "Javanese Speech Levels." *Indonesia* 6 (1968): 54–81.

K

KALAGANS   The Kalagans, who live on the southern island of Mindanao in the Philippines, are Tagakaolos who have become Muslim by virtue of contacts and/or intermarriage with their Maguindanao neighbors. Their name, sometimes spelled Calagan or Karagan, connotes "imitators" and has reference to the fact that some Tagakaolos have adopted the dress, customs and religion of the Philippine Muslims (see Maguindanao).

There are about 8,000 Kalagans, found mainly in various municipalities along the coast and in the hinterland to the west of the Davao Gulf. They are agriculturalists, and a few in Tagum, Davao del Norte, are plantation laborers. Kalagans living on the coast are also fishermen.

There have been Kalagan Muslims for generations, but Islamization is still occurring among the Tagakaolo pagan hillsmen. One sometimes meets Kalagans whose fathers or grandfathers were not Muslim. Younger Kalagans report that the "old folks" still talk of belief in *enkantos, diwatas* and the divine spirits in trees, fish and other objects. The Kalagans retain their ancestral Tagakaolo language (related to Mansaka), a Central Philippine subgroup.

BIBLIOGRAPHY

Book

Lebar, Frank M. *Ethnic Groups of Insular Southeast Asia.* Vol. 2. *Philippines and Formosa.* New Haven: Human Relations Area Files, 1975.

Article

Gowing, Peter G. "The Growing List of Filipino Muslim Groups." *Dansalan Research Center Reports* 1:2 (1975): 5–6.

Peter G. Gowing

KALIBUGANS   The term "Kalibugan" means "mixed breed." The Kalibugans are people of Subanon in the Philippines who have intermarried with Tausug or Samal and thus acquired the name. They identify themselves as Muslim.

The Kalibugans (or Kolibugans) are a peaceful people found scattered in hamlets along the coasts of the Zamboango del Norte and Zamboanga del Sur provinces in western Mindanao. Numbering about 15,500, they are farmers and fishermen who do some trading, ironworking and matmaking as subsidiary activities. Their language is Subanon, but culturally they are a blend of their Tausug and Sama kinsmen, both of whom tend to look down upon them socially.

BIBLIOGRAPHY

Book

Lebar, Frank M. *Ethnic Groups of Insular Southeast Asia.* Vol. 2. *Philippines and Formosa.* New Haven: Human Relations Area Files, 1975.

Article

Gowing, Peter G. "The Growing List of Filipino Muslim Groups." *Dansalan Research Center Reports* 1:2 (1975): 5–6.

Peter G. Gowing

KAMBERI   Ethnic survival and the use of Islam to gain advantages distinguish the Muslim Kamberi of Nigeria. The Kamberi, most of whom are traditionalists in religion, live in the tropical savanna in an area encompassing the states of Kwara, Niger and Sokoto. Including related groups, they number more than 700,000; however, the core Kamberi number only about 100,000, of whom some 10,000 are Muslim. Being spread over such a large area, their minority status is assured wherever they live. Kamberi are increasingly turning to Islam.

The Kamberi claim to be the original rulers of the ancient Yauri emirate in Sokoto State. That claim is recognized in the special relationship prevailing between the current Emir of Yauri, a Hausa, and Kamberi from the Ngaski District. The only Hausa with tribal marks in Yauri are members of the royal family. Their marks are Kamberi ones featuring a rising sun on the stomach and pectorals.

The Kamberi language belongs to the Plateau division of the Benue-Congo branch of the Niger-Congo language family. Two other languages of that division are centered in Yauri, Reshe and Dukawa (see Reshawa).

Like the Dukawa, with whom they share a joking relationship and a common origin myth, the Kamberi were in Yauri quite early. Some authors claim they were there before the thirteenth century and were, in fact, Yauri's first inhabitants. Certainly they had a centralized government by the time of the Mali and Songhay invasions after the thirteenth century.

Before that time, the Kamberi say that their ancestors came from Mecca in Arabia. There, a leader named Kisra led a resistance movement against the Prophet Muhammad. After his defeat, Kisra fled across Africa, and either he or his followers founded a number of states. Finally, depending upon the myth's version, either he or his followers stopped at the Niger River. The Kamberi trace their direct descent from Lata, one of the Kisra's sons, and still maintain a shrine to him at Agwarra, Borgu Division, Kwara State.

Not surprisingly, Kamberi have special relationships with other ethnic groups that claim similar descent. Thus their joking relationship with the Dukawa, with whom they share many ties of culture and language. They also hunt with the Reshawa.

Whatever their origin, the Kamberi have proved highly adaptable. They were left alone for lengthy periods of time in their history and became reknowned horticulturists and adequate hunters. They showed no desire to develop either the trading or fishing resources of the Niger River. Rather, they used their farm surpluses to develop relationships with other ethnic groups, leaving it to others to be commercially enterprising.

In the late seventeenth century a Muslim became Emir of Yauri, a turning point in Yauri's history, as the coming of Islam meant the rise to power of the Hausa in this area of Nigeria. The Hausa and Hausa-ized rulers of Yauri did not immediately turn everyone into Muslims. Some, such as the Reshawa, began to be included as members of the ruling elite through a process that ultimately included changing their ethnic identity. The Kamberi, however, kept their distance while enjoying their special relationship with the Hausa. As newcomers, the Hausa sought to increase their legitimacy by marrying the older elite. Kamberi women were in demand, and one mode of survival was for Kamberi to allow their women to marry into the ruling groups.

The nineteenth century proved to be one that tested Kamberi adaptational skills. The period was one of almost constant civil war and slave raiding, both of which affected the Kamberi harder than any other group as they had a centralized self-governmental system and were non-Muslim. To survive, the Kamberi decentralized, and in place of patrilineages they created autonomous clans. In place of a state organization, they created independent homesteads. In place of participation in the fighting, they fled to the forests where possible. The Kamberi became known as a meek and docile people and became the butt of jokes—a price of survival.

As the prestige of Islam increased in the nineteenth century through the *jihad* of Uthman dan Fodio, the great Fulani religious leader, the plight of non-Muslims worsened. Increasingly they had to make themselves invisible while building alliances with the powerful by contributing their women in marriage to dominant groups.

British rule in the late nineteenth century "froze" the political system. Colonial officials supported Islam, the Hausa and the tax system. Kamberi and other subordinate groups found themselves locked into a system that was far from "traditional" but sanctified as being so.

Kamberi live in a patriarchal, patrilateral society. All property belongs to the men. A woman only has use of property, including that which she may have brought to the marriage. She is given sufficient land on which to raise "women's crops"—dry rice or anything close to the compound, including economically useful trees. Unlike the land, however, on which men grow their crops, her land does not pass to her heirs; only to her husband or sons.

Kamberi women are regarded as an economic asset. They are famed for their chastity and faithfulness, at least in interethnic marriages. And with their reputed gentleness in raising children, they are prized as wives by members of Yauri's other ethnic groups.

Kamberi culture includes a wrestling (for Muslims, boxing) and brideservice complex common to groups in this part of Africa. Wrestling serves to tie males from the same village closely together while bringing them to the notice of eligible young ladies and their parents. Wrestling groups also become work groups. Brideservice is time and labor given by a groom to the father of the bride, a period that might last up to seven years. During that time the groom and his work team go from farm to farm as a unit working for one prospective father-in-law after another.

The Kamberi are exceptional farmers, a fact noted in 1976 at an "Operation Feed the Nation" ceremony in Yauri, when Kamberi were honored guests. They performed the acrobatic dances for which they are famous, sang, played music and then addressed the Emir in a rather cheeky manner: "We are glad to see that you advanced people have decided to follow we poor backward Kamberi by becoming humble farmers." The line drew great laughter and applause and displayed some of the biting wit that Kamberi usually keep hidden.

The Kamberi are magnificent physical specimens, male and female. They eat well. Their farms produce guinea corn, millet and dry rice, while sorghum crops provide the staples. The Kamberi are willing to experiment and participate in various government schemes to try new crops and techniques. Some raise cattle, employing Fulani to care for them. They seem to have no food taboos (except Muslims, who do not eat pork) and otherwise are noted for eating any kind of meat, including a rat-like creature and dogs.

Muslim Kamberi engage in the modern sector and have influential educational and governmental positions. Some also engage in trade. They are careful to observe all Islamic proscriptions, including abstinence from alcohol.

Cooperation with the group and adherence to its rules are of paramount importance to the Kamberi. Behaving in a non-threatening manner is essential to smooth living. Witchcraft, for instance, is the worst possible crime because it strikes at the trust which is essential for Kamberi survival as an ethnic group.

Survival as a major Kamberi value also plays a role in the conversion to Islam. Kamberi are hostile to the ruling Muslim Hausa (many have not forgotten that Muslims made slaves of non-Muslims), although they have a special relationship with the ruling family and marry Hausa women and men. Many adopt Islam to preserve their ethnic identity and are careful to live a scrupulously Islamic life to counter the reputation that Hausa are the only good Muslims. The presence of non-Hausa Muslims in high positions in Yauri offers a new distinction between ethnicity and Islam not readily available before.

In Yauri, Muslim Kamberi have retained their social diffidence. Since they are upwardly mobile, such behavior is instrumental to their purposes. They act politely to Hausa and Fulani despite their hidden antagonism towards them.

Kamberi Muslims are often mistaken for Hausa by Hausa students, who sometimes call them Hausa for the way they act, evidence, perhaps, of Kamberi dissimulation.

In neighboring Agwarra in Kwara State, Kamberi converts behave differently. There, Muslim converts do not act deferentially towards Hausa but are much more assertive. Translated into behavioral terms, "not acting like Kamberi" means they do not display timidity.

Kamberi Muslims do not intend to "become Hausa" and strive to prove that one can be an enterprising Muslim and still be Kamberi. Their ethnic goal is survival in a sea of assimilating Hausa. So far they have been successful at their game.

BIBLIOGRAPHY

Books

Gunn, Harold, and Conant, Francis. *Peoples of the Middle Niger*. London: International African Institute, 1960.
Harris, P. G. *Provincial Gazetteer of Sokoto Province*. London: Waterlow, 1938.
Salamone, Frank A. *Gods and Goods in Africa*. New Haven: HRAFlex, 1974.

Articles

Bertho, J. "Le groupe Kamberi." *Bulletin de l'Institut Français d'Afrique Noir: Section B (Bulletin IFAN)* 14:1 (1952): 264–266.
Harris, P. G. "Notes on Yauri, Sokoto Province, Nigeria." *Journal of the Royal Anthropological Institute of Great Britain and Ireland* 68 (1930): 283–334.
Hoffman, C. "The Noun Class System of Central Kambari." *Journal of West African Language* 2:3 (1963): 160–169.

————. "A Word List of Central Kambari." *Journal of West African Language* 2:2 (1965): 7–31.

Salamone, Frank A. "Children's Games as Mechanisms for Easing Ethnic Interaction." *Anthropos* (1979): 201–210.

————. "Competitive Conversion and Its Implications for Modernization." *Anthropos* 75 (1980): 383–404.

————. "Dukawa-Kamberi Relations of Privileged Familiarity." *Ethnicity* 6:2 (1979): 123–136.

————. "Structures, Stereotypes and Students; Implications for a Theory of Ethnic Interaction." *Council on Anthropology and Education Quarterly* 8:2 (1976): 6–13.

————, and Swanson, Charles. "Identity and Ethnicity." *Ethnic Groups* 2 (1979): 167–183.

Frank A. Salamone

KANEMBU   For centuries the northern part of the Lake Chad basin has been divided between the people of Te in the north and the Kanembu in the south, an area which today is Kanem Province of the Republic of Chad. The Kanembu occupy almost completely the banks of the northern half of Lake Chad with a concentration around the city of Mao (pop. 5,000), the home of their leader, the Alifa. Their territory spreads north to Chitati, where it meets that of the Daza (see Tebu). In the south, their neighbors are the Kanuri of Borno, Nigeria, the Buduma and Kuri of Lake Chad and the various Chadian Arabs of the Dagana country (see Arabs, Chadian; Buduma; Kanuri; Kuri).

It is estimated that the Kanembu number approximately 331,000, with 190,000 in Chad, 135,000 in Nigeria and 6,000 in Niger. They are divided into about 40 lineages, of which the most important are the Dalatoa around Mao, the Ngigim of Dibinentchi, the Kadjidi north of Bol, the Ngaltuku around Ngelea, the Kubri in Liwa, the Tumagri in Ngigmi, Niger and the Magimi in Nigeria.

Kanembu speak a Nilo-Saharan language, Eastern Saharan group, which is also the language of the Tebu, Daza, Zaghawa and especially the Kanuri (see Beri). Despite dialect differences, the Kanembu understand the Kanuri when they visit Nigeria. A distinction can be made between the Kanembu dialect of Lake Chad and that of central Kanem. The Buduma know this dialect difference as they call speakers of the Lake dialect Nganai and speakers of the second Kanurna. Kanembu is not a written language; those who are literate read and write Arabic.

The numerical size of Kanembu and the large territory they occupy indicate that they were once a more powerful people. This is supported by oral traditions and written genealogical lists collected by the great explorers of the nineteenth century, which show that the Kanem empire was indeed significant.

Legend traces Kanembu origins back to a great leader who reigned in Arabia shortly before the arrival of the Prophet Muhammad. When he was converted he took the name Tubba Lawal. A princess of his family had sons who became the eponymic ancestors of the main Kanembu (and Kanuri) lineages. Saif (Sayf) was the ancestor of the Magimi; Derman, ancestor of the Kubri; Tama the ancestor of the Tumagri; Man, ancestor of the Kanku; and two slave sons, Ndjidi and Ngal, became ancestors of the Kadjidis and Maaltuku, respectively, who consider themselves the only true Kanembu.

To reach Kanem from Yemen, where these ancestors were raised, there were two possible roads: the northern road through Fezzan, Tibesti and Kawar; and the eastern road through Kordofan, Darfur and Wadai. Ngal's people took the northern route and Saif's the eastern, and from each derive today's factions, all considered descendants of Tubba Lawal.

Primarily herdsmen, the Kanembu's ancestors migrated to their present locations for a number of reasons. Drought in the north sent many south seeking greener pastures. They were encouraged by the rise of warrior groups such as the Tuareg, themselves claimed descendants of Tubba Lawal. It is known that by the eighth century the Kanembu were beginning to form an empire; this reached its height in the thirteenth century. Their armies occupied Fezzan in the north, Bornu in the west, the lower Chari River areas and the borders of Wadai. With an army of 100,000 men and a strong political and administrative structure based on the Arab models, the Kanem Empire became the most important power in sub-Saharan Africa. It was totally Sunni Muslim.

The empire enriched itself by importing technology. Construction with baked bricks, an innovation, permitted the creation of original architecture in different Kanem capitals, the first being Njima, near present-day Mao. Camel caravans introduced wheat, cotton, horses and camels, which broadened the base of the economy.

Relations with north and northeastern Africa were close, the lingua franca being Arabic. Ibn Khaldun reported that the Kanem sent a giraffe as a gift to the Sultan of Tunis in 1257. Islam was rigorously observed, and in 1243, the Emir built a *madrasa* in Cairo specifically for Kanembu Quranic students.

But the Kanem Empire began to decline under the growing strength of vassals such as the Bululas. The Saif leadership with a vast following moved to Bornu; eventually they became the Kanuri. By the sixteenth century the Bornu Empire controlled the area and Kanem remained only a distant province.

When the French arrived to colonize this part of Africa towards the end of the nineteenth century, they found Kanem ruled by the Alifa of Mao, who, within Bornu hegemony, dominated a few vassal districts and collected a variety of taxes. Kanembu culture, traditions and political organization had been consolidated by then.

Kanem is a Sahelian region, arid (less than 12 inches of annual rainfall), with a landscape of thin, thorny bushes and seasonal vegetation. It rains only in July and August. Villages, composed of houses built of straw with domed roofs, are built midway between the tops of sandy hills and the wadis where water can be found. Each house stands with its back to the east to provide protection from the *harmattan*, a dust-laden wind that blows fiercely in the dry season.

The Kanembu are farmers and stockbreeders. In the north, they practice a short semi-nomadism with their cattle. In the center and south, they are sedentary, raising livestock, cultivating millet on ground fertilized by the manure of their cattle. Many families keep small gardens in the wadis (depressions between sand dunes once or occasionally watered by streams, hence somewhat fertile). In good wadis, farmers can harvest corn twice a year and wheat once.

While the Kuri claim to have invented it, all people living around Lake Chad today make use of the polder, a wadi artificially created by damming a small arm of the lake which then becomes a moist, fertile soil for agriculture. Underground water is less than ten feet away in most polders. Frequently, Kanembu farmers have a surplus of grain, which they export north by camel and across Lake Chad to Nigeria by pirogue.

The Kanembu are enterprising businessmen. The region of Liwa contains natron (sal soda, used in washing and bleaching textiles), which is extracted by Haddad laborers and exported (see Haddad). Many Kanembu are fishermen and operate the fish trade between Kanem and Borno (the current name for Bornu). But the dynamism of commercial life has not led to any significant urbanization in Kanem. The markets, although animated and busy, are in modest villages; the capital, Mao, shows no signs of development. It is a small market town which at most grows only through the arrival of a few hundred refugees when climatic conditions are bad in the Sahel.

The Kanembu have a stable social structure. Each village has a secular chief and a religious leader who between them provide for material and spiritual guidance. Families are large; polygyny is practiced by perhaps 13 percent of the men.

Islam is strong among the Kanembu. The only schools they attend are the *madrasas*, not the secular French schools. Many young Kanembu boys travel to Borno to attend Quranic high schools. The Tijaniyya and Qadiriyya Sufi orders are active among the Kanembu, who generally are orthodox, following only Islamic procedures with the exception of a few agrarian rites. Drinking of alcohol is rare.

The Kanembu people were deeply involved in the struggle for independence from France. While not openly involved in the Chad rebellion since independence, the third dissident army was stationed in Kanem in 1979, and its recruiting office was in Maiduguri, Borno, naturally with the support of the Kanembu.

Nigerian ambitions in Kanembu country are not without foundation. Lake Chad and its fresh water will irrigate thousands of acres now lying non-productive. There is wealth in the fertile wadis and polders. Finally, oil has been discovered around Rig Rig in Chad and was to be exploited when the first civil war broke out in 1979.

The Kanembu people, although still 95 percent illiterate, lacking in modern schools and health care and hindered by the absence of arterial roads, can have a prosperous future. This will not happen, however, until the disturbances shaking Chad have ceased.

BIBLIOGRAPHY

Books

Bouquet, C., and Cabot, J. *Atlas pratique du Tchad*. Paris: I.G.N. 1971.
————. *Le Tchad*. Paris: P.U.F., 1973.
Carbou, H. *La Région du Tchad et du Ouaddaï*. Paris: Leroux, 1912.
Chapelle, J. *Le Peuple tchadien*. Paris: L'Harmattan, 1981.
Lange, D. *Chronologie et histoire d'un royaume africain*. Wiesbaden: F. Steiner, 1977.
LeBeuf, A. *Les Populations du Tchad au nord du 10ème parallèle*. Paris: P.U.F., 1959.
————. *Les Principautés kotoko*. Paris: C.N.R.S., 1969.
Le Rouvreur, A. *Sahéliens et sahariens du Tchad*. Paris: Berger-Levrault, 1962.
Tilho, J. *Documents scientifiques de la mission tilho*. Paris: Imprimerie Nationale, 1914.
Urvoy, Y. *Histoire de l'empire du Bornou*. Paris: Larose, 1949.
Zeltner, J. -C. *Pages d'histoire du Kanem*. Paris: L'Harmattan, 1980.

Christian Bouquet

KANURI   The people who refer to themselves as Kanuri, a name whose etymological roots are not known, live chiefly in Nigeria on the arid plains west and south of Lake Chad in what is now Borno State. The Nigerian census has not been updated officially since 1963, but it is estimated that there are about 4 million Kanuri in Nigeria and perhaps another 376,000 in other countries, with all but a few thousand of these in Niger. The Kanuri language is part of the Nilo-Saharan group of languages and is unrelated (except for loan words) to the major neighboring languages (see Hausa).

All but a few Kanuri are Sunni Muslim. Although farming is the principal source of livelihood for Kanuri (crops include rice, millet, guinea corn, groundnuts and maize), the economy is complex, with commerce, transportation and construction constituting the other main elements of the private business sector. Government and public service jobs provide another major source of employment today. Manufacturing and industry play a relatively minor role in the economy.

While there are semi-legendary views about early roots in Yemen, little is known of the earliest phases of Kanuri society. Contemporary Kanuri (narrowly defined) are the descendants of the ruling family of the Kanem Empire. As a result of civil war, this family (the Saifawa) left Kanem in the fourteenth century and, after nearly a century of internal strife, established a new empire southwest of Lake Chad. This empire was and is known as Bornu, although "Borno" is now the official rendering of the name. The area to which the Saifawa moved was inhabited by various peoples about whom little is known. Now they are known collectively as the Sao—reputedly a race of giants. Regardless of their size, it may be assumed that for a period of several centuries the efforts of the Saifawa to consolidate their power and expand their kingdom's boundaries led to the incorporation of many distinctive groups within Kanuri society. This process of incorporation has not ended. Intermarriage, commerce, politics and other factors have combined to produce a people who, although identified by the term "Kanuri," are in fact culturally heterogeneous. Manga, Marghi, Kwoyam and other groups speak what usually are considered dialects of Kanuri. Other groups have maintained linguistic and ethnic distinctiveness but have been incorporated very closely into contemporary political and social life in Borno. For example, the Shuwas, who are traditionally Arabic-speaking nomadic cattle herders (see Arabs, Chadian), have prominent positions in the traditional political system and today are closely integrated with the mainstream of Kanuri society (many having given up their nomadic life-style). There are many people who call themselves Kanuri who, a few years ago, would have been considered members of other ethnic groups. There are others who consider themselves Kanuri (and are so considered by others) with parents neither of whom is Kanuri. And there are some who would be considered Kanuri in most contexts but, if pressed, could produce other legitimate ethnic labels. The complexity of the situation needs to be stressed; there is considerable variation in language and other aspects of culture within the category of people known and referred to as Kanuri.

The major unit in Kanuri life is the household. Headed by males, composed ideally of a husband, his wives and concubines, his unmarried children, some servants and employees and a scattering of other relatives and followers, the household is a vital socioeconomic unit. Descent is reckoned bilaterally—that is, individuals consider persons linked biologically through their fathers *and* mothers to be kinsfolk ("blood" and "milk" relatives, respectively). In matters of law and economics, however, kinsfolk linked to individuals through fathers are more important.

In accordance with Muslim law, polygyny is permitted. Concubinage is also practiced, although far less commonly than polygyny. Ideally, married Kanuri women are secluded. This practice is rare in rural areas where the economic role of women is vital, but it is rather common in large cities, such as Maiduguri (one study found that 10 percent of married women "never" left their houses, and 60 percent left only for medical treatment or chaperoned visiting).

The major events of the life cycle, including circumcision, marriage and death, are marked by Islamic rituals. Boys are circumcised between 7 and 12 years of age (female circumcision is not practiced). Marriage for men usually occurs first at about the age of 20 and for women, about 14. The rate of divorce is extremely high, approaching 80 percent of all completed marriages.

Social inequality is evident in Kanuri society. In the past the principal contrast was between the nobility and royalty on the one hand and commoners on the other. Today this contrast is being transformed to one between the modern, educated, bureaucratic elite and the traditional, illiterate peasantry.

Occupations related to politics and religion have high status, while occupations associated with things thought to be dirty have low status. Thus, Quranic scholars and individuals with political position have high status; barbers, blacksmiths, well diggers, tanners and butchers, very low status. In between are the great bulk of commoners (or peasantry) who are farmers, craftsmen and traders. Musicians (classed as beggars) and moneylenders (who, since they charge interest, are viewed as violators of Muslim law) hold the lowest status of all.

The patron–client relationship—relationship between social unequals where each has diffuse obligations to and expectations of the other—is the backbone of social interaction in the society at large. This is as true today in an era dominated by wealthy merchants and contractors as it was in the past with titled nobility. Research conducted in Kanuri society, as well as in other similarly organized African states, has led some to predict the early demise of such social systems in the face of rapid Westernization and modernization. Not all available evidence, however, points to this. Indeed, there is every reason to expect that patron-client-based social systems (modified somewhat, to be sure) will endure, regardless of the magnitude of other changes.

Another major dimension of social inequality in Borno is between men and women. In a pattern reflecting Islamic law as interpreted locally, women are legally and socially inferior to men, and they are considered a major source of social instability. Accordingly, various civil and social rights are denied to women.

During the agricultural season, much of family life centers around the fields, which are located in open areas around villages. Women, men and older children all work in the fields at times. In the remaining six to seven months of the year, activity centers in the family compound. Women and girls spend the bulk of their time in food preparation and related activities; men engage in various manufacturing and maintenance tasks. Craft specialists typically have their workshops in front of their compounds. In this way they carry out their art while greeting neighbors, friends and passersby. Children are expected to assume tasks suitable to their age, including water carrying, goat and sheepherding, caring for younger siblings and running errands.

The workday begins at dawn (naming ceremonies, weddings and funerals are held then, too) and continues until dusk, when the main meal of the day is usually eaten. Men and favored children eat together in groups, sharing a communal tray of food. Women and the lesser favored children eat later in an inner part of the compound. In the evenings children attend Quranic schools, sitting around open fires and repeating the verses over and over, following the exhortations of their *mallam*. Men sit outside their compounds in groups of four to eight, discussing public affairs; women remain inside, talking with visitors or entertaining the younger children with songs and stories.

Islam has been a part of Kanuri culture from sometime in the eleventh century and a strong force since at least the fifteenth century. As with other kingdoms in the Sudanic region, Islam came to Borno with the trans-Saharan trade. So little is known about the shape of politics, law and social order in Kanem-Borno in the pre-Muslim period that it is difficult to judge the extent of changes brought about by the advent of Islam. However, pre-Islamic religious and secular beliefs and values were not obliterated overnight, and Kanuri culture is best understood as an amalgamation of Islamic and varied local traditions.

Today, Islam is unquestionably the central ideological force in the daily lives of Kanuri, affecting the thinking and behavior of its people in every way. The full ritual calendar of the Muslim year is followed, the fast is faithfully kept by all who are required to do so by traditional laws and the other pillars of Islam are religiously followed by the great majority. Despite the strength of this orthodoxy, a few superimposed superstitious practices, such as the wearing of charms and amulets, are considered by most of the populace as acceptably Islamic. There is not now, however, nor does there ever appear to have been, a Kanuri equivalent of the Hausa *Bori* cult. Of the various Sufi brotherhoods in Nigeria, the dominant one in Borno appears to be the Tijaniyya.

Many of the principal values of Kanuri society have to do with aspects of interpersonal style. Certain behavioral modes are expected or required in some contexts and are to be avoided in others. Taken collectively, these values encourage a degree of restraint that contrasts greatly with the norms expected in similar contexts in the West. Patience, fortitude, respect, shame, tolerance, formality and solemnity are key interpersonal values for Kanuri. Levity, familiarity, hostility and impatience are rarely appropriate, and even when they are (e.g., the joking relationship of certain affines, and between grandparents and grandchildren), the degree of familiarity is relatively limited in its expression.

Another axis in the value system is generosity and hospitality. All societies have norms for dealing with strangers, visitors and guests. Serving tea and such small foods as dates and kola nuts is a minimal gesture of welcome in Borno. Making social visits and attending funerals, weddings, namings and other ceremonies constitute a major part of the Kanuri daily round. Hospitality is intimately linked to social mobility goals, where the amassing of followers is more important than the amassing of wealth. Kanuri say that a man who is not in debt after his wedding has no friends. It is expected, moreover, that the more money a person has, the more demands he will have to meet, in the form of providing jobs, food, housing, school fees and marriage costs to those with financial restrictions. Hospitality and generosity are two sides of a coin in Borno; they are essential to social, political and economic success.

A third dimension of the value system, and the one that crosscuts the others, has to do with authority. For Kanuri, the ultimate authority is the Islamic tradition. God is the highest but not the only context for displaying strict obedience to duly constituted authority. Husbands in relation to wives, parents in relation to children, teachers in relation to pupils, political officials in relation to the populace—these are authority relations to which Kanuri respond with complete respect and obedience. Islam teaches obedience, and Kanuri have learned the lessons well.

Most Kanuri live in non-urban settlements ranging in size from hamlets consisting of three or four families to large towns of up to 10,000 people. Urban traditions, however, are not new to Kanuri, as a succession of capital towns of relatively great size have been the political and social foci of Borno for centuries. From the air the landscape appears evenly dotted with villages connected by winding paths and narrow roadways. With the construction of new hard-surfaced highways, villages along the roads have grown rapidly; other villages have relocated along the roads in order to take advantage of the improved transportation and communication. Commerce in the rural areas continues to focus on weekly markets held in selected villages. These markets meet on given days, and, ideally, it is possible for professional marketers to move from one market village to another throughout the week. Agricultural and locally manufactured products are available in such markets. In Maiduguri the market place is huge and meets daily, but retailing is also carried out in numerous shops throughout the city.

BIBLIOGRAPHY

Books

Botting, Douglas. *The Knights of Bornu*. London: Hodder and Stoughton, 1961.

Brenner, Louis. *The Shehus of Kukawa*. Oxford: Clarendon Press, 1973.

Cohen, Ronald. "Bornu and Nigeria: Political Kingdom in a Troubled Nation." In *Communalism in Nigeria*, edited by H. Volpe and R. Melson. East Lansing: Michigan State University Press, 1970.

———. "Brittle Marriage as a Stable System." In *Divorce and After*, edited by Paul Bohannan. New York: Doubleday, 1970.

———. *Dominance and Defiance: A Study of Marital Instability in an Islamic African Society*. Washington, D.C.: American Anthropology Association, 1971.

———. "Incorporation in Bornu." In *From Tribe to Nation in Africa*, edited by Ronald Cohen and J. Middleton. San Francisco: Chandler, 1970.

———. *The Kanuri of Bornu*. New York: Holt, Rinehart and Winston, 1967.

———. "Social Stratification in Bornu." In *Social Stratification in Africa South of the Sahara*, edited by Arthur Tuden and L. Plotnicov. New York: Free Press, 1970.

Low, Victor N. *Three Nigerian Emirates: A Study in Oral History*. Evanston: Northwestern University Press, 1972.

Murdock, George P. *Africa: Its People and Their Culture History*. New York: McGraw-Hill, 1959.

Schwartz, F.A.O., Jr. *Nigeria: The Tribes, the Nation or the Race*. Cambridge: MIT Press, 1965.

Tessler, Mark A.; O'Barr, William M.; and Spain, David H. *Tradition and Identity in Changing Africa*. New York: Harper & Row, 1973.

Trimingham, J. Spencer. *Islam in West Africa*. London: Oxford University Press, 1959.

Articles

Cohen, Ronald. "The Analysis of Conflict in Hierarchical Systems: An Example from Kanuri Political Organization." *Anthropologica* 4 (1962): 87–120.

———. "Family Life in Bornu." *Anthropologica* 9 (1967): 21–42.

———. "The Just-so So: A Spurious Tribal Grouping in Western Sudanic Culture." *Man* (1962): 153–154.

———. "Slavery Among the Kanuri." *Trans-action* (1967): 48–50.

Peshkin, Alan. "Education and Modernism in Bornu." *Comparative Education Review*
14 (1970): 283–300.
Rosman, Abraham. "Social Structure and Acculturation Among the Kanuri of Bornu
Province, Northern Nigeria." *Transactions of the New York Academy of Science*
21 (1958): 620–630.

Unpublished Manuscripts

Brenner, Louis. "Concepts of Legitimacy in Bornu as Manifested in Various Forms of
Literary Expression and Behavior." Paper presented at the fifteenth annual meeting
of the African Studies Association, Philadelphia, November 1972.
Cohen, Ronald. "The Structure of Kanuri Society." Ph.D. dissertation, University of
Wisconsin, 1960.
Hutchison, John P. "Aspects of Kanuri Syntax." Ph.D. dissertation, Indiana University,
1976.
Low, Victor N. "The Border States: A Political History of Three Northwest Nigerian
Empirates, ca. 1800–1902." Ph.D. dissertation, University of California, Los
Angeles, 1967.
Rosman, Abraham. "Social Structure and Acculturation Among the Kanuri of Northern
Nigeria." Ph.D. dissertation, Yale University, 1962.
Spain, David H. "Achievement Motivation and Modernization in Bornu." Ph.D. dissertation, Northwestern University, 1969.

David H. Spain

KARACHAI   The colorful Karachai can trace their origins to the eleventh-to-
thirteenth-century merging of nomadic Kipchak Turks (Kuman, Kipchak and
Polovtsy) with autochthonous tribes of the northern foothills of the Greater
Caucasus Mountains. Best known among their neighbors as Alans—a misnomer
which applies directly to ancient Asiatic nomads who ultimately settled in Spanish
Catalonia—the Karachai refer to themselves as Kiarachaly (Kiarchal). They are
Caucasian by race and claim to be related historically to the Huns, Bulgars and
Khazars, although, in fact, the last group is allied most directly with the lineage
of the Daghestani Kumyk. Traditionally, they have been Sunni Muslims of the
Hanafi rite (see Kumyk).
   In the Soviet Union today, the Karachai number around 141,000. They also
live in Turkey, but the Turkish Karachai are indiscernible from other ethnic
groups in the census. It is known, however, that the majority of Karachai were
deported by the Russians to Turkey in 1864 during the Caucasian wars. It may
be that the vast majority of extant Karachai now live outside the U.S.S.R. in
Turkey and other Middle Eastern countries, where they commonly are lumped
together with other former North Caucasians as "Circassians." Over 95 percent
(130,000) of the Soviet Karachai live in the Russian republic, where 121,000
reside in the Karachai-Cherkessian Autonomous Oblast', an administrative sub-
unit which they share with the Cherkess (former Circassians).
   The Karachai might just as well be combined with the Balkar, for the same

language, a variant of Kipchak Turkic, is spoken by both peoples. Not only do the Karachai and Balkar speak the same language, but at one time they were one Karachayevo-Balkar people. In the wake of the Russian Revolution, in an effort to "divide and conquer" the truculent North Caucasian mountaineers, Stalinist henchmen slyly gave administrative recognition to numerous, but related, tribes and clans in order to stave off any possibility of a recrudescence of North Caucasian unity, which almost became reality during the nineteenth century. If Soviet officials truly had been interested in maintaining ethnic integrity by way of their administrative organization, they would have combined the Karachai and Balkar, who are virtual "latitudinal" neighbors, into one autonomous region. Instead, the subdivision was made longitudinally, joining the linguistically disparate Cherkess (Central Circassians) with the Karachai and, similarly, the Kabard (Eastern Circassians) with the Balkar. This ethnically illogical "gerrymandering" of minorities was perpetrated elsewhere in the Soviet Union as well as in the North Caucasus (see Balkar; Circassians; Daghestanis).

The Karachai were united with Russia in 1828. A mountain warrior people, they frequently rose up, along with other North Caucasian groups, against the colonialist policies of czarist Russia. The unending oppression of the Karachai by czarist authorities led, in the 1860s and 1870s, to a powerful movement in favor of resettlement in Turkey. Deep-seated prejudices between the Russians and Karachai survived at least until the 1950s, and probably still exist. In November 1943, the entire Karachai population was deported from its native lands and shipped in closely guarded freight cars to "special settlements" in Central Asia and Kazakhstan. In the process, their autonomous region was abolished. The reasons surrounding the deportation were at best debatable. At least one analyst suggests that the Karachai, Balkar, Crimean Tatars, Chechen and Ingush were deported from their homelands because of Soviet designs on Turkey and western Iran, the latter of which was occupied by Soviet armies in the immediate postwar years. The Stalinists alleged that the Karachai had collaborated with the Nazis during the brief German occupation. Undoubtedly, some Karachai had served the Reich in some way, but the overwhelming majority of the population had not. This was borne out by Premier Nikita Khrushchev in his famous speech delivered at the Communist Party Congress of 1956. In that speech, he granted total amnesty to deportees of all nationalities; by that time, one-third or more Karachai had died in exile or, simply, had "disappeared." A small number of former Karachai deportees still live in Kirghizia, but most of them have returned to their homeland, which was granted autonomous status again in February of 1957.

Karachai live in the southern, most mountainous and least accessible part of the autonomous region which they share with the lowland Cherkess. Within their province, better than four-fifths of the Karachai are rural. (Most certainly, this also would be true in Turkey.) Elsewhere in the U.S.S.R., Karachai are more urban (40 percent).

Karachai are extremely devoted to clan. They, along with the Balkar, Chechen and Ingush, have been described by experts as pre-feudal patriarchal clanic. This means that they together with most of the groups of North Caucasia by tradition have married strictly within clans. This in part explains why there are so many linguistically separate ethnic groups within the isolated corridors of the North Caucasus. At latest count there are more than 40 languages there.

Before the revolution, mixed marriages were rare even between Muslims, and, except among the highest grades of nobility, Turks did not marry Ibero-Caucasians. Today, Karachai, among peoples of their region, tend to intermarry with other Muslims. Intermarriage with Russians is rare indeed, and almost always such intermarriages are between a male Karachai and a female Russian; very few Karachai women would even consider marriage with a Russian. At any rate, intermarriage occurs most often among urban dwellers, meaning these marriages take place at a higher pace outside of the autonomous region, where Karachai urban shares are greater.

Among city residents, Karachai–Russian intermarrieds find ethnic composition counts for little. The cooking is a mixture of Russian and native dishes. The children bear Russian and Muslim first names indifferently; however, Russian is the sole language of the family, and children attend Russian schools. As of 1958, Karachai children were taught in Karachai between grades 1 and 4, but as of 1972, the language was not used. Now it is taught as a separate subject between grades 1 and 10.

In rural areas, the situation is quite different. There the non-Karachai wife, unless she is Russian, loses touch with her community and devotes herself entirely to the customs and language of her husband. The (Karachai) father's tongue becomes the speech of the family, even if the children frequently acquire and retain certain elements of their mother's language.

If the wife is Russian or Ukrainian, she learns her husband's language but retains her own tongue and teaches it to her children. In such marriages, some children will bear Russian names and some will have Karachai names. Often, the children will receive two names: the first being Russian and the second Muslim or vice versa. Cooking in Karachai-Slavic households usually is a compromise mix. Furniture and household management also are a composite of the two cultures. Muslim customs are allowed to lapse. For instance, patriarchy rapidly fades.

Karachai are a transhumant people. Unlike the Central Asian Turks (see Kazakhs, for instance), who use mobile yurts as temporary dwellings during their movements between pastures, the Karachai have long possessed permanent cabins (*koshi*) in their alpine summer pastures. In winter the livestock are driven downslope to warmer forest clearings, lowland pastures or livestock shelters. The herdsmen return to their permanent abode residences on state or collective farms. In further contrast to other nomadic groups, Karachai men traditionally allow at least some of their women and children to accompany or follow them to the summer grazing areas, where the women maintain the cabins and process various livestock products.

Before 1917, the alpine shelters were primitive stone structures with thatched roofs, but today these have been replaced with more contemporary camps. The latter include wood-frame adobe houses and iron- or tile-roofed stucco dormitories, each with male and female sleeping quarters, kitchens and dining rooms. The old ways no doubt persist, however, in at least isolated corners of the Karachai realm.

The Karachai are less involved in industry than almost any other North Caucasian peoples. Where it exists at all, light industry (meat processing, dairying, sewing and baking) prevails. Some coal mining and rock quarrying are carried out in the region, as are electric power production and timber processing, but these activities are patently subordinate to agriculture, and especially pastoralism. Of the total agricultural income, for instance, animal husbandry accounts for almost 75 percent; grain cultivation makes up the balance. Karachai livestock include beef cattle (roughly 50 percent of the agriculture product), sheep, pigs and poultry. Less than one-third of the land available to agriculture is devoted to crops; the great bulk of these resources are relegated to hayfields, pasture and other rangeland.

The Karachai were converted to Islam by the Kabardinians in the eighteenth century. Because of its late arrival and the nomadic habits of the Karachai, Islam was never observed very devotedly among them. While driving their flocks, the Karachai could not very often perform their formal religious duties. Making matters worse was the Kabardinian practice of taxing persons who did not attend the mosque; consequently, Karachai were taxed often and severely. Thus, some Karachai clans even into this century refused to accept many Islamic traditions and prohibitions. Currently, some continue to raise pigs, to eat pork and to save the hides and bones as good luck charms. This may account for the relatively large hog population that exists in this region. (Elsewhere in the U.S.S.R., hog populations decline dramatically in Muslim-dominated areas.)

Because Islam did not obtain total acceptance among the Karachai before the revolution and because it is almost inevitably weaker among nomads than among sedentary people, the Karachai retain numerous pre-Islamic shamanist and demonological traditions. In addition to Allah, tribes had and probably still have a whole spectrum of deities, including gods and goddesses of the hearth, fertility, harvest, rain, trees, rocks and pastures.

In spite of Soviet efforts to abolish existing loyalties of tribe, clan and joint family through the establishment of a Karachai (and Cherkess) autonomous region, extended family relationships continue on state and collective farms. Nomadic groups are familial in organization to this day and generally live in the same collective or state farm village or dormitory. The farm includes one or several related clan entities.

Despite the patrimonial character of the family, Karachai women never wore veils and, among the North Caucasians, were relatively free. They always have played an active income-earning role and, because they join in the annual migrations, have been relatively mobile. They often hold jobs at local dairies or meat-processing plants.

Karachai dietary habits include a strong preference for food of livestock origin. *Ayran* (a yogurt- or fermented milk-based drink) takes the place of all other liquids, including water, tea and soup. Meat is cooked on a spit, shish-kebab style (*shashlik*). Sausage is made from various meat by-products, and a meat loaf is produced from tripe. A common second course at mealtime is a meat soup topped with *ayran*. This is eaten along with the more familiar diamond-shaped Arab bread. Another popular food is a potato pastry similar to the Russian *pirozhek*. Special Karachai condiments include wild mushrooms, apricots and plums. These ethnic dishes have been maintained throughout the Soviet period, but they have been enhanced by more sugar, candy, porridges, fruits and vegetables.

As befits their nomadic way of life, Karachai ride horses on the job, but as mountain roads replace trails, they also drive trucks and cars. Otherwise, asses remain important pack animals, and, even on modern highways, donkey carts are not unusual sights.

The political influence of the Karachai in Soviet state and republican government is probably nil. As residents of an autonomous *oblast'*, they merit five positions, which they share with the Cherkess and others in the Soviet of Nationalities. The latter body has never been important on matters of public policy. Karachai membership in the local Communist Party is not known, but because they make up only 28 percent of the population of their region, even if their share in population was duplicated by party membership, their influence would be meager.

Despite the insidious Soviet efforts to discourage the use of native languages in North Caucasia, Karachai has been remarkably resilient. Around 98 percent of the Karachai still consider their speech as their primary language. Customarily, North Caucasians have had high percentages of language retention (over 90 percent overall). The Karachai rank sixth among the 40-odd groups in this category. Three-quarters of them speak Russian as a second language, having been taught in Russian from at least the fifth grade for several generations.

BIBLIOGRAPHY

Books

Chew, Allen F. *An Atlas of Russian History*. New Haven: Yale University Press, 1967.
Conquest, Robert. *The Nation Killers*. London: Macmillan, 1970.
D'Encasse, H. C. *Decline of an Empire*. New York: Newsweek, 1982.
Horak, Stephan M., ed. *Guide to the Study of the Soviet Nationalities*. Littleton, Colo.: Libraries Unlimited, 1982.
Luzbetak, Louis J. *Marriage and the Family in Caucasia*. New York: Johnson Reprint, 1966.

Nekrich, A. M. *The Punished Peoples*. New York: Norton, 1978.

Symmons-Symonolewicz, K. *The Non-Slavic Peoples of the Soviet Union*. Meadville, Pa.: Maplewood Press, 1972.

Wixman, Ronald. *Language Aspects of Ethnic Patterns and Processes in the North Caucasus*. Chicago: University of Chicago Press, 1980.

Articles

Baytugan, B. "The North Caucasus." *Studies on the Soviet Union* 11:1 (1971): 1–34.

Bennigsen, Alexandre. "Mixed Marriages in the Caucasus." *Central Asian Review* 16:3 (1968): 217–222.

————. "The Problem of Bilingualism and Assimilation in the North Caucasus." *Central Asian Review* 15:3 (1967): 205–211.

Shuiskii, S. A. "Muslims in the Soviet State: Islam, a Privileged Religion?" *Oriente Moderno* 60: 7–12 (1980): 383–402.

Silver, Brian. "The Status of National Minority Languages in Soviet Education: An Assessment of Recent Changes." *Soviet Studies* 26:1 (1974): 28–40.

Wixman, Ronald. "Ethnic Nationalism in the Caucasus." *Nationalities Papers* 10:2 (1982): 137–154.

Victor L. Mote

KARAKALPAK   The land of Khorezm (Khiva), legendary khanate of Tamerlane's splintered empire, today environs the Karakalpak of Central Asia, a people of complex origin related in part to the ancient Sacs, Oguz, Pechenegs, Kipchaks and Turkicized Mongols. The tribal name may have originated with a Turkic people who lived on a tributary of the Dnieper River in the twelfth century. Whatever its origin, the ethnonym earlier known as *chernyye klobuki* in Russian and *kara-borki* in Kipchak eventually became "Karakalpak." All three words mean "black hat," alluding to the traditional headwear of the tribe.

The Karakalpak are relatively few in number, with some 326,000 residing in the Soviet Union, some 52,000 in Turkey, over 25,000 in Iran and traditionally more than 3,000 in Afghanistan. In the U.S.S.R., the great majority of the group (300,000) lives on or near oases of the Karakalpak Autonomous Soviet Socialist Republic (A.S.S.R.) within the northern confines of the Uzbek Soviet Socialist Republic (S.S.R.), consisting of the lower reaches of the Amu-Darya (Oxus River) flood plain and the adjacent Kyzyl-Kum Desert. Outside their own officially designated administrative unit, several thousand Karakalpak live in nearby Tazhauz Oblast' in the Turkmen Republic, in the Zeravshan and Fergana valleys in Uzbekistan and in neighboring Kazakhstan. The Turkish Karakalpak are concentrated high in the mountains of eastern Turkey near the headwaters of the Murat River. Their Iranian relatives dwell on the southern shore of Lake Urmia in the northwest corner of the country, where during the Khomeini takeover, they rebelled temporarily. Before the Soviet occupation of Afghanistan, they were found in the vicinity of Jalalabad on the Kabul River east of the capital.

No doubt, some Karakalpak have fled along with other Afghan tribespeople to Pakistan.

The Karakalpak are first mentioned as a distinct tribal entity in the Central Asian chronicles of the sixteenth century, and their ethnogenesis appears to have culminated two centuries later. Until the Russian Revolution, they were composed of the same tribal formations as the Uzbek and Kazakhs. Indeed, even today only a special dialect distinguishes the Karakalpak from their neighbors to the south and east. Because the Karakalpak lacked a national consciousness before 1917, Western ethnographers have criticized the Soviet decision to give the group an autonomous republic. Their literary heritage took form only in the last century, much later than most of their neighbors.

Linguistically, the Karakalpak belong to the Northwest Turkic (Kipchak) branch of the Altaic family of languages. Chiefly Mongoloid by race and Sunni-Hanafi by religion, they are predominantly sedentary by occupation and live in flat-roofed, tamped-earthen houses in winter. They often shift to traditional yurts, which are set up next to the permanent dwelling, in summer. Roughly 30 percent of the Soviet Karakalpak live in cities, where they gin cotton, mill cotton-seed oil, process fish and generally engage in other light industrial activities. The rural majority is organized onto state and collective farms, all of which are based on irrigation. The bulk of the farms are specialized in the raising of cotton, but they grow rice, alfalfa, muskmelons, hemp and sorghum as well. Collectivized livestock raising of karakul sheep, beef cattle, horses and Bactrian camels is conducted in the Oxus River delta region. A few Karakalpak are fishermen in the Aral Sea basin.

Before this century, the Karakalpak were semi-sedentary, combining irrigated agriculture with nomadic herding. Even today at least some tribes of the Fergana Valley, Turkey, Iran and Afghanistan practice transhumance (seasonal mountain–valley nomadism).

Despite Soviet attempts to abolish existing loyalties of tribe, clan and joint family through the creation of a Karakalpak ''nation,'' extended family relationships persist under the framework of the collective farm. The social structure remains patriarchal with a strong emphasis on past genealogical organization. To this day, many older people know their ancient clan affiliations. Traditionally, these have been understood so well that ethnic maps based on Karakalpak clan divisions could be compiled in the 1940s and 1950s.

Though patrimony prevails within the tribal structure, Karakalpak women have never worn veils, and in some areas, the Fergana Valley, for instance, the inferior position of women is disappearing faster than among other Central Asian tribes. Nevertheless, responsibility for making the felt superstructure of the occasional yurt plus the erection and dismantling of the dwelling in summer remain ''women's work.'' Although some girls are allowed to attend middle, technical and, on occasion, high schools, many withdraw upon their eighteenth birthday or shortly thereafter to be married. Indeed, girls are still expected to marry young (upwards of a third between 16 and 19 during the 1960s)—sometimes, as in the past, by prior arrangement (child marriage)—and to subordinate themselves to the wills of their husbands and fathers-in-law. In this sense the woman has few rights and privileges except her dowry, an Islamic tradition not proscribed by the Soviets because it is also a European custom. There have been reports of parents intentionally refraining from registering the birth of daughters because they would like to be able to claim—in the future—that the girls are older than they really are, since Soviet law forbids the marriage of minors. Some schoolgirls have been sent away to distant relatives in regions where the children's ages are not known, again to circumvent the law.

Today, clan genealogical exogamy has been replaced by collective farm exogamy. (Overall, the Karakalpak remain endogamous.) As is the case with most Central Asian cultures, Karakalpak almost never intermarry with Russians, and, if they must marry outside the tribe, it is usually with Kazakhs (see Kazakhs). Wedding feasts remain week-long celebrations at the home of the groom and usually occur in the fall when meat is plentiful. The only post-revolutionary change is that the bride is brought to the groom's house in a car or truck instead of on horseback.

The majority of Karakalpak readily respect Islam, although the role of the religion was weakening among them even at the end of the nineteenth century. In 1972, only 23 percent of the men and 20 percent of the women reported that they were atheists. This exists despite Soviet suppression of the religion, which has included among other things laws against polygyny, propaganda against pilgrimages (to local shrines) and Muslim festivals—they interrupt work—and the closing of mosques. The day of rest and bazaar day have been shifted from Friday to Sunday. Traditional folklore and music are tolerated only on a limited basis. Authorities also have placed strict limits on the number of *madrasas* and *madrasa* graduates (a mere 50 per year from Tashkent and Bukhara), meaning the population of the active clergy lags behind the number of potential faithful.

If current regional estimates are correct, there may be as many as 20 registered and unregistered mosques in the Karakalpak republic. A Karakalpak reportedly holds his mosque in higher esteem then does a neighboring Uzbek or Kazakh. This has been ascribed to the homogeneous ethnicity of their geographical region, where entire villages and towns may represent composites of only one or two clans. Clans have their own *mullahs*, pilgrimage shrines and cemeteries. Mosque-going takes on an ethnocentric flavor. Whole clans may shun mosques administered by *imams* who are not Karakalpak. In more ethnically diverse regions, Karakalpak faithful flock to mosques run by *imams* of their own kind.

Observance of the five pillars is rather subdued among the Karakalpak, as it is with most Soviet Central Asians. There are no restraints on the repetition of the *shahada*, but frequency data are obviously difficult to obtain. Praying is not especially evident, but it was rare even before 1917. Alms, more like gifts, are rendered to the Tashkent *muftiyat* because of Soviet laws against begging. Similarly supported are the local shrines. Fasting at Ramadan persists despite official condemnation. And pilgrimages are conducted only locally. Even now, less than

100 token faithful from the entire U.S.S.R.—all aged 60 or more—are permitted to perform the Haj each year, and even they go disguised as officially sanctioned "tourist groups" and not as pilgrims.

Some Karakalpak youth, even those who are Komsomol or Communist party members, observe the ancient national customs as formerly, and much more actively than in Stalin's time. One witness notes that the "majority of non-believers are still convinced that because of their nationality they are obliged to fulfill certain rites and observe customs which upon closer inspection turn out to be religious." According to the same source, the vast majority of young people continue to celebrate marriage in the Muslim way. "Even Communists behave in this way."

Where childbirth, weddings and funerals, especially, are concerned, Karak-alpak still practice shamanistic rituals and ceremonies. Often considered deriv-atives of Islam, rituals and festivals associated with mourning and childbirth have no basis in the holy books. Nevertheless, a few villages (*auls*) yet practice complicated year-long funeral rites and 40-day celebrations after the birth of a child. All villages observe these rites at least to some degree. Gone is the splendor associated with anniversary observances, and banquets are restricted today to invited guests only. Young people normally do not participate in the events, and intellectuals eschew them as superstitious relics.

Associated with rituals and feasts, circumcision is practically universal. Kur-ban Bayram, commemorating the sacrifice of Abraham, continues to be observed, as some Karakalpak are absent from work on that occasion. To combat absen-teeism, Soviet authorities have introduced substitute festivals. However, the celebrations no longer are marked by dancing boys and troops of professional entertainers.

Alcoholic beverages, of course, continue to be forbidden by Muslim law, although young people and intellectuals are fond of cognac and wine. Officially encouraged by the Soviet regime as a means of disseminating information (and propaganda), teahouses are located in almost every oasis, *aul* or town. The teahouses serve as chatty environments where people smoke cigarettes—and not water pipes—and take a kind of snuff. (During the 1960s, snuff-taking was alleged to cause mouth cancer among Karakalpak men.) Chess is also a popular pasttime in the teahouses.

Soviet officials reportedly have been upset by the amount of time squandered by Central Asian men, and an occasional woman, in teahouses. "From morning to late evening there is no end to the customers, the great majority of whom are men. They crowd in the tea shops around the braziers and are obviously in no hurry to go anywhere." During harvests and other periods of job deadlines, the great majority of harvesters and other workers are women and adolescents. "The men, in striped robes and black skull caps, sit in the tea shops and drink green tea. . .a sip at a time."

To avoid eating "forbidden" Russian fare, the Karakalpak generally dine at home rather than in the cafeterias at their place of work. Although now household utensils are used at mealtime and European furniture has appeared in their residences, some families continue to eat at low tables and to sleep on the floor. Like most Muslims, Karakalpak do not eat pork, and visitors rarely see pigs in the republic.

Despite Soviet restrictions, tribal groups inside the U.S.S.R. have experienced a much faster overall rise in standard of living than their Turkic relatives. Although they are much freer to practice their religion and customs, Turkish, Iranian and Afghan Karakalpak are worse off economically than their kinsmen in the Soviet Union.

Politically, representatives of the Karakalpak, including 2 percent of the population of the Uzbek S.S.R., compose more than 2 percent of the Uzbek Supreme Soviet and almost the same percentage of the Uzbek Communist Party. Insofar as such political representation means anything in the Soviet Union, the Karakalpak fare as well as can be expected. They send the A.S.S.R. standard 11 representatives to the Soviet of Nationalities.

Among the major Turkic language groups in the Soviet Union, the Karakalpak are undergoing the most rapid adoption of Russian as a second language; between the latest (1970, 1979) censuses, they experienced a slight decline in the number of their own tribespeople who considered Karakalpak their native language. In 1970, 1 out of 10 Karakalpak spoke Russian as a second language. In 1979, the ratio had risen to almost 1 out of 2. This ''Russianization'' process was similarly matched by a 300 percent increase in the number of people who spoke other languages (probably Uzbek and Kazakh) as a second tongue. These seemingly radical linguistic turns, after 60 years of Karakalpak entrenchment, strongly relate to the efficiency of the Soviet school system and, possibly, to the artificiality of the concept of Karakalpak nationhood. There is no doubt that knowledge of Russian improves one's standing in the U.S.S.R., and Karakalpak young people appear to be getting the message, no matter how unwillingly.

Distinguishing themselves among other Central Asian cultures, the Karakalpak are fine craftsmen. Unlike their neighbors, they adorn their yurts far more luxuriously with decorative rugs, wall-hangings, macrame and wide-fringed belts, currently emphasizing brown, green and blue patterns on a red and yellow backdrop (in the Soviet Union). In contrast, pre-revolutionary, and possibly contemporary Turkish, Iranian and Afghan, designs are brown, pink, light green and yellow on a white background. Additionally, Karakalpak tribesmen are recognized for their excellence in work with leather, wood and bone. However, as is the case throughout Central Asia, machines are replacing handiwork, and ever fewer young persons possess the know-how to perform traditional crafts.

BIBLIOGRAPHY

Books

Bacon, Elizabeth. *Central Asians Under Russian Rule*. Ithaca: Cornell University Press, 1966.

Caroe, Sir Olaf K. *Soviet Empire: The Turks of Central Asia and Stalinism*. New York: St. Martin's Press, 1967.

Coates, W. P., and Coates, Zelda K. *Soviets in Central Asia*. Westport, Conn.: Greenwood Press, 1969.

D'Encansse, H. C. *Decline of an Empire*. New York: Newsweek, 1979.

Katz, Zev; Rogers, Rosemarie; and Harned, Frederic. *Handbook of Major Soviet Nationalities*. New York: Free Press, 1975.

Krader, Lawrence. *Peoples of Central Asia*. Bloomington: Indiana University Press, 1963.

Symmons-Symonolewicz, Konstantin. *The Non-Slavic Peoples of the Soviet Union*. Meadville, Pa.: Maplewood Press, 1972.

Wheeler, Geoffrey. *The Modern History of Soviet Central Asia*. New York: Praeger, 1964.

Wixman, Ronald. "Recent Assimilation Trends in Soviet Central Asia." *The Nationality Question in Soviet Central Asia*, edited by Edward Allworth. New York: Praeger, 1973.

Articles

Caferoglu, Ahmet. "The Literary Scene: Past and Present." *Studies on the Soviet Union* 8:1 (1968): 46–58.

Esbergenov, Kh. "On the Struggle Against Survivals of Obsolete Customs and Rites (The Karakalpak 'As' Memorial Feast)." *Soviet Anthropology and Archaeology* 3:1 (1964): 9–20.

Shuiskii, S. A. "Muslims in the Soviet State: Islam, a Privileged Religion?" *Oriente Moderno* 7–12 (1980): 383–402.

Tolstova, L. S. "The Karakalpak of Fergana," *Central Asian Review* 9 (1961): 45–52.

Victor L. Mote

KASHMIRIS There are several Muslim groups, in all numbering more than 4 million in the state of Jammu and Kashmir, now divided unequally between India (where it is the only state with a Muslim majority–68 percent) and Pakistan (where it is called Azad Kashmir). The largest Muslim group, numbering some 2.5 million, speaks Kashmiri, an Indo-Iranian language. Its members are culturally distinguishable and think of themselves as distinct not only from Hindus, Sikhs and Buddhists but also from other Muslims of the region who speak Punjabi, Pashto, Dogri, Pahari and Shina.

Kashmiri speakers, who are 95 percent Muslim, are heavily concentrated in the Vale of Kashmir, the heart of the former princely state located high in the Himalayan Mountains of north India. The 1961 census of India reported Muslims to be 95 percent of the population of the three districts composing the vale. While there are nearly 1 million Muslims in Azad Kashmir, only a few are Kashmiri speakers who fled the vale during the time of Partition in 1947.

The key to understanding the Muslim Kashmiri, both in the context of Indian domestic politics and in the international context of the Indo-Pakistani dispute over their territory, is that, like the Bengali but unlike the north Indian and Pakistan Muslims, they do not have a former ruling elite outlook. Although there was an independent Muslim sultanate in Kashmir for two centuries (1346–1586) and it was a province of the Moghul empire for another century and a half (1586–1752), its more recent history is one of subjugation, first to the Pushtun of Afghanistan (1752–1819), then to the Sikh kingdom of Ranjit Singh (1819–1846) and lastly to the British, ruling through a Hindu Dogra dynasty from neighboring Jammu State (1846–1947). Under these three sets of alien rulers, the Muslim ruling class disappeared, and the peasantry and artisans were systematically exploited through oppressive taxation, forced labor and usurious debts. Kashmiri Muslims were excluded from the state's army, civil service and education in favor of outsiders, so they naturally developed a deep suspicion of all governments. Only Hindu Pandits (Brahmins) among the Kashmiri-speaking subjects of the maharaja had some opportunity in the later years of Dogra rule to join the ruling elite. Thus, there has been, until the generation which entered politics in 1931, no Muslim leadership comparable to the Muslim aristocracy and professional upper middle class of the United Provinces in British India which played such a conspicuous part in the founding of Pakistan. It was this difference in elite, in conjunction with the fear of plundering Pushtun tribesmen, which probably accounts for the unwillingness of most Kashmiri Muslims to take the side of Pakistan in the three wars that country has fought with India over this territory (1947–1948, 1965, 1971).

Since the overthrow of Dogra rule in 1947, power has shifted to the largely Muslim National Conference Party (Prime Ministers Shaikh Abdullah, Bakshi Ghulam Mohammed, and G. M. Sadiq). Now it is the turn of the Hindu Dogras of Jammu and the Hindo Pandits of Kashmir to charge that they are discriminated against in government employment. Some have even emigrated to Delhi for employment.

In a different respect, nevertheless, Muslim Kashmiris do resemble their co-religionists in pre-Partition Pakistan and Bangladesh more than those in India. They are disproportionately rural (90 percent) and agricultural in residence and occupation. Hindus, by contrast, are almost one-third of the urban population.

Like Muslims all over South Asia, Kashmiris exhibit ranked, caste-like divisions which show some similarities to the *varna* and *jati* categories among Hindus. This is not surprising in that most of them are probably descendants of converts from Hinduism since the fourteenth century. The boundaries of these groupings among Muslims, however, are much less rigid than among Hindus because they not only are not supported by the formal theology of Islam but are actually in violation of Islamic egalitarianism. There is, for instance, no element of ritual pollution, except perhaps regarding the lowest rank which handles night soil. Endogamy is observed only in the highest and lowest categories, the Sayyids and Shaikhs at the top and the Hanjis at the bottom. Sayyids claim descent from the Prophet and Shaikhs from his disciples. The former monopolize the religious functions and offices associated with religious learning. The Shaikhs tend to be traders. Moghuls and Pathans (Pushtun), who occupy the next rank in north India, do not have the same high status in Kashmir because they are still feared as outsiders and, unless Kashmiri-speaking, do not really belong to the Kashmiri. The lowest of the occupational subcastes are the Teli (oil pressers), Lohar (blacksmiths), Kumiar (potters), Hanji (boatmen and fishermen), Hajjam (barbers) and Machi (leatherworkers). In the middle, much like a Hindu dominant cultivator subcaste, are the Kashmiri proper, numbering 40 percent of the whole.

Crosscutting these quasi-caste groupings is the sectarian split between Sunnis (95 percent) and Shias (5 percent), which are more strictly endogamous than the "castes." The Shias, as a minority sometimes persecuted by Sunni rulers, have proven more adaptable to non-Muslim rule than the Sunnis and have therefore enjoyed more urban residence and prosperity. The Sunnis are in their turn divided by the revivalist movement, which leads some of them to reject the syncretistic Sufi saint worship and other superstitions and practices of traditional Kashmiri Islam. Earlier, this puritan tendency was represented by the Wahhabi sect. Now it is spearheaded by the Jama'at-i-Islami, which was active in propagating Islamic education in the state until it was banned under the Indian emergency in 1975. Ironically, it was the theft of a sacred hair of a saint from the Hazratbal shrine in 1964 which enabled more orthodox Muslim forces to riot and bring about the downfall of former Prime Minister Bakshi Ghulam Mohammed.

Kashmir continues to be a battleground between competing tendencies within Islam: traditionalist, revivalist, modernist and secularist, and it is to be suspected that these conflicts underlie much of Kashmiri politics since leaders from the Muslim majority achieved dominance a generation ago. As in India, an incongruous alliance between traditionalists and secularists has kept the state within the Indian union against the claims and subversive efforts of Pakistan. One manifestation of this anomaly is that the Shariah still governs in matters of marriage, divorce, adoption and inheritance for Muslims in Kashmir as in the rest of India, despite the secularist posture of the rulers.

Muslim Kashmiris distinguish themselves from Hindus by subtle nuances of dress, the wearing of beards, dialect, method of salutation and name. Pandits and Muslims practice various degrees of mutual avoidance, such as not interdining, but for lack of Hindu service castes, the Pandits must surreptitiously accept physical contact with Muslim barbers, midwives and even butchers. The Pandit stereotypes Muslims as "dirty, polluted, unprincipled and lustful," while the Muslims reciprocate with stereotypes of the Hindu *kafirs* as "faithless, double-dealing, mean, cowardly and corrupt," but this does not prevent amiable relationships of mutual dependency.

Since Muslim quasi-castes are not well organized except for artisan guilds in urban wards, the extended family is the most salient social unit for Kashmiri Muslims. While some marriage customs reflect Hindu-Muslim syncretism, practices, such as first cousin marriage and dowry, owe more to Islam than to Hinduism. As in neighboring India and Pakistan, polygyny is permitted but seldom practiced because of the expense. There is no bar to widows remarrying.

Artisans in Srinagar have historically been organized along guild lines (apprentices, journeymen, masters), selling their famous shawls, embroidery, rugs and carvings to a dealer who supplies raw materials, markets the product and garners most of the profit. Working conditions in the homes and shops are traditionally crowded, ill lit and unhealthy. Cooperative and cottage industries emporia have improved these conditions and exports in the past generation.

Other changes brought about by the Muslim National Conference Party government have ameliorated the depressed income and status of Kashmiri Muslims. Chief of these was the land reform of 1950, which abolished *jagirdari* (landlordism), in effect without compensation, and made the bulk of the poor tenants landholders in their own right. Simultaneously, their burden of indebtedness to landlords and moneylenders was removed by a moratorium. Since most of the former and many of the latter were Hindus, this brought about a social revolution in the relative status of the two communities comparable to that which occurred at about the same time in East Pakistan. By a series of five-year plans, heavily subsidized by the government of India in order to win the loyalty of the Muslim majority, large investments were made in free education, irrigation, transportation, electrification and some industries. The cultural activities of the Jammu and Kashmir governments have emphasized music, art and poetry which facilitate Hindu-Muslim integration. All of these policies must be having an effect on the life, culture and values of the once-submerged Muslim majority, but due probably to the political sensitivity of the area, no general survey of Muslim ethnography in Kashmir has been undertaken since 1956, so that the direction and measurement of these changes is as yet unknown.

On the Pakistani side of the cease-fire line in Azad Kashmir, the opposite cultural policies and influences are at work on Kashmiri Muslims, assimilating them into the Urdu and Islamic culture of the Punjab. In its competition with India for Kashmiri allegiance, the government of Pakistan has also subsidized economic development in the less fertile fringe of the state which it acquired, and it too eventually carried out a land reform. As with other politically divided peoples in the world since World War II, the Kashmiri Muslims may over the years become ethnically distinct, closer to the cultures of India and Pakistan, respectively, than they are to each other.

BIBLIOGRAPHY

Books

Aslam, Mohammed. *Social Implications of Technological Change in Rural Kashmir.* New York: Humanities Press, 1981.

Bazaz, Prem Nath. "Progress in Cultural Fields." In *Kashmir in the Crucible.* Bombay: Pearl, 1967.

Crane, Robert I., ed. *Area Handbook on Jammu and Kashmir State.* Chicago: University of Chicago for Human Relations Area Files Press, 1956.

Gupta, Sisir. *Kashmir: A Study in India-Pakistan Relations.* Bombay: Asia Publishing House, 1966.

Korbel, Josef. *Danger in Kashmir.* Princeton: Princeton University Press, 1954.

Quraishi, Zaheer Masood. *Elections and State Politics of India: A Case Study of Kashmir.* Delhi: Sundeep Prakashan, 1979.

Raza, Moonis, et al. *The Valley of Kashmir: The Land.* Vol. 1. Durham: Carolina Academic Press, 1978.

Article

Madan, Triloki Nath. "Religious Ideology in a Plural Society: The Muslims and Hindus of Kashmir." *Contributions to Indian Sociology* n.s. 6 (1972): 106–141.

Theodore P. Wright, Jr.

KAZAKHS   The Turkic Kazakhs are the descendants of nomadic horsemen who helped Genghis Khan sweep across Central Asia and much of Russia in the thirteenth century. Today, most of them live peaceful lives in the Kazakh Soviet Socialist Republic. Their 1983 population exceeded 8 million, with some 6 million in their republic, another million in other Soviet republics, nearly a million in the People's Republic of China, about 70,000 in the Republic of Mongolia and perhaps 20,000 in Afghanistan.

Their language, also called Kazakh, belongs to the Kipchak group of Turkic languages within the Altaic language family. Until the 1930s it was written in the Arabic script, and then for a few years in Latin letters. Thereafter, as part of the Russification program, it was and continues to be written in Russian Cyrillic letters.

The etymology of the name "Kazakh," which is used by the people for themselves, is uncertain. According to some scholars, "Kazakh" derives from a Turkic word meaning "wanderer" or "independent man." These meanings conform to the reputation the Kazakh steppe nomads enjoyed among their neighbors. The people's own folk etymology traces the name to the Turkic words *kaz* (goose) and *ak* (white). Among some Kazakhs, there is a charter myth to support this. Historically, the name most probably referred to a political entity before it took on its present ethnic significance. Prior to the fifteenth or sixteenth centuries, there is no evidence of a Kazakh ethnic identity. Further complicating historical study was the Russian practice of referring to the Kazakhs as "Kirghiz" until 1925, in order to avoid confusion with the Cossacks.

Although their Turkic and Mongolian ancestors roamed the Central Asiatic steppes for hundreds of years, the Kazakhs did not acquire a distinct identity until the late fifteenth and early sixteenth centuries during a chaotic political period characterized by short-lived separatist and succession states. Early in the sixteenth century, a group of khans and their followers broke away from the Uzbek confederation (see Uzbek) and united under the rule of Kaysym Khan. Soon other Turkic nomadic groups joined them to form what became known as the Kazakh Orda, or Confederation. Henceforth, the term "Kazakh" took on an ethnic significance and has been applied to the Turkic people occupying the area roughly between the Caspian Sea in the west to Lake Balkhash in the east, and from the Syr Darya River in the south to the Siberian lowlands in the north.

Soon after the death of their first great khan, the Kazakhs divided into three main hordes: the Great Horde (Ulu Yüz), east of the Aral Sea to Lake Balkhash; the Little Horde (Kshi Yüz), west of the Aral Sea; and the Middle Horde (Orta Yüz), between them. These three hordes reunited only once for a brief period in the late seventeenth and early eighteenth centuries under the great Khan Tevke. During the nineteenth century, the hordes were absorbed into the Russian empire according to their proximity to Europe. Russia conquered the Little Horde first and the Great Horde last.

Like practically all other Turkic peoples, the Kazakhs are Muslims. They had converted to Islam by the sixteenth century, but the details of their conversion process are not known. Because Islam was spread in the steppes largely by Sufi mystics and unorthodox preachers, Muslims there have commonly displayed a flexibility of belief and a laxity in orthodox ritual. Generally, Turks adopted the comparatively liberal Hanafi school of Islamic law. Certain dress and social customs, such as the veiling and seclusion of women, although common among sedentary Muslims, were not practiced by Kazakh nomads.

Physically, most Kazakhs are of medium build, with black hair, swarthy complexions and Mongol features. Their basic clothing was fashioned from sheepskin and felt, which the women wove expertly. The men valued horse-manship, freedom of movement and prowess. The steppe Kazakhs lived in the typical Turkic-Mongol yurt, or circular tent of felt or skins on a framework of wooden poles. Their diets consisted of meat and milk products from their herds supplemented by grains and vegetables acquired from settled peoples. Their preferred drink was and still is a fermented mare's milk called *kumyss*.

The details of early Kazakh social organization are unclear. Eighteenth- and nineteenth-century observers' accounts vary somewhat by writer and location, but it is evident that the hordes ideally were comprised of clans and patrilineages, all united by agnatic (through males) descent ties. Each clan had its own dis-tinctive earmark for livestock and war cry by which its members identified themselves in battle or large gatherings. In reality, the Kazakhs were probably organized into territorial tribes of related and unrelated people who employed somewhat fabricated genealogies as charters to legitimize their rights to pasture and water and to justify their internal alignments. The fission and fusion of tribal components and the incorporation into existing geneologies of newly accepted migrants were probably fairly common practices.

Many clans had at least one constituent patrilineage of noble status. Its mem-bers claimed descent from the great khans of the past, such as the Mongol Genghis Khan. These noble lineages constituted the "white bone" (*ak süök*) or aristocratic stratum of society, while the others, the "black bone" (*kara süök*) lineages, formed the common stratum. Generally, the white bone lineages were wealthier and their male heads became the khans of the Kazakh tribes and tribal confederations.

Theoretically, each horde was headed by a great khan and was composed of tribal divisions led by lesser khans. Seldom, however, was the great khan able to command all the tribes in his horde. The constituent tribes followed his directives only when they all recognized a common threat from the outside, such as military invasion. The khans coordinated tribal movements so as to prevent overgrazing and to avoid internal conflicts over migratory routes, pasturage and water. The khans also represented their tribes or confederations to outsiders and when necessary directed them militarily for purposes of defense and offense. In return, the khans had the right to levy taxes on tribal members, who usually paid in animals. The courts of the khans consisted of relatives, councillors, bodyguards, servants and slaves. Through their agents, many khans actively pursued commercial interests with merchants outside their tribes. They traded animals derived from taxes for agricultural produce, textiles, metal products, weapons and other goods.

The day-to-day, effective socioeconomic unit among the Kazakhs was the nomadic encampment (*aul*), which included families that tented together and moved their herds as a unit. During the dispersal season of summer, the *auls* were small, consisting of from 5 to 20 tents. They moved from pasture to pasture along an established route. In the winter, a number of *auls* joined together at one place, commonly in a river valley to be sheltered from the cold wind. The winter *auls* ranged from 50 to over 1,000 tents. Grazing rights were assigned to each *aul*, and the *aul* headman, called *ak sakal* (white beard), supervised their utilization by *aul* members. The *ak sakal* was a wise and experienced leader, selected more or less by consensus from an *aul*'s dominant clan or lineage. Not all *aul* members were necessarily related.

The most common stock in the Kazakh herds were sheep and goats, horses and camels, in that order. The herdsmen traded meat, cheese, leather and wool with the oases dwellers to the south and the Russians to the north. In return, they received grain, textiles and metal products. Adverse weather conditions of high frequency, including droughts and severe blizzards, often caused sharp reductions in herd sizes. This in turn compelled the Kazakhs to raid commercial caravans and sedentary populations to survive until herds could be rebuilt.

Kazakh tentholds consisted of both nuclear and patrilineally extended families. The ideal post-marital residence rule was patrilocal; hence, married sons commonly resided in the same *aul* as their fathers, economic conditions permitting. These nomads practiced clan and probably *aul* exogamy, thereby creating marital alliances between large kin groups and encampments. On occasion, a Kazakh judge (*bii*) would recommend that two disputing parties establish affinal ties of marriage between them so as to end their adversary relationship. The Kazakhs further promoted marital links between groups by practicing the levirate and sororate. Divorce was uncommon. Some rich men, such as khans, married polygynously, and those people with white bone or aristocratic status usually married among themselves. At the time of marriage, the bride's family supplied her with a dowry of jewelry, utensils and clothing, while the groom's family paid the bride's parents a bridewealth (*kalym*) in horses and/or other animals.

In the traditional system of Kazakh law, each family had sole jurisdiction over its internal affairs. Even if one family member murdered another, outside authorities could not initiate a legal proceeding. In the instance where a family member killed the family member of another, the entire family of the murderer was responsible for the payment of the *wergeld* (blood money).

Most of the family's wealth passed intergenerationally through the patriline. Sons received most of the paternal estate. As each son married, his living father paid the bridewealth and outfitted his son with a tent, felts and herd animals in proportion to his wealth. The youngest son remained with the father and eventually inherited the father's tent and the remainder of his herd and possessions. He was obligated to care for his surviving mother and unmarried sisters.

The occupying Russians dissolved the Kazakh khanships and divided and administered the region in ways which broke up established migratory routes and destroyed historic tribal-territorial identities. Large-scale colonization programs involving Russian and Ukrainian peasants converted steppe pasturage into farmland. Many Kazakhs were forced to settle and become peasants also. The Russians introduced railroads, factories and roads into the steppe, employing mostly non-Kazakhs in the process. They transfigured the area economically, politically, demographically and culturally despite the opposition of most Kazakhs.

During the Russian Revolution, a Kazakh faction called the Alash Orda Party proclaimed an autonomous Kazakh region. In this period of political storm, however, the Kazakhs were too divided internally by feuds to establish a cohesive state. Pro-Bolshevik and anti-Bolshevik forces used the steppe as a battle theater. Many Kazakhs were killed and their herds destroyed by war. A large number escaped to neighboring China and Afghanistan. Of those who remained, about 1 million died of starvation during the 1921–1922 famine. With the victory of the Russian Red Army over the Whites, the Kazakhs were forced to recognize Soviet dominance. In 1920, Lenin decreed the establishment of the ''Autonomous Kirghiz'' (i.e., Kazakh) Soviet Socialist Republic. Stalin reconstituted it as a union Republic in 1936.

Soviet government-promoted industrialization and urbanization forced Kazakh sedentarization. The collectivization of farming intensified the transformation of Central Asia. Continued colonization programs reduced the Kazakhs to a minority status. Today, most Kazakhs continue to reside in rural areas, whereas the majority Russian population and other non-Turkic peoples concentrate in cities. The population of the capital, Alma-Ata, for example, is less than 15 percent Kazakh.

Most Kazakhs continue to be Muslims. With literacy and settlement, their Islamic religion has become more orthodox than it was formerly. Their rate of intermarriage with non-Muslims is low. The traditional white bone–black bone system of social stratification has been erased, and large kinship units, such as clans, have lost their former meaning and function. In the rural areas, the effective social units are the family and the collective farm group. The latter has taken on some of the characteristics of the *aul*, in that its director is called *ak sakal*, and for purposes of marriage it constitutes the exogamous unit.

Kazakhstan is interlaced by a network of public schools from the elementary to the university levels. In the Kazakh-dominated rural areas, the language of instruction at the primary levels is Kazakh. At the higher levels and in the cities it is Russian. According to the 1970 census, 40 percent of Kazakhs spoke Russian as a second language, but the percentage was much higher for urban areas.

Through time, the Kazakhs have increased their participation in Soviet politics. Their membership in the Kazakhstan Communist Party rose from 8 percent in 1924 to 40 percent in 1970. During the 1960s, about 50 percent of the party's province, city and district secretaries were Kazakhs.

Mass literacy and a popular press developed among the Kazakhs only in the twentieth century. In 1980, almost 40 percent of the 425 newspapers published in Kazakh S.S.R. were in the Kazakh language. The same was true for 31 of the republic's 114 periodicals. The major radio and television stations broadcast primarily in Russian and Kazakh.

The Kazakhs did not have a classical written heritage, but they developed a tradition of rich oral literature. During the eighteenth century, folk poets created and recited epics glorifying their nomadic conquest traditions. In the early 1900s, poets devoted their works to the Kazakh rebellion against czarist Russia. Later, they praised the Soviet victory in Central Asia.

Education, literacy and the general standard of living among the Kazakhs have risen under Russian rule. The Kazakhs have, however, played only a minor role in determining their own destiny. The Red Army, central planning agencies, Russian settlers and the improbability of outside assistance have combined to compel the Kazakhs to accept their fate without open rebellion. The degree of nationalism among them today is difficult to determine.

Paul Magnarella

BIBLIOGRAPHY

Books

Bacon, Elizabeth E. *Central Asians Under Russian Rule*. Ithaca: Cornell University Press, 1966.
Benningsen, Alexandre, and Lemercier-Quelquejay, Chantal. *Islam in the Soviet Union*. New York: Praeger, 1967.
Clem, Ralph Scott. "The Impact of Demographic and Socio-Economic Forces Upon the Nationality Question in Central Asia." In *The Nationality Question in Soviet Central Asia*, edited by Edward Allworth. New York: Praeger, 1973.
Coates, W. P., and Coates, Zelda K. *Soviets in Central Asia*. Westport, Conn.: Greenwood Press, 1969.
Demko, George J. *The Russian Colonization of Kazakhstan, 1896–1916*. Uralic and

Altaic Series, 99. Bloomington: Indiana University Press, 1969.

Dunn, Ethel, and Dunn, Stephen P. "Ethnic Intermarriage as an Indicator of Cultural Convergence in Soviet Central Asia." In *The Nationality Question in Soviet Central Asia*, edited by Edward Allworth. New York: Praeger, 1973.

Hudson, A. E. *Kazak Social Structure*. New Haven: Human Relations Area Files Press, 1964. (1938 study.)

Krader, Lawrence. *Peoples of Central Asia*. Uralic and Altaic Series, 26. Bloomington: Indiana University Press, 1963.

———, and Wayne, Ivor. *The Kazakhs*. Washington, D.C.: George Washington University Human Resources Research Office, 1955.

Menges, Karl H. *The Turkic Languages and Peoples: An Introduction to Turkic Studies*. Wiesbaden: Harrassowitz, 1968.

Moseley, George. *A Sino-Soviet Cultural Frontier: The Ili Kazakh Autonomous Chou*. Cambridge: Harvard University Press, 1966.

Procyk, Anna. "The Search for a Heritage and the Nationality Question in Central Asia." In *The Nationality Question in Soviet Central Asia*, edited by Edward Allworth. New York: Praeger, 1973.

Shorish, M. Mobin. "Who Shall Be Educated: Selection and Integration in Soviet Central Asia." In *The Nationality Question in Soviet Central Asia*, edited by Edward Allworth. New York: Praeger, 1973.

Winner, Thomas G. *The Oral Art and Literature of the Kazakhs of Russian Central Asia*. Durham: Duke University Press, 1958.

Articles

Abramzon, S. M. "Reflections of the Process of the Coming Together of Nations in the Family Life and Daily Habits of the Peoples of Central Asia and Kazakhstan." *Soviet Sociology* 1:2 (1962): 41–52.

Dunn, Stephen P., and Dunn, Ethel. "Soviet Regime and Native Culture in Central Asia and Kazakhstan: The Major Peoples." *Current Anthropology* 8 (1967): 147–208.

Wiens, H. H. "Change in the Ethnography and Land Use of the Ili Valley and Region, Chinese Turkestan." *Association of American Geographers* 59:4 (1969): 753–775.

Winner, Irene. "Some Problems of Nomadism and Social Organization Among the Recently Settled Kazakhs." *Central Asian Review* 11:3 and 4 (1963): 355–373.

KÉDANG   The Kédang (locally pronounced "édang") are a small ethnic group of some 30,000 persons at the extreme east of the island of Lembata (Lomblen) in the Solor Archipelago of eastern Indonesia. Together with the much more numerous Lamaholot, they make up the East Flores Regency in the Province of East Southeast Islands. Census reports for 1980 show 52 percent of the Kédang as Muslims and 48 percent as Catholic, but these figures deliberately disguise the number of those who maintain traditional practices. Locally available census records of 1970 show that around 45 percent professed Islam, 28 percent were Catholic and some 27 percent retained the traditional religion. The language of the Kédang, called Tutuq-nanang Wéla ("the language of the mountain"), is a member of the Austronesian or Malayo-Polynesian family and is distinct from the neighboring and related Lamaholot language (see Lamaholot).

Unlike the Lamaholot, the Kédang enter only rarely and fleetingly into historical records prior to the twentieth century. The log of Magellan's ship *Victoria*, which passed the island in January 1522, records the name of Kalikur, a politically important village on the north coast which offered some harbor facilities. Towards the end of the nineteenth century, the Dutch threatened Kalikur with two gunboats, forcing the leading family to acknowledge itself as a vassal of the Raja of Adonara. The Dutch then recognized the head of this family as the leader of all the Kédang and employed their military strength to insure that the Kédang accepted him as such.

Islam appears to have had little impact on Kédang until early in the nineteenth century, when Muslim Lamaholot settlers from Lamahala, Adonara, established a colony at Dololong. The religion was largely confined to Dololong and principal families of Kalikur until around 1931, when Muslims from Kalikur began proselytizing in the interior.

Catholic missionaries first started working in Kédang in the early part of the 1920s; Islamic proselytizing efforts were a direct response to their advances. Whereas initially Catholicism was spread by Europeans of various nationalities in the Divine Word Society, Islam (Sunni) came to Kédang through the agency of the Lamaholot and perhaps other Indonesians.

Most Kédang practice subsistence horticulture on swidden fields. The staples are maize and dry rice, but the fields also produce many varieties of vegetables. The Kédang are well known for their citrus fruit. They also produce coconuts and candlenuts. A few people living at the shore are itinerant merchants or practice artisanal fishing. Cash has only a small role in the economy.

Differences in social class are very little marked among the Kédang. Until the Indonesian government removed political power from the ruling family of Kalikur in the 1960s, persons from this village exercised a sometimes harsh supremacy over others; however, this circumstance is now changed. Kédang may have been a supplier of slaves in the past, but little is known of this trade.

The Kédang are very like the neighboring Lamaholot. Each village is comprised of a number of named groups, membership in which derives from descent through males. These patrilineal clans are linked by a pattern of prescribed asymmetric marriage alliance. This rule is more clearly expressed in the social classification, ritual and behavior of linked families than it is in the overall configuration of marriages. The Kédang expect the wife-giving allies will be distinct from the wife-taking affines.

The wife-givers are superior to the wife-takers. A person regards his or her mother's close male relatives as being superior, exercising complete control over health and well-being. Wife-givers take a central place in life-cycle rituals, especially those dealing with birth and death. Wife-givers receive a regular series of gifts, usually gongs or elephant tusks, and return tie-dyed decorated sarongs. There is a traditional prohibition in Kédang on weaving, now broached to the extent of producing coarse clothing. The Kédang purchase cloth for marriage gifts from the Lamaholot. They show great interest in the exchange of these marriage gifts, and they always complete the payments even though it may take more than one generation to do so.

Village government is now arranged with elected head, treasurer and clerks as part of the national administrative apparatus. In the past, the oldest clan in each village provided a lord of the land, *léu-auq wala*, whose leadership was primarily ceremonial and concerned with community rituals now largely defunct. Unlike elsewhere, in Kédang this officer seems to have exercised only slight power over control of agriculture.

Many traditional rituals are still performed, even by some who acknowledge themselves to be Muslim or Catholic. Most villages, and even many families, contain Muslims, Catholics and traditionalists. Persons in each of these categories still take part in rituals and feasts associated with alliance. Any large festivity brings together people of each orientation, and the Kédang take steps to accommodate their respective religious sensitivities. They will prepare goat meat and water for Muslims, pork and palm wine for the others. Many villages have both a church and a mosque. These are usually small and temporary structures; but recently with outside assistance they have erected several large, modern buildings.

Kédang villages are situated rather evenly around the sides of the extinct Uyo Léwung volcano. This mountain (5,000 feet) holds a central place in Kédang culture and mythology. Mankind's original village, marked by stone constructions, is situated at the top of the mountain. The traditional centers of each village are usually located high on the mountain's slopes. Some of these are still inhabited. The Kédang regard them as places of pronounced ceremonial significance, intimately linked with their spiritual well-being. The Dutch and Indonesian governments have persuaded most villagers to relocate in new hamlets in more accessible places, but the older village sites, even when uninhabited, have not lost their importance. In recent years clans have refurbished ancestral temples on these sites. Christians and Muslims participate in these activities to the extent that they think compatible with their religion. The traditional Kédang High God bears several names, among them Ula-Loyo (Moon-Sun), Loyo Buyaq (White Sun), Loyo Rian (Great Sun), Lia Rian (Great Morning Star), Lia-Loyo (Morning Star-Sun). Kédang of any religious persuasion typically identify these names with the Arabic Tuhan Allah, Lahatala. Both Muslims and Christians employ the last expression for their conception of Divinity.

BIBLIOGRAPHY

Books

Barnes, R. H. "Concordance, Structure and Variation: Considerations of Alliance in Kédang." In *The Flow of Life: Essays on Eastern Indonesia*, edited by James J. Fox. Cambridge: Harvard University Press, 1980.
———. *Kédang: A Study of the Collective Thought of an Eastern Indonesian People*. Oxford: Clarendon Press, 1974.

Articles

Barnes, R. H. "Mancala in Kédang: A Structural Test." *Bijdragen tot de Taal-, Land-en Volkenkunde* 131 (1975): 67–85.
———. "Number and Number Use in Kédang, Indonesia." *Man* 17 (1982): 1–22.

R. H. Barnes

KHO   In the mountain valleys between the Hindu Kush and Hindu Raj ranges of northernmost Pakistan lies the district of Chitral, a formerly independent state dominated by an Indo-Aryan-speaking people who call themselves Kho. Until 1970 Chitral was ruled by a succession of hereditary kings called *mehtars*. Since Britain asserted control over Chitral in 1895, the *mehtars'* powers were somewhat curtailed, but the kingdom retained an eroding autonomy even after it joined Pakistan in 1949. When the *mehtar's* powers were abrogated in 1970, Chitral was incorporated as a district of Pakistan's North-West Frontier Province, and it is currently governed by a federally appointed district commissioner.

Chitral covers the 180-mile-long upper basin of the Chitral River, down to the point where it crosses the Afghanistan border and becomes known as the Kunar. The physical barrier of the surrounding mountain ranges and the political barrier of the Afghanistan border tend to isolate Chitral. Overland communication is possible only when the high mountain passes are not blocked by snow; during the winter, scheduled airline service, frequently interrupted because of inclement weather, is the only link with the outside.

The climate and steep ruggedness of the terrain allow irrigated agriculture only within the main valley and its major tributaries. The lower quarter of the basin can support rain-fed fields in addition to irrigated ones, but the remaining area is arid and relies totally on irrigation fed by glacial runoff. Major crops include barley, wheat, maize, millet and rice, supplemented by legumes and potatoes. In addition to agriculture the Kho rely to a lesser extent on the transhumant herding of dairy goats and cattle. An increasing population and limited resources make much of Chitral chronically short of food.

The roughly 287,000 Kho constitute four-fifths of the population of Chitral; the remaining population consists of numerous ethnic minorities primarily inhabiting higher valley enclaves. The Kho extend eastward from Chitral over the Hindu Raj range, where they inhabit the Ghizar and Yasin valleys of Gilgit and the upper Ushu Valley of Swat Kohistan.

Most Kho are Sunnis of the Hanafi legal school; however, a minority living in Upper Chitral are Ismailis. Although the latter sect arrived in Chitral from the north before the former arrived from the south, the Ismailis occupy an inferior social position.

Kho society is divided into three classes: an aristocracy, a landed gentry and a lower class of ethnic minorities and generally landless tenant farmers and laborers. The aristocracy descends from linguistically absorbed foreign conquerors of the region. It includes the agnatic descendants of Baba Ayub and

Sumalik, the founders of the current and previous dynasties. Sumalik's descendants, the Rais Mehtars, apparently came from the east and ruled over portions of the area until 1595. From their names it appears that they were Muslims at least since the early fourteenth century. The descendants of Sumalik are today known as the Zodre. Baba Ayub, reputedly an eighth-generation descendant of Tamerlane (Timur-i-Lang), established himself in Chitral in the early sixteenth century after immigrating from Khorasan. His great-great-great grandson, Muhtaram Shah Katur, supplanted the last of the Rais Mehtars and founded the current royal line, the Kature.

Baba Ayub's descendants traditionally marry only endogamously or to foreign ruling families, whereas the Zondre reportedly marry their women to men of the gentry, also. Aristocrats may marry women of the gentry. The *mehtars* took concubines freely from the commoners; the sons of such unions often gained princely titles and estates but were not considered legitimate heirs to succession.

Under the *mehtars* the administrative organization of Chitral consisted of a hierarchy of provincial, district and village officials responsible primarily for mustering revenue and conscripts. The *mehtar's* court consisted of ministers, ambassadors and retainers. Courtly ritual expressed the sociopolitical status of those in attendance and was embellished by music, poetry and sports.

The *mehtar* could also determine the sociopolitical status of his sons and close supporters by allotting them usufruct rights to his estates throughout the country. Princes residing on such estates were charged with settling disputes arising in the surrounding region. Occasionally, the *mehtar* would redistribute the right to his estates, matching the needs or amenities of individual estates to the talents of his sons. Redistribution also assured that a single son could not consolidate a local following that would back him in an attempted usurpation.

Since 1970 the traditional administrative system has been replaced with the formal Pakistani system of district administration. The higher posts of the bureaucracy have been filled by Pushtun (Pathans) from outside Chitral (see Pushtun). When the *mehtar*-ship was abolished, the ownership of royal estates was fixed to the heirs of the princes who held them. In addition to owning the estates, the princes retain rights to surrounding highland grazing areas, from which they gain lease fees. The princes are generally held in high regard and are still invited to mediate disputes. Many have held military rank and civil service posts.

Among the Kho, descent is reckoned agnatically. The precise nature and functions of the numerous patrilineages, as well as the kinship system in general, are poorly understood. Inheritance is patrifilial; the share entitled to a daughter under Shariah law is counted as her dowry.

Fosterage is a common Kho institution. Among the nobility infants are often raised in households far from those of their parents, and in later life members of the foster family act as the foster child's retainers. The families of foster mothers and those whom they suckle reckon each other as kinsmen, just as if the foster mother were the child's biological mother. Marriage between members of such families is considered incestuous.

Although the Kho language, Khowar, is unwritten, native poetry and songs enjoy high esteem, even beyond Chitral. Under the *mehtars*, poetry contests were held regularly.

As Chitral undergoes further integration into the mainstream of Pakistani national life, Kho culture and society will continue to undergo the radical changes that began with the abolition of the *mehtar*-ship. An extensive road-building project currently underway promises to accelerate the influx of Pushtun into Chitral from the south. The Pushtun minority in Chitral has grown rapidly in the last few generations, and their expanding influence, abetted by the Pushtun-dominated bureaucracy of the district government, is engendering a growing resentment among the Kho. Only through judicious planning will interethnic conflict be averted.

BIBLIOGRAPHY

Books

Barth, Fredrik. *Indus and Swat Kohistan: An Ethnographic Survey*. Oslo: Forenede Trykkerier, 1956.
Biddulph, John. *Tribes of the Hindoo Koosh*. Reprint ed. Karachi: Indus, 1977. (Originally published 1880.)
Nagel, Ernst. "Der Reisbau bei den Kho in Chitral." In *Vergleichende Kulturgeographie der Hochgebirge des Sudlichen Asien*, edited by Carl Athjens, Carol Troll, and Harald Uhlig. Erdwissenschaftliche Forschung, 5. Wiesbaden: Franz Steiner, 1973.

Article

Staley, John. "Economy and Society in the High Mountains of Northern Pakistan." *Modern Asian Studies* 3:3 (1969): 225–243.

Richard F. Strand

KHOTON   The Khoton are one of a very few Muslim peoples found to the east and north of the Gobi Desert in Mongolia. Although they are of Turkic origin, probably of the same stock as the Kazakhs and Kirghiz, they have lost their original language and adopted the Mongol Dorbet dialect. There were about 2,400 Khoton in 1930, the most recent figures available for them. They are no longer listed separately in Mongol census records.

In 1930, the Khoton nomadized in two separate groups, the Bayan Mandal and Altan Degeli camps, in northwest Mongolia around Ulangom and Lake Ubsu.

Islam was still found among the Khoton in 1930, with *mullahs* still practicing. The faith, perhaps because of isolation and strong influences of Mongol life surrounding it, had become corrupted by shamanist nature cults, such as those of earth, water, fire and sheep sacrifice. Nothing is known of current religious practice among the Khoton.

BIBLIOGRAPHY

Article

Moses, Larry W., trans. "The Khotons: Muslims of Mongolia." *Mongolia Society Bulletin* 6:1 (Spring 1967): 11–14.

Larry W. Moses

KIRGHIZ The etymology of the ethnonym "Kirghiz" is not clear, but most Turkologists believe it to be a compound of two Turkic words: *girgh* (forty) and *qiz* (girl, daughter), which means, according to the Kirghiz, "descendants of the 40 maidens." Since about the middle of the eighteenth century they have occupied the Pamir-Altai ranges in the Soviet Union and Afghanistan and the Kunlun and the Tien Shan in China.

There are approximately 2.2 million Kirghiz, nearly all of whom live in the Soviet Union. Close to 88 percent of the Soviet Kirghiz live in Kirghiz Soviet Socialist Republic (Kirghizia). Some 120,000 live in Uzbekistan, and smaller numbers are found in the Tajik and Kazakh republics. About 110,000 reside in the Xinjiang Uygur Autonomous Region of the People's Republic of China. Until 1978 about 2,000 Kirghiz occupied the Pamirs of Afghanistan in the Wakhan Corridor. Following the 1978 Marxist military coup in Kabul, more than 1,000 of them fled to Pakistan. In 1982 they were resettled in eastern Anatolia in Turkey.

Kirghiz is a Turkic language that belongs to the northwestern group of Turkic languages and has close affinities with Kazakh, Karakalpak, Tatar and Kipchak-Uzbek. Until about the turn of this century Kirghiz was not written, and literate Kirghiz used a written form of Uzbek and Uygur popularly called "Turki" throughout Turkic Central Asia. Since the 1930s, Kirghiz, like other Central Asian languages, has been written in Cyrillic and is the official language of Kirghizia.

The Kirghiz are numerically one of the smallest of the Turkic-speaking populations in Central Asia. Historically the demographically and politically more powerful Uzbek, Kazakhs, Uygur and Mongols have pushed them to marginal and often harsh, cold mountain regions. They have had little access to the fertile, low-lying agricultural valleys, and as a result very few of them have been farmers. Their traditional subsistence system has been nomadic pastoralism involving raising sheep, goats, horses, common cattle, yak and camels, including the Bactrian. For the large majority of Kirghiz, their lot has changed little under Russian, Chinese and Afghan domination. In their own titular republic, where they make up less than 48 percent of the population, nearly 80 percent of them are engaged in collectivized nomadic pastoralism. They are the exclusive inhabitants of the 85 percent of the republic's territory that lies more than 5,000 feet above sea level.

In the traditional Kirghiz way of life, the most significant independent economic and political unit was the *oey*, or family-household. Ideally this consisted of a man, his wife or wives, their unmarried children and married sons and their children. Often the Kirghiz *oey* consisted of other close blood relatives, adopted members and even some unrelated dependents. The *oey* was headed by an adult male, although on the death of a husband or in the absence of mature sons a woman could also become the head of the household. Members of an *oey* generally owned and occupied a single yurt, the round, felt-covered Central Asian tent with a collapsible wooden lattice frame. Only the very rich had an extra yurt to use as a guest house or a residence for a second wife. The domestic unit owned its own herd and shared pasturage rights with other patrilineal kinsmen. A number of households belonging to the same *kechek orug* (patrilineage) camped together and cooperated with one another in migration, trade, herding and ritual occasions. Although the size of family-owned herds differed depending on their access to good pasturage and the availability of adequate labor, extremes of poverty and wealth were rare.

The Kirghiz social structure was organized on agnatic descent principles, and all Kirghiz claimed common descent from the same male ancestor, whose name and identity were unknown to the majority. Kirghiz were divided into numerous named kinship groups and categories called *chung oruq* or *orow* (clan or tribe) and *kechek oruq* (lineage). The ability to trace ancestry for seven ascending generations in the male line was crucial to the Kirghiz as proof of identity and as claim to membership in a particular *oruq*. Those unable to do so were considered *qul* (slaves), as were children of those born of mixed marriages between Kirghiz and non-Kirghiz/non-Kazakh. As a result, Kirghiz marriages were highly endogamous within extended families between all kinds of first cousins and within lineages and clans. Marriage with non-Kirghiz and non-Kazakh, including those of the sedentary Turkic groups such as Uzbek and Uygur, was strongly discouraged. In fact, the Kirghiz referred to the dominant Uzbek and Uygur as *sart*, a derogatory term which also included all the non-Turkic peoples in the area, especially the Tajik (see Tajik).

All forms of kinship ties, blood, marriage and fictive, played an important role in the organization of Kirghiz economic, social and political relations. Important local leaders were generally senior members of *oruq* groups. Leadership qualities entailed bravery (military prowess), honesty, abilities in public persuasion and oratory, sound judgment, being a good Muslim, membership in a large *oruq* and success as a herdsman, with large flocks and wealth in other tangible goods. What was significant about wealth in this regard was not its possession but rather how it was used to help the community of kinsmen. Hospitality, generosity and the offer of help to one's relatives and to the needy and poor stood out as signs of being a good Muslim and were all personal qualities desired among the politically ambitious in Kirghiz society.

The organization of the Kirghiz household varied considerably, depending upon its size, composition and access to herds and pastures. Generally, both the structure of authority and the division of labor were flexible. The eldest adult male (or in his absence the eldest female) acted as head of the domestic unit, representing its interest in the community. The head of the household enjoyed respect but did not exercise absolute authority. All significant decisions affecting marriages, herd management, labor and resource allocation, camp membership and migration were reached through agreements among adult members of the herding family group. The Kirghiz women were quite assertive in all matters of importance to the domestic unit.

Kirghiz women did not wear the veil or avoid contact with non-kinsmen. Some women owned considerable herds of their own and became head of their households after the death of their husbands. Although most marriages were arranged by parents and other adult members of the household, courtship before marriage was common and often influenced the choice of partners.

The Kirghiz marked births, circumcisions, weddings, deaths and major Islamic religious holidays with festivities. However, for politically ambitious and wealthy families, two occasions—weddings and the first anniversary of the death of an important member—provided the context for considerable celebrations and the gathering of large numbers of tribesmen for public festivities.

The Kirghiz had embraced Islam by the sixteenth century, becoming Sunni followers of the Hanafi school of Shariah law. Because of their nomadic way of life, Western writers have often considered the Kirghiz to be nominally religious and their Islam full of Central Asian shamanistic beliefs and rituals. However, the Kirghiz commitment to Islam and their practice of Islam prior to the Bolshevik Revolution seems to have been as strong as that of any other sedentary or nomadic people in the Muslim world.

Until 1978 the small number of Kirghiz in Afghanistan were probably the only Kirghiz who were able to continue their traditional pastoral nomadic mode of subsistence and to perpetuate their social organization without any significant direct outside interference. They had been able to create a rather stable niche for themselves within the pre-1978 context in Afghanistan. Following the Marxist coup, they decided to leave their mountain retreat in the Afghan Pamirs. Resettled in eastern Turkey, they are now confronted by the challenge to build a new future.

In China, Communist government policies towards all pastoralists has been, and remains, their eventual sedentarization and transformation into agricultural communes. The policies towards the minorities envisage their eventual assimilation into the larger Han culture and politics. However, in practice, government policies regarding minorities and nomads in Xinjiang have been determined both by the social realities in the area and by the changing nature of Soviet and Chinese political relations in the past three decades.

Three distinct phases have marked Chinese policies towards the peoples of Xinjiang. First, from 1949 to 1957 the Chinese were confronted by strong anti-Communist and anti-Han resistance in Xinjiang from the Muslim populations, nomadic and sedentary alike. The Chinese response was moderate and gradual, aimed at strengthening state power by pacifying or eliminating the resistance leadership. Only in 1955 did the government begin to organize the Kirghiz into mutual aid teams and cooperatives organized along the traditional *oruq* (patrilineage) structure.

The second phase coincided with Mao's Great Leap Forward of 1958–1960. The principal aim of this policy was the formation of communes and a socialist upsurge. No special economic or ethnic peculiarities of people were tolerated, and the anti-Islamic and anti-nomadic campaign was strong. The Great Leap Forward policy caused a great influx of Hans into Xinjiang. Reaction towards the radical policies resulted in a grain crisis, and the authorities decided to put some of the pastoralists' pasture lands under the plow. The nomadic population reportedly slaughtered large numbers of livestock during this phase, and in the face of growing political disputes between the Chinese and the Soviets a large number of pastoralists in northwestern Xinjiang, among them some Kirghiz, joined in the exodus across the border to the Soviet Union, causing the "Ili Crisis" of 1962.

The third phase of the Chinese policies was particularly influenced by the Sino–Soviet split. In many instances a reversal in their Great Leap Forward policies occurred. The pastoral communes are believed to have remained as nominal enterprises, although they were nothing more than earlier forms of cooperatives located near various settlement points. Kirghiz *oruq* once again became the basic unit of the production brigades, who enjoy certain material incentives and partial ownership of the herds. Undoubtedly, the Kirghiz have benefitted to some extent from Peking's laissez-faire approach to ruling its ethnic minorities along the Xinjiang–Soviet frontier.

By the eve of the Bolshevik Revolution, the Kirghiz in Central Asia had lost much of their land to Slavic colonists, and their alienation and resentment towards the Russians led to a major rebellion in 1916. When the Bolsheviks established control over the area in 1918, the Kirghiz territories were incorporated with various other provinces in Turkestan. As in the earlier period, Kirghiz lands were expropriated and given to Russian settlers. Confronted with the anti-Communist armed resistance of the so-called Basmachi movement in the area, the Bolsheviks adopted a more conciliatory policy, and during the land reform of 1920–1921 some of the Kirghiz lands were returned to them. In 1924 a Kirghiz Autonomous Oblast' was created, a number of leading Kirghiz intellectuals were recruited into the administration and the traditional structure of Kirghiz society and pastoral nomadic economy was left intact. In February 1926 the Kirghiz Oblast' was elevated to an autonomous Soviet socialist republic, and ten years later, in 1936, it was accepted as Kirghiz S.S.R.

Despite the concessions offered during the early 1920s, the Russians dominated all aspects of government and party structure. When Kirghiz intellectuals openly expressed their frustrations, many of them were incarcerated or exiled. The real change of policy came about in 1928, when Stalin set out to "de-nomadize" and collectivize the Kirghiz. This agrarian revolution of 1927–1928 was met by widespread slaughter of livestock and the exodus of large numbers of Kirghiz and Kazakhs into Xinjiang in China. Despite the turmoil, significant progress was made in the development of education and health care during this period.

Industrial development in Kirghizia expanded after World War II. However, the industrial economy, which emphasizes power production, nonferrous metallurgy, construction material, fossil fuel extraction, woodworking, textiles, sugar refining and meat packing, is dominated by the Slavs. The great majority of the Kirghiz are still herding through pastoral collectives.

More than six decades of Soviet rule over the Kirghiz has produced significant changes in the Kirghiz way of life. The traditional form of nomadic pastoralism has been modified. The *oruq* structure and other kinship ties have been weakened but still play an important role in funerals, ceremonial rites, mutual aid practices, residential patterns and attitudes towards non-Kirghiz. The patrilineal extended family has remained strong and in most instances simply incorporated into herding brigades. The families apparently also are able to own some of their own livestock. The Kirghiz endogamous marriage practices are still favored, and marriage of Kirghiz women to Russians discouraged. Although some urbanized Kirghiz men have married Russian women, the reverse seems not to have occurred. The Kirghiz exchange of bridewealth, *qalen* (*kalym*), and dowry upon marriage has also persisted. The practice of polygyny is also reported to continue among some influential leaders of collectives. Like other Central Asian populations, the Kirghiz birthrate has remained high. The increase in Kirghiz population is attributed not only to the high birthrate but also to in-migration of Kirghiz from the other republics and China.

The most critical development among the Soviet Kirghiz has been in the field of education. In 1967–1968 it is reported that nearly 280,000 pupils in grades 1 through 10 were enrolled in schools, with Kirghiz as the medium of instruction in their titular republic. There is increasing evidence that large numbers of Kirghiz are learning technical, intellectual and professional skills and are competing with Slavs and other Europeans for better paid positions. Increasing numbers of them now hold higher positions in the party and administration and places of work, although party membership still remains low. This development, coupled with an increased sense of Kirghiz nationalism and kinship loyalties, has produced a momentum that may lead to a greater role for the Kirghiz in both government and positions of authority.

A strong component of the heightened national consciousness of the Kirghiz, and an important factor influencing Kirghiz attitudes towards others, is Islam. This is so despite the fact that the outward institutional apparatus of religious practice (mosques, *madrasas*, *mullahs*) has been reduced to a minimum. The extent of knowledge of Islam among the younger generations may have decreased, but the intimate relationships of Islam with Kirghiz ethnic and national identity has remained strong through family structure, pro-natalism, marriage, observance of life-crisis rituals, the rites of transition and the continuation of Islamized folk belief and practices in the domestic and kinship domains. Islam continues to help shape the content of a socialist form that has been externally imposed upon their society. Nationalistic-religious resistance has occurred in a very subtle and calculated manner. There are some indications that Islamic nationalism may have been expressed in a more violent manner in the December 1980 assassination of Sultan Ibrahim, the prime minister of Kirghizia. The Islamic sentiments openly expressed by the (Kirghiz) foreign minister of Kirghizia, Mrs. Sahin Begmatova, in 1980 towards Russian policies in Afghanistan resulted in a major political shake-up in the republic. The Soviet Kirghiz have slowly gained in education and as a result have become more assertive and conscious of their rights.

BIBLIOGRAPHY

Books

Allworth, Edward. *The Nationality Question in Soviet Central Asia*. New York: Praeger, 1973.

Azrael, Jeremy, ed. *Soviet Nationality Policies and Practices*. New York: Praeger, 1978.

Bacon, Elizabeth. *Central Asians Under Russian Rule*. Ithaca: Cornell University Press, 1980.

Bennigsen, Alexandre, and Lemercier-Quelquejay, Chantal. *Islam in the Soviet Union*. New York: Praeger, 1967.

Bennigsen, Alexandre, and Wimbush, Enders. *Muslim National Communism in the Soviet Union: A Revolutionary Strategy for the Colonial World*. Chicago: University of Chicago Press, 1979.

Caroe, Sir Olaf K. *Soviet Empire: The Turks of Central Asia and Stalinism*. New York: St. Martin's Press, 1967.

Carrere d'Encausse, Helene. *Decline of an Empire: The Soviet Socialist Republics in Revolt*. New York: Newsweek Books, 1979.

Hetmanek, Allen. "Kirgizistan and the Kirgiz." In *Handbook of Major Soviet Nationalities*, edited by Zev Katz. New York: Free Press, 1975.

Mote, Victor. "Kirgiz." In *Muslim Peoples: A World Ethnographic Survey*, edited by Richard V. Weekes. Westport, Conn.: Greenwood Press, 1978.

Novosti Press Agency. *Kirghiz Soviet Socialist Republic*. Moscow: Novosti Press Agency Publishing House, 1972.

Shahrani, M. Nazif. *The Kirghiz and Wakhi of Afghanistan*. Seattle: University of Washington Press, 1979.

Articles

Abramzon, S. M. "The Kirghiz of the Chinese Peoples' Republic." *Central Asian Review* 11:2 (1963): 196–207.

"Down in Kirghizia Something Stirs." *The Economist*, January 17, 1981, p. 48.

Karklins, Rasma. "Nationality Power in Soviet Republics: Attitudes and Perceptions." *Studies in Comparative Communism: An International Interdisciplinary Journal* 21:8 (1981): 70–93.

M. Nazif Shahrani

KOHISTANIS   The remote valleys of the Indus, Swat and Dir Kohistan regions of northern Pakistan are a haven for numerous ethnic groups called by outsiders Kohistanis, "people of the mountains." The unwritten Indo-Iranian languages spoken by these peoples indicate a common phylogenetic relationship, but beyond the scanty linguistic evidence little is known of their historical interrelationships. Some ten generations ago, they were converted from their polytheistic Aryan beliefs to Sunni Islam by Pushtun from Swat, who also displaced many of them from a formerly wider territory. Since then, the Pushtun have continued to exert considerable cultural, economic and political influence over the less numerous (perhaps 100,000) Kohistanis (see Pushtun).

The Kohistanis occupy two distinct ecological areas: the upper basins of the Swat and Panjkora rivers, and the tributary valleys of the Indus River roughly from the town of Besham north to the Kandia Valley. Hemmed in to snowy alpine valleys by lowland Pushtun, the inhabitants of Swat and Dir Kohistan can grow only a single crop of irrigated maize or millet annually. They occupy permanent villages, from which they drive their cattle, goats and sheep to alpine pastures in the summer.

In contrast, the peoples of Indus Kohistan utilize the entire lengths of the tributary valleys, from the formidable Indus River gorge to the alpine pasturelands lying on the Indus watersheds. They follow an annual transhumant cycle, planting rice in late winter close to the Indus, then moving up the tributary valleys in the spring to plant maize, wheat and barley on higher, terraced fields. From there they drive their cattle, buffalo, goats and sheep to the alpine pastures for the summer. In early autumn they return to harvest the crops planted in the spring, and by late autumn they arrive at the Indus to harvest the rice. During this cycle the Indus Kohistanis occupy seasonal dispersed settlements at the higher altitudes. Only during the winter do they reside together in their compact villages along the Indus River.

Two ethnic groups, each with its own language, occupy Swat and Dir Kohistan. The uppermost valleys of the Swat and Panjkora basins are home to speakers of the Garvi language. These people are politically subdivided into regional groups that center on the upper Panjkora basin in Dir and the village of Utror, the village of Kalam, and the Ushu Valley in Swat. In Bahrain and a few smaller villages of the Swat basin below the Garvi speakers live the speakers of the Torwali language.

A more complex ethnic situation exists in Indus Kohistan, where the people of each major valley consider themselves politically distinct and speak dialects that are often mutually unintelligible. From south to north on the west bank of the Indus River reside the inhabitants of the Duber, Jijal and Patan valleys, the village of Seo and the Kandia Valley. On the east side of the Indus from north to south, Kohistanis inhabit the valleys that open out at the villages of Jalkot, Palas, Kolay and Bhatera. The ethnic mosaic is further complicated by an admixture of Shina-speaking inhabitants in Jalkot, Palas and Kolay (see Shina-speaking Peoples). In addition, there are families of Pakhto-speaking craftsmen and saintly descendants scattered throughout the area. Linguistically the people of Duber and Kandia constitute one dialect group, the inhabitants of Jijal, Patan, Seo and parts of Jalkot and Palas form another group, those of Bhatera form a third group and the people of Kolay apparently constitute a fourth group. A definitive statement of the phylogenetic relationships of the peoples and languages of Indus Kohistan awaits further research.

Agnatic kinship is the basic organizing principle of Kohistani society, which is divided into segmentary patrilineages. Within the patrilineages of the Indus Kohistani there is a tendency towards endogamy. Landholdings and rights to pasturelands are inherited patrifilially. The right to blood vengeance devolves on the closest agnatic inheritors of a murder victim, unless blood payment is negotiated.

The traditional governmental body of the Kohistani peoples is the council, which is composed of landholding men from the village or region. Among the Indus Kohistanis, councilmen usually represent entire patrilineages, while among the Garvi and Torwali speakers, representatives are drawn from agnatic extended families. The councils traditionally met to consider administration of community affairs, but their function is apparently being supplanted by the current Pakistani system of district administration.

Recently the Kohistanis' isolation from the mainstream of Pakistani society has been lessened by the completion of roads into their territories. In Dir and Swat the commerce brought by such roads threatens to increase the economic and cultural dominance of the down-country Pushtun, who control the motor transport industry in the region. Better transportation and communications may enhance the Kohistanis' access to the political arenas of the Swat and Dir district governments. The newly opened Karakorum Highway follows the difficult Indus River valley through the heart of Indus Kohistan and promises to open the region to exploitation of its timber and mineral resources. To demonstrate its commitment to the development of the Indus region, the government of Pakistan has created a new Kohistan District, giving the Indus Kohistanis their own administrative area within the North-West Frontier Province. The effect of commercial development on the cultures and living standard of the Kohistanis remains to be seen.

BIBLIOGRAPHY

Books

Barth, Fredrik. *Indus and Swat Kohistan: An Ethnographic Survey. Studies Honouring the Centennial of Universitetets Ethnografiske Museum, Oslo, 1857–1957.* Oslo: Forenede Trykkerier, 1956.

Biddulph, John. *Tribes of the Hindoo Koosh*. Reprint ed. Karachi: Indus, 1977. (Originally published 1880.)

Stein, Aurel. "Note on Torwal and Its People." In *Torwali: An Account of a Dardic Language of the Swat Kohistan*, edited by George A. Grierson. London: Royal Asiatic Society, 1929.

Article

Barth, Fredrik, and Morgenstierne, Georg. "Vocabularies and Specimens of Some S. E. Dardic Dialects." *Norsk Tiddskrift for Sproguidenskap* 18 (1958): 118–136.

Richard F. Strand

KOREANS   Islam was introduced to Korea by the contingent of Turkish troops who fought under the United Nations flag during the Korean War, 1950–1953. Two Turkish *imams* accompanying the troops responded to the interest of a small group of South Koreans living near their encampment. The *imams* instructed them in religious knowledge and the practice of Islam, setting aside a special tent to serve as a mosque and school. In September 1955, some 30 Koreans officially embraced Islam.

The new converts, in turn, attracted other followers among their countrymen. A temporary mosque was constructed near Seoul in 1957, and by 1959 the first Korean Muslims had made the Haj, visiting various Islamic countries on the way to and from Mecca to spread the news of the growing community of Muslims in Korea. In 1963 Malaysian officials visiting the Republic of Korea made contact with Korean Muslims, resulting in the Malaysian prime minister donating funds to support the continued propagation of the faith. Before long, religious teachers from South Asia and the Middle East joined the missionary work.

The Korean Muslim Federation was organized in 1965 and was officially registered with the government's Ministry of Culture and Information two years later. At that time the federation had nearly 3,000 members, and one of the earliest converts, Hadji Sabri Suh, was its first president. In June 1967, the federation began publishing the *Korean Islam Herald*, a bimonthly and bilingual (Korean and English) newspaper, as an important instrument for the promotion of Islam. The Korean government in 1970 donated land on the outskirts of Seoul for the construction of an Islamic Center and Mosque, and a year later a delegation of Korean Muslims traveled abroad to raise funds for the proposed building. Contributions came from Saudi Arabia, Kuwait, Abu Dabi, Libya, Morocco, Qatar and the World Muslim League. By May 1976 the beautiful and impressive center was completed, and 55 delegates from 21 Islamic countries attended the opening ceremony.

Since its opening the Islamic Center in Seoul has been the headquarters of the Korean Muslim Federation and the base for a variety of outreach activities such as preaching, teaching, publishing and social work. It has attracted many inquirers, a large percentage of whom have become Muslims. Today there are more than 50,000 Korean Muslims, and the faith is winning new adherents daily. Some of the new Muslims (about 7,000) are to be found among the more than 100,000 Korean workers in the Arab world. Indeed, the Korean Muslim Federation has opened branches in Saudi Arabia and Kuwait.

One of the most dramatic instances of growth in Korean Islam is the conversion of almost the entire village of Ssan Ryung in the Kyung-gi District, some 30 miles southeast of Seoul. A native of the village, Abdullah Jeun Duck Lin, embraced Islam in 1977 while teaching in a Seoul secondary school. He returned to Ssang Ryung filled with quiet fervor to share his new faith with his relatives and neighbors. Today just about all of the 123 households (nearly 700 people) are Muslim. There is a new mosque under construction, and the village boasts an Islamic school bursting with young students.

In September 1980 the Korean Muslim Federation opened another impressive Islamic Center and Mosque in Pusan, Korea's second largest city. Like the center in Seoul, this center is proving an effective base for spreading Islam.

In 1980 there were some 53 young Muslims studying in Islamic centers of learning abroad (in Pakistan, Saudi Arabia, Libya, Egypt, Morocco, Indonesia and Malaysia) on religious scholarships. As the future *ulama* of Korean Islam, they will be important in tying Korean Islam to the universal and normative beliefs and practices of world Islam. While the growing community of Korean Muslims remains culturally Korean, new converts reportedly find Islam's prohibition of alcohol and pork particularly difficult to follow. The spiritual discipline of five daily prayers is especially hard to maintain in a culture which has nothing comparable to it. Another difficulty is the image in the minds of many Koreans that Islam is the religion of "backward" or "unprogressive" or "fanatical" countries—hence Koreans becoming Muslims are seen to be something of an oddity. Still, the fact that more than half of South Korea's 37 million population espouses no particular religion means there is a large field for the propagation of Islam among those not attracted to the traditional shamanist, Buddhist or Christian faiths to which the rest of the population adheres. Moreover, nearly all of the Korean Muslims are literate and employed skilled workers or professionals, many of them university and college students and teachers.

Two major projects in progress under the Korean Muslim Federation are the translation of the Quran into Korean and the construction of a Korean Islamic university. The translation project is expected to take 10 to 20 years as it is the work of a Committee of Korean Muslims which seeks to become knowledgeable in the teaching of Islam as well as fluent in Arabic. The university, which is being built on land provided by the government some 12 miles from Seoul, will have 4 academic colleges and 15 departments, including a College of Islamic Studies and History. It will admit students regardless of religious preference but will offer its education program in an "Islamic educational atmosphere." It also aims to be a center of Islamic learning for the Far East, offering scholarships to Muslim students from Japan, China, Taiwan and Hong Kong. Saudi Arabia is giving major financial assistance in the construction of the university.

BIBLIOGRAPHY

Books

Korean Muslim Federation. *The Project of Islamic University in Korea.* Seoul: K.M.F.,
    1980.
————. *Silver Jubilee Photo History of Islam in Korea.* Seoul: K.M.F., 1980.

Articles

Abbas, M. Y. "Islam in South Korea." *Institute of Muslim Minority Affairs Bulletin* 4–
    5 (1977): 14.
"The Mosque in Seoul." *Korea Calling* 15:5 (1976): 1–2.

Peter G. Gowing

KOTOKO   The Kotoko, primarily a riverine townspeople, number about 72,000,
with 36,000 in Cameroon, 18,000 in Chad and 18,000 in Nigeria. They live
along the Logone River from Bongor to Kusseri, the Chari River below Lake
Chad and such rivers and tributaries as the Makari, Mani, Kusseri, Logone-Birni
and Logone-Gana. There are three Kotoko villages near the Chadian capital of
N'Djamena, and a member of the group is prominent in the government, but his
power is limited because his ethnic backing is relatively small.

Kotoko country is bounded on the north by the Buduma, on the east by the
Arabs, and on the west by the Kanuri (see Arabs, Chadian; Buduma; Kanuri).
Frequently they are outnumbered by surrounding Arabs and Fulani herdsmen.
The word "Kotoko" probably is of Arab origin, but its sound is similar to the
noise made by the fishermen as they corral fish into nets from their pirogues by
beating the water and yelling. The Kanuri call them Moria, the Barma call them
Bara and the Mului call them Mamaka. The Kotoko usually call themselves by
the name of their geographical home, such as Mandagé (on the Makari River),
Msar around Kusseri and Dâa in the south.

The Kotoko language belongs to the Chadian group of the Nilo-Saharan family
of languages, the same group as the languages of the Buduma, Kanuri, Kuri and
Kanembu. Linguists recognize three distinct dialects: Mandagé, Lagwané and Dâa.

The Kotoko appear to be descendants of the Sao; at least, the Sao were there
before them—and about everyone else in this part of Africa. The Sao are said to
have been giants with extraordinary strength who apparently settled in the Chari
River region as far back as the fifth century. Archaeologists have found some 637
settlements in mounds, complete with ceramics, tools, weapons and statuettes. It
appears the Sao were able to resist attacks by migrating groups and did not disappear
until the rise of the Bornu Empire in the sixteenth century.

The modern history of the Kotoko is blended with that of the Bornu Empire,
of which they were vassals or, sometimes, allies. In their fortified towns (with
enormous walls sometimes 30 feet high and miles in length) along the Chari

River they were able to defend themselves against the encroachments of outsiders. They claim ownership to all the land around, each city controlling its lands (and charging fees for its use) and traffic on the river, for which they charge tolls.

Legends, usually involving mythical Sao hunters, are rife about the founders of the various Kotoko towns. The leader of one town was presumably a snake whose accession to power symbolized the failure of the Sao. In Gulfei, women, led by a queen mother (*magira*) took over the land; *magira* remains an important element in Kotoko traditions. Elsewhere, as in Afade, Wulki and Maltam, there are similar legends, each symbolized by existing rituals and shrines. These phenomena ended with the coming of Islam, and only the older generations today recite the legends.

Islam came to the Kotoko probably in the sixteenth century during the rise of the Bornu Empire with its many Muslim traders and *mallamai* (clerics). The Kusseri (those who live along the Kusseri River) only adopted Islam in the eighteenth century.

The organization of society, from the family to municipal government, reflects imperial traditions. There is a class of nobles, who generally live on the northern side of each city, from which the rulers are selected. The head of the family, *geifun*, is the grandfather, *akaba*, with a loose structure below him, guaranteeing him significant power. So, too, the chief of a town, the *mé*, is similar to a sultan, assisted by civil servants belonging to the nobility (*megum-dmo*); their task is to manage the wealth of the town and control foreign settlements, most of which, recently, have been Arab.

Studies among Arab and Kotoko groups in the 1960s indicated that demographically the Kotoko appeared to be a stagnated group while the Arabs were increasing rapidly, yet without political power, a situation which could lead to political problems. More recent studies, however, show that, far from being stagnant, the Kotoko have an average growth rate of 4.8 to 6.1 percent, while the Arabs increased only 2.7 to 3.1 percent. This increase by the Kotoko may reflect a "Kotoko-ization" of the Arabs, improved health through urbanization and out-migration of the Arabs, or all three. In any case, the Kotoko appear to be considerably more dynamic in the 1970s than previously.

Parallel to the changes in demography have come changes in the economic life of the Kotoko. Where once they had been mostly fishermen, hunters, gardeners and craftsmen, especially potters, now they are turning to trade and commercial stockbreeding through contracts with Arab pastoralists. This change in economic emphasis also reflects a change in social structure. Involvement in commercial life inevitably erodes status of individuals based upon kin relationships. New status symbols appear in which material wealth and occupational identity create a non-traditional social hierarchy.

BIBLIOGRAPHY

Books

Bouquet, Ch., and Cabot, J. *Atlas pratique du Tchad*. Paris: I.G.N., 1971.

————. *Le Tchad*. Paris: P.U.F., 1973.
LeBeuf, A. *Les Principautés kotoko*. Paris: C.N.R.S., 1969.
Nelson, Harold D., et al. *Area Handbook for Chad*. American University FAS, DA Pam
    550-159. Washington, D.C.: Government Printing Office, 1972.

Christian Bouquet

KUMYK The largest Turkic group in the Daghestan Autonomous Soviet Socialist Republic is the Kumyk, whose territory includes the northeast Caucasus
Mountains between the Terek and Samur rivers. Their population is estimated
at 245,000 (they constitute 13 percent of the republic). While most remain
agriculturalists, many have moved to the cities, especially the capital of the
republic, Makhachkala, on the Caspian Sea.

The Kumyk (Kumuk, Kumik, Kumih, Qumuq) are surrounded by Ibero-
Caucasian speakers as well as some 6 million Turkic-speaking Azeri to the south.
Many are trilingual in Kumyk, Azeri, Russian and indeed sometimes in other
Turkic and Ibero-Caucasian languages as well. Their own language is the only
Turkic language broadcast in Daghestan. Kumyk belongs to the Northwestern
or Kipchak group of Turkic languages. This group is referred to as Kipchak
because it was the language of the great Kipchak Empire located in the vast
steppes of southern Russia from the eleventh to the sixteenth century (see Turkic-
speaking Peoples). Kirghiz, Kazakh, Karakalpak, Karachai, Balkar, Tatar and
Bashkir are from the same language group, while Azeri and Ottoman Turkish
belong to the Southwestern group of Turkic languages. The proximity of Kumyk
and Azeri speakers has rendered these two dialects mutually comprehensible.
The Kumyk literary language is influenced greatly by Azeri. It is recorded that
the great Caucasian leader, Shah Shamil, who led the attacks against the Russian
advances in the middle of the eighteenth century, spoke Kumyk to his chief
aides-de-camp in spite of the fact that nearly all of them, including Shah Shamil,
were Avars (see Daghestanis).

The Kumyk appear to have their origins in the large waves of Turkic and
Mongolian peoples who began pushing westward across the great steppes of
Central Asia as early as the fifth century A.D. As early as the middle of the
eighth century, they located where many of them live today. It is possible that
the Kumyk were part of the Kazi-Kumyk (Lak) Confederation, which had its
capital in the town of Kumuk. Prior to their Islamization, the Kumyk were
pagans, shamanists, Jews and Christians. The Arab geographer, Mas'udi, recorded that a Christian Kumyk state existed under Khazar domination in the
ninth and tenth centuries.

The Kumyk were part of the Kuman-Polovtsi-Khazar-Kipchak-Turkic Confederation, which occupied the great steppes north of the Black and Caspian
seas from the eighth to the sixteenth century. They separated from these larger
confederations and were pushed to the lowlands of the North Caucasus steppes
in the eleventh to the thirteenth centuries. This is also the same time that their
language was imposed as the second or third language among the indigenous

peoples. In the thirteenth century as the Golden Horde empire was consolidating in the southern steppes of Russia, the Kumyk were pushed into the areas where they live today. Forced into geographically more cramped quarters and among non-Turkic peoples, the Kumyk began to emerge as a community with a distinct sense of identity, if not yet a nationality. Also at this time the Kumyk began to convert to Islam, again largely through the influence of the Golden Horde. The pressure from the Golden Horde on the Kumyk to become Muslims became particularly intense after Ozbek, the Khan of the Golden Horde, converted to Islam in 1313.

During the fifteenth and sixteenth centuries, the Kumyk were part of the Kazi-Kumyk (Lak) principality, one of the three feudal principalities controlling Daghestan. When the leader, Shamkhol Choban, died in 1578, the Laks refused to accept the rule of his son, Sultan-But, and the center of government was moved to Buynaksh (Boynak), a major city of the Kumyk. This development further strengthened the Kumyk and allowed them to play an important role in the ensuing battles between the sons of Shamkhol Choban as well as against the advances of the Russians in the last decades of the sixteenth century, forcing the Russians to retreat temporarily in 1604. In 1640, Makhachkala became the capital of the principality. In spite of and because of the persistent Russian invasions, the Kumyk-centered principality acknowledged the sovereignty of the Safavid dynasty of Persia throughout the sixteenth and seventeenth centuries. Oddly enough, it was not the direct threat and conquests of the Russians which weakened the Kumyk-centered principality but its involvement in wars with fellow Caucasians, the Kabardins and the Georgians. As a result of these intra-Caucasus wars, the Kumyk principality lost control of the lands between the Terek and Sulak rivers and lands which were largely settled by Kumyk themselves. Throughout the seventeenth century, the Kumyk participated in the wars between Russian and Ottoman empires as vassals of the Crimean Khanate.

Peter the Great (1689–1725), the first great Russian czar who sought to modernize the Russian Empire, occupied Derbend in 1722 and defeated the ailing Safavid dynasty of Persia. Peter the Great defeated the Ottomans as well, and by the Treaty of 1724 Russia secured rights to the western littoral of the Caspian Sea, which in effect ended the independence of the Kumyk principality. From this date onwards, the fortunes of the Kumyk began to decline, and by 1765 they controlled only the long strip of land along the coast. Nevertheless, despite the demise of their independence, the inability of any successor to consolidate power in Persia and the dire straits of the Ottoman empire after the shattering rebellion of Patrona Halil in 1730 allowed the Kumyk to maintain a good deal of autonomy over their affairs.

The most significant event of nineteenth-century Caucasian history was the heroic resistance of Shah Shamil (d. 1871), often referred to as the Imam, a title which reflected the messianic furor with which he fought against the Russian advances into the Caucasus during the years 1834 to 1869. The increase in the strength of the Naqshbandiyya, a militant Islamic brotherhood, in the nineteenth century additionally served as a rallying point for the forces of Shah Shamil. While the main leaders of the Shah Shamil rebellion were Avars and Chechens, many other peoples of Caucasus joined his cause, notable among them the Kumyk. The Shah Shamil resistance movement to the Russians was the greatest Islamic and Turkic response to the Russians until the Basmachi rebellions against the Soviets after the Russian Revolution. At times Shah Shamil tied up the entire Russian armed forces. During the Crimean War (1853–1856) the Russians were forced to station nearly 250,000 men in the Caucasus, which greatly contributed to their defeat. In fact, during the Crimean War, when Turkey, France and Great Britain attacked Russia, Shah Shamil surrendered to the Russians on September 6, 1859, and this date also marks the incorporation of the Kumyk and other Daghestani peoples into the Russian empire.

Some Kumyk played a role in the early revolutionary movements which occurred in Russia in 1904–1905, especially in Derbend. Kumyk participation in workers' movements was influenced by the urbanization and industrialization which the Caucasus was undergoing during the twentieth century, especially in Makhachkala and Derbend and the oil-related industries in those two cities. In spite of some Kumyk participation in these revolutionary movements, most Kumyk preferred an Islamic/Turkic nationalism to communism or national socialism. On the eve of the Russian Revolution, the Kumyk played an important role in the North Caucasus peoples' move for independence. Influenced by their deep involvement in the industrialization of the western coast of the Caspian Sea, most Kumyk favored a Turkic independence movement over an Islamic one. The common language to be adopted was Kumyk or Azeri, which would have given the Turkic peoples of the Caucasus solid linguistic ties and access to the literature of the Pan-Turanism movements centered in Baku, Kazan and the Crimea. By April 1918, after a protracted conflict with the Islamists, the Turkic group of nationalists proved successful and consolidated their ranks with the Bolsheviks, which shortly thereafter were defeated by General Bicherahov's White Army equipped by the British in Iran. In 1920, the Bolsheviks reestablished themselves in Daghestan, where the Eleventh Army defeated General Denikin's White Army and forced the Islamists led by Imam Gotinski to retreat to the mountains. The Kumyk on January 20, 1921, became part of the Soviet system of government, and they have remained so to the present.

The vast majority of Kumyk are Sunni Muslims of the Hanafi school. Some, however, especially in the cities of Makhachkala and Derbend who have had close contact with the Azeri, are Shias. Despite rapid urbanization during the last two or three decades, Islam has remained a fairly strong force. This is true not only in the cities but also among those Kumyk still engaged in agriculture, whether traditional or mechanized.

Kumyk by tradition are farmers and fishermen living in small villages in mountain valleys or along the seacoast. During the past two decades, they have been engaged in large-scale production of cereals and cotton. There are also several large collective farms run by Kumyk. Despite mechanization, many

Kumyk are still engaged in traditional agriculture; some smaller owners even possess tractors. In the traditional and smaller villages, Kumyk supplement their livelihood by the production of handicrafts. Chief among Kumyk wares and crafts are woollen goods and carpets. Gold, silver and iron work are also still among the major traditional crafts which are practiced profitably.

Traditional Kumyk and Islamic values seem to prevail among most of the Kumyk despite an occasional marriage with a Russian or non-Kumyk Daghestani. The stress on family, kinship ties and endogamous marriage continues among the Kumyk, whether city or country dweller. Improved communication between city and country Kumyk has enabled them to keep strong family ties. It is possible to speculate that the pressure to replace Kumyk by Avar as an inter-ethnic language has increased the sense of self-identification of the Kumyk, especially since the Avar are the major non-Russian Daghestani group competing with the Kumyk.

Urbanization is rapid among the Kumyk, many thousands having migrated to the cities. They have engaged actively in the oil industrialization centered in Makhachkala, as well as the chemical-related industries, machine building, tool and die industries and construction trades. Most are employed as workers, engineers and technicians.

A sense of community remains among the Kumyk despite urbanization. Immigrants to the cities tend to cling to traditional patterns in new situations. The smallness of the area in which Kumyk live, together with good communication and transportation systems, and increased ownership of cars, which allow for frequent visits between city and country village, have worked to keep the Kumyk united. Family ties remain strong.

One of the greatest strengths of the Kumyk which has helped resist dramatic governmental and social pressures has been their language, which has survived changes in script from the Arabic to Latin to Cyrillic and contributed immensely to the Kumyk sense of nationality. The Kumyk were one of the first Turkic peoples of the Caucasus, other than the Azerbaijanis, to be influenced by the Turkic literary renaissance in Istanbul, the Crimea and Kazan, especially the latter city because of language closeness.

Yirchi Kazak (born in 1830 or 1839) is considered the father of Kumyk literature. Some of his original work is incorporated in a volume of poetry and letters edited by the Kumyk author, Osmanov Muhammad (1840–1904) and published in 1873 in St. Petersburg under the title, *Collection of Nogay and Kumyk Folksongs*. His volume includes pieces written after the Crimean War and reflects ideas of Kumyk scholars in the latter nineteenth century. The Kumyk established a press in Buynaksk early in the twentieth century, which contributed to strengthening the Kumyk language. Two of the most important and significant prose writers were Nuray Batirnurzayov and his son Zeynel-abid, both of whom wrote many works before they were shot by the White Russian forces on September 18, 1919. The literary journal *Tang-Cholpan* (Morning Star) which they established had a lasting effect on Kumyk literature.

The strong literary tradition of the Kumyk is the main reason that of the nine literary languages of Daghestan, Kumyk is one of five languages in which a newspaper is published, the others being Avar, Dargin, Lak and Lezgin. Radio and television broadcasts are only in these languages (other than Russian) as well. Kumyk thus remains the only Turkic language which is used on the airwaves, the others being Ibero-Caucasian languages. This seems to indicate that the Kumyk will remain one of the most important ethnic and language groups in Daghestan and in the Caucasus and will inevitably dominate the smaller Turkic groups such as the Karachai, Balkar, and Nogai and the smaller Ibero-Caucasus groups.

BIBLIOGRAPHY

Books

Barthold, W., and Bennigsen, A. "Daghestan." In *Encyclopedia of Islam*. New ed. Vol. 2. Leiden: Brill, 1965.
Barthold, W., and Kermani, David. "Kumuk." In *Encyclopedia of Islam*. New ed. Vol. 2. Leiden: Brill, 1965.
Bennigsen, Alexandre. "Muslim Conservative Opposition to the Soviet Regime: The Sufi Brotherhoods in the North Caucasus." In *Soviet Nationality Policies and Practices*, edited by Jeremy R. Azrael. New York: Praeger, 1978.
Geiger, B., et al. *Peoples and Languages of the Caucasus*. The Hague: Mouton, 1959.
Menges, K. H. *Turkic Languages and Peoples: An Introduction to Turkic Studies*. Wiesbaden: Harrassowitz, 1968.
Scherer, John, ed. *USSR Fact and Figures Annual*. Gulf Breeze, Fla.: Academic International Press, 1981.

Robert Olson

KURDS   The Kurds are a nation without a politically recognized homeland, a people numbering nearly 10.4 million with an urgent sense of common ethnic identity overriding long established patterns of diversity in tribal affiliation, ways of life and religious practice. An essentially Muslim people, although locally adhering to different sects and orders, they are widely distributed throughout central Southwest Asia. Nowhere do they dominate or even reflect their numbers in a national political system. (There are a number of Kurdish-speaking Jews, many of whom have migrated to Israel. Ed.)

Precise population figures are lacking for most areas. Such official figures as are available have to be regarded with skepticism. Most commonly, they are prepared by officials in countries where the Kurds constitute a substantial minority whose efforts for increased political autonomy are viewed as a threat. Fairly conservative estimates would place 2.9 million Kurds in Iraq and 3.4 million in Turkey. In both countries, Kurds are the largest minority ethnic grouping. In Iran the Kurds are thought to number 3 million and in Syria, 800,000.

The Kurds of Kurdistan occupy a rugged mountain system, formed by the Anti-Taurus and Zagros mountain ranges. With the exception of communities on the edges of the Syrian steppe, in the lowlands of southeastern Turkey and on the lower fringes of the Mesopotamian Valley, climate is characterized by heavy snows during the winter months followed by spring rains and heavy runoff down the slopes. Although the region is relatively well watered, rainfall is seasonal and varies greatly from year to year. Thus agriculture is often risky and in many places depends on intricately constructed systems of mountain terracing, utilizing small-scale systems of runoff irrigation. The terrain is also one in which communications are difficult and where the day-to-day control by remote governments has been tenuous at best. In this sense, it has been a refuge zone for religious and politically dissident groups, and for the same reason, it is understandable that local tribal politics have been historically important among settled and nomadic populations alike. Although there is an increasing sense of national Kurdish identity, the history of Kurdish politics and foreign domination would not be complete without reference to the frequent alliances of expediency made by the Kurdish tribes and rulers with Arabs, Turks and Persians directed against rivaling Kurdish factions and tribes.

Kurdish, an Indo-Iranian language, is grammatically and lexically distinct from Persian and is thought to have developed separately over a long period of time. It is spoken in two mutually intelligible major dialects: Kermanji in northern and western Kurdistan, and Kurdi (Sorani) in the south and southwest. Members of the Qizilbash sect in Turkey speak Macho-Macho, a third dialect. Although Kurdish nationalists sometimes refer to Luri as a Kurdish dialect, it is not so regarded by the Lurs themselves, and linguists classify it as Persian (see Lur). The primary literary language today is Kurdi (Sorani), largely because it is the dialect of most of Iraq and Iran, where it has been possible to publish relatively freely. Kermanji was more widely published prior to World War I. The Arabic alphabet is employed except for some Kurdish publications in the Soviet Union and underground publications in Turkey.

Kurdish people differ greatly in local economic, social and political organization. As a rule, this diversity reflects the general cultural patterns of the particular region in which they are found. Kurdish populations in Turkey, Iraq and Iran closely resemble non-Kurdish groups among whom they live in terms of many, if not most, marriage, kinship and familial practices. In Ankara, for example, Kurdish porters in the markets arrive regularly from the same eastern villages as did their fathers to pursue a traditional means of supplementing the incomes of their land-poor families. This is so, too, for their non-Kurdish neighbors. At the same time, at Ankara University, Kurdish students from the same villages, perhaps even the same families, are preparing themselves for careers in government, computer technology and engineering. This situation is repeated throughout countries where Kurds live. They participate actively, despite numerous political problems, in the educational and economic life of the nation-states where they live as minorities. The increasingly urban character of Kurdish peoples is part of a general transition taking place throughout the Middle East. Significant rural population growth, increased use of advanced agricultural technology and increased educational and job opportunities at the national level have encouraged urban migration.

Despite varied life-styles, tribal identity is still important for the majority of Kurds. It is common to distinguish between still traditional tribal villages and nomadic communities in the upland areas, as opposed to detribalized feudal or landlord-centered villages of the more fertile plains and valleys. While there is a difference in political organization along these lines, most people, urban and rural alike, associate themselves with specific, named tribal groupings. What is changing is the nature of these political systems and the extent to which the tribe is the exclusive vehicle for political organization. For urban professionals, artisans and merchants in predominantly Kurdish cities, such as Kirkuk, Mosul and Sulaymaniyah, tribal identity is of limited economic and social importance. However, even for such urban classes it may be the basis for their allegiance to particular regional or national political parties or factions. In Turkey, before the coup of 1980, elected Kurdish officials, although affiliated with national parties, often drew locally on tribally defined constituencies. In Iraq, local factions within the nationalist independence movement are organized in units along tribal lines. In Iran, following the Khomeini-led revolution in 1979, large armed revolts by the largely Sunni Kurds of the west were apparently organized along tribal divisions.

Villages in the lowlands tend to be more productive agriculturally and are socially characterized by class stratification based on control of land and water resources.

Village society varies greatly according to local ecology, and the three countries with most of the rural Kurdish population differ in terms of the provision of village schools and health care and even in basic patterns of land tenure. Physically, villages are relatively uniform in tightly nucleated patterns, with houses close to one another and kinship groups clustered together. Patrilineal ties are everywhere important, and often dwellings will be located to form a compound shared by the households of brothers or the married sons of brothers. The villages in mountainous regions are usually situated on hillsides, with the houses built into the slope and the flat roofs forming an accessible terrace-like work area. The roofs are used for drying fruits and preparing bulgur. While small one-storied dwellings of mud, timber and stone construction are typical of central Kurdistan, most villages are distinguished by one or two houses of markedly different construction: much larger in size, often two-storied with an outward-facing balcony on the second floor. These are the residences of principal landlords, *shaikhs* or tribal leaders. They serve as meeting places for the adult males, with local factions indicated by patterns of informal meetings and tea drinking.

The primary unit of Kurdish social life for all classes in both urban and rural communities is the co-residing family or household. In rural Kurdistan, households are fundamental units of production and consumption. Sometimes expenses will be shared and labor pooled among two or more households, usually those of brothers. More commonly, each household functions as an autonomous social and economic unit, although cooperating closely in numerous ways with other households related by kinship and marriage. The closest external ties are agnatic, and these are reinforced by marriage. Throughout Kurdistan, close cousin marriage and marriage within the tribal section is preferred. Father's brother's daughter marriage is the ideal, and many groups recognize the right of a girl's paternal uncle to claim her hand in marriage for his son. Actual incidence of such marriages varies, with a higher frequency occurring in tribal areas than in non-tribal ones. Such marriages are nonetheless accompanied by the payment of brideprice, a substantial sum of money paid to the father of the bride. A dowry of less value than the brideprice is commonly, but not uniformly, given by the bride's family to their daughter.

Socially, the household is referred to in terms of its oldest male member and ideally includes a male head of house, his wife or wives, his sons (although never the sons of wives by former husbands), his sons' wives and other unmarried agnatic descendants. Kurds everywhere are patrilocal regarding post-marital residence, and even should married sons subsequently leave their father's household in his lifetime, there is a tendency for them to establish a new residence in close proximity to that of their father. Brothers and the sons of brothers often form the basis for wards, or *mahalle*, within villages.

Within the household, there is a clear division of labor by age and sex. Co-wives are ranked by order of marriage. The senior wife directs a clearly demarcated arena of household activities to be carried out by other wives, daughters-in-law and unmarried daughters. The men of the household are similarly ranked, with older brothers taking precedence over younger ones. Inheritance rules differ slightly for Shia and Sunni groups, and practice differs a great deal according to local community and the wealth and education of the family. In general, males share to the exclusion of their sisters in the family estate. Anticipatory inheritance is common in Turkey among pastoral tribes, with each son taking a share of the herd when he sets up a new independent domicile, but anticipatory inheritance is not common among farmers. Daughters may attempt to exercise their claim, recognized in civil and religious law, to their father's estate if they are willing or able to tolerate the resulting animosity of brothers. Among the educated, it is more common for daughters to share in the estate. In general, it is often noted that Kurdish women enjoy more freedom and a wider participation in public life than do Turkish, Arab and Persian women. And, as with tribal women of all ethnic groups in Southwest Asia, Kurdish women are freer in their interaction with males than are traditional townswomen, who are more apt to be secluded from public activities.

Religion in Kurdish society is of great importance. The large majority of Kurds are Sunni of the Shafi school of law, except in Iran and parts of Iraq, where many are Shia. The division between the two sects is significant politically.

Further, many Sunni communities are adherents of various Sufi orders, such as the Qadiriyya and the Naqshbandiyya found throughout Kurdistan or the Qizilbash in Turkey and the Ahl-i-Haqq in Iraq and Iran. Approximately 100,000 Kurds are Yezidis, living near Mosul. Religious leaders, or *shaikhs*, have political and social influence at the local level throughout the region, although their orders are outlawed in Turkey. There are two main routes to achieving a position of religious influence. One is through study with an already acknowledged *shaikh*, at the completion of which one becomes a *mullah*. A successful *mullah* may attract a substantial following and be able to sustain himself through their offerings. Most, however, are also engaged in agriculture. The other route to religious leadership is through purported descent from the Prophet. These families, called Sadaat (sing. Sayyid), often form a rich and influential segment of local society, resembling in some cases an endogamous landowning caste.

Presently, the Sunni Kurds of Iraq are committed to a protracted struggle for local autonomy or independence, although this struggle is in a period of quiescence during the Iran–Iraq war. The immediate origins of this effort lie in the nationalist movements of the late nineteenth and early twentieth centuries. With the division of Kurdistan within the Ottoman empire between Anglo-French spheres of influence in 1918, Kurdish nationalist agitation became more militant and better organized. In Iran, Kurdish uprisings occurred from 1920 to 1925, in part coordinated with nationalist efforts in Iraq. By 1930, Reza Shah was able to pacify the region around Lake Urmiyah, partly by organizing local Turkish resistance to Kurdish rule. Kurdish tribal leaders were exiled and their land confiscated. However, in 1945, following the collapse of Iranian authority in the area, the Kurdish republic of Mahabad was established, only to fall in 1946 with the withdrawal of Soviet support. In 1979 most of the Kurdish population of Iran boycotted the national referendum establishing the Islamic Republic. Shortly thereafter a series of uprisings, notably in 1979 and 1981, were met by strong resistance. Fighting is said to continue, although the government is able to maintain control over urban areas in Iranian Kurdistan.

In Turkey, shortly after that country became a republic in 1924, the Kurdish populations of Diyarbakir and Elazig provinces revolted but were rapidly subdued. Armed conflict between Kurdish units and the Turkish army persisted sporadically until 1946. Local Kurdish unrest and political resistance have continued, but on a small scale, and have been effectively countered by the Turkish government. Kurdish participation in the national party system in Turkey has given high priority to the economic and educational development of the eastern provinces.

Kurds in Iraq have long had more formal political recognition than elsewhere, but the struggle for independence has nevertheless continued. The recent bitterness engendered by this struggle makes it likely that Kurdish nationalism will persist. Also, it is likely that the out-migration of educated individuals from Kurdistan will accelerate.

BIBLIOGRAPHY

Books

Al-Kanaani, Nauman M. *Limelight on the North of Iraq*. Baghdad: Dar al-Jumhuriya, 1965.

Arfa, Hassan. *The Kurds: An Historical and Political Survey*. London: Oxford University Press, 1966.

Barth, Fredrik. "Father's Brother's Daughter Marriage in Kurdistan." In *Peoples and Cultures of the Middle East*, edited by Louise E. Sweet. Vol. 1. Garden City, N.Y.: Natural History Press, 1970.

————. "Nomadism in the Mountain and Plateau Areas of South-West Asia." In *The Problems of the Arid Zone*. Paris: UNESCO, 1960.

————. *Principles of Social Organization in Southern Kurdistan*. Oslo: Brodrene Jorgensen A/S, 1953.

Bates, Daniel, and Rassam, Amal. *Peoples and Cultures of the Middle East*. Engelwood Cliffs, N.J.: Prentice-Hall, 1983.

Coon, Carleton S. *Caravan: The Story of the Middle East*. New York: Holt, Rinehart and Winston, 1958.

Cronin, Vincent. *The Last Migration*. London: Hart-Davis, 1957.

Douglas, William O. *Strange Lands and Friendly People*. New York: Harper, 1951.

Eagleton, William. *The Kurdish Republic of 1946*. New York: Oxford University Press, 1963.

Edmonds, C. J. *Kurds, Turks, and Arabs*. London: Oxford University Press, 1957.

Francisse, A. E. *The Problems of Minorities in the Nation-Building Process: The Kurds, The Copts, The Berbers*. New York: Vantage Press, 1971.

Ghareeb, Edmund. *The Kurdish Question in Iraq*. Syracuse: Syracuse University Press, 1981.

Ghassemlou, Abdul Rahman. *Kurdistan and the Kurds*. Publishing House of the Czechoslovak Academy of Sciences. London: Collet's, 1965.

Hamilton, A. M. *Road Through Kurdistan*. London: Faber & Faber, 1958.

Hansen, Henny H. *Daughters of Allah: Among Muslim Women in Kurdistan*. London: Allen & Unwin, 1960.

————. *The Kurdish Women's Life*. Copenhagen: Nationalmusetts, 1961.

Keddie, Nikki R. *Roots of Revolution: An Interpretive History of Modern Iran*. New Haven: Yale University Press, 1981.

Kinanne, Derk. *The Kurds and Kurdistan*. London: Oxford University Press, 1964.

Leach, E. R. *Social and Political Organization of the Runwanduz Kurds*. London: London School of Economics, 1940.

Nyrop, Richard F., et al. *Area Handbook for Syria*. American University FAS, DA Pam 550-47. Washington, D.C.: Government Printing Office, 1971.

————. *Area Handbook for the Republic of Turkey*. American University FAS, DA Pam 550-89. Washington, D.C.: Government Printing Office, 1973.

O'Ballance, Edgar. *The Kurdish Revolt: 1961–1970*. London: Faber & Faber, 1973.

Safrastian, Arshak. *Kurds and Kurdistan*. London: Harvill Press, 1948.

Smith, Harvey H., et al. *Area Handbook for Iran*. American University FAS, DA Pam 550-68. Washington, D.C.: Government Printing Office, 1971.

———. *Area Handbook for Iraq*. American University FAS, DA Pam 550-31. Washington, D.C.: Government Printing Office, 1971.

Van Niewenhuijze, C.A.O. *The Sociology of the Middle East: A Stocktaking and Interpretation*. Leiden: Brill, 1971.

Zelter, Moshe. "Minorities in Iraq and Syria." In *Peoples and Cultures of the Middle East*, edited by Ailon Shiloh. New York: Random House, 1969.

Articles

Aristova, T. F., and Vasil'yeva, G. P. "Kurds of the Turkmen SSR." *Central Asian Review* 13:4 (1965): 302–309.

Bates, Daniel G. "The Role of the State in Peasant-Nomad Mutualism." *Anthropological Quarterly* 44:3 (1971): 109–131.

Bazarov, K. "The Kurds and Their Overlords." *Venture* 22:5 (1970): 20–23.

Burton, H. M. "The Kurds." *Journal of the Royal Central Asian Society* 31 (1944): 64–73.

Edmonds, C. "Kurdish Nationalism." *Journal of Contemporary History* 6:1 (1971): 87–107.

Fields, Henry. "Mountain Peoples of Iraq and Iran." *American Journal of Physical Anthropology* 9 (1951): 472–475.

Galloway, J.P.N. "A Kurdish Village of Northeast Iran." *Geographical Journal* 124 (1958): 361–366.

Harik, I. "The Ethnic Revolution and Political Integration in the Middle East." *International Journal of Middle East Studies* 3 (1972): 303–323.

Kinsman, J. "The Changing Face of Kurdish Nationalism." *New Middle East* 20 (1970): 19–22.

Magnarella, P. "Jewish Kurds of Iran." *Jewish Digest* 15:7 (1970): 17–20.

Vinogradov, Amal R. "Ethnicity and Power Mediators in Northern Iraq: The Case of the Shabak." *American Ethnologist* 1:1 (1974): 207–218.

Unpublished Manuscript

Masters, William M. "Rowandus: A Kurdish Administrative and Mercantile Center." Ph.D. dissertation, University of Michigan, 1953.

Daniel G. Bates

KURI Within 50 years the Kuri may no longer exist as an ethnic group. A small, dynamic, insular people living on and around Lake Chad, their future appears to be one of immersion and disappearance within the neighboring Buduma (see Buduma).

The Kuri number no more than about 12,400 and live on the islands and peninsulas of eastern Lake Chad, totally in the Republic of Chad. Even today, they are often wrongly considered to be Buduma because they speak Yedina, the Buduma language. In fact, however, the Kuri are closer to the Kanembu, of which, according to legend and oral tradition, they are a branch (see Kanembu).

The word "Kuri" means "the ones who live on islands," as opposed to the meaning of "Buduma": "the ones who live in grass." Old Kuris tell this story of their origin:

During a halt in the village of Sulu, near Rig Rig, a Kanembu chief's daughter died. Like all Kanembu women, she was wearing silver rings about her ankles. Unable to remove them, the father buried his daughter with the rings. During the night, his son, Diledim, exhumed her body, broke her ankles and took the rings. In the morning, the father discovered the act and expelled his son, who fled to the islands, where eventually he married a Buduma girl. His descendants were called Kuri and populated the eastern islands.

According to legend, Diledim's five sons, Kura, Kalia, Medi, Yakudi and Ngadji, left home. Medi took the road to Bornu (he had been accused of being a *kindra*, or sorcerer). The others settled near Isseiron and fought among themselves; Kalia, Yakudi and Ngadji opposing Kura, who was joined by Medi.

The two contending groups, each headed by a strong *mai* (chief), recognize this cleavage today, Kalia groups in the south, Kura and Medis, called Midias, in the north. Each group is divided into clans. Among the Kuras there are 5 clans: Dagila, Tojima, Doria, Maradalla and Kallameida. There are 2 among the Medis: Fetra and Dalla. There are 12 among the Kalia: Bodalla, Kola, Yerima, Tcharigiria, Marcudia, Baraya, Karia, Killakada, Tcharmaya, Gallao, Mullumtchilloum and Wadjirima. The Yakudi have 4: Mallumia, Kallamia, Kanoa, Kwallia; the Ngadji, 5: Issia, Batuma, Bellerama, Tchukulia and Kongurama.

In the process of settling the islands, the Kuri came into contact with the Buduma, who were there before them. From this contact, the Kuri learned Yedina, the Buduma language, one of the Chadian languages of the Nilo-Saharan family, akin to Kotoko (see Kotoko).

The Kuri consider themselves a distinct ethnic group, possessing a "country" with specific boundaries: Ira on the north, Kuludia on the south, Kangalom on the west, Isseirom on the east. Their neighbors are the Buduma, Kanembu and Asale Arabs. Despite their insularity, they have maintained close relations with the Kanembu and share aspects of the Kanembu culture such as a strong sense of Islam, a well-structured community organization and an openness to outsiders in spite of language barriers.

The Kuri are a dynamic, adaptable people. In the past they have been fishermen, cultivators and stockbreeders, fishing the arms of the lake in all seasons, cultivating millet on the sands of the islands during the rainy season and growing corn on the beaches when the lake subsides. They bred the famous "Kuri cattle," known for their bulbous horns and the quality of their milk and meat. The herds often swim from island to island for new pasture.

In 1956, an exceptional rise in Lake Chad decimated the herds and reduced the number of islands. Many Kuri withdrew to dry land to await subsidence and became interested in the polders which the colonial administration was promoting. Indeed, Kuri claim they invented the Lake Chad polders when, at the end of the last century, they blocked the arm of the lake with two dams and when the water subsided, farmed the fertile lake bottom. Polders are now a prime economic asset around Lake Chad.

Since 1956, the Kuri have lived on both the main islands and on the edge of the lake around polders and in temporary villages where each family cultivates wheat and corn. Fishing has been of decreasing interest to them. Stockbreeding continues its importance, but cross-breeding has reduced the purity of the Kuri cattle.

The Kuri are a pious people whose leaders are the keepers of tradition and religion in the area. About 12 percent of the Kuri are polygynous. They have produced many religious leaders, *mallamai*, some of whom are respected beyond Kuri borders. In the district of Isseiron some Kuri have adopted the Tarrabia sect, a somewhat fanatical group which more or less rejects classical Islam.

While Kuri are economically and religiously active, it is questionable how long they can remain a distinct group. Increasingly, they are being assimilated by the Buduma, who, in perhaps the next half century, will obliterate Kuri identity.

BIBLIOGRAPHY

Books

Bouquet, Ch., and Cabot, J. *Atlas pratique du Tchad*. Paris: I.G.N., 1971.
————. *Le Tchad*. Paris: P.U.F., 1973.
Chapelle, J. *Le Peuple tchadien*. Paris: L'Harmattan, 1981.
Nelson, Harold D., et al. *Area Handbook for Chad*. American University FAS, DA Pam 550-159. Washington, D.C.: Government Printing Office, 1972.

Christian Bouquet

L

LABBAI   The Tamil-speaking Muslims of Tamilnadu State, India, are collectively known as the Labbai. They are divided into four distinct groupings: the Rawther, Labbai, Marakkayar and Kayalar. Since the generic name for the community is the same as one of the four subgroups, the term "Labbai" is used here only for the subgroup, the whole group being termed Muslim Tamils. Slightly less than 5 percent of Tamilnadu's population is Muslim, with perhaps 80 percent of these (approximately 2 million) being Muslim Tamils. The remaining Muslims, most of whom live in Tamilnadu's cities, belong to various other communities including the Mappillas (see Mappilla), who are Malayalam speakers, and Urdu-speaking communities including the Shaikh, Sayyid, Sharif, Pathan, Ismaili, Navayat, Daudi Bohra, Wahhabi and a catch-all group, the Deccani (see Deccani).

The Muslim Tamils are descendants of Arab traders and local converts. They are an autochthonous population which bears the stamp of Tamil culture and the political heritage, not of conquest and rule such as northern Muslims have experienced, but of mercantilism and integration. Since they are the indigenous population, they speak Tamil as their household language. Among those living in cities, Urdu is also frequently used, although it is less commonly claimed as a first language. Under the influence of Arab culture in certain coastal towns, such as Nagappattinam and Kayalpatnam, some Muslims write Tamil and occasionally publish in Tamil using Arabic script.

The Muslim Tamils follow the Sunni sect of Islam; the majority of Labbai and Rawther follow the Hanafi school, while the Kayalar and Marakkayar follow the Shafi. The importance of this difference is slight and reflects more the differences in their origin than it does religious differences. The Kayalar and Marakkayar live predominantly along the Coromandel coast and claim to have converted to Islam under Shafi Arab influence. The Rawther and Labbai, in contrast, live primarily in the interior of the state and owe their religion to the influence of non-Arab Muslims. The majority of Indian Muslims are Hanafi. The Muslim Tamils consider themselves and are considered by other Indian Muslims to be devout and orthodox.

Muslim Tamil family life reflects their orthodoxy. Except among the very wealthy and the poor, *purdah* (the seclusion of women) is practiced. Muslim houses, reflecting this, are inwardly oriented and lack the public veranda which typifies the homes of their Hindu neighbors. Men and children attend prayers in mosques. Women pray in their homes.

Muslim Tamils are patrilineal, and their extended, patrilocal households are organized around two to three generations of agnates, who form a coparcenary (joint ownership) group known as a *pangaali*. Following Dravidian custom, mother's brother's daughter marriage is prescribed, and many will say that it is their right to marry such a woman, if one of appropriate age is available. In fact, such marriages are infrequent, but marriages between classificatory matrilineal cross-cousins (classificatory cousins to whom one is linked through one's mother) are common. Parallel cousin marriages (father's brother's daughter or mother's sister's daughter), although allowed by Islamic law, do not occur, since in Dravidian culture these cousins are classified as siblings and so such marriages are thought incestuous.

Muslim Tamil lineages are known in the Tamilian manner by family names (*kudambam peer*). These names typically designate a grandfather's place of origin, a legendary or humorous characteristic of this ancestor or his former occupation. Family names are bilateral so that each person is known by his father's and his mother's name and may be referred to by one or the other in situations where one or the other family name is better known. Typically a person will be known by his father's family name in his place of residence, but when he visits his mother's kin, will be referred to by their name. Alternatively, if the mother's family is more famous than the father's, then her family name may be the standard. When a man's son has children, they become known by an attribute of their grandfather or great-grandfather. In this manner family names change every third to fourth generation. The paternal side of a Muslim Tamil's family has more economic importance than the maternal side, since it dictates patterns of ownership and inheritance, but as naming practices suggest, both sides are socially important and determine a person's identity within a community.

The Muslim Tamils are known throughout Tamilnadu State as skillful, shrewd shopkeepers and traders. Indeed, they are one of the important merchant communities of the state. Their prominence in trade is associated with their comparatively high degree of urbanization. In 1961 approximately 55 percent of the Muslim population of Tamilnadu was urban, compared with 26.7 percent of the total state population. This latter figure is commensurate with a society based on an agricultural economy. The 55 percent figure is high and reflects the non-agricultural basis of the Muslim's livelihood.

Associated with the urbanism are two far-reaching characteristics of the Muslim Tamil population. First, and as a consequence of their mercantile interest, the Muslim Tamils are widely scattered over much of the Asian world. For example, for centuries they have been an important economic and political force in Melaka. They are found in numbers in Malaysia, Thailand and Singapore.

Prior to World War II, some made their way as far as Japan. Muslim Tamils in recent years are to be found in the Arab cities of the Middle East, as well as Africa. Wherever they go, they are primarily merchants.

Despite their far-flung wanderings, India remains a homeland for them, and ties are maintained with kinsmen in India. Often, overseas Muslim Tamils maintain households and families in India to which they periodically return and/or remit money. Regardless of their wanderings and attachment to Islam, they identify themselves as Tamilians.

Although as merchants the Muslim Tamils find their kin widely dispersed, they exhibit a cohesive social organization in which "kin centers" form focalizing locations. These are the ancestral towns and villages which the Muslims commonly name as their native places. A Muslim may never have lived in or even been in his kin center, but he considers it the nexus of kin-centered activities and the hub of an extensive kin-based network.

Rural kin centers are often remarkable in appearance. Large, well-maintained houses proclaim their merchant owner's affluence, while the house's vacancy, except in festival times, produces an aura of abandonment. Centers such as these are found in many places in Tamilnadu, and other Indian Muslim communities appear to have them elsewhere in the subcontinent. Muslim Tamil merchants periodically return to their centers with their families to attend annual festivals associated with the celebration of saints' death anniversaries. These festivals are much like the annual temple festivals of their Hindu neighbors, and in a similar fashion Muslims' joint sponsorship and participation in the festival defines them as a local community with a corporate identity. This joint identity is reinforced during the saint's festival by the nightly processions which slowly circumambulate the Muslims' residential area and bring blessings upon it. The visiting Muslims use their visits to arrange marriages, to perform life crisis ceremonies such as circumcisions and to participate in a few intense days of interaction with their kinsmen before they scatter again to their places of business. Businessmen exchange information about enterprises and learn of business opportunities in different regions, of the businesses which are most successful and of new sources of wholesale supplies. They arrange to hire new employees and assess one another's successes and failures, while judging each other's moral stature as merchants who adhere appropriately to Islamic business precepts. Kin centers, therefore, act as hubs of communication interlinking the villages' dispersed descendants.

Although Muslim families vary among themselves, genealogies reveal that a majority, between 60 and 80 percent, of Labbai marriages are between kin and are performed at kin centers. These marriage alliances form the ties which interlink kin and maintain the kin centers as the hub of the mercantile networks.

Muslim Tamils have lived for the most part in harmonious syncretism with their Hindu neighbors. As an integrated population the Muslims identify the bulk of their cultural traditions with those of the Tamil population. They proclaim their Tamilian origin, speak the Tamil language as their language, dress in the rural areas in much the same way as Hindu Tamilians and even refer to Muslim contributions to Tamil literature, the *sine qua non* of the locals' view of Tamil culture.

The second characteristic associated with the Muslims' urbanism is their view of society, which differs from the Hindus' in several significant ways. Urban Muslims stress an egalitarian ideology, while Hindus embrace an ideology of hierarchy and inequality. Following Islamic values, Muslim Tamil view caste as inappropriate, although they do recognize individual differences in rank and are aware of the Hindu system. Muslim ethos stresses economic independence, for, they argue, only the independent can be equal. Hindu ethos stresses inter-dependence, subordination, and superordination as a concomitant of the inter-locking Hindu caste system. Since the Muslim Tamil groups do not occupy interdependent economic statuses among themselves in their urban settings, this aspect of caste ranking is absent. All four of the Muslim Tamil groups occupy approximately the same rank in urban society and do not rank themselves. All interact equally in the mosque and are buried in the same graveyard. Further, intermarriages do occur among the different Muslim Tamil groups without social ostracism. Consequently, caste in the usual sense of ranked, endogamous groups is absent among Muslim Tamils in the cities, although in the countryside Muslim Tamils are treated as a caste by Hindus and are endogamous. Because the Muslim Tamil groups occupy different territories in the countryside, more than one group is not usually found in any single village, and so Muslim caste ranking is infrequent. The extent to which it occurs is unknown, but the use of Hindu caste names among Muslims in Ramanathapuram District points to its presence there.

The third unique feature of Muslim ethos is its stress on work as a means to success and the association of success with frugality and hard work. Work and frugality are highly valued. Hindus, in contrast, associate success with the ability to command and with leisure and associate low status with work. A consequence of their differing views is that, while the Muslims identify with Tamilians, they also see their differences and recognize that culturally they are fully integrated into neither the Tamilian population nor the greater Muslim population. They are somehow caught in the middle, wanting to be both but, as a result, being neither.

In recent years, the Muslim Tamils, especially of the northern Tamilnadu cities, have undergone a process of Islamization. This process has been char-acterized by a differentiation of the Muslim Tamil population from their Hindu neighbors and a shift in religious practices. The most striking feature of this process has been the acquisition of Urdu as a household tongue. This has occurred within the last couple of generations and, in part, has been in response to the political currents of pre-independent India and Pakistan, when Muhammad Ali Jinnah, then head of the Muslim League, attempted to unify all Indian Muslims with Urdu as their language. Subsequent identification with the Muslim popu-lation rather than the local population led considerable numbers to adopt Urdu as their language. In addition, Muslim Tamils have changed their style of dress, giving up the Hindu *dhoti* for the Muslim *lungi*, (a sarong-like garment) and donning the characteristic Muslim hat or *topi*. More important, Islamic ritualism in the countryside has a strong tradition of Sufi-inspired saint worship. While this continues as an undercurrent in the cities, it is clear that this is viewed ambiguously at best by the urban religious leadership, whose stress on austerity and orthodoxy replaces the pomp and music of the rural saint-worship festivals. All in all, Islamization has resulted in a differentiation of the Muslim Tamils from the local Hindu population and the creation of an ethnic identity.

The causes of Islamization are multiple. Identification with the Muslim movement prior to Independence undoubtedly was important during the early stages of its development, but political and economic reasons are no longer the cause for continued differentiation. Instead, internal needs arising within the Muslim community to acquire status and a sense of social position inspires Islamization. In the city the Muslim Tamil's identity is based on his group identity as a Muslim and on his personal prestige and status; but in no case is his identity a purely ascribed appellation. It is something which he establishes in his relationships with others and in the way that they perceive and evaluate him. Among urban Muslims, what kind of a Muslim a person is is particularly important because it determines how they relate with one another. Since all the Muslim Tamils are Sunni, they evaluate one another in terms of their orthodoxy and perceived behavior, the standards for which are set by the leaders of the Muslim community. Urban ethnicity arises from their desire to be good Muslims. When urban Muslim Tamils visit their home villages, they often go in part in order to attend saint festivals. Concern about orthodoxy is temporarily put aside, as are other features of their urban ethnicity. Tamil again is the language of the household as well as the mosque, and some visitors revert back to the Hindu *dhoti*. Muslim ethnicity is contextual, arising out of the particular needs for identity and status in the urban contexts where these needs are defined in terms of Muslim behavior. This kind of identity is less significant in the Muslims' home villages, where their identity as a Muslim is assumed and status is achieved on the basis of such things as wealth, occupation and personal character. Accordingly, in the village Muslim Tamils are able to relax their concern about orthodoxy. Yet when they return to the city, they don the garb of Muslim orthodoxy again.

In several ways the Muslim Tamil population is unique among Muslims in India. They have had the advantage of largely harmonious relationships with their Hindu neighbors and as a result do not view themselves as a threatened population. Unlike many northern Muslims, they have never had a tradition of rule in India and accept their minority status in a predominantly Hindu society. For them it has always been that way. Further, the Muslim Tamils who reside in the cities are not organized into castes or subcastes as Muslims are elsewhere in India. Mercantilism, urbanism in combination with Muslim values and the separate origins of the Muslim Tamil groups combine to deemphasize caste. Clearly, the example of the Muslim Tamils or Labbai proves yet again how wrong it is to view Indian Muslims as a homogeneous population.

BIBLIOGRAPHY

Books

Mines, Mattison. "Islamization and Muslim Identity in South India. In *Islam in Southern Asia: A Survey of Current Research*, edited by Dietmar Rothermund. Beitrage zur Sudasein-forschung, Sudaisien Institut, Universitat Heidelberg. Vol. 16. Wiesbaden, Germany: Franz Steiger, 1975.

————. *Muslim Merchants: The Economic Behavior of an Indian Muslim Community.* New Delhi: Shri Ram Centre of Industrial Relations and Human Resources, 1972.

————. "Social Stratification Among Muslim Tamils in Tamilnadu, South India." In *Caste and Social Stratification Among the Muslims*, edited by Imtiaz Ahmad. Delhi: Manohar Book Services, 1973.

————. "Tamil Muslim Merchants in India's Industrial Development." In *Innovation in Traditional Societies: The Modernization of Occupational Cultures in South Asia*, edited by Milton Singer. Durham: Duke University Press, 1973.

Ryan, N. J. *The Making of Modern Malaysia: A History from Earliest Times to 1966.* Kuala Lumpur: Oxford University Press, 1967.

Articles

Mayer, Peter B. "Tombs and Dark Houses: Ideology, Intellectuals and Proletarians in the Study of Contemporary Indian Islam." *Journal of Asian Studies* 40:3 (1981): 481–502.

McPherson, Kenneth. "The Social Background and Politics of the Muslims of Tamil Nadu, 1901–1937." *The Indian Economic and Social History Review* 6:4 (1969): 381–402.

————. "Yakub Hasan: Communalist or Patriot?" *University Studies in History* 5:4 (1970): 72–84.

Mines, Mattison. "Islamization and Muslim Ethnicity in South Asia." *Man* 10:3 (1975): 404–419.

————. "Kin Centers and Ethnicity Among Muslim Tamilians." *Papers in Anthropology* (University of Oklahoma) 18:2 (1977): 259–274.

————. "Muslim Social Stratification in India: A Basis for Variation." *Southwest Journal of Anthropology* 28:4 (1972): 333–349.

————. "The Potential Role of the Tamil-speaking Muslim Merchant as a Force in India's Industrial Development." *Indian Journal of Industrial Relations* 8:3 (1972): 403–410.

Wright, Theodore P., Jr. "The Muslim League in South India Since Independence: A Study in Minority Group Political Strategies." *American Political Science Review* 60 (1966): 579–599.

Mattison Mines

LAMAHOLOT   Nearly all the people who live in the Solor Islands and the eastern portion of Flores—called the East Flores Regency in the Indonesian province of East Southeast Islands—speak Lamaholot, today their ethnic designation. The Dutch called them Solorese after the Solor Island, the smallest, driest and most impoverished of the islands in the archipelago, which includes Adonara and Lembata (Lomblen on maps).

The official census of 1980 listed the total Lamaholot population of 227,750 as comprised of around 40,000 Muslims, 188,000 Catholics and a small number of Protestants, Hindus and Buddhists. Apparently some 30,000 did not acknowledge affiliation with any of these religions. In fact, these figures surely exaggerate the number of practicing Catholics and possibly Muslims, while underrepresenting those who maintain traditional Lamaholot religious orientations.

A second ethnic group, the Kédang, lives on the extreme eastern portion of Lembata. They speak a language related to but distinct from Lamaholot (see Kédang). Other ethnic groups in the regency are immigrants such as the Chinese, Arabs, Europeans and Bajau Laut (see Bajau).

There are three dialects of the Lamaholot language, a member of the Austronesian or Malayo-Polynesian family. West Lamaholot, influenced by the neighboring Sika language, is spoken near the Sika border on Flores. Middle Lamaholot is spoken on the rest of eastern Flores, Adonara, Solor and parts of Lembata. East Lamaholot is spoken by those living in the interior of Lembata.

Long before Islam became established on Java and elsewhere in Indonesia, Muslims had brought their religion to the Lamaholot. A Jesuit, Father Baltasar Diaz, who visited Solor in 1559, discovered there a mosque and many Muslims. In 1561, Portuguese Dominicans opened a mission on Solor and erected a palisade of lontar palm trunks as protection against the Muslims. In 1563 a fleet, said to be Java Muslims, attacked and burned the palisade, but the fortuitous arrival of a Portuguese galleon, which surprised their boats, saved the priests. This stroke of good fortune so impressed the Lamaholot that many of them abandoned Islam and became Christians.

Prior to the coming of the Portuguese the Lamaholot had been influenced by Hindu Javanese. A Majapahit fleet conquered Larantuka, Flores, in 1357, and the Negarakertagama listed Solor as a Majapahit dependency. In the sixteenth century some Lamaholot recognized the suzerainty of the Sultan of Ternate, and on at least one occasion they sent him envoys requesting military assistance (see Ternatan-Tidorese). The straight between Solor and Adonara is narrow, shallow and protected from the winds. It was a favorite harbor, especially during the storms of December and through March at the height of the wet monsoon, for ships trading in sandalwood and beeswax acquired principally on Timor. The ships could remain safe while awaiting calmer winds. Before the Portuguese took control of the sandalwood trade, it was plied by Malays, Javanese, Chinese, Indians, Arabs and others. During the sixteenth and part of the seventeenth centuries, the harbor and the access it provided to sandalwood gave the Lamaholot region a relative importance which it has never again held.

In 1566 the Portuguese erected a stone fort at Lohayong (Lawayong), Solor, and soon had converted several thousand persons to Catholicism, including the villages of Lamakera, Solor, and Lamahala, Adonara. The Muslim village of

Trong, Adonara, attacked its neighbor, Lamahala, in 1590. Thereafter Lamahala became and remained Muslim. In 1598 villagers at Lohayong and Lamakera temporarily overthrew their Portuguese masters, but in reestablishing themselves the following year, the Portuguese burned Lamakera to the ground. The 2,000 former Christians of Lamakera soon rebuilt their village, and thereafter they adhered to Islam. So, too, did the young man who succeeded to the principal position of leadership among the Lamaholot, Kaichil Partani, known as Dom Diogo. But he did not do so openly until the Dutch captured the fort from the Portuguese in 1613.

Eventually, the Portuguese retired to Larntuka, Flores, but retained influence on east Solor and parts of Adonara. For most of the seventeenth century and later, the Portuguese and Dutch faced each other in the region in a relative stalemate. One party or another on several occasions burned, plundered or sometimes abandoned the fort, and the Dutch twice took it from the Portuguese. Two severe earthquakes devastated it in 1648, and it ceased to have real importance, although the structure still stands. In 1653 the Dutch shifted the center of their interest to Timor.

The split between the two European powers eventually coincided with a division in the Lamaholot community. There were two groups, Demonara and Pajinara, descendants of two mythical brothers named Demon and Paji. Each lived in different villages and were set against each other by a fissure of hatred passed on from generation to generation. Their villages were distributed in an irregular pattern across the four islands, being mixed among each other in places on Adonara but dividing Solor roughly in half, Demon to the east, Paji to the west. Those called Pajinara (today usually simply Paji) either retained traditional Lamaholot religious forms or adopted Islam. The Demonara (today, Demon) frequently accepted Christianity.

Ironically, the Portuguese first established themselves among the Paji and tried to convert them. When these reverted to Islam the Portuguese found themselves supported by the Demon. The Dutch were left with an uneasy alliance with the predominantly Muslim Paji. For a variety of reasons the Portuguese and Dutch were not particularly active in this part of Indonesia during the eighteenth century. In 1859 the Portuguese ceded their rights in the Solor Archipelago to the Dutch as part of a general regulation of the holdings of these powers in the vicinity, much to the anguish of the Raja of Larantuka, who did not regard himself and his people as property subject to sale.

Through a series of military actions toward the close of the nineteenth century and the beginning of the twentieth, the Dutch established for the first time direct control throughout the islands. Subsequently they consolidated Paji villages under the Raja of Adonara and Demon villages under the Raja of Larantuka. The present structure in which all groups are part of the same regency does not recognize the division, and the government takes steps to diminish the confrontation. The underlying patterns of affairs today cannot, however, be understood without knowledge of this history.

Conversion to Islam and Christianity has greatly increased in the twentieth century, with both sides stepping up their efforts at proselytizing; there are now many villages, especially Lambeta, where both religions are represented. Nevertheless many people, particularly in more remote communities, have resisted efforts to convert them from more traditional means of religious expression. In some villages as many as a third of the population may keep to the older practices.

Until the twentieth century no education was available beyond a small elementary school at Larantuka. During the 1920s the Dutch began to subsidize elementary education provided by the Catholic mission, and the Muslim communities responded by setting up schools of their own. Today elementary education is available to all children. There are also junior and senior high schools and Islamic teacher training schools in the regency. Some Lamaholot go on to higher education elsewhere in Indonesia.

Most of the Lamaholot practice subsistence horticulture on swidden fields, with maize and dry rice the staples. Villagers near towns sometimes grow vegetables for the market. Muslim villages along the shores of the Solor Strait continue an ancient tradition of small-scale trading, purchasing among other things deer antlers and shark fins for export to Ujung Pandang and elsewhere. Others fish using artisanal techniques to supply regional markets. The Muslim village of Lamakera, Solor, and the Catholic village of Lamalera, Lembata, hunt whales and other sea mammals, as well as manta ray, shark and other fish. The first village hunts the fin whale but avoids the sperm whale. The second village hunts the sperm whale, killer whale and some lesser cetaceans but avoids all baleen whales.

Lamaholot increasingly are employed as schoolteachers, as carpenters and at other skilled or semi-skilled occupations, though percentages vary from district to district. Cash remittances and other kinds of gifts sent home by Lamaholot who have acquired an education and taken employment as clerks or other wage-paying jobs elsewhere in the nation now play an important role in domestic finance. Village economies are quite mixed, with some sectors regulated by barter exchange and others by cash.

Despite the many significant changes which the Lamaholot have experienced, they still have a distinctive culture in which there are many variations from place to place. The general culture pattern is followed everywhere regardless of religious orientation, occupation or education. There is ideally one family per house. Houses are made of bamboo with grass or palm leaf roofs or in the new form of brick and wooden frames often with tin roofs.

Every Lamaholot belongs to a descent group, to which he inherits his right of membership via his father. These patrilineal clans and descent groups are linked to each other by a pattern of marriage alliance. The clans, which are exogamous, provide other clans with women and spiritual influence. Such alliances lead to permanent ritual obligations between the two groups. Each clan may have several allies, but it must maintain an asymmetric pattern in which its wife-giving allies are distinct from its wife-taking allies. Wife-giving allies are superior, and a clan owes them deference and respect and is bound to them by a series of obligations. It must also give them a series of expensive gifts according to formal agreement. These usually consist of elephant tusks, but some communities have substituted modern goods such as cement for building houses. The payments may take two or more generations to complete. They are reciprocated by counter gifts, usually decorated tie-dyed cloth of local manufacture. There is a good deal of regional variation in how these payments are handled. Some communities insist that they are made; others regularly substitute a period of brideservice, and in others the expectation that marriage gifts will be exchanged is rarely actually fulfilled so long as both parties belong to the same or nearby village.

Wife-giving allies must perform several ritual services for the children of their sisters and daughters, usually connected with life-cycle rites such as those at birth, name giving and death. They also attend modern festivities having to do with educational achievements or religious training.

Formerly each village had a *tuan alat*, or lord of the land, drawn from the oldest clan. This person was responsible for the well-being, primarily spiritual, of the community and had certain powers in regulating ritual and agriculture. On Flores and in places on Solor and Adonara, he was the superior of four traditional officers, who together governed the village. Widespread conversions to Islam and Catholicism have robbed him of the opportunity to plan community rituals, and modern administrative procedures have displaced him from village government. He usually retains some residual prestige and power, though. Slavery was once widespread but no longer occurs. Some land-owning clans are wealthy and powerful. Except for some former ruling lineages, such as those of the rajas of Adonara and Larantuka, however, there is no nobility, and social distinctions based on wealth are not clearly marked.

Lamaholot Muslims are Sunni and follow the Shafi school of law. Less than half of the population of 210,000 are Muslim, the rest being divided about equally between Catholic and traditional.

Community government formerly was closely linked to religion. Now individual rites survive frequently where community ceremonials have disappeared. The Lamaholot High God is Lera (Rera) Wulan (Sun/Moon). His female complement is Tana Ekan (Earth). Many now associate Lera Wulan with the Christian or Muslim God. Both Christian and Muslims still display in varying degrees a tendency towards religious syncretism. Some Catholic villages on Flores have rebuilt the village temple, which missionaries had once persuaded them to destroy. On Adonara one local Catholic priest has led a movement to revive some pre-Christian practices. Many rituals, particularly those involving alliance ties, remain in Muslim or Christian guise. Though these matters are primarily controlled by men, on Flores each clan also has a woman ritual specialist who plays an essential role. On the whole the Lamaholot exhibit a variegated pattern of allegiances between the orthodox beliefs and one or other of the two world religions, syncretism and out and out traditionalism.

BIBLIOGRAPHY

Books

Arndt, Paul. *Religion auf Ostflores, Adonara und Solor.* Studia Instituti Anthropos, Vol.
     1. Wien-Modling, Austria: Missionsdruckerei St. Gabriel, 1951.
———. *Soziale Verhältnisse auf Ost-Flores, Adonara und Solor.* Anthropos, Interna-
     tionale Sammlung Ethnologischer Monographien, Vol. 4. Munster i. W., Ger-
     many: Aschendorffsche Verlagsbuchhandlung, 1940.
Barnes, R. H. "Marriage, Exchange and the Meaning of Corporations in Eastern In-
     donesia." In *The Meaning of Marriage Payments*, edited by John Comaroff.
     London: Academic Press, 1980.
Kennedy, Raymond. "Flores." In *Field Notes on Indonesia, 1949–1950*, edited by Harold
     C. Conklin. New Haven: HRAF, 1953.
Keraf, Gregorius. *Morfologi Dialek Lamalera.* Ende-Flores, Indonesia: Arnoldus, 1978.
Vatter, Ernst. *Ata Kiwan: unbekannte Bergvölker im Tropischen Holland.* Leipzig, Ger-
     many: Bibliographisches Institut, 1932.

Articles

Barnes, R. H. "Alliance and Categories in Wailolong, East Flores." *Sociologus* 27
     (1977): 133–157.
———. "Lamalerap: A Whaling Village in Eastern Indonesia." *Indonesia* 17 (1974):
     137–159.

                                                                      R. H. Barnes

LIMBA   The oldest but third largest ethnic group in the Republic of Sierra
Leone (after the Temne and Mende) are the Limba, who number some 270,000.
Perhaps 70 percent of them are Muslims. Except for a handful in Guinea, all
live within Sierra Leone's borders.

Limba territory is in the Northern Province, embracing large sections of the
Bombali, Kambia and Koinadugu districts, with small portions in the Tonkolili
District. Rural–urban migration, particularly towards Freetown, the capital, have
led to a widespread distribution of Limba.

There are five major subgroups among the Limba: the Tonko, Biriwa, Wara
Wara, Safroko and Sela. There are no accurate figures for the size of each group,
but the largest is the Tonko, the smallest the Sela. A 1977 estimate put the
Safroko Limba at 14,450.

Limba is one of the Mel group of languages found generally along the West
Atlantic coast, part of the Niger-Congo family. It has basic similarities in pattern
among the subgroups, but dialects are so distinct that they are not always mutually
intelligible. The Wara Wara in the north can barely understand the Safroko in
the south. The variations of the Limba language are often partly due to relations
with neighboring peoples. The dialect of the Sela has been influenced by the

Soso (Susu), while the Safroko dialect has a large percentage of loan words from the Temne. Literature among the Limba is largely oral, and only recently have attempts been made to translate parts of the Bible into Limba. A regional conference in 1981 in Sierra Leone met to standardize the orthography of Limba, among other languages.

Limba country is hilly and has two major rivers, the Scarcies and the Rokel, and numerous streams. They provide much needed water and drainage, especially in the dry season, the second of two major seasons in Sierra Leone. The area is well suited for agriculture. The Limba have traditionally built their houses on hilltops, and many of their ritual traditions surround caves in the Wara Wara Mountains, the point of dispersal of all Limba people.

Limba traditions connect them with archaeological discoveries dating back to the seventh and eighth centuries. Limba claim they originated from roughly what is Limba country today. But the original Limba clan, which appears to have been the Kamara, gradually expanded with infusion from Manding-speaking peoples coming from the north, from the direction of the Mali Empire in about the eighteenth century. This gave rise to new ruling families among the various Limba subgroups, who now hold the positions of paramount chiefs, as the traditional rulers, usually descended from pre-colonial kings and rulers, are now called. Among the Wara Wara, the Mansaray clan holds this position. Among the Biriwa, it is the Conteh (or Konde, as it is called in Francophone areas). The Safroko have the Bangura as the ruling clan, while the Kargbo clan dominates the Tonko Limba (see Mandinka).

These Mandinka-related clans were bearers of at least rudimentary elements of Islam as they migrated southward. Some, like the Conteh of Biriwa, were said to be Muslims when they reached Limba country, though they quickly abandoned Islam. Some Islamic words and elements like *baraka* (blessing) and *almamy* (chief) were thus initially brought into Limba culture. Traders, clerics and *karamokhos* (Islamic teachers and sometimes charm makers) visiting these areas also contributed to the Islamization process.

Large-scale conversion to Islam, however, occurred in the late nineteenth century with the wars of expansion of the Mandinka conqueror, Samory Touré of Konyan country, presently in the Republic of Guinea. Samory's empire, in 1886, embraced the entire Limba country, and one element of his control was conversion to Islam. Today, although Christianity has taken some root, especially among the Tonko and Sela Limba, the majority of Limba are Muslims.

The family structure among the Limba is dominated by the household, which usually occupies one dwelling unit. The average size of a household is 7 persons, although there are smaller households and others with as many as 20 people. The household is basically composed of a man and his wife or wives and their children. Society is polygynous, regulated among the Muslim Limba to not more than four wives, though some Limba take more than this number. Most households have two wives. Other dependents in the household may include aged parents, younger brothers and/or sisters of the household head, sometimes children of near relations who may perhaps have migrated to the bigger towns. The household head is usually male among the Limba, and he invariably makes major decisions concerning his dependents. Women are subservient to their husbands or the head of the household, although they sometimes own separate farms and have a major say in the use of the proceeds of those farms. The women do housework, work on farms and look after children.

The Limba trace their descent, and property is acquired, through the male line. Succession to property and position is usually collateral, running from one brother to the next younger in line and back to the eldest son of the oldest brother. Wives are also inherited. If a husband dies, his wife is inherited by the brother. This can only be broken if the brother acquiesces or if the woman's family pays back all that had been expended on the woman by way of dowry. These traditions are observed more strictly in the more rural Limba setting than in the larger settlements, which have been affected by Western values imported from Freetown.

Within the rural village, day-to-day life revolves around the household. There is always a headman of the village (*gbaku bamet*) who calls together the male heads of households to pass on information from higher authority like the district heads, or to hold council on matters affecting the entire community. The headman is usually chosen by the elders but often comes from the most prominent family in the village, sometimes from the oldest family. A number of rural settlements in Sierra Leone are grouped in chiefdoms, which sometimes bear some relationship to pre-colonial provinces of states or petty states. The Tonko, Biriwa and Wara Wara Limba are three such entities. The present paramount chiefs of these areas, referred to as *gbaku*, still wield some influence in national politics as the local rulers of their areas. Their positions have, however, been tampered with by the central government of Sierra Leone, which seeks to control their authority. Thus paramount chiefs in some instances are not direct descendants of "ruling houses" but mere puppets of some prominent person in the central government. But Limba influence in Sierra Leone is strong. The President of Sierra Leone (in 1982), Dr. Siaka Stevens, has a Limba father, and the second vice-president in the central government is from, and represents, one of the Tonko Limba constituencies.

Contact between subgroups of the Limba and their neighbors is not dictated by ethnocentrism but by proximity and other interests such as farming or local trade. For example, the Wara Wara Limba could be considered closer to their immediate northern neighbors, the Yalunka, than to the Safroko Limba (see Yalunka).

Limba country is agricultural, largely subsistence farming, chiefly rice, with peanuts and cassava as secondary crops. In Wara Wara country, some cattle raising is significant as that area has strong connections with the Fulani, West Africa's traditional pastoralists. Limba country is also important as a source of fruits and vegetables for the local market in Freetown.

Labor is communal. The household/family unit is the primary work force. The task of clearing the farm bush is done by the men. Hoeing and planting is done by both sexes. Weeding is almost entirely women's work, while children frighten away birds and the men set traps or build fences. In some instances, cooperative work groups comprising several different families in a community are formed, and they work each other's farms in turn. In the larger settlements, these work groups, called *kune* or *maworiso* among the Safroko Limba, are formed by young men in the settlement and are available for hire.

Subsidiary crops like cassava or peanuts are planted after a piece of land has been used for rice. After they are harvested, the land is left fallow for a period of six years or more, depending on the availability of land. The fallow period forms a rudimentary calendar for indicating the passage of years. Thus, if land is left fallow for six years in a particular area, the number of times it has been used for rice farming multiplied by six indicates the age of an individual.

The period of major harvesting of the rice crop and immediately thereafter, between November and March, is the time of festivity. Post-funeral ceremonies, like the fortieth-day feast, which is sometimes postponed with poor families, would take place at this time. Societies for the initiation of girls and boys into adulthood, accompanied by feasts, also carry out their major activities during this period. After an especially good harvest, young men come together from nearby villages and hold singing and dancing festivals. This is controlled by the Limba secret society called the *gbangbani*. Participants sing songs of praise for outstanding leaders and blacksmiths (who are important figures in Limba society). There is much conspicuous consumption, and concerns for the provision of food for later, more difficult periods are not given much attention.

Indeed, during the "hungry season" (June to August), when food supplies are low, some families are reduced to seeking wild roots in the forests. Others pledge land not currently in use or obtain loans on rice at high interest rates. This often places them deeply into debt and perpetuates the crisis of hunger over the years.

Local political, social and semi-religious life among the Limba is dominated by the secret society, *gbangbani*. It has been erroneously suggested in the past that the *gbangbani* society is for social and moral purposes only and has no political function. Recent investigation has demonstrated otherwise.

The *gbangbani* is a strictly male organization in which all male members of the community are expected to participate. Young Limba boys who go to Western-type schools in the large urban centers and sometimes pursue higher education and take jobs in those areas do not join. But those who later want to identify with their culture, perhaps for political reasons, go back to their village and get initiated into the *gbangbani*.

One major requirement for initiation is that the individual must have been circumcised. The youth is then given various tests of endurance to determine his acceptability. The young man is then taught by special tutors in various traditional songs, codes of conduct and the adult language spoken by members of the society. At the end of this training, the neophyte is bonded by oath to take up his responsibility as a full member of the society and to abide by its rules and regulations. There are penalties for infraction of these rules.

The *gbangbani* society performs chiefly at night, though on special occasions, like the death of a prominent member, it may perform during the day. When the spirit, *gbangbe* (usually called "the devil"), is performing in the village, all women and non-members must stay indoors and lock all doors and windows.

The *gbangbani* society is part of the religious tradition of the Limba. Formerly, all Christians and Muslims felt the *gbangbani* was opposed to their religion and would not join the society. This feeling was reciprocated by the *gbangbani* members, and they forbade the Muslim Fulani from joining the society. This is no longer a rigid rule as people of all religious persuasions join the *gbangbani* today.

Islam as practiced among the Limba does not place emphasis on a particular sect or Sufi order. Observing the Five Pillars of Islam is the major concern. The Ahmadiya sect, relatively new in Sierra Leone, has not penetrated Limba country. One important feature of Islam is its receptive attitude toward traditional belief patterns. Thus the *alfa*, the ritual leader, is also a charm maker. Islamic words are written on a writing board and washed off with water, which is given to adherents to drink or rub about the body for good luck or to ward off evil. Islamic verses from the Quran are written on pieces of paper, sewn into small leather pouches by the *alfa* and worn around the neck or hips (the latter particularly among the women). This is called *sebe*, a practice observed by Sierra Leone Muslims.

The major Muslim festivals among the Limba are the same as those celebrated in Sierra Leone by all Muslims. There is the celebration of breaking the fast at the end of the month of Ramadan, Id al Fitr, Id al Adha or the feast of Abraham's sacrifice and the birthday of the Prophet Muhammad (Maulud). For all non-Christian Limba, Friday is the day of rest when no work is done.

The Limba believe in one god called Kanu Masala. Within this pattern Islam and Christianity have been accommodated. But a good number of Limba especially in the remote villages retain a strong attachment to their traditional belief practices, identifying lesser gods and building shrines to them. Considerable ritual and sacrifice is associated with these beliefs; for instance, pieces of animal horns are stuffed with small items and hung about the house for protection.

Western education has penetrated Limba country, but the *karanthe* or Muslim school is still a very strong tradition. There children learn some Arabic sections of the Quran as a prerequisite to being good Muslims. Demands of an agricultural society and in some instances poverty often militate against children being sent to Western-type schools, which involve far more expenditure than the *karanthe*. With the Islamic education, payment can be in kind, with the pupils sometimes assisting on the *karamokho's* (teacher's) farm.

BIBLIOGRAPHY

Books

Finnegan, R. "Limba Chiefs." In *West African Chiefs*, edited by M. Crowder and O. Ikime. New York: Africana, 1970.

———. *Limba Stories and Storytelling*. Oxford: Clarendon Press, 1967.
———. *Survey of the Limba of Sierra Leone*. London: Her Majesty's Stationary Office, 1965.
Fyle, C. Magbaily. *Almamy Suluku of Sierra Leone*. London: Evans, 1979.
———. "The Kabala Complex: Koranko–Limba Relations in 19th and 20th Century Sierra Leone." In *Topics in Sierra Leone History*, edited by A. Abraham. Freetown, Sierra Leone: Nyakon, 1978.

Articles

Berry, J. "A Note on Voice and Aspect in Hu-Limba." *Sierra Leone Studies* 13 (1960): 36–40.
Dorjahn, V. R., and Tholley, A. S. "A Provisional History of the Limba, with Special Reference to Tonko Limba Chiefdom." *Sierra Leone Studies* 12 (1959): 273–283.
Finnegan, F. "The Traditional Concept of Chiefship Among the Limba." *Sierra Leone Studies* 17 (1963): 241–253.
Glanville, R. R., and Bangura, Ibrahim. "Palm Oil Extraction in the Sherbro Country with Notes on Wara Wara Palm Oil." *Sierra Leone Studies* 11 (1928): 59–63.
Moseley, K. P. "Land, Labour and Migration: The Saffroko Limba Case." *Africana Research Bulletin* 8:2–3 (1978): 14–44.

C. Magbaily Fyle

LUR   The Lur of Iran, numbering nearly 580,000, are concentrated in three major areas: Lurestan, Bakhtiari and Kuhgiluyeh, located along a northwest-southeast axis of the Zagros range and its southern foothills. These mountains, from 100 to 200 miles wide, extend southeastward from Lake Van in Turkey to near Bandar Abbas in southern Iran, a distance of about 1,000 miles. Throughout the system the intermontane valleys hold seasonally rich pastures, which have made possible the development of several nomadic pastoral societies such as the Kurds and Lur (see Kurds).

There is a plethora of historical speculation as to the origins of the Lur people. One widely accepted theory is that they were Kurds similar to their present neighbors, who migrated from Syria into the western Zagros Mountains sometime after the Arab invasion of Iran in the seventh century A.D. Another somewhat more plausible theory claims that since early times the area was inhabited by an indigenous people who were nomadic herders and spoke an Indo-Iranian language. This territory served as no man's land between the Medes, whose hegemony extended from Lake Urmia to the north of Kermanshah, and the area of the Persians, including present-day Khuzistan, Kuhgiluyeh, and Fars Province. The Achaemenians, the Sassanians and finally the Arabs held intermittent control over this rugged land and its warlike inhabitants.

Around the tenth century, perhaps for administrative reasons, the whole region was broken into what became known as the Lurestan-e-Bozorg ("the large

Lurestan''), the present Bakhtiari territory, and the Lurestan-e-Kuchak (''the small Lurestan''), the present province of Lurestan. Presumably, owing to internecine conflicts among the constituent tribes, each of the two Lurestans was subsequently further subdivided into smaller political units. Today the Lurestan-e-Kuchak consists of two ecological and cultural zones: Pusht Kuh (''behind the mountain'') and Peesh Kuh (''in front of the mountain'').

Pusht Kuh is actually a transitional zone between the Lurestan proper and central Kurdistan. The population, estimated at 120,000, is a mixture of Kurds, Lur and Arabs and has strong cultural and linguistic affinities with the more dominant Kurdish populations to the north. This segment also exhibits a rather high degree of religious diversity in contrast to the other Lur populations. The major religious groups here are 1) Muslim Shia Ithna Ashari, which is the sect of most of the Lur, 2) Ali Allahi, a sect which believes that Ali is God, 3) Sunni Muslims, which includes most Kurds and Arabs, and 4) Christian Assyrians. There is no statistical information on the exact number of followers of each branch.

Culturally and ethnically, the Lur of Peesh Kuh or Lurestan proper (population estimate, 230,000) are much more homogeneous and, as such, resemble their southeastern neighbors, the Bakhtiari. There is also a greater degree of linguistic similarity between them (see Bakhtiari).

The Bakhtiari of Lurestan-e-Bozorg also experienced a split into two tribal blocs: Haft Lang and Chahar Lang. While the latter, by virtue of close proximity, resemble the northwestern Peesh Kuh Lur in culture and language, the former have more in common with the Kuhgiluyeh Lur to their immediate southeast.

Kuhgiluyeh, an administrative district in southwest Iran, is the home of roughly 270,000 Lur. It covers an area of some 5,800 square miles and is bounded by Fars Province to the east, the province of Khuzistan and Bakhtiari region to the west, Isfahan to the north and the Persian Gulf coast to the south. The region lies within the southwestern segments of the Zagros arc.

There are three principal languages spoken in this area. First, Luri, a dialect of Farsi and a major Indo-Iranian language in Southwest Asia, is spoken by almost 90 percent of the inhabitants of Kuhgiluyeh. Despite a good deal of Arabic and Turkic elements, Luri is fairly close to Pahlavi or Middle Persian, the language of the Sassanian period. Middle Persian lost much of its grammatical complexity and evolved into New Persian or modern Farsi. Although somewhat different from the Luri spoken by the Bakhtiari, the two dialects are mutually intelligible. The second is a Turkic language which seems to be intrusive to the region and is spoken almost exclusively by the Qashqa'i pastoral nomads (mainly of the Dareshuri tribe), who annually migrate to this region and spend the winter months grazing their flocks in the southern foothills. Some Turkic-speaking Qashqa'i farmers have settled permanently in a few large nucleated villages in the lowlands (see Qashqa'i).

The third language is standard Farsi, the official language of government bureaucracies and non-Lur civil servants. However, because of a spate of government-sponsored regional development programs including compulsory education, Farsi is gaining in importance and popularity. Generally, however, since men play a dominant role in regional markets and have extensive contacts outside their communities, they are often bilingual in Luri-Farsi and Turkic-Farsi. Women, on the other hand, who seldom leave their community, are usually monolingual. Through the region, these speech differences help to maintain the ethnic and cultural identity of the groups.

Irrespective of linguistic variation, the Shia sect of Islam is almost the sole religious belief among these mountain people. Judged by the pragmatic orientation of their belief system and the simplicity of their religious observances, however, the kind of Islam practiced can be distinguished from the highly esoteric and literate Islam of the urban centers. In Kuhgiluyeh, most religious practitioners belong to a segment of the population who are called Sadaat (singular, Sayyid), that is, those who claim descent from the Prophet Muhammad. Only a handful of Sadaat have ever achieved eminence through scholarship and training. Others, sometimes barely literate, are self-proclaimed practitioners who rarely rise above the level of petty *mullah* and charm writers.

Scattered throughout the region are shrines dedicated to holy men who were the founders of various Sadaat descent groups. Special powers are attributed to each shrine. Supplicants visit these shrines to seek cures for a variety of physical and psychological ailments. Other uses of shrines include oath taking by disputants in legal cases in order to solemnize their testimonies.

Although Islamic tradition provides the basic framework for the system of Lur values, a host of other cultural elements contribute significantly. These include specific accounts glorifying the past of each group and a rich body of folklore which keeps alive the exploits of cultural heroes, in some ways reminiscent of the epic poetry of Ferdowsi's *Shahnamah* (The Book of Kings), the best-known literature among the Lur. The dominant theme extols such personality traits as honor, loyalty, generosity and, above all, bravery in battle.

Although agriculture, mostly the cultivation of wheat and barley, is becoming increasingly important in the economy of Kuhgiluyeh, pastoralism is the predominant form of subsistence activity. More than half the population is engaged in nomadic herding of sheep and goats. Consistent with the migratory pattern prevalent among other nomads of the Zagros, the Lur herders of Kuhgiluyeh spend six to eight months (usually October to April) utilizing the low-lying pasture lands, coupled with some farming to meet consumption needs. With the onset of the dry season (May to September), the pastoralists move to the high mountain pastures, a distance of up to 150 miles. The longest migration takes about 25 days. The other half of the population also maintains a dual economy but emphasizes agriculture over herding and tends to live in permanent villages and hamlets. The residence pattern of the nomadic groups when in their winter quarters also consists of permanent dwellings made of adobe bricks or stone. For about eight months of the year the nomads live in black goat-hair tents, which, like so many things of their material culture, are produced by women.

For the sale of agricultural and pastoral surpluses and the purchase of goods manufactured elsewhere in the country, the Lur have access to two major market towns, Behbahaan in the south and Ardekaan to the north. Itinerant traders and merchants from these centers have established longstanding commercial relations with the Lur, especially with the pastoralists. They extend credit to their trading partners during the fall and winter slump season and collect the debts in summer, when the surplus dairy products and animals born in the previous winter become available for the market. However, the exorbitant interest rates, often as high as 100 percent semiannually, and other illegal practices by these urban traders are threatening the economic viability of the average nomadic household. It has been estimated that nearly 30 percent of the region's herds of sheep and goats are owned outright by the urban-based merchants. It is indeed an exceptional household that is not burdened with perpetual indebtedness. Despite the systematic exploitation, the nomads of Kuhgiluyeh, like other pastoral groups in Iran, continue to make substantial contributions to the nation's supply of meat, dairy products, wool and hides.

The Lur of Kuhgiluyeh are organized into six tribal societies, of which the largest and most populous (125,000) is the Boyr Ahmad and the smallest is the Choram, with a population of about 9,000. Others include Bavi, Behmei, Tayebei and Doshmanziari. The tribe, or *il*, is the most inclusive political unit and is composed of a number of genealogically and territorially distinct subtribes, or *tirah*. Structurally, a *tirah* is a federation of several localized kinship groupings called *oulad*. *Oulad* members trace descent through the male line to an ancestor whose name has become the referent or the label for the whole group. *Oulad*, in turn, is an aggregate of several migratory camp units or hamlets, in the case of the settled agriculturalists, the size of which varies from three to eight tent households. The tent household, comprising a man, his wife and their children, with a flock of sheep or goats, is the basic social and economic unit.

Traditionally, each tribe is headed by a hereditary chief, or khan, who is recruited by a special *oulad*. He functions in a number of important ways. Aided by an army of retainers, the khan ensures peace and security within his jurisdiction by maintaining a balance of power among the component subtribes. He acts as the highest court of appeal for the potentially disruptive disputes which cannot be resolved at the local level. He also represents the tribe in matters involving the state or the neighboring sedentary communities. The financial support of the khan's administrative apparatus is the general annual tax on grain and animals collected in kind.

The recent history of relations between the central government and the tribal groups in this region has been fundamental changes in many areas of tribal life. During the early part of Reza Shah's reign (1925–1942) pacification and elimination of tribes received priority. The tribes, often mutually hostile and disunited, proved no match for the Shah's relatively modernized army. The oath of loyalty by the defeated chiefs was not sufficient to placate the Shah; nearly all central leaders met summary executions. To force the transformation of the nomads into permanently settled farming peasants, annual migrations between the winter and summer pastures were banned. In little more than 12 years the nomads lost about 90 percent of their livestock with untold human suffering.

The abdication of Reza Shah in 1942 and the ensuing political vacuum presented the long-awaited opportunity for the nomads to resume annual migrations and rebuild their vitiated pastoral economy. With few exceptions, the new tribal leaders, perhaps naively, envisioned a smooth and constructive integration of the tribal societies into the national structure, with shared rights and responsibilities as full citizens.

The tribal policies of Mohammed Reza Shah (1942–1979) were scarcely less ruthless than those of his father. The decade between 1953 and 1963 witnessed a renewed reign of terror for the tribes, as indeed for the entire country. This is often attributed to 1) the Shah's personal insecurity, which was heightened after the coup of 1953, which overthrew the nationalist government of Muhammad Mossadeq and reinstituted monarchic absolutism, and 2) his much revitalized army and his intelligence apparatus, the SAVAK.

From 1963 to 1978 the Pahlavi regime adopted a reformist strategy to deal with the tribes, introduced under the aegis of the Shah's "White Revolution." Despite much publicity and fanfare, in reality the main objective of the planners was not so much modernization and development as the resurrection of the panacea of settling the tribes.

The much celebrated land reform, for example, created ecological disasters when impoverished nomads began a frantic conversion of steep mountain pastures into farmlands in order to qualify for individualized ownership of land. Meanwhile, the introduction of the national system of education undermined the normative foundation of the traditional social and economic systems. After 12 years of a primary and secondary education, the price of literacy is often alienation from the only available life-style.

The revolution of 1978–1979 ended the Pahlavi regime and brought a halt to at least some of the tragic waste of human and natural resources in the tribal enclaves. Although it is too early to offer a definitive judgment, it seems that some progress have been made in resuscitating the pastoral economy by eradicating the exploitive commercial practices of the town merchants while making interest-free loans available to nomads. Health clinics, electrification of villages and sanitization of drinking water seem to have received some attention from the authorities. The educated tribesmen seem to enjoy a relatively more equal opportunity in finding employment in the local government agencies, although the higher-echelon positions are still the exclusive purview of the nontribal Persian-speaking bureaucrats. Tribal education still suffers from a heavy emphasis on indoctrination at the expense of a pragmatic approach which could in time ameliorate the material conditions of life.

These post-revolutionary changes are proceeding in the context of the Islamization of society along strict lines laid down by the central government. As a consequence the tribal religious figures have emerged from relative obscurity to play a decisive part in supervising and implementing Islamic guidelines in education, bureaucracies, the commercial sector and aspects of social behavior and relationships. More significantly they are now the adjudicators of the Shariah courts, presumably the sole legal apparatus in Iran today. Time and considerable research are needed to study and to evaluate the magnitude and effects of these changes.

BIBLIOGRAPHY

Books

Barth, Fredrik. "Nomadism in the Mountain and Plateau Areas of South West Asia." In *Problems of the Arid Zone*. Paris: UNESCO, 1960.

Douglas, William O. *Strange Lands and Friendly People*. New York: Harper, 1951.

Fazel, G. Reza. "Economic Bases of Political Leadership Among Pastoral Nomads: The Boyr Ahmad Tribe of Southwest Iran." In *New Directions in Political Economy: An Approach from Anthropology*, edited by M. B. Leons and F. Rothstein. Westport, Conn.: Greenwood Press, 1979.

————. "The Encapsulation of Nomadic Societies in Iran." In *The Desert and the Sown: Nomads in the Wider Society*, edited by Cynthia Nelson. Berkeley: University of California Institute of International Studies, 1973.

————. *Tribes and State in Iran: From Pahlavi to Islamic Republic*. In press.

Articles

Fazel, G. Reza. "Social and Political Status of Women Among Pastoral Nomads: The Boyr Ahmad of Southwest Iran." *Anthropological Quarterly* 50:2 (1977): 77–89.

Hole, Frank, and Flannery, Kent V. "The Prehistory of Southwestern Iran: A Preliminary Report." *The Prehistoric Society* (Yale University), no. 9 (1976): 167–207.

Unpublished Manuscripts

Afashar-Naderi, Nader. "Sedentarization and Culture Change." Paper presented at the conference on Psychological Consequences of Sedentarization, University of California at Los Angeles, December 12–14, 1974.

————. "The Settlement of Nomads and Its Social and Economic Implications." Report prepared for the Ad Hoc Consultation on the Settlement of Nomads in Africa and the Near East, sponsored by the FAO, Cairo, December 6–12, 1971.

Fazel, G. Reza "Economic Organization and Change Among the Boyr Ahmad: A Nomadic Pastoral Tribe of Southwest Iran." Ph.D. dissertation, University of California, Berkeley, 1971.

Golamreza Fazel